The Complete Guide to
EVERYDAY
LAW

*The Complete Guide to*
# EVERYDAY
# LAW

*by*
## Samuel G. Kling

THIRD EDITION

FOLLETT PUBLISHING COMPANY
CHICAGO

# Preface to the Third Edition

The aim of this greatly expanded edition is to make *The Complete Guide to Everyday Law* the most comprehensive book of law for the layman ever published in a single volume.

To this end I have not only revised and updated existing material but have added four entirely new chapters: Small Claim Courts, Credit Cards and Credit, Handling Your Own Accident Case, and Your Income Tax Return.

In addition, I have included extensive new material in the chapters on Your Marriage, Parent and Child, Divorce, Real Estate, Landlord and Tenant, and Criminal Procedure. The legal glossary has been expanded and additional legal forms provided. The chapter on Social Security has been updated and Veterans' Benefits completely rewritten.

In this third edition of a book that has had a number of printings I have again been guided by the fact that a knowledge of the law is increasingly indispensable to every citizen. Whether we like it or not, the truth is that the law regulates our lives from the moment we are born until the day we die.

My book is intended for the layman and is based on some forty years experience both as a practicing lawyer and as a writer on legal topics. My choice of material includes those subjects which I believe of most interest to the average reader, whether he resides in New York or California, Maine, Kansas, or Florida.

I have also avoided legal jargon as much as possible. To make the book more interesting and more readable the contents are presented in question and answer form. However, like every other profession, the law has its own special vocabulary and meaning. Although most of the legal terms are explained within the context of the various chapters, the glossary at the end of the book is a helpful and handy explanation for words and phrases most likely to baffle the reader.

Finally, my purpose is not to make lawyers out of laymen but to provide basic, useful information about the law—on the theory that a person aware of his legal rights is much less likely to lose them.

SAMUEL G. KLING

*Baltimore, Maryland 21218*

# Contents

# CONTENTS

THIS BOOK IS AFFECTIONATELY DEDICATED
TO THE MEMORY OF MY PARENTS.

## CHAPTER 1

# THE COURTS AND HOW THEY WORK

*What is "the law"?*

The law is the body of rules of conduct prescribed by the supreme power of a state. These rules command the citizen to do what the state says is right and forbid him to do what the state says is wrong. Law is divided into substantive law and adjective law. Substantive law tells the citizen the nature of his rights and duties and of any violation or breach of those rights and duties. Adjective law deals with the methods of legal procedure and points out how the citizen may enforce his rights, fulfill his duties, and redress wrongs.

*What is the chief purpose of the law?*

The chief purpose of the law is to regulate human conduct. Law consists of the state-imposed rules of society, for violations of which the individual is punished. Without law there would be anarchy and violence. A system of law only comes into existence when a centralized police authority appears to enforce the rules laid down by the governing body of the society.

*What is "written law"?*

Written law is based on constitutions, treaties, and statutes or laws drawn up, ratified, or enacted by the state or federal governments. The Constitution of the United States takes precedence over all state constitutions, and is thus the supreme law of the land. State constitutions, in fact, must conform to the federal constitution.

*What is "unwritten law"?*

Historically, the unwritten law was formulated by priests, rulers, and prophets and handed down verbally from one generation to the next. In modern times the unwritten law refers to precedent, or judicial decisions, transcribed and published by court reporters. The phrase "unwritten law" is really a misnomer.

*What is "common law"?*

Common law refers to the earliest branch of the unwritten law as founded in ancient English usage and custom. It was brought to this country by the earliest English colonists, who adopted the common law to meet their specific, changing needs. The common law also refers to the great body of law that consists of judicial decisions, as distinguished from legislation.

*What is "civil law"?*

Civil law is a modern legal system based on ancient Roman law. In modern usage, however, civil law denotes the rules that govern private legal affairs, as distinguished from criminal law, which concerns acts against the state as such, rather than mere grievances between private citizens. The law of contracts, for example, is a part of the civil law, since it lays down the rules and regulations governing contractual obligations between individuals. In criminal law it is the state that is the aggrieved party, and in its name action must be taken. However, the distinction between criminal law and civil law is not always a clear one. An action may be both a public crime and a private wrong, as is the case with assault and battery. Thus a person who beats another may be prosecuted by the state for having committed the crime of assault and battery; and the victim may also institute a civil suit for damages resulting from the beating.

*What is "statutory law"?*

A statute is a law passed by a legislative body. A law passed by Congress is called an act; a law passed by a state legislature is called a statute; and a law passed by a city council or other municipal legislative body is called an ordinance.

*What is "admiralty law"?*

Admiralty law—otherwise known as maritime law—is that system of law governing navigation and overseas commerce. It is largely based on ancient customs and usages, modified by American usages, statutes, and judicial decisions. In the United States exclusive jurisdiction is vested in the federal courts; state courts are completely without jurisdiction to try maritime cases.

*What is "international law"?*

International law is the body of rules, regulations, customs, treaties, and decisions of the international tribunals that are supposed to regulate the conduct of nations. Because there is no sovereign supernational body to enforce international law, some persons deny that it is actually true law. Private international law, on the other hand, governs the rights of citizens that may be acquired in one country and enforced in another through what amounts to international reciprocity. Such law may be enforced, and often is, not only internationally but by the fifty states in the American Union.

*What is a treaty?*

A treaty is a solemn contract or compact entered into between two or more nations. Once adopted, a treaty constitutes binding international law, not only on the signatory nations, but on their respective citizens.

*How is the law enforced?*

In civil law the processes of the law are set in motion by the aggrieved party, the person who feels that his legal rights have been breached or violated. He may do this by acting as his own attorney or, more generally, by employing an attorney to act on his behalf. In criminal cases—as already indicated—the legal machinery is set in motion by the state or by its representative—by whatever name he is called, state's attorney, prosecuting attorney, or district attorney.

*What is the function of a court of law?*

The function of a court is to provide a governmental intermediary whereby the law of a particular state may be applied to controversies or disputes coming before it.

*What are the principal duties of a judge presiding at a trial?*

If the judge is hearing a case without a jury, his function is to apply the law to the facts in a particular case and to render a decision that is fair and just. If he presides at a trial where a jury has been empaneled, his function is to instruct the jury on the applicable law, the jury being the sole judge of the facts. In either case, a judge decides which evidence is admissible and which is not, hears and decides points of law raised by counsel, passes on motions and on requests for new trials, and determines who is eligible to sit on the jury. The ultimate goal of the judge who hears a legal matter is to administer justice in a fair and impartial manner.

*What is the function of an attorney engaged in the trial of a case?*

His chief function is to present the issues to be tried before the judge—with or without a jury—until a verdict or decision has been reached.

*What role does the clerk of the court play in a trial?*

The clerk keeps and maintains the records of all cases tried before his particular court.

*What purpose does the bailiff serve?*

The bailiff's job is to carry out the orders of the judge and to maintain order in the court.

*How many kinds of courts are there?*

Two. All courts—state and federal—may be divided, generally, into courts of original jurisdiction and courts of appeal.

*What is a court of original jurisdiction?*

A court of original jurisdiction is one in which a case is tried for the first time, witnesses heard, evidence introduced, and a verdict handed down, either in favor of the plaintiff (the party suing) or in favor of the defendant (the party sued). The losing party has the opportunity to appeal his case to a higher court.

*What happens in a court of appellate jurisdiction?*

The original case is argued, but not retried, on the written record of the trial in the court having original jurisdiction. No witnesses are heard, and no additional evidence is presented. Briefs containing a transcript of the original testimony, together with citations from appropriate and pertinent legal authorities, are included in the record and turned over to the clerk of the court of appeals.

The clerk in turn sees that the copies of the record are submitted to each of the judges of the court of appeals. In such a court, counsel for both sides may, if they wish, submit oral arguments based on the written records already submitted. After reading the transcript of the record and applying what each judge believes to be the applicable law, the appeal is either sustained or denied. If denied, that is usually the end of the matter. If the appeal is sustained, the court may reverse the decision of the court of original jurisdiction by granting a new trial, cutting down the amount of any award, or doing whatever else it deems necessary in order that justice be done.

*Which courts handle probate and estate matters?*

These courts are called probate courts, orphan's courts, or surrogate courts.

*What are equity courts?*

Equity courts, sometimes known as circuit courts, are courts of general jurisdiction that evolved originally to correct a too technical system of law. When legal remedies for wrongs would not otherwise exist, equity courts supply suitable remedies.

*What kinds of cases are heard in state equity courts or circuit courts?*

As a general rule, if an adequate remedy can be had in a law court, courts of equity will not assume jurisdiction. But to this rule there are a number of exceptions. The cases most frequently heard in equity courts concern divorce, fraud, accident or mistake, imperfect consideration, and the cancellation or reformation of legal documents such as contracts or deeds. Such courts also have the power to grant injunctions to force or restrain an individual or corporation to do or not to do a specific act. Relief will also be granted if mischief would result if the court did not interfere, as when contracts are made in restraint of trade, public offices are bought and sold, and agreements are founded on corrupt considerations.

*What other cases are heard in equity courts?*

When, from a relation of trust and confidence, the parties do not stand on equal ground in dealing with each other, as in the case of parent and child, guardian and ward, attorney and client, principal and agent, executor and legatee, equity courts will assume jurisdiction. They will also hear cases involving trusts, account, partition, dower, and land boundary disputes.

## What are federal courts?

The federal courts are those established under Article III, Section I, of the United States Constitution, which provides that "the judicial Power of the United States, shall be vested in one supreme Court, and in such inferior Courts as the Congress may from time to time ordain and establish." Under this authority Congress has created the Supreme Court of the United States, comprising the Chief Justice of the United States and (at present) eight Associate Justices, and a system of inferior courts. The trial courts with general federal jurisdiction are the district courts. Coming between the district courts and the Supreme Court are the various courts of appeal, one for each of the eleven judicial circuits in the United States. In addition to these courts Congress has from time to time created certain special courts: the Court of Claims, the Customs Court, the Court of Customs and Patent Appeals, the Court of Military Appeals, and various territorial courts comparable in jurisdiction to the district courts. Congress has also established a Tax Court, which, however, is an executive agency and not a direct part of the federal judicial system.

## What cases are heard by the Supreme Court of the United States?

The judicial power of the Supreme Court extends to all cases arising under the Constitution, laws, and treaties of the United States; to cases involving foreign diplomats and admiralty practice; to diversity cases (those between citizens of different states); and to cases to which the United States or a state is a party. The Supreme Court has original jurisdiction in cases to which foreign diplomats or a state of the Union is a party. In all other federal cases the Supreme Court hears cases only on appeal from the lower federal courts. The Supreme Court determines the constitutionality not only of state laws thought to be in conflict with the federal Constitution, but of acts of Congress as well. When the Supreme Court rules against the constitutionality of a statute or an executive action, its decision can only be reversed by an amendment to the Constitution or by the Court itself—if it later overrules or modifies its previous opinion. The Supreme Court thus potentially wields the highest power in the federal government, since it can veto the acts of both the legislative and the executive branches.

### What is a United States district court?

A district court is the court of original jurisdiction under the federal system. Such courts have exclusive jurisdiction over admiralty, maritime, and prize cases. They may try cases relating to patents, copyrights, and trademarks, as well as all matters pertaining to bankruptcy. District courts also have original jurisdiction to try all civil cases in which the matter in controversy exceeds $10,000 and the dispute arises under the Constitution or treaties of the United States. They also have original jurisdiction over all civil cases in which the matter in controversy exceeds $10,000 and the action is between citizens of different states, between citizens of a state and a foreign state or citizen or subject thereof, and between citizens of different states and to which foreign states or citizens are additional parties. District courts also have jurisdiction over criminal matters in which a federal statute is alleged to have been violated, as, for example, over violations of the income tax laws.

Appeals from the decisions of the judge in a district court are taken, generally, to the court of appeals having jurisdiction over the circuit in which the district court is located. In certain instances the decisions of the district court may be appealed directly to the Supreme Court.

### What cases are heard by the federal courts of appeals?

These courts are intermediate appellate courts in the federal judicial system. They review all decisions of the district courts (with certain exceptions), and are empowered to review and enforce the orders of many federal administrative bodies. The decisions of the courts of appeals are final except as they are subject to discretionary review or appeal in the Supreme Court.

### What cases are heard by the Court of Claims?

This court allows individuals an opportunity to sue the federal government for certain designated claims. Appeals from the decisions of the court are heard by the Supreme Court.

*What cases are heard by the Customs Court?*

The Customs Court reviews appraisals of imported merchandise and all decisions of collectors of customs, including orders on rate of duty, exclusion of merchandise, and liquidation of entries.

*What cases are heard by the Court of Customs and Patent Appeals?*

This court hears appeals from the decisions of the Customs Court and of the Board of Patent Appeals, the Board of Patent Interferences, and of the examiners of the Patent Office. It has jurisdiction to review decisions of the Commissioner of Patents on trademark applications. It may also review questions of law of the United States Tariff Commission on unfair practices in import trade. The Supreme Court may hear appeals taken from the Court of Customs and Patent Appeals.

*What function does the Court of Military Appeals serve?*

It is the final appellate court for convictions by military courts.

*What cases are heard by the Tax Court?*

The Tax Court reviews the decisions of the Bureau of Internal Revenue on income tax matters.

*What are the steps in a civil lawsuit?*

1. Every person sued is entitled to notice of the nature of the suit so that he can properly defend himself. The first step, usually, is the issuing of a summons to the party being sued. The summons, issued by the sheriff, briefly states the nature of the suit and when the defendant must enter his appearance, or the date and time when he is to appear in court. Upon receiving the summons, the defendant should immediately get in touch with his counsel or take steps to engage counsel if he has none. While state rules vary widely, the usual practice is to have the summons served personally on the defendant by the sheriff or one of his deputies at the place where the defendant resides or is employed. (In some states, especially in suits arising in municipal, people's, or small claims courts, service may be had by registered mail.) The defendant is

usually handed, with the summons, a copy of the declaration drawn by the plaintiff's attorney. The declaration states the plaintiff's complaint and sets forth his demand for damages if damages are involved. (Damages may be requested in a variety of legal matters.) If the defendant wishes to contest the suit, he engages counsel who, after one or more conferences with his client, draws up an answer to the declaration. In this answer the defendant may specifically deny or admit each of the individual points raised by the plaintiff's attorney. In addition, there may be a further exchange of what are known as legal pleadings, or documents that narrow down the issues of the case so that they may be properly tried.

2. On the other hand, if the defendant's counsel believes that the declaration of the plaintiff (the party suing) has failed to set forth a valid legal action, he will file what is known as a demurrer, which will then be heard by the trial judge merely on the legal merits of the case. If the demurrer is sustained, the plaintiff either loses his case completely or is allowed to amend his declaration to conform with the rulings of the judge.

3. The third step in a civil suit is the actual trial. The trial may be held with or without a jury, usually at the option of the plaintiff. A jury is chosen from a list of prospective jurors handed both attorneys at the trial table. The foreman is usually the first juror chosen. Once a jury has been selected, counsel for the plaintiff has the right to make an opening statement in which he outlines, as briefly and as clearly as possible, the basis for his client's claim and states the amount of damages he seeks. The attorney for the defendant then proceeds to make his opening statement, in which he generally denies the plaintiff's claim. Witnesses are then called by the plaintiff to substantiate the claim set forth in the declaration. These witnesses are cross-examined by defendant's counsel in order to discredit their testimony and weaken the plaintiff's case. The witnesses for the defendant are next called to further destroy the plaintiff's case or minimize the amount of damages or both. Such witnesses, of course, are also subject to cross-examination by counsel for the plaintiff.

4. After all the testimony has been heard by the court and jury, or by the court sitting as a jury, counsel for the defendant or for the plaintiff may ask for a "directed verdict," which means that the case will be taken away from the jury and decided solely by the judge. The granting of a directed verdict on behalf of counsel for the defendant indicates that the plaintiff has failed to make out a

legal case sufficient even to be considered by the jury or by the judge sitting as a jury. An additional point must be made: when a case is heard by a jury, it is the latter that is exclusive judge of the facts, while the judge merely instructs the jury on the law applicable in the particular case.

5. If the trial judge dismisses the motion for a directed verdict, the counsel for the plaintiff sums up his case in an oral argument before the court and jury. Counsel for the defense then has the opportunity of rebutting the defendant's allegations in his closing argument. In many states the attorney for the plaintiff closes the case by attempting to rebut the arguments brought forth by the defendant's counsel.

6. After the jury returns its verdict for plaintiff or defendant, either counsel may request the court for a judgment "not withstanding the verdict." If, for example, a jury brings in a verdict of $10,000 in a negligence suit, defendant's counsel may request the trial judge to set the verdict aside on the ground that there was no legal evidence to support such a verdict.

7. If the motion to set aside the jury's verdict fails, judgment is entered for $10,000 against the defendant. However, the defeated party still has the opportunity to move for a new trial. If this motion is granted, a special day is set aside for the hearing before the same judge who heard the original trial, with only the counsel for both sides present to argue the legal merits of the case. If the request for a new trial is denied, the defeated party has the further right of appeal to a court of appellate jurisdiction.

*What are the steps in legal procedure in criminal cases?*

The procedure in criminal cases is roughly comparable to that in civil lawsuits. Criminal procedure is treated in detail in chapter 29.

*What happens if a defendant refuses to pay the amount of a judgment?*

The plaintiff—the party suing—may, through his counsel, direct the sheriff or marshall to execute upon the judgment; the latter makes a seizure or levy upon the judgment debtor's property, sells it at public auction, and applies the proceeds in payment of the judgment. If any money is left over from the proceeds of the sale, the balance is turned over to the defendant or judgment debtor, less costs of the sale.

*Suppose an automobile is owned jointly by the defendant and his wife, but the judgment is only against the husband. May the plaintiff enforce his judgment against the automobile?*

No. The judgment may be only enforced against property belonging exclusively to the defendant. If, after judgment, the defendant transfers his property to another person, including his spouse, the transaction may be set aside on the ground of fraud.

*What if the defendant has no property, but merely a salary. Can the salary be attached?*

Yes, in most cases.

*Is all property of a defendant subject to execution or seizure?*

No. Certain items are usually exempt by statute. These items include wearing apparel, tools of one's trade, livestock, household goods, and all but a given percentage of an employee's salary, usually ten percent.

*Is a sheriff allowed to break into a house to effect a levy?*

No. The sheriff or marshall must gain entry peacefully. Once in, however, the officer may use whatever force is necessary to effect an execution.

*Within what period must a plaintiff bring suit in a commercial transaction?*

If the creditor fails to bring suit within the period prescribed by state law, the right of action is said to be barred by the statute of limitations. This means that the creditor or plaintiff cannot recover. Following are the periods, by states, within which a creditor must bring suit:

STATUTES OF LIMITATIONS IN THE VARIOUS STATES AND TERRITORIES

| State or Territory | Open Accounts | Notes and Written Contracts | Judgments |
|---|---|---|---|
| Alabama | 3 yrs. | 6 yrs. | 20 yrs. |
| Alaska | 6 | 6 | 10 |
| Arizona | 3 | 6 | 5 |
| Arkansas | 3 | 5 | 10 |
| California | 4 | 4 | 5 |
| Colorado | 6 | 6 | 20 |
| Connecticut | 6 | 6 | None |
| Delaware | 3 | 6 | None |
| District of Columbia | 3 | 3 | 12 |
| Florida | 3 | 5 | 20 |
| Georgia | 4 | 6 | 20 |
| Hawaii | 6 | 6 | 10 |
| Idaho | 4 | 5 | 6 |
| Illinois | 5 | 10 | 20 |
| Indiana | 6 | 10 | 20 |
| Iowa | 5 | 10 | 20 |
| Kansas | 3 | 5 | 5 |
| Kentucky | 5 | 15 | 15 |
| Louisiana | 3 | 5 | 10 |
| Maine | 6 | 6 | 20 |
| Maryland | 3 | 3 | 12 |
| Massachusetts | 6 | 6 | 20 |
| Michigan | 6 | 6 | 10 |
| Minnesota | 6 | 6 | 10 |
| Mississippi | 3 | 6 | 7 |
| Missouri | 5 | 10 | 10 |
| Montana | 5 | 8 | 10 |
| Nebraska | 4 | 5 | 5 |
| Nevada | 4 | 6 | 6 |
| New Hampshire | 6 | 6 | 20 |
| New Jersey | 6 | 6 | 20 |
| New Mexico | 4 | 6 | 7 |
| New York | 6 | 6 | 20 |
| North Carolina | 3 | 3 | 10 |
| North Dakota | 6 | 6 | 10 |
| Ohio | 6 | 15 | 21 |
| Oklahoma | 3 | 5 | 5 |
| Oregon | 6 | 6 | 10 |
| Pennsylvania | 6 | 6 | 20 |
| Rhode Island | 6 | 6 | 20 |
| South Carolina | 6 | 6 | 20 |
| South Dakota | 6 | 6 | 20 |
| Tennessee | 6 | 6 | 10 |
| Texas | 2 | 4 | 10 |
| Utah | 4 | 6 | 8 |

| State or Territory | Open Accounts | Notes and Written Contracts | Judgments |
|---|---|---|---|
| Vermont | 6 | 6 | 8 |
| Virginia | 3 | 5 | 10 |
| Washington | 3 | 6 | 6 |
| West Virginia | 5 | 10 | 10 |
| Wisconsin | 6 | 6 | 20 |
| Wyoming | 8 | 10 | 5 |

*When does the period fixed by the statute of limitations begin?*

Generally, at the time the wrong was committed or the contract breached. Thus, in New York, if a contract was violated on January 10, the judgment creditor has six years from that date within which to file suit, else his claim is forever barred; and if he fails to execute on the judgment within twenty years, he can no longer recover.

## CHAPTER 2

## SMALL CLAIMS COURTS

*What exactly are small claims courts?*

They are courts of limited jurisdiction, variously known as courts of justices of the peace, municipal courts, small claims courts, traffic courts, and, more recently, district courts.

*What kinds of cases are tried in such courts?*

They involve consumer complaints concerning defective products, damages as a result of injuries sustained in an automobile accident, suits between landlords and tenants, breaches of contracts, and other civil suits.

*What sort of consumer complaints are heard in such courts?*

Quite a variety. They include deposits wrongfully witheld by landlords, breaches of warranties concerning defective merchandise, damage done by movers, clothing or laundry lost or damaged by cleaners and laundries.

*What is the philosophy behind such small claims courts?*

To allow the average person to prosecute or defend a claim without the expense of an attorney or costly and time-consuming litigation.

*How do you go about filing a claim in such a court?*

The procedure is simple. The first step is to determine whether your claim falls within the monetary jurisdiction of such a court. (Dollar limits covered later in chapter.) If it does, go to the clerk of such a court, under whatever name it calls itself, describe your claim to him, and he will help you file a simple statement of your legal grievance. If you are being sued, he will help you file your answer.

*Is formal legal procedure observed in such courts?*

No, at least not to the extent observed in higher courts. Rules of evidence are relaxed and the parties are allowed to state their respective sides with as little interference as possible. In the typical case the plaintiff, the person suing, testifies first. He may present witnesses and written evidence to substantiate his claim. Both the plaintiff and his witnesses may be cross-examined by the defendant. After the plaintiff presents his case in full, the defendant is allowed to give his side of the case and to present any evidence, oral or written, to back up his contentions. The plaintiff has a similar right to cross-examine the defendant and his witnesses. Unlike courts of higher jurisdiction, there is usually no summing up on the part of the litigants.

*How long does it take for a case to be heard before such a court?*

Usually it is a matter of weeks rather than months or even years.

*Is a decision made immediately after trial or is there a waiting period before a verdict is handed down?*

Normally a decision is handed down immediately after the case is heard. In cases where a difficult point of law is involved, the judge may wish to take a few days or even a few weeks in which to make up his mind, but this is unusual.

*Can you give an example of a case that might be filed in such a court?*

You purchase a dining room table and upon its arrival from the store you find it defective. You notify the store, and they refuse to do anything about the defect, claiming the table was perfect when delivered. All else having failed, you can go to the small claims court and file a suit for damages. The clerk will help you file the proper claim. Since the burden of proof is on you—the plaintiff or party suing—you will have to supply some corroborative evidence that the table was indeed defective upon arrival. You can establish this with either a photograph of the defect or by a witness, including a member of your household. It will then be up to the court to render a verdict favorable either to you or to the store.

*Do you have a right to appeal a verdict from a small claims court?*

Yes, in most states. A right of appeal is normally granted to the one dissatisfied with the decision, usually thirty to sixty days after the verdict is handed down. When an appeal is contemplated to a higher court, it is usually wise to retain legal counsel.

*How are parties notified that suit has been filed?*

A summons goes to the defendant, served either by registered mail, a deputy sheriff, or someone else acting for and on behalf of the small claims court. Together with the summons are the allegations providing the basis of the legal action so that the defendant is advised what the suit is all about. If he fails to answer within the prescribed time—usually thirty to sixty days—the court may hear the case *ex parte*, that is from the plaintiff's point of view. If the plaintiff makes out a prima facie case, a judgment will be entered against the defendant. Even so, the defendant may have a right of appeal when he did not actually receive any summons, was out of town at the time the summons was mailed, or has some other valid reason.

*What is the maximum amount you can sue for in small claims courts in the fifty states, and what does it cost?*

**Alabama**    $200–$1500; suit costs $3 to $5. Called county court, court of common pleas or civil court, and located in the county seat.

**Alaska**    $3,000; suit costs $11 to $15. Known as the district court and located in the larger towns.

**Arizona**    $500; suit costs $5 to $10. Filed in justice court in the county seat.

**Arkansas**    $300; suit costs $15. Filed in municipal court in most towns.

**California**    $300; suit costs $5. Filed in small claims branch of municipal or justice court in most of the larger towns.

**Colorado**    No small claims courts.

**Connecticut**    $750; suit costs $3. Filed in small claims division of circuit court in many towns.

**Delaware**    $1500; suit costs $10. Filed in justice of the peace or magistrate's courts in most towns.

**District of Columbia**    $750; filing fee $2. Filed in small claims branch of Court of General Sessions in Washington.

**Florida**    $250 to $1500; suit costs $3 to $10. Filed in small claims court, court of record, or magistrate's court in county seats and larger towns.

**Georgia** $100 to $1000; suit costs $2 to $15. Filed in small claims court, justice of the peace court, or recorder court in county seats.

**Hawaii** $300; suit costs $7 to $8. Filed in the district court of each island.

**Idaho** $200; suit costs $5. Filed in small claims court or justice court or magistrate's division of district court in county seats.

**Illinois** $1000; suit costs $7.50. Filed in circuit court of county seats.

**Indiana** While Indiana has no statewide system of small claims courts, it does have in Greenfield an experimental county court which is authorized to hear claims of $10 to $750 on an informal basis.

**Iowa** $100; suit costs $3. Filed in conciliation or small claims court, division of municipal court, in larger cities.

**Kansas** $500 to $3000; suit costs $5 to $15. Suits filed in magistrate's court in larger cities.

**Kentucky** $500; suit costs $3. Filed in magistrate's court, justice court, or before justice of peace in most towns.

**Louisiana** $1000; suit costs $1 to $20. Filed in city court or parish court in parish seat.

**Maine** $200; suit or filing costs $3. Filed in small claims division of district court in county seats and larger towns.

**Maryland** $2500; suit costs $4 to $13. Filed in small claims division of district court in county seats and larger towns, including Baltimore City.

**Massachusetts** $300; suit costs $1.78. Filed in district court of larger towns.

**Michigan** $300; suit costs $8.50. Filed in conciliation division, Detroit Court of Common Pleas, and district court of larger towns.

**Minnesota** $300 to $550; suit costs $2. Filed in conciliation court of county seats.

**Mississippi** $200; suit costs $6.50. Filed before justice of the peace in larger towns.

**Missouri** $3500; suit costs $11. Filed in magistrate's court in larger towns.

**Montana** $300; suit costs $7. Filed in justice court in most towns.

**Nebraska** There are no small claims courts.

**Nevada**    $300; suit costs $7. Filed in small claims division of justice court in county seats and larger towns.

**New Hampshire**    $200; suit costs $2.68. Filed in district or municipal court of most towns.

**New Jersey**    $200, and up to $500 for rent security cases; suit costs $4. Filed in small claims division of district court in county seats.

**New Mexico**    $2000; suit costs $14. Filed in small claims or magistrate's courts in Alburquerque and larger towns.

**New York**    $500; suit costs $3. Suits filed in small claims branch of city courts. In large cities parties may choose arbitration instead of trial, the decision of the arbitrators being binding.

**North Carolina**    $300; suit costs $3 to $6. Filed in small claims division of district court in county seats.

**North Dakota**    $200; suit costs $3. Filed in small claims court of county seats.

**Ohio**    $150; suit costs $2.75. Filed in county seats; tried in conciliation court, where most are settled; those not settled go to small claims courts.

**Oklahoma**    $400; suit costs $8 to $10. Filed in small claims division of county court in county seats.

**Oregon**    $200; suit costs $2 to $5. Filed in small claims court in county seats.

**Pennsylvania**    $500; suit costs $7.50 to $15. Filed in district justice court in most towns, municipal court in Philadelphia, and county court in Pittsburgh. Arbitration is compulsory in Philadelphia, but arbitrator's decision can be appealed.

**Rhode Island**    $300; suit costs $1.57. Suits filed in small claims division of district court in larger towns.

**South Carolina**    $100; no filing fee. Filed in magistrate's court in most towns.

**South Dakota**    $500; filing fee $2. Filed in municipal court, justice of the peace or district courts of county seats.

**Tennessee**    $3000; suit costs $8.75. Filed in civil division of general sessions in county seats.

**Texas**    $200; suit costs $5 to $7.50. Filed before justice of the peace in most towns.

**Utah**    $200; filing fee $6. Filed in city court or before justice of the peace in larger towns.

**Vermont**    $250; filing fee under $5. Filed in small claims division of district court.

**Virginia** $300 to $3000; filing fee $5. Filed in civil or county court in most towns.

**Washington** $200; filing fee $2 to $5. Filed before small claims division of justice court in county seats.

**West Virginia** $300; filing fee $5. Filed before justice of the peace in most towns.

**Wisconsin** $500; filing fee $4.50. Filed before small claims branch of county court of county seats.

**Wyoming** $200; filing fee $6. Filed in county courts of county seats.

*Can you still engage a lawyer to represent you before a small claims court?*

Yes, except in California, Idaho, Michigan, Nevada, Oregon, and Washington.

## CHAPTER 3

## YOUR LAWYER AND YOU

*Why is the choice of a lawyer important?*

The wise choice of an attorney can be one of the most important acts of your life. He may be the difference between your success or failure in business; his counsel and experience may help you avoid many of the legal pitfalls to which virtually all laymen are subject from time to time. A good lawyer can be both friend and counselor. Like your family physician, he should be chosen carefully and wisely and should be discarded only for the most persuasive reasons, that is, when he has proved to be incompetent or dishonest.

*What qualities should one look for in an attorney?*

1. A good lawyer should enjoy an excellent reputation both in the community in which he lives and among his fellow lawyers.

2. A good lawyer should be thorough. He should prepare his legal documents and cases with care and deliberation, so that no unforeseen development will impair his client's case.

3. A good lawyer should have a sound grasp of legal principles. While it is impossible for even the best lawyers to know all the law, a successful attorney not only has a firm grasp of basic fundamentals but has the legal mind capable of wrestling with an involved set of facts and coming up with a conclusion that makes legal sense. Thus a keen, analytical mind is one of the chief qualities of any lawyer.

4. A good lawyer should be tenacious. He does not give up readily, nor is he easily discouraged. If he represents a client in an accident case, he makes a thorough investigation of all the facts; he interviews witnesses, he obtains and examines copies of police

and traffic accident reports, and he does whatever else is necessary to determine the strength and weakness of his client's case. Only when an attorney is in possession of all the relevant facts is he in a position to evaluate his client's case properly, whether it be for damages as a result of an automobile collision or a suit for libel or slander.

*Is an older attorney to be preferred over a younger one?*

As with individuals in general, mere age is no guarantor of a lawyer's ability or wisdom. Although an older lawyer may have had more experience than a young attorney, he may have been unable to profit by it. He may also lack the intelligence, training, background, and resourcefulness of the younger man. The chronological age of the attorney employed is not so important as his maturity, competence, and sagacity. Equally as important is the client's confidence in the integrity and ability of his counsel. For if that confidence is impaired, though the counsel be the best obtainable, the relationship between attorney and client is apt to deteriorate rapidly.

*To what extent should a client shop around for an attorney?*

Many laymen are likely to seek an attorney merely in terms of price. If one attorney asks a $1000 fee for representation in a divorce case, the client may engage another attorney who promises to represent him for $500 or even less. In this respect the client may be penny-wise and pound-foolish. What he should consider is not so much the attorney's fee, but his experience, intelligence, perseverance, character, and reputation.

*Should one choose a specialist over an attorney with a general practice?*

Like physicians, lawyers of late have tended to specialize. There are attorneys who specialize in labor law. There are those who engage primarily in divorce or criminal law, and there are, among many other specialists, those who engage primarily in negligence work, that is, who represent claimants involved in automobile accidents or other damage suits. But the fact than an attorney handles a great many negligence cases does not mean that he cannot handle divorces or write wills; he often does, though usually not with the flair of the specialist who has devoted almost his entire legal life to one special part of the law. Obviously the specialist in divorce, everything else being equal, is more likely to achieve better results in a divorce case than the specialist in labor law. Just as obviously the attorney who has successfully handled many automobile accident cases is more likely to obtain better settlements than the general practitioner who only occasionally handles a damage suit for negligence.

*Do specialists exist in all communities?*

No. Most legal specialists practice in the larger cities. In the smaller towns the lawyer in general practice is very much similar to the old-time family physician or to the modern general practitioner. But even in the larger cities, such as New York, Chicago, Los Angeles, and Philadelphia, the majority of attorneys are engaged in the general practice of law, and are usually competent to deal with almost every variety of legal matter.

*In engaging an attorney, is it wiser to choose a firm of lawyers or an attorney in practice for himself?*

Much depends on the nature of the legal business and the temperament and personality of the individual. A large corporation is likely to engage the services of a firm having twenty or more attorneys as associates or assistants. Many large legal firms also have members who specialize in various fields of the law. One member may represent insurance companies. A second may handle labor relations for large business accounts. A third may handle the trial work for the entire firm. The advantages of hiring a large firm is that you are buying a "name" and the prestige that usually goes along with it. In addition, the firm, because it is successful, is likely to have the respect of other members of the bar, of the judges, and of the business community as well. Many clients employ large firms, however, not because they need them for their legal business, but because the association bolsters the client's ego and provides a status symbol. The disadvantages of engaging a large firm are, first, that the fees are likely to be much higher, and second, that the client may not get the personal attention he might receive from an attorney practicing on his own.

*How should one actually go about choosing an attorney?*

A strong recommendation from a friend or relative who has encountered a legal problem similar to the one now confronting you is as good a reason as any for choosing that particular attorney. But beware of "ambulance chasers" and "friends" who recommend a particular lawyer only because they expect a part of the attorney's fee for the recommendation. Many lawyers obtain clients, especially when negligence is involved, in this unethical manner. Under the code of ethics of the American Bar Association no attorney is permitted to solicit business directly or indirectly; nor is he allowed to pay those who refer legal business to him.

## What exactly is an "ambulance chaser"?

An ambulance chaser is an unethical attorney who solicits negligence cases, usually those of persons involved in automobile accidents. He may do this directly and brazenly or indirectly through an organization. If the former, the attorney may go to see the prospective client and request that he be permitted to represent him. He will inform the client that he has had wide and varied success with this particular type of accident, and then he will proceed to reel off impressive amounts he claims he has obtained, either as a result of settlement or of a trial by jury. He will then and there suggest that the client sign a power of attorney authorizing the lawyer to proceed with the case. Obviously, no client should ever consider engaging such an attorney. To the contrary, the name of the soliciting lawyer should be given to the local bar association for disciplinary action.

## How do "ambulance chasers" work indirectly?

Through the intermediary of men in key positions who are ready to turn over business to the attorney, with the understanding that the "ambulance chaser" and the "contact" are to share in whatever fee is ultimately obtained. The contact, who may be an orderly in the hospital in which the client is confined, first obtains the client's confidence and then tells him that he knows a very successful "accident" lawyer who has made a specialty of handling just his type of case. The contact will impress the patient with his narration of verdicts that the lawyer is alleged to have secured. He will suggest to the prospective client that he see the attorney for an interview. If the client is naive or gullible, he may readily agree.

Some ambulance chasers maintain elaborate organizations. They arrange with tavern owners, with orderlies and attendants in hospitals, and with whomever else they may come in contact, to have legal business referred to them—with the assurance that these individuals will get a portion of the final fee. Some ambulance chasers, on the other hand, prefer to pay their contacts immediately in cash rather than await the results of the case.

*Is there any objection to signing a power of attorney in an accident case?*

Not as a rule. No client should ever sign such a power when it is presented by an ambulance-chasing attorney. But there is otherwise no objection when an attorney whom the client has chosen requests that he sign such a power. A power of attorney simply authorizes the lawyer to represent the client in a given matter, usually a negligence case, under certain terms which are defined in the contract.

*What are those terms?*

They usually authorize the attorney to represent the client in negotiating a settlement or, if the latter is impossible, in instituting a suit on behalf of the client against defendant. The attorney's fee for services to be rendered is also set forth in the power.

*How is such a power of attorney usually worded?*

A simple power of attorney may read as follows: "I, John Smith, hereby authorize my attorney, William Johnson, to represent me in my claim for personal injuries as a result of an accident which occurred on or about January 15, 1973, at the corner of Baltimore and Calvert Streets, Baltimore, Maryland, when the automobile I was operating was struck by the automobile owned and operated by Francis Jones, as a result of which I sustained personal injuries, loss of time from my employment, and property damage to my car. I authorize my attorney to settle or compromise this claim and, if a satisfactory settlement cannot be effected, I authorize him to institute suit against the defendant and to try the case on my behalf. I agree to pay my said attorney a fee of twenty-five per cent of the gross amount of the settlement, and a fee of one-third in the event suit is instituted and the case tried.

_____Claimant."

*Does a client have to pay an attorney a retainer for representation in an accident case?*

No. Negligence lawyers take accident cases on what is known as a contingent basis. The attorney receives a fee only if he is success-

ful in obtaining a settlement or, if the case must be tried, in procuring a favorable verdict. If he fails to obtain a satisfactory
settlement or if he is unable to obtain a favorable verdict, the attorney gets no fee whatever. In short, since a contingent fee is
based on the successful efforts of the lawyer employed, the client
has nothing to lose and everything to gain by employing counsel
on this basis.

*Who determines whether a settlement is satisfactory or not?*

Usually the attorney, but he rarely ever makes a settlement without the express consent or approval of his client. When a settlement is finally negotiated, the attorney will consult with his client,
who will advise him whether or not to accept the final offer of the
defendant, usually the insurance company.

*What happens if the client is not satisfied with the amount settled
for?*

He can ask his attorney either to reopen negotiations or to file
suit. He can also, if he wishes, dismiss his attorney, provided he
compensates him for legal services already rendered.

*Is switching attorneys in the middle of negotiations for a settle-
ment a desirable thing to do?*

Not usually. If, however, the client feels strongly that his attorney
is not, for one reason or another, properly representing his interests, he has a legal right to discharge him and to engage other
counsel. But he may only do so, usually, after the attorney has
been paid for legal services rendered up to the date of dismissal.
Until he has been paid the attorney has a right to retain all papers
and correspondence of the client.

*Suppose a client wishes to employ counsel in a nonnegligence
matter but has no funds at all. What can he do?*

He can seek assistance from one of the many Legal Aid Societies
throughout the country. To be eligible for Legal Aid, a client
must prove that his income and assets are so inadequate that he
cannot afford to pay *any* fee. Legal Aid services are free. There is
no charge for advice or counsel. Most Legal Aid Societies are
community service agencies, and are supported by contributions
from the city or the state.

*What is Lawyers' Referral?*

The Lawyers' Referral service provides a means whereby any person who needs the services of an attorney and can afford to pay for one, but who does not have one and is too unsophisticated to find one on his own, may be referred to an attorney through the local bar association. Typically, the applicant pays a registration fee of one dollar for the referral and pays the counsel a fixed fee of five dollars for the initial consultation, which may last up to thirty minutes. The attorney makes a normal charge for any additional services. Periodic reports are required of the attorneys.

When a dispute arises between attorney and client, they agree to arbitration by the Lawyers' Referral Committee. Lawyers' Referral is a sort of halfway house between free legal aid and private legal counsel. The legal fees charged for divorce, for example, are much less than normal, since clients who use Lawyers' Referral are apt to come from low-income groups. Many clients are directed to Lawyers' Referral by Legal Aid societies if their incomes suggest that they can afford to pay some fee.

*Does Legal Aid handle all kinds of legal cases?*

No. Legal Aid will not handle criminal and divorce cases.

*What about Lawyers' Referral?*

All kinds of legal matters are handled by Lawyers' Referral, including criminal and divorce cases.

*How does Lawyers' Referral actually work?*

Lawyers' Referral consists of a pool of lawyers who serve in rotation and provide a sort of potluck of legal assistance. A client cannot have the lawyer of his choice; he must take the lawyer whose name currently heads the list. If the client is dissatisfied with the lawyer chosen, he is eligible, by paying another consultation fee, to use the services of the attorney next in line.

*What about representation in a criminal case if the defendant is without funds?*

If the accused is without funds and charged with a serious crime such as murder, rape, robbery, larceny, embezzlement, or manslaughter, the judge of the criminal court will appoint counsel to represent the defendant at the state's expense. In many communities the practice has been extended to those charged with misdemeanors or less serious crimes.

*Is it good practice to retain counsel by the year?*

Yes, if the business of the client so warrants. Many businessmen retain an attorney on an annual basis, paying either a flat fee for all the legal work likely to come up during the year or a combination of flat fee, for routine legal matters, and special fees for non-routine matters that require extra work. By far the best arrangement is for client and counsel to have a written contract specifying the work to be done by the attorney or firm, so that there will be no misunderstanding about what the retainer actually covers.

*How confidential is the relationship between an attorney and his client?*

The most confidential known to the law. No lawyer is permitted to disclose information communicated to him by his client, even when the lawyer is called as a witness. For violation of his trust, an attorney may be subject to disciplinary action by his local bar association and to suit if damage occur from a breach of the privileged communication.

*What responsibility does a lawyer have to his client?*

An attorney is both an officer of the court and the agent of the client who employs him. He has an obligation to be fair and honest with both. When an attorney accepts a client, he undertakes to exercise ordinary care, skill, and diligence in handling the client's affairs. In general, any agreement by the attorney within the scope of his authority, and, in particular, any agreement respecting procedure or the conduct of the trial, binds the client. The attorney must keep his client informed of the state of his business and of what is being done so that the client can keep abreast of what is going on concerning the matter for which he retained counsel. This does not mean, of course, that the lawyer must give his client a blow-by-blow description of everything that takes place. It does mean that he must keep his client posted on the major legal steps taken on his behalf.

*What does a client owe his counsel?*

The duty to give a full and fair disclosure of all the facts relevant to his case. When you consult an attorney, therefore, be sure to tell him the truth, the whole truth, and nothing but the truth, even if the facts seem damaging to your case. There is a practical reason for this: only when the attorney is in full possession of all the facts can he act intelligently on the matter at hand. No sensible patient conceals information that may help a physician effect a diagnosis and cure. Yet many clients withhold facts in the mistaken belief that the less a lawyer knows about the real situation the better. Given all the facts, an attorney is able to determine which are relevant and which are not, which are useful and which are harmful to his client's interests. No layman can possibly do this. Presented with damaging information, a careful attorney prepares his defense accordingly, in order not to be caught unawares by the opposition. It is far worse to have the opposition bring out the damaging information when the attorney is least prepared for it.

*May an attorney be discharged before the conclusion of a legal matter?*

Yes. An attorney may be discharged at any time, provided the client compensates counsel for services performed to the day of dismissal. Failing to receive adequate compensation, an attorney can file suit against the client to recover reasonable compensation.

*As a general rule, when is it best to engage counsel?*

As soon as an important legal matter arises. Many cases, especially suits to recover damages for personal injuries as a result of an automobile accident, have been lost by the client's delay in employing an attorney. For example, in an automobile accident case, it is often imperative that an investigation into the facts be instituted as quickly as possible. Witnesses must be questioned and their statements reduced to writing and signed. Photographs showing the damage to the automobile or to the point of impact may have to be taken, as well as photographs revealing personal injuries. In addition, reports from the Traffic Accident Bureau or from the police department will have to be obtained in order for counsel to have all the facts in his possession. What the client must remember is that the defendant, usually represented by an insurance company, makes a prompt and thorough investigation with the idea of relieving the defendant of liability, or at least of minimizing the client's claim. That is why the client should employ competent counsel as soon as possible after a serious automobile accident.

*When else should one employ counsel promptly?*

It is a good idea to consult an attorney whenever a legal paper is served on an individual; when he becomes involved in a personal injury or property damage claim; when he is arrested in a criminal action; when he wants to sue or is being sued; when he contemplates going into business; when he buys or sells real estate; and, finally, when he writes a contract, a deed, or any other important legal document.

## CHAPTER 4

## THE MATTER OF FEES

*What determines a lawyer's fee?*

1. The nature and extent of the services to be performed.

2. The difficulties of the case.

3. The novelty and doubtfulness of the question involved.

4. The amount of time it is necessary to devote to the matter, including conferences, telephone calls, research, etc.

5. The sum involved.

6. The importance and magnitude of the case.

7. The results attained by the lawyer's efforts and the benefits and advantages they bring to the client.

8. The attorney's experience, skill, and standing in his profession.


*Are cases other than negligence suits handled by attorneys on a contingent basis?*

Contingent fees are usually confined to negligence suits and to cases contesting a will. This means that the lawyer's fee depends upon whether or not he wins his case. If he wins, he gets a share of whatever is recovered, depending on the agreement entered into between client and counsel. If the attorney loses, there is usually no charge.


*What is a retainer?*

A retainer is a portion of the total fee paid by the client to his attorney; it is paid upon the latter's acceptance of a case. It binds the attorney to act for and on behalf of the client and by the same token prevents him from accepting any business antagonistic to his client's interests. In addition, a retainer assures the lawyer of at least part payment for the services he is about to render.

*What do lawyers usually charge the average client for obtaining a reduction on real or personal property assessments?*

The usual fee is about one-half of the first year's tax savings. Such cases are generally handled on a contingent basis, with the attorney obtaining a fee only if he is successful. To make certain that the case is to be handled on a contingent basis, it is good practice for the client to obtain a letter from the lawyer to that effect.

*What do lawyers generally charge to collect commercial debts?*

Many attorneys charge 21 percent of the first $1000, 15 percent on amounts over $1000. There is usually a minimum commission of $25, and on claims of $42 or less, attorneys usually charge 50 percent of the amount collected. Collection cases are also usually handled on a contingent basis, so that the client has nothing to lose in case the debt is uncollected.

*What are the average fees if an attorney has to file suit on small claims?*

Suit fees are not contingent. On claims of $100 or less, most lawyers charge a suit fee of $7.50, provided the total compensation does not exceed 50 per cent of the amount collected. This fee is in addition to commissions. It might be added that the above is intended to apply to current commercial claims. On difficult claims, the schedule of fees is likely to be higher. Of course, an attorney and client may agree to any fee in collection matters, unless the fee requested is actually unconscionable.

*What other contingent fees are there, and in what kinds of cases are they encountered?*

1. Condemnation suits involving land. If the suit is settled before trial, the fee is 25 per cent of the amount above the initial offer; if there is a trial, one third of the amount procured, if there has been no offer or one third of the amount above the initial offer.

2. Contracts and will contests. If the case is settled before suit is brought, the fee is 25 per cent of the amount procured; if settled after suit, one third; if settled after trial and appeal, 40 per cent.

3. Personal injury cases. The fee is one fourth to one third if the case is settled before suit. If settled after suit, one third—unless

the case is appealed or retried, in which case the fee might be 40 per cent.

4. Workmen's Compensation cases. The fee is usually 10 to 20 per cent of the amount awarded.

*What do lawyers normally charge for the drawing of contracts?*

Many lawyers charge $50 for writing a simple contract, chattel mortgage and note, a conditional sales agreement, or a power of attorney. For a simple prenuptial or antenuptial agreement the average fee is likely to be around $250.

*What do lawyers generally charge for organizing a corporation?*

For complete corporate organization work, including articles of incorporation, corporate organization minutes, including the first shareholders' meeting, first directors' meeting, together with original issuance of stock and conferences, the minimum fee is likely to be $250. If the corporate organization or reorganization is complex and involves large sums of money, the fee can easily go into the thousands, or tens of thousands.

*What do lawyers generally charge to take an appeal from one court to another?*

The minimum fee to take an appeal to the U.S. Supreme Court is usually $2,000 or more; to a U.S. circuit court of appeals, $1,000; to the U.S. Tax Court, $500; to a state's highest court of appeal, $500—unless the appeal concerns personal injury, negligence, or workmen's compensation, in which case the appeal is often handled on a contingent basis.

*What fees are payable in bankruptcy matters?*

For preparing and filing a voluntary petition, schedule, and statement of affairs, there is usually a minimum fee of $250; for preparing and filing an involuntary petition, there is a minimum fee of $250; for preparing and filing an objection to discharge, there is usually a minimum fee of $25 an hour and/or a minimum fee of $100. It is always good practice in bankruptcy, as well as in all other legal matters, for both attorney and client to agree as to precisely what the fee and court costs will be, so there will be no subsequent misunderstanding.

*What do lawyers generally charge in adoption proceedings?*

The usual minimum fee in an uncontested adoption proceeding is $250. If the adoption is contested and the attorney has to try the case, the minimum fee for the trial is likely to be $350 a day for each day in court.

*What is the minimum fee lawyers usually charge to try a case in a U.S. district court?*

Two hundred dollars for each day spent in court.

*What is the usual minimum fee for a preliminary hearing before a United States commissioner?*

One hundred twenty-five dollars if the hearing takes place in the city; $200 if it takes place out of town. If the case is tried, there is usually an additional fee of $200 a day.

*What do lawyers normally charge to represent clients in the criminal courts?*

If the client is charged with murder in the first degree, the minimum fee is likely to be $1,500; if the attorney represents two men at the same murder trial, the usual fee is $2,500; if the lawyer represents a client charged with second degree murder, the minimum fee is usually $1,250. For manslaughter cases, a fee of $750 is generally charged; for representation in other felony cases, including one day of trial, a fee of $250 may be charged; for misdemeanors, the usual minimum fee is $200.

*What is the usual fee for representation in a parole or probation matter?*

Approximately $150.

*What about representation in traffic courts?*

The amount will vary with the gravity of the charge. If the violation is a serious one, such as drunken driving, the fee may be $1,000 or more, since conviction may lead to the imprisonment of the driver or to the revocation of the driver's license. For traffic violations that do not carry a jail sentence, the fee is much less, ranging from $25 to $100. In all cases, the wisest procedure is to ask the attorney in advance what his fee will be.

*What do attorneys usually charge in divorce cases?*

In the average uncontested divorce case, the usual fee is likely to be anywhere from $250 to $500, depending on the status of the attorney and the wealth of the parties. If the parties are wealthy and the property settlement complicated, the fee may range from $1,000 to $100,000, again depending upon the time and effort required to reach a property settlement, the wealth of the parties, the status of the lawyers involved, and the time and effort expended.

*What about contested divorce cases?*

Contested divorce cases are usually expensive, since they involve much time in court. Here again, much depends on the property involved, the time consumed in the preparation and trial of the case, and the status of the attorneys involved. If the husband earns a modest salary, the fee, in the average contested divorce case, may be about $500. But if the stakes are high and the trial lasts for days, the fee may range from $1,000 to $50,000.

*What do lawyers charge for drawing an agreement for the sale of real estate?*

The fee depends on the value of the property. For the average house the fee is likely to be anywhere from $100 to $150. If the value of the house is higher, the fee is likely to be larger.

*What does an attorney usually charge to represent the seller at a settlement for a house?*

The average fee runs anywhere from $150 to $200.

*What do attorneys charge to draw up a residential or apartment lease?*

Fifty dollars. For drawing a commercial lease the usual fee is $150.

*How about partnership agreements?*

A simple partnership agreement is likely to cost around $150. Limited or more complicated agreements, from $250 to $500.

*What do lawyers charge for drawing up a simple will?*

The usual fee is $50. If the will is more complicated and involves larger sums of money, the fee is likely to range from $100 upwards. However, if the attorney drawing the will or trust agreement is made either the executor, co-executor, trustee or co-trustee, he may waive the fee for preparing the agreement, since he will receive commissions as executor or trustee of the estate.

*What do lawyers charge for an office consultation?*

The usual fee is $25 to $50 an hour.

*What do attorneys charge for complete representation in the sale of a business?*

A usual fee is 3 per cent of the sale price of the business.

*What do lawyers charge for consultations about tax matters, such as tax consequences of contracts, pension plans, etc?*

Approximately $25 to $50 an hour.

*What does an attorney charge to represent one who is under investigation for income tax evasion?*

Much depends on the work involved. For a hearing or conference with an agent of the Internal Revenue Service, many tax consultants charge $200 a day. When an attorney actually defends the accused in a federal court, the fee is usually negotiated privately between the attorney and his client. The fee will depend, of course, on the complexity of the charges, the amount of time and labor involved, and the skill and success of the attorney. Whenever possible, a client should attempt to ascertain in advance what the fees are likely to be.

*What do attorneys generally charge for the title examination to real estate?*

If the property involved is valued at $3,500 or less, there is generally a minimum charge of $60; if between $3,500 and $8,000, the fee is usually one per cent plus $25; if between $8,000 and $50,000, the fee is generally one half of one per cent plus $65; if between

$50,000 and $300,000, the fee is likely to be $4 a thousand in excess of $50,000, plus $315; if between $300,000 and $500,000, the fee is usually $3 a thousand in excess of $300,000, plus $1,315; if more than $500,000, the fee is usually $2.50 a thousand in excess of $500,000, plus $1,915.

## CHAPTER 5

## YOUR MARRIAGE

*Is marriage a contract?*

Only in part. Marriage is a status fixed by law. A marriage differs from a contract in several important respects. In an ordinary contract the parties, if they so wish, may modify the terms of the agreement, or even cancel it. Thus a landlord and tenant may, by agreement, modify the terms of an existing lease. In marriage, the husband and wife may not modify the terms of the nuptial contract. They cannot, for example, mutually agree to dissolve the marriage and wed other spouses except in accordance with the law. In the average contract, again, the only test is one of mental capacity. Did the parties at the time of the agreement understand the nature of their act? In marriage much more is required. The husband, for example, must be physically able to consummate the union; that is, he must be able to have sexual intercourse with his wife. If he is impotent at the time of marriage, the marriage may be dissolved by annulment. There is also the question of age. The contracts of those under legal age, usually twenty-one, may be rescinded or voided when the youngster reaches his or her majority. This is not true of marriage. Children of sixteen may lawfully marry in a number of states if they have their parents' consent.

*What are the marriage requirements in the various states?*

**Alabama**    Age of consent for males seventeen, females fourteen. Personal or written consent of parents and bond for $200 required where male is under twenty-one or female under eighteen, unless such minor has previously been married. However, marriage is not invalid if license is issued without parents' consent. A blood test is required, but there is no waiting period either before or after a license is issued. Common law marriages are not recognized.

**Alaska**    Male between eighteen and nineteen and female between sixteen and eighteen require written, verified consent of parents or guardian before license is issued. There is a three-day waiting period before marriage. Common law marriages are not recognized, but a medical test is required. If the bride is eighteen and the groom twenty-one, no parental consent is required.

**Arizona**   Males under eighteen and females under sixteen may not marry; consent of parents is required where male is under twenty-one or girl under eighteen. A blood test must be taken. There is no waiting period between issuance of license and wedding ceremony. Common law marriages are forbidden but, if legal in state where performed, will be recognized in Arizona.

**Arkansas**   Age of consent with parental approval is eighteen for males and sixteen for females. If either party is under minimum age, marriage is void unless bride is pregnant; parental consent required if male is under twenty-one and female is under eighteen; blood test required; common law marriages not recognized unless legal in state where performed. There is a three-day waiting period between intention to marry and issuance of license. However, failure to comply does not make marriage void.

**California**   Written consent of parent or guardian must be filed with court clerk where male is under twenty-one and female under eighteen; approval and court order also required where boy is under eighteen and girl under sixteen; blood test necessary; common law marriage valid if consummated before 1895; out of state common law marriages legal if valid in state where contracted; no waiting period before or after issuance of marriage license.

**Colorado**   Parental consent required if male is under twenty-one and female under eighteen; common law marriages are recognized; blood test obligatory; no waiting period for marriage license.

**Connecticut**   Marriage of persons under sixteen allowed only under exceptional circumstances; marriage without parental consent allowed if male is twenty-one and female eighteen; blood test required; common law marriages not recognized; there is a four-day waiting period between issuance of license and ceremony.

**Delaware**   Minimum age for marriage is eighteen for males and sixteen for females; where either party is under nineteen, written consent of parents or guardian required; medical examination is obligatory; there is a waiting period of twenty-four hours before ceremony, or ninety-six hours where both parties are nonresidents; common law marriages are invalid but will be recognized if valid in state where contracted.

**District of Columbia** Parental consent required where male is under twenty-one and female is under eighteen; blood test required; there is a four-day waiting period between application and issuance of marriage license; common law marriages are recognized.

**Florida** Parental consent needed if either party is under twenty-one with certain exceptions; there is a three-day waiting period before issuance of license; physical examination and blood test both required; common law marriages consummated are invalid.

**Georgia** Parental consent required if applicants have not passed their nineteenth birthday; blood test required; there is a three-day waiting period except where both parties are over twenty-one or, regardless of age, the woman signs affidavit of pregnancy; common law marriages are recognized.

**Hawaii** Parental consent required if boy is under twenty and girl is under eighteen; no waiting period for license; blood test required; common law marriages are not recognized.

**Idaho** Parental consent required if male is under twenty-one and female is under eighteen; blood test mandatory except on proof that an emergency exists; common law marriages are recognized.

**Illinois** Parental consent required if male is under twenty-one and female is under eighteen; no waiting period for license; common law marriages are void until solemnized; blood test necessary.

**Indiana** Parental consent necessary if groom is under twenty-one and bride under eighteen; there is a three-day waiting period between application and issuance of marriage license; blood test necessary; common law marriages void after January 1, 1958.

**Iowa** Parental consent required if male is under twenty-one and female is under eighteen; there is a three-day waiting period between application and issuance of marriage license; a blood test is necessary; common law marriages are recognized.

**Kansas** Parental consent necessary if groom is under twenty-one and bride is under eighteen; blood test mandatory; there is a three-day waiting period between application and issuance of marriage license but this may be waived by judge; common law marriages are recognized.

**Kentucky**  Parental consent required where either party is under eighteen unless one of the parties has previously been married; blood test necessary; there is a three-day waiting period between application and issuance of license; common law marriages not recognized.

**Louisiana**  Parental consent required if male is under eighteen and female under sixteen, but marriages between minors without parental consent are nonetheless binding; blood test necessary; there is a three-day waiting period between issuance of license and marriage ceremony; common law marriages are not recognized.

**Maine**  Parental consent required if male is under twenty and female is under eighteen; there is a five-day waiting period between application and issuance of license; blood test necessary; common law marriages probably not recognized in state, but probably would be recognized if contracted in state where they are legal.

**Maryland**  Parental consent required if boy is under eighteen and girl under sixteen; no consent required if girl is eighteen and boy twenty-one; there is a forty-eight-hour waiting period between application and issuance of license; no blood test required; common law marriages not permitted but will be recognized if valid where contracted.

**Massachusetts**  Parental consent required if boy is under twenty-one and girl is under eighteen; there is a three-day waiting period before marriage; a blood test is required; common law marriages are not recognized.

**Michigan**  Parental consent not required if both parties are over eighteen; blood test necessary; there is a three-day waiting period before marriage; common law marriages not recognized since January 1, 1957.

**Minnesota**  Parental consent required if bride is under eighteen and groom under twenty-one; there is a five-day waiting period before marriage; common law marriages are not recognized; no blood test is needed.

**Mississippi**  Parental consent necessary if male is under twenty-one and female is under eighteen; three-day waiting period unless parties receive waiver from court; blood test is required; common law marriages no longer valid.

**Missouri**  Parental consent needed if male is under twenty-one and female is under eighteen; there is a three-day waiting period before marriage; blood test is required; common law marriages are no longer valid.

**Montana**   Those over nineteen may wed without parental consent; there is a five-day waiting period before marriage; blood test is necessary; common law marriages are recognized.

**Nebraska**   Parental consent needed if either party is under twenty-one; blood test required; common law marriages no longer recognized; there is no waiting period after marriage license is issued.

**Nevada**   Parental consent required if groom is under twenty-one and bride is under eighteen; there is no waiting period nor blood test; common law marriages are not recognized.

**New Hampshire**   Males of twenty and females of eighteen do not require parental consent; there is a five-day waiting period before marriage; a blood test is needed; common law marriages are not recognized.

**New Jersey**   Parental consent required for males under twenty-one and females under eighteen; blood test required; there is a three-day waiting period before marriage; common law marriages are no longer recognized.

**New Mexico**   Parental consent required if bride is under eighteen and groom under twenty-one; there is a three-day waiting period before marriage can be performed; medical examination required; common law marriages not recognized.

**New York**   Parental consent needed if bride is under eighteen and groom is under twenty-one; blood test required; there is a three-day waiting period; common law marriages are now prohibited.

**North Carolina**   Parental consent needed if bride is under eighteen and groom is under twenty-one; blood test required; there is no waiting period; common law marriages not recognized unless contracted in state where such marriages are valid.

**North Dakota**   Parental consent needed if bride is under eighteen and groom is under twenty-one; there is no waiting period before marriage; a medical test is required; common law marriages are not recognized.

**Ohio**   Parental consent needed if either party is under twenty-one, with certain exceptions; there is a five-day waiting period; a medical test is required; common law marriages are recognized.

**Oklahoma**   Parental consent required if male is under twenty-one and female is under eighteen; blood test necessary; there is no waiting period; common law marriages are recognized.

**Oregon**   Parental consent needed if girl is under eighteen and boy is under twenty-one; blood test is required; there is a seven-day waiting period before marriage; common law marriages do not exist in Oregon but will be recognized if valid in state where contracted.

**Pennsylvania**   Parental consent required if either party is under twenty-one; there is a three-day waiting period before marriage; a blood test is necessary; common law marriages are recognized.

**Rhode Island**   Parental consent not required if either party is over twenty-one; there is no waiting period before marriage; a blood test is required; common law marriages are recognized.

**South Carolina**   No parental consent required if either party is over eighteen; there is a one-day waiting period; common law marriages are recognized; a blood test is required.

**South Dakota**   No parental consent required if both parties are over twenty-one; there is no waiting period before marriage; a medical test is required; common law marriages are not recognized.

**Tennessee**   Parties eighteen years or more do not need parental consent; there is a three-day waiting period; a blood test must be taken; common law marriages are not recognized unless legal in state where contracted.

**Texas**   Parental consent required if bride is under eighteen and groom under nineteen; no waiting period; common law marriages recognized; medical test required.

**Utah**   Parental consent required if male is under twenty-one and female is under eighteen; there is no waiting period; common law marriages are not recognized; blood test required.

**Vermont**   Parental consent required if either party is under eighteen; no waiting period; a medical test is required; common law marriages are not recognized.

**Virginia**   Parental consent required if either party is under twenty-one; no waiting period; common law marriages are not recognized; a blood test is required.

**Washington**   Parental consent necessary if either party is under eighteen; there is a three-day waiting period; no blood test required; common law marriages not recognized in Washington but are valid if recognized in state where contracted.

**West Virginia**   Parental consent necessary if either party is under twenty-one; three-day waiting period; common law marriages are not recognized; a medical test is required.

**Wisconsin** Parental consent required if bride is under eighteen and groom is under twenty-one; blood test necessary; there is no waiting period; common law marriages are not recognized.

**Wyoming** Parental consent necessary if either party is under twenty-one; no waiting period before ceremony; common law marriages are not recognized; a blood test is required.

*Is the subsequent marriage invalid if the boy or girl falsifies his or her age in the application for marriage and marries without parental consent?*

Yes, in most states. However, a few states—such as Alabama— provide that a marriage is still binding if the license is procured without parental consent, even in those states where such consent is required.

*What is a common-law marriage?*

A common-law marriage is one in which a man and woman represent themselves as husband and wife in the community in which they live, even though they were never actually married by a minister, judge, or other official.

*Does a common-law marriage have to be in writing?*

No. It may be entered into verbally. What is important is the intention of the parties that they be considered man and wife by the community in which they live.

*Are witnesses necessary to a common-law marriage?*

No.

*Are the children of such marriages legitimate?*

Yes, in those states that recognize such marriages.

*Are common-law marriages recognized as valid everywhere?*

Yes, in many states under the principle that a marriage valid where performed will be recognized as valid everywhere else.

*May a man or woman legally remarry without obtaining a divorce from his or her common-law spouse?*

No. Since the marriage is considered binding in those states which recognize common-law marriages, a divorce is necessary before either party may lawfully rewed; otherwise the man or woman runs the risk of prosecution for bigamy.

*What is a proxy marriage?*

A marriage in which the presence of both the man and the woman is not required at the ceremony. Proxy marriages were quite common during World War II, but have been abolished since.

*Are such marriages legal?*

Yes, if provided for by statute in the state in which the proxy marriage is sought to be arranged. The vast majority of states no longer make provisions for such marriages.

*What is community property?*

Community property comprises all property acquired by either spouse after marriage.

*Who owns community property?*

Each spouse owns an undivided half interest in such commonly held property. For example, if, after marriage, a husband purchases a piece of real estate valued at $50,000, this becomes community property, with the wife owning an undivided half interest.

*What happens to community property on the death or divorce of either party?*

Upon divorce the community property is equally divided between the ex-spouses. At the death of one, the community property goes to the heirs and representatives of the deceased instead of to the surviving spouse.

*What about property acquired before the marriage?*

This remains separately owned by the individual.

*Which states have community property laws?*

Arizona, California, Nevada, Texas, and Washington.

*What is an antenuptial agreement or property settlement?*

A contract or agreement made between a man and a woman before marriage but in contemplation and in consideration of marriage. In such an agreement the property rights and interests of either the prospective husband or wife, or both, are determined in advance of the marriage. Marriage settlements, in a word, are designed to protect the prospective spouse in the control of his or her property.

*Who generally draws up such agreements?*

The usual and best procedure is for both parties to be represented by legal counsel. Such agreements may provide that the property of each spouse is to be separate and independent from the other; that neither spouse is to acquire any interest in the estate of the other; that each spouse is to control separate property and contribute proportionately to the family expenses; that the wife is to hold her property to her separate use; or that the property of both spouses is to be held jointly. Any other arrangement, of course, may be made between the contracting parties and will be upheld unless fraud is shown.

*May such an agreement be entered into only before the marriage?*

No. It may be entered into either before or after the marriage ceremony.

*Does a wife acquire an immediate interest in the property of her husband after marriage? Does a husband acquire a similar interest in his wife's property?*

Yes. Immediately upon marriage husband and wife have a reciprocal interest in each other's property, usually one third. The only way to avoid such an interest is by means of an antenuptial agreement or marriage settlement. Many wealthy men and women, especially in a second or third marriage, have their attorneys draw up such an agreement in order to make certain that the individual is not marrying the prospective spouse for his or her money; such agreements are also frequently drawn to provide protection for children of the first marriage.

*What is a suit for breach of promise?*

A suit for damages. A suit for breach of promise is most often brought by a woman who alleges that a given man offered to marry her and subsequently refused to go ahead with the wedding.

*Can a man be sued for breach of promise even though at the time he had a wife living?*

Yes. This is true even though performance of the contract was impossible, provided the woman did not know of the marriage at the time.

*What are the defenses against a suit for breach of promise?*

1. That either party has been convicted of an infamous crime.

2. That the intended wife is sterile or is infected with a venereal disease.

3. That either party has a bad character generally, and the other party was ignorant of it at the time of the engagement.

4. That the woman committed fornication, and the man had no knowledge of it at the time of the engagement.

5. That false representations were made by the woman, or by her friends in collusion with her, about her circumstances and situation in life.

*Must a couple actually be engaged before a breach of promise suit can be maintained?*

No. A promise to marry may be inferred by showing the conduct of the party and the general circumstances, such as visiting, understanding among friends and relations, and preparations for marriage. There need not be a formal engagement to maintain an action.

*May a breach of promise action be filed in all states?*

No. Many states now frown on such suits because they have often been used by unscrupulous women for financial gain.

*What is meant by alienation of affections?*

By alienation is meant the stealing of the affections, society, and fellowship of one of the spouses in marriage. Formerly, suits for alienation of affections were common, but like breach of promise suits, they have been discouraged by laws enacted in a number of states, usually the same states that discourage actions for breach of promise.

*Who has the right to determine where the couple shall live?*

The husband, but he must not be unreasonable or arbitrary about his choice. Since the husband is still nominally the head of the household, he still has the right to determine the permanent residence of the family. If he decides, for example, that for reasons of health or business, he must move to another community within the state, or even to another state, it is the legal obligation of the wife to follow. In fact, her willful failure to do so may constitute legal desertion on her part and thus provide the husband with grounds for divorce.

*May the wife refuse to follow her husband on the ground that it would be a hardship on her parents?*

No. The first obligation of a wife is to her husband and children, not to her parents.

*What if the wife refuses to move with her husband on the ground that to do so would be injurious to her health?*

If the wife has medical evidence to support her view, she may rightfully refuse to follow her husband into another community or state. Should the husband still move, it would be he who would be guilty of desertion, not the wife.

*Does a husband have the right to beat his wife?*

No. Physical violence inflicted on a wife—or on a husband, for that matter—is a crime punishable by a fine or imprisonment or both, and may give the injured party the right to sue for divorce on the ground of cruelty.

*To what extent is a husband obliged to support his wife and family?*

The husband must provide his wife and children with food,

clothing, shelter, medical and dental care, and the other essentials of living.

*Does this mean that the husband may provide only the bare necessities?*

No. It means that he must support them in accordance with his financial ability. Thus a husband who earns $50,000 a year cannot live or make his wife live as if he earned only $100 a week.

*Does the wife share in the ownership of property acquired by the husband during the marriage?*

No. The single exception is property that is placed in both names or is purchased with money actually belonging to both.

*What can a wife do if her husband willfully deserts her and the children?*

Any husband who willfully and without legal cause deserts his family may be subject to criminal prosecution. The wife may obtain relief by going either to the local police department or to the state's attorney's office for assistance in apprehending the husband. If the husband has fled to another state and the wife knows his whereabouts, she may, through the county prosecutor's office, seek to have him extradited. Under the Uniform Dependent's Support law, enacted in many states, it is no longer necessary for the deserted wife to have the husband arrested in the state in which he is located. She may obtain support by notifying the authorities in her own community, and they will arrange for the husband's hearing in the community to which he has fled. The authority to be notified to obtain such action is the local county prosecutor's office.

*Is the husband entitled to property which the wife acquired before marriage?*

No. Such property continues to belong to the wife, and she may do with it what she pleases.

*After marriage, may a wife enter into written agreements without the consent or approval of her husband?*

Yes. She may also sue and be sued in her own name.

*Can a wife insist that the husband provide her with a weekly allowance?*

No. A wife cannot insist that a husband give her an allowance as long as the husband provides her with the necessaries of life, in accordance with his financial status.

*May a husband insist on having sexual relations with his wife as often as he wishes?*

Yes, provided such intercourse does not affect the health or well-being of the wife. Obviously, however, the sex life of the couple, if it is to be rewarding, will depend on their feelings toward each other rather than on what the law allows. Thus a husband would be foolish to insist strictly on his marital rights if the wife isn't agreeable. A more sensible procedure would be to work out a compromise wherein the health and well-being of both parties are taken into consideration.

*May a wife arbitrarily refuse to engage in sexual relations with her husband?*

No. One of the purposes of marriage is to provide a legal outlet for a couple's sexual desires. For a wife continuously to frustrate a husband's sexual drive may constitute legal cruelty and so entitle the husband to a divorce.

*May a husband or wife insist that the other indulge in so-called sexual perversions?*

No. In the eyes of the law both husband and wife are entitled to enjoy "normal" sexual intercourse with each other. By normal is meant the insertion of the male penis into the female vagina. This is the legal definition. Physiologically and psychologically, however, any deviation from the norm is permissible, provided both parties agree to it.

*Are marriages between whites and negroes illegal under miscegenation laws?*

No. The U. S. Supreme Court has held such laws unconstitutional, so it is now permissible for the two races to inter-marry.

CHAPTER 6

## PARENT AND CHILD

*At what age does one reach his majority?*

The age varies according to the laws of the individual states. The legal age for voting is now eighteen for both sexes. As we have already seen, the age at which one may marry without parental consent is generally twenty-one for males and eighteen for females, though here, too, there are exceptions.

In contract law the general principle is that a youngster attains his majority when he is twenty-one; at that time he becomes fully responsible for his contractual obligations.

*Who is responsible for the support of a child?*

The father. It is his primary obligation to feed, clothe, and shelter the child to the best of his ability or, at the very least, in accordance with his financial position. On the death of the father the duty of support falls on the mother.

*Who has the final decision on the education of a youngster?*

Since the father is legally the head of the family, responsible for its support, he has the last word on his youngster's education. This is also true of the child's religious education. If, in an interfaith marriage, for example, the mother wishes the child reared as a Catholic and the father wishes him raised as a Protestant, the father's wishes will prevail if the matter goes to court for settlement.

*Who is entitled to a child's earnings?*

The father. At the father's death the mother becomes entitled to those earnings. In the event of divorce, the parent having custody of the child is normally entitled to whatever the child earns.

*What happens if a parent refuses to support his child?*

50

A parent who refuses to support a child or otherwise neglects him may be subject to criminal prosecution.

*Is a husband legally bound to support his wife's children by another marriage?*

No, unless he voluntarily assumes the obligation by taking the youngsters into the family.

*Is a parent obliged to send a youngster to college if he cannot afford it?*

No. A parent is only bound to do what he can financially.

*How may a child be free or "emancipated" from control by his parents so as to retain his own earnings?*

A child becomes emancipated by the consent of his parents, either orally or in writing. He is also entitled to retain his earnings when the parents fail to support him, when he reaches the age of twenty-one or, in some states, in the case of girls, eighteen, and when the child contracts a valid marriage, either with or without the parents' consent.

*May a father chastise his child?*

Yes, but the father, or mother for that matter, must not be unreasonable in exercising this right. For any unnecessary violence inflicted on a child the parent may be arrested and subject to either a fine or imprisonment or both.

*What obligation does a child have to support his parents?*

Under the laws of the various states, a child may be legally compelled to support a parent who is unable to support himself. If the child is derelict in his legal duty, he may be criminally prosecuted.

*If there are several children and one or more of them refuses to support an indigent parent, what may the other children do?*

They may institute civil or criminal proceedings to compel their siblings to contribute to the support of the parent. Of course, if any of the children are financially unable to contribute to the support of the parents, not much can be done about it.

*A youngster under twenty-one purchases an automobile, falsifying his age. After making a few payments, he decides to return the car. What are his rights?*

He is entitled not only to return the automobile but also to the return of the payments he has already made. The guiding principle is that a minor may be held accountable only for his necessaries, like food, clothing, and medical and dental care. Most other contracts made by him are voidable at his option; that is, he has the right to repudiate his agreements when he reaches his majority or to rescind them after purchase, no matter what his age, as long as he is still a minor. In short, a businessman who deals with a minor does so at his own risk and should demand strict proof (such as a birth certificate) that the buyer is twenty-one.

*Is a parent liable if his child injures someone or destroys property?*

No. A parent is not liable for the negligence of his child unless the act is performed with the parent's knowledge and consent. However, this does not relieve the child of responsibility. The youngster may be sued for damages and a judgment obtained against him. The judgment may be satisfied if, when, and as he later acquires any property.

*Can a parent be held responsible for the crimes of his child?*

In many states the statutes punish parents who contribute to the delinquency of a child.

*What rights does a parent have if a daughter is seduced?*

The father or, if there is no father, the mother has a right to sue for damages.

*Can a child be convicted of a crime?*

A child under the age of seven cannot be convicted of any crime. A child between the ages of seven and seventeen is legally presumed to be incapable of committing a crime, but this presumption may be rebutted by the prosecuting attorney's showing that the child had sufficient intelligence and understanding to comprehend the nature and consequences of his act. To escape responsibility, the child has the burden of satisfying the court or jury that he lacked sufficient intelligence to really know what he was doing.

*What is a bastardy suit?*

A bastardy suit determines the paternity of a child.

*Are paternity blood tests conclusive evidence that a given man is the father of a child?*

No. Such blood tests are evidence to be considered by the court in arriving at a decision as to who the child's father really is. The tests usually prove who is *not* the father rather than who is.

*When are such blood tests taken?*

They are usually taken shortly after the birth of the child. If the blood of the mother, the alleged father, and the child match, there is presumptive evidence that the man could be the father. If they do not match, the paternity suit against the alleged father is usually dismissed. However, even if the blood types do agree, it by no means follows that the accused is the father of the child, since there are millions of men with similar blood types. What has to be proved is that the accused had sexual access to the mother.

*Who is obligated to support an illegitimate child?*

The father. The amount of support is usually determined by the judge of the criminal court or by a branch of the prosecuting attorney's office. The amount of support is based on what the father earns. The father is also liable for medical and hospital bills, but not until the child is actually born.

*Can the stigma of illegitimacy be removed from a bastard child?*

Many states now have provisions whereby the stigma of illegitimacy may be sealed in the court's records, so that not even the child may be aware of the fact when he later grows up. In most states now the subsequent marriage of the man and woman legitimizes the child.

*Who has the right to custody of an illegitimate child?*

The mother. She also determines its residence and controls its education and rearing.

*What are the general legal requirements for the adoption of a child?*

To adopt a child legally it is necessary for the adopting parents to obtain the formal consent, expressed in writing and in the form required by law, of the child's natural parents or of other persons having the legal control of the youngster. It is also usually necessary to obtain the consent of both living parents if they are living together. If they are living separate and apart, the consent of the one who has the legal custody of the child only is required. The same principle is applicable to the adopting parents. If the adopting parents are living together, the consent of both is usually required. If they are living separate and apart, the consent of the adopting parent only is necessary. It is essential, too, that the adopting parents give evidence that they are of good character, are sober and industrious citizens of the community, and are financially and morally able to give the child the care and affection to which it is entitled. An additional requirement, applicable in cases where the child is fourteen years of age or over is that the youngster give his formal consent to the adoption. All this is done in a court proceeding handled by attorneys for both sides.

*May one spouse adopt a child without the consent of the other spouse?*

Most states require that both husband and wife sign the adoption papers. In a few states it is possible for one spouse, the wife, to adopt a child without the consent of the husband, but her action will not impose any legal obligation on the husband to support the child.

*May an unmarried woman adopt a child?*

Yes.

*Can you adopt a person who is over twenty-one years of age?*

Yes, in most states.

*What is the effect of legally adopting a child?*

Adoption creates for the adopting parents the same duties, rights, and responsibilities that exist with a natural-born child.

*What is a guardian?*

A guardian is one who legally has the care and management of the person or estate, or both, of a child during its minority, the child being the ward.

*How are guardians appointed?*

Guardians are most often appointed by the court in conformity with statutes. If the child is over fourteen years old, he may name the person he desires, but the court may reject the choice for good reason, and the child will be entitled to choose again.

*Does a ward under the age of fourteen have a choice in replacing his court-appointed guardian?*

Yes. If the guardian is appointed when the child is less than fourteen years of age, the ward may, in most places, on reaching fourteen, select another guardian with the approval of the court.

*May a guardian be appointed for a child even when the father or mother is living?*

Yes, if the court believes it is in the best interests of the child.

*Must a guardian accept his appointment?*

No. The usual procedure is for the guardian to be notified by the court of his appointment. He then has a right to accept or refuse. If he accepts, he must take an oath on assuming his duties and post a bond as security unless he is otherwise excused by the court.

*Must a guardian maintain and support his ward at his own expense?*

No.

*Is a guardian allowed to make a profit from his ward's estate?*

No. Instead, he must account to the ward for all profits made, and the ward may elect either to take the profits or to charge interest on any capital of his that the guardian may have used.

*May a guardian spend the principal of the ward's estate for the ward's education?*

Yes, but only if he first obtains the approval of the court.

*Is a guardian, like a parent, entitled to his ward's services and earnings?*

No.

*May a guardian determine the religious upbringing of his ward?*

As a general rule, courts insist that the ward be reared in the faith of his natural parents.

*Is a guardian empowered to direct his ward's education?*

Yes. A ward is entitled to an education suitable to his station in life and in conformity with his finances. He is thus entitled to the best education under all the circumstances, the ward's wishes, of course, being taken into consideration.

*Is the guardianship affected by the marriage of the ward?*

Yes. If the ward is a girl, the guardianship usually terminates upon her marriage. If the ward is a boy, the guardian still has control over his estate and property, but not over his person, until the term of the guardianship ends.

*Is a guardian empowered by law to forbid his ward's meeting and accompanying certain individuals?*

Yes. For example, a guardian may forbid a female ward to go out with a certain man. However, the guardian must not be unreasonable or arbitrary in his objections.

*May a guardian forbid his ward to marry a certain person?*

Yes. But here again he must not be capricious or arbitrary. Like a parent, a guardian may withhold his consent to a marriage when such consent is required.

*What must a guardian do with his ward's funds?*

He must invest them within a reasonable time in prudent securities, or he will be charged with interest. If there is real estate, he must do everything possible to see that the buildings are leased or rented, that rents are collected, and that repairs are made in order to avoid unnecessary depreciation of property.

*May a guardian sell his ward's real estate?*

Yes, if he secures the prior approval of the court.

*May a guardian purchase his ward's property at an auction sale?*

No.

*May a guardian retain profits made as a result of speculating with his ward's money?*

No. A guardian should not speculate with his ward's money, but if he has done so, any profits made by such speculation must be turned over to the ward.

*What happens if a guardian, speculating with his ward's money, sustains losses?*

Not only will the guardian have to make up such losses from his own pocket, but he may be removed from the guardianship. To protect himself and his ward, a guardian should only invest his ward's money in stocks and bonds approved by the court.

*What happens if, in the exercise of ordinary care, the guardian loses money on behalf of his ward?*

Since a guardian has only to exercise ordinary care, he will not have to make up the losses.

*How may a ward compel his guardian to give an accounting of the ward's property?*

By petitioning the court, through his attorney, for such an accounting. Under the law, a guardian must provide two kinds of accounting: one, an annual accounting of the ward's property, and two, a final accounting when the guardianship comes to an end.

*How are guardians paid?*

By fees fixed by the courts. The fees are deductible from the ward's estate.

*How is a guardianship ended.*

A guardianship is terminated when the ward reaches his majority or by the death of the ward, by the death of the guardian, by the marriage of a female ward, by the guardian's resignation, or by the guardian's removal by the court.

*What are the obligations of a stepparent to a stepchild?*

Generally speaking, a stepfather is under no obligation to support the children of his wife by another marriage unless he voluntarily assumes such support by receiving the youngsters into his family or by adopting them. If he adopts them, he is as much obliged to support them as he would be if they were his own children. Even when a stepfather voluntarily assumes the duty of supporting the children, he need not do so after the death of the mother. Nor must he continue to support them if he leaves the mother or is divorced from her.

*What happens if a child leaves home without parental consent?*

Such a child is considered a runaway, and the police will do everything possible to apprehend the youngster and return him or her to parental control. The first time the child is caught he is usually reprimanded; the second time he may be placed on probation. For a child to run away repeatedly may result in his being turned over to juvenile court authorities who may sentence him to a term in a training school for youngsters.

*What if a youngster runs afoul of the law?*

Each state and many cities have their own definitions of what constitutes delinquency. In some states the age of jurisdiction of juvenile courts is eighteen, in some sixteen. If your youngster runs afoul of the law, your first step should be to engage competent counsel.

Originally, juvenile courts were designed to separate the young, first offender from the adult, hardened criminal and to treat the former on a less formal, more sympathetic basis. The juvenile court judge was usually selected because he had some special rapport with youngsters, and he was aided by a battery of psychologists, sociologists, and social workers who had the youngsters' interests at heart. The proceedings themselves, unlike the more formidable criminal court, were usually much more relaxed, often without lawyers, stenographic records, and jury trials. Much of this has now changed. Juvenile courts are overworked and understaffed. Many judges lack the temperament to deal with delinquents, with the result that some youngsters have gotten the short end of the judicial stick.

Obtaining counsel for a child who has run afoul of the law is just as important as it is for an adult. The youngster has the right to be represented at every stage of the juvenile court proceeding. He has the right to remain silent. He has the right not to incriminate himself. He may even have the right to a jury trial, and he may have the right of appeal. Where the youngster's parents are too poor to engage counsel, they may have the right of having the court appoint an attorney to defend the minor against the charges leveled against him.

## CHAPTER 7

## ALTERNATIVES TO DIVORCE

*What are the alternatives to divorce?*

The first is to remain unhappily wed; a second is to seek to improve the marriage; a third is to attempt to have one's cake and eat it too, by having an affair; and a fourth is to separate without obtaining a divorce.

*What is to be said for remaining unhappily married?*

You at least know what you have, which is possibly more than you may expect in the next marriage. An unhappy marriage may also offer compensatory advantages in terms of status, prestige, finances, and acceptance by the community. It is often the line of least resistance, since it requires little energy or exertion. Moreover, remaining unhappily wed may satisfy some masochistic impulse on the part of the husband or the wife or both. Some people are gluttons for punishment; they would be miserable, paradoxically, if they were *not* unhappy.

*What are the arguments against remaining unhappily married?*

The chief argument is that life is too short to bear unnecessary burdens; that if a marriage overwhelmingly produces more pain than pleasure, then it's time to call a halt. What the final decision will be depends on the individual's age, temperament, personality, and background. Each person must arrive at his or her own decision. For one individual, adherence to the tenets of his religion may outweigh the advantages of obtaining a divorce. For another, the children or finances may be more important. In short, each person must seek his own way to salvation, solving his or her problems the best way possible, knowing full well that there is no perfect solution to any marital problem.

*How does one go about improving a marriage?*

The best method is to seek outside assistance. This means enlisting the services of a qualified marriage counselor, clinical psychologist, psychiatric social worker, psychiatrist, or clergyman with a background in pastoral psychology.

*How does one locate a "qualified" marriage counselor?*

Perhaps the safest procedure is to write to the American Association of Marriage Counselors, Inc., 27 Woodcliff Drive, Madison, New Jersey, for the name of a qualified marriage counselor in your community. However, since the association has only a few hundred members, the chances are slim that you will find one in your community, unless you live in a fairly large city. In addition, many smaller communities, as well as larger cities, have branches of the Family Service Association. Social workers attached to the branch staff provide marriage counseling for very modest fees.

*How successful is marriage counseling?*

On the whole, the chances are about one in four that marriage counseling will improve a marriage. A good marriage counselor is interested only in keeping a marriage together if the end result seems worthwhile; that is, if the husband and wife will emerge much richer emotionally in terms of each other. If, as a result of the counseling, they learn to understand each other better, discover new areas of interest, and so become much more compatible, both mentally and physically, the counseling experience can be an emotionally rewarding one. Certainly, whenever possible, especially when there are children, a couple should do whatever they can to improve the marriage, before going ahead with plans for a divorce.

*What about having one's cake and eating it too?*

This is one of the traditional escape hatches for unhappy marriages. According to the late Dr. Alfred C. Kinsey, about one half of all husbands engage in extramarital affairs, and about one third of all wives. But having an affair can be catastrophic for a married man or woman. It can lead to financial disaster, blackmail, divorce on the ground of adultery with large alimony payments or property settlements, emotional disturbances of one kind or another, all sorts of psychosomatic symptoms, and a variety of other afflictions. Despite these and other hazards, many unhappy husbands and wives do engage in adulterous relationships. Doing so, however, rarely solves the real problem. It merely postpones the solution.

*What is the difference between a divorce and an annulment?*

A divorce is a judicial decree that a previously existing valid marriage has been legally dissolved. An annulment is a judicial declaration that an alleged marriage never legally existed, the court declaring the marriage to be void from its very inception.

*What are some of the practical consequences in obtaining an annulment?*

In an annulment, since no marriage ever validly existed, the wife is not entitled to alimony or to separate maintenance. Nor is she entitled to support for any children, since the children of an annulled marriage are bastardized. A further consequence is that there are no restrictions on the right to remarry, as there sometimes are in cases of divorce. Finally, after a marriage has been annulled, the ex-husband or ex-wife may testify against each other, since they were never lawfully wed.

*In which state is it just as easy—if not easier—to obtain an annulment as it is to obtain a divorce?*

New York.

*What is the most popular ground for an annulment?*

Fraud. Since marriage is a contract, any misrepresentations that go to the very essence of the contract may be used to annul the marriage. To end a marriage on the basis of fraud it must be shown:

1. That there was a false representation.

2. That the plaintiff (the party suing) had no knowledge that the representation was false.

3. That the defendant (the party being sued) intended that the representation be relied upon.

4. That the party suing relied on the representation and that he would not have married the defendant had he known the facts.

5. That there was resulting damage.

*Is Lesbianism or homosexuality a ground for an annulment?*

Yes, if the facts were unknown at the time of the marriage.

*Is the refusal to have children a ground for an annulment?*

Yes, provided there was an understanding before marriage that the couple would have children afterward. The law assumes that marriage is entered into for, among other things, sexual intercourse so that children may be born. The refusal of one of the parties to fulfill the promise would be sufficient to void the marriage. This was one of the more popular grounds for annulment in New York.

*Can an annulment be obtained if the only purpose of the marriage is to give the child a name and not for the parents to live together as man and wife?*

Yes.

*Can an annulment be procured if one of the parties to the marriage was drunk?*

Yes, if one person was so intoxicated that he or she did not know the nature, meaning, and consequence of the marriage contract. To obtain relief, legal proceedings should be instituted promptly, usually within a few days or weeks.

*Can an annulment be obtained if both parties to the marriage are under the age of parental consent?*

Yes. In such a case either party, or the parents of either party, may institute annulment proceedings.

*Suppose only one of the parties is under the age of parental consent?*

In this case the party under the age of parental consent can often procure an annulment. The person over the age of parental consent, usually the boy, will not generally be allowed to file annulment proceedings.

*What is impotence as the basis of an annulment?*

Impotence is the inability to achieve an erection or to have normal sexual intercourse. In women impotence is known as frigidity. However, the impotence or frigidity must have been unknown to the other party at the time of the marriage.

*Can an annulment be procured if a middle-aged or elderly couple enter into a marriage solely for companionship.*

No. A couple may marry for any reason it wishes. Having married for that reason, neither party can later change his or her mind and claim not to be getting what had been bargained for.

*Can a marriage be annulled if, as a result of an accident or disease, the husband becomes impotent?*

No. The impotence must have existed at the time of the marriage. The proper remedy would be a divorce in those states in which impotence is a ground for divorce.

*May a husband have his marriage annulled if his wife concealed that her pregnancy was induced by another man?*

Yes, since this is the kind of fraud that goes to the very essence of the marriage contract.

*Can a marriage be annulled if a wife tries to pass off an illegitimate child as one born in lawful wedlock?*

Yes, provided the husband institutes proceedings promptly after discovering the facts.

*Can a marriage be annulled if, after a man and a woman have entered into a written agreement in which the husband agrees to convert to his wife's religion and to rear the children in his wife's faith, the husband later repudiates the agreement after the children are born?*

Yes.

*Suppose a husband deserts his wife and children and flees to another state. Is it necessary to have him extradited in order to compel him to support the family?*

No. The Uniform Support of Dependents Act, adopted in all states, now makes it possible for an abandoned wife to obtain help without going to the trouble of having the errant husband extradited. Under this act the wife goes to the prosecuting attorney in her home city or county and states the basis of her complaint. The court will then hold a hearing to determine all the facts and circumstances of the case, including the amount of money necessary to support the family unit. The court in the community in which the husband is located files proceedings against the deserting spouse. If the husband agrees to pay the amount stipulated by the court in the wife's home state, the threat of extradition and of a jail sentence is dropped. If the husband refuses to pay the amount so stipulated, the chances are he will be extradited and compelled to stand trial.

*In what way are criminal proceedings an alternative to divorce?*

A criminal proceeding against either husband or wife does not legally dissolve a marriage, but it may lay the foundation for a subsequent divorce. It may be indicated when the husband beats his wife, when he fails to support his wife and children, when he is habitually drunk, or when he abuses the youngsters. It is a remedy frequently resorted to by people in the lower income brackets.

*Can a wife compel her husband to support her and the children even if she leaves home?*

Yes, provided she is legally justified in leaving the home. She may be so justified when the husband is a habitual drunkard, when he physically assaults the wife or children, or when he refuses to support the family.

*What is a suit for separate maintenance?*

Such a suit is a civil proceeding instituted by the wife, in which she seeks an award of alimony without obtaining a divorce. To obtain such separate maintenance she must usually have grounds for a divorce.

*Under what circumstances will separate maintenance be awarded?*

Usually in those cases where the husband has forced his wife to leave the home because of his own misconduct. The husband may be a habitual drunkard. He may have threatened the lives of the wife or children. He may have refused to support them. Unable to tolerate conditions at home, the wife leaves and finds an apartment or home for herself and the children. Not wanting a divorce, she may engage an attorney to file a suit for separate maintenance. If, after a hearing, the court is satisfied that the facts are as the wife sets them forth, an order will be granted allowing the wife a certain amount of money for the support of herself and the children. In all cases, however, the wife must prove by satisfactory evidence that she herself was not at fault in breaking up the marriage.

*May a wife request separate maintenance if she remains in the home or apartment, but lives apart from her husband?*

Yes, if she can prove there is such an acute housing shortage that she can find no other place to live.

*Can a suit for separate maintenance be successfully maintained by the wife if she has sufficient funds of her own?*

Not usually. A prime requisite for a separate maintenance suit is that the wife is unable to support herself and her children. If it can be proved that, just before leaving her husband, the wife cleaned out the joint checking account and so provided herself with adequate funds, the action will be defeated. It will also be defeated if the wife is financially independent, has a private income of her own, or holds a job that pays her a salary adequate to the support of herself and the children.

*Can the courts compel a man to marry a woman whom he has made pregnant?*

Rarely. A man is most likely to be forced to marry the woman if he has been convicted of rape or seduction. He may then be given the choice of marrying her or facing a prison term. If he marries the woman, the chances are he will not be able to have the marriage subsequently voided.

*Can a woman compel a man to marry her if he has made her pregnant?*

No. Except in the rare cases mentioned above, no one can force another into marriage. When a woman has become pregnant, she can, after the birth of the child, compel the father, through the courts, to support the child until the latter attains majority.

*What is a partial divorce?*

A partial divorce is the same as a legal separation, and is known as a divorce *a mensa et thoro*, "from bed and board." Under such a divorce the husband and wife live separate and apart. Neither can remarry until an absolute divorce is granted. As a general rule there is no great advantage to a partial as distinguished from an absolute divorce, except that the former may lay a foundation for the latter. Where the law requires that the parties be separated for at least eighteen months before being allowed to file for an absolute divorce, a bill for a partial divorce can be filed if they have lived apart for only three months. It will be granted after a proper case has been made. But often a partial divorce is a needless expense and burden, since after the requisite eighteen months have expired, a new bill for an absolute divorce will have to be filed, with additional counsel fees and court costs. In most cases, it is best to wait such a period as will enable the party suing to obtain an absolute divorce.

*What is the difference between a voluntary separation and a legal separation?*

When a husband and wife agree to live separate and apart, without going into court, the separation is said to be voluntary. Spouses living apart under such circumstances may enter into a separation agreement arranged by respective counsel. Such an agreement may contain any terms agreed upon by the parties. If the agreement is violated, the wife may bring the husband into court and have the contract enforced. For the husband's refusal to pay the judgment, however, the wife cannot have him sent to jail as she can in a legal separation.

A legal separation, on the other hand, is the result of litigation in court brought by one spouse against the other. Its terms are embodied in the court's decree, and for violation of those terms the husband may be committed to jail. A legal separation is similar to a partial divorce. Either party may procure a separation upon showing just cause. Under such a separation the parties, though living apart, remain man and wife and may not remarry. When the wife procures the legal separation, the husband, by court order, is usually under an obligation to support her and the children. When the husband obtains the decree, he is viewed as the "innocent" party, and is usually under no such obligation to support his wife, but he is compelled to support the children until they reach their majority. The husband, in fact, is always obliged to support the children, regardless of who obtained the separation or divorce.

*How useful is the husband's notice in the local newspaper that "My wife having left my bed and board, I will not be responsible for my wife's debts?"*

Such a notice is usually worthless. Under the law a husband is responsible for his wife's necessaries, despite the fact that they are living apart. Such necessaries include food, medical and dental care, clothing, and shelter.

*Is it wise for a husband to close out his charge accounts after his wife has wrongfully left him?*

Yes. If the husband is fearful that the wife will run up extravagant bills on charge accounts in his name, he should immediately notify by letter, as well as by phone, all concerns with whom he has charge accounts that he is having domestic difficulties and request that the charge account be closed. Such concerns should include department stores, filling stations, drug and liquor stores, and any others that might extend credit to the wife.

*May a husband and wife have sexual intercourse either with each other or with third parties during a legal separation?*

No. If they do, they forfeit whatever rights they may have had during the separation.

*What is a separation agreement?*

It is an agreement entered into by the husband and wife, usually as a prelude to an absolute divorce, which settles such important matters as the division of property, the amount of alimony, and the custody of the children and their support.

*Is it necessary to have a lawyer draw up such an agreement?*

It is certainly highly advisable that both parties to a separation agreement be represented by separate counsel in order to protect their respective interests.

*After a separation agreement has been signed, can either party date other individuals?*

It is not advisable. Even after the separation agreement is signed, the parties remain husband and wife until an absolute divorce is obtained. To prove adultery, it is not essential that the adulterer be caught in the act. All that must be proved is that the husband or wife had an adulterous disposition and that the surrounding circumstances were such as to lead a reasonable person to believe that the act did take place.

*What is the effect of a husband or wife's committing adultery after a separation agreement is signed?*

Although the agreement would still be enforceable, the innocent party would have the right to seek an absolute divorce on the ground of adultery. In addition, if the wife committed the act, her rights to her husband's property may be adversely affected.

*Is it wise to entertain in one's home during a legal separation?*

No. Such entertainment may make the other party to the separation feel that there existed both the disposition and the opportunity to commit adultery. Should this be proved, the innocent party may be able to obtain an absolute divorce.

*How does a court determine the amount of money to be awarded to the wife and children during a separation?*

The amount to be paid to the wife is determined by the husband's income, as well as by the financial resources of the wife. Usually the wife and children are allotted—depending on the number of children—between one third and one half of the husband's net income.

CHAPTER 8

DIVORCE

*What are the grounds for an absolute divorce in the fifty states?*

Variously, depending upon the state, adultery, alcoholism, cruelty, desertion, drug addiction, felony conviction, fraud, impotence, imprisonment, incompatibility, indignities, insanity, nonsupport, pregnancy, separation, sodomy, sterility, vagrancy, venereal disease, and irreconcilable differences leading to breakdown of marriage.

*Must the person who seeks an absolute divorce fulfill certain residence requirements.*

Yes. Each of the states has a specific requirement. The party who seeks a divorce under the laws of one state must actually have resided in the state or county where the divorce suit is filed for the time required by statute.

*Are there any restrictions on remarriage by the parties to a divorce?*

In some states the parties to a divorce cannot remarry within a certain period of time—unless they remarry each other.

*What are the specific grounds for divorce in each state?*

**Alabama**
  Absolute divorce:
  1. Incapacity.
  2. Adultery.
  3. Physical violence.
  4. Abandonment for one year.
  5. Imprisonment in penitentiary for two years under sentence of seven years or more.
  6. Crime against nature before or after marriage.

70

7. Five successive years in insane asylum after marriage, the person so confined being hopeslesly and incurably insane when divorce is filed.

8. Final decree of partial divorce in effect for more than two years.

9. Husband may obtain divorce on ground of wife's pregnancy at time of marriage without his knowledge.

10. Wife may obtain divorce for husband's nonsupport for two years.

11. Habitual drunkenness or drug addiction contracted after marriage.

12. Incompatibility.

Partial divorce:

Cruelty or any cause justifying divorce, if plaintiff desires separation only.

*Residence:* Plaintiff must have resided in state at least one year if defendant is a nonresident. No specific residence of plaintiff is required where court has jurisdiction of both parties and one party is domiciled in Alabama. *Remarriage restrictions:* Neither party may remarry (except each other) within sixty days after decree or pending appeal. Guilty party in divorce may not remarry without court's permission.

## Alaska

Absolute divorce:

1. Impotency at time of marriage continuing until commencement of legal action.

2. Adultery.

3. Felony conviction.

4. Willful desertion for one year.

5. Cruelty impairing health, endangering life, or personal indignities rendering life burdensome.

6. Incompatibility of temperament.

7. Habitual and gross drunkenness, begun after marriage and continuing for one year.

8. Willful neglect by the husband to provide necessaries of life for the wife for twelve months when he is able to do so, or when failure is because of his idleness, profligacy, or dissipation.

9. Incurable mental illness when spouse is confined to an institution for at least eighteen months prior to the filing of the divorce.

10. Addiction, after marriage, to habitual use of drugs.
Partial divorce:
Not granted in Alaska.

*Residence:* Plaintiff must have been resident of state at least one year before divorce bill can be filed. *Remarriage restrictions:* None.

### Arizona

Absolute divorce

1. Adultery.
2. Physical incompetence at time of marriage continuing until time of suit.
3. Conviction of felony and prison sentence.
4. Willful desertion for one year.
5. Habitual intemperance.
6. Extreme cruelty.
7. Husband's neglect to provide wife with common necessaries of life for one year, he having the ability to do so but failing because of idleness, profligacy, or dissipation.
8. Felony conviction before marriage unknown to other party at time of marriage.
9. Wife's pregnancy by another man at time of marriage unknown to husband.
10. Failure of husband and wife to have lived or cohabited together as such for five years or more for any reason.

Limited divorce:
Any ground for absolute divorce or such conduct of husband as may make it unsafe or improper to cohabit with him.

*Residence:* One year for plaintiff. *Remarriage restrictions:* None.

### Arkansas

Absolute divorce:

1. Adultery.
2. Impotency at time of marriage continuing until bill of divorce is filed.
3. Desertion for one year without reasonable cause.
4. Husband or wife by former undissolved marriage living at time of marriage.
5. Felony conviction or infamous crime.
6. Habitual drunkenness for one year.
7. Cruel and barbarous treatment endangering life of innocent party.
8. Indignities to person making his or her life unbearable.

9. Parties living apart for three consecutive years without cohabitation, whether or not by mutual consent.

10. Willful nonsupport.

11. Insanity in which the spouse must have been continuously confined in an institution for at least three years or have been adjudicated insane for more than three years before filing of suit.

*Residence:* Plaintiff or defendant must have lived in the state for at least sixty days before filing bill of divorce. Nonresident establishing residence to obtain divorce must prove bona fide residence, or domicile, both at time suit is filed and at time of final decree. *Remarriage restrictions:* None.

## California

Absolute divorce or legal separation:

1. Irreconcilable differences which have caused irremediable breakdown of the marriage.

2. Incurable insanity.

*Residence:* Six months by either plaintiff or defendant. *Remarriage restrictions:* None after final decree.

## Colorado

Absolute divorce or legal separation:

Irretrievable breakdown of marriage relationship.

*Residence:* Ninety days. *Remarriage restrictions:* None.

## Connecticut

Absolute divorce or legal separation:

1. Adultery.

2. Fraudulent contract.

3. Willful desertion for one year with total neglect of duty.

4. Seven years absence where spouse has been unheard from.

5. Sentence for imprisonment for life.

6. Any infamous crime involving a violation of conjugal duties and punishable by imprisonment for more than a year.

7. Legal confinement because of mental illness for an accumulated period of at least five years within the six-year period next preceding filing of complaint.

8. Habitual intemperance.

9. Intolerable cruelty.

*Residence:* Plaintiff must have resided in state for one year unless cause of divorce arose after removal to state; or plaintiff was domiciled in state at time of marriage and has returned with intention of remaining permanently; or defendant has lived in state for one year and has actually been served. *Remarriage restrictions:* None.

### Delaware

Absolute divorce:

1. Adultery.
2. Bigamy.
3. Conviction of crime with imprisonment for two years.
4. Extreme cruelty.
5. Willful desertion for one year.
6. Inability and failure to support family.
7. Habitual drunkenness for two years.
8. Complaining party was under age of consent at time of marriage.
9. Adjudication by court appointed commission that spouse is mentally ill and has been under supervision or care of a mental clinic for five years.
10. Voluntary separation for eighteen months.
11. Incompatibility for two years.

Legal separation:

1. Adultery.
2. Bigamy.
3. Conviction of crime or punishment for two years.
4. Extreme cruelty.
5. Willful desertion for two years.
6. Habitual drunkenness for two years.
7. Hopeless insanity of husband.

*Residence:* For adultery or bigamy action may be brought if either party was a bona fide resident of the state at the time the cause of action arose. For any other ground divorce proceedings may be instituted if either party has been a bona fide resident of Delaware for two years. *Remarriage restrictions:* None.

### District of Columbia

Absolute divorce:

1. Adultery.
2. Desertion for one year.
3. Voluntary separation from bed and board for one year without cohabitation or living together.

**4.** Final conviction of a felony and sentence for not less than two years, partly or wholly served.

Legal separation:

**1.** Any ground justifying absolute divorce.
**2.** Cruelty.

*Residence:* One year. *Remarriage restrictions:* None.

## Florida

Absolute divorce:

**1.** Irreconcilable differences.
**2.** Mental incompetency for three years.
Partial divorce or legal separations: Not granted.

*Residence:* Six months. *Remarriage restrictions:* None.

## Georgia

Absolute divorce:

**1.** Relationship between parties such that marriage is prohibited.
**2.** Mental incapacity at time of marriage.
**3.** Impotency at time of marriage.
**4.** Force, menace, duress, or fraud in obtaining marriage.
**5.** Pregnancy at time of marriage unknown to husband.
**6.** Adultery.
**7.** Desertion of either party for one year.
**8.** Conviction of offense involving moral turpitude where penalty is two or more years in prison.
**9.** Habitual intoxication or drug addiction.
**10.** Extreme cruelty.
**11.** Incurable insanity.

Partial Divorce: None.

*Residence:* Six months before action is brought. *Remarriage restrictions:* Subject to judge or jury hearing case.

## Hawaii

Absolute divorce:

**1.** Adultery.
**2.** Desertion for six months.
**3.** Imprisonment for life or for more than seven years.
**4.** Habitual drunkenness or drug addiction for more than one year.
**5.** Mental cruelty for more than sixty days which makes life of other spouse burdensome and intolerable and further living together insupportable.

6. Failure to provide suitable support for wife, when husband is able to do so, for more than sixty days.

7. Expiration of term in decree of partial divorce without reconciliation having been effected.

8. Living separate and apart for more than two years without a reconciliation having been effected.

9. Extreme cruelty.

Partial divorce:

May be granted for not more than two years for any cause for which absolute divorce may be allowed.

*Residence:* One year. *Remarriage restrictions:* None.

### Idaho

1. Adultery.
2. Extreme cruelty.
3. Willful desertion.
4. Willful neglect.
5. Habitual intemperance.
6. Conviction of felony.
7. Permanent insanity.
8. That parties have lived separate and apart without cohabitation for at least five years.
9. Irreconcilable differences determined by court.

*Residence:* Six weeks. *Remarriage restrictions:* None.

### Illinois

Absolute divorce:

1. Impotency.
2. Another spouse living at time of marriage.
3. Adultery.
4. Desertion for one year without reasonable cause.
5. Habitual drunkenness for two years.
6. Attempt on life of spouse by poisoning or other means showing malice.
7. Extreme and repeated mental or physical cruelty.
8. Conviction of felony or infamous crime.
9. Communication of venereal disease.
10. Excessive use of addictive drugs for two years.

*Residence:* One year unless marital offense occurred within Illinois, in which case party filing bill for divorce need be resident for only six months. *Remarriage restrictions:* None.

**Indiana**

Absolute divorce:

1. Adultery.
2. Impotency existing at time of marriage.
3. Abandonment for two years.
4. Cruel and inhuman treatment.
5. Habitual drunkenness.
6. Failure of husband to make reasonable provision for his family for two years.
7. Conviction after marriage of infamous crime.
8. Five years' commitment for incurable insanity in a hospital or asylum.

Legal separation:

1. Adultery.
2. Desertion on nonsupport for six months.
3. Habitual cruelty or intolerable, recurring strife.
4. Habitual drunkenness or drug addiction.
5. Neglect of conjugal duty for six months.

*Residence:* One year. *Remarriage restrictions:* None except where divorce is obtained by default on notice by publication only, in which case the plaintiff's right to rewed is restricted for two years.

**Iowa**

Absolute divorce:

1. Breakdown of marriage with no reasonable likelihood that relationship can be preserved.

*Residence:* One year. *Remarriage restrictions:* Unless permission is given in divorce decree, neither party may remarry within one year after divorce is obtained except to each other.

**Kansas**

Absolute divorce or separate maintenance:

1. Abandonment for one year.
2. Adultery.
3. Extreme cruelty.
4. Habitual drunkenness.
5. Gross neglect of duty.
6. Conviction of a felony and imprisonment after the marriage.
7. Confinement in a mental institution for three years, which need not be continuous.

8. Incompatibility.

*Residence:* Six months. *Remarriage restrictions:* Prohibited for sixty days after divorce becomes final.

### Kentucky

Absolute divorce or legal separation:

1. Impotency or malformation which prevents sexual intercourse.
2. Living apart without cohabitation for five consecutive years.
3. Abandonment for one year.
4. Adultery.
5. Felony conviction.
6. Concealment from other spouse of loathsome disease existing at time of marriage or contracted afterwards.
7. Fraud, duress, or force in obtaining the marriage.
8. Habitual drunkenness for one year.
9. Extreme cruelty.
10. Pregnancy of wife by another man without husband's knowledge at time of marriage.
11. Insanity for not less than five successive years.

*Residence:* One year. *Remarriage restrictions:* None.

### Louisiana

Absolute divorce or legal separation:

1. Adultery.
2. Conviction of felony and sentence to death or to imprisonment at hard labor.
3. Habitual intemperance, excesses, cruelty, or outrages if such conduct makes living together impossible.
4. Public defamation.
5. Abandonment.
6. Attempt on life of other spouse.
7. Flight from justice after felony conviction.
8. Intentional nonsupport.
9. Spouses living apart voluntarily for one year.
10. Living separate and apart for two or more years, which allows either party to sue for absolute divorce.

*Residence:* One year with certain exceptions. *Remarriage restrictions:* A wife may not remarry until ten months after a preceding marriage has been dissolved.

### Maine

Absolute divorce:

1. Adultery.
2. Impotency.
3. Extreme cruelty.
4. Utter desertion for three years.
5. Habitual drunkenness or drug addiction.
6. Cruel and abusive treatment.
7. Husband's failure to support wife when he is able to do so.

Legal separation:

1. Desertion for at least one year.
2. When one spouse is living apart from other spouse without just cause for at least one year.

*Residence:* Six months. *Remarriage restrictions:* None.

## Maryland

Absolute divorce:

1. Impotence at time of marriage.
2. Any cause making marriage null and void from the beginning under Maryland law, such as fraud or duress.
3. Adultery.
4. Abandonment for eighteen months without reasonable expectation of reconciliation.
5. Voluntary separation without cohabitation for at least eighteen consecutive months with no reasonable expectation of a reconciliation.
6. Conviction of crime and sentence of at least three years or an indeterminate sentence in a penal institution, eighteen months of which have been served.
7. Uninterrupted separation without cohabitation for five years.
8. Permanent and incurable insanity provided insane spouse has been confined to mental institution for not less than three years before filing of bill.

Legal separation:

1. Cruelty.
2. Excessively vicious conduct.
3. Abandonment and desertion.

*Residence:* One year. *Remarriage restrictions:* None.

## Massachusetts

Absolute divorce:

1. Adultery.
2. Impotency.
3. Utter desertion for two consecutive years.

4. Habitual and gross intoxication or drug addiction.
5. Cruelty.
6. Gross and cruel failure on part of husband to support wife and family.
7. Sentence to prison for five years or more.

Legal separation:

1. Nonsupport of wife without just cause.
2. Desertion.

*Residence:* Two years with certain exceptions. *Remarriage restrictions:* None.

## Michigan
Absolute divorce:

Breakdown of marriage.

*Residence:* One year with exceptions. *Remarriage restrictions:* None unless provided in divorce decree.

## Minnesota
Absolute divorce:

1. Adultery.
2. Impotency.
3. Cruel and inhuman treatment.
4. Prison conviction.
5. Willful desertion for one year.
6. Habitual drunkenness for one year.
7. Three years' commitment for mental illness.
8. Continuous separation under decree of limited divorce for more than five years.
9. Continuous separation under order or decree of separate maintenance for two years before filing bill of divorce.

Legal separation:

Action for separate maintenance allowed.

*Residence:* One year. *Remarriage restrictions:* Remarriage within six months after divorce is forbidden except to each other.

## Mississippi
Absolute divorce:

1. Natural impotency.
2. Adultery.
3. Prison sentence.
4. Desertion for one year.

5. Habitual drunkenness or drug addiction.
6. Habitual cruelty.
7. Insanity or idiocy at time of marriage.
8. Prior undissolved marriage.
9. Pregnancy at time of marriage unknown to husband.
10. Consanguinity within prohibited degree.
11. Incurable insanty if spouse has been under regular treatment and confined in an institution for preceding three years.

*Residence:* One year. *Remarriage restrictions:* Court may prohibit remarriage of guilty party in adultery.

## Missouri
Absolute divorce:

1. Impotence at time of marriage continuing until divorce is sought.
2. Prior undissolved marriage.
3. Adultery.
4. Desertion for one year.
5. Conviction of felony or infamous crime during marriage or before marriage if innocent party was unaware of act.
6. Habitual drunkenness for one year.
7. Cruel or barbarous treatment endangering life.
8. Personal indignities making life intolerable.
9. Husband's vagrancy.
10. Pregnancy of wife by man other than husband at time of marriage unknown to husband.

*Residence:* One year with certain exceptions. *Remarriage restrictions:* None.

## Montana
Absolute divorce and legal separation:
1. Adultery.
2. Extreme cruelty consisting of infliction or threat of infliction of grievous bodily injury or personal violence; repeated publication or utterance of false charges against wife's chastity; and infliction of grievous mental suffering.
3. Willful desertion.
4. Willful neglect.
5. Habitual intemperance.
6. Felony conviction.
7. Incurable insanity, provided insane spouse has been confined

in mental institution for five years before filing divorce proceedings.

NOTE: Grounds for mental suffering, desertion, neglect, and intemperance must have continued for one year or more.

*Residence:* One year. *Remarriage restrictions:* None.

## Nebraska

Absolute divorce:

1. Adultery.
2. Physical incompetency at time of marriage.
3. Sentence to prison for three years or more.
4. Abandonment or desertion for two years.
5. Habitual drunkenness.
6. Incurable insanity where spouse has been confined to institution for at least five years.
7. Extreme cruelty.
8. Gross neglect to provide for wife when husband is able to do so.

Legal separation:

1. Cruelty.
2. Desertion for two years.
3. Willful nonsupport when husband is able to provide.

*Residence:* One to two years with exceptions. *Remarriage restrictions:* None after decree becomes final.

## Nevada

Absolute divorce:

1. Impotency at time of marriage continuing until time of divorce.
2. Adultery.
3. Willful desertion for one year.
4. Conviction of felony or infamous crime.
5. Habitual gross drunkenness since marriage of either party which prevents spouse from contributing his or her share to the support of the family.
6. Extreme cruelty.
7. Willful nonsupport on the part of the husband not the result of his poverty or which he could not avoid by ordinary industry.
8. Insanity for two years.
9. Incompatibility.
10. Husband and wife living apart for one year without cohabitation.

Legal separation: None.

*Residence:* Six weeks. *Remarriage restrictions:* None.

## New Hampshire

Absolute divorce or legal separation:

1. Impotency.
2. Extreme cruelty.
3. Imprisonment for more than one year.
4. Adultery.
5. Treatment which seriously endangers health or reason.
6. Absent unheard of for two years.
7. Habitual drunkenness for two years.
8. Joining any religious sect which professes to believe the relation of husband and wife unlawful, and refusal to cohabit for six months.
9. Abandonment and refusal for two years to cohabit together.
10. Willful absence for two years of either party without the consent of other party.
11. Willful desertion and nonsupport for two years.

*Residence:* One year with certain exceptions. *Remarriage restrictions:* None.

## New Jersey

Absolute divorce or legal separation:

1. Adultery.
2. Willful desertion for one year.
3. Extreme cruelty for three months.
4. Separation for at least eighteen months.
5. Habitual drunkenness or drug addiction for one year.
6. Institutionalization for mental illness for twenty-four consecutive months after marriage.
7. Imprisonment for eighteen or more consecutive months after marriage.
8. Deviant sexual conduct.

*Residence:* One year with certain exceptions. *Remarriage restrictions:* None.

## New Mexico

Absolute divorce or legal separation:

1. Adultery.
2. Impotency.
3. Cruel or inhuman treatment.

4. Pregnancy of wife at time of marriage by other than her husband without husband's knowledge.
5. Abandonment.
6. Felony conviction.
7. Drunkenness.
8. Incurable insanity for five years.
9. Incompatibility.
10. Failure of husband to support wife according to his means and station in life.

*Residence:* Six months. *Remarriage restrictions:* None.

### New York
Absolute divorce:

1. Cruel and inhuman treatment which endangers physical or mental well-being of plaintiff.
2. Abandonment for two or more years.
3. Imprisonment of defendant for three consecutive years.
4. Adultery.
5. Living apart for one year as a result of separation agreement or judicial decree.

Legal separation:

1. Extreme cruelty, either mental or physical.
2. Abandonment.
3. Husband's failure to provide support for wife.
4. Adultery.
5. Imprisonment of defendant for three consecutive years after marriage.

*Residence:* One to two years depending on circumstances. *Remarriage restrictions:* None.

### North Carolina
Absolute divorce:

1. Adultery.
2. Natural impotency at time of marriage continuing to time divorce is filed.
3. Pregnancy of wife by another man at time of marriage without knowledge of her husband.
4. Separation for one year.
5. Separation for three or more years by reason of insanity.
6. Crime against nature.
7. Bestiality.

Legal separation:

1. Abandonment.
2. Maliciously turning other spouse out of doors.
3. Cruel and barbarous treatment endangering life.
4. Indignities to the person, making life burdensome and intolerable.
5. Habitual drunkenness or drug addiction.

*Residence:* Six months. *Remarriage restrictions:* None.

## North Dakota

Absolute divorce or legal separation:

1. Adultery.
2. Extreme cruelty.
3. Willful desertion for one year.
4. Willful neglect for one year.
5. Habitual intemperance for one year.
6. Felony conviction.
7. Insanity for five years.
8. Irreconcilable differences.

*Residence:* One year. *Remarriage restrictions:* Neither party may remarry except as permitted by decree of court granting the divorce.

## Ohio

Absolute divorce:

1. That either party has spouse living at time of marriage.
2. Willful absence of spouse for one year.
3. Adultery.
4. Impotency.
5. Extreme cruelty.
6. Fraudulent contract.
7. Any gross neglect of duty.
8. Habitual drunkenness.
9. Imprisonment in penitentiary.

*Residence:* One year. *Remarriage restrictions:* None.

## Oklahoma

Absolute divorce or legal separation:

1. Abandonment for one year.
2. Adultery.
3. Impotency.

4. Pregnancy of wife at time of marriage by man other than husband.

5. Extreme cruelty.

6. Fraudulent contract.

7. Incompatibility.

8. Habitual drunkenness.

9. Gross neglect of duty.

10. Imprisonment for felony.

11. Insanity for five years.

12. Procurement of divorce outside Oklahoma which does not release the other party from the obligation of the marriage.

*Residence:* Six months. *Remarriage restrictions:* Remarriage forbidden for six months after divorce decree or thirty days after disposition of appeal.

## Oregon
Absolute divorce:

1. Irreconcilable differences causing breakdown of marriage.

Legal separation:

1. Adultery.

2. Separation.

3. Willful desertion.

4. Refusal to support wife for six months.

5. Habitual drunkenness for one year.

6. Cruelty or personal indignities.

*Residence:* Six months with certain exceptions. *Remarriage restrictions:* Neither party may remarry for sixty days after decree or until appeal has been disposed of.

## Pennsylvania
Absolute divorce:

1. Incapability of procreation.

2. Existing prior marriage.

3. Adultery.

4. Desertion for two years.

5. Cruel and barbarous treatment endangering the life of other spouse.

6. Indignities to spouse making life burdensome and intolerable.

7. Unforgiven force, fraud, or coercion.

8. Conviction of certain crimes resulting in sentence of two years or more.

9. Consanguinity or affinity.

Legal separation:

1. Abandonment of wife.
2. Turning wife out of doors.
3. Cruel and barbarous treatment endangering wife.
4. Indignities to wife's person.
5. Adultery.

*Residence:* One year with certain exceptions. *Remarriage restrictions:* Either party may remarry except that defendant guilty of adultery may not marry other party to adultery during lifetime of the plaintiff.

## Rhode Island

Absolute divorce or legal separation:

1. Impotency.
2. Adultery.
3. Extreme cruelty.
4. Willful desertion for five years or for other periods at discretion of court.
5. Continued drunkenness.
6. Habitual, excessive, and intemperate use of certain drugs.
7. Nonsupport for one year, the husband being able to provide.
8. Other gross behavior committed by either spouse, at court's discretion.
9. Living separate and apart for ten years.

*Residence:* Two years with certain exceptions. *Remarriage restrictions:* None.

## South Carolina

Absolute divorce:

1. Adultery.
2. Desertion for one year.
3. Physical cruelty.
4. Continuous separation for three years.
5. Habitual drunkenness.
6. Drug addiction.

*Residence:* One year. *Remarriage restrictions:* None.

## South Dakota

Absolute divorce or legal separation:

1. Adultery.
2. Extreme cruelty.
3. Willful desertion for one year.

4. Willful neglect for one year.

5. Habitual intemperance for one year.

6. Felony conviction.

7. Incurable chronic mania or dementia for at least five years.

*Residence:* One year with certain exceptions. *Remarriage restrictions:* Where divorce is granted for adultery, guilty party cannot marry any person except the innocent party, until the death of the other party.

### Tennessee

Absolute divorce:

1. Impotency.

2. The existence of a prior marriage not legally dissolved.

3. Adultery.

4. Willful desertion for one year.

5. Conviction for an infamous crime.

6. Felony conviction and sentence to prison.

7. Attempt on life of other spouse showing malice.

8. Willful refusal by wife to move to Tennessee with husband and willfully absenting herself from him for two years.

9. Wife's pregnancy at time of marriage by another man, unknown to husband.

10. Habitual drunkenness contracted after marriage.

Legal separation:

1. Extreme cruelty.

2. Husband's indignities to wife.

3. Husband's desertion of wife, and refusal to provide for her.

*Residence:* One year. *Remarriage restrictions:* A defendant guilty of adultery may not marry person with whom act was committed, during lifetime of former spouse.

### Texas

Absolute divorce:

1. When one spouse is guilty of excesses, cruelty, or outrages against complaining spouse, if such ill treatment makes living together insupportable.

2. Desertion for one year.

3. Adultery.

4. Living separate and apart without cohabitation for three years.

5. Felony conviction.

6. Confinement in mental institution for five years.

7. Irreconcilable differences.

*Residence:* One year with certain exceptions. *Remarriage restrictions:* Neither party may remarry (except themselves) within six months after divorce.

## Utah

Absolute divorce:

1. Impotency at time of marriage.
2. Adultery.
3. Willful desertion for more than one year.
4. Willful neglect to provide common necessaries.
5. Habitual drunkenness.
6. Felony conviction.
7. Mental or physical cruelty.
8. Permanent insanity, legally adjudged.
9. Separation for three years under decree of separate maintenance.

Legal separation:

1. Desertion.
2. Nonsupport.

*Residence:* Three months. *Remarriage restrictions:* None after time for appeal has run out.

## Vermont

Absolute divorce or legal separation:

1. Adultery.
2. Confinement in state prison at hard labor for three years.
3. Intolerable severity.
4. Willful desertion or absence for seven years without being heard of.
5. Husband's nonsupport without valid reason.
6. Insanity for at least five years, including confinement in mental institution for that period of time.
7. Couple have lived separate and apart for two consecutive years without reasonable expectation of a reconciliation.

*Residence:* Six months with certain exceptions. *Remarriage restrictions:* None.

## Virginia

Absolute divorce:

1. Adultery.

2. Sodomy or buggery.
3. Natural or incurable impotency at time of marriage.
4. Sentence to a penitentiary.
5. Conviction of infamous offense before marriage unknown to other party.
6. Willful desertion for one year.
7. Pregnancy of wife by another man unknown to husband.
8. Prostitution of wife before marriage unknown to husband.
9. Continuous separation for two years without cohabitation.

Legal separation:

1. Cruelty.
2. Reasonable apprehension of bodily hurt.
3. Desertion.

*Residence:* One year. *Remarriage restrictions:* Court may forbid guilty party in adultery to remarry for six months after decree.

## Washington

Absolute divorce:

1. Consent to marriage obtained by force or fraud.
2. Adultery.
3. Impotency.
4. Abandonment for one year.
5. Cruelty or personal indignities making life burdensome.
6. Habitual drunkenness.
7. Husband's willful nonsupport.
8. Imprisonment in federal or state penal institution.
9. Parties have lived separate and apart for two or more years.
10. Insanity for at least two years.

*Residence:* Six months preceding filing of bill. *Remarriage restrictions:* None.

## West Virginia

Absolute divorce:

1. Adultery.
2. Felony conviction.
3. Abandonment for one year.
4. Cruelty or inhuman treatment.
5. Habitual drunkenness.
6. Drug addiction.
7. Where parties have lived separate and apart for two or more years without any cohabitation.

8. Permanent and incurable insanity.

*Residence:* One year with certain exceptions. *Remarriage restrictions:* None.

## Wisconsin
Absolute divorce or legal separation:

1. Adultery.
2. Imprisonment for three years or more.
3. Willful desertion for one year.
4. Cruelty.
5. Habitual drunkenness for one year.
6. Voluntary separation for five years preceding commencement of action.
7. Pursuant to a court judgment have lived entirely apart for five years.
8. Nonsupport of wife.

*Residence:* Two years. *Remarriage restrictions:* One year after divorce is granted.

## Wyoming
Absolute divorce or legal separation:

1. Adultery.
2. Physical incompetency at time of marriage continuing to time of divorce.
3. Conviction of felony and sentence to imprisonment.
4. Willful desertion for one year.
5. Habitual drunkenness.
6. Extreme cruelty.
7. Neglect of husband for one year to provide common necessaries, unless due to poverty not preventable by ordinary industry.
8. Indignities rendering condition of other party intolerable.
9. Vagrancy of husband.
10. Conviction of felony or infamous crime prior to marriage when facts unknown to other party at time of marriage.
11. Pregnancy of wife at time of marriage by person other than husband and unknown to husband.
12. Incurable insanity.
13. Husband and wife have lived separate and apart for two consecutive years without cohabitation.

*Residence:* Sixty days before filing suit, unless marriage was solemnized in Wyoming and petitioner resided therein from time of marriage until filing of petition. Married women may obtain necessary residence although her husband resides in another state. *Remarriage restrictions:* None.

*What is adultery?*

Adultery is the voluntary sexual intercourse of one married person with another person who is not his or her spouse.

*A wife confesses to her husband that she has committed adultery. He forgives her, continues to live with her, and has sexual relations with her. Later he changes his mind and seeks to obtain a divorce. Will he succeed?*

No. In "condoning" or forgiving the adultery, the husband forfeited his right to a divorce on this ground. However, should the wife again commit adultery after the forgiveness, the husband would have an action, since the forgiveness is merely conditioned on the wife's future behavior. Of course, what is true of the wife is also true of the husband.

*In what way is cruelty a ground for divorce?*

Cruelty may be physical or mental. Physical cruelty is conduct by one spouse that either actually or apparently endangers the physical safety or good health of the other spouse to a degree that makes it physically impractical for the endangered party to continue with the marriage. It is not necessary that the spouse be physically assaulted; a mere threat to assault or beat the spouse may be sufficient, provided there is some corroboration by a third party. Evidence sufficient to establish physical cruelty includes testimony of medical treatment, photographs of the blows and lacerations, and when possible, the testimony of a disinterested third party, undenied by the defendant.

Mental cruelty, on the other hand, is an act that injures or threatens to injure the mental health of the complainant. It may include the husband's refusal to provide medical care for the wife, the husband's or wife's declaration that the other is a philanderer or adultress, or continued insulting or rude remarks either about the spouses or their relatives. Even persistent nagging has been held to be mental cruelty. Mental cruelty is thus an extremely elastic term and covers a multitude of marital sins. It is a common ground for divorce in California.

*How is violence defined as a ground for a divorce?*

Violence, as a ground for divorce, is akin to extreme cruelty. It is either the physical beating of one spouse by the other or a threat to beat the spouse that places him or her in genuine fear of his or her health or safety.

*What constitutes desertion?*

Desertion, also known as abandonment, is the voluntary separation of one spouse from the other without the intention of returning. The desertion must be the deliberate act of the party complained against. "Constructive" desertion takes place when the spouse by his or her misconduct brings the cohabitation to an end, regardless of which spouse left the home. In short, "constructive" desertion takes place when one spouse wrongfully forces the other to leave either the house or apartment.

*For business reasons, a husband wishes to move from one state to another. The wife refuses because her elderly parents are dependent on her. Will the husband be entitled to a divorce on the ground of desertion?*

Yes, in those states where desertion is a ground for divorce. Generally speaking, the husband has the right to establish the family residence. The wife's refusal to follow her husband into another state constitutes desertion on her part, unless the refusal is justified because the wife's health or that of the children would be seriously affected or impaired by the move.

*What constitutes nonsupport?*

Nonsupport is the failure of the husband to provide the wife and children with financial support consistent with his means. In many states the husband's willful failure to support his family is a ground for an absolute divorce. It may also give rise to a divorce action based on desertion.

*Can the wife insist that the husband provide her with a weekly allowance?*

No. A wife cannot insist that a husband give her such an allowance as long as he provides her with the necessaries of life, such as food, clothing, shelter, and medical and dental care.

*What constitutes habitual drunkenness as a ground for divorce?*

Constant indulgence in stimulants such as wine, brandy, beer, and whisky. The drunkenness must be habitual, and the habit must be actual and confirmed. The fact that the wife knew of her husband's alcoholism prior to the marriage would bar her from obtaining a divorce on this ground.

*What constitutes "gross" personal indignities?*

Personal indignities usually consist of a course of conduct calculated to make the life of the complaining party intolerable. They may consist of acts of rudeness, vulgarity, unmerited reproach, haughtiness, studied neglect, humiliating insults, intentional incivility, obvious disdain, abusive language, malignant ridicule, and every other sign of settled hate and estrangement. In mental cruelty, the act complained of is dangerous to the health or life of the spouse; in personal indignities, all that is necessary is to prove that the acts of one spouse make the other's life unbearable.

*What is impotence?*

Impotence in the male is the inability to achieve an erection for normal sexual intercourse with the wife. By ordinary and normal intercourse is meant the insertion of the male penis into the female vagina, with a view toward having an orgasm. Fellatio and cunnilingus are not considered "normal" intercourse in the eyes of the law. Both these forms of sexual deviation derive pleasure from the application of the mouth to the sexual organs. When the wife does it to the husband, it is known as fellatio. When the husband does it to the wife, it is called cunnilingus. Many competent sexologists and psychiatrists believe that there is nothing wrong with an occasional act of oral coitus, provided both husband and wife are agreeable. It is only when there is an insistence on fellatio or cunnilingus to the complete exclusion of normal intercourse that the oral method can be said to be a perversion. The law to the contrary, oral coitus is widely practiced in this country and even more in Europe, which has a generally more civilized attitude toward sex. The practice of fellatio or cunnilingus may constitute a ground for divorce by the spouse who refuses to indulge in such practice. The specific ground is cruelty, where cruelty is a ground for divorce.

*Is premature ejaculation by a husband a form of impotence?*

Yes. Premature ejaculation is ejaculation that occurs too soon for satisfactory expression of the mutual love of husband and wife. It often occurs prior to the introduction of the penis into the vagina. If it does, it may be considered a legal form of impotence. If the premature ejaculation occurs within a few seconds after the penis enters the vagina, it probably would not be considered impotence and would not entitle the wife to a divorce. Psychologically, impotence, whether in the male or in the female, is considered a form of rejection of one spouse by the other.

*What is incompatibility or irreconcilable differences which have caused marital breakdown?*

In any of the states where either of these is a ground for divorce, a decree will be granted when it is conclusively shown that the married couple is incapable of existing together in peace and harmony. The incompatibility may be sexual, intellectual, financial, religious, or temperamental. Basically, incompatibility or irreconcilable differences should be the only grounds for divorce in a civilized society, since they go to the very essence of marriage validity.

*What does the law mean by "loathsome disease"?*

The courts generally construe loathsome disease to mean a venereal disease, such as syphilis or gonorrhea.

*What is vagrancy?*

By vagrancy is usually meant idle wandering from place to place with no visible means of self-support.

*In what way is fraud a ground for divorce?*

Fraud, as a ground for divorce, is the use of any deceitful practice or device to induce one person to marry another.

*What is insanity?*

As a ground for divorce, insanity usually means a mental disorder or illness so severe as to eliminate a person's legal responsibility for his actions or behavior.

*What is separation without cohabitation?*

In separation without cohabitation a husband and wife live separate and apart and have no sexual relations with each other. Theoretically, a husband and wife can be separated in the same house—if they occupy separate bedrooms and do not have sexual intercourse with each other.

*Are Mexican divorces still available to Americans?*

Now that Mexico has virtually outlawed quickie divorces, Haiti and the Dominican Republic have stepped in to fill the breech.

*What are the requirements in Haiti and the Dominican Republic?*

In both cases husband and wife must consent to the divorce, usually on ground of mutual incompatibility, and only one spouse need attend the court hearing. The other party may be represented by a local lawyer. Any separation agreement must be drawn up in the United States before the foreign proceedings begin.

*Is a Haitian or Dominican divorce worth obtaining if one party objects?*

Like most Nevada divorces a Haitian or Dominican divorce is valid only if both parties consent to it. If there is no bona fide consent, the chances are that the divorce decree, whether in Nevada, Haiti, or Santo Domingo, can easily be upset.

*How expensive are divorces in Haiti and the Dominican Republic?*

The fee in both countries varies between $300 and $500. This does not include the American lawyer's fee or the cost of the flight to the Caribbean or the hotel in Santo Domingo or Port-au-Prince. The American lawyer's fee may range from $500 to $25,000 or more depending on the client's financial status, the work involved, the nature and complexity of the property settlement or separation agreement, and the time consumed.

*Will Haitian and Dominican divorces be recognized in this country?*

There is no reason to assume they will not. Under the principle of "comity of nations" a country will normally recognize a divorce as valid if it was valid in the country where procured.

*Which are the so-called easy divorce states?*

At one time Arkansas, Idaho, and Nevada were the only so-called easy divorce states both because they required little actual residence and because they liberally interpreted the grounds for divorce. In those states dissolving a marriage became a relatively painless affair instead of, as with most other states, an adversary proceeding in which a great deal of dirty linen was washed in public.

Today a few states have adopted the no-fault doctrine of divorce, in which the basic ground is either incompatibility or irreconcilable differences in which the marriage has broken down without regard to the fault of either party. Alaska, California, Delaware, Florida, Kansas, Michigan, Nevada, New Jersey, North Dakota, Oklahoma, and Texas have adopted relatively enlightened divorce laws.

Residence requirements have also been lowered in several other states, including Utah and Wyoming. For out of state residents Nevada still remains the easiest state in which to obtain a divorce both because of its six-weeks residence requirement and because, among other grounds, incompatibility is a legal basis for terminating a marriage.

*Is a Nevada divorce recognized as binding in other states?*

Yes, if the divorce is uncontested and both parties are represented by legal counsel.

*What does a plaintiff have to testify to in a Nevada divorce case?*

The plaintiff's case is brief, simple, and direct, and takes no more than ten or fifteen minutes, after which the judge hearing the case signs the divorce decree. Either party may marry minutes afterward.

*How many witnesses are necessary to obtain a divorce in Nevada?*

Only one. The landlord or landlady who houses the client testi-fies merely on the matter of the plaintiff's residence. Such arrange-ments are usually taken care of by the attorney who handles the divorce in that state.

*Are Nevada divorces expensive?*

The average Reno or Las Vegas divorce, including the six-weeks' stay, costs between $1,500 and $2,000. The usual agreement in such uncontested divorce cases is that the husband will pay the bills including legal fees. But where the woman is anxious to obtain the divorce, other arrangements are made. As for legal fees, there is one to be paid to the attorney in the home state, and this may vary from $500 to $10,000 or more, depending on the wealth of the clients, the complexity of the case, and any property settlement. There is also the fee to be paid to the Nevada attorney. The usual practice is for the local attorney to charge a single fee that will include the Nevada attorney. The client should get a definite statement from his local counsel, preferably in writing, of exactly what the fee will be and what it will include.

*On what grounds are Nevada divorces usually obtained?*

The usual one in Nevada is either mental cruelty or incompati-bility.

*Are witnesses to the acts of a defendant required in a divorce pro-ceeding in states other than Nevada?*

Yes, with the exception of such states as California, Iowa, Michi-gan, and Texas, where no-fault divorce laws are in operation. In most states if the divorce is sought on the ground of adultery, a witness will have to be found who can testify that the defendant had both the opportunity and the disposition to commit adultery. Any credible witness, even a relative, will suffice, especially if the divorce is uncontested. If the ground is desertion or cruelty, a witness will have to testify of his own knowledge about the facts leading up to the actual desertion or cruelty. In short, there has to be some corroboration of the plaintiff's testimony.

*What about states like California, Florida, Iowa, and Michigan where no-fault divorce laws are in effect?*

California, which is typical of those states which have discarded the often irrational, historical concept of divorce law, has discarded the use of corroborating witnesses as being irrelevant to the legal point at issue: whether or not there exists irreconcilable differences between the parties which make a viable marriage impossible. This is a question which only the spouses themselves can settle. If, for example, the husband claims that the differences between him and his wife are so irreconcilable as to make the marriage a nightmare, it is completely immaterial whether his views are confirmed by outside witnesses or even by the wife, for that matter. The fact that one of the parties is convinced that the marriage has irretrievably broken down is sufficient.

Under the old system in existence in most of the states it is still necessary for the plaintiff to prove that the defendant is exclusively at fault for the failure of the marriage. That this assumption often runs counter to the known facts is of little interest either to judges or lawyers. By proving fault or guilt on one side, the "innocent" victim achieves considerable material advantage. The truth of the matter is that it is often difficult or impossible to determine who is actually at fault when a given marriage breaks up. Usually responsibility is shared by both parties, which is why no-fault divorce laws are becoming increasingly popular.

*Can a divorce decree be set aside?*

Yes. Even after a divorce has been granted, it may be set aside if the defendant can prove that the plaintiff obtained the decree by fraud or duress. The fraud may consist of perjured testimony given in favor of the plaintiff, as, for example, when a witness testifies falsely as to an alleged adultery or when the plaintiff swears that she was a resident of a certain state for the required period of time when actually she was not such a resident.

*Are there any states that do not require a corroborating witness?*

In Connecticut divorces will not ordinarily be granted on uncorrobated evidence of parties in uncontested divorce cases, but they may be granted on the uncorroborated testimony of a party in a contested case. In Pennsylvania a divorce decree may be granted on the unsupported testimony of the complainant, but if the plaintiff's testimony is contradicted and shaken by the defendant, the divorce may not be granted.

*When is it unnecessary to retain counsel after one has been served with divorce papers?*

When the defendant has no desire, for one reason or another, to contest the divorce; when the wife does not wish support for herself or the children, and when no property rights are involved.

*What are the defenses to a divorce action?*

The defenses are (1) a general denial of the allegations contained in the bill of complaint or divorce, (2) condonation or forgiveness, (3) connivance and procurement, (4) collusion, (5) recrimination, (6) agreement for separation, (7) invalidity of the marriage, (8) antenuptial knowledge of cause, (9) a want of capacity to commit the marital offense alleged, and (10) a countersuit, or cross-bill.

A general denial contradicts the plaintiff's assertion as to the existence of a fact. If a husband asserts that his wife committed adultery at a certain time and place with a certain man, the wife may show that she never had sexual relations with the alleged corespondent and that she had neither the inclination nor the opportunity to commit adultery.

Condonation is the conditional forgiveness of a matrimonial offense on condition it will not be repeated. For condonation to be an effective defense, there must be knowledge on the part of the spouse of all the facts on which the divorce action is based; a genuine reconciliation must have taken place; and the offending spouse must have been restored to all his marriage rights. For example, a husband commits adultery. The wife, with full knowledge of the facts, forgives the husband and resumes living with him. A few months later the husband again commits adultery. Under the theory of condonation, the original forgiveness is revoked and the wife may obtain her divorce.

Connivance is the legal doctrine that declares that he who seeks relief must come into court with "clean hands"; that is, he must himself be blameless.

Collusion is an agreement between husband and wife whereby one of them, for the purpose of enabling the other to obtain the divorce, commits a matrimonial offense or fabricates or suppresses evidence. Divorces based on collusion are void, if discovered.

Recrimination is the doctrine that one who seeks redress for a violation of a contract must have himself performed the obligations on his part. Thus if both husband and wife are equally at fault, as when both have committed adultery or cruelty, a divorce will be granted neither.

A countersuit occurs when a defendant, having been served with divorce papers charging him with a matrimonial offense, denies the said charges in his own suit, in which he charges the plaintiff with a matrimonial offense. For example, a wife charges her husband with adultery. Believing himself wrongly accused, the husband, through his counsel, files a countersuit denying the allegations and brings charges against the wife. The case will then be heard on its merits, with the court determining which party, if any, is entitled to the divorce.

In those states where the principle of no-fault divorce has been established the traditional defenses have been abolished.

In Arkansas recrimination is no longer a defense for cruel and barbarous treatment endangering life of innocent party, when the parties have lived apart for three years.

In Colorado the only defenses are failure to establish cause and lack of jurisdiction.

In Florida condonation, collusion, recrimination, and laches have been abolished.

In Iowa the defense of recrimination has been eliminated.

In Michigan the defenses of collusion and condonation have been specifically abolished.

In Minnesota recrimination has been abolished.

In Mississippi court has discretion on the use of recrimination as a defense.

In New Jersey recrimination, condonation, and the "clean hands" doctrine have been abolished.

In New York all defenses abolished except where ground for divorce is adultery.

In Oregon doctrines of fault and *in pari delicto* (where parties are equally at fault) have been eliminated.

In Texas recrimination has been abolished. Condonation is still a valid defense only if it is proved that there is a reasonable expectation of reconciliation.

*How important is it whether the wife or husband files for the divorce?*

As a rule, a wife has considerable advantage if she files first. In the first place, if she can show need, she is entitled, pending litigation, to alimony to support herself and the children, and to a reasonable counsel fee. Since the overwhelming majority of divorce cases are uncontested and privately arranged, what is even more important is that the client be the "innocent" party to the divorce proceedings. For one thing, the innocent party generally wins a more favorable settlement. If a woman is the innocent party, she will get alimony for herself as well as custody of the children. In addition, she will by court order receive a counsel fee which the husband will have to pay. If the husband is the innocent party, he will be relieved of alimony for the wife, though he will have to support the children.

There is also the question of stigma. The guilty party may have to explain to his children or to a prospective second wife or husband that he was guilty of wrongdoing in the legal sense of the term. He may have to explain to his children, for example, that he committed adultery or that he was guilty of cruelty toward their mother. He may also have to explain things away to a prospective second wife. The innocent party to a divorce has, naturally, much less explaining to do, even though, as often happens, it may have been the wife's nagging or frigidity which drove the husband into adultery or compelled him, in self-defense, to resort to acts of mental or physical cruelty.

### What is alimony?

Alimony is the allowance a husband is compelled to pay, by order of court, for his wife's maintenance while she is living apart from him, or after they are divorced. It includes money for her living expenses and is allowed when absolute or partial divorces are granted. Temporary alimony, also known as alimony *pendente lite,* is an allowance to the wife made by the court during pendency of a suit for legal separation or divorce. The award is more or less routinely made if the wife is without separate means and the husband is able to support her.

### What do courts usually award the wife as temporary alimony?

Generally about a third of the husband's net income. However, if the wife has some income of her own, but not enough to support herself, the court will compel the husband to make up the difference. The granting of temporary alimony is a matter of discretion for each court, depending on the circumstances, though most courts grant such payments almost routinely.

*What can a husband do if the wife deliberately delays bringing the case to an issue in order to prolong alimony payments?*

Through his counsel, the husband can explain the facts to the court. If the court is convinced that the wife is using delaying tactics, it may end all temporary alimony payments.

*Will the wife be refused temporary alimony if the husband can show that she has the capacity to earn money but refuses to do so?*

Courts, in awarding alimony, will not go into the question whether the wife should or should not work. It suffices the court if the wife shows that she does not work and lacks the means to support herself.

*If the wife has sufficient money to enable her properly to prosecute or to defend a divorce action, will she be awarded a counsel fee?*

No. What is important is the wife's income rather than the fact that she has securities that do not bring in an income. A wife may also be awarded expenses in connection with a pending divorce case. It has been held that she is entitled to meet expenses incurred in investigating and acquiring information as to her husband's adulterous behavior; that she is entitled to an allowance to prove the grounds of divorce; expenses incurred in investigating the character of nonresident witnesses; the expense in taking depositions; expenses in taking a transcript of testimony; and the cost of printing the wife's record on appeal.

*How is the wife's counsel fee determined?*

Among the factors taken into consideration are the nature of the services to be performed, the practice of the court, the finances of the parties, the wife's needs, the husband's ability to pay, the relative responsibility or fault of the respective parties, the amount of time and preparation involved in the case, the ages of the parties, and the assistance, if any, of the wife in the cumulation of the husband's estate.

*What is permanent alimony?*

These are usually payments to the wife imposed by the court, after the divorce is granted, continuing during the joint lives of both parties. In most states alimony automatically ceases upon the re-marriage of the wife. In no-fault states such as California the court may order either party to pay support to the other for as long as the court thinks just and reasonable. In determining the amount and duration the court takes into consideration the length of the marriage and the ability of the supported spouse to engage in gainful employment without interfering with the proper interests of the children. With the ascent of "women's lib," courts are less likely to favor wives at the expense of husbands.

*Under what circumstances is a husband under no obligation to support his wife?*

A husband is relieved of such support when he can prove that the wife refused or refuses to have sexual relations with him without just cause; when she has unjustifiably left the husband's home and insists on living apart; when the wife has left her husband for some sound legal cause such as drunkenness or cruelty, but lives in open adultery with another man; when the husband wishes in good faith to move to another city, but the wife refuses to accompany him; when the husband and wife live separate and apart as a result of a separation agreement and the husband is fulfilling his obliga-tions; when it has been judicially determined that neither the hus-band nor the wife is entitled to either an absolute or partial di-vorce and the wife refuses the husband's bona fide invitation to return to the home; and, finally, when the separation is by agree-ment and the fault is as much the wife's as the husband's.

It should be noted, however, that a wife may be entitled to ali-mony if she leaves her husband without just cause but later offers in good faith to return and he will not allow her to do so.

*What determines the amount of alimony a husband will have to pay?*

His age, education, professional training, income, means, and prospects; his physical and mental health; the wife's reasonable needs in relation to the husband's capacity to work; the wife's own means and income; the wife's age, ability to work, and potential earning capacity; the parties' station in life; the husband's reason-able needs; the length of the marriage; whether it is a first, second, or third marriage; the conduct of each party during the marriage;

which party actually caused the collapse of the marriage; the number and ages of the children; and the effect of income taxes on the parties.

*How much alimony do husbands have to pay?*

The usual amount is from one third to one half of the husband's income for the support and maintenance of the wife and children. But the amount varies. A second wife in a marriage of brief duration will generally get less than a first wife who has been married fifteen or twenty years. A wife without children will usually get less than a wife with three or four small youngsters.

In Pennsylvania and Vermont the husband does not have to pay alimony after the divorce has been procured, even if the wife obtained the divorce.

Alimony payments, since they are subject to the jurisdiction of the court, may be increased or reduced, as new circumstances warrant. Thus a husband may apply for a reduction if his income is reduced or if his health becomes seriously impaired. A wife, on the other hand, may apply for an increase in alimony payments if the husband's income increases or if she or the children become seriously ill. Even the remarriage of the husband may entitle him to a reduction in alimony payments.

*What happens if a husband falls in arrears in his almony payment?*

A failure to pay court-awarded alimony is contempt of court, for which the husband may be jailed. Of course, the husband may plead extenuating circumstances, which may or may not be taken into consideration. Such circumstances would include inability to obtain a job, serious impairment of health so that he is unable to work, the fact that the ex-wife is now working or has inherited money.

*What are the advantages and disadvantages of arranging for a lump-sum settlement instead of alimony payments?*

There may be special advantages if the marriage has been of short duration, and the wife is young, has no children, and already plans a second marriage. A lump-sum agreement writes the end to a marriage. There is no need for further communication on money matters, and the wife is completely on her own. She need not

worry whether in the future the husband's income will be reduced or his estate dissipated.

The biggest disadvantage to a wife is that she may so dissipate
the lump sum that she will be left without visible means of support, leaving herself and her children stranded.

The advantage to the husband is that he may fulfill his financial
obligation to his wife in one fell swoop. By giving her a lump
sum he will not have to increase payments if in the future his income increases or he falls heir to a fortune.

The disadvantages to the husband are that he cannot deduct the
lump sum for income tax purposes as he can ordinary alimony
payments, and that, if there is no divorce within two years, the
lump-sum settlement may be set aside and the sum declared a
gift subject to tax by Uncle Sam, so defeating the intentions of
both parties. Finally, not all states recognize the validity of a lump-
sum settlement agreement. In those states which do not, the wife,
after spending the lump sum, may apply to the court for periodic
payments, especially if children are involved and cannot be supported by the wife. In all cases, of course, an attorney should be
consulted as to the course to be pursued.

*May a lump-sum settlement be paid in installments?*

Yes. A husband who agrees to pay his wife $50,000 as a lump sum
in lieu of all other claims she may have, may, with his wife's approval, pay the sum in five equal installments or according to
whatever other arrangement is mutually agreed upon. Should the
wife die after entering into a lump-sum settlement with periodic
payments, the wife's estate may recover any balance still due.

*Can a husband be extradited if he moves to another state in order
to avoid alimony payments?*

For failure to pay alimony few states will order the extradition of
a man from one state to another. The ex-wife, however, does have a
remedy under what is known as the Uniform Reciprocal Enforcement of Support Act, adopted in all fifty states. Under this act the
ex-wife files a petition or complaint in the court of her own state
(usually the domestic relations court or prosecuting attorney) alleging her ex-spouse's failure to pay. The proper authorities in her
own community then get in touch with officials of the state to

which the ex-husband has fled. If after a hearing the husband still refuses to pay the alimony, he may be held in contempt in the state in which he now resides. Unhappily, the remedy is more theoretical than practical, since many prosecuting attorneys plead they lack the necessary time and money to make more than a superficial compliance with the law.

*Can a husband and wife agree as to the amount of alimony payments?*

Yes, but the agreement is still subject to the approval of the court. If the court determines that the amount of alimony is inadequate for the wife, it will not hesitate to make the necessary changes. It should be noted that a wife may attach her husband's automobile for nonpayment of alimony, and the court may even compel a husband to put up security for alimony payments when it suspects that the husband may attempt to flee into another state.

*Who gains custody of the children in a divorce case?*

In general, the mother obtains custody of the children, unless she is proved morally unfit. If the court finds that both parents are unfit, the court may award custody either to a third party or to an institution. Before deciding the question of custody the court will consider the following: the fitness of the parents, as revealed by their past record; which parent was at fault in breaking up the home; whether the wife, if awarded custody, would remove the children from the state; whether there have been any violations of the court's orders, as in the payment of temporary alimony; the financial position of the parties; their love for the children; the religion of the parents; and, finally, the preferences of the children. The most important consideration of all, of course, is the welfare of the youngsters.

*Under what circumstances will a court allow a parent to remove a child from one state to another?*

Removal is most likely to be granted when the spouse having custody of the child remarries and her new husband lives outside the state. Under such circumstances the court may disregard the clause in a separation agreement forbidding the removal of a child to another state. The two other most important reasons are health and business. In each case, however, the court will scrupulously go into all the facts in order to determine the validity of the applicant's claim.

### Under what circumstances may a custody order be changed?

When the custodial parent alienates the child's affection from the other parent; when there is serious interference with the other spouse's visitation rights; when the custodial parent is unable to keep the child in school; when the custodial parent unlawfully removes the child from the state; when the custodial parent has become mentally ill; and finally, when the custodial parent leads an immoral and dissolute life.

### May a child refuse to see a visiting parent?

Yes, especially if the child has some basis in fact for his refusal. A court may compel a child to allow the parent to visit him, especially if the child's behavior is arbitrary or has been influenced by the custodial parent. Many mothers who have custody of the children often subtly turn them against the father. For that matter, fathers who have custody often attempt to influence the child against the mother. The courts often intervene to prevent such hostility from continuing.

### Does a father's obligation to support his children cease with the wife's remarriage?

No. The father is obligated by law to support his children until they attain majority, no matter how many times the mother remarries. He must also support the children even if they are abusive and insulting to the father's second wife. Moreover, the ex-wife may refuse to allow the father the right to visit the children if the father refuses to make regular payments for their support. The marriage of an eighteen-year-old daughter, however, usually relieves the custodial parent of his obligation to support her. Nor must the ex-husband continue to support his children if the ex-wife remarries and the second husband adopts the children into the family.

### How can a father make certain that the money he contributes to his child's support is actually going to the child and not to the mother?

He may require the mother to post a bond or other security to see that she fulfills her obligations. Or he may call the matter to the attention of the court.

*What is the most practical method of dividing marital property?*

By far the best method is for each party to employ counsel to work out a fair settlement and then set forth the agreement in legal form, as in a separation agreement. To allow the court to make a property settlement, even in those states where it is permitted, is a costly, time-consuming process, and often grossly unfair to one of the parties. Lawyers are far better equipped for the job, since they are more likely to be aware of the real causes for the divorce, rather than the purely legal grounds. Moreover, they are more apt to know what each party actually contributed to the marriage financially.

*Are women who commit adultery affected in their property rights?*

Yes, and not only in community property states. In Maine a husband is entitled to one third of his wife's estate if she had sexual relations with another man, even though the husband's indifference or neglect drove her to adultery. Divorce is an adversary proceeding, with the court pinning a label of guilt or innocence on the husband or wife, with dire consequences often attached thereto. In Illinois and Massachusetts the wife, if she obtains the divorce, retains her dower interest in her husband's estate, usually one third. In Arkansas the wife who is successful in divorce proceedings is entitled to a one-third interest in her husband's land for life.

*To whom do jewelry and furs belong when purchased with the husband's own money?*

The wife.

*To whom do the television set and the stereo equipment belong?*

If the husband bought these items with his own funds and has receipts for them in his name, they belong to him. If they were bought with the funds of both husband and wife, they belong equally to both and should be divided if there is to be a separation or divorce; or if division is not feasible, a monetary allowance should be made for them, depending upon who retains possession of them.

### To whom does the household furniture belong?

To both husband and wife. In practice, attorneys attempt to make some sort of equitable distribution, taking into consideration who actually paid for the furniture and the needs of the husband, wife, and children. Here, too, an allowance is often made to the husband if he gives all or nearly all of the furniture to his wife.

### To whom do the wedding presents belong?

After the breakup of a marriage, all gifts in contemplation of marriage, unless specially earmarked for either the bride or the groom, are the property of both and should be equally divided. This principle applies to all money given the married couple.

### What about money in savings accounts and checking accounts?

The presumption is that the husband and wife hold the money as joint tenants, which means that each has an undivided interest in the entire account and that there is a right of survivorship. Neither, therefore, can withdraw the money without the consent of the other. However, this presumption may be rebutted if the husband can show that all the money in fact belonged to him. The right of survivorship, in a joint tenancy, means that, upon the death of one of the tenants, the money goes directly to the surviving spouse.

Funds may also be held by the husband and wife as tenants by the entireties. As with a joint tenancy, there is a right of survivorship; when one spouse dies, the money goes directly to the survivor. One spouse may legally withdraw all the funds held in a tenancy by the entireties, and an unscrupulous spouse often does so when he or she contemplates a divorce.

### Will the law compel a husband and wife to sell their home, before the divorce, and divide the proceeds?

No. The ownership of a house during marriage is technically known as a tenancy by the entireties. This means that the property is not subject to partition during the marriage. It also means that both spouses must join in the sale or conveyance of such properties. Upon the death of either spouse the entire property goes to the survivor.

When the marriage ends in divorce, the tenancy by the entirety is terminated, and the ex-spouses become tenants in common, after which the court may decree partition and divide the proceeds.

When the wife holds property in her own name, but the property was acquired by funds belonging solely to the husband, the husband may regain possession of such property, unless the wife can prove by strong evidence that a gift to her was intended.

*Is it possible in a community-property state for one party to waive his or her rights by a written agreement?*

Yes.

*Under what circumstances will a wife forfeit her rights to community property?*

When she willfully and adulterously lives with another man.

*May a husband deduct alimony payments from his gross income to determine his income taxes?*

Yes, if he meets certain basic requirements. To avoid paying taxes on such alimony the husband must show that a written separation agreement was completed after August 16, 1954; that the payments have been periodic; that they are required under the terms of a court decree of divorce or separation or a written agreement providing for such payments; that alimony payments have been made after the divorce decree; and that the payments have been made in discharge of a legal obligation based on marriage.

If the husband meets these requirements, it is the wife who must pay the income tax on the alimony payments. Such payments are considered part of the wife's gross income and are taxable as such.

Periodic payments are those made at fixed intervals. Payments to a wife on a weekly, semimonthly, monthly, quarterly, semiannual, or annual basis are all considered periodic payments.

*May a husband deduct, for income-tax purposes, money paid to a wife under an annulment decree?*

No. Since an annulment renders a marriage null and void from the very beginning, there is no valid marriage within the meaning of the Internal Revenue Act. Nor does the wife have to pay a tax on the money she obtains from her ex-husband. But when the wife receives a sum of money monthly, without any part of it specifically earmarked for the wife's support or for the children's support, the entire sum is regarded as income to the wife and is taxable to her. To avoid this, it is advisable that the attorney set forth in the divorce decree or separation agreement exactly how much is to be paid to the wife as alimony and how much is to be paid to the children as support.

*Are lump-sum settlements deductible for income tax purposes?*
No.

*Are temporary alimony payments deductible by the husband?*
Yes.

*Are attorney's fees deductible in divorce and separation cases?*
No, since they are not considered business expenses.

*From a tax viewpoint should a husband under an installment lump-sum agreement attempt to pay off the entire obligation at one time?*
No. If he does, he gains no tax benefits, since the Internal Revenue Service will only allow him to deduct 10 per cent of the principal sum.

*May a husband deduct alimony payments under an interlocutory decree?*
Yes.

*Is it advisable for a husband and wife, while living separate and apart or while awaiting the divorce decree, to file separate income tax returns or a joint return?*
A joint return whenever possible. Such a return may save both husband and wife considerable money, since they can take advantage of the split-income tax rates.

*Does bankruptcy discharge a husband's obligation to support his wife and children?*
No.

CHAPTER 9

# CONTRACTS

*Why is the law of contracts important?*

Because it forms the basis of all business transactions. Contracts are very much a part of everyday life, and they occupy a major place in everyday law. When you purchase an automobile or house, you do so by means of a contract; when you become a passenger on a bus, steamship, train, or airplane, you enter into a contractual arrangement with the carrier. All employment is regulated by the law of contracts. Understanding contracts, then, can be of vast practical importance, not only in everyday business but in everyday living.

*What is a contract?*

A contract is a definite agreement between two or more competent parties, based upon a lawful consideration, to do or not to do some lawful thing. For a contract to be binding and enforceable, it must fulfill four legal requirements: there must be *mutual assent* or *consent, competent parties, lawful consideration,* and *valid subject matter.*

*How are contracts classified?*

A contract may be valid, unenforceable, voidable, or void.

*Valid contract:* A contract that fulfills all four legal requirements.

*Unenforceable contract:* A contract that cannot be enforced by court action.

*Voidable contract:* A contract in which one of the parties has the option not to perform. For example, a contract made by an infant (that is, a person under twenty-one years of age) or by a person induced through fraud or misrepresentation is a voidable contract. An infant may, as we shall see, accept or reject the contract at his option. A person whose consent has been obtained by fraud may

113

either elect to stand on the contract or to repudiate it at his option.

*Void contract:* A contract that is a nullity and has no legal effect. A contract to murder someone is void as against public policy.

Contracts are also classified as *formal* or *informal* (or simple).

Formal contracts are those under seal. They must be in writing, sealed by the promisor, and delivered. Negotiable instruments, such as checks and promissory notes, are also considered formal contracts.

Contracts are *executory* or *executed*. Contracts are executed when nothing more remains to be done.

Contracts are also called *express* or *implied*. If all the terms of the agreement are stated, either verbally or in writing, the contract is expressed. A contract may be implied from the conduct or behavior of the parties. An implied contract exists, for example, when a passenger boards a train without a ticket: he will have to pay the fare.

*What is meant by mutual assent or consent?*

To establish a valid contract there must be a meeting of the minds. The parties must be in complete agreement as to what is being offered and what is being accepted. If you offer your 1963 Chevrolet for sale to a friend who believes it is a 1964 model, there is obviously no meeting of the minds as to the thing being sold, and no contract is consummated. The elements of mutual consent, therefore, are offer and acceptance.

*What is an offer?*

An offer is a promise intended to create a legal obligation. A promise to attend a dance, a dinner, or a social gathering is not legally binding, and is not a legal offer. Nor is a promise to do something in the future an offer. An offer to sell your house "one of these days" at a certain price is not binding. Neither an offer made in jest nor a vague, ambiguous offer, such as a promise to pay a salesman "a fair share of the profits," or a promise to pay more "if I can afford it," is binding. However, an offer to sell merchandise or goods at a future date, at the prevailing market price, is neither vague nor indefinite, since the future market price can be readily ascertained on the date of delivery.

*Are price lists, catalogs, circular letters, and advertisements of sales considered legal offers?*

No. They are merely invitations to trade, like a government's invitation to receive bids.

*When does an offer become effective?*

An offer becomes effective when the offerer (the person making the offer) communicates the proposal to the offeree (the person to whom the offer is made). An offer may be communicated orally, in writing, or by conduct. An offer is communicated orally or verbally when you attend an auction and make a bid. It is communicated in writing when you send in a written bid to construct a school or other public building. It is communicated by conduct when you pay the taxicab driver the amount indicated on the meter.

*Is failure to read a written offer a valid defense?*

No. A person is bound by what he signs. An exception is when the person signing a written offer is induced to do so by fraud or trickery.

*Are printed notices on receipts and documents considered part of the communicated offer?*

Yes. For example, you sign an order for merchandise. At the bottom of the order blank is the notation, in red ink, that "no claims will be accepted for defective merchandise unless made within twenty-four hours after receipt." You fail to read the notation, but forty-eight hours after delivery you notice that the merchandise is defective and attempt to return the goods. In this case you will be liable for the goods. However, if the written offer contained terms so inconspicuous that the average person would not take notice of them, you would not be bound, especially if no reference to them is made in the body of the writing.

*What may be done about an offer?*

It may be accepted, rejected, revoked, or allowed to lapse. An offer may be accepted only by the person to whom it is made, the offeree, or by his duly authorized agent. The act of an agent is considered the act of the principal; knowledge by the agent is considered knowledge by the principal; and delivery to the agent is considered delivery to the principal. An offer made by mail is accepted when the letter of acceptance, properly addressed and posted, is dropped into the letter box. It need not be actually received by the person who made the offer. In this instance the Post Office becomes the agent of the offerer, the dropping of the letter into the mail box constituting acceptance on the part of the offerer's agent, the Post Office Department. The same principle holds true of telegrams. For example, you wire Smith an offer. Smith receives the telegram at 10 A.M. and wires his acceptance a half hour later. Through some error the wire is not received by you until the following morning. In this case the offer was accepted by Smith at 10:30 A.M., and you will be legally bound.

*When does an offer terminate if no time for acceptance is stated?*

The offer terminates on the lapse of a reasonable time, which depends on the circumstances of each case. An offer to sell real estate at a certain price must be accepted within a matter of days. An offer of a reward for the capture of a criminal may be open for acceptance for a very long time.

An offer, unless under seal or given for a consideration, may be revoked at any time before acceptance. However, if the offerer wishes to revoke his offer, he must communicate his revocation to the offeree. In all but four states—California, Montana, North Dakota, and South Dakota—a letter, telegram, or message of revocation is not effective until received by the offeree. In these four states, the revocation is effective when dispatched.

An offer to the general public is made by making a general announcement of the offer. This may be made by radio, television, newspapers, or any other means suitable to the purpose. Once made, the offer may only be revoked in substantially the same way as that used to announce the offer. If the offer is made by newspaper, it should be revoked by that medium; if by television, then by that medium. An attempt to accept after the publication of the withdrawal is ineffective.

An offer may be rejected. If it is, any later attempt to accept it is inoperative. A counteroffer is a rejection of the original offer. So is a conditional acceptance of an offer. An offer to sell an automobile for $2,500 is rejected when the buyer says he will pay only $2,300, the counteroffer. It is also rejected when he demands additional equipment for the car.

An inquiry by the prospective purchaser regarding the terms of the offer is neither a counteroffer nor a conditional acceptance, and will not terminate the offer.

An offer is terminated by the death or insanity of either party. This is true even though the offeree has no notice of the actual death or insanity.

An offer is also terminated with the destruction of the subject matter, provided the offer has not previously been accepted and the subject matter has been destroyed without the knowledge or fault of either party.

### How can an offer be kept open?

By obtaining an option. An option is a promise, for a consideration, to keep an offer open for a certain length of time. If the offer is not accepted within the time allowed, the offerer may keep the consideration—the money given for the option.

### Does silence imply acceptance of an offer?

Not as a general rule. The fact that one writes to another, "If I do not hear from you within ten days, I shall assume that you accept my offer," does not mean that the offeree has to do anything about the offer. Silence indicates rejection. To this general rule there is an important exception, as when the offeree accepts benefits although it is clear they are not conferred as gifts. If, for example, a tie company sends you a half dozen ties through the mail without your having ordered them, you are under no obligation to return them. But if you use the ties, you become obliged to pay the sales price.

### Do infants, or those under twenty-one, have the right to enter into contracts?

Yes, but the businessman who deals with those under the age set as the majority in the various states does so at his peril, for the law considers that the young are too immature to be held fully responsible for their contracts and provides them with special safeguards for their protection.

The contracts of an infant, therefore, are not void, but merely voidable at his option; that is, the infant has the right to affirm or disaffirm his contracts, either during his minority or within a reasonable time after he reaches his majority, except for those contracts involving necessaries, and for these he must pay, not the contract price, but merely their fair value.

The right to affirm or repudiate the contract belongs to the infant only. The adult contracting party is bound by the terms of the agreement and cannot defend on the basis that the other party was an infant.

*At what age does an infant become an adult for contractual purposes?*

For both sexes the age is twenty-one in Alabama, Alaska, Arizona, California, Colorado, Connecticut, Delaware, District of Columbia, Florida, Georgia, Illinois, Indiana, Iowa, Kansas, Kentucky, Louisiana, Maine, Maryland, Massachusetts, Michigan, Minnesota, Mississippi, Missouri, Nebraska, New Hampshire, New Jersey, New Mexico, New York, North Carolina, Ohio, Oklahoma, Oregon, Pennsylvania, Rhode Island, South Carolina, Tennessee, Texas, Utah, Vermont, Virginia, Washington, West Virginia, Wisconsin, and Wyoming.

In Arkansas, Idaho, Montana, Nevada, North Dakota, and South Dakota the age is twenty-one for males and eighteen for females.

In Hawaii the age is twenty for both sexes.

*What special rights and obligations are infants under in the various states?*

**Alabama**    The right to repudiate contracts terminates for a woman at eighteen, if married.

**Alaska**    The right to repudiate contracts terminates for a woman at her marriage.

**Arizona**    The right to repudiate contracts terminates upon marriage, if eighteen, as to community property only.

**Arkansas**    An infant, if fifteen years old, may not repudiate a contract for life, health, or accident insurance.

**Connecticut**    The law is the same as in Iowa.

**Florida**    The right to repudiate terminates upon marriage. An infant may not repudiate the transfer of a negotiable instrument, but he is not bound by endorsement.

**Iowa**   An infant may not repudiate a contract if he represents that he is an adult and the other party has good reason to rely thereon. The right to repudiate a contract terminates on marriage.

**Kansas**   The law is the same as in Iowa.

**Kentucky**   The right to repudiate a contract terminates upon marriage.

**Maine**   The right to repudiate a contract for real or personal property ends at marriage.

**Maryland**   A contract not beneficial to a minor is void and may not be ratified.

**Michigan**   A contract not beneficial to a minor is void, and other contracts are voidable. The minor may not repudiate a contract if he represents that he is an adult and the other person has good reason to rely thereon. A minor, if sixteen years old, may not repudiate a contract for life, accident, and health insurance, but is not liable for note given on a premium.

**Minnesota**   The right to repudiate a contract for real property transfers terminates for a woman when she marries.

**Nebraska**   The right to repudiate a contract terminates for a woman when she marries. A minor may not repudiate the transfer of a negotiable instrument, but is not bound by endorsement.

**New York**   An infant, if fifteen years old, may not repudiate a contract for life, health, or accident insurance. If he is eighteen, and in business, he may not repudiate business transactions unless improvidently made.

**North Carolina**   An infant may not repudiate the transfer of a negotiable instrument, but he is not bound by endorsement.

**Oklahoma**   An infant, if under the age of eighteen, may not contract as to personal property not in immediate possession, and any contract as to real property is void. If married, he may not repudiate any contract for real property acquired after marriage.

**South Dakota**   The contracts of an infant, if under eighteen years of age, for real property or personal property not in immediate possession are void.

**Utah**   An infant, if sixteen years old, may not repudiate a contract for life, accident, or health insurance. An infant, if in business, may not repudiate business transactions unless the other party is given notice of minority. He may not repudiate the transfer of a negotiable instrument, but he is not bound by endorsement.

**Washington**   A married woman may not repudiate a contract if her husband is an adult. An infant may not repudiate a contract if he represents that he is an adult and the other party has good reason to rely thereon. If he is in business, he may not repudiate business transactions.

*How long after a minor reaches his majority does he have to repudiate contracts he made as a minor?*

A reasonable time, depending upon the circumstances of the individual case.

*For what contracts are minors liable?*

For what the law considers necessaries. These include food, clothing, shelter, medicine, and an elementary or vocational education. For the minor to be held responsible for payment, the articles furnished must be suitable to his station in life. But even for necessaries the minor is only liable for the reasonable value of goods or services furnished, not for the actual contract price. To recover payment for a minor's necessaries, the seller must prove that the goods were suitable to the condition in life of the infant and that he did not at the time have an adequate supply from other sources.

A minor, therefore, cannot bind himself even for necessaries if he lives with a parent or guardian, unless it can be proved that the parent or guardian is unable or unwilling to furnish him with necessaries.

Generally excluded from the term "necessaries" are liquor, expensive foods for parties, diamonds, violins, guns, saddles, horses (except where riding is necessary to the health of the minor), automobiles, and motorcycles.

Cars and motorcycles are not considered necessaries even though they are used by a minor to carry on a business operated by him. This follows the theory that the law views with disfavor any minor who engages in a business involving a variety of contracts, since he doesn't normally have sufficient discretion to engage in a business or trade.

A minor may disaffirm or avoid any contract at any time during his minority or within a reasonable time after reaching his majority. He may not, however, repudiate contracts involving real estate until after he reaches his majority. The repudiation may be either verbal or written, and it must be of the entire contract, not of a part only. Repudiation is any action, express or implied, showing the minor's intention not to abide by the contract.

If the minor does not repudiate an executed contract (an agreement in which nothing further remains to be done), he is assumed to have ratified the contract and decided to elect to claim its privileges. Since repudiation requires some positive action, silence constitutes affirmation of an executed contract after a lapse of a reasonable time. A longer time is allowed to repudiate a real estate transaction than for one involving personal property.

*Does the minor have to restore the consideration or money before he can repudiate a contract?*

All courts agree that if the minor can restore what he has received, or any part of it, he must do so before he can recover the amount paid by him. Most courts hold that even if the goods are injured, depleted, or entirely lost, the minor may repudiate the contract and recover his consideration, on the theory that he would not otherwise be protected by the laws which were specifically designed for that purpose, since any other rule would limit his repudiation to his foresight in keeping the goods.

Nor does a minor lose all his rights even if he fraudulently misrepresents his age; though if he does, the adult may have a claim against him in damages for deceit. A minority of states provide that when an infant returns property in a depreciated state, he may be charged with the value of its use and its depreciation for the time he had it.

*Are the contracts of intoxicated persons binding?*

No. Intoxication is a defense regardless, no matter whether it was voluntary intoxication or intoxication produced by the intervention of another. The important question concerns the capacity of the contracting party; namely, was he in such a condition that he was unable to understand the nature and effect of the instrument? If he was, his contracts are voidable and may be repudiated within a reasonable time after he becomes sober. Promptly upon recovering his judgment, the individual must elect either to affirm or repudiate the agreement.

*What about insane persons?*

The general rule is that notes, contracts, and conveyances of an insane person, even though he has not been adjudged insane, are voidable like those of minors and may be ratified or repudiated when the infirmity is removed. Similarly, if the contract is for necessaries or for the benefit of the insane person, the contract may be enforced against him.

If the contract is an executory one (one in which something remains to be done), it will not be enforced.

The weight of authority is to the effect that, when a contract with an insane person has been entered into in good faith, without fraud or imposition, for a fair consideration, without notice of insanity, and has been executed in whole or in part, it will not be set aside unless the parties can be restored to their original position. However, if the sane party to the contract knew of the other's insanity, or if the circumstances were such that a reasonable and prudent person should have known of it, the contract may be repudiated at the option of the lunatic or his representative without regard to the fairness of the contract.

After a person has been adjudged insane by a court, any acts, contracts, or conveyances entered into thereafter are void.

### Does a convict forfeit his contractual rights?

An inmate in a jail or prison or a person convicted of a crime does not lose his right to make a valid will, contract, or deed. However, he cannot enforce any contract on his own behalf, because his civil rights are suspended; hence, he cannot sue for breach of contract, though his creditors may reach any property that belongs to him.

### What mistakes make contracts defective?

Mistakes as to the identity of the subject matter; mistakes as to the existence of the subject matter; mistakes as to the nature of the agreement; and mistakes as to the identity of the parties.

For example, a mutual mistake concerning the identity of the subject matter may arise when one party agrees to sell to another a lot on a street with a certain name in Baltimore, Maryland. Unknown to both parties is the fact that there are two streets with that name in Baltimore. The seller has in mind a lot on one street and the prospective buyer has in mind a lot on the other. The agreement is defective because of the mutual mistake about which lot is the subject matter of the contract.

A mutual mistake as to the existence of the subject matter may arise when the one party agrees to buy a specific pair of racing dogs from the prospective seller. Unknown to both parties, both dogs have died from poisoning the day before. The agreement is defective because of the mutual mistake as to the existence of a particular pair of animals.

A mistake as to the nature of the agreement may arise when one party is handed a document which is represented as a lease to a certain property, but which in reality is a deed to it. Instead of reading the document himself, Jones asks that it be read to him. It is read in a way that indicates that the paper is a lease rather than a deed. The agreement to sell the property rather than to lease it is defective because Jones does not know the nature of the paper he has signed. If, however, Jones reads the paper himself and then signs it, he can be charged with negligence and will not be able to disaffirm the contract.

A mutual mistake as to the identity of the parties may arise when contracts are negotiated by mail, telegram, or telephone, as when each party believes the other to be someone else.

*What agreements are considered illegal and therefore unenforceable?*

Gambling and wagering contracts are both illegal and void. So are agreements that charge interest at usurious rates, that is, at rates the law considers excessive. These rates vary from state to state (see the accompanying chart).

All agreements that the law considers to be against public policy are invalid and unenforceable. Such contracts include those which unreasonably restrain trade, those which interfere with public service, and those which obstruct the administration of justice.

*You bet $100 on the outcome of a football game. The man with whom you made the bet refuses to pay. Can you recover?*

In most states, no—since the courts will refuse to aid either party to a gambling transaction.

*You borrow $500 from a friend at 10 per cent interest, agreeing to repay the loan in three months. When you discover that the legal rate of interest in your state is only 6 per cent, you refuse to pay the additional 4 per cent. What are your legal rights?*

All states prescribe both a legal rate of interest and a contract rate. The contract rate is the rate of interest specified by the parties and included in the agreement. When no contract rate is specified, the legal rate is binding. However, if the contract rate exceeds that allowed by the state, the law allows the forfeiture of interest, and, in some cases, the principal amount also. In the above example, the borrower would have to pay the 10 per cent interest, assuming 10 per cent was the lawful contract rate of the state in which both parties resided.

*What are the interest rates in the various states?*

| State | Legal Rate | Contract Rate | Does usury result in forfeiture of interest? |
|---|---|---|---|
| | Per Cent | | |
| Alabama | 6 | 8 | Yes |
| Alaska | 6 | 8 | Yes |
| Arizona | 6 | 8 | Yes |
| Arkansas | 6 | 10 | Yes, and principal, too |
| California | 7 | 10 | Yes |
| Colorado | 6 | No Limit | No |
| Connecticut | 6 | 12 | Yes, and principal, too |
| Delaware | 6 | 6 | Yes, above the legal rate |
| District of Columbia | 6 | 8 | Yes |
| Florida | 6 | 10 | Yes |
| Georgia | 7 | 8 | Yes |
| Hawaii | 6 | 12 | Yes |
| Idaho | 6 | 8 | Yes |
| Illinois | 5 | 7 | Yes |
| Indiana | 6 | 8 | Yes, above the legal rate |
| Iowa | 5 | 7 | Yes |
| Kansas | 6 | 10 | Yes, above the contract rate, plus penalty of same amount |
| Kentucky | 6 | 6 | Yes, above the legal rate |
| Louisiana | 5 | 8 | Yes |
| Maine | 6 | No Limit | No |
| Maryland | 6 | 6 | Yes, above 6% |
| Massachusetts | 6 | No Limit | No |
| Michigan | 5 | 7 | Yes, if unpaid |
| Minnesota | 6 | 8 | Yes, and principal, too |
| Mississippi | 6 | 8 | Yes. If greater rate of interest than 20% per year is charged, principal and interest are forfeited. |
| Missouri | 6 | 8 | Yes, above the legal rate |
| Montana | 6 | 10 | Yes, double interest paid |

| State | Legal Rate | Contract Rate | Does usury result in forfeit-ure of interest? |
|-------|-----------|---------------|-----------------------------------|
| | Per Cent | | |
| Nebraska | 6 | 9 | Yes |
| Nevada | 7 | 12 | Yes, above rate allowed |
| New Hampshire | 6 | No Limit | No |
| New Jersey | 6 | 6 | Yes |
| New Mexico | 6 | 10 | Yes |
| New York | 6 | 6 | Yes, and principal, too, on certain debts |
| North Carolina | 6 | 6 | Yes |
| North Dakota | 4 | 7 | Yes, plus 25% of principal |
| Ohio | 6 | 8 | Yes, above legal rate |
| Oklahoma | 6 | 10 | Yes, double interest |
| Oregon | 6 | 10 | Yes, and principal, too |
| Pennsylvania | 6 | 6 | Yes, above legal rate |
| Rhode Island | 6 | 30 (on amounts over $50) | Yes, and principal, too |
| South Carolina | 6 | 7 | Yes |
| South Dakota | 6 | 8 | Yes |
| Tennessee | 6 | 6 | Yes, and principal, too, un-der certain conditions |
| Texas | 6 | 10 | Yes |
| Utah | 6 | 10 | Yes, and principal, too |
| Vermont | 6 | 6 | Yes, above the legal rate |
| Virginia | 6 | 6 | Yes, above the legal rate |
| Washington | 6 | 12 | Yes, above the contract rate |
| West Virginia | 6 | 6 | Yes, above the legal rate |
| Wisconsin | 5 | 10 | Yes |
| Wyoming | 7 | 10 | Yes |

*You borrow $600 from a finance or small-loan company for a period of one year, agreeing to pay 4 per cent on the first $100 and 3 per cent a month on the balance still due, the entire $600 to be repaid in equal monthly installments of $50 each. After paying for four months, you refuse to make any further payments, claiming that you are being charged an unlawful rate of interest. How valid is your claim?*

Since most states have laws forbidding small loan companies to charge in excess of 3½ per cent a month interest, you would be in such states within your legal rights in refusing to make further payments.

*But isn't 3½ per cent interest a month in itself usurious?*

No, since the rate is applied each month only on the balance still due.

*What are the statutory small-loan rates in the various states?*

| State | Monthly Rate | Maximum Loan | Maximum Allowable Rates |
|---|---|---|---|
| Alabama | — | $ 300 | 8% a year |
| Arizona | 3% | $ 600 | 3% on first $300; 2% on remainder |
| Alaska | 4% | $1,000 | 4% on first $300; 2½% on next $300; 2% above $600; 5% on loans not exceeding $50; default fee of $3. |
| Arkansas | No Law | | 10% a year |
| California | 2½% | $5,000 | 2½% on first $100; 2% on next $400 (if security insured); 5 to 6% on next $4,500; no maximum above $5,000 |
| Colorado | 3% | $1,500 | 3% on first $300; 1½% on next $200; 1% above $500 |
| Connecticut | 3% | $ 600 | 3% on first $100; 3 to 4% on next $300; 12% a year after 20 months |
| Delaware | No Law | | 6% a year discount; 2% service fee; 5% fine; various limitations; industrial law; loan size based on capital and surplus |
| District of Columbia | 1% | $ 200 | |
| Florida | 3% | $ 600 | 3% on first $300; 2% on next $300; 10% a year 12 months after maturity |
| Georgia | — | $2,500 | 8% a year; fee of 8% on first $600 and 4% of excess; charged on initial balance as discount for 18 months as add-on for longer maturities; plus other charges |
| Hawaii | 3½% | $ 300 | 3½% on first $100; 2½% on remainder |
| Idaho | 3% | $1,000 | 3% on first $300; 2% on next $200; 1% above $500 |
| Illinois | 3% | $ 800 | 3% on first $150; 1% on remainder |
| Indiana | 3% | $ 500 | 3% on first $150; 1½% on remainder |

| State | Monthly Rate | Maximum Loan | Maximum Allowable Rates |
|---|---|---|---|
| Iowa | 3% | $ 300 | 3% on first $150; 2% on remainder |
| Kansas | 3% | $2,100 | 3% on first $300; 5 to 6% on remainder; 10% a year 6 months after maturity |
| Kentucky | 3½% | $ 300 | 3½% on first $150; 2½% on remainder |
| Louisiana | 3½% | $ 300 | 3½% on first $150; 2½% on remainder; 8% a year, one year after maturity |
| Maine | 3% | $2,500 | 3% on first $150; 2½% on next $150; 1½% on remainder; 25¢ minimum |
| Maryland | 3% | $ 300 | |
| Massachusetts | 2% | $ 300 | 2% for one year; thereafter 6% a year |
| Michigan | 3% | $ 500 | 3% on first $50; 2½% on next $250; 3 to 4% on remainder |
| Minnesota | 3% | $ 300 | |
| Missouri | 2.218% | $ 400 | 8% above $400 |
| Montana | No Law | | 10% a year |
| Nebraska | 3% | $3,000 | 3% on first $150; 2½% on next $150; 3 to 4% on remainder |
| Nevada | 3% | $1,500 | 3% on first $300; 1% on remainder; $5 a year minimum; other charges |
| New Hampshire | 2% | $ 300 | $1 fee on loans up to $50; $2 fee on loans up to $300 |
| New Jersey | 2½% | $ 500 | 2½% on first $300; ½% on remainder |
| New Mexico | 3½% | $1,000 | 3½% on first $150; 3% on next $150; 1% on remainder; 10% a year one year after maturity and in certain other cases |
| New York | 2½% | $ 500 | 2½% on first $100; 2% on next $200; ½% on remainder |
| North Carolina | No Law | | 6% a year |
| North Dakota | No Law | | 7% a year |

| State | Monthly Rate | Maximum Loan | Maximum Allowable Rates |
|---|---|---|---|
| Ohio | 3% | $1,000 | 3% on first $150; 2% on next $150; 2 to 3% on remainder |
| Oklahoma | — | $ 300 | 10% a year plus service charge not exceeding $2 a month |
| Oregon | 3% | $1,500 | 3% on first $300; 2% on next $200; 1% on remainder |
| Pennsylvania | 3% | $ 600 | 3% on first $150; 2% on next $150; 1% on remainder; 6% a year after 24 months |
| Rhode Island | 3% | $ 300 | |
| South Carolina | No Law | | 7% a year |
| South Dakota | 3% | $2,500 | 3% on first $300; 3 to 4% on remainder, $2 minimum; 8% a year 6 months after maturity |
| Tennessee | — | $ 300 | ½% plus fees not exceeding 1% a month |
| Texas | No Law | | 10% a year |
| Utah | 3% | $ 600 | 3% on first $300; 1% on remainder |
| Vermont | 2½% | $ 500 | 2½% on first $125; 2¼% on next $175; 1% on remainder |
| Virginia | 2½% | $ 600 | 2½% on first $300; 1½% on remainder; 6% a year after 23 months and in certain other cases |
| Washington | 3% | $ 500 | 3% on first $300; 1% on remainder; $1 minimum |
| West Virginia | 3½% | $ 300 | 3½% on first $150; 2½% on remainder |
| Wisconsin | 2½% | $ 300 | 2½% on first $100; 2% on next $100; 1% on remainder |
| Wyoming | 3½% | $1,000 | 3½% on first $150; 2½% on next $150; 1% on remainder; plus $1 fee on loan of $50 or less; $1 record-fee |

*What is meant by an agreement in unreasonable restraint of trade?*

An agreement is considered unreasonable when it is not reasonably limited in time and space. You agree, for example, to sell your drug store for $25,000 and also agree, at the insistence of the purchaser, not to open another drug store in the United States for a period of ten years. Within six months you decide to open a store within three blocks of your competitor. You would be within your legal rights, since the agreement would be considered an unreasonable restraint of trade. Had the buyer merely insisted that you not open a drug store within a specified area of the city for a certain period of time, the contract would have been enforced in the courts.

*What agreements are invalid as interfering with public service?*

1. An agreement to pay money to legislators in order to influence legislation.

2. An agreement to pay money to a public official for an appointment to public office.

3. An agreement to pay money for public employment.

*What agreements are illegal because they obstruct the administration of justice?*

Those which encourage lawsuits and those which provide for the concealment of a crime, for the false swearing of witnesses, and for the bribing of jurors are all illegal and unenforceable. In addition, they may subject both parties to criminal penalties.

*What is "consideration" in contracts?*

Consideration is that which binds the parties to a contract. It is the price, motive, or inducement that leads one party to do something he is not otherwise bound to do, or to forbear or refrain from doing something he is otherwise free to do.

*You ask an auto salesman the price of a certain car. He replies, "$1,500 if sold today." You agree to this price and ask that the car be delivered at your home at 3 P.M. Is this a valid contract?*

Yes. The consideration which binds the promise is $1,500.

*You tell your nephew that you will give him $3,500 if he obtains his law degree by the time he is twenty-three. Your nephew does so. Can he demand the $3,500?*

Yes. The consideration in this case is the nephew's doing something he is not otherwise bound to do.

*You promise your eighteen-year-old son that if he quits smoking for six months, you will give him $1,000. Is such a promise legally enforceable?*

Yes. Here the consideration is the son's promise to refrain from smoking for six months. Having carried out the promise, the son is entitled to the father's $1,000.

*You promise to donate $1,000 to the Community Chest. Can you be sued on your failure to make good the contribution?*

Probably, especially if the Community Chest has relied on your promise in planning its budget.

*You have a diamond ring worth $1,000, but you need money badly. You finally accept an offer of $300, because it is the highest offer made. After accepting the offer, but before turning the ring over to the buyer, you receive and accept an offer of $500. The man who made the first offer sues you to obtain the ring. Your defense is that the consideration of $300 was inadequate. Is this a good defense?*

No. The law will not step in to aid a person who has made a bad deal or bargain. In this case you will be liable in damages if you refuse to turn over the diamond ring to the person who made the original offer.

*You give an expensive automobile to a friend as a gift. Later, having some second thoughts about the matter, you demand the return of the car on the ground that there was no consideration for your act. Is this a good defense?*

No. Contracts which have been fully executed on both sides will not be disturbed by the courts. Had you failed to deliver the car to your friend, however, you could not be legally compelled to do so.

*You promise a police officer in your neighborhood that if he will keep an eye on your store you will give him $50. Is your promise binding?*

No, since there is no legal consideration for your promise. The rule is that policemen are bound to protect the lives and property of citizens in their community. A promise to pay someone for something he is already bound to do is void as against public policy.

*You receive a bill from your dentist in the amount of $217. You believe the bill should be $200, and you send a check for that amount, marked "Paid in full," to the dentist. The dentist cashes the check, and a month later he demands the $17. Do you have to pay?*

The general principle in most states is that when an undisputed amount is owed, a promise to pay a lesser amount than is due, or the payment of a lesser amount, will not discharge the debtor's liability for the balance. In this case, there seems to be a genuine dispute as to the exact amount, so that you would be liable for the balance of $17. If you had marked the check "Paid in full re disputed amount" and if the dentist had then cashed it, you would have been relieved of further liability.

*You owe Smith $500. When the debt is due, you ask for an extension of three months, to which Smith verbally agrees. The next week, however, Smith sues you for the $500. What are your rights?*

None. A verbal promise to extend the time of payment of a debt is not binding unless the debtor gives the creditor something as a consideration. Since there is no consideration for the extension, Smith is not bound and can enforce his rights any time he pleases. Had the agreement to extend the time been in writing, and signed by both parties, it would have been recognized as binding in some states.

*You become involved in an automobile accident that inflicts injuries on a pedestrian. To avoid having suit filed against you, you promise to pay the injured party $1,500 within sixty days. When you discover witnesses favorable to your version of the accident, you refuse to pay. What are your legal rights?*

None. Here the consideration for the avoidance of the suit was the payment of $1,500. The injured party therefore refrained from doing what he had a right to do, that is, to file suit. Your failure to pay the $1,500 within the time limit could be enforced in the courts.

*Which contracts are required to be in writing?*

Whenever possible, *all* contracts should be in writing in order to provide written proof of what the parties actually agreed to in case of a dispute.

Certain contracts, by law, are required to be in writing. If they are not, they are unenforceable. The Statute of Frauds, which has been adopted by every state of the Union, provides that the following contracts must be in writing:

1. A contract which by its terms cannot be performed within one year from the date it is made. If, for example, you enter into a contract of employment for more than one year, such contract must be reduced to writing. If the contract is merely a verbal one, you can be fired without any legal redress. If the contract is in writing, you may have a claim for damages as a result of the contract's breach.

2. A contract for the sale of real property, or of any interest in real property, or for the lease of real property for more than a year. Suppose, for example, you agree to buy one hundred acres of land. Before the contract can be reduced to writing, the land is sold to someone else. Do you have a claim? No. The fact that the agreement was not in writing makes it unenforceable.

3. A contract to answer for the debt or default of another person. A friend of yours owes money to a third person. You tell that person that if your friend does not pay the debt, you will. When your friend defaults, you are sued. Can there be a recovery against you? No, since the agreement was merely a verbal one. Had you signed a written promise, you could have been held.

4. Agreements made in consideration of marriage. A verbal promise made before marriage to make a settlement after marriage is unenforceable. The promise must be in writing.

5. A contract for the sale of goods, wares, and merchandise for a stated value, or over, unless the buyer accepts part of the goods and actually receives the same or gives something in part payment,

or unless some note or memorandum is made in writing and signed by the party to be charged by such contract or his authorized agent. The Statute of Frauds in most states specifies the minimum amount for which a sale of goods must be made in writing, the amount varying from $50 to $2,500 (in Ohio). (For further discussion of this see the chapter on Sales.)

*To what extent may contracts be assigned?*

In general, all contracts involving money or property may be transferred or assigned to third persons. The person who assigns a contract is known as the assignor. The person to whom the contract is assigned is known as the assignee. Unless prohibited by some statute or by the original contract itself, assignments may be either oral or written.

*What happens if the person to whom the contract has been assigned fails to live up to the agreement?*

Liability then falls on the assignor.

*You employ a prominent trial attorney to represent you in a suit. On the day you go to court, you find you are represented by that attorney's assistant. What are your rights?*

Contracts involving special skill, knowledge, or judgment cannot be assigned or transferred without the consent of both parties to the contract. In the example above, you are under no obligation to accept the services of the trial attorney's assistant.

*What are the rights of the assignee of a contract, that is, the person to whom the contract has been assigned?*

An assignee legally stands in the shoes of the assignor, having no better title or rights than had the assignor. He can enforce whatever rights the assignor had, and would be subject to whatever defenses the assignor could raise had he been sued.

*As a landlord, you assign your rent claim of $300 from one of your tenants to a third party. Not having been notified of the assignment, the tenant pays you the sum due, and subsequently you* *leave town. What are the rights of the third party, to whom the assignment was made?*

Since the assignee (the third party) failed to notify the tenant of the assignment, he has no legal claim against the tenant.

### Do contracts terminate on death?

All contracts, not of a personal nature, are performed by the deceased's executor or administrator. This is known as assignment by operation of law. A similar disposition is also made when a person becomes a bankrupt, in which case a trustee takes over the bankrupt's contracts and enforces them for the benefit of creditors.

### How are contracts terminated?

1. By performance, or the rendering of services.

2. By a subsequent impossibility of performance, for example, by a strike, by a change of law, or by the death or serious illness of the contracting party when the contract is for personal services, as in the serious illness of a lecturer or star performer in a show.

3. By the agreement of both parties to end the contract.

### What is meant by a breach of contract?

A breach is the failure of one party to perform his part of the contract.

### What are the remedies for a breach of contract?

1. The injured party may sue for damages, provided he can show loss. But he must also minimize damages. Thus an employee wrongfully discharged is entitled to recover as damages the salary fixed by the agreement, less whatever money he has been able to earn in other employment. If the contract breached is for the payment of money, the injured party is entitled to recover interest at the legal rate from the time the debt is due in addition to the full amount of the debt.

2. The injured party may have a right to sue for the reasonable value of the services actually performed by him.

3. The injured party may have a right to sue for specific performance. If, for example, you contract to sell your house for $20,000 and later change your mind, the buyer may petition the court to

compel you to go through with the sale, instead of seeking money damages. Specific performance is a special remedy and is granted only in cases involving real property and such personal property as valuable paintings and jewels unobtainable elsewhere.

4. There may also be a right to enjoin another person. While it is true that contracts for personal services will not be enforced, an injunction will prevent the performer's accepting employment elsewhere during the term of the contract if his services are rare and unique.

5. A contract may also be dissolved by proper arbitration proceedings. Arbitrators are usually businessmen experienced in the kind of work in which the contracting parties are engaged. The decision of the arbitrators is binding and may not be disturbed except on the ground of fraud or obvious errors in computation. The decision of the arbitrators is final, and from it no award may be taken to the courts, except in the case of fraud or error.

*What happens if one of the parties to an arbitration proceeding refuses to comply with the award?*

The aggrieved party may then apply to the appropriate court to make the award into a judgment of the court, so that the award may be judicially enforced.

## CHAPTER 10

## SALES

*What is the subject matter of the law of sales?*

The buying and purchase of goods, wares, and merchandise. Each year American consumers spend billions of dollars on such tangible, personal property goods as automobiles, jewelry, radio and television sets, and countless other items. So important is the subject of sales that most states have adopted the Uniform Sales Act, which attempts to standardize and regulate the purchase and sale of goods throughout the country.

*Who are the parties to a sale?*

The seller, sometimes known as the vendor, and the buyer, sometimes known as the vendee.

*What is the consideration for a sale?*

The consideration is the price of the article involved.

*When must a contract for the sale of goods be in writing?*

As we saw in the chapter on contracts, certain contracts must be in writing to come within the Statute of Frauds. Among these are agreements for the sale of goods valued at more than $50. But to the rule that all sales agreements over a certain amount must be written, there are certain exceptions. In brief, a sales agreement may be oral, provided:

1. The buyer has received and accepted part of the goods sold to him.

2. The buyer has made part payment to bind the bargain.

3. Some note or memorandum of the agreement between the parties is made in writing and signed by the party to be charged; that is, by the party who is going to be held liable on the contract or by his authorized agent.

*You order a suit of clothes from a custom tailor, designed to your individual specifications and measurements, for $150. After receiving the suit, you find it unsatisfactory and set up as a defense that the agreement was not in writing as required by the Statute of Frauds. Can you refuse payment?*

No. Under the Statute of Frauds "if the goods are to be manufactured by the seller especially for the buyer and are not suitable for sale to others in the ordinary course of the seller's business, the provisions of this section shall not apply." Hence, the agreement to purchase the suit need not be in writing, and you would be liable for the full amount, provided the suit was satisfactorily made.

*What are the minimum amounts for which sales must be made in writing under the Statute of Frauds?*

| | |
|---|---|
| Alabama | $ 500 |
| Alaska | 50 |
| Arizona | 500 |
| Arkansas | 30 |
| California | 500 |
| Colorado | 50 |
| Connecticut | 100 |
| Delaware | 500 |
| District of Columbia | 50 |
| Florida | All |
| Georgia | 50 |
| Hawaii | 100 |
| Idaho | 500 |
| Illinois | 500 |
| Indiana | 500 |
| Iowa | All |
| Kansas | None |
| Kentucky | 500 |
| Louisiana | None |
| Maine | 500 |
| Maryland | 50 |
| Massachusetts | 500 |
| Michigan | 100 |
| Minnesota | 50 |
| Mississippi | 50 |
| Missouri | 30 |
| Montana | 200 |
| Nebraska | 500 |
| Nevada | 50 |
| New Hampshire | 500 |

| | |
|---|---|
| New Jersey | 500 |
| New Mexico | 50 |
| New York | 50 |
| North Carolina | None |
| North Dakota | 500 |
| Ohio | 2500 |
| Oklahoma | 50 |
| Oregon | 50 |
| Pennsylvania | 500 |
| Rhode Island | 500 |
| South Carolina | 50 |
| South Dakota | 500 |
| Tennessee | 500 |
| Texas | None |
| Utah | 500 |
| Vermont | 50 |
| Virginia | None |
| Washington | 50 |
| West Virginia | None |
| Wisconsin | 50 |
| Wyoming | 50 |

NOTE: In the states of Florida and Iowa, all sales, regardless of amount, must be in writing. Remaining states with designation "None" have no requirement, and all sales of personal property in these states may be made orally.

### What is "title"?

Title is evidence of the ownership of goods. In the purchase or sale of goods, title passes from the seller to the buyer. Thus the question of ownership of the goods, and so responsibility for whatever losses may occur, rests on the determination of when title passes.

### Answering an ad in the newspaper, you buy, for $500, a diamond ring, which later turns out to have been stolen. Do you have to return the ring to the true owner?

Yes. Since a thief does not obtain title to the goods he steals, he cannot convey title to anyone else. Under the circumstances, your only recourse is to sue the seller for the purchase price of the ring. The loss actually will fall on the one to whom the thief sold the ring in the first place.

### What is a warehouse receipt?

A warehouse receipt is a document certifying that goods, wares, or merchandise have been deposited in a warehouse by a certain person. A warehouse receipt is either negotiable or nonnegotiable. If the goods stored are to be delivered only to the person named in the document, the warehouse receipt is nonnegotiable. If the receipt asserts that the goods are to be delivered to the *order* of some person named in the document, the receipt is negotiable and may be sold, transferred, or discounted to a third party.

*What is a bill of lading?*

A bill of lading is similar to a warehouse receipt, except that the former also represents a contract for the shipment of goods. When goods are shipped by rail, the bill of lading is mailed to the consignee, the person to whom the goods are shipped. This procedure allows the consignee to receive the goods described in the bill of lading when he presents the bill at the freight station. If the goods are consigned to the order of a specified individual, the document is known as an *order* bill of lading, and is negotiable: the consignee may sell, transfer, or otherwise dispose of the goods while the latter are still in the possession of the carrier. If, however, the goods are consigned to a specific person, the straight bill of lading is not negotiable, and the goods may not be disposed of until the consignee has physical possession of them.

*What is a bill of sale?*

A bill of sale transfers formal ownership of personal property from the seller to the buyer. It is especially important to have a bill of sale for an automobile, for without such a document, neither a registration card nor license plates will be issued.

*When does title pass in a cash sale?*

Upon payment.

*You buy a television set on credit. Before the set can be delivered to you, it is destroyed by a fire in the store. On whom does the loss fall legally?*

On you, the buyer. Technically, title passed to you at the time the sale was made, even though payment or delivery or both are postponed to some future date. The fact that the store extended credit is an indication that it intended to part with title immediately. As a practical matter, however, you would not suffer any loss at all. The store would simply replace the destroyed set with another and recover its own loss from its insurance company.

*You order a set of valuable books to be paid for C.O.D. When does title pass to you?*

Title passes to you as soon as the books are delivered to the express company or carrier for delivery to you. Should the books be destroyed, mutilated, or lost while in transit, you will have to bear the loss, since you have legal ownership.

*You purchase an expensive mink coat with the understanding that if either you or your husband does not like it, you can return it to the store within thirty days. While you have the coat in your home, it is stolen. Upon whom does the loss fall?*

You. In sales with the privilege of return, title passes on delivery of the item. When you return the coat within the stipulated time, title reverts to the seller.

*What if no stipulated time for the return of the coat had been mentioned?*

The same principle prevails, except that the coat would have to be returned within a reasonable time. What constitutes a reasonable time depends upon the facts of the individual case. In any event, should something happen to the coat while it is in your possession, you would have to bear the loss.

*When does title pass on an F.O.B. sale?*

A sale F.O.B. (free on board) means that the shipper will pay all the costs up to and including the placement of the goods in the car of the carrier. Title normally passes to the buyer at the time the goods are placed in the hands of the carrier. If the goods are sold F.O.B. destination, title does not pass to the buyer until they have reached their destination, the risk of loss, if any, being borne by the seller. If the goods are sent F.O.B. shipping point, the risk of loss in transit is assumed by the buyer.

*Much to your surprise, you receive a set of books through the mail which you did not order. What are your obligations?*

If you use them, you must pay for them. If you have no intention of using them, you should either mark the package "rejected" or "return to sender" and deliver it to the postman or to the local post office; or you may hold the package and notify the sender to send for it. You are under no obligation to return the package at your own expense.

*You sell your package liquor store and give to the purchaser an inventory of your stock, together with a list of creditors. Shortly after the sale, one of your creditors, a wholesale whisky house, sues to have the sale set aside because he has not been notified of the sale. What are your rights and what are those of the creditor?*

To protect creditors against fraud, the states have enacted what are known as Bulk Sales Laws. These laws provide, in effect, that:

1. Not less than ten days before the sale, the seller must deliver to the buyer a full and detailed inventory, showing the cost price to him of each article to be included in the sale, which the buyer must retain for ninety days for inspection by the creditors of the seller.

2. The buyer may demand and receive from the seller a written list of the names and addresses of his creditors and the amount of the seller's indebtedness to each, with the list being certified under oath by the seller.

3. At least ten days before the sale (the number of days varies from state to state), the buyer must notify every creditor, either personally or by registered mail, of the proposed sale and of the price and terms.

Since, in the example, the seller failed to comply fully with the requirements of the Bulk Sales Law, the creditor may have the sale set aside. As the owner, you will have to satisfy your creditors before you can proceed with the sale.

*What is a conditional sale?*

A conditional sale is one in which the buyer makes a down payment and agrees to make weekly or monthly payments until the balance is paid. In the typical conditional sales agreement:

1. The buyer obtains immediate possession of the goods, with title remaining in the seller.

2. A down payment is made at the time of sale, with the balance payable in installments.

3. The risk of loss falls on the buyer.

**4.** Title passes to the buyer only when the last installment is paid.

**5.** The seller has the right to repossess the goods if the buyer fails to meet his payments.

**6.** The buyer has no right to redeem the goods after the seller gives notice before retaking them, but if the seller fails to provide such notice, the buyer generally has ten days in which to redeem them.

**7.** After retaking the goods, the seller has the right to dispose of them at public auction or at private sale and to credit the buyer with any balance left over from the sale; however, if there is any deficiency, the seller may procure a money judgment against the buyer.

**8.** Finally, the buyer, in a conditional sales agreement, pledges not to dispose of the goods without the prior written consent of the seller.

*Should conditional sales agreements be recorded?*

Yes. A seller's failure to record a conditional sales contract gives a third-party purchaser good title to the chattel, the loss falling on the original owner, since he failed to comply with the statute's requirement that such agreements be recorded.

*You buy a television set under a conditional sales agreement and, without notice to the seller, sell it to a third party. What are the rights of the respective parties?*

The sale of the television set to the third party is void, since you do not have legal title to it. The original owner can recover the set from you, and the third party can sue you for damages.

*What happens in a conditional sales agreement when the buyer is unable to meet installments?*

Generally, the seller has the choice of two remedies: he may either retake the goods or sue the buyer for the unpaid balance.

*What is a chattel mortgage?*

A chattel mortgage is a written instrument by which one person, the mortgagor, transfers his title to, but not possession of, the chattel to another person, known as the mortgagee, as security for the repayment of a debt. If the mortgagor fails to meet his obligations or payments, the mortgagee may sell the property, through proper legal proceedings, to satisfy his claims.

*Who has title under a chattel mortgage?*

The mortgagee. Title is returned to the mortgagor when the loan is paid.

*Why should chattel mortgages be recorded?*

Because the recording of a chattel mortgage is notice to all that the person using the property does not have title to it. The chattel mortgage should also be recorded to protect the interests of the mortgagee. If, after the chattel mortgage is properly recorded, the mortgagor sells the article, the third person will not obtain a valid title.

*You buy an automobile under a chattel mortgage. May you remove the car to another state?*

No. To do so constitutes a breach of the mortgage, giving the mortgagee the right to reclaim the car or to sell it. If the car is sold, after proper notice, any balance must be turned over to the mortgagor.

*For how long a period are chattel mortgages filed?*

For three years, usually, but they may be renewed if the debt is not satisfied within the time limit.

*What precautions should every installment buyer observe?*

1. If in doubt about the agreement or contract, consult an attorney. In the long run, this may well turn out to be the least expensive method of protecting yourself.

2. Make certain you read the entire agreement, including the small print.

3. Be sure you understand the penalties involved if you cannot make the necessary payments on time.

4. Be sure you notify the seller before the date of the next installment if you run into financial difficulties and cannot make the payment.

**5.** Never allow the seller to fill in any spaces after you sign the agreement unless he does so in your presence.

**6.** Do not allow the seller to demand excessive security for the debt.

*What is a warranty?*

In the sale of personal property a warranty is a statement of fact concerning the quality or character of goods sold; it is made by the seller to induce the sale and is relied on by the buyer.

*Your stockbroker tells you that the stock of the XYZ Company will advance ten points within three months. On the strength of his statement you purchase the stock, which, instead of advancing, declines five points. Do you have any recourse against the broker?*

No. The law considers that the salesman's representation amounts to mere sales talk, or "puffing," and does not constitute a warranty.

*You purchase three shirts with the understanding that the fabric will neither fade nor shrink. After you have the shirts washed, you find that they have faded. Do you have a claim against the store?*

Yes. The statement by the salesman, acting on behalf of his employer, constitutes a warranty on which you have a right to rely.

*A used-car salesman informs you that a certain automobile is the best buy in the city. Relying on that statement, you purchase the car. After using it for a few days, you find you have bought a lemon, and that the car was overpriced. Do you have any recourse?*

No. Here, too, the law regards the salesman's statement as mere puffing, or sales talk.

*What is the difference between an express and an implied warranty?*

An express warranty is one made either orally or in writing by the seller to the buyer. An implied warranty is one imposed by law; it has nothing to do with any statement made by the seller.

*What implied warranties does the law infer?*

**1.** That if the seller has possession of goods he also has title. If it later turns out that the seller, in fact, did not have title, he may be sued for breach of warranty by the one to whom he sells the article.

**2.** That food is fit for human consumption. If, for example, you order dinner in a restaurant and come down with ptomaine poisoning, the implied warranty of fitness for human consumption has been breached, and you will have a claim in damages against the owner of the restaurant. By extension, there is also an implied warranty that drugs and cosmetics are fit for human consumption. Under the federal Food, Drug and Cosmetics Act, it is a criminal offense to manufacture or sell harmful products.

**3.** That goods are fit for the specific purpose for which they have been ordered. This applies only when the buyer relies on the experience and judgment of the seller. If, for example, you decide to air-condition your apartment or house, the company may tell you that certain equipment is needed to fully cool the premises. If you then rely on that judgment, the law will imply a warranty that the equipment ordered is fit for the purpose. If it turns out that the equipment is inadequate or ineffective, you have a right to sue for damages for breach of the warranty.

*In such a breach do you also have the right to sue the manufacturer of the equipment?*

Yes. Courts have recently ruled that the manufacturer of the faulty device may also be sued.

*You buy a television set from a discount house. When the set is finally delivered and installed, you discover it does not work properly. What are your rights?*

You have a right either to return the set and get your money back or to sue the discount house for breach of the implied warranty that the set was merchantable.

*Does an implied warranty exist when the buyer has the opportunity to examine the goods and fails to notice any defects?*

No. In such cases the rule of *caveat emptor* (let the buyer beware) is generally applicable.

*You buy a loaf of bread and, while eating a slice, cut your mouth on a piece of glass imbedded in the bread. Do you have a claim, and against whom?*

You have a claim against the storekeeper for breach of the implied warranty of merchantability. You may also have a claim against the baker of the bread.

*What other rights does the buyer have for a breach of warranty?*

1. He may, if he has paid for the goods, accept and keep them and maintain an action for damages for the breach.

2. If title has not passed, he may refuse to accept the shipment and bring an action for damages.

3. He may cancel the contract and refuse to accept the shipment. If he has received the shipment, he may return it to the seller and recover the price he has paid for it.

*Must the buyer give notice to the seller of his intention to rescind the contract?*

Yes.

*What is the measure of damages for a breach of warranty?*

The damages are the difference between the contract price of the goods and their market price at the time and date of delivery.

*What remedy does the seller have against the buyer?*

When title to the goods has passed to the buyer and he refuses to pay the agreed price, the seller may sue for the contract price.

*Suppose title has not passed to the buyer, what can the seller do in case of nonpayment?*

He can sue for the price, if the price is to be paid on a specified date and the buyer wrongfully refuses to pay, or he can hold the goods for the buyer.

*You order a television set from a discount house and pay cash for it. It is agreed that the set is to be delivered the next day. Instead, you are advised that the sale is cancelled since the clerk was not authorized to sell you that particular set at that price. What are your rights?*

When the buyer has title and the seller fails to deliver the goods, as in this case, you have two choices; you may sue to obtain either possession of the set or the money value of the goods at the time of the seller's refusal to deliver—known as an action for conversion.

*You buy an original painting for $1,500. You later discover that the painting is not an original, but an imitation. What are your rights?*

You can return the painting and sue for the recovery of the $1,500. You may also have an action for fraud or deceit.

*What is "stoppage in transit"?*

It is the right of an unpaid seller to regain possession of goods while they are being transported by the common carrier. The seller can stop goods in transit:

1. When the goods have been sold on credit and the price is unpaid.

2. When there has been notice that the buyer is insolvent or bankrupt.

3. When the common carrier or express company still has possession of the goods.

*When does a seller lose his right to stop goods in transit?*

1. When the purchase price of the goods has been fully paid.

2. When the buyer has a negotiable bill of lading from the seller and has delivered it to another bona fide purchaser.

*You sell Jones a bill of goods on credit, to be shipped F.O.B. Chicago to New York. You ship the goods via railroad, the bill of lading being made out to Jones. While the goods are in transit, Jones goes into bankruptcy. What can you do?*

You may stop the goods in transit; if you do, the trustee in bankruptcy cannot claim them as part of Jones' estate. An unpaid seller, generally, has a lien against the goods for the agreed price, unless he agrees to sell on credit; if the buyer becomes insolvent, an unpaid seller may stop goods in transit, even after their delivery to the carrier. He has a right also to resell the goods and, finally, a right to rescind the sale. The unpaid seller has these rights even though title has passed. If title has not passed, the goods are his, and he may treat them as such upon nonperformance by the buyer. He may even sue the buyer for damages occasioned by the breach.

### When is time considered to be the essence of a contract?

In business contracts and in the law of sales, stipulations as to the time when an agreement shall be performed are generally of the essence: for example, when a contract stipulates that one hundred fall suits are to be delivered by September 1 and they are delivered September 5, the buyer need not accept them.

Time may be made the essence of a contract by the express stipulation of the parties, or it may be construed to be such from the nature of the transaction.

### A buyer purchases one hundred cases of marshmallow cream. When the order arrives, he finds that ninety cases are good, nine are broken, and one is missing. The seller offers to allow the purchaser a credit for the missing case as well as for the nine broken ones. The buyer, however, refuses to accept any part of the shipment. Is he legally justified in doing so?

Yes. The delivery of goods in an unsound condition is the same as a delivery of goods of a different quality or character. Even though the deterioration is slight, though only one case out of a large number is unsound or missing and the seller is willing to allow full credit, the buyer may refuse delivery.

### You agree to sell Brown five hundred bushels of May wheat. No particular lot of wheat is specified as the subject matter of the sale. You have five hundred bushels of wheat on hand. Before the sale takes place, the five hundred bushels are destroyed. Are you still bound to deliver the five hundred bushels of wheat?

Yes. In this case the destruction does not relieve you, the seller, for you can still perform the agreement by selecting out of other stock, or by going out in the open market to buy.

### In need of money, you agree to sell your first edition of David Copperfield to Jones for $5,000. Jones pays the price and arranges to

*pick up the book the next day. You now refuse to deliver the book and offer to refund Jones his money. Are you guilty of breach of contract?*

Yes. Since such a book is not obtainable elsewhere, it being an original manuscript, Jones can demand specific performance and can bring a suit in equity to compel you to deliver the book. In this case money damages would not be adequate compensation for the injured party because the subject matter cannot be duplicated. Jones can demand specific performance, which means he can compel you to carry out the exact terms of the agreement.

*John and George are negotiating for the sale of oranges but reach no agreement. The next day John phones George and orders five boxes of oranges. That same day George ships fifty boxes of oranges. Is John bound to accept the fifty boxes?*

No. When a larger quantity of the goods is delivered than the quality acceptable, the buyer can keep the quantity ordered and return the others. Under such an agreement it is possible to divide the units, as in a divisible contract, and John would not be liable for the boxes he returned.

*Smith, by a written agreement, promises to deliver six hundred tons of coal to Jones on November 12, at $20 a ton. Jones refuses to accept the goods and Smith brings action for breach of contract. Is Smith entitled to recover on this breach of contract?*

Yes. It is the duty of the buyer to accept and pay for the goods ordered and delivered. Smith is entitled to damages, which would be the difference between the market price on the date of delivery and the contract price. If Smith resells the coal at a higher price, he will not be entitled to damages.

CHAPTER 11

CREDIT CARDS AND CREDIT

*How important is credit in the American economy?*

Chances are that if everyone were compelled to pay cash for goods and services, the entire economy would collapse overnight. More than any other nation in the world, the United States is credit-oriented. Virtually everything is bought on credit, from gas in your car to travel overseas.

*Does everyone who applies for credit obtain it?*

No. Obtaining a line of credit depends on how trustworthy you are financially. Before you can open a charge account in a department store, you have to answer a questionnaire. The store has a right to investigate your financial and moral standing in the community to determine whether or not you are a good risk. If, based on objective data, the credit bureau determines you are a bad risk, the store or finance company may either decline to grant you any credit or place a limitation on the amount of your credit.

*Are you legally bound to answer all pertinent questions to enable a creditor to determine whether credit should be granted you?*

Yes. The creditor has a right to know whether or not you are a good risk. He has a right to know whether you have a savings account and/or a checking account, whether you rent or own your own home, where and how long and by whom you have been employed, as well as your salary. To give false or misleading information may subject you to charges of fraud or of obtaining goods under false pretenses.

*What if you are credit-worthy but the credit bureau says otherwise?*

Under the Federal Fair Credit Reporting Act of 1971 you have a right to request the credit bureau to reveal the basis for denial of your credit. This means, in effect, that you have a right to make the bureau open its file on you. If it claims that you gave false and misleading information, you have a right to tell your side of the story and rebut the allegation. If the bureau insists that you are a deadbeat, you have a right to produce any evidence to the contrary. In short, you can, by filing a complaint with the credit bureau, make it prove to your satisfaction that your right to credit has been denied arbitrarily.

*What if the credit bureau still refuses to change its records even after you have refuted its charges?*

You have several alternatives. You can take up the matter with the Federal Trade Commission, your local consumer agency or commission, or the attorney general of your state. If all these fail, your next step is a suit for damages against the offending bureau and any individual who gave false, malicious evidence on the basis of which credit was denied.

*What about credit cards?*

Under present law credit card companies are no longer allowed to send out unsolicited credit cards. In addition, there are now limitations in case your credit card is either lost or stolen. When a card has been lost or stolen, you are now obliged to notify the credit card company or bank immediately, preferably by registered letter with return receipt requested. Once this is done, you are no longer responsible for purchases made with your card by an unauthorized individual. However, until the company is properly notified, your maximum liability is $50 for each lost or stolen card which is used by an unauthorized person.

*What is the penalty for the fraudulent use of a credit card?*

If the transaction involves interstate or foreign commerce and the accused uses any counterfeit, ficticious, altered, forged, lost, stolen, or fraudulently acquired credit card to obtain goods or services or both having a retail value of more than $5,000, the convicted accused shall be fined not more than $10,000 or imprisoned for not more than five years or both. This is the federal penalty. However, where the offense is intra-state, a state may also prosecute for obtaining money or goods under false pretenses.

*What types of credit are covered under the Truth in Lending and Consumer Credit Disclosure Acts?*

Generally, any credit extended to people for personal, family, household or agricultural uses not exceeding $25,000. However, all real estate credit transactions are covered regardless of amount.

*What is the purpose of the Truth in Lending Act and Regulation Z?*

The aim is to let borrowers and customers know the cost of credit so they can compare the cost with other sources and avoid the uninformed use of credit. However, the Act does not fix maximum, minimum, or any charges for credit. It seeks only to provide full disclosure, so the customer may know what he is getting and shop around, possibly, for more favorable credit terms.

*What businesses are affected?*

Regulation Z applies to banks, savings and loan associations, department stores, credit card issuers, credit unions, auto dealers, consumer finance companies, residential mortgage brokers, and craftsmen such as plumbers and electricians. It also applies to physicians, dentists, and other professional people, and hospitals. In fact, the Act is applicable to any individual or organization that extends or arranges credit for which a finance charge is or may be payable or which is repayable in more than four installments.

*What protection does the Truth in Lending Act provide the consumer?*

It is supposed to provide the consumer with precise information—spelled out plainly, simply, and clearly—of the terms of the agreement where credit is involved. Concealed finance charges are forbidden. Under the law you must be told the price of the article, the amount of annual interest, how and when the interest charges must be paid, what extras are included in the agreement, what, if anything, you will save by making payments in advance, and what, if anything, you will save by paying the entire balance in one fell swoop. In addition, the Act provides for a "late date," which is part of the agreement. This means that you must exceed a stated period, usually twenty or more days grace, before you can be penalized with additional charges for not making a payment on time.

*What protection is the consumer afforded if he is presented with an erroneous bill?*

Your only recourse is to have the mistakes corrected at the source. If, for example, your charge account shows an erroneous balance, you must take the matter up promptly with the source that made the error—merchant, store, company, or credit bureau. This is true whether you purchased an automobile on time and the balance is in error, or whether you are billed for medical or dental services you have not received or for an incorrect amount not in your favor.

*What is the liability of a co-maker or co-signer to an agreement or note?*

The same as that of the maker or signer himself. Some companies, to protect themselves, insist that another perhaps even more financially responsible individual sign the installment contract or promissory note. If he does, and the maker defaults in his payment, the company has the right to sue the co-maker for the entire balance due. This is the so-called acceleration clause in action. In brief, many installment agreements provide that if any one payment is not made within a specified time, the entire agreement is breeched and the promissory note becomes payable immediately, both from the maker of the note and the co-maker.

*What is the balloon payment which is usually mentioned in installment agreements?*

A balloon payment is a final payment which is more than twice the amount of the equal monthly installments. Although legal, it must be mentioned in the retail installment agreement.

*How long must the creditor keep records?*

Evidence of compliance must be kept for at least two years.

*What exactly is the finance charge?*

It is the total of all costs a customer must pay, directly or indirectly, for obtaining credit.

*What costs must be included in the finance charges?*

1. Interest.

2. Loan fee.

3. Finders fee or similar charge.

4. Time price differential.

5. Amount paid as a discount.

6. Service, transaction, or carrying charge.

7. Appraisal fee (except in real estate transactions).

8. Premium for credit life or other insurance, if this is made a condition for credit.

9. Points.

10. Investigation or credit report fee, except in real estate transactions.

*In what form must the finance charge be shown the customer?*

It must be clearly typed or written, stating the dollars and cents total and the annual percentage rate. The words "finance charge" and "annual percentage rate" must stand out clearly. In the sale of dwellings the total dollar finance charge need not be stated, although the annual percentage rate must be included.

*What is the annual percentage rate?*

The relative cost of credit in percentage terms.

*Are maximum or minimum rates specified under the acts?*

No. The law does not fix either maximum or minimum rates but does require that the rate charged be disclosed.

*How accurate must the annual percentage rate be?*

It must be accurate to the nearest one-quarter of one percent.

*How is the annual percentage rate computed?*

It depends on whether the credit is open-end or other than open-end credit.

*What is open-end credit?*

Typically it covers most credit cards and revolving charge accounts in retail stores, where finance charges are usually made on unpaid accounts each month.

*What must an open-end credit card customer be told under the law?*

If it is a new account, the customer must receive these specific items in writing to the extent applicable.

1. The conditions under which the finance charges may be imposed and the period in which payment can be made without incurring a finance charge.

2. The method used in determining the balance on which the finance charge is calculated.

3. How the actual finance charge is calculated.

4. The periodic rates used and the range of balances to which each applies.

5. The condition under which additional charges may be made along with details of how they are calculated.

6. Descriptions of any lien which may be acquired on a customer's property.

7. The minimum payment that must be made on each billing.

*What sort of information must accompany a monthly statement?*

1. The unpaid balance at the start of the billing period.

2. The amount and date of each extension period and identification of each item bought.

3. Payments made by a customer and other credits, including returns, rebates, and adjustments.

4. The finance charge shown in dollars and cents.

5. The rates used in calculating the finance charge plus the range of balances to which they apply.

6. The annual percentage rate.

7. The unpaid balance on which the finance charge was calculated.

8. The closing date of the billing cycle and the unpaid balance at that time.

*Where must this information appear?*

Some items must appear on the actual face of the statement. Others may be shown on the reverse side or on a separate form enclosed in the same envelope.

*How is the annual percentage rate determined on open-end credit?*

The finance charge is divided by the unpaid balance to which it applies. This gives the rate per month or whatever time period is used. The result is multiplied by twelve or the number of times used during the year. A typical charge of one and a half percent is made on an unpaid balance where bills are sent out monthly. The annual percentage rate would be twelve times one and a half percent or 18 percent.

*What about credit other than open-end?*

This includes loans and sales credit—in every case for a specified period of time where the total amount, number of payments, and due dates are agreed upon by the seller and buyer. Typically, it is used in buying or financing the purchase of "big ticket" items. A good example is a loan from a finance company to buy an automobile.

*What must the credit customer be told in these types of transactions?*

The customer must be presented the following written information plus additional information relating to the type of credit extended.

1. The total amount of the finance charge, except in the case of a credit transaction to finance purchase of a dwelling.

2. The date on which the finance charge begins to apply, if this is different from the date of the transaction.

3. The annual percentage rate.

4. The number, amounts, and due dates of payments.

5. The total payments—except in the case of first mortgages on dwelling purchases.

6. The amount or the method used for calculating the amount charged for any default, delinquency, etc.

7. Description of any security that will be held.

8. Description of any penalty charge for prepayment of the principal.

9. How the unearned part of the finance charge is calculated in the case of prepayment. Charges deducted from any rebate or refund must also be stated.

*Are there any other things customers must be told?*

That depends on the transaction—whether it is a loan or a credit sale.

*In the case of a loan what must be told customers?*

In addition to that previously indicated, the following information must be provided a customer:

1. The amount of credit to be given. This includes all charges which are part of the amount of credit extended but not part of the finance charge. This information must be itemized.

2. Amounts that are deducted as prepaid finance charges and required deposit balances.

*Regarding credit sales, what additional information must be given customers?*

1. The cash price.

2. The down payment, including trade-in.

3. The difference between the two.

4. All other charges, itemized, that are included in the amount financed but not part of the finance charge.

5. The unpaid balance.

6. Amounts deducted as prepaid finance charges or required deposit balances.

7. The amount financed.

8. The total cash price, finance charge, and all other charges. (This does not apply to the sale of a dwelling.)

*When must customers receive all this information on loan or credit sales?*

Before the credit is extended.

*Must this information be given to customers in writing?*

Yes. It must be included in the information on the face of the note or other instrument evidencing the obligation, or on a separate sheet that identifies the transaction.

*Are monthly statements required?*

No. But if monthly statements are sent out, they must show clearly the annual percentage rate and the period in which a payment must be made to avoid late charges.

*How is the annual percentage rate calculated on loans or credit other than open-end?*

By the actuarial method—payments are applied first to interest due and any remainder is then applied to reduce principal.

*What are examples of the actuarial method?*

Here are two simple examples:

1. A bank loan of $100 repayable in equal monthly installments over one year with a 6 percent add-on finance charge. The annual percentage rate would be 11 percent. The borrower would repay $106 over one year. He would have use of the full $100 only until he made his first payment, and less and less each month as payments were made. The effect is that the actual annual percentage rate is almost twice the add-on percentage rate.

2. The same example as above with the 6 percent finance charge discounted in advance. The annual percentage rate would be 11½ percent because the customer would receive only $94 but have to repay $100. He would have use of only $94 of the loan and that only up to the time he made his first payment.

*But isn't the actuarial method very complicated?*

Yes, it is. Recognizing this, the Federal Reserve Board has prepared tables showing the annual percentage rate based on the finance charge and the number of weekly or monthly payments to be made. These tables are available from the Federal Reserve Board and Federal Reserve Banks at a nominal cost.

*Must one use the Board's Annual Percentage Rate tables?*

No. One can purchase specially prepared tables for special types of business from one of several table or chart publishers. Trade associations and financial institutions can be helpful also.

*Must the creditor always show the annual percentage rate?*

Generally yes, except that on credit other than open-end credit the finance charge need not be shown if it is $5 or less on credit of $75 or less. The same exception applies to a finance charge of $7.50 or less on credit of more than $75.

*Is real estate credit covered under Truth in Lending?*

Yes. All real estate credit to an individual in any amount is covered under this regulation when it is not for business purposes, unless the business purpose is agriculture.

*Does real estate credit cover more than mortgages?*

Yes, very definitely. Any credit transaction that involves any type of security interest in the real estate of a consumer is covered.

*Are there any special provisions that apply to real estate credit?*

Two basic points:

1. It is not necessary to show the total dollar amount of the finance charge on a credit sale or first mortgage loan to finance the purchase of the customer's dwelling.

2. In many instances a customer has the right to cancel a credit arrangement within three business days if his residence is used as collateral for credit.

*Must a creditor inform his customer of the right to cancel?*

Yes. He must furnish the notice prescribed by the regulation.

*What must the customer do to cancel a transaction under the regulation?*

A customer may cancel a transaction in three ways:

1. By signing and dating the notice to customer required by Federal law, which he receives from the creditor, and either
   a) mailing the notice to the creditor at the address shown on the notice, or
   b) delivering the notice to the creditor at the address shown on the notice either personally or by messenger or other agent.

2. By sending a telegram to the creditor at the address shown on the notice. A brief description of the transaction which the customer wishes to cancel should be included in the telegram.

3. By preparing a letter (or other writing) which includes a brief description of the transaction which he wishes to cancel, and either

a) mailing the letter to the creditor at the address shown on the notice, or

b) delivering the letter to the creditor at the address shown on the notice either personally or by messenger or other agent.

*What if the customer telephones that he is going to cancel?*

A telephone call to the creditor may not be used to cancel a transaction; WRITTEN notice of cancellation is required. If the customer takes one of the above steps to cancel within the three day period, he has effectively cancelled the transaction.

*What if the notice of cancellation has not been received in three days?*

Time should be allowed by the creditor for a mailed letter or telegram sent within the three day period to be delivered, and he should determine that the customer has not cancelled the transaction.

*Does this right of cancellation apply to a first mortgage on a residence?*

A first mortgage to finance the purchase of a customer's residence carries no right to cancel. However, a first mortgage for any other purpose and a second mortgage on the same residence may be cancelled.

*What happens regarding cancellation in the case of a mechanic's lien or similar security interest acquired by a craftsman who works on credit?*

Take a craftsman, for example, who charges his customers a finance charge or allows payment in more than four installments. His customer does have a right to cancel, but only within three business days. Unless there is an emergency, the craftsman should wait three days before starting work.

*Suppose a customer needs emergency repairs and cannot wait for three days?*

A customer may waive his right to cancel a credit agreement if credit is needed to meet a bona fide personal financial emergency and if failure to start repairs would endanger him, his family, or his property.

*What are the penalties under the Truth in Lending Act?*

If a creditor fails to make disclosures as required under the act, a customer may sue for twice the amount of the finance charge— for a minimum of $100 up to a maximum of $1,000—plus court costs and attorney fees. Anyone willfully or knowingly violating the law or Regulation Z may, upon conviction, be fined up to $5,000 or be imprisoned for one year or both.

*What happens if you are unable to meet your credit obligations on time?*

The normal procedure is for the creditor to contact the debtor first by letter, then by telephone. When all other means have been exhausted, including possible credit-cutoff, the next step is turning over the account to a collection agency and/or a collection attorney. Collection agencies usually charge from one-third to one-half the amount collected, depending on the size of the debt. The larger the debt the smaller the fraction. Under guidelines in current practice collection agencies are forbidden to use threatening or scare tactics or physical force. Nor may a creditor enter a home without the invitation of the homeowner or exert pressure on the debtor's employer in order to force him to pay his debts.

*What rights does a purchaser have if he enters into a transaction which results in a lien, mortgage, or other security interest on his home?*

Under federal law the customer has a right to rescind the transaction within three business days either from the date the agreement was entered into resulting in a lien or mortgage, or from any later date on which all material disclosures required under the Truth in Lending Act were given the buyer. As a matter of fact, the rule now requires that the seller inform the purchaser of this right to rescind at the time the transaction is made. The required notice is as follows:

## NOTICE TO CUSTOMER REQUIRED BY FEDERAL LAW

You have entered into a transaction on _____

date

which may result in a lien, mortgage, or other security interest on your home. You have a legal right under Federal law to cancel this transaction, if you desire to do so, without any penalty or obligation within three business days from the above date or any later date on which all material disclosures required under the Truth in Lending Act have been given to you. If you so cancel the transaction, any lien, mortgage, or other security interest on your home arising from this transaction is automatically void. You are also entitled to receive a refund of any downpayment or other consideration if you cancel. If you decide to cancel this transaction, you may do so by notifying _____

name of creditor

at _____ by mail or telegram sent

address of creditor's place of business

not later than midnight of _____. You may

date

also use any other form of written notice identifying the transaction if it is delivered to the above address not later than that time. This notice may be used for that purpose by dating and signing below.

I hereby cancel this transaction.

_____        _____

date                                    customer's signature

## CHAPTER 12

BAILMENTS

*What is the subject matter of bailments?*

For the most part, bailments deal with the *temporary* transfer of personal property and with the performance of certain services. A *bailor* is one who transfers possession of property. The one to whom possession is transferred is called the *bailee.* Actually, a bailment is a contract, and the usual elements of a valid contract must be present: mutual consent, competent parties, consideration, and valid subject matter.

*How does a bailment differ from a sale?*

In a sale, title passes from the seller to the buyer. In a bailment, there is merely the *transfer* of possession of personal property. In short, the bailee must return the article or property whenever the purpose of the bailment is accomplished.

In a sale, the buyer is generally responsible for any loss or damage to the goods bought. In a bailment, the bailee is not the owner of the goods, and his rights and liabilities are limited, as we shall see.

Another distinction is that, in a sale, the purchaser may sell, transfer, or otherwise dispose of the things purchased. In a bailment, the bailee may not so dispose of the goods, because he is not the owner but the mere temporary custodian.

A bailment contract may arise either from agreement between the parties or by operation of law.

There are three types of bailments. The first is for the sole benefit of the bailor. The second is for the sole benefit of the bailee. The third confers benefits on both parties.

*You have a gold watch which you ask a friend to take to the jewelers for repair. On the way the friend drops the watch, making the cost of repairs about five times as expensive as it normally would have been. Is your friend liable in damages?*

This case is an example of a bailment contract for the sole benefit of the bailor, in this instance, yourself. In such bailments, the bailee (the friend to whom the watch was entrusted) need only exercise reasonable or slight care. He is responsible, however, for any gross negligence committed by him. Since it is doubtful whether you could prove gross negligence by your friend, you could not recover for the damage to your watch.

*Going out of town, you ask a friend to leave your car in his garage for a couple of days until you return. Your friend agrees. An emergency arises and your friend uses your car and an accident occurs in which your automobile is damaged. Would your friend be liable in damages?*

Yes. Unless your friend had your express permission to use your car, he has no right to use it for his personal benefit, even if he used it to make an emergency call. Since the car was damaged, he would be liable in damages.

*You give your neighbor permission to use your car in order to make a trip twenty miles from town. The neighbor, on his way back, runs into another car, causing considerable damage to yours. What are your rights?*

Since this is a bailment for the sole benefit of the bailee, he must exercise great care in the use of the car, and is held responsible even if he is only slightly negligent. Since, presumably, your neighbor ran into another driver's car because of his own carelessness, he could be sued for damages to your car.

*Suppose your neighbor, instead of going on the agreed trip, had gone off on some venture of his own and had had an accident. What would be his liability?*

Since such use of the car would be unauthorized, the neighbor would be held responsible no matter whether he was negligent.

*Planning a trip, you ask your neighbor to care for your dog for a few days, which he agrees to do. While you are away, the dog be-*

*comes ill, and your neighbor spends $25 for a veterinarian. Do you have to reimburse him?*

Yes. Since the bailment was for your benefit, you are obligated to pay the ordinary expenses of taking care of the dog. Had the bailee insisted on taking the dog during your absence, he would have been liable for whatever expenses were incurred, since the bailment was for his benefit.

*On one or two occasions your dog has shown vicious propensities. Nevertheless, you ask your neighbor to care for him for a few days while you are away on a trip. You forget to warn your neighbor, however, of the dog's tendency to bite. While in your neighbor's care, the dog attacks a third person. Are you liable in damages?*

Yes. Your failure to warn the bailee would make you responsible for injuries inflicted by the dog on any person. Had you warned your neighbor, you would have been absolved, and he would have been liable in damages.

*You pawn your watch. When you come to redeem it, the pawnbroker informs you it is missing. What are your rights?*

In a bailment which is of mutual benefit to both parties—as in this illustration—the pawnbroker need only exercise ordinary care, and is liable only for ordinary negligence. If you can prove that the watch is missing because of the pawnbroker's carelessness, you may recover the value of the watch.

*You park your car on a parking lot. Through no fault of the owner of the lot, a fire takes place and your car is completely destroyed. Do you have a claim against the owner?*

No. Since the bailment was for your mutual benefit, the bailee has only to exercise ordinary care. Since the fire started through no fault of his own, he will be relieved of liability. If the fire had started because of some carelessness on his part or on the part of his employees, he would have been liable.

*You take your automobile into a garage for repairs, but the mechanic is so inept that the car comes out worse than when it went in. What are your rights?*

If you can really prove that the mechanic is a bumbling idiot, you will have a claim for damages. But, as a practical matter, incompetence is very difficult to prove, for often another expert mechanic will be needed to testify on your behalf.

*You leave your watch at your jeweler's for repair. When you come to call for it, you find you do not have enough cash to pay the jeweler. You insist that you be allowed to take the watch and that you will pay the jeweler later. He refuses. What are the rights of both parties?*

A mutual-benefit bailee has a lien for services on the goods in his possession until all reasonable charges are paid. Since you cannot pay for the repairs when you call for the watch, the jeweler is entitled to retain possession until you do.

*What rights does a pawnbroker have to articles pledged with him?*

The person who pledges an article is known as the pledgor. The person who receives the pledge—the pawnbroker—is known as the pledgee. Pawnbrokers are allowed to charge interest for loans ranging from 2 per cent to 10 per cent a month, the law varying from state to state. They are forbidden to sell any unclaimed property for at least a year. The unclaimed property is usually sold at public auction after due notice in the newspapers. In some states, surplus proceeds must be turned over to the pledgor. A pawnbroker who is unable or unwilling to return redeemed pledges may be sued for damages.

*Is a hotelkeeper obliged to accept all who apply for accommodation?*

Yes, with certain exceptions. A hotel or motel keeper does not have to accept guests when all accommodations are already taken; nor need he accept a drunken or disorderly guest, or one who is obviously not ready, willing, and able to pay for hotel or motel services.

*What are the responsibilities of a hotel to its guests?*

1. The hotelkeeper must exercise ordinary care in providing for the comfort and safety of his guests.

**2.** He must maintain the hotel and its conveniences in proper condition.

**3.** He must protect his guests from assault or abuse by his employees, or by other guests, for that matter.

**4.** He must provide a safe in the office of the hotel for the valuables of his patrons, and he is required, by the law of most states, to post a notice to this effect in the room of each guest.

*What is a common carrier?*

A common carrier is one who undertakes for hire to transport persons or goods for anyone who may choose to employ him. In contrast, a private carrier, such as a private delivery service or moving van, undertakes to supply transportation in special instances and upon special arrangements.

A common carrier is one whose business is affected by a public interest. Thus, unlike a private carrier, a common carrier is much more subject to public regulation and control, either on a state or federal level. If the carrier is engaged in interstate commerce, it is regulated by the Interstate Commerce Commission.

A private carrier is liable only as an ordinary bailee for hire; it is liable for loss or injury only if there is negligence. A common carrier, such as a railroad or shipping line, is liable for the loss of goods regardless of negligence.

*When does the liability of a common carrier begin?*

When the goods are delivered to it or to its authorized agent at the proper place for the purpose of transportation.

*Under what circumstances is a carrier relieved from such liability?*

When the shipper fails to give proper shipping directions; when he directs the carrier to hold the goods until further notice; or when he fails to prepay the freight.

*Are common carriers insurers of passengers, as well as freight?*

No. However, a common carrier is under a duty to exercise the highest degree of care consistent with the nature of its undertaking.

*When is a common carrier excused from liability as the insurer of goods?*

A carrier is excused from liability if loss or damage results from the following causes:

1. Acts of God. Such acts include floods, snowstorms, hurricanes, cyclones, lightning or fires caused by lightning, and any other extraordinary natural causes beyond the control of the shipper.

2. Acts of public enemies. These include civil war, riots, insurrections, etc.

3. Acts of public authorities. These include the seizure of goods by law enforcement or health officers or by due process of law, as by attachment, stoppage in transit, etc.

4. The inherent nature of the goods. Perishables, livestock, and merchandise subject to natural deterioration are in this category.

*May a carrier limit liability for loss of goods due to negligence?*

Yes, under certain circumstances. Under amendments to the Hepburn Act, a common carrier, although it cannot exempt itself completely from liability, may, by agreement, limit its liability, provided:

1. The shipper receives consideration for the limitation, which usually means a lower rate.

2. The shipper is given an option to ship the goods without such limitation, though at a higher rate.

3. The limitation is reasonable and just and bears a fair relation to the reduced rate.

*What is an express receipt?*

An express receipt acknowledges receipt of the goods by the carrier from the shipper. When the receipt contains provisions for transportation, it constitutes the contract between shipper and carrier. An express receipt limits the carrier's liability for loss to specific contingencies.

*What is a uniform express receipt?*

It is a receipt prescribed by the Interstate Commerce Commission for transportation of goods in interstate commerce. Many states have similar receipts for the transportation of goods within a state. Such receipts often limit the shipper's liability for damage or delay caused by acts of God, strikes and riots. To know in advance the carrier's liability, the shipper should become familiar with the meaning and terms of shipping receipts.

### What is a bill of lading?

A bill of lading is a contract between shipper and carrier in which the freight to be shipped is described and the terms of the contract for its transportation stated. Every bill of lading must include the date of issue, the name of the person from whom the goods have been received, the place where the goods have been received and the place where they are to be shipped, the name of the person to whom the goods are to be shipped, as well as the destination, a description of the goods, and the signature of the carrier or his agent. If the bill of lading is to be negotiable, the words "order of" must be printed or written immediately before the name of the person upon whose order the goods are deliverable.

### What is the effect of a bill of lading?

A bill of lading in the hands of the shipper is evidence of title or ownership. If the bill is negotiable, the owner can sell, transfer, or assign the bill without actually receiving possession of the goods from the carrier.

If the bill is nonnegotiable, the owner may still sell his interest in the goods without having actual possession of them.

### How do negotiable bills of lading differ from ordinary bills of lading?

In a nonnegotiable bill of lading, the transferee acquires only such title as the transferor has. On the other hand, a bona fide (good faith) transferee of a negotiable bill of lading—one to whom a bill is negotiated for value, without notice—acquires a good title even though the transferor's title is defective, as when the original owner of the bill has lost possession of it because of theft, fraud, accident, mistakes, duress, or conversion.

Once goods are shipped via a negotiable bill of lading, they cannot be attached or levied upon in legal proceedings against the shipper—while the goods are in possession of the carrier or other bailee—unless the bill of lading is first surrendered, or the negotiability of the bill enjoined by legal proceedings. This is not the case with nonnegotiable bills of lading.

A third distinction is that once a negotiable bill has been issued, the unpaid seller cannot defeat the rights of a purchaser for value in good faith by stopping the goods in transit. Nor is the carrier obliged to deliver the goods or justified in delivering them unless the bill is first surrendered for cancellation. This is not true of a nonnegotiable bill of lading.

A fourth distinction is that liens or claims of a seller, shipper, or prior transferor are invalid against a purchaser in good faith to whom a bill of lading has been negotiated. This is not true in the case of a nonnegotiable bill of lading.

### What is the liability of a connecting carrier?

Connecting carriers of interstate commerce are agents of the initial carrier, and are liable for any loss or damage. The rule is somewhat different as to intrastate shipments. The New York rule, followed in a number of other states, is "that any one of two or more corporations owning or operating connecting roads within this state, or partly within and partly without the state, shall be liable as a common carrier, for the transportation of passengers or delivery of freight received by it to be transported by it to any place on the line of a connecting road; and if it shall become liable to pay any sum by reason of neglect or misconduct of any other corporation it may collect the same of the corporation by reason of whose neglect or misconduct it became liable."

### Does a common carrier have a right to eject passengers?

Yes, under certain circumstances. A railroad has a right to eject a passenger who does not have a ticket or refuses to pay his fare. A passenger may also be ejected for annoying a fellow passenger. But in all cases the carrier must use only proper and reasonable means. A passenger wrongfully ejected may resist such ejectment by using whatever force is necessary. He also has a right to sue the carrier for wrongful ejectment.

### What is the liability of a carrier for the passenger's baggage?

A carrier is an insurer of a passenger's baggage or luggage entrusted to its care, except as to acts of God, etc. But a carrier may limit the amount for which it may be liable for such loss.

*Before purchasing a ticket at the railroad station, a prospective passenger stumbles and falls on a defective step that is poorly illuminated. Is the railroad liable in damages for the passenger's injuries?*

Yes, if negligence can be proved. The fact that the passenger has not yet purchased a ticket is immaterial. The same principle would hold true if the passenger's slipping on a greasy surface were caused by the carrier's failure to remove the grease promptly.

CHAPTER 13

## INSURANCE

*What is the purpose of insurance?*

Insurance is a means by which one party (the insurer) indemnifies or guarantees another (the insured) against a specified loss. Insurance is a contract (the policy) between the two, and the consideration for the contract is regular payments (premiums) made by the insured to the insurer. In the event the specified loss occurs, the insured is indemnified from a fund to which many individuals exposed to the same risk have contributed. The payment of a loss, divided among many policyholders, does not fall heavily upon any one of them. The essence of an insurance contract is mutuality; that is, the existence of reciprocal rights and obligations between the company and the policyholders.

*What is the difference between a mutual insurance company and a stock insurance company?*

Stock insurance companies are corporations that issue stock to stockholders, who are separate and apart from the policyholders. The stockholders are entitled to any profits available for dividends. (Stock insurance companies are frequently listed on the Stock Exchange or traded over the counter.)

A mutual company, on the other hand, issues no stock. Policyholders automatically become owners in part of the company, and any surplus is distributed to the members as dividends.

*What is the difference between a premium and an assessment?*

A premium is what the prospective policyholder pays the company as the consideration for assuming the risk. An assessment is the amount levied by a mutual company to meet its needs.

*On whom does the risk of nondelivery fall when premiums are sent by mail?*

On the insured, unless the company by its duly authorized agent requested or directed the payment of the premium by mail or, through long practice, acquiesced in such payment.

172

*What is meant by insurable interest?*

Unless a policyholder has an interest in the subject matter of the insurance—that is, stands to gain by its preservation or to lose by its loss or destruction—the policy constitutes a mere gamble and is unenforceable.

*You take out an insurance policy to indemnify you against loss by rain on October 23, the night you are promoting a prize fight. Do you have an insurable interest?*

Yes. Obviously you stand to lose in receipts if the fight is called off because of rain. Had you merely taken out a policy as a wager that it would rain on a certain night, the policy would have been unenforceable, and you would not be able to collect the specified sum.

*Does a corporation have an insurable interest in any of its officers or stockholders?*

Yes, so long as the officer or principal stockholder continues with the company.

*What if the officer severs his connection with the company or the principal stockholder relinquishes his control?*

Some states take the position that the company no longer has an insurable interest in the officer and so must relinquish the policy. Other states take the contrary view.

*In general, what persons have an insurable interest in the lives of others?*

Anyone related by blood, marriage, or business who stands to gain by the continued life of another and to lose by his death has an insurable interest. A husband and wife have an insurable interest in each other's lives. So do parents and their children. A creditor has an insurable interest in the life of his debtor and a partner has an insurable interest in the life of his fellow partner or partners.

*May a policyholder make a beneficiary of a third party who has no insurable interest in the policyholder's life?*

Yes.

*May a sister insure the life of her brother?*

Only if she is dependent on him. Otherwise she has no insurable interest in his life.

*May a person insure the life of another without his consent?*

Ordinarily a person cannot insure the life of another unless he has both an insurable interest and the consent of the insured. However, most states allow a wife to obtain insurance upon the life of her husband without such consent; an employer is allowed to insure his employees collectively against sickness, accident, or death; and a person liable for the support of a child is permitted to obtain a policy graded in amount according to the age of the child.

*Who has an insurable interest in property?*

Anyone who has a right, interest, or relation in property in which he stands to profit if the property is preserved and to lose if the property is destroyed. Thus the purchaser of real property has an insurable interest in the property even though title has not yet passed to him.

*Are losses caused by the deliberate acts of the insured recoverable?*

No. However, if a policy is silent on the question of suicide, or even if the policy provides that the company will not be liable in case of suicide, recovery may be permitted under certain conditions.

*Must all insurance contracts be in writing?*

No. Since the happening of the event covered by the policy may take place within a year, the insurance contract may be made orally and need not be in writing as the Statute of Frauds requires for contracts that cannot be executed within a year. However, Georgia and New York expressly require insurance contracts to be in writing.

*What is the difference between an insurance agent and an insurance broker?*

An insurance agent usually represents the company; an insurance broker usually represents the insured and may represent more than one company.

*An insurance broker receives a policy from the company at his request; he collects the premium, but neglects to forward it to the company. The insured dies after the premium is collected by the broker but before it is forwarded to the company. The company refuses to pay the face amount of the policy on the theory that the broker was the insured's agent. Is the company justified in refusing payment?*

No. In mailing the policy to the broker, the broker became the company's agent. The failure of the broker to forward the premium falls on the company, not on the insured. The company must seek recourse against the broker.

*What notice and proof of loss is required in life insurance?*

A certificate of death is all that is usually necessary. Prompt notice, as required by the policy, should be rigidly complied with.

*What proof of loss is required in fire insurance?*

A schedule of the items damaged or destroyed, with their monetary value.

*On what grounds may an insurer cancel a policy?*

1. Fraud.
2. Concealment.
3. Breach of warranty, representation, or condition.

*What is marine insurance?*

It is insurance against the hazards known as perils of the sea— fire, shipwreck, and piracy. Perils of the sea do not include the ordinary action of wind and wave, wear and tear, or loss due to delays occasioned thereby.

*What is meant by a "time policy" in marine insurance?*

A time policy sets the duration of the risk at a fixed period, as from February 4, 1966 to March 1, 1966. A voyage policy, on the other hand, fixes the duration of the risk for the length of the specified voyage.

*What is a "lost or not lost" provision in a marine policy?*

Such a phrase covers not only the risk of future loss of vessels, but the risk of loss that may have already occurred. However, an insured who is aware that a vessel has already been lost and who conceals his knowledge from the insurer cannot recover.

*What proof of loss is required in a marine insurance policy?*

Before payment will be made, the owner of the vessel must give full particulars as to the nature, amount, and cause of damage, and his statement must be sworn to by the master and crew of the vessel. Bills of lading and similar documents must be submitted to prove title. When there is a disagreement about the amount of damaged goods, they are sold at public auction and the realized value taken into consideration in the actual payment.

*What is inland marine insurance?*

Inland marine insurance provides an indemnity against loss of tourist baggage, motor truck cargoes, express and parcel post packages, and a large variety of other goods in transit. The insured is indemnified for all loss or damage to personal property, except loss from those risks specifically excluded by the policy.

*What risks are covered under standard fire insurance policies?*

The insured is protected from any loss directly or proximately caused by what is known as a "hostile" fire. A hostile fire is one that has escaped its natural bounds.

*You place some furniture too close to a stove and it becomes scorched. Will you recover under a fire insurance policy?*

No. The theory is that the fire in the stove is a "friendly" fire, that is, one within its natural bounds. Should the fire escape from the stove to scorch or burn the furniture, the fire is then "hostile," and the insured may recover.

*More damage is caused to a storekeeper's goods by the firemen's attempts to extinguish the blaze than by the fire itself. May the insured recover for such water damage?*

Yes. He may also recover for loss caused by falling parts of a building or for loss caused by the removal of his property from the burning building or from premises endangered by the fire.

*After a blaze has been extinguished, some looting takes place on the premises. May the insured recover for such loss?*

No. An insured may not recover for indirect or remote damages caused by a fire.

*A few months after you take out a fire insurance policy, you vacate the premises. The next day a fire breaks out. Can you collect from the insurer?*

Yes. The standard forms of fire policies provide that the policy will be suspended if the premises are left vacant or unoccupied for more than sixty days.

*Can you "overinsure" premises under a fire policy?*

No. If, for example, you take out two separate policies covering your residence and sustain a fire loss, you will not be paid the full amount of damage twice by each of the companies. Each company will pay only a proportionate share of the loss sustained.

*What should you do if you increase the hazard of fire by storing inflammable materials on the premises?*

Obtain the written consent of the company; otherwise, in case of fire, you will not be able to recover.

*Is the insured entitled to a refund of the premium when he cancels his fire policy?*

He is entitled to be paid for the unexpired term of the policy an amount based on a table that is included in the policy.

*You take out a five-year fire insurance policy, paying $50 for the full term. At the end of one year you decide to cancel by giving written notice. Must the insurer refund your premium at the short rate or at the regular rate?*

At the regular rate, which would be $40. Under the short rate you would have received less.

*What is coinsurance?*

It is the amount of insurance, expressed as a certain percentage of the value of a property, that the insured must carry. Because most fires do not totally destroy a property, most owners do not insure it for its full value. Coinsurance is used to induce them to insure the property at a higher percentage of its value, generally 80 per cent.

*You insure your store with one company against fire loss in the sum of $6,000. A coinsurance clause in the policy provides that you must at all times carry insurance with either your present company or with another insurance company to the extent of 80 per cent of the value of the goods. When a fire breaks out, your inventory amounts to $10,000. You have not, however, increased your insurance. The actual loss caused by the fire amounts to $4,000. How much will you be able to recover?*

Eighty per cent of $4,000, or $3,200. Had there been a total loss, you would have collected $6,000.

*May a fire insurance policy be assigned?*

Not without the written consent of the insurer.

*When must notice and proof of loss be given in fire insurance policies?*

Immediate notice is required, considering all the circumstances. Proof of loss must usually be given within sixty days after the fire.

*What is "additional coverage"?*

For an added premium the insured may obtain protection against loss by wind, hailstorm, hail, riot, fallen aircraft, automobile damage to property, and smoke damage. This added protection is provided by means of an endorsement or rider, attached to the fire insurance policy, called the extended-coverage endorsement.

The insured may also obtain extended additional coverage against such specific hazards as malicious mischief, vandalism, boiler explosion, glass breakage, falling trees, and collapsing floors, walls, or roofs.

*How can an individual best determine his insurance needs?*

By obtaining the services of a reputable insurance broker. To obtain the all-round protection you need it is better to deal directly with a reputable broker than to obtain insurance on a piecemeal basis.

*Will every misrepresentation by the insured allow the insurer to avoid payment on the policy?*

No. There are two kinds of misrepresentations. One kind includes representations deliberately made to mislead the insurer; the other, those of the innocent variety. Since the insurer has the right to rely on the statements of the insured, before determining whether or not it will assume the risk, a deliberate misrepresentation will avoid the policy.

An innocent misrepresentation, however, will usually only avoid the policy if the falsity is material; that is, if the misrepresentation either contributes materially to the risk or contributes directly to the loss. What constitutes such an innocent misrepresentation depends on the facts of the individual case.

When a statement of fact is made a part of the insurance contract, it is called a warranty. If, for example, you tell the insurer that you have had no surgery during the past five years, and as a matter of fact you have, the insurer, as soon as it learns the facts, may cancel the policy.

*Through no fault of your own, you meet with an automobile accident in which you suffer serious injuries. Unfortunately, the other motorist is not insured, but he lives in a state where a "financial responsibility" law has been enacted. What are your rights?*

States having such financial responsibility laws provide that the owner of a car post either money or securities in the event of an accident or a violation of certain traffic regulations. When the motorist has automobile insurance, he need not post such evidence of financial responsibility. When the motorist has neither insurance nor financial responsibility, the state may suspend the owner's and operator's license and car registration and, in addition, require proof of financial responsibility covering future accidents.

*What is a "100/200 limit" automobile insurance policy?*

The figures specify the maximum amounts that the insurer will pay for the happening of specific injuries or deaths. In this case the insurer will pay a maximum of $100,000 on any just claim involving one person and a maximum of $200,000 on all claims for which the owner or operator may become liable in a single accident.

*How much liability insurance should one carry?*

A wise precaution is to take out automobile liability insurance roughly covering one's net worth, especially since the premium rates for a higher amount are only a few dollars more than for a lower rate.

*You take out a 100/200 limit automobile insurance policy. Shortly afterward, as a result of your negligence, you knock down a pedestrian and cause him extremely serious injuries. Unable to settle the claim, the pedestrian sues you and recovers a judgment against you in the amount of $150,000. What is the liability of the insurance company?*

The company is only liable for $100,000, and you will have to make up the difference.

*Is the insured protected in case of an accident if the car is driven by another person or by a member of the insured's family?*

Yes, if the car is driven with the express permission of the insured. Some policies, however, provide that the company will not be liable if the car is driven by a person under a specified age, or under the age prescribed by law for driving cars.

*What does automobile property damage insurance protect?*

It protects the insured for any obligation he may be under as a result of an automobile accident in which he injures or destroys the property of another, including that person's automobile. Such coverage does not protect the insured against loss to his own car or property, property that he leases or rents, property in his custody, or property that he is transporting.

*What coverage is provided by medical-payments insurance?*

A good feature of many automobile insurance policies—a feature that should be included in the coverage—is payment for medical, surgical, and hospital expenses for automobile accidents, regardless of fault. Such payments are made to the operator of the car and to any passenger therein, as well as to any pedestrians injured, and to guests, owners, and operators of the vehicle in collision with the insured's automobile. Payment is made up to the limit of the medical-payments coverage, which should be the maximum obtainable.

*What is collision insurance?*

It is insurance that protects the insured against any loss from damage to, or destruction of, his own automobile when caused by an accidental collision with another car or object or by an upset of the vehicle. When the insured has collision insurance, he receives the amount of the damage less whatever the deductible clause. If the damage done is $100 and there is a $50 deductible clause, the insured receives only $50. If the damage done is $500 and the deductible amount is $100, the insured will receive $400.

*What does comprehensive insurance provide?*

Such insurance protects the insured against loss or damage to his car caused by fire, windstorms, floods, riots, glass breakage, theft, robbery, and pilferage. Notice of loss must be made immediately to the insurance company; there must also be a sworn proof of loss as a prerequisite to recovery. If the car has been stolen or the tires removed, the police should be notified promptly.

*What is the liability of the insurer?*

The insurer is liable for the actual cash value of the car at the time of loss, not exceeding the stated liability on the face of the policy.

*Does the theft coverage include packages left in the car?*

No. Nor does it include tools and repair equipment unless the entire car is stolen. Coverage does include payment for loss of use of the automobile at the stated rate in the policy. If his car is damaged or stolen, the insured may rent another car at a certain sum per day, for which he will be later reimbursed by the insurer. No payment is made, usually, for the first seventy-two hours after the theft has been reported to the police and insurance company.

*What is public liability insurance?*

It is insurance which protects the insured against claims arising in his home, on his grounds, or even away from his home.

*Your dog bites your neighbor. Does public liability insurance cover such accidents?*

Yes. Much else is also covered. For example, a guest stumbles and falls over a defective step in your home. With public liability insurance, you would be protected against any claim for injury or damage.

*What is an ordinary life (straight-life) policy?*

An ordinary life policy calls for regular premium payments throughout the life of the insured. He is fully protected only while payments are being made.

*What is a limited-payment life policy?*

This policy calls for a limited number of premium payments, the insured being fully protected not only during the period of payments but for the rest of his life.

*What is an endowment policy?*

An endowment policy provides for the payment of premiums by the insured for a given period. At the end of the period of payments, the sum is payable to the insured himself; but if he should die before the period of premium payments expires, the sum is payable to his beneficiary immediately.

*What is a term policy?*

A term policy provides insurance for a fixed term of years. Because of the low premium, the policy does not provide for any accumulations or allow the holder to take out a paid-up policy at the end of the term. A term policy is usually taken when the insured has not decided upon a permanent form of insurance, but wishes to be covered in the meantime.

*What is a tontine policy?*

It is a policy in which the holder agrees, in common with every other policyholder, not to take dividends or premiums or to surrender the policy for cash for a certain period of years. Under such a plan the accumulated surplus is divided at the end of the term among all those who have maintained their insurance in force.

*What is group insurance?*

It is insurance offered at lower premium rates to professional or business associations operating on a group basis. When a member leaves the group, he loses his group coverage, but he is allowed to convert to an individual policy.

*What is a "grace" period?*

Life insurance policies allow an additional thirty-day period in which to pay the premium, the grace period beginning at the date the premium was due.

*Which risks may or may not be excluded from coverage by an insurer?*

Generally, the only risks that may be excluded from life insurance coverage are military service, suicide (within two years from the date the policy is issued), and aviation accidents.

*What is an "incontestable clause" in a life insurance policy?*

This clause provides that after a policy has been in effect for a given time, usually two years, the policy cannot be contested by the insurer for the insured's misstatements or for any reasons other than those specified in the policy, usually the nonpayment of premiums or the breach of some other specified condition.

*Can an insurance company, in spite of the incontestable clause, claim fraud as a defense?*

If the policy becomes incontestable at its date of issue, fraud is a good defense. If the policy becomes incontestable after a given period elapses, fraud is not a good defense, since the company can have learned of the fraud during the interval.

*What other defenses may a company set up despite the incontestable clause of the policy?*

1. That the risk is not covered by the policy.
2. That the policyholder lacks an insurable interest in the insured.
3. That proof of death has not been filed within a required time.
4. That the insured committed suicide.

*Will suicide by the insured while insane defeat recovery?*

No, in the absence of a suicide clause in the policy.

*What if the self-destruction took place while the insured was sane?*

In most jurisdictions, self-destruction while the insured is sane bars recovery, unless the policy is payable to beneficiaries other than the insured's family or personal representatives.

*What if it can be proved that the insured intended to commit suicide at the time he took out the policy, that he intended to defraud the insurer?*

There can be no recovery under the policy. However, after a specified period of incontestability, suicide will not bar recovery, unless the incontestable clause excludes death from suicide. A few states hold that suicide shall not constitute a defense unless the insured contemplated suicide when he took out the policy. This is obviously a matter of proof.

*You apply for a life insurance contract, making some false statements on the application blank, which, however, do not appear in the policy issued to you. After your death, the company refuses to pay the beneficiary on the ground that you made fraudulent statements; it produces the original application blank to that effect. Is the company justified in refusing payment?*

No. The application was not made a part of the original policy, and all policies contain a clause that the policy constitutes the entire contract between the parties. Under the circumstances the company would be required to pay the face amount of the policy.

*In your application for insurance you willfully misstate your real age. After your death the company refuses to pay the face amount of the policy on the ground of fraud. Is it justified in so doing?*

No. Many states allow the company an offset for the amount of premiums that should have been paid had the age been correctly stated. Other states hold the company liable for the amount of insurance that the premium paid would have bought at the correct age.

*What happens if a policyholder defaults in the payment of his premium?*

A policyholder usually has three options: (1) He can obtain the cash surrender value of his policy, as specified in the policy, less handling expense. (2) He can obtain extended insurance, usually in the form of term insurance, for as long a period as the surrender value of his policy will buy. (3) He can obtain paid-up insurance for an amount that the reserve or surrender value of the policy will buy.

*What loan value is provided in a standard life insurance policy?*

The usual provision is that, after premiums have been paid for three full years, the policyholder may borrow up to the amount of the policy reserve, less proper charges and deductions, upon assignment of the policy to the company. The loan values during each of the first twenty years are shown in a table set forth in the policy.

*What happens if a policyholder dies while a loan is still unpaid?*

Provided the policyholder keeps up the premium payments, an insurer will pay the face amount of the policy less the amount of the loan, with an adjustment for interest both prepaid and accrued.

*Under what circumstances will a policy be reinstated after non-payment of the premium?*

Most policies contain this typical provision: "The policy will be reinstated at any time within three years from the date of default, unless the cash surrender value specified in the policy has been exhausted by payment or unless the period of extended insurance has expired, upon the application of the insured and the production of evidence of insurability, including good health, satisfactory to the insurer and the payment of all overdue premiums and the payment or reinstatement of any other indebtedness to the insurer upon said policy with interest. . . ."

*Is an insurance company legally bound to notify a policyholder when a premium is about to become due?*

Yes. Notice must be given in writing not less than fifteen nor more than forty-five days prior to due date, or the policy will remain in force for at least a year after default. In addition, the notice must also state the penalty for failure to pay the premium on the due date or within the grace period. Such notice applies to all policies.

*May a life insurance policy be assigned?*

Yes, under certain circumstances. An assured may assign his policy:

1. If he has named himself as beneficiary and has paid the premiums.

2. If he has named another as beneficiary, but has reserved the right of revocation.

3. If he has not reserved the right of revocation, but has first obtained the consent of the beneficiary.

4. If, having an insurable interest in the life of another, he has insured such life for his own benefit and has paid all the premiums.

Under no circumstances, however, can an assignment take effect without written notice and approval by the company.

*How may a life insurance policy be terminated?*

1. By expiration (as of a term policy).

2. By lapse (as by a default in premium payment).

3. By payment of the loss by the insurer.

4. By forfeiture or cancelation by the insurer.

*What should you look for in health and accident policies?*

1. What is covered by the policy and what is not.

2. How much the policy will pay.

3. How long the policy will go on paying.

4. How much it costs.

*What is meant by "accidental injury" in a health and accident policy?*

An accidental injury is one over which you have no control, even though you may have been careless or negligent. An accident occurs, for example, if you cut yourself with a knife or if you stumble on a step and sprain your ankle.

*What is meant by "total disability" in a policy?*

Unless otherwise defined in the policy, total disability means the permanent inability of the injured to earn a living at his usual and regular calling, business, occupation, profession, or vocation. A pianist who permanently injures his right hand is totally disabled under a health and accident policy.

*What is "double indemnity"?*

Double indemnity provides for double the face value of the policy when the death of the policyholder occurs through an accident.

*Can creditors claim a life insurance policy?*

Yes, if the policy is payable to the estate of the insured. If the policy names someone other than the insured as the beneficiary, it cannot ordinarily be attached by creditors.

*You use your car to transport some fellow workers to the office, each one contributing $.75 for the round trip. Returning home one evening, you carelessly become involved in an automobile accident. The property damage to your car is $150. You have a $50 deductible collision policy, and you ask your insurer to reimburse you for $100. The company refuses on the ground that no liability is incurred, since the car was used as a public conveyance for carrying passengers for hire in violation of the policy. Is the company correct in refusing your claim?*

No. Your main business is your employment, the transporting of riders being merely incidental to it.

*What does burglary insurance cover?*

Burglary insurance protects property owners from loss by burglary. To discourage "inside jobs," payment under such policies is usually made only when the loss results from unlawful, violent, and external entry into buildings where the property is kept, of which violent and external entry there must be some mark or evidence. Such evidence includes the breaking of a window or the forcing of a lock.

*How can a purchaser of real property protect himself from loss due to defective title?*

By taking out title insurance in advance of the title closing.

*What is reinsurance?*

Reinsurance is a procedure by which underwriters reinsure their risks in whole or in part with other companies in order to avoid a concentration of risk beyond the point of safety.

# Chapter 14

# AGENCY AND EMPLOYMENT

*What is the subject matter of the law of agency?*

Agency plays an important part in the business world. Virtually every business operates by means of agents. An insurance company, for example, employs agents in dealing with prospective and actual policyholders. When you buy an automobile, you buy through a salesman (agent) acting on behalf of the automobile dealer (principal). A lawyer acts as an agent for his client, the principal. Agency, in fact, represents delegated authority and, in the world as we know it, plays an increasingly important role, in affairs both domestic and foreign.

*What is the central principle from which the law of agency is derived?*

That when a person deals with an agent, salesman, or representative, he is in fact dealing with the principal; that the agent has the legal power to act on behalf of the principal, to commit his principal to definite acts; that the principal is legally bound by the acts of his agents and representatives, as if he, the principal, had made those acts himself.

*What is the difference between a general agent and a special agent?*

A general agent has broad authority to bind his principal. A special agent's authority is limited to a specific task or to a series of special assignments, after which his authority ceases. Agency is a contractual relationship between the parties and may be either written or oral.

The personnel manager of a large factory may hire more men than are actually needed. If he does, the owners of the factory are responsible for the salaries, not the personnel manager, because the latter is a general agent with very broad powers.

An agent who is merely authorized to make one call on a cus-

189

tomer and return to the office is not authorized to make other stops. If, in doing so, he meets with an accident, he will be held personally responsible, not the firm, since he has exceeded the scope of his limited authority.

*What is the difference between an agent and an independent contractor?*

An agent is subject to the control and supervision of the one employing him. An independent contractor is not. In a relationship of principal and agent, it is the principal who is liable for the agent's contracts and torts (wrongs independent of contracts). An individual who is an independent contractor is himself liable for his own contracts and negligence.

*What is the difference between an agent and a trustee?*

1. An agent has no title to the property he handles, while a trustee has the legal, or administrative title, but not the equitable.

2. An agent acts on behalf of his principal, and in his name. A trustee acts in his own name.

3. An agency may be revoked, usually, at any time by the principal. A trustee cannot be dismissed until the purposes of the trust have been fulfilled. He may, however, be removed for cause.

*What is the difference between an agent and an escrow holder?*

1. An agent acts for a principal in dealing with third parties. He cannot represent both his principal and a third party if there is a conflict of interests. An escrow holder, on the other hand, can represent conflicting interests, since he is merely a stakeholder whose principal function is to hold money, securities, deeds, or something else of value until the happening or fulfillment of some event or condition.

2. An agent's authority may be revoked by his principal. The authority of an escrow holder is revocable only by the consent of all parties.

*What is the difference between an attorney at law and an attorney in fact?*

The former is a duly qualified and registered lawyer. The latter is merely an agent who acts under some special instrument or deed, such as a power of attorney. Another name for an attorney in fact is agent by procuration.

*May a minor be a principal in order to appoint agents?*

In most states, yes. A minor may appoint agents, but the appointment is voidable—not absolutely void—at the minor's option. Hence the need of caution by anyone who accepts appointment by a principal who is under age. However, if the agent's appointment is a necessity—not a luxury—the minor will be bound by the acts of his agent.

*Does a married woman have the same rights to appoint an agent as her husband does?*

Yes.

*Can an insane person appoint an agent?*

Not if he has been judicially declared insane.

*Can unincorporated clubs and other voluntary associations appoint agents?*

Since neither group is a legal entity, they cannot employ legal agents. However, their members may be held as joint principals if they have acted in the appointment of an agent.

*Who may act as an agent?*

Aside from infants, lunatics, and imbeciles, anyone may serve as an agent. The only requirement is that the agent have sufficient physical and mental capacity to exercise the authority delegated to him. What should be remembered is that one may be legally incompetent to make a valid contract, yet act as an agent, since an agent's contracts are not his own, but his principal's.

*When is a person disqualified from acting as an agent?*

1. When the agent has a personal interest adverse to or conflicting with that of his principal.

2. When the agent acts for several principals with conflicting interests.

3. When the agent and the third party have mutual interests that might conflict with that of the principal.

4. When the agent lacks the necessary qualifications or licenses required by law for the performance of the agency, as for lawyers, auctioneers, stockbrokers, etc.

### How is an agency created?

An agency may be created by (1) appointment, (2) ratification, (3) estoppel, or (4) necessity.

### What is agency by appointment?

Agents may be appointed either orally or in writing, in which case the agency is said to be express. An agency may be implied by the conduct or behavior of the parties. A power of attorney, for example, is written evidence of an agent's authority. It may be a formal power of attorney, as in the case of a duly acknowledged instrument under seal; or it may be a simple power of attorney, as in a letter addressed to an agent authorizing him to collect rents for and on behalf of the landlord.

### What is the difference between a general and special power of attorney?

The difference basically concerns the extent of the authority conferred on the agent. In a general power the agent is invested with complete and exclusive authority to do everything for the principal that the latter could do for himself. Such general powers of attorney are rare. They are only given under unusual circumstances, as when the principal leaves on an extended journey during which he is likely to be without the means to communicate with others.

A special power of attorney is restrictive in purpose and authority. For example, an owner of securities may give his stockbroker discretionary power to buy and sell stocks on his behalf.

### For what purposes are powers of attorney usually given?

1. To execute commercial paper.
2. To collect the debts of a business.
3. To collect dividends.

4. To manage, lease, and sell real estate.

5. To sell shares of stock.

6. To solicit and accept subscriptions and to collect the proceeds thereof.

7. To acknowledge documents.

8. To institute suit or to be represented by an attorney.

9. To appoint subagents.

10. To sign receipts.

*Are most agents appointed orally or in writing?*

By far the larger number are appointed as a result of an oral agreement.

*Does marriage create an agency, so that one spouse is authorized to act on behalf of the other?*

Except for the implied agency of the wife in binding her husband for household necessities, no implied agency is created by the mere fact of the marriage. However, by conduct and circumstances, a husband may be bound by his wife's acts, and a husband may be bound by his wife's behavior.

*When must an agency contract be in writing?*

When it comes within the Statute of Frauds discussed in the chapter on Contracts. Thus if the Statute of Frauds in a particular state provides that a contract to sell real estate must be signed by the party to be charged or by his duly authorized agent, the contract authorizing the agent to act need not be in writing. The agency must be in writing, however, if the statute reads "or his lawful agent thereunto authorized in writing." Additionally, an agency that cannot be performed within one year from the date of the making of the agreement must also be in writing.

*What is agency by ratification?*

In agency by ratification an act by the agent, previously unauthorized, or an act beyond the scope of the agent's authority, may be approved by the principal so as to bind the principal and not the agent. Such ratification may be express (oral or written) or implied, as when the principal accepts the benefits of the agent's previously unauthorized conduct.

*One of your employees forges your name to a check and cashes it. Can you ratify your employee's act and so relieve him of criminal prosecution?*

No. However, your ratification will relieve your employee of being civilly responsible for the amount of the check.

*An insurance company dismisses one of its employees. Nevertheless, the insurance agent continues, with the knowledge of the company, to collect premiums and to turn them over to the company. At the end of the month the company refuses to pay the agent his commission on the ground that the latter was dismissed and therefore was not authorized to collect any premiums at all. Is the company justified in its refusal?*

No. This case illustrates what is meant by agency by estoppel. Since the company acquiesced in the conduct of the agent, it is estopped or precluded from denying the agency.

*Under what circumstances is agency implied by necessity?*

An implied agency may be created under the following conditions:

1. When one spouse pledges the credit of the other for household necessities.

2. When a child pledges a parent's credit for necessities when the parent fails to supply them.

3. When, as a result of emergencies, the master of a vessel obligates the ship's owner for repairs, for towage, or even for jettisoning part or all of a ship's cargo.

4. When, as in the case of a railroad wreck, it becomes necessary for the conductor, trainman, or other individual to contract for hospital or medical expenses, it being impossible or difficult to obtain consent from the railroad itself.

*What are the major duties and obligations that a principal owes an agent?*

1. To compensate the agent.

2. To reimburse him for expenses.

3. To indemnify him against risks.

4. To pay damages for breach of the agency contract.

*What compensation is due an agent when none has been agreed upon?*

In the absence of an agreement, written or oral, the amount an agent may recover depends on the reasonable value of his services as determined by custom and by the nature of the services performed.

*You enter into an agreement to sell your house, it being understood that if the deal falls through, the broker will not receive a commission. The broker succeeds in finding a person ready, willing, and able to buy, but the deal cannot be consummated because your title to the property is defective. Must you pay the agent's commission?*

Yes, since the deal was canceled because of your fault, and not that of the agent's.

*A salesman is guaranteed a drawing account of $100 a week against commissions. He earns no commissions. Is the agent required to reimburse the drawing account?*

Only if the contract provides that the drawing account is to be considered nothing more than an advance or loan that is to be returned in any event.

*While performing the duties of his employment, a salesman runs through a red traffic signal. Can he compel his employer to reimburse him for the fine?*

No. Since what the salesman has done is illegal, he must bear the risk, not the principal.

*A salesman holding a one-year contract is dismissed after six months. He makes no attempt to find other employment within the range of his capacities. May he recover damages for the breach of contract for the entire six months?*

No. Although an agent has a right to damages for breach of contract, he is also under an obligation to mitigate or minimize such damages by attempting to obtain other employment as quickly as possible. Had the salesman made a reasonable effort to obtain such employment and failed, he would be entitled to the balance of his salary.

*What duties and obligations does an agent owe his principal?*

1. He must be loyal and show good faith.

2. He must be obedient to his principal's instructions.

3. He must exercise skill, care, and diligence in carrying out the principal's instructions.

4. He must give the principal an accounting of his agency, whenever called for.

*What degree of loyalty and good faith does an agent owe his principal?*

The highest degree, since the relationship between a principal and his agent is a confidential or fiduciary one. Thus an agent may not serve two principals with conflicting interests. If he does, he not only loses his right to compensation, but he may be sued in damages.

*May an agent represent both buyer and seller?*

Yes, if the agent has nothing to do with the price but merely brings the parties together, as do many real estate brokers.

*A principal instructs an agent to buy a certain property. The agent does so, but he takes title in his own name instead of in the name of the principal. What are the rights of the principal?*

He may either sue the agent for damages or institute suit to have the property reconveyed to him.

*May an agent carry on a business that competes with his principal's business?*

Not unless he does so with the principal's knowledge and consent.

*Due to the carelessness of the accountant who prepares your income tax return, a number of stock dividends are not included, as well as income from some property. Several years later the Inter-*

*nal Revenue Service finds the discrepancy and penalizes you with a fine and interest. Can you hold your accountant liable in damages?*

Yes. There is an implied warranty when a person undertakes a particular agency that he has the necessary skill and that he will exercise the necessary care and diligence to perform properly the task assigned. His failure to do so, as in the case of the accountant, will make him liable to the principal for any loss.

*Is an agent permitted to intermingle his funds with those of his employer or principal?*

If he does, he does so at his own risk, and is responsible for whatever loss occurs, even though he may not have been negligent.

*May an agent retain secret profits earned directly or indirectly by his agency?*

No. An agent may not derive a secret profit or take advantage of the agency. If he does, he must turn over the proceeds to his principal.

*When is a principal liable to third parties on contracts made by his agent?*

1. He is liable when the contract is expressly or implicitly authorized.

2. He is liable when the contract, though originally unauthorized, is later ratified.

3. He is liable when the circumstances in which the contract is made warrant a third party's assuming that the agent is duly authorized.

There is an important distinction between contracts made by a general agent and those made by a special agent. If the contract is made by a general agent, a principal is liable even when the agent exceeds his actual authority, if the agent had *apparent* authority to commit the principal. The test of apparent authority is whether similar agents usually have authority to perform similar specific acts. A second criterion of the binding of the principal by the acts of the agent is whether the third party is unaware that the agent has exceeded his authority.

*Does mere authority to sell or to solicit carry with it a presumption of authority to make collections?*

Not unless the agent has possession of the goods or other indicia of authority.

*A door-to-door salesman calls and persuades you to buy a vacuum cleaner at a greatly reduced price, but he does not show you any machine at this time. The next day he brings the machine and you pay him cash. The salesman absconds with the money. The company refuses to supply a new machine. Do you have any claim?*

No. Since the salesman did not have any machines with him or any other "indicia" of authority that he represented the company when he first called on you, your only recourse would be against the salesman, either criminally or by way of a civil suit.

*You authorize a rental agent to collect rents for various properties that you own. One fine week the agent, having obtained numerous checks from the tenants, endorses your name and cashes them. What are your rights as the landlord?*

You can sue the bank for the amount lost by you through the fraudulent endorsements. An agent authorized to make collections has no implied authority to collect anything but money. If he is given authority to take checks, he has no implied authority to cash them.

*You desire a divorce and consult an attorney in New York who advises that you do not have legal grounds in that state, but that he can obtain a Nevada divorce for you. You agree to the Nevada divorce. Without your knowledge or consent, the attorney employs counsel in Reno. After the divorce, the New York attorney presents you with a bill for $500 for services rendered by the Reno lawyer. Are you obligated to pay?*

Yes. In this case, your attorney had implied authority to hire a subagent, the Reno attorney. In general, whether an agent has such authority depends on the nature of the duties to be performed, the need to hire skilled assistance, the trade usage, the status of the agent, and the agent's location in relation to the place where the services are to be performed.

*Under what circumstances may an agent not delegate his duties or responsibilities?*

When the services to be performed are special or unique. If you employ a certain attorney to represent you, he cannot have an assistant or associate try your case without your express consent. If you hire a surgeon to perform an operation, he cannot delegate those duties to someone else without your express approval.

*What is the difference between a "disclosed" and an "undisclosed" principal?*

A disclosed principal is one whose identity is revealed by the agent to the third party at the time of the making of a contract. An undisclosed principal is one whose identity is not revealed at the time of the agreement.

*At the signing of a contract the name of the principal is undisclosed. Later, the third party learns the name of the principal for whom the agent was presumably working. What may the third party do?*

The third party has the option of holding either the agent or the undisclosed principal for any breach, but he cannot hold both.

*As the agent for the purchase of a piece of real estate, you give the seller your personal notes, which he accepts. The seller does not know the name of the principal for whom you are acting. When the notes fall due, you are unable to pay. May the undisclosed principal be held by the seller?*

The general legal principle is that a principal is not liable on a contract which has been fully executed by an agent, even though the principal received the benefit of the transaction. Since, in the above illustration, the contract was fully executed, the undisclosed principal cannot be held, though the agent can be.

*An agent signs a contract, under seal, for an undisclosed principal. Is the latter bound in case of default?*

No. As a rule, a principal cannot be bound by a contract under seal unless his name is on the document.

*Is a principal liable for his agent's negligent acts against third parties?*

Yes, if such acts are committed during the course of the agent's duties and within the scope of his actual or apparent authority or employment.

*Would a principal be liable if the agent, a bill collector, threatened unlawful imprisonment if the debtor did not pay?*

Yes.

*Would a principal be liable if an employee followed a customer out of the store and wrongfully accused her of shoplifting?*

Yes.

*Would an owner of a property be liable if the caretaker, becoming involved with a trespasser, wrongfully killed him?*

Yes.

*Would the owner of a vacuum cleaner company be liable if a salesman made fraudulent statements about the machine, even though warned not to do so by the owner of the business?*

Yes.

*Would a principal be liable if, in collecting a disputed amount, the agent willfully and maliciously assaulted the debtor?*

No. Here the agent is acting beyond the scope of his authority, express or implied.

*Would the head of a contracting firm be held liable if one of his employees, without the knowledge of the principal, attempted to bribe a state official?*

No.

*A department store advertised the services of a chiropodist as a feature of the store. The chiropodist actually was on his own, though he rented space from the department store owner. As the result of the chiropodist's negligence, a customer's foot became painfully infected. Is the department store liable?*

Yes. In a similar case the court held that the store was estopped, or prevented, from denying that the chiropodist was the owner's agent.

*Is a principal liable for the crimes committed by his agents?*

Only if the crime is committed by the express authority of the principal or performed in his presence or if the agent is directed and aided by the principal.

*When is notice to the agent binding on the principal?*

When such notice is received by the agent on matters within the scope of his authority.

*How may an agent become liable to third parties?*

An agent may become personally liable if:

1. He acts for a nonexistent or incompetent principal. Thus an agent becomes personally liable if he acts on behalf of a minor who wishes to purchase a luxury such as an automobile.

2. He acts for an undisclosed principal.

3. He misrepresents the extent of his authority.

4. He receives money wrongfully paid to him through fraud or mistake or for any other reason.

5. He personally assumes or guarantees the principal's obligation.

6. He willfully commits a fraud on behalf of his principal.

*What is the liability of a third party to the principal?*

Just as a principal is bound by his agent's contracts, so the third party is bound to the principal by the same contracts.

*A third party stipulates in the agreement that the person with whom he is dealing represents that he is acting as principal, not as agent. Is the third party liable if the agent is really acting for an undisclosed principal?*

No.

*What is the liability of the third party to the agent?*

Basically, the liability is the principal's on whose behalf the agent works. However, should the third party assault, slander, or libel the agent, the agent would have recourse against the third party for any wrongs against the agent personally.

*A real estate broker engages to sell a piece of property. Just before the sale is completed, his real estate license expires. Is the broker still entitled to his commission?*

No. For the broker to be entitled to his commission, the license must be in force throughout the entire period during which services are rendered.

*Does a real estate broker have a lien for an unpaid commission?*

No. His only recourse is to sue for breach of contract.

*Does a seller's inability to give good title to a buyer excuse the former from paying a commission to the real estate broker?*

No.

*Does an attorney have a lien on a client's papers to secure payment of fees?*

Yes. However, a client may secure the return of such papers when he pays the fee for services due the attorney.

*Does an accountant have a lien on the books and records of his clients?*

No. A client owns only the papers, records, or books that originated in the client's home or office. An accountant owns all his working papers.

*How is an agency terminated?*

By act of the parties or by operation of law.

*How is an agency terminated by act of the parties?*

An agency may be terminated:

1. By original agreement between the parties, as when a contract calls for its termination by a specified date.

2. By the resignation of the agent, even if it means he may be sued for breach of the agency contract. An agent has the right to resign, without being subject to penalties, when the principal refuses to pay the compensation called for or otherwise violates the agency agreement; when there is no consideration for the agency, as when an agent performs a service for and on behalf of his principal without making any charge; or, finally, when the agency may be discharged at the will of either party.

*Under what circumstances is an agency terminated by operation of law?*

An agency may be so terminated when:

1. The subject matter of the agency is illegal.

2. The subject matter is lost or destroyed.

3. Either of the parties dies or is incapacitated.

4. The business is dissolved.

5. The principal becomes bankrupt or insolvent.

*What notice is required to terminate an agency?*

If no notice is mentioned in the contract or agreement, then reasonable notice must be given, depending on the circumstances of each case. Third parties must also be given notice, preferably in writing, else they will not be bound by the termination of the agency and will still be able to hold the principal liable for the acts of his agent.

*Is it necessary to notify third parties of the death of the principal?*

Most states hold that an agency is terminated with the death of the principal and that thereafter the third party deals with the agent at his peril. Thus a tenant, unaware of the landlord's death, who continues to pay rent to the agent is still liable if the agent absconds with the rent or otherwise refuses to turn it over to the landlord's estate.

*What is the difference between an agent and an employee?*

There are usually three parties to an agency: the agent, the principal, and the third party. In the usual employment there may not be a third party involved at all, as when a person is hired to drive a truck or to act as a clerk. In many cases, of course, an employee may also be an agent, for example, a salesgirl in a department store who deals with customers. When the employee is also an agent, the law of agency applies. When he is strictly an employee, other legal principles are involved.

*Is an employee entitled to be paid for overtime?*

Only if the local law so provides or there is an agreement to that effect between employer and employee.

*May an employer demand the tips received by an employee?*

No, unless there is an agreement to the contrary.

*Under what circumstances may an employer withhold compensation to his employee?*

Since compensation depends basically on performance, an employer may lawfully withhold payment of salary or wages if the employee fails or refuses to discharge his duties or is dishonest, disloyal, or otherwise guilty of serious misconduct.

*What compensation, if any, is an employee entitled to if he quits while on the job?*

His right to compensation will depend on the amount earned up to quitting time, less any damage sustained by the employer if the quitting was wrongful.

*Suppose the damage or loss exceeds any compensation earned?*

In such a case, nothing will be due the employee.

*What rights and duties does an employer owe an employee?*

An employer must provide an employee:

1. A safe place to work.

2. Safe tools and equipment.

3. Proper instruction and training.

4. Competent co-workers. Thus if an employee is assaulted by a fellow employee known by the employer to be a troublemaker, the employer as well as the fellow employee may be liable for damages.

*What rights and obligations does an employee owe his employer?*

1. He must use reasonable care in the exercise of his employment. This means that if he is careless or negligent in the performance of his duties to the extent of injuring someone, he may be held liable by the employer for such negligence, as well as by third parties.

2. He must obey the employer's instructions.

3. He must be diligent.

4. He must be loyal to the firm's interests.

*May an employee divulge the trade secrets of his employer?*

No. He may not do this even after the employment is terminated.

*May a salesman, after discharge, solicit the customers of his former employer?*

Yes, provided he did not appropriate a written list of names while working for his employer. If the employee solicited customers from a list he had memorized, he would not be prevented from such solicitation.

*As between employer and employee, who is entitled to inventions and shop rights?*

In the absence of an agreement or understanding to the contrary, an employee is entitled to his inventions, even if he created them on company time. To protect himself, the employer must provide in the contract of employment that any inventions by the employee shall become the property of the employer.

*What are shop rights?*

This term designates those rights an employer has when an employee invents, improves, or perfects a method of doing his work while working for his employer and using his employer's time and equipment. Although the employee has the right to the invention itself, the employer has the right to use the improvement in his shop or business. Of course, if the employee made the improvement on his own time and with his own equipment, the employer has no shop right.

*What is the employer's liability for industrial injuries?*

Under workmen's compensation laws enacted in practically every state, the burden for industrial injuries falls on the employer, regardless of whether the employee was negligent. Compensation laws rest on the theory that the injured workingman or employee is entitled, as a matter of right, to pecuniary relief from the distress caused by his injury, unless his own willful act, such as intoxication, is the proximate cause.

*Are all employments covered by workmen's compensation laws?*

No. The laws are designed to provide compensation for accidental injury arising from, and in the course of, extrahazardous tasks. Most workmen's compensation acts preclude the employee from recovering only in cases of drunkenness or the willful self-infliction of injury.

*Suppose the employment as a whole is considered nonhazardous, as in the publishing industry, will an employee still be covered by workmen's compensation laws?*

Yes. Truck drivers may have to be covered by workmen's compensation, even if the business as a whole is exempt.

*Are casual employees and independent contractors covered under such acts?*

Only regular workers are protected. Those employed for a limited time to accomplish some particular task are known as casual employees and are not covered by workmen's compensation laws. Nor are independent contractors, who are not technically employees at all.

*What happens if a casual employee is injured on the job?*

His only recourse is to sue the employer, provided he can prove that his injuries were caused by the employer's negligence.

*What medical and surgical benefits are afforded an employee under workmen's compensation?*

Nearly every state allows injured employees a certain amount of medical and surgical care. In about half the states such benefits range from two months to one hundred months.

*Who determines the benefits that an injured employee receives?*

The Workmen's Compensation Commission of the individual state. Compensation is based:

1. On the amount of wages the employee has received.

2. On the extent of injury or incapacity.

3. In case of death, on the decedent's wage scale and the number and status of his dependents.

*What methods for insuring risks are available to an employer?*

An employer has the option of:

1. Insuring with a stock or mutual insurance company.

2. Insuring with a state insurance fund.

3. Self-insuring, when the employer can furnish proof of his financial ability to pay the compensation, accompanied by the deposit of adequate security with the state commission to support such proof.

*Is it always advisable for an injured employee to retain counsel, or will he do just as well if he allows the Workmen's Compensation Commission to determine the nature and extent of his injury, if any, and the award that shall be made by way of compensation?*

In all cases where the employee or claimant has sustained an accidental injury or acquired an occupational disease arising from, and in the course of, his employment, he should immediately engage the services of an attorney. The attorney will promptly file the necessary papers so that the claim will not be barred because it was filed too late. Actually, no claimant or employee should attempt to settle his claim without first engaging the services of a lawyer. To do so may mean that the claimant may jeopardize his legal rights or receive inadequate compensation for his injuries.

*What fees do attorneys charge for handling compensation cases?*

The fee, usually set by the Workmen's Compensation Commission, is between 15 and 25 percent of the amount awarded. There is no obligation to pay if the claimant fails to win an award. In all cases the fee must first be approved by the Commission.

*How soon after an industrial accident must an employee, his representative, or beneficiary give notice to an employer?*

**Alabama**   Written notice of an accident must be given to the employer within five days unless the claim is prevented by physical or mental incapacity, youth, fraud, deceit, or other good reason. In any event, notice must be given ninety days after the accident, or if death results, within ninety days after the employee's death. If the employer has actual knowledge of the accident, no notice is required.

**Alaska**   Notice of beneficiary's claim is required, but the statute is liberally construed.

**Arizona**   The provisions of the law are compulsory on both employer and employee, and the remedies provided are exclusive, except that an employee, prior to an injury, may reject the act and retain his right to sue by filing written notice with the employer.

**Arkansas**   Notice of injury or death must be given to the employer and to the Commission within sixty days, but the Commission may excuse noncompliance with the law.

**California**   Written notice of an accident must be given to the employer within thirty days of the injury. If death results from the injury, written notice must be given within thirty days of death.

**Colorado**   The employee or someone in his behalf must report the injury to the employer within two days, unless the employer or the person in charge has actual notice of the injury or the employee is physically or mentally unable to report the accident. The employer must give notice of the injury to the Commission within ten days thereafter, or in case of death, immediately. If notice is not given by the employer, any person may give notice, which the employee or his representative may disclaim within a reasonable time. The worker's right to compensation or benefits is barred unless notice is given within six months after the injury or within one year after death resulting therefrom, but such limitations do not apply if the Commission finds within two years after the injury or death that a reasonable excuse for failure to file existed and the employer's rights have not been prejudiced thereby.

**Connecticut** Proceedings for compensation may not be maintained unless written notice of a claim is given to the employer or the Commissioner within one year from the date of the accident or from the first manifestation of disease; but if death results within two years of the above dates, a dependent may make a claim within the said two-year period. No claim for disease may be made against the employer except while the employee is still in employ or within five years of his leaving employ. If a hearing, or request therefor, or a voluntary agreement is submitted, or if the employer furnishes medical service, within one year of the accident or first manifestation of disease, no want of notice is a bar. A claim must contain a statement of date, place, and nature of injury and the name and address of the employee. A defect or inaccuracy of notice is a bar to recovery only to the extent that the employer has been prejudiced thereby. Compensation is payable only if the injury incapacitates the employee for more than seven days from earning full wages at his customary employment. If the incapacity continues for more than seven days but less than two weeks, compensation begins at the end of seven days. If the incapacity continues for two weeks, compensation begins on the day of the injury, which day is not counted as a day of incapacity and for which the employee is entitled to full wages.

**Delaware** A claim must usually be filed within thirty days after an injury. When death results, a claim must be filed within ninety days of death.

**District of Columbia** The law is the same as in Delaware.

**Florida** A claim for disability must be filed within three years after the time of the injury, and a claim for death within two years after death, except that when compensation has been paid without an award on account of such injury, a claim may be filed within three years after the date of the last payment and two years after death.

**Georgia** Notice of an accident must be given in person and in writing by an employee or his representative, as soon after the accident as practicable, to the employer, his agent, or representative, the foreman, or the employee's immediate superior. The employee is not entitled to any physicians' fees or compensation that accrued prior to the giving of notice. No compensation is payable unless the prescribed notice is given within thirty days after death resulting from an accident, unless the employee was prevented from notifying the employer because of physical or mental incapacity or fraud or deceit; or unless the employer, his agent or representative, the foreman, or the employee's immediate superior had knowledge of the accident; or unless there is some other reasonable excuse and the employer has not been prejudiced by the delay.

**Hawaii**   A claim must usually be filed within thirty days after an injury. When death results, a claim must be filed within ninety days of the employee's death.

**Idaho**   The law is the same as in Hawaii.

**Illinois**   Notice of an injury must be given to the employer within forty-five days (fifteen days in hernia cases), and an application for compensation filed with the Commission within one year of the injury or the last payment of compensation.

**Indiana**   A claim under the terms of the act must be filed within two years of the date of accident or death.

**Iowa**   Both master and servant have the right to accept or reject the terms of the law by complying with certain forms of notices. Acceptance is conclusively presumed unless a notice of rejection is given in a manner provided by statute.

**Kansas**   To entitle injured workman to compensation, notice of an accident must be given to the employer within ten days of same, but no notice is necessary if the employer or his agent has actual knowledge of the accident.

**Kentucky**   A claim must usually be filed within thirty days of an injury. When death results, the claim must be filed within ninety days of the employee's death.

**Louisiana**   An employee may claim compensation without affecting his claim for damages against a third person for the amount that he has paid or become obligated to pay as compensation. The parties to the case have a right to compromise the dispute under the supervision of a court.

**Maine**   Notice of an accident must be given to the employer, foreman, or official in charge of the work, if the employer or his agent had no knowledge of the accident, stating the time, the place, the cause of the accident, and the nature of the injury, together with the address of the person injured, within thirty days of the injury, or there can be no proceedings under the act. Any time during which the employee is unable by reason of physical incapacity to give said notice, or fails to do so on account of a mistake of fact, is not included in the thirty-day period. If the employee dies within the thirty-day period, three months after such death are allowed for giving the said notice.

**Maryland** Written notice of an injury should be given to the employer within ten days of the accident, or in case of death, within thirty days of death. A claim should be filed with the Industrial Accident Commission within sixty days of the disability or, in the event of the worker's death, within one year of death. The claim must be on the form prescribed by the Commission.

**Massachusetts** No proceedings for compensation may be maintained unless the injured employee serves notice upon the employer or insurer as soon as practicable after the happening thereof and unless the claim is filed within six months after the happening thereof. The notice must be in writing, signed by the person injured or, if the worker has died, by his legal representatives or beneficiary, and must give the time, place, and cause of injury. A want of proper notice or a delay in filing the claim will not bar recovery by the employee if it is found that the insurer was not prejudiced thereby.

**Michigan** An employee's right to compensation is barred unless the employer is given notice of the injury within three months, and unless the claim is made orally or in writing within six months after the injury or death, or within the first six months during which the employee is not physically or mentally incapacitated to make the claim. If the employer is given notice or knowledge of the injury within three months, but the disability does not develop within six months, a claim may be made but not later than three years after the injury. The time allowed for making a claim does not run during physical or mental incapacity, nor, if the employer has notice or knowledge of the injury within three months and fails to report it to the Compensation Department, until the report is filed.

**Minnesota** The employee must sue within two years after giving notice to the Commission of the accident and within six years of the accident. If the employee dies, his dependents may bring suit within two years after giving notice to the Commission and within six years of the employee's death. In the case of persons under a disability, the limitation is extended for two years from the date of the removal of the disability.

**Mississippi**    An employer's notice or knowledge of the accident is notice or knowledge of the insurer. Jurisdiction of the employer by the court is jurisdiction of the insurer. Any order of the Commission or the court that is binding on the employer is binding on the insurer.

**Missouri**    The Act applies to all major employers (those with more than ten employees) unless the employer files a written notice of specific intent not to accept the act. Such notice becomes effective on receipt by the Division. Notice by the employee affects only the employment at which he may then be employed. Notices of rejection are furnished by the Division and must be conspicuously placed on the employer's premises.

**Montana**    If the employee fails to sue within six months, the employer may prosecute an action.

**Nebraska**    Employers and employees are presumed to accept the terms of the compensation schedule, as outlined in the statute, for injuries arising out of and in the course of the employment, unless they give notice that they elect not to be bound by the schedule of compensation.

**Nevada**    An employee is presumed to have accepted the benefits of the act unless he gives written notice of rejection to his employer and to the Industrial Commission. When the employee rejects the act, the employer, if under the act, may plead practically all common-law defenses to the employee's claim.

**New Hampshire**    No proceedings for compensation (other than medical care, hospital services, other remedial care, or property damage) may be maintained unless notice of the accident has been given to the employer as soon as practicable after the happening thereof, and before the workman has voluntarily left the employment in which he was injured, and within ninety days of the occurrence of the accident; or in case of the death of the workman, or in the event of his physical or mental incapacity, within ninety days after such death or the removal of such physical or mental incapacity; or in the event that weekly payments have been made under the act, within ninety days after such payments have ceased. No want, defect, or inaccuracy of a notice is a bar to the maintenance of proceedings, unless the employer proves that he is prejudiced by such want, defect, or inaccuracy; but the employee's claim is barred unless said notice is given to the employer within one year from the date of the accident. For the purpose of giving notice of a disease, the date of disablement shall be deemed the date of the accident. Notice by the employee of the accident in writing on blanks to be approved by the Commissioner of Labor must apprise the employer of the claim for compensation under the act and must state the name and address of the workman injured and the date and place of the accident. Notice may be served personally or sent by registered mail addressed to the employer at his last known residence or place of business.

**New Jersey** With certain exceptions, an employee's claim for compensation must be made within two years of the injury.

**New York** Written notice of injury must be given to the employer within thirty days thereafter, and in case of the death of such employee resulting from the injury, within thirty days after such death. A failure to give such notice, unless excused by the board, is deemed a waiver of such objection.

**North Carolina** A claim must be filed within one year of the accident.

**North Dakota** A claim for disability or death must be made within sixty days after injury or death, but for reasonable cause the bureau may allow a claim to be made at any time within one year.

**Ohio** A claim is barred unless it is presented within two years of injury or death.

**Oklahoma** Notice of an injury must be given to the employer and to the Commission within thirty days, and notice of an occupational disease within eighteen months of last exposure or within three months from disablement; an employee's failure to do so, unless excused by the Commission for cause of want or prejudice, bars recovery, and a failure to present a claim for injury within one year, or a claim for occupational disease within three years, is a permanent bar.

**Oregon** An employee's claim must usually be filed within thirty days of an injury. When the employee's death results, the claim must be filed within ninety days after death.

**Pennsylvania** An employee's claim for compensation must be preceded by notice in specified form to the employer within ninety days of the accident and must be filed with the Workmen's Compensation Board within one year. In hernia cases, notice to the employer must be given within five days after the occurrence of the accident.

**Puerto Rico**   An employee's claim must usually be filed within thirty days of the injury. When death occurs, the claim must be filed within ninety days of death.

**Rhode Island**   All agreements for compensation must be filed with and approved by the Director of Labor.

**South Carolina**   An employee's claim for compensation must be made within one year of an accident or death from an accident.

**South Dakota**   An employee is required to give the employer written notice of the injury immediately, or as soon as practicable thereafter; and unless the employer or his agent or representative had knowledge thereof, or unless notice was prevented by physical or mental incapacity, etc., no benefits accruing before notice are payable. Unless there is a reasonable excuse to the satisfaction of the Commissioner, a claim is barred by a failure to give notice to the employer within thirty days of the injury or death of the employee. The notice should state the name and address of the employee, the time, the place, the nature, and the cause of the injury, or death; it should be signed by the employee or by a person in his behalf, or if he is dead, by one or more of his dependents or by a person in their behalf. The notice may be served personally or by registered mail, and unless the employer is prejudiced thereby, an inaccuracy or defect in the notice does not bar compensation.

**Tennessee**   Written notice of an injury is required within thirty days of the accident, unless the employer has actual notice. Claim is barred within one year, except where payments have been made, and then one year from last payment.

**Texas**   An employee may retain his right of action at the common law and under state statutes by giving notice thereof to his employer at the time he is hired, but such right of action is subject to all defenses previously existing under common law and state statutes. If the employee does not give such notice, the common-law right of action is waived.

**Utah**   Notice of an accident must be given to employer within one year. If the employee fails to report the accident, a deduction of 15 per cent is made on adjustment of compensation.

**Vermont**   The workman must give notice of an injury and of a claim for compensation in the form prescribed by statute and as soon as practicable after the happening of the injury. The claim for compensation must be made within six months from the date of the injury or, in case of death, within six months after such death. The claim must be in writing, contain the name and address of the employee, and state in ordinary language the time, the place, the nature, and the cause of the injury. It must be signed by the employee or by a person in his behalf, and be delivered or sent by registered letter addressed to the employer at his or its last known residence or place of business.

**Virginia** Written notice of an accident must be given to the employer within thirty days.

**Virgin Islands** Written notice of a claim is required within forty-eight hours of the injury, unless reasonable cause is shown why it could not be so made.

**Washington** A claim must usually be filed within thirty days of an injury. If death occurs, the claim must be filed within ninety days of death.

**West Virginia** A claim, except for silicosis, must be filed within one year of injury or death, and proofs of dependency must be filed within one year of death. A claim for silicosis must be made within two years of the last injurious exposure or, in case of death, by a dependent within one year of the employee's death.

**Wisconsin** Notice of an injury must be given to the employer within thirty days of the injury, but a failure to give notice does not bar the claim unless employer is prejudiced thereby. The amount of the award is determined by the extent of the injury, and in case of death, the employer pays reasonable expense of burial not exceeding $300. Increased liability is provided for injuries to minors illegally employed.

**Wyoming** A report of an injury must be made by the employee within twenty-four hours thereafter, and a report of death must be made within twenty days. An employer must likewise report both injuries and death within twenty days. An employee's claim for an award must be made within one year. The notice must contain the following information about the injury and injured workman: (1) the employee's name; the time, the cause, and the nature of the accident and injury; the disability; (2) the relation of the accident to employment; (3) the nature of the employment and the length of service with the employer; (4) whether injury was due to the culpable negligence of the employee; (5) the marital status and dependents of the employee; (6) the employee's intention in claiming compensation.

*What can be done if an employer withholds or delays the payment of the employee's wages?*

He can be sued for the wages due; in some states, he may also be criminally liable.

*Must an employee join a union before being hired?*

No. Under the Taft-Hartley Act of 1947, employees may join or refrain from joining any union, without restraint or intimidation. Under the Act, the closed shop, in which only union members are employed, is banned. However, an employee must join the union when such arrangement is supported by a majority vote of the workers.

*What unfair labor practices are banned under the Taft-Hartley Act?*

1. Coercion by unions or employers in the selection of bargaining representatives.
2. Discrimination against nonunion employees.
3. Union refusal to bargain.
4. Illegal strikes and boycotts.
5. Discriminatory or excessive initiation fees for joining a union.
6. "Featherbedding," or forcing an employer to pay for services that are not performed or not to be performed.

*What other benefits does the Taft-Hartley Act provide?*

1. Free speech is guaranteed to employers in expressing their views of labor problems to their employees, so long as they contain no threat of reprisal or force or promise of benefit.

2. Unions must file reports on money taken in, and give an accounting thereof.

3. Communists cannot hold union office.

4. Compulsory check-offs are abolished. Employers are not compelled to deduct union dues from the wages of employees and turn them over to the unions; each worker now has the right to decide for himself whether he will permit a check-off on his wages.

5. Threatened strikes which may create national emergencies are subject to study by a board of inquiry appointed by the President of the United States. The board's report, which is made public, is coupled with the President's authority to procure an injunction against the strike, followed by a sixty-day period for collective bar-

gaining and, if necessary, a further fifteen-day period for a secret ballot under the auspices of the National Labor Relations Board.

6. When there is a danger of a work stoppage toward the expiration of a collective bargaining contract, the Taft-Hartley Act provides for a "cooling off" period of sixty days prior to such work stoppage. When such a situation exists, neither party to the dispute may terminate or modify it without:

a. First serving written notice on the other party sixty days prior to the expiration of the contract of the proposed termination or modification.

b. Offering to meet and confer with the other party for the purpose of negotiating a new or modified contract.

c. Notifying the Federal Mediation and Conciliation Service and corresponding state agencies of the existence of the dispute.

d.. Continuing, without work stoppage, under all the terms and conditions of the existing contract for at least sixty days after serving the written notice.

## CHAPTER 15

## NEGOTIABLE INSTRUMENTS

*What is the subject matter of negotiable instruments?*

Checks, bills of exchange, bills of lading, letters of credit, promissory notes, and bonds. To an extent not often realized, the business world rests on credit, which in turn revolves around negotiable instruments. If, for example, Congress tomorrow passed a law making it mandatory that all sales be paid for in cash, our free enterprise system would collapse within twenty-four hours. Since everyone would need cash, there would be a run on the banks that would lead to their complete ruin; merchants would close their stores, and factories would soon be idle; starvation and unemployment would stalk the land. Both business and the government are run on credit—which means borrowed money in one form or another—and credit makes up a good part of the subject matter of negotiable instruments.

*What is meant by negotiability?*

A written instrument such as a check or promissory note is negotiable when it passes freely from hand to hand as a credit instrument or substitute for money. A negotiable instrument is thus acceptable on its face.

*What is the difference between a negotiable instrument and an ordinary contract?*

Not all contracts may be assigned. A negotiable instrument is transferred by endorsement and delivery, or by delivery alone. In a contract, the rights of an assignee can never be greater than the rights of the assignor or the one who has assigned the contract. A transferee by "negotiation" is not disadvantaged in this way. A contract also differs from a negotiable instrument as to consideration. In the first place, in an ordinary contract there is no presumption that there is a consideration. If, for example, you filed suit for breach of contract, you would have to prove that there was a lawful consideration for the contract. Failure to adduce such proof would mean dismissal of the lawsuit. When it comes to negotiable instruments, there is a legal presumption that the check or note was given for a valuable consideration. Again, the usual contract is unenforceable if given for a past consideration, which is not the case with a negotiable instrument. In the third place, one to whom a contract has been assigned (the assignee) acquires no greater rights than his assignor. This is not true when a check or a note has been acquired by a holder in due course.

*What makes an instrument negotiable?*

According to the Uniform Negotiable Instruments Law, adopted in all states, an instrument:

1. Must be in writing and signed by the maker or drawer.

2. Must contain an unconditional promise or order to pay a sum certain in money.

3. Must be payable on demand, or at a fixed or determinable future time.

4. Must be payable to order or to bearer.

5. If addressed to a drawee, must name him or otherwise indicate him therein with reasonable certainty.

All five elements must be present for the instrument to be negotiable.

*When is an instrument payable on demand?*

An instrument is payable on demand:

1. If the instrument itself so states.

2. If it is payable on presentation or at sight.

3. If it expresses no time for payment.

4. If it is accepted or endorsed after it is overdue. (Thus if you endorse a note today that was due three years ago, the note is payable on demand.)

*When is an instrument payable to bearer?*

1. When it is payable to a person or bearer.

2. When it is payable to cash.

**3.** When it is intentionally made payable to a fictitious or nonexistent person, such as "Payroll" or "Petty Cash."

**4.** When the payee's name does not purport to be the name of any person.

**5.** When the only or last indorsement is in blank, that is, when it consists merely of writing one's name on the back of the instrument.

*What do the words, "to order" and "to bearer" mean on a negotiable instrument?*

They mean that the instrument is transferable at the will of the holder and that the maker of the instrument will pay any holder the sum of money mentioned therein.

*You endorse a check by writing "Pay to bearer, John Jones" above your signature. Is this check negotiable?*

No, since it is payable only to the bearer, and not to his order.

*Is an instrument negotiable if the date is omitted?*

Yes.

*Is an instrument negotiable if the words "value received" are omitted?*

Yes.

*Is an instrument negotiable if the place where the instrument was drawn is omitted?*

Yes.

*Is an instrument negotiable if the place where the instrument is payable is omitted?*

Yes.

*Is an instrument negotiable if there is no provision for interest?*

Yes.

*You sign a note agreeing that thirty days after you arrive in Paris you promise to pay to the holder, William Warren, the sum of $1,500. Is this note negotiable?*

No. It is not negotiable because the condition of arrival may never occur and, second, because it is payable not to order or bearer, but merely to William Warren.

*You make out a check payable to the order of John Smith for the sum of $100, correctly writing out the words "One hundred dollars." However, you set down the figure "$10.00" instead of "$100.00." Is the check negotiable?*

Yes. When the sum payable is expressed in words and also in figures and there is a discrepancy between the two, the sum denoted by the words is the sum payable; but if the words are ambiguous or uncertain, reference may be had to the figures to fix the amount.

*Suppose the instrument provides for the payment of interest, without specifying the date from which interest is to run. Is the instrument negotiable?*

Yes. The rule is that interest runs from the date of the instrument or, if the instrument is undated, from the date the instrument was issued. The date of issue may be proved by circumstances.

*What if the instrument is not dated?*

It will be considered to be dated as of the time it was issued.

*An agent signs a note "William Brown, agent." Will this relieve the agent of liability?*

No. To relieve himself of liability, the agent should sign the instrument "Henry Folsom, by William Brown, agent."

*Suppose a signature is so placed on an instrument that it is not clear in what capacity the person making it intended to sign?*

The person so signing the instrument is presumed to be an endorser.

*What if there is a conflict between the written and printed provisions of the instrument?*

The written provisions prevail.

*Who is the key party to a negotiable instrument?*

The holder in due course, who may acquire rights greater than those held by the transferor who turned over the instrument to him. For example, a holder in due course is not concerned with the claims or counterclaims of prior parties to the instrument. Nor is he concerned that the maker of a note gave it to the payee without consideration. A holder in due course is in the driver's seat merely because he is able to enforce his legal rights.

*When is a person a holder in due course?*

A holder in due course is one who acquires a negotiable instrument under the following conditions:

1. *The instrument is complete and regular on its face.* Thus the taker of a promissory note in which some material item, such as the amount, maturity, or signature, is omitted, incomplete, or irregular, is not a holder in due course. Actually, the holder of paper with such omissions is put on notice, and takes his chances if he fails to inquire.

2. *The holder took the instrument before it was due and without notice that it had been previously dishonored, if such was the fact.* Thus one who takes a note on February 4 when it was due on February 3 is not a holder in due course.

3. *The holder took the instrument in good faith and for value.* A person who takes a check or note, knowing that it was procured through fraud or that it lacks consideration, is not a holder in due course. Value is any consideration sufficient to support a simple contract.

4. *At the time the instrument was negotiated to the holder, he had no notice of any infirmity in the instrument or defect in the title of the person negotiating it.* Infirmities include erasures, omissions, or errors on the instrument itself. Defect in the title has reference to fraud, duress, or any other unlawful means by which the holder acquired the check, bill, or note.

*Can there be a holder in due course of a nonnegotiable instrument?*

No. Title to a nonnegotiable instrument passes by assignment, and is subject to any defenses by prior parties.

## What is a promissory note?

A note in which one party, the "maker," promises to pay a sum of money to another party, the "payee," or to his order, or to bearer. A note may be signed by a single individual, jointly, or jointly and severally, with corresponding liability.

## What is the difference between a simple note and a collateral note?

A simple note is an ordinary, unsecured note. A collateral note is one which recites that it is secured by some form of collateral. It allows the payee, on default, to sell the collateral and apply the proceeds to the payments of the note.

## What is a bank note?

A note issued by a bank or banker, payable to bearer on demand. A bank note is intended to circulate as money.

## What is a mortgage note?

A note secured by a mortgage, which may be foreclosed if the note is unpaid.

## What is a judgment note?

A note that authorizes the holder to have judgment entered for the amount of the note without trial, plus interest, attorney's fees, and costs.

## What is a certificate of deposit?

It is a written acknowledgment by a bank that a certain sum of money has been deposited payable to the depositor or to his order at a time specified in the certificate.

## What is a bond?

A bond is a sealed acknowledgment of an obligation to pay a fixed sum of money either to bearer or to a named obligee on demand or on a certain day, with interest to be paid at fixed intervals.

## What is a bearer bond?

A bearer bond, usually with interest coupons attached, is negotiable by delivery. If lost or stolen, a bearer bond passes good title to an innocent purchaser for value.

*What is a registered bond?*

It is a bond transferable only by endorsement and by registration of the transferee's name on the books of the government or corporation.

*What is a debenture bond?*

It is a bond unsecured by any assets of the corporation, except as a charge on its earnings.

*How is a bearer bond transferred?*

Simply by delivery from one person to another, much as one hands or transfers a dollar bill to another.

*How is a registered bond transferred?*

For a transferral to be effective, a registered bond must be both delivered to another person and endorsed by the original holder of the bond.

*What is a bill of exchange?*

A bill of exchange, or draft, is a direction in writing, by the person who signs it, to another to whom it is addressed, to pay to a third person a definite sum of money at a specified time.

*What is a two-party draft?*

It is a draft made payable by the drawer to himself as payee, for collection purposes.

*What is a domestic, or inland, bill or draft?*

It is a draft drawn and payable in the same state. All other bills and drafts are "foreign."

*What is a sight draft?*

It is a draft or bill payable "at sight" or on demand. A sight draft is distinguished from a time draft, which is payable at a fixed time after date or "after sight"; that is, at a fixed time after the instrument has been presented to the drawee for acceptance.

*What is a documentary sight draft?*

If a sight draft is accompanied by documents such as bills of lading or warehouse receipts in connection with which the draft is drawn, the instrument is known as a documentary sight draft.

*What is a bank draft?*

It is a check drawn by one bank on another.

*What is a letter of credit?*

A letter of credit is an instrument containing a request, either general or special, to pay money to the bearer or person named therein, and looks to the drawer of the letter for compensation. It is frequently used by travelers who, upon presenting the letter to express offices or banks, may obtain funds as and when needed, up to the full amount specified in the letter, by signing checks or drafts for the particular amounts needed.

*What constitutes endorsement?*

Endorsement means writing one's name, with or without additional words, either on the instrument itself or, if that is too crowded, on a paper attached to the instrument.

*Are typewritten endorsements valid?*

Yes. So are stamped endorsements.

*A check is made payable to you, but your name is misspelled? How should you endorse the bill or note?*

It should be signed the way it is written, misspelling and all. You may then, if your wish, sign your name correctly.

*What is the effect of endorsing a check or note?*

First, you guarantee that the check or note is genuine and in all respects what it purports to be. Second, you guarantee that as the endorser you have good title to the paper. Third, you guarantee that all other holders of the check or note will be paid when the instrument is duly presented; that if it is not paid and proper proceedings are taken by the holder, you will pay the amount of the check or note to the holder or to any later endorser who has been compelled to make it good.

### What is a blank endorsement?

The endorsement of a bill of exchange, promissory note, or check by merely writing the name of the endorser or transferor on the back of the instrument is known as an endorsement "in blank." Such an endorsement makes the instrument payable to bearer. The instrument is negotiated by delivery; it can be cashed without further endorsement. Thus a check made payable to John Doe is endorsed in blank when he signs his name on the back of the check.

### What is an endorsement in full?

It is an endorsement in which the transferor mentions the name of the person in whose favor the endorsement is made: "Pay to Thomas Smith, John Doe" or "Pay to Thomas Smith, or order, John Doe." Further negotiation requires the endorsement of the holder. A check endorsed in full cannot be cashed without the signature of the transferee. Thus such an endorsement is a protection against loss if a check is lost or stolen.

### What is a restrictive endorsement?

In a restrictive endorsement the transferor designates another as the only person to whom payment will be made, or appoints another his agent for a special purpose: "Pay to Thomas Smith only, John Doe," or "For Deposit Only, John Doe." A restrictive endorsement prohibits further negotiation. A lost or stolen check, endorsed restrictively, can only be used for the purpose indicated by the endorsement.

### What is a qualified endorsement?

By this endorsement the endorser merely passes title to the instrument. He has no liability as an endorser for payment should the maker fail to pay. The endorser is liable, however, for certain warranties. He warrants that the check or note is genuine, that he has good title, that all prior parties were competent, and that the instrument is valid. An endorsement is qualified when it is signed "Without recourse, John Doe."

*What is the liability of an endorser?*

An endorser is secondarily liable. He warrants that he will pay the face amount of the check or note if the maker, the person primarily liable, does not.

*May a minor endorse a check or note?*

Yes. A minor may pass title to an instrument by endorsement even if, from lack of capacity, he may not be liable on it.

*On what two things does liability depend in a negotiable instrument?*

1. The instrument itself, including the amount, date of making, date when due, and so on.
2. The capacity in which a party signs his signature to the instrument.

*Who is primarily liable on a negotiable instrument?*

The maker of a note, to whom it must first be presented; and the acceptor of a bill or check. The drawer and endorsers are secondarily liable on a bill; the endorsers on a note.

*What is the liability of a general endorser?*

A general endorser warrants to all subsequent holders in due course:

1. That the instrument is genuine and in all respects what it purports to be.
2. That he has good title to it and that all prior transferors had good title.
3. That all prior parties had capacity to contract.
4. That the instrument was valid at the time he endorsed it.
5. That on due presentment the instrument will be accepted, paid, or both.
6. That if the instrument is not accepted or paid, and the necessary proceedings on dishonor are taken, he will pay the instrument.

*What is the liability of a qualified endorser?*

A qualified endorser warrants everything a general endorser does, except that he does not guarantee that the instrument was valid, nor does he warrant that the instrument will be paid at maturity.

*What is the order of liability among endorsers?*

Endorsers are liable, in the absence of agreement, in the order of their endorsements. If there are five endorsers, the first one is primarily liable. If the first one defaults, the second endorser becomes liable, and so on down the list of endorsers.

*What is an accommodation party?*

One who gives a note or other form of negotiable instrument made for the purpose of enabling the payee to obtain credit. Such a note has no validity until it passes into the hands of a holder for value. Accommodation paper is any type of bill or note to which an accommodation party puts his name.

*Under what circumstances is an accommodation party liable?*

1. If the instrument is payable to the order of a third person, he is liable to that person and to all subsequent parties.

2. If the instrument is payable to the order of the maker or drawer himself, or is payable to bearer, he is liable to all parties who sign after the maker or drawer.

3. If he signs for the accommodation of the payee, he is liable to all parties who sign after the payee.

*What is meant by "dishonoring" a check or note?*

"Dishonor" consists in the nonacceptance of a bill or nonpayment of a note by the maker.

*What is meant by "protest"?*

A protest is a formal attestation of dishonor and consists of a certificate signed by a notary public, attested by his seal, certifying that the presentment of the check or note has been duly made to a given person at a given time and place and that payment has been refused.

*What is "notice of dishonor"?*

When an instrument has been dishonored, notice must be given by the holder to the drawer and to each endorser to allow each of them to meet his obligation or protect his interests or both.

*Who must be given notice of the dishonor?*

Notice of dishonor must be given to all parties secondarily liable on a check or note.

*What happens if notice is not given?*

Failure to give such notice will discharge that person's obligations.

*How is notice of dishonor given?*

Notice may be given orally or in writing (preferably in writing) to all persons secondarily liable on the instrument.

*Where must notice of dishonor be sent?*

If the drawer's or endorser's address is on the instrument, notice must be sent to that address. If no address appears on the instrument, notice must be sent either to the residence or business address of the individual involved. If the person to be notified is dead, notice should be sent to the executor or to the administrator of the deceased. If there is no executor or administrator, notice should be mailed to the last known address of the decedent.

*When must notice of dishonor be given if the parties live in the same community?*

1. If notice is given at the place of business of the person who is to receive such notice, it must be received before the close of business and, in any event, not later than the day following the day the check or note is dishonored.

2. If notice is given at his residence, notice must be received before the usual hours of rest, and at all events, not later than the day following the day of dishonor.

3. If notice is sent by mail, it must be deposited in the post office in time to reach the person who is to receive the notice not later than the day following the day the instrument is dishonored. This

usually means that notice should be mailed on the day the instrument is actually dishonored.

### When is delay in giving notice excused?

When the delay is caused by circumstances beyond the control of the holder of the note or check and not due to his misconduct, neglect, or default.

### Under what circumstances is a party excused from liability on an instrument?

He is excused from liability or responsibility when he is able to set up what are known as "personal" defenses, by which are meant defenses personal to the original parties to the negotiable instrument, but which are unavailable against a holder in due course. Since a negotiable instrument is a contract, the parties to the instrument have more or less the same defenses they would have if the instrument was a simple agreement rather than a promissory note or check. Among the personal defenses available are lack of consideration, failure of consideration, breach of contract, counterclaim, fraud, duress, blank spaces wrongly filled in, nondelivery of complete instrument and payment.

### In what way is lack of consideration a personal defense?

If you give a friend a promissory note without any consideration, you can refuse payment against either your friend or any subsequent holder, except a holder in due course.

### In what way is failure of consideration a personal defense?

If, for example, you sold a used automobile with a sixty-day warranty, accepting a ninety-day note in payment, and the car proves worthless after a few days' trial, the buyer may resist payment on his note because the car did not live up to its warranty; in short, the consideration failed. Had you discounted the note to a third party, he could have compelled the buyer to make good on the note.

### In what way is a counterclaim a personal defense?

If you are obligated on a promissory note to Jones and Jones is obligated to you on a promissory note, you may set off your obligation against his, or that of any subsequent holder, except a holder in due course.

## In what way is fraud a personal defense?

As we have already seen in the chapter on contracts, any fraud used to induce the making of a contract makes the contract voidable at the option of the party defrauded. The same principle holds true in the law of negotiable instruments. If you give your promissory note for a used automobile that is warranted as having been driven only five thousand miles and it subsequently appears that the car was actually driven ten thousand miles, you do not have to pay the promissory note. However, if the automobile agency discounts the note to a holder in due course, you will be liable to the third party, your recourse then being a suit against the agency for breach of warranty. And what is true of fraud is equally true of duress, as, for example, the signing of a promissory note under the threat of exposure.

## In what way is a failure to fill in blank spaces a personal defense?

If, for example, you purchase an automobile and the salesman informs you he will fill in the blank spaces after you have signed the note, and he subsequently fills in the price incorrectly, you have a valid defense, except against a holder in due course.

## How do personal defenses differ from real or absolute defenses?

Real or absolute defenses may be maintained against any holder of a negotiable instrument, including a holder in due course. Such defenses include forgery, alteration, incompetence, illegality, fraud in the execution and nondelivery of an incomplete instrument.

## Your name is forged to a check for the amount of $100. The check is negotiated to a holder in due course who endorses it and has it cashed at the bank. Can the bank or holder in due course proceed against you for the collection of $100?

No. Forgery is an absolute defense, good against all parties, including a holder in due course.

*How does a check differ from a bill of exchange or draft?*

1. A check is always drawn on a bank or banker, unlike a bill.

2. A bill may be drawn when there are no funds on deposit. To write a check when there are no funds on deposit is fraudulent and in some states a criminal offense.

3. Unlike a bill, a check need not be presented for acceptance or certification.

4. The death of the drawer of a check revokes the authority of the bank to pay. The death of a drawer of a bill of exchange does not.

5. Failure of a holder of a check to present it promptly for payment discharges the drawer, provided the latter sustained injury by the delay. Such failure does not discharge the holder of a bill of exchange.

6. Certification of a check discharges the drawer and all endorsers from liability and makes the bank responsible. This is not true of a holder of a bill of exchange.

*Does the mere writing of a check impose an obligation on a bank?*

No. Until a check is presented to the bank, and either certified or paid, the bank is under no obligation. Thus a child who receives a substantial check from his father as a birthday gift cannot recover from the estate of the father if the father dies before the check is presented for payment.

*Who has the right to compel payment of a check, the drawer or the payee?*

The drawer. There is no privity of contract between a bank and a payee. If a bank refuses to pay a check, the drawer has a claim against the bank, and the payee has a claim against the drawer or maker of the check.

*What is an overdraft?*

An overdraft is a draft or check drawn on a bank in excess of the amount on deposit. When there is an overdraft, the law implies that the excess has been loaned by the bank to the drawer of the check, who may properly be charged with the difference.

*Within what time must a check be presented for payment?*

Within a reasonable time, usually a matter of days; otherwise the drawer will be discharged from liability to the extent of the loss caused by the delay. If no loss is occasioned by the delay, the drawer remains liable.

*What is the effect of a check being certified?*

Certification makes the drawee bank primarily liable to the holder. Certification means that the bank guarantees the genuineness of the drawer's signature and, moreover, that it has set aside funds to pay the check. The drawer of a check cannot stop payment after a check is certified.

*Who may certify a check?*

The holder, that is, the person in possession of the check, or the drawer, the person making the check.

*If the holder of a check has it certified, and the bank later fails, is the drawer released from liability?*

Yes, since the holder elected to have it certified.

*When may the drawer of a check stop payment?*

At any time before the check is paid, certified, or passed on to a holder in due course.

*What happens if the bank cashes a check after it has been told to stop payment?*

The bank becomes liable to the drawer of the check, who in turn becomes liable to the holder of the check.

*You sign a blank check which, through your carelessness, is stolen. The check is completed, negotiated, and presented to and paid by your bank. Can you recover from the bank?*

No. The legal rule is that between two innocent parties the liability should be borne by the one who made the loss possible, in this case, you.

*Is a bank liable for the payment of a check after the death of the drawer?*

Yes, if it had reasonable opportunity to learn of the death. The legal principle is that the death of a drawer automatically revokes any outstanding drafts on his account with a bank.

*Is a check drawn in pencil valid?*

Yes.

*What is a cashier's check?*

It is a check drawn by an officer of a bank on his own bank payable to some other person.

*You give a check in payment of a bill, the check coming back marked "Insufficient Funds." Are you subject to criminal prosecution?*

No. You can only be sued for the amount of the bill.

*You buy a typewriter and give a check in payment. You have no account with the bank on which the check is drawn. Can you be held criminally liable?*

Yes. In most states, however, you are allowed a certain number of days in which to make the check good.

*You give a check to your dentist for services rendered three months previously. You have no account in the bank on which you draw the check. Can you be prosecuted criminally?*

No. To be held criminally liable there must be a present consideration. Since the services have already been performed, you can only be sued civilly.

*Must all partners of a firm sign their names to a check in order to make it valid?*

No. The signature of any one partner binds the entire firm.

*You give a check for $50 to your physician for medical services rendered. However, he does not deposit the check until about a* *year later, when you no longer have any account in that bank. Are you relieved of liability?*

No. The physician will still have a claim against you for the amount due.

*You issue a check but fail to date it. Does the omission of the date affect the validity of the check?*

No, since a check will be considered dated as of the time it was issued. The payee has implied authority to fill in the correct date.

*You give a note that falls due on a Sunday or holiday. Is the note payable on that day?*

No. It is due the next succeeding business day.

## CHAPTER 16

# PERSONAL PROPERTY

*What is personal property?*

Personal property is all property not fixed or immovable; it is distinguished from real property, which is fixed, permanent, and immovable. Articles of personal property are generally called chattels.

*How is personal property classified?*

Broadly speaking, personal property is classified as to lands, tangibility, income, and origin of title.

*How is personal property related to land?*

Natural products of the soil (which is real property) such as trees and crops become personal property on being severed from the soil. Other examples of personal property related to land are mortgages, leases, chattels personal, such as a watch or an automobile, and emblements.

*What are emblements?*

Emblements are growing crops. A tenant has a right to the emblements of crops planted by him but maturing after his tenancy terminates.

*How is personal property further divided?*

Into tangibles (choses in possession) and intangibles (choses in action).

*Of what does tangible personal property consist?*

Tangible personal property consists of all things physical, such as money, gold, silver, and merchandise; in brief, of all personal property subject to physical possession. The most common *chose in possession* is money.

236

*Of what do intangibles, or choses in action, consist?*

Intangibles comprise all things personal not susceptible to physical possession, but requiring some form of action to reduce them to possession. Contracts, promissory notes, stocks, bonds, and bank accounts are examples of intangibles. Other intangibles are insurance policies, legacies, and bills of lading.

*You find a wallet containing money, but nothing in it identifies the owner. Must you advertise for the owner before you can consider the wallet yours?*

No. It is up to the loser to advertise for the finder of his property.

*While in a drugstore, you notice a $10 bill lying on the floor. As you pick up the money, the pharmacist strolls over and asks you for the bill, on the ground that you found it in his store. May you keep the money or must you turn it over to him?*

You may retain it, providing the real owner is not in the store to claim it. The law takes the view that the money has been lost, not mislaid, and that you have a better claim to it than anyone except the person who lost it. Should the owner later return to ask for the money, the druggist would not be responsible. However, if he has your name and address, he should refer the owner to you.

*While riding in a bus, you notice a purse on one of the seats. You pick it up and, as you are about to step off, the bus driver, having seen you take the purse, requests that you turn it over to him for safekeeping. Must you do so?*

Yes. When property is mislaid on a chair or counter in a store, hotel, or bus, the one in possession of the premises, in this case the bus operator, is the proper custodian of the mislaid article, not the person who discovers it.

*While walking through the woods with some friends, you stumble over a cardboard box. You and your friends take turns in kicking the box around until it bursts open and $500 in bills come tumbling out. You claim possession of the entire amount. Who is entitled to the money?*

All of you are entitled to an equal share, even though you were the first to notice the box. Had you opened the box yourself after stumbling over it, the money would have been yours.

*You find a wallet containing $120 in bills, together with an identification card bearing the owner's name and address. Hurrying to the address stated on the card, you inform the owner that for a reward of $35 you will be glad to return his wallet. The owner refuses to offer any reward at all and threatens to call the police if you do not instantly deliver the wallet to him. What are your rights?*

Legally, none. There is no obligation on the part of the owner to give any reward at all. Should you refuse to return the wallet, the owner may properly have you arrested.

*A newspaper advertises the following: "Liberal reward will be paid to finder of wrist watch bearing the initials S.G.K. Address Box 125." Having found a wrist watch answering this description, you hasten to the owner's address (which you have learned) and offer to return the watch for the promised reward. The owner offers you $10, an amount that you do not consider liberal. You refuse to return the watch unless you are given $25. What are your legal rights?*

None whatever. Legally, the reward advertised must be definite and specific in regard to the sum to be paid before you can have a lien against it. If a definite amount is not mentioned, the person returning the lost article has no recourse but to accept the amount offered.

*Before checking your coat in a restaurant, you put your gloves in the pocket. Later the coat is returned to you, but the gloves are missing. Is the restaurant owner liable?*

No, since the gloves were concealed in the coat without the knowledge of the checkroom attendant. Had the attendant seen the gloves placed in the coat, the restaurant owner would then be responsible for the gloves as well.

*A sailboat, which was sunk a year ago, is raised from the sea by you. You find $200 in a tin can hidden on the boat. Both you and the owner of the boat claim the money. Who is entitled to it?*

You, on the legal theory that the owner had abandoned it.

*You park your car in a parking lot, paying $.75 for the privilege, and receive a ticket which states that it must be surrendered be-*

*fore the car can be taken away. At the request of the parking lot attendant, you leave the ignition key in the car. Later, when you return for the car, you find that it has been stolen. Is the parking lot owner liable?*

Probably. There are two theories of liability. One is that you merely rented parking space, in which case the parking lot owner would not be liable for the theft of the car. The other theory is that the transaction amounted to a "bailment," in which case the parking lot owner would be obliged to exercise reasonable care. His failure to return the car establishes a prima-facie case of liability on the part of the parking lot owner. In the present example, the fact that the key was left in the ignition so that control of the car was surrendered to the parking lot attendant would be strong evidence to hold him and the owner of the lot liable.

*You go into a restaurant for lunch and hang your hat and coat on a hook on the wall. When you finish your meal, the coat is missing. May you recover the value of the coat from the restaurant owner?*

No, since the coat had not been placed under the care of the restaurant owner or a waiter. A waiter is not expected to guard unchecked coats and hats on hooks about the room. Whenever possible, ask for a check to fix liability on the owner of the restaurant.

*You deposit a suitcase in the parcel room of a railroad station and receive a check on which is printed a notice that the railroad's liability for loss is limited to $25. When you call for the suitcase, you are told that it is missing. Actually, the contents and case are worth $150. You have not read the printed notice. May you recover the value of the case and the contents instead of the $25?*

Yes. The failure of the stationmaster to return your luggage charges him with negligence. It is true that the parties to a contract may generally limit their liability, but without your actual consent, such a limitation is not binding. The fact that you failed to read the printed notice, if such were really the case, indicates that you never gave your approval to such an agreement and will not be bound by it. However, you will have to prove by proper evidence that the suitcase and contents were actually worth $150.

*A garage has a sign posted on the wall which says: "Not responsible for damage to automobiles entrusted to our care." You have never read the sign. May you recover against the garage owner for damage to your automobile by one of the attendants?*

Yes. Unless you have actually read the notice, you are not bound by it. The question of whether you actually did read or see the sign then becomes a question of fact to be determined by a jury or by a court sitting as a jury.

*You register in a New York hotel and take to your room several valuable diamond rings and watches. The hotel has posted notices that it has provided a safe for the deposit of valuables. Is the hotel liable if the jewelry is stolen from your room?*

No. In New York and other states where such notices are posted, the failure of the guest to deposit valuables in the designated safe relieves the hotel of liability. Here the question is one of statute law. You may not plead ignorance, since ignorance of the law is no excuse.

*A railroad posts a notice stating that it will not be liable as an insurer for more than $1,000. You read the notice and ship goods worth $3,000. The goods are destroyed in transit. Is the railroad liable for more than $1,000?*

Yes. A railroad must exercise reasonable care consistent with the nature of the goods it undertakes to handle.

*You deliver fruit to a railroad for shipment to a company in Boston. The fruit is transported to New Haven and placed in a warehouse. Before an agent of the company in Boston can call for the fruit, it is destroyed by rain, which comes through a defective roof in the warehouse. Is the railroad liable?*

Yes. A railroad must store goods in a safe place.

*You go to a hotel, hand your luggage to a porter, and go to lunch in the grill. Your luggage is misplaced and cannot be found. Is the hotel liable?*

Yes. When the porter took charge of your luggage, you became a guest of the hotel, even though you had not signed the hotel register.

*You deliver a coat to your tailor for repairs. When the work is completed, you refuse to pay the bill on the ground that the charge is exorbitant. May the tailor sell the coat to obtain payment?*

No. The tailor has only the right to retain possession of the coat until he is paid or some agreement is reached. If there is no agreement, his proper recourse is to file suit.

*You are called to a home to repair a piano. The customer claims your bill is excessive and refuses to pay you for your services. Do you have a lien on the piano?*

No, since the piano was always in the customer's possession. You have, however, a claim for services rendered.

*You take your suit to a cleaner. You later lose your receipt for this suit, and it is found by a stranger who presents it to the cleaner and obtains the suit. May you recover the value of the suit from the cleaner?*

Yes. The cleaner is under a strict obligation to make certain that the right suit is turned over to the right owner.

*You deliver an overcoat to a cleaner who agrees to clean, repair, and deliver the garment to you by Tuesday of the following week. The garment is not delivered on time. Do you have a claim against the cleaner?*

Yes. The failure to deliver on time constitutes a breach of contract. The question then resolves itself to one of credibility—that is, whether the cleaner is to be believed or the person delivering the overcoat. The burden of proof, as in all damage suits, is on the plaintiff, the party suing, to make out a case. Naturally, the plaintiff makes out a stronger case if he can corroborate his story by means of a witness, if there is no written evidence to support his claim.

*A tailor accepts a suit for cleaning, to be delivered when finished. He sends his employee to deliver the suit, and the latter disappears, taking the suit with him. The customer demands a new suit. Does he have a claim?*

Yes, on the theory that a breach of contract has been committed.

*Accompanied by a friend, you leave some laundry in a drop box outside a laundry. The bundle contains shirts, hose, handkerchiefs, and collars. When you call for the finished work, you are told that the laundry never received it. May you collect the value of your laundry?*

Yes. If you testify that you dropped the bundle in the drop box and your friend corroborates the testimony, you have established a strong case, which will be difficult to defeat. The fact that the box is outside the laundry is an implied invitation to drop bundles in it, and the laundry assumes responsibility. If you had no witness, your case would be that much weaker.

*Your laundry leaves your bundle outside your apartment door. The bundle is stolen. Is the laundry responsible?*

Yes, unless you have given instructions for the bundle to be left outside. In that event, you assume the risk; otherwise, the laundry does.

*A customer leaves some bundles at his laundry. Later, the establishment is broken into and the laundry stolen. Is the laundry owner liable?*

No, unless the customer can prove that the theft was caused by the laundry's negligence. Showing that the laundry carelessly left the door open at night might suffice.

*A fire breaks out in the laundry and destroys all the garments, yours included. Is the laundry responsible?*

Not unless you can prove that the fire was caused by the laundry owner's negligence. A laundry is not an insurer against theft or loss by fire.

*You rent a safe deposit box in a bank, placing five savings bonds therein. The bank gives you one key and retains the master key itself, both being necessary to open the box. Burglars enter the vault, break open your safe deposit box, and take your bonds. Can you recover the value of the bonds from the bank?*

No. If the bank exercises reasonable care, it is not liable; it does not guarantee loss of property against theft.

*A friend of yours, a watchmaker, undertakes to repair your watch free of charge. He does it so carelessly, however, that it is damaged. Is he liable?*

Yes, irrespective of whether he was to be paid or not.

*You borrow a friend's automobile. While the car is in your garage, it is struck by lightning and is totally destroyed. Are you liable?*

No. While you owe the highest degree of care toward the automobile, you are not liable for any loss not caused by your negligence.

*You erect a ten-story brick building on your land. You sell the land to Johnson. You claim title to the building. Are you right?*

No. The sale of the land passes title to Johnson, not only to the land but also to the building on it.

*A tenant installs a new electric light fixture in his apartment. Upon the termination of the lease, he desires to take the fixture with him. The landlord protests, on the ground that the removal of the fixture will ruin the wallpaper. Who is entitled to the fixture?*

The tenant. The general rule is that unless the fixture is so firmly attached as to be incapable of removal without great injury to itself or the landlord's property, it may be removed by the tenant. Hangings, tapestries, window blinds and curtains, stoves, cupboards, sheds, grates, steam radiators and their valves, and electric refrigerators may be removed by the tenant—assuming, of course, that they are his own.

*You promise Mary a ring for her birthday. You buy the ring in her presence; but later you give the ring to someone else. Does Mary have a legal claim to the ring?*

No. Until the ring is actually delivered to Mary, you have a perfect right to change your mind as often as you please.

*You write a number of letters to your wife, saying that you are giving her certain furniture stored at the time in a warehouse. You later change your mind and refuse to turn over the furniture to your wife. Can you be compelled to carry out your promise?*

No. There was no gift because there was no delivery. Had you delivered the furniture, there would have been a valid gift, and you would not later have been able to secure the furniture.

*Having had a heart attack and expecting to die, you give Johnson your car. You recover, go about your business, and die eight months later. Your estate now claims the automobile. Does Johnson have to give it up?*

Yes. Your recovery automatically revokes the gift; your estate may rightfully claim the car. Had you died within a few days after giving the automobile to Johnson, it would have been a valid gift and Johnson could then have kept it.

*You have money and bonds in a metal box. You deliver the box to John, telling him that you are about to go to the hospital for a serious operation and that, if you should die, John is to keep the box. Your operation is successful. Shortly thereafter, however, you die suddenly of a disease other than that for which the operation was performed. May John retain the box?*

Yes. Your gift is called *causa mortis*, or "on account of death," and is completed with your delivery of the box with its contents. A gift of this sort is recognized when death is anticipated from an impending disease or peril, but it is not necessary that you, the donor, die of the disease from which you apprehended death. The theory is that causa mortis enables the donor to dispose of personal property under circumstances in which the writing of a will is impracticable and yet regain title of the thing or article disposed of if he recovers.

*You are engaged to Alice. In anticipation of the marriage you give her jewelry, furs, and a diamond engagement ring. Alice breaks the engagement and marries another man. May you get back your gifts?*

Yes. Such gifts are legally said to have been made upon condition that the marriage takes place. Should the marriage not take place, you may recover the presents.

*You give Dorothy a wrist watch for a Christmas present. Later, after a quarrel, you demand the return of the watch. Must Dorothy give it up?*

No. Such a gift is made merely to secure the lady's favor and is an unconditional gift.

*You sign a pledge to give a church or charity a contribution of $50. Can this promise be legally enforced?*

No, unless the church or charity incurs obligations on the strength of your promised contribution. If it does, your promise can be legally enforced.

*What rights does one have to a wild animal?*

Rights depend upon possession. To prove possession, the claimant must show that at the time in question his control over the animal was sufficiently complete to satisfy this concept of possession. One is considered to be in possession if actual possession is practically inevitable. Thus a claimant's rights will be sustained if it is shown that he fatally wounded a wild animal and was in fresh pursuit when another person intervened and completed the capture. In the whaling industry, prior rights are acquired by the one who first harpoons a whale. A landowner is entitled to a wild animal captured on his land by a trespasser.

*On a safari a hunter wounds a tiger, which is later killed by another hunter. Who is entitled to the animal?*

The one who actually kills the tiger. There is a clear distinction between merely wounding an animal and wounding it so severely as to deprive it of its natural liberties.

*You want to change your name from Peter Gorinsky to John White. May you do so without going into court?*

Yes. You may change your name as often as you like, so long as there is no intention to defraud.

*What objects may be patented?*

Federal law provides that "any person who has invented or discovered any new and useful art, machine, manufacture, or composition of matter, or any new and useful improvement thereof, not known or used by others in this country and not patented or described in any printed publication in this or any other foreign country, before his invention or discovery thereof, and not in public use or on sale for more than two years prior to his application, unless the same is proved to have been abandoned, may, upon payment of the fees required by the law, and other due proceedings had, obtain a patent therefor."

*In an invention or discovery, what two things are essential before a patent will be granted?*

It must have novelty and utility, or usefulness.

*How does one go about obtaining a patent?*

The inventor or discoverer must make written application to the Commissioner of Patents in Washington, D.C., and file what is known as a "specification," or written description of the invention or discovery "and of the manner and process of making, constructing, compounding, and using it, in such full, clear, concise, and exact terms as to enable any person skilled in the art or science to which it appertains, or with which it is most nearly connected, to make, construct, compound, and use the same." It is further provided that "in case of a machine, he shall explain the principle thereof, and the best mode in which he has contemplated applying that principle, so as to distinguish it from other inventions, and shall particularly point out and distinctly claim the part, improvement, or combination which he claims as his invention or discovery." Both the specification and the claim must be signed by the inventor and witnessed by two persons.

*What is the next step after the filing of the specification?*

The applicant must furnish a drawing, specimen, or model to illustrate his claim. He must also make oath that he believes himself to be the original and first inventor or discoverer of the art, machine, manufacture, composition, or improvement for which he seeks a patent; that he does not know and does not believe that the same was ever before known or used; and he must also state of what country he is a citizen. All this information, together with the necessary fees, is filed with the Patent Office in Washington, usually through an attorney. A patent is then granted if it appears that the claimant is entitled to one.

*Who issues patents?*

They are issued in the name of the United States of America, under the seal of the Patent Office, signed by the Secretary of the Interior and countersigned by the Commissioner of Patents.

*For how long a period is a patent issued?*

A patent is granted for a term of seventeen years to the patentee, that is, to the person who applies for the patent, and gives him the exclusive right to make, use, and sell the invention or discovery throughout the United States and its territories. An ordinary patent is not renewable. A design patent covering "any new, original, and ornamental design for an article of manufacture" is granted for terms of three and one half years, seven years, or fourteen years, at the option of the applicant.

*Suppose an inventor dies before a patent is issued but after the application is made?*

The right to apply for and obtain the patent passes to the heirs of the patentee.

*May a patent be assigned or transferred by the inventor to a third party?*

Yes. Not only the patent, but any legal interest in it may be assigned or transferred to a third person, provided the assignment is made in writing. As a precaution and protection, such assignment should be recorded by the assignee in the Patent Office within three months from its date.

*What happens when two persons file an application for a patent for the same invention and both inventions are pending in the Patent Office at the same time?*

The Commissioner of Patents may compel the two interested persons to appear before him and offer evidence as to which was really the first inventor.

*What is a copyright?*

A copyright is a grant to an applicant of the sole right to print, publish, or sell his literary, musical, or artistic compositions. The law provides that the application for copyright shall specify to which of the following classes the work belongs: (a) books, including composite or other cyclopedic works, directories, gazetteers, and other compilations; (b) periodicals, including newspapers; (c) lectures, sermons, addresses prepared for oral delivery; (d) dramatic or dramatic-musical compositions; (e) musical compositions; (f) maps; (g) works of art; (h) reproductions of works of art; (i) drawings of plastic works of a scientific or technical character; (j) photographs; (k) prints and pictorial illustrations; (l) motion picture plays; (m) motion pictures other than motion picture plays.

*How do you go about securing a copyright?*

First, print the work with the copyright notice on it. For example, "Copyright 1973 by John Brown"; or in the case of works specified in (f) to (k) above, the notice may consist of the letter *c* enclosed in a circle, thus ©, accompanied by the initials, monogram, or symbol of the owner, provided his name appears on some accessible part of the copies.

Second, send to the Register of Copyrights, Library of Congress, Washington, D.C., two copies of the work, together with an application for registration. The copies deposited must be accompanied by an affidavit stating that the typesetting, printing, and binding of the book, etc., have been performed within the United States.

*Where do you secure such affidavit forms and application blanks?*

From the Copyright Office, Library of Congress, Washington, D.C.

*For what period of time does a copyright protect the author or owner?*

Twenty-eight years. However, within one year prior to the expiration of the twenty-eight years, the owner, or the next of kin, may secure a renewal for another twenty-eight years.

*May a copyright be assigned to another?*

Yes, provided the assignment is made in writing.

*What is the fee for a copyright?*

Six dollars. This fee includes the certificate from the Register of Copyrights under seal.

*What does the expression "in the public domain" mean in copyright law?*

It means that the work is not now, has not been, or cannot be copyrighted. Works that fall into the public domain may be freely used by anyone.

*How does a literary work fall into public domain?*

A work may fall into the public domain (1) by expiration or lapse of copyright, (2) by failure to conform to the copyright law or by failure to have the work copyrighted at all, (3) by government publication, or private publication, of the works of government officials that are usually not copyrighted.

*What rights to a personal letter does the addressee acquire?*

One to whom a letter is delivered acquires, by gift, ownership of the letter, including the paper, envelope, and stamp. He has the right to destroy the letter or to recover it from one who wrongfully takes it from his possession. However, the contents of the letter may not lawfully be published without the consent of the writer.

*What is a trademark?*

A trademark is a distinctive word, emblem, symbol, or device, or a combination of these, used on goods actually sold in commerce to indicate or identify the manufacturer or seller of the goods.

*Where are trademarks registered?*

With the Commissioner of Patents, Patent Office, Washington, D.C.

*How does one register a trademark?*

Under the law, the Commissioner of Patents is required to establish classes of merchandise for the purpose of trademark regulation and registration. There are forty-nine different classes. One application for the registration of a trademark will cover only goods belonging to one class. If the applicant desires to register his goods for trademark under any other class, he is required to file another application.

The fee is $10 for each application.

The application must consist of a drawing of the trademark to be registered, made in India ink on sheets of Bristol board of a particular size and shape.

Five specimens or facsimiles of the mark must be filed with the application, together with the applicant's affidavit. After the registration is filed, it is examined, and if it appears to the examiner to be a mark that can properly be registered, the Commissioner of Patents gives public notice in the Official Gazette for Registration that such a mark has been applied for.

*For how long a period is a trademark registered?*

Twenty years; and the registration may be renewed.

*What are the rights of one whose copyright, trademark, or patent is infringed?*

The aggrieved party may sue in a United States district court for an injunction, together with an accounting for profits and damages. A suit for violation of a copyright is a suit in plagarism. The aim of copyright, trademark, and patent laws is to encourage literature, science, and invention by allowing to the writer or inventor the exclusive enjoyment of the fruits of his labor for a certain period of time.

## CHAPTER 17

# REAL ESTATE

*What is real property or real estate?*

All land, with everything permanently affixed thereto, either natural or artificial, is known as real property. Real property consists not only of the land on the surface but of everything above it within a reasonable distance and everything beneath it.

*How may real property be owned?*

Real property may be owned by an individual person or it may be owned by several persons together. The manner of ownership may affect the manner in which the property may be disposed of. Among the various ways in which real property may be held are: for life, in fee, in severalty, jointly, and in common.

*What is a life estate?*

A life estate is an ownership in lands the duration of which is measured by a person's life.

*What is an estate in fee?*

It is an estate belonging to a person and his heirs forever.

*What is an estate in severalty?*

When real property is owned by one person it is said to be owned in severalty. An individual man or woman who owns property is thus an owner in severalty. The estate may have been an inheritance, a gift, or a purchase.

Marriage may affect an estate in severalty. If the estate is purchased before marriage, it must remain separate from the couple's community property; if it is commingled with community property, it becomes community property. If the estate is purchased after marriage, it must be purchased from separate income if it is to be held in severalty.

*What is a joint estate?*

A joint estate is one held by two or more persons who acquired an interest at the same time from the same person. If one of the joint tenants dies, the surviving tenant takes title without probate, and becomes the sole owner. This is known as the right of survivorship. A joint tenancy has two important features: a property held by joint tenancy cannot be willed while both owners are living; and upon the death of one of the joint tenants, the property automatically goes to the survivor, with all of the rights of ownership.

*What is an estate in common?*

An estate in common is one held by two or more persons who may have acquired the interest at different times and from different persons. The ownership need not be equal, for example, a husband may own an undivided two-thirds interest and his wife an undivided one-third interest. Each person may sell his interest regardless of the interest of the other, and each has the right to bring action to divide the property. If community money was used to purchase the property, as in the case of a husband and wife, each will have an undivided one-half interest in the property. There is no right of survivorship in a tenancy in common; each may will his portion of the property as he may choose.

*What is dower?*

It's the interest, usually one third, that a wife has in her husband's real estate during her life.

*What is curtesy?*

Curtesy is the life estate a husband has in his wife's real estate, usually one third.

*What is community property?*

All property acquired by a husband and wife during marriage is community property. The husband and wife have equal rights, although the husband may have control of the property. The property cannot be sold without the wife's consent and signature on the deed. On the death of either husband or wife, the surviving member is entitled to one half of the community property, the other half being distributed according to the terms of the will of the deceased. Some state laws permit a married person to own separate property. Such property includes that property owned before marriage, that acquired during marriage by inheritance or gift, and the income and rents from such property.

*What happens to separate property that is mixed or commingled with community property?*

It loses its identity and becomes community property.

*Suppose a neighbor of yours has on his land an apple tree whose branches protrude onto your property. Can you cut them off?*

Yes.

*Suppose the same tree sat squarely on the boundary between your property and your neighbor's, could you cut the limbs off?*

Here the tree would be owned in common by your neighbor and yourself, and neither he nor you could cut the branches without the permission of the other.

*Suppose you and another man own a building as joint tenants and the person holding the joint interest with you dies. Who owns the property?*

You do; his interest automatically passes to you.

*You and Black own property together as tenants in common. Black dies. What becomes of Black's interest in the property?*

It passes to his heirs.

*What does the word "title" mean when referring to any property?*

"Title" signifies ownership.

*How may real property be acquired?*

1. By contract.
2. By law.
3. By acts of the parties.

4. By eminent domain.
5. By occupancy.
6. By tax sale.

*How is real estate acquired by contract?*

Real estate is acquired by contract when the buyer pays the agreed contract price to the seller.

*How is real property acquired by law?*

Real property may be acquired by succession, as by will or inheritance; by marriage, as by community property or dower; by accretion, as when land is added by water deposits or other natural causes; by bankruptcy, as when land is given to the creditors; by tax or judicial sale.

*How is real property acquired by acts of the parties?*

It may be acquired by gift, as when one is given a piece of land or real estate; by dedication, as when land is conveyed for public use as a park; and by deed, which conveys title to the property to another person.

*How is real property acquired by eminent domain?*

Eminent domain is the right of a government to take private property for public use.

*How is real property acquired by occupancy?*

By what is known as a homestead entry; that is, the entry of a settler upon public lands of the United States under provisions of an act of Congress.

*How is real estate most often acquired?*

By purchase or inheritance.

*What is title by devise?*

Title by devise is a distribution of real property by will.

*What is title by prescription?*

This is a right acquired by a person or persons because of prior use or enjoyment of property for a period of time fixed by law, usually fifteen to twenty years. For example, for fifteen years the public indiscriminately crosses a neighbor's lot openly, without his permission. At the end of the statutory period, by prescription, there arises a public right of way over the neighbor's lot; if an individual similarly crossed the neighbor's lot, a private easement would arise in favor of that individual alone.

*What is a deed?*

A deed is a written instrument under seal granting the right to real property. Of the several types of deeds, the most common are:

1. Warranty deed. A warranty deed is one in which the seller makes certain covenants or guaranties.

2. Bargain and sale deed. A bargain and sale deed is one in which the seller transfers title but makes no warranties respecting title to or use of the property.

3. Quit-claim deed. In a quit-claim deed the seller releases the claim to property without transferring title. No guaranties or warranties of any sort are made by the seller. A quit-claim deed is generally used to clear some defect of the title, as in a mortgage that has been paid but not removed from the land records.

4. Grant deed. A grant deed warrants that the property is free from encumbrances, including taxes, assessments, and all liens, building restrictions, easements, and rights of way, except as shown and recorded in the deed. Warranties carried by this deed are not usually expressed in the deed form, but are "implied warranties," since the law requires them to be effective whether expressed or not and since the seller warrants that he has title to the property. California and some other states use this type of deed quite commonly.

*What methods are commonly used to describe land?*

1. Metes and bounds, a reference to natural objects that are more or less permanent and well known, such as trees, mountain ranges, rocks, and so forth.

2. A system of meridians and parallels extending north and south,

and east and west. These meridians and parallels divide the region into townships, each township being divided into thirty-six sections one mile square. This system is based upon surveys made by the United States government.

*How is a real estate transaction handled?*

The seller can offer the property for sale himself by advertising it in the local newspapers or by placing a "For Sale" sign on the property. Alternatively, if he does not wish to be bothered by details, he can place the property in the hands of a real estate agent or broker, giving the latter an "exclusive" right to sell the property within a limited period of time, usually ninety days, for a commission of five or six percent of the selling price of the property. Another possibility is to request the seller's attorney to find a buyer with or without a real estate broker. Attorneys often know those actively engaged in buying and selling real estate.

*What is the function of a real estate broker?*

He serves as an intermediary in bringing the buyer and seller together.

*What must a real estate broker prove before he is entitled to his commission?*

That he was properly licensed; that he had a contract of employment; and that he was the efficient and procuring cause of the sale.

*Who usually employs a real estate broker?*

The seller, though the buyer can also employ a broker to help him purchase a home.

*What do real estate brokers usually charge?*

Though commissions vary, the usual charge is five or six percent; there is no reason, however, why the prospective buyer or seller cannot negotiate for a commission agreed upon between the parties, as in any other contract.

*What is meant by multiple listing?*

This is an arrangement between brokers that, when a sale results, the commission is divided between the broker having the listing and the broker making the sale at no additional cost to the buyer or seller.

*If property is in the name of both husband and wife, must both sign the listing with the broker?*

Yes. If the broker finds a buyer ready, willing, and able to buy on the husband's terms but without the wife's authority, the broker can not collect his commision because he cannot convey a good title.

*May a broker, without the knowledge or consent of the property owner, purchase the property for himself?*

No. Before the broker may purchase the property for himself he must make a full disclosure to the principal who has employed him.

*You sign an agreement to purchase a home on a Friday, giving your check as a deposit. Over the weekend, you change your mind. Is the broker entitled to his commission?*

Yes; however, the seller has a right to sue you for breach of contract or for specific performance of the agreement, i.e., compelling you to go ahead with the original contract.

*Who is entitled to the down payment if the buyer defaults in performance?*

The seller, not the broker. The broker's commission is based on the fact that he has someone ready, willing, and able to buy on the seller's terms. If the buyer is unwilling to go ahead with the arrangements, the broker has not met his responsibilities and hence is not entitled to his commission.

*A listing contract provides that "a deposit made if forfeited by the buyer, shall first apply to the broker's commission; the balance, if any, shall belong to the owner." Suppose a broker obtains a buyer for a $25,000 piece of property, receiving a deposit of five percent or $1,250.00. The buyer defaults and forfeits the deposit money. Is the broker allowed to retain the entire $1,250.00 for his efforts?*

No. The forfeited deposit is usually divided equally between the seller and the broker. The theory is that it would be unfair to place the entire burden on the seller which may involve costly litigation, attorney's fees, and perhaps an uncollectible judgement.

*You sign a listing contract with a broker allowing him to sell your home for $30,000. Your broker is able to find a buyer who is willing to pay $35,000. Is the broker entitled to the $5,000 excess?*

No. Whatever the broker realizes over and beyond the minimum net sale price set by the seller, belongs to the seller, not the broker. Of course, the seller owes the broker a commission on the $35,000, not the $30,000. In all cases, of course, the listing agreement should be carefully read by the seller so that he understands exactly the nature and extent of the agreement.

*You list a piece of property for sale with a broker at $10,000, the broker to receive a commission of five percent. The broker obtains a buyer who refuses to pay more than $8,000. Three months later, after the listing has expired, you approach the broker's buyer and sell him the property for $8,000. Is the broker entitled to his commission?*

Yes. The broker is entitled to a five percent commission based on the sale price of $8,000 even though you executed the sale yourself. This is on the theory that the agent laid the groundwork and introduced you to the eventual buyer.

*Is a broker's commission dependent upon the seller's transfer of a good title to his property?*

Yes. If the title turns out to be defective, the owner is still liable to the broker since there is a presumption that the owner, in listing his property, has a good, merchantable title.

*In dealing with real estate brokers what one thing should you insist upon?*

That you be furnished with an exact copy of the listing agreement. This should contain, among other things, the date, the conditions, the commission, the minimum price, the furnishings which go with the house, and the termination of the listing, signed by the broker or his authorized agent.

*May a broker represent both buyer and seller in a real estate transaction?*

No, since the interests of buyer and seller are conflicting and may lead to fraud and double dealing at the expense of either party.

*What is a condominium?*

A condominium represents an individual ownership of a single unit in a multi-family structure. It may be either of the hi-rise or garden type. In a condominium the owner has title to his own unit and, with the owners of other units, has an individual interest in the common areas and facilities that serve the development. Common areas include land, roofs, floors, main walls, stairways, lobbies, parking space, and community and commercial facilities. These common areas and facilities are maintained by an association of owners. Each unit owner makes a monthly contribution to the Association covering his share of the cost of maintaining and operating the common properties. In a condominium you own your apartment much as you would a private home. All taxes and special assessments are levied against the individual units, separately, and not against the whole project or building. Each unit must be capable of bearing its own mortgage. Thus an owner's title is not endangered by default on the part of owners of other units in meeting mortgage and real estate tax payments, nor is the owner subject to call to meet deficiencies in such payments. The owner of a condominium has a right to sell his unit without reference to other owners in the project.

*What are the chief differences between a condominium and a cooperative apartment?*

In a condominium each owner takes title to his unit; in a cooperative individuals have a stock ownership in the cooperative and the right of occupancy to a specific unit. In a condominium individuals vote on a proportionate basis; in a co-op each individual has one vote regardless of the size of his unit. In a condominium each individual is taxed separately on his unit; in cooperatives individuals pay their share of taxes on the project in their monthly carrying charges. In a condominium an individual is responsible only for his own mortgage indebtedness and taxes involving his own property and has no mortgage indebtedness or tax liability for the other properties; in a co-op each individual is dependent on the solvency of the entire project, which makes it riskier than a condominium. Finally, the owner of a condominium has the right to sell his own unit without reference to other owners in the condominium. The owner of a co-op usually requires the approval of fellow members of the cooperative before he can sell his unit.

*What tax advantages accrue to the purchaser of a condominium?*

For one thing, interest paid on mortgages is an income tax deduction. In addition, there are other income tax benefits such as depreciation and lower tax liability on the land since it is spread among a large number of owners.

*How is financing done on a condominium?*

Much like a private home. Condominiums vary in price from $15,000 or $20,00 to $200,000 or more. There is of course a down payment, taxes, and a mortgage on which interest is paid, plus a monthly maintenance fee.

*May your property be sold for failure to pay real estate taxes?*

Yes. Even failure to receive a bill is no excuse. As owner you are obliged to pay real estate taxes when due even though you receive no notice.

*What is a contract of sale?*

A contract of sale is an agreement between a seller and a purchaser describing the real estate purchased and the terms thereto. A contract of sale, in short, is an agreement to convey title. A deed is the conveyance itself.

*What is a "binder?"*

A binder is a written memorandum between a buyer and a seller containing the terms of the proposed real estate transaction, including the amount of the broker's commission. A simple written statement that does not go into all the details of the transaction is preferable until the actual contract is negotiated. Since a binder is often prepared by the buyer or his agent or attorney, the seller should not sign one without proper legal advice.

*What is the first precaution a buyer should take before paying for real estate?*

He should make sure the seller has a good merchantable title free and clear of all liens and encumbrances. To do this it is important that the buyer be represented by counsel.

*What is a title search?*

A title search is the process by which an attorney or a title company discovers whether the seller of the property has title and whether there are any claims against the property.

*What is involved in a title search?*

In many states it is customary to let a third party—a title company, attorney, bank, or escrow officer—handle the details of transferring title to a property. The property owner delivers the deed to the escrow officer, and the purchaser deposits the money. An escrow is a grant deposited by the grantor with a third person to be delivered on the performance of a condition, and is completed when all of the terms of the escrow instructions have been met and performed.

One of the duties of the escrow officer, title company, or attorney is to search title before it is transferred to the buyer. This search reveals:

1. The legal owner of the property.

2. Recorded mortgages or trust deeds.

3. Liens against the property, such as unpaid taxes.

4. Easements granted on the property, right-of-way, etc.

5. Reservations, as when the former owner reserves the oil rights to subsurface area.

6. Restrictions, as on fences, size of building, etc.

7. Judgment liens recorded against the property.

*What are the obligations of the seller?*

1. To prove title to the property.

2. To provide a legal description of the property.

3. To state the sales price and conditions of payment.

4. To indicate any liens, taxes, or encumbrances against the property.

5. To pay his share of the escrow costs.

### What are the obligations of the buyer?

1. To pay the purchase price according to the terms of the agreement.

2. To accept the property subject to the easements, restrictions, etc.

3. To pay any prorated expenses, such as taxes, insurance, etc.

4. To indicate how the title is to be held, whether as separate property, community property, etc.

5. To pay his share of the escrow costs.

### What are the obligations of the escrow agent, title company, bank, or attorney?

1. To search the title for flaws and to reveal unpaid taxes, liens, etc.

2. To draw the necessary deeds and releases.

3. To act as a depository for holding possession of money, mortgages, or deeds until the transaction is completed.

4. To pay the seller the money due, less expenses.

5. To deliver to the buyer the deed to the property.

6. To issue a policy of title insurance which insures the buyer against loss due to forgery and other defects of the records.

7. To record the deed or mortgage with the county recorder.

### What is an abstract of title?

An abstract of title is a condensed version of the title deed or history that is taken from the legal records. It summarizes, or by reference indicates, the encumbrances, reservations, easements, etc., that may affect the title. If you wish to know what these restrictions are exactly, you must look up the legal records in the county clerk's office or, better still, have your attorney do so. The abstract is made by the attorney or title company on behalf of the buyer.

*Should one close a title without having an attorney present at the time of settlement?*

No. For the relatively small fee involved, an attorney affords the best type of insurance that a buyer is getting what he bargained for. At the time of settlement, the buyer—and the seller, for that matter—will both receive a closing statement, or settlement sheet, which indicates the account between the buyer and seller. Stated simply, the closing price is the purchase price due the seller less the payments made by the buyer, less the amount of the existing mortgage. In addition, there will be the difference in adjustment totals, including U.S. excise taxes as well as other stamps affixed to the deed, usually supplied by the seller, or borne equally by buyer and seller, after which the deed is recorded in the county where the property is situated. An attorney will see that the arithmetical calculations are correct, that his client is not being overcharged, and that his legal rights are protected in every phase of the transaction. The fee the buyer or seller pays for the attorney's services is small compared to the total sum involved and the protection afforded.

*I agree to sell you my house for $40,000, but you do not sign an agreement to that effect. If I later decide I do not want to sell my property, will I have to go through with the deal?*

No, since all contracts for the sale of real estate must be in writing to be enforceable.

*You buy a house from Black, record your deed, and after a time get it back from the register of deeds and misplace it. Have you lost the title to the land?*

No. The actual possession of the deed is not necessary as long as it is recorded. The same rule applies when property is transferred in escrow: the deed is recorded in the name of the new owner.

*You sell a piece of property to Johnson for cash. In the contract of sale, nothing is said about the type of deed to be used. What kind of deed should you offer at the time of settlement?*

A bargain and sale deed will be sufficient.

*When is a deed effective?*

A deed is effective when it is delivered to the grantee or purchaser.

*Black enters into a contract of sale to sell you his property. Your attorney discovers a flaw in the title which makes it unmarketable. Can you recover your deposit?*

Yes, as well as any reasonable expenses you incurred.

*What is "delivery in escrow"?*

Delivery in escrow is the delivery of a deed or other instrument to a third party to be held until the performance of some act.

*What should you do when you receive a deed to property?*

Record it immediately, usually at the record office, county court house, or register of deeds.

*What is the purpose of recording a deed?*

It puts everyone on notice that the purchaser has title to the property.

*You sell your property in the morning to Black. Later the same day, you give a deed for the same property to Johnson. Johnson records the deed at once. Black doesn't record his deed until the next day. Who owns the property?*

Johnson. As between two innocent purchasers, each of whom obtains a deed to the same property, that person will have better title who records his title first. Black's remedy would be an action against you for money damages for fraud. You may also be criminally liable.

*What rights does an owner of property have?*

During his lifetime he has the right to use and enjoy the property, sell it, give it away, or dispose of it. He also has the right to dispose of the property after his death, by will.

*What limitations are there on the ownership of real property?*

Even though one may own a parcel of real estate absolutely, the law imposes a number of limitations. The chief ones are the following:

1. Right of eminent domain. The government—federal, state or local—has the right to take private property for public use, as in

the construction of schools, roads, county and state buildings, etc. The property is possessed by condemnation and by the payment of a fair price to the owner. When the government and the owner are unable to agree on a fair price for the land, the issue may be submitted to a jury.

2. Easements. An easement is an interest in land belonging to another, and the owner of an easement has the right to use the other's property. An easement may be public or private. Easements are generally granted for electric and telephone lines, gas lines, sewer lines, public highways, etc. Private easements may also be granted; for example, an individual may be granted the right to drive across another person's property in order to get to his own property.

3. Unpaid taxes or debts. Property may be sold by the government to pay taxes due or to obtain payment of debts.

4. Deed restrictions. An owner may place certain restrictions on the use of land by recording the restrictions in the deed to the property. Most subdivisions of land developments have deed restrictions concerning the height of fences, the number and kinds of animals that may be kept on the premises, whether the property is to be used for a single family residence, etc.

5. Liens. Mortgages, trust deeds, unpaid bills, all become a lien on property and may force the owner to sell the property to pay the debts.

6. Air rights. A person cannot build on his property in a manner that deprives his neighbor of air and light, nor can he prevent airplanes from flying over his property.

7. Police powers. The state or federal government has the right to take temporary possession of private property to protect the public interest—in the case of riots, floods, forest fires, etc.

8. Water rights. A person does not have the right to change the course of a river on or abutting on his property, to dam it, or to pollute it. In some cases he does not have even the right to use the water, for others below him may have prior rights to its use, as for irrigation purposes. He does have the right to use the water for domestic purposes.

9. Assessments. Assessments- for such improvements as roads, streets, sewers, curbs, etc., are a lien on the property, and if they are not paid, the property may be sold to pay the assessments.

10. Land use ordinances. Cities and counties have ordinances that restrict the use one may make of property. These ordinances regu-

late the location of factories, business, apartments, private homes, etc., so that each owner may have the quiet enjoyment, pleasure, and use of his property without interference from noises, odors, nuisances, early and late hours of business, etc.

*Can a property owner refuse to sell to a Negro?*

Only if the private owner of a dwelling house sells or rents his home without a real estate agent or broker.

*What is a license?*

A license in real property is a permission, oral or written, granted by the owner to another, to use the land for some purpose, and is revocable at will.

*How is an easement different from a license?*

An easement is a definite interest in land, whereas a license is a mere permission or privilege.

*How may an easement be acquired?*

An easement may be acquired in writing or by uninterrupted use, usually for a period of twenty years. It may be terminated by the expiration of the terms granted in the original easement.

*The town needs a piece of your property as a site for a firehouse. Can the town take the property?*

Yes. By the right of eminent domain, the federal or state government, or any subdivision thereof, may take private property for a public purpose upon just compensation.

*You purchase a piece of ground at a winter resort. The deed you receive contains a provision that you may not construct a house on the lot costing less than $10,000. You plan to build a cottage costing $5,000. Can you be prevented from doing this?*

Yes. Such a deed restriction is valid and enforceable.

*What is a lien?*

A lien is a right against specific property as security for a debt. A mortgage against real estate is the most common type of lien.

*You are a contractor and have supplied material and labor to build a side porch for Black's house. If Black refuses to pay, what are your legal rights?*

You have a right to a mechanic's lien for the amount due against the property which you made improvements on.

*What are taxes and assessables?*

They are liens on the specific property so taxed or assessed and they take priority over all other liens.

*What is a judgment?*

A judgment is a declaration in a court of law of the legal rights and obligations of the litigants.

*You sue Black and obtain a judgment against him in the amount of $3,000. Is this a lien against his real estate?*

Yes.

*Suppose Black doesn't pay the judgment. What can you do?*

His real estate may be sold to satisfy the judgment.

*What is a real estate mortgage?*

It is a lien on property given by the owner as security for a debt.

*What is a mortgagor?*

A person who makes a mortgage in order to borrow money.

*What is a mortgagee?*

A mortgagee is the lender of the money.

*Why should mortgages be recorded?*

To serve notice that the lender or mortgagee has a claim or lien against the property.

*Black executes a mortgage to Jones, who fails to record the instrument. Black then sells the property to Murphy. Murphy borrows*

*$5,000 from Johnson, secured by a $3,000 mortgage against the property. Murphy executes and delivers the mortgage to Johnson who immediately records it. Both Murphy and Johnson are unaware of Jones's mortgage. Is the deed to Murphy and the mortgage to Johnson subject to Jones's mortgage?*

No, because Jones failed to record his mortgage.

*What is a purchase-money mortgage?*

A purchase-money mortgage is a mortgage given as a part of the purchase price at the time the property is bought.

*What are the rights of a mortgagor?*

A mortgagor may sell, lease, or assign the property subject to the rights of the mortgagee.

*What are the rights of the mortgagee?*

The mortgagee may require the mortgagor to pay interest on the mortgage, insure the property, maintain it in good condition, pay taxes and assessments, and repay the mortgage.

*Suppose you borrow money from a loan company and give as security a mortgage on your home. If you fail to pay your debt, what may the mortgagee do?*

He may bring foreclosure proceedings and sell the property at auction.

*Suppose the property does not bring enough at auction to pay the mortgagee's claim. What can he do?*

He can hold the mortgagor or borrower responsible for the difference between what the property brought at sale and the balance due on the mortgage.

*What does one do when purchasing a property if there is an existing mortgage?*

Either pay off the mortgage or purchase the property subject to the mortgage.

*What does one do if foreclosure is threatened?*

Either make whatever payments are called for under the mortgage or allow the property to be sold under a foreclosure sale, made pursuant to the authority of a court of law. When a mortgagee (the person holding the mortgage) forecloses, he seeks a judicial decree and judgment shutting out all interests but his own. The suit is brought in a court of equity; and if the mortgagee is successful, the judgment directs that a foreclosure sale be conducted by an auctioneer under the direction of a referee or master of the court. Should the property sell for more than the amount of the mortgage (plus interest, legal fees, court costs), the surplus is turned over to the owner, the mortgagor or person who made the mortgage. If the property sells for less than the amount due, a deficiency judgment is entered and the mortgagor is required to make good the deficit.

*What do water rights include?*

*Surface water.* The property owner has a right to a reasonable use of the water for domestic and agricultural purposes. He may divert the flow through his own land, but it must enter the land of an adjacent owner only in its natural channel. Water falling upon the land is surface water and belongs to the owner, who may control it in any way he sees fit, provided he does not intentionally use it to injure another person.

*Underground water.* Underground water was formerly considered to belong to the owner of the land. But in some states the landowner only has a common right to the water and can only take a reasonable share for beneficial purposes.

*Riparian rights.* In most states all of the water or the use of water within the state is the property of the people of that state. The right to the use of the water flowing in a river or stream, however, may be acquired by appropriation, so that all riparian owners have the right to the reasonable use of waters flowing past their lands. The water appropriated must be for some useful or beneficial purpose, but the water cannot be used on other noncontiguous land nor diverted from one watershed to another for use there. The owner of land bordering upon a nonnavigable stream has no absolute ownership of the water.

One wishing to use the running water must apply to the proper authorities for a specified amount of water and give the purpose and the place of the intended use, as well as the means by which he intends to divert the water for that use. If the applicant complies with the statutory requirements, his rights are permanent.

Since the system of prior rights prevail, the first person to apply gets his allocation, then the second, and so on.

In some states each property owner along a stream has a right to use the water for domestic purposes, but he cannot divert the water in a manner that diminishes the flow.

Anyone who pumps water to supply a neighbor becomes a public utility, and such person cannot be deprived of the continued use of the water. The person receiving the water must pay a reasonable price for it.

If the body of water is entirely on your land, you have the exclusive right to the water and may use it for whatever purpose desired such as fishing, swimming, irrigation, etc.

### To whom do mineral rights belong?

The general rule is that the minerals underground belong to the owner of the land above. The rule works well for solid minerals and metals, such as gold and silver, but oil rights have been somewhat confusing, since oil moves. In general, mineral rights belong to the landowner, unless reserved by deed. Although oil is considered a mineral, it has special regulations relating to its ownership. Oil or water pumped from a well belongs to the man who owns the well, even if it is drained from a neighbor's land or from beneath his land. Decisions by the state and federal courts have reconciled rules of ownership whereby each property owner gets his share of the oil produced in a given lease or field, regardless of the location of the producing wells.

*A man bought water from a canal company for several years and made regular payments for the water used. The company, to conform to a new state regulation, advanced the date of payment several months. One of the users refused to make payment at the advanced date set under the new schedule, the company shut off the water, and the user lost his entire crop. The man sued the canal company for failure to supply water as provided in his contract. Was he right?*

No. The man could have paid the assessment, even though the time of payment was advanced several months, and thus saved his crop and trees. By making the payment he could have reduced his loss to a minimum, which it was his duty to do.

*A neighbor built a dike that, by interfering with the natural flow of flood water, would force this water over on your land. Could this be prevented?*

Yes. Any interference with the natural flow of flood waters would make the neighbor liable for damages or injury done to your property. You might even get an injunction to stop him before any damage is done.

## Chapter 18

## LANDLORD AND TENANT

*With what is this chapter concerned?*

This chapter deals with the nature and essentials of the relationship between landlord and tenant; the various kinds of tenancies; the rights, duties, and obligations of the landlord and tenant; the nature and form of a lease; and the ways in which a tenancy may be ended.

*How did the landlord-tenant relationship arise?*

It arose as an outgrowth of the feudal system, under which the serf or peasant held lands from the lord of the manor.

*Is a lease a contract?*

Yes, and a lease must contain all the contractual requisites. The parties to a lease are the landlord and the tenant, who must be capable of entering into a valid contract. There must be a valid consideration, the consideration being the rent paid by the tenant and the possession of the premises given by the landlord. There must be a valid or lawful subject matter. A contract to lease premises for prostitution or some other illegal activity is void as against public policy.

*Can a lease become void after it is made?*

Yes, as in the case of a building that has been condemned after the lease has been entered into.

*Who are the parties to a lease?*

The lessor who rents the premises (the landlord) and the lessee to whom the premises are rented (the tenant).

*What kinds of tenancies are there?*

1. Tenancies for a fixed period or estate for years.
2. Tenancies at will.

3. Tenancies by sufferance.

4. Periodic tenancies.

### What is a tenancy for a fixed period?

All tenancies, no matter how brief, for which the term or duration is definite and fixed. A tenancy of six months, a year, or five years is a tenancy for a fixed period.

### What is a tenancy at will?

This is a tenancy for an uncertain period, held at the will of either the tenant or landlord. Either party may terminate whenever he pleases, and unless the tenancy is so terminated, it continues indefinitely. The common-law rule has been modified to require written notice by either party (usually thirty or sixty days, depending on the individual state).

### What is a tenancy by sufferance?

This differs from a tenancy at will in that it can be terminated only at the end of a given period, and not at any time the tenant desires. Tenancies by sufferance are made from year to year, six months to six months, and month to month. In actual practice there is little difference between a tenancy at will and a tenancy by sufferance.

### How are the rights, obligations, and incidents of the landlord-tenant relationship determined?

By the covenants expressed in the lease or by those implied by law, or both.

### What points should be included if you are writing or drawing a lease and a lawyer is not available?

The lease should contain:

1. The names and addresses of the parties.

2. The consideration, price, or rent of the premises to be leased.

3. A description of the premises to be leased, listing whatever exceptions and reservations have been agreed upon by the parties.

4. The terms and period for which the property is to be leased.

5. The purpose for which the property is to be leased.

6. A clause providing for landlord's re-entry on nonpayment of rent or other nonperformance of covenents on the part of the tenant.

7. The signature of the parties to the lease.

*What does the landlord implicitly warrant, even if premises are rented without a written lease?*

When a landlord rents premises, he implicitly warrants or guarantees that he has the right to rent such premises and that he will not disturb the tenant's right to absolute possession of the premises. These are warranties of "quiet enjoyment," for the breach of which the tenant may cancel the lease or sue for damages, or both.

*Is everyone who occupies premises considered a tenant?*

No. To be a tenant one must have exclusive possession, which means that one must have an estate or interest in the land. For example, a contractor who erects a structure is a mere licensee, not a tenant; the same is true of boarders and lodgers who merely occupy but do not possess the premises.

*How may a tenancy be terminated?*

1. By expiration of the lease.

2. By forfeiture.

3. By eviction.

4. By destruction or substantial injury to the premises.

5. By condemnation.

6. By surrender.

7. By operation of law.

*What happens if a tenant remains after the expiration of his lease?*

The landlord, at his option, may treat the tenant as a trespasser, sue him for damages, and remove him by legal proceedings, or he may treat the tenant as obligated for an additional period depending on the term of the lease.

*What happens if a tenant is unable to move, after the expiration of his lease, because of illness?*

The remedies provided in the paragraph above do not exist in such a case. All the tenant may be liable for is the period of his illness, if that.

*What is forfeiture?*

Forfeiture results from the violation or infraction of some provision in a lease, such as nonpayment of rent. When forfeiture does occur, the landlord may institute eviction proceedings or proceedings for the nonpayment of the rent, or both.

*What is eviction?*

Eviction is the ousting of a tenant from the premises by a landlord.

*How may a tenant be evicted?*

A landlord may evict a tenant:

1. By expelling him forcibly.
2. By locking him out.
3. By leasing the premises and giving possession to another tenant.
4. By preventing the tenant's using the halls, elevators, or other means of access to the premises.
5. By permitting the existence of a nuisance that forces the tenant to move, such as failing to furnish heat or water, allowing noisy tenants to remain in the building, or permitting odors or stenches to remain without making a bona fide attempt to remove them.

*When can the landlord evict you?*

He may do so if you damage the premises, fail to pay the rent on time, or create or maintain a nuisance. A landlord has several options: he may write you a letter informing you to make necessary repairs according to the lease, that your rent is overdue, or that playing your TV loudly at 3:00 A.M. is a nuisance to other tenants. If you fail to comply, he may obtain a court order directing you to leave the premises. Before the order is actually carried out, however, there is generally notice of a court hearing so that you can present your side of the issue. If, for example, the landlord claims that you are in arrears for rent, all you need do is prove that you

did pay the rent; even in cases where you actually are in arrears—
unless you have a long record for nonpayment, the court will usually allow you to stay on if you tender payment at the time of
hearing.

### What is "surrender"?

This is a mutual agreement between the tenant and the landlord
to cancel the tenancy, either by agreement of the parties or by
operation of the law. It occurs by operation of law when the parties
enter into a new lease to take the place of the old.

### How is a tenancy ended by operation of law?

A tenancy is so ended by either the death of a tenant or landlord
or by the bankruptcy of either. The death of a tenant automatically
ends a tenancy at will, but not a periodic tenancy or a tenancy by
years. In the two latter cases, the death of the tenant will make his
estate liable for the balance of the rent due. The death of a landlord has no effect on a lease. The death merely substitutes one
landlord for another, with the tenant still being liable for the rent.
The bankruptcy of either tenant or landlord discharges either's
obligations under the lease.

### What duty does a tenant have on vacating the premises?

He must remove his belongings within a reasonable time after
vacating the premises. If he does not, the landlord may remove
them at the tenant's expense.

### What remedy does a tenant have if, after moving in, he is forced
out by someone else who proves he has a superior title to the landlord who rented the premises to the tenant?

The tenant has a right to sue for damages as a result of the breach
of the convenant of quiet enjoyment.

### What if a tenant is forced out by a mortgage foreclosure?

If, as a result of a third party's foreclosure, the tenant is forced
out, he has a right of action for damages against the landlord. An
exception is made when the premises are leased subject and subordinate to a mortgage. In such a case the tenant forfeits whatever rights he might otherwise have and may be evicted as a

result of the mortgage foreclosure. However, the tenant is still subject to such eviction if he had actual knowledge of the mortgage or knew that it had been recorded.

### What is a deposit?

It is a sum of money paid by a tenant to the landlord as a condition to leasing the premises.

### May a landlord always demand a deposit?

Yes, but this is subject to negotiation between the parties.

### You make a deposit on an apartment or house; later you change your mind about it and demand the return of your deposit from the owner. Must he return it to you?

No.

### You sign a lease for one year for an apartment. You give a deposit as evidence of good faith. Under the terms of the lease you are not to move in until thirty days after signing the lease. A few days after you have signed the lease you ask the landlord to return your deposit because you have decided the apartment is not adequate to your needs. Is the landlord obliged to return your deposit?

No. The landlord not only need not return your deposit—he can also sue you for breach of contract, holding you liable for the entire year's rent.

### Must a deposit be returned?

Not unless expressly provided for in the receipt. If so provided, the tenant has an action against the landlord for the return of the deposit.

### What if a tenant vacates the premises before the termination of the lease? May the deposit be used in lieu of the last month's rent?

Yes.

### What is rent?

Rent is compensation, either in money or other value, paid by a tenant for the leased premises. If no rent is mentioned, the law implies that the tenant agrees to pay a reasonable value for the use and occupation of the premises.

*When is rent due?*

A lease usually provides that rent is due in advance.

*If rent falls due on a Sunday, must it be paid that day?*

No. It may be paid on the next business day. This is not true if rent falls due on any other holiday—it must be paid that day.

*If a lease begins on the second day of January, rent commencing from that day, when is the next rent due, assuming rent is payable monthly?*

February 1.

*If a lease provides that rent is to be payable "either quarterly or monthly," who determines when it shall be paid?*

The landlord.

*What are the rights of a landlord when a tenant fails to pay rent?*

1. The landlord may sue for rent, as for any other debt.
2. He may dispossess the tenant.
3. In some states he may do both.

*May a landlord seize, attach, or levy upon a tenant's household goods or chattels for nonpayment of the rent?*

Not until he has first brought suit and obtained a money judgment against the tenant.

*By a written lease, a tenant agrees to pay $70 a month for the use of the rented premises. Later he persuades the landlord to reduce the rent to $65 monthly. After taking the reduced rental for several months, the landlord changes his mind; he tells the tenant that the rent is again $70 a month. May the tenant refuse to pay the original rent?*

No. There is no legal consideration for the reduced rental.

*Who has the duty to make repairs to the leased premises, the landlord or the tenant?*

The tenant ordinarily. To this rule there are certain exceptions. A landlord is bound to make the repairs (1) when he assumes the duty under a lease, (2) when it is imposed on him by statute, as by emergency rent legislation, (3) when he has exclusive control of portions of premises used in common, such as common stairways, hallways, and roofs, and (4) when the repairs are of a structural nature, as when a ceiling collapses or a wall caves in. Plumbing is not ordinarily covered, except as provided by lease or statute.

*Because of the inconvenience and expense suffered by a tenant during the making of repairs, he requests his landlord to reduce the rent. The landlord agrees. Later the landlord changes his mind. May the tenant continue to pay the reduced rent?*

Yes. There is now a legal consideration for the reduction, binding on the landlord.

*May a tenant refuse to pay rent if the plumbing and drainage of his leasehold are defective, although no provision in the lease is made therefor?*

No. Nor may a tenant refuse to pay rent if the house is unhealthful or infested by vermin.

*Though the lease provides that a landlord shall provide adequate heat, he consistently fails to do so. What may the tenant do?*

He may sue the landlord for damages; he may heat the premises himself and deduct the cost from his rental; or he may terminate the lease and move to another place.

*Black's house, which he has rented from Jones, is temporarily made unsuitable for occupancy, due to the making of repairs by the landlord. May Black refuse to pay rent until such time as the house is once again habitable?*

No. If, however, the landlord fails to exercise diligence in carrying repairs through to completion, thus depriving the tenant of the use of the premises, the tenant may be entitled to suspend payment of rent.

*Not long after you rent a house, a bowling alley is erected adjacent to it. The noise from the bowling alley disturbs your sleep at night. May you break your lease and avoid payment of rent due under it?*

Yes. With the rental of premises there is an implied covenant that the tenant will have "the quiet enjoyment" of these premises, meaning simply that he will not be disturbed in his use of the property. When, as in the above case, something occurs that disturbs the tenant's "quiet enjoyment," he may vacate the premises and file suit for breach of his lease.

*You rent a store, signing a lease for a year, with an option to renew. At the end of six months, before the expiration of the lease, you find that the business you do does not warrant your staying and you move from the store. What rent will you be liable for?*

You will be liable for the remaining six months on the lease. If the owner succeeds in re-renting the store, your obligation will be reduced proportionately. If the lease you signed is for five years and you stay for only six months, you will be liable for the rent for four and a half years.

*Black leases a store. It is provided that the landlord shall give his written consent to the use of the premises as a liquor store when Black applies for a liquor license. After Black takes over the store, the landlord changes his mind and willfully refuses to give his consent. May Black refuse to pay his rent?*

Yes, if he abandons the premises. Black could then file suit against the landlord for breach of contract.

*You rent a store for a period of one year, the rent to be paid in twelve equal monthly installments. As required by your lease, you give the landlord written notice of your intention not to renew the lease. Instead of moving on the day your lease expires, you stay for another week or so. What can the landlord do?*

He can treat you as a tenant "holding over," compelling you to continue payment of rent for an additional year. Or he can sue you as a trespasser—that is, as one wrongfully in possession of his property.

*A tenant, without the landlord's knowledge, uses the leased premises for an illegal purpose, gambling. What can the landlord do when he discovers the illegal purpose?*

A number of states by law provide that in such cases the lease shall be void and that the landlord may recover possession, even when the tenant has paid the rent in advance. In the absence of a state law, however, the landlord has no right to terminate the lease. He may sue merely for its breach or obtain an injunction prohibiting such illegal use.

*A landlord leases a house to a tenant who, with the knowledge of the landlord, uses it as a house of prostitution. The tenant refuses to pay rent and the landlord files suit to recover rent for the premises. May he?*

No. If a lease is made with the intention that the premises shall be used for an illegal purpose, a landlord cannot recover rent.

*Does your landlord have a right to enter your apartment without your permission?*

Yes. He may enter to demand payment of rent, when due, to prevent waste, or to do anything to save himself from liability for negligence in connection with the premises. For example, an owner may, without the consent of his tenant, tear down walls when the building has become unfit and unsafe by reason of fire or other defect.

*Suppose a landlord, without authority or permission, forces himself into the tenant's premises. What can be done?*

A landlord may be sued for damages for an unauthorized entry. The unauthorized entry is called a trespass.

*How much heat is a landlord required to furnish in an apartment?*

Generally, an amount that will make the temperature of the rooms reasonably comfortable for the average person during the time the premises are usually occupied.

*After being in your rented house for a few months, the defective heating system becomes unable to furnish 60° Fahrenheit. The lease provides that the landlord shall furnish the heat. You have sublet a few rooms in the house, but because of the defective heating system, your tenants move out. What damages may you recover?*

You may recover the loss of rental of rooms which you sublet and any expenses to which you may be put if you yourself have to leave the house.

*In his lease, a landlord agrees to provide the premises with sufficient heat. As a result of his negligent failure to do so, the tenant contracts tuberculosis. May the tenant hold the landlord liable?*

Yes, if it can be proved that such neglect is the proximate cause of the tuberculosis or that it made an already existing tubercular condition worse.

*You rent a beauty parlor. After being in possession for a few months, the landlord fails to provide hot water for use in your business. What can you do?*

You may cancel the lease and file suit for damages. What you will get by way of damages will be the difference between the rent agreed on in the lease and the rent the beauty parlor would bring without hot water. The damages, of course, would include only the period for which you were deprived of hot water.

*In renting you an apartment the landlord assures you that the rooms are "clean." Shortly after you move in, you discover that the apartment is bug-ridden. You seek to cancel the lease. May you do so?*

No. A statement that an apartment or house is "clean" means only that it has been swept and scoured after the last tenant moved out. It is not a guaranty that the place is free of insects or vermin.

*You rent a house. Shortly after moving in, you notice that it is so infested with rats that it is uninhabitable. Can you cancel the lease?*

Yes, providing you have not created the condition and have made every effort to destroy the rats.

*You rent an apartment or house, the lease being silent on the ques-*

*tion of who is to make repairs. A few months after you have been living in the apartment or house, the plumbing fails. You ask the landlord to make the necessary repairs. He refuses. Is he right in refusing?*

Yes. In the absence of an express agreement, the landlord is not bound to make ordinary repairs—nor is he bound to pay for such repairs made by the tenant.

*Suppose, in the above example, there is no lease; the apartment or house is rented on a monthly basis. Would the same rule hold true of the tenant's liability for repairs?*

Yes.

*The sidewalk in front of your house is defective. Must you or the landlord make the repairs?*

You, in the absence of an express agreement to the contrary.

*You rent a five-room apartment from Black and, in turn, you sublet one of your rooms to Jones. The window in Jones's room becomes broken. Who must replace the window?*

Jones, since he is the subtenant and you the tenant—unless an express agreement has been made by you to assume the obligation.

*A lease provides that the landlord agrees to keep the house in good repair. The tenant, at his own expense, hires a caretaker to keep the walks clean and to rake, mow, and seed the grounds. May he recover the expense from the landlord?*

No. Such work does not constitute repairs.

*A tenant agrees in a lease to keep the plumbing and heating plant in good repair. A few weeks after he takes over the property, the tenant discovers that the heating plant was defective when he rented the property. May he compel the landlord to make the necessary repairs?*

No, unless the landlord practiced some fraud or deception on the tenant by concealing the defect.

*A tenant leases a motion picture house, agreeing in the lease to keep the theater in good repair. The theater, through no fault of the tenant's, is totally destroyed by fire. Who must rebuild, the tenant or landlord?*

The tenant. Keeping premises in repair has often been held to mean restoring the property after a fire.

*A tenant leases a retail clothing store, the lease providing that the landlord is to make all necessary repairs. Shortly afterward, the plate-glass front is broken by burglars. The landlord refuses to make repairs. What can the tenant do?*

He can replace the front at his own expense and sue the landlord for reimbursement.

*A lease by which you have rented a building provides that the landlord is to make the repairs. After a severe rain, the basement of the building is flooded; you call in a crew to clean out the mud and water, paying them out of your own pocket. You later notify the landlord that you wish to be reimbursed for the money you paid out, advising him that, under the lease, he is required to make the repairs. Upon the landlord's refusal to return you the money, you file suit. Can you recover?*

No. In order to recover, you must first give the landlord notice of the flood and provide him with an opportunity to make the necessary repairs. The failure to give the landlord such notice and opportunity relieves him of liability, even when the lease provides that the landlord shall make the repairs.

*Though the lease does not mention the party who is to make the repairs, the landlord agrees to repair the tenant's roof. However, the tenant's property is damaged by rain falling through openings negligently left by the landlord while doing the work. Is the landlord liable?*

Yes. Although a landlord is not under any obligation to make repairs, if he does undertake to make them, he is liable for any injuries which may result to the tenant from the negligent manner in which the work is done.

*Suppose, in the above example, the landlord has employed a workman to do the work instead of doing it himself. Would the landlord still be liable?*

Yes, on the theory that the landlord controls or directs the work. The landlord, in turn, may recover against the one doing the work.

*An office building is heated by the landlord's engines. As a result of the latter's negligence, the heating apparatus explodes, causing damage to your office. Is the landlord liable?*

Yes. A landlord is liable for injuries to a tenant, as he is to any other person rightfully on the premises, caused by the former's neglect to remedy defects in, or by his improper management of, appliances of which he retains control. Landlords have been held liable for injuries caused by leakage of water pipes or other plumbing attachments in their control, elevators carrying freight or passengers, dumb-waiters, machinery transmitting power, etc.

*A tenant who has leased a warehouse places therein a reasonable weight of goods, not suspecting that the floor structure cannot bear this weight. The floor gives way and the landlord seeks to hold the tenant liable. Can he?*

No. The tenant would be liable for injuries caused by placing an unreasonable and extraordinary weight in the building. In this case the weight was reasonably related to the structure of the floor; the tenant therefore would be absolved of responsibility.

*A state law provides that a landlord shall maintain lights in the hallways of all apartment houses occupied by two or more families. As a result of the landlord's failure to provide such lights, a tenant stumbles on the stairs and breaks a leg. Is the landlord liable for damages?*

Yes. The tenant is under no obligation to install bulbs or lights in hallways. For any injuries sustained by him or his family, or by persons coming upon the premises for business with or at the invitation of the tenant, the landlord would be held responsible.

*You rent an apartment, the lease being silent concerning who shall make repairs. Your mother-in-law, while visiting you for the first time, stumbles and falls on a broken step. Can the landlord be held responsible?*

No. A landlord who has not agreed to repair, and is without knowledge of hidden defects, is not liable for personal injuries sustained on the rented premises—unless the premises contained some defect known to the landlord at the time of the rental and not disclosed to or discovered by the tenant.

*Suppose, in the above example, that the landlord agrees to repair the defective step after it is called to his attention and that, as a result of his negligent failure to do so, the mother-in-law stumbles and falls. Is the landlord then liable?*

Yes.

*You are living in a rented house. A stranger, walking by, slips and falls on the ice you have neglected to remove. Who is liable, the owner of the property or you?*

You, unless there is an express agreement to the contrary.

*A landlord rents an apartment with the knowledge that the timbers in a floor are defective. A few weeks later, a member of your family falls through the rotted floor and sustains injuries. Is the landlord responsible?*

Yes. The rule is that if there is some hidden defect which is known to the landlord at the time the lease is made, but which is not apparent to the prospective tenant, the landlord is bound to inform the tenant. Failing to do so, he is liable for injuries sustained by the tenant or his family.

*You lease a floor of a building to Smith for warehouse purposes, knowing it to be too weak to be safely used for such purposes. The floor collapses, causing personal injuries to the tenant below and damage to his goods. Who is liable in damages to the tenant?*

You, the landlord. A landlord who rents premises to be used for a particular purpose, having reason to believe that this use of the premises is likely to injure a stranger, is liable to that person.

*A market company leases you a fruit stall but reserves control over the passageway. A customer stumbles over a defective plank in the passageway and sustains personal injuries. Who is liable in damages, the market company or you?*

The market company, since it reserved control of the passageway.

*Your lease provides that, at its expiration, you are to return the apartment to the landlord in as good a condition as when you received it, natural wear and tear excepted. When you vacate the apartment, you remove some of the fixtures and leave some of the windows broken. What can the landlord do?*

He can sue you for breach of the lease and collect damages.

*If a tenant installs fixtures in his apartment, may he remove them after he vacates the premises?*

Basically, the test is the intention of the parties. If at the time the fixtures were installed the tenant intended that they be merely temporary, he may remove them, provided they do not materially alter, disfigure, or permanently damage the leased premises. Some fixtures, such as a bathtub in an apartment or a passenger elevator in an office building, are clearly intended for permanent use and cannot be removed, even if installed by the tenant. Other fixtures, such as a lighting fixture, draperies, curtains, or electric motors, are so clearly intended for temporary use that they can be removed by the tenant after he leaves the premises. Trade fixtures, in general, can be removed, while machinery and heating and cooling systems are generally considered permanent fixtures unless, from the intent of the parties or the provisions of the lease, it is clearly intended that they are to be regarded as temporary fixtures.

*Must the landlord or the tenant maintain insurance on the leased premises?*

Unless the lease expressly so provides, there is no obligation on the part of the tenant to maintain insurance on the leased premises. Most business leases, however, provide that a tenant must either insure the premises for the benefit of the landlord or maintain insurance already in force.

*A lease provides that the tenant is to make all repairs. The store leased is destroyed by fire. To what extent is the tenant obligated?*

He is usually bound to rebuild the store. He will also be bound to rebuild if the premises are destroyed by lightning, flood, or tornado. As a precaution, the tenant should always insert in a lease a clause relieving him from liability in such cases or carry sufficient insurance to protect himself against such loss.

*In the absence of a contract to that effect, is the tenant under any obligation to insure the buildings and other improvements on the premises for the benefit of the landlord?*

No, but it is generally a good idea to do so, since, in case of destruction of the premises, the tenant will be held liable.

*A lease provides that the tenant shall insure the building for the landlord's benefit. He takes out a policy for a year, but he does not renew it. A fire occurs after the expiration of the policy. Is the tenant liable?*

Yes. He must keep the premises insured for the entire tenancy.

*A tenant agrees in his lease to insure the buildings on the premises and, in case of loss, to apply the proceeds of the insurance to the restoration of the buildings. After the fire he assigns his lease to a third party. Must the third party apply the proceeds of the insurance to the restoration of the building?*

Yes.

*In the absence of a provision in the lease to the contrary, may a tenant sublease the premises without the consent of the landlord?*

Yes. Most written leases, however, contain a clause prohibiting subletting, except by and with the consent of the owner.

*You lease premises known as the Black Building and now wish to change the name to the Jones Building. May you do so without the consent of the landlord if there is no provision in the lease?*

Yes.

*After you lease a store, you desire to cover the outside walls with signs advertising your business. Your landlord objects. The lease itself is silent about such signs. May you use the outside walls?*

Yes. A tenant is entitled to use the outside walls, unless there is an express agreement to the contrary. Of course, he cannot use the walls in any way that will injure the property or for purposes inconsistent with the reasonable enjoyment of the property.

*In the absence of an express agreement, may a tenant alter the premises without obtaining the consent of the landlord?*

A tenant generally has no right to make material or permanent alterations in the rented premises. If a tenant has a long lease, however, he usually has the right to make such changes as the business established requires, provided the value of the building is not impaired.

*A tenant leases a house and land, and plants some trees, bushes, and shrubs. At the expiration of his tenancy, he seeks to remove that which he has himself planted. May he?*

Yes. The tenant may remove what he has planted.

*What are the obligations of a tenant who rents farming land?*

He must use the land as such and see that no waste is permitted, that the land is farmed in a husbandlike manner, that the soil is not unnecessarily exhausted by negligent or improper tillage, and that repairs are made.

*You rent a stock farm from Black. Who is entitled to the natural increase of the stock?*

In the absence of an agreement to the contrary, the increase belongs to the tenant.

*Who is entitled to the fruit of the trees on leased land?*

The tenant.

*As between the landlord and tenant, who is entitled to the annual crop on leased property?*

The tenant, providing the crop has ripened or is severed from the soil during the term of the tenant's lease.

*Black rents a house and a barn where he keeps a number of horses. He tells the landlord that he may have the manure to be made at the barn if he furnishes the straw there. This the landlord refuses to do. Later, the landlord claims the entire manure. Who is entitled to it?*

The tenant. Manure made in livery stables, or in buildings unconnected with agricultural property, belongs to the tenant, unless, of
course, there is a contract to the contrary.

*Black leases a piece of farm land from Hall. Black is unable to pay
his rent and Hall re-enters, taking possession of the premises. Who
is entitled to the growing crop planted by the tenant?*

Hall. Black's rights are lost by nonpayment of rent.

*At the expiration of his lease, a tenant farmer seeks to remove ma-
nure made during his tenancy and from his own crops. May he do
so?*

No. This is done as a matter of public policy to prevent the deterioration of land.

*You agree to cultivate Johnson's land on shares. Before the culti-
vation of the crop is completed, you abandon the land without
justification. Are you still entitled to your share of the crops?*

No. The landlord is entitled to take the whole crop. He may also
hold you liable in damages for breach of contract to cutivate. However, you do not lose your right to a share of the crop by abandoning the cultivation of the land if you are justified in doing so; if for
example, the behavior of the landlord provokes you into leaving.

*You enter into a written agreement to rent an apartment at $100
a month for a period of one year. You give the prospective landlord
a deposit as evidence of your good faith and obtain a receipt.
Your family, living in another city, is brought to town and you ship
the furniture by express. The day before you are to move in, the
landlord notifies you that he has rented the apartment to someone
else. What can you do?*

You can sue the landlord for breach of contract. You may recover,
usually, damages which are the natural, direct, and necessary consequence of the landlord's failure to give you possession of the
apartment; specifically, you may recover the expense you and
your family have been put to—railroad fare, shipping charges for
household furniture and belongings, etc. You may not, however,
recover for the inconvenience to which you and your family have
been put.

*You obtain a cigar concession in a hotel. A few months after you acquire possession, the hotel is forced to close for lack of business. What are your rights?*

You have a claim against the landlord for damages.

*After renting you a house, your landlord acts disagreeably to you, makes all sorts of insulting remarks, threatens to forcibly dispossess you, and finally advertises the house for rent. What are your rights?*

You may rightfully abandon the house, refuse to pay rent, and file suit against the landlord for damages.

*A tenant leases an apple orchard but fails to take care of it properly. May the owner cancel the lease?*

Yes. This is permitted so that further waste and destruction may be prevented.

*You and your wife rent a $350 per month apartment on a two-year lease. How can you protect yourself in case of the death of one of the parties?*

By requesting the landlord to insert a death clause in the lease. With such a clause the survivor of the tenants is allowed to terminate the lease if he or she wishes relief from further liability under the lease.

*How does such a death clause read?*

The following rider is attached to and made a part of the lease.

Provided that lessee (tenant) is not in default of any of the terms of this lease, upon the death of either Mr. or Mrs. _____
co-tenants
lessee may terminate this lease by giving written notice to the lessor (landlord) within ninety days after such death. The written notice shall also be executed by the decedent's administrator or executor and shall designate a termination date between seventy and one hundred days after the date of such notice. The said termination date shall be on the last day of a calendar month, provided said notice shall be accompanied by payment to lessor of all the rent due or to become due as of said termination date; and, further, provided that the premises shall be vacated and sur-

rendered to the lessor at least sixty days prior to the said termination date. Said termination shall not release lessee from any liabilities or obligations under said lease for the period prior to said termination date."

*What if I have a lease which does not contain such a death clause?*

While the landlord is under no obligation to insert one in your old lease (or in your new one for that matter), there is no harm in trying. Some landlords are willing to cooperate.

*Who prepares such a clause?*

It can be prepared by you, your attorney, or the landlord. The clause can cover not only a husband and wife but any two co-tenants, e.g. parent and child or just two individuals who live in one apartment sharing expenses.

*How do you determine the net income from an apartment house?*

From the gross income—the rents received—you deduct the insurance on the apartment house, repairs, taxes, license fees, depreciation on building, reserve for replacement, cost of utilities, collection of back rents, furniture depreciation, and management expenses.

*What is the difference between a sublease and an assignment of a lease?*

In a sublease the premises are rented to another person by the lessee or original tenant; an assignment is the transfer of the lessee's rights under the terms of his lease to a third person.

*In renting out an apartment what information should you have about the prospective tenant?*

The size of his family, his income, occupation, previous address, and a credit report.

*May a landlord insist that a tenant pay two or three months rent in advance?*

Yes. Where the landlord has doubts about the prospective tenant's ability to pay, he may require a surety bond or advance payment of the rent to be applied to the last few months of the lease.

*What is a percentage lease?*

This is a lease where the tenant, in addition to paying the rent called for in the lease, agrees to pay a percentage of the gross income of the leased premises, varying in amount from three to fifteen percent or more of the business.

*Does a tenant have a right to keep a pet in his apartment?*

It all depends on the agreement entered into between the landlord and tenant. If there is a lease and the lease is silent as to pets, there is no reason why you cannot have one in your apartment. However, if your pet is a nuisance to other tenants, the landlord may force you to get rid of the offending animal. If the lease forbids pets in the apartment or allows them under certain conditions, you are bound by the written lease. If you fail to comply with those conditions, the landlord may terminate the lease.

*What happens if the apartment house in which you live is sold to a third person?*

The new owner takes title subject to all the leases in existence at the time of sale. As each tenant's lease expires, he may enter into new arrangements and new leases.

*If you sublet your apartment, who is responsible for the rent, you or the subtenant?*

You, the original tenant.

*You lease an apartment under your own name. Later, you ask someone to move in and share both the apartment and the expense. May you do so?*

Most leases do not allow this without the express written consent of the landlord. Even if there is no written lease, the lessor may still refuse such permission.

*Does a tenant have an automatic right to stay on in his apartment after his lease expires?*

No. Most leases have a termination date after which the tenant must vacate the premises in the same condition he found them, normal wear and tear excepted. A tenant should always make certain that the lease allows him an option to renew at a certain rental for a certain period. Otherwise he may forfeit whatever rights he has.

*After you rent an apartment in a hi-rise, you discover that the walls are so thin that you can hear not only the flushing of the toilet but the heated arguments of your next door neighbor. What rights do you have?*

Virtually none. The law says you should have discovered these refects before you rented the apartment.

CHAPTER 19

PARTNERSHIPS

*What is a partnership?*

A partnership is an association of two or more persons to carry on as co-owners a business for profit.

*What are the essential characteristics of a partnership?*

**1.** It is an association of individuals.

**2.** It is voluntary, in the sense that no person can be forced into a partnership. For example, one partner may assign or sell his interest in a partnership, but he can only become a partner by being accepted by the other partners.

**3.** There is co-ownership. Each of the partners must have a proprietary interest not only in the profits, but also in the enterprise itself.

**4.** The association must be for profit. Nonprofit organizations cannot be partnerships.

**5.** There is mutual agency of partners. Each partner is the agent of the others and of the firm for all partnership acts. Since there is mutual agency, the relationship between partners is a fiduciary or confidential one, which means that there must be good faith and full disclosure among all the partners.

**6.** There is mutual liability of partners. Each partner is liable for all partnership acts. This means, in effect, that each partner may become exclusively liable for partnership debts and obligations if the firm and/or other partners become insolvent.

*Who may be a partner?*

Any person competent to make a binding contract may become a partner.

*How about minors, or those under twenty-one?*

295

Since the contracts of an infant are voidable, an infant has a right to disaffirm his partnership agreement. Once partnership debts have been incurred, however, an infant may not withdraw his investment until creditors are paid, unless the remaining assets are sufficient to pay such debts.

*May one partnership become affiliated with another partnership?*

Yes, provided all the members of both partnerships agree.

*What is the true test of whether or not a partnership has been created?*

The intent of the parties, expressed either by an agreement—written or oral—or implied by the circumstances.

*Does the fact that two persons own an apartment house make them partners?*

Not necessarily. Mere co-ownership does not of itself establish a partnership, even though the co-owners share profits or gross returns. However, the sharing of net returns or profits is prima-facie evidence of an intent to form a partnership.

*Under what terms and conditions will money or credit advanced in consideration of a share of the profits be considered a loan rather than an inference of partnership?*

1. When the money advanced is returnable in any event.

2. When the party advancing the money is given no control over the business, except as security to protect the advance.

3. When a note is taken for the amount of the advance.

4. When there is a stipulation against liability.

*Under what circumstances will such advancement of money or credit be construed as a partnership?*

1. When the repayment of the money is contingent upon profits made by the firm.

2. When the party advancing money or credit is given managerial control, including duties.

3. When there are no instruments or evidence of debt.

4. When there is no stipulation against liability for losses.

*A manager is hired at $20,000 a year plus 10 per cent of the profits. Is he considered a partner of the firm?*

No. He is still merely an employee.

*What can an employee of a partnership do to protect himself from liability to creditors of the firm?*

The contract of employment should stipulate that:

1. The employee is hired as such and not as a partner.

2. The employee is not required to contribute to capital or losses.

3. Compensation is received as salary or bonus or both, and not as profits.

4. The employee's name is not to appear on firm stationery.

5. The employee is not to be represented as a partner either to other employees or to the business world.

6. The employee is to receive a minimum guaranteed salary irrespective of the profits or losses of the firm.

*What constitutes documentary evidence of a partnership?*

1. The partnership agreement, which should disclose the names of all partners.

2. Books of account, which should show the relationship of the parties.

3. The stationery of the firm, which should indicate the firm names as well as the names of those comprising the partnership.

4. Contracts, business orders, and invoices, which often indicate the nature of the proprietary interest.

5. Leases, which should be signed by all members of the firm.

6. Letters and other correspondence, which often indicate how the parties regard themselves.

7. Bank accounts, which disclose who is authorized to issue checks and in whose individual names the funds are listed.

8. Law suits, which disclose the individual names of the partners who file or defend a suit.

*How may a partnership be established by circumstances?*

The Uniform Partnership Act provides, in part: "When a person, by words, spoken or written, or by conduct, represents himself, or consents to another representing him to any one, as a partner in an existing partnership or with one or more persons not actual partners, he is liable to any such person to whom such representation has been made, who has, on the faith of such representation, given credit to the actual or apparent partnership, and if he has made such representation or consented to its being made in a public manner he is liable to such a person, whether the representation has or has not been made or communicated to such person so giving credit by or with the knowledge of the apparent partner making the representation or consenting to its being made."

*How does a partnership differ from a corporation?*

1. A partnership may be dissolved by mutual consent of the partners; a corporation only by the fulfillment of statutory requirements.

2. A partnership is an association of individuals. A corporation is an entity, separate and apart from the incorporators who form it.

3. Partners are liable personally for debts of the firm when the firm assets are insufficient to pay the firm's creditors. Stockholders of a corporation are not liable for the corporation's debts, except in certain special cases.

4. Unless otherwise provided for in the partnership agreement, a partnership is dissolved upon the death or bankruptcy of a partner or upon the sale of a partner's interest. This is not the case with a corporation.

5. Members of a partnership may bind one another by acts within the scope of the firm business. Corporate members or stockholders cannot bind the corporation merely because they are stockholders.

6. A partner's interest in the firm cannot be readily transferred; and if the interest is transferred, the transferee has no voice in the firm. A stockholder may transfer his interest or stock in a corporation at will, since the corporation is an impersonal entity.

7. A partnership may engage in any legitimate business it desires. A corporation may do only those things allowed by its charter.

8. A partnership may conduct business throughout the United

States. A corporation may do business only in the state in which it is incorporated, unless it first obtains a license in those states in which it seeks to do business.

### What are the advantages of a partnership?

1. Partners may be better able to expand a business through the individual contribution of ideas and capital.

2. Partners are better able to share responsibility and decisions, as well as losses.

3. Partners will probably pay less taxes than if they were incorporated.

4. The partners will probably be able to obtain more credit.

5. Supervision is likely to be better, since there will be more than one manager to keep an eye on business affairs.

### What are the disadvantages of a partnership?

1. A partnership is dissolved by the death of any partner.

2. Profits are shared.

3. Unless the partners know each other well, the partnership may encourage bickering and dissension, and these may lead to failure of the partnership.

4. Each partner becomes liable as the principal of the other partners and as his agent as well. There is unlimited liability in a partnership.

### What is a general partner?

A general partner has ownership of the partnership property, or a share in such property, full powers of management within the partnership purposes, and full personal liability. A general partner may also be a member of a limited partnership.

### What are some of the rights and obligations of a general partner?

1. The acts of any partner are the acts of every partner.

2. Each partner is an agent of the firm and of the other partners.

3. All are liable, as partners, upon contracts made by any of them with third persons within the scope of the partnership business.

**4.** Not only is the partnership property liable for debts incurred by the partnership, but the individual property of each partner is also liable, each partner being individually liable for the acts of the partnership.

*What is the extent of a general partner's liability?*

He is liable for all debts regularly contracted by the firm.

*What is the difference between a limited and unlimited partner?*

The difference is in the extent to which partners may be liable. In the usual general, or unlimited, partnership, the partners are liable to creditors for the debts of the firm, since, in partnership law, they are individual debts. Limited partnerships are organized to permit all or some members to limit their liability to creditors.

*What is a special partner?*

A special partner is an investor who receives a share of the property or profits, but has no power of management and no personal liability beyond the amount of his investment.

*What is an ostensible partner?*

An ostensible partner is one who, though not actually a partner, represents himself as being one, or consents to being so represented by those who carry on the business. As far as third persons are concerned, who act on such representations, an ostensible partner is liable as if he were an actual partner.

*What is a dormant, silent, or undisclosed partner?*

One whose name is not used and who is so inactive in the partnership that his relationship to it is generally unknown. A dormant or silent partner is liable for all partnership obligations while he is a member of the partnership. So is a secret or undisclosed partner.

*What is an incoming partner?*

An incoming partner is one brought into a going business as a new partner. He is not personally liable on old obligations, unless he actually assumes them. He is liable, however, for his capital contribution to the partnership property.

## What is a retiring partner?

A retiring partner is one who, after a partnership is dissolved, ceases to be a partner in the business, which is carried on by others. He remains liable for partnership obligations incurred while he was a partner, but is not liable for new obligations unless he fails to give the necessary notice of withdrawal. He should give actual notice, in writing, to all parties who have extended credit to the firm. He should give constructive notice, by inserting an advertisement in a newspaper, that he is retiring from the firm on a specified date.

## What are continuing partners?

Those who continue a business after dissolution are called continuing partners.

## What is a surviving partner?

A surviving partner is one who remains after the dissolution of the partnership or death of a partner or partners. A surviving partner succeeds to the ownership of the partnership property and is charged with the duty of liquidation—unless, by agreement, the business is to be continued.

## What is the liability of a deceased partner's estate?

His individual property is subject to levy for all obligations of the partnership firm while the deceased was a partner. However, it is subject to such levy only after the firm assets are first applied, and after the decedent's estate has paid off his personal liability exclusive of his liability to the firm.

## How is a partnership formed?

A partnership is formed by the drawing up of an agreement between the future partners setting forth the terms of the partnership.

## What should be included in the partnership agreement?

1. The date when the partnership is to become effective.
2. Names and addresses of the partners.

**3.** The firm name, or the name under which the partnership will operate.

**4.** The nature, purpose and scope of the partnership. The more detailed the description of the proposed activities, the better.

**5.** Where the business is to be located.

**6.** How long the partnership is to last.

**7.** Whether or not interest is to be paid on invested capital.

**8.** How profits and losses are to be shared or divided. If there is no specific provision to the contrary, it is presumed that profits and losses are to be shared equally.

**9.** What salaries or drawing accounts are to be provided each of the partners.

**10.** How much time each partner is to devote to the partnership business.

**11.** The power of each of the partners, especially the power to sign checks, buy goods, etc.

**12.** How the business is to be managed and controlled.

**13.** Provisions for proper bookkeeping.

**14.** Provisions for the retirement of each of the partners.

**15.** Dissolution of the partnership, especially provisions for the right to continue the business upon withdrawal of any partner.

**16.** How the surplus is to be distributed upon dissolution.

**17.** How the firm's name and good will are to be disposed of after dissolution.

**18.** Provision for arbitration in case of disputes between partners.

*Is the drawing up of a partnership agreement all that is required in law?*

Yes, except in the case of a limited partnership agreement, which must be registered with the clerk of a court.

*Must there be witnesses to the agreement?*

There need be no witnesses to any partnership agreement, though witnesses are always advisable.

*May the partners use a fictitious name in organizing a partnership?*

Yes. They may use any name—the actual names of the partners or any other name—so long as there is no intention to mislead the public.

*What if the firm uses a name similar to one already in existence?*

The one already in existence may procure an injunction to restrain the new firm from using a similar name.

*May a partnership sue or be sued in the name of the firm?*

No. A partnership must sue and be sued in the individual names of the partners. If there are two or more partners, each of them must join in the suit.

*After a partnership is dissolved, who is entitled to the name of the firm?*

In the absence of an agreement to the contrary, any partner may use the firm's name, provided the public is not misled, or the name may be sold as an asset of the firm, or a retiring partner may give or sell to a continuing partner the right to the firm name; or, finally, the court may order a sale of the firm's good will and assets, which includes the sale of the firm name.

*What is good will?*

Good will is the benefit arising from the successful conduct of business by a certain person or firm, at a certain place. It has been defined as the probability that "the old customers will return to the old place of business."

*What is the capital of a partnership?*

It is the sum total of money or agreed value of property contributed by the partners for the transaction of partnership business.

*Are there any restrictions upon the nature of a partner's contribution to the capital of a partnership?*

Yes. A general partner may contribute capital in the form of cash, property, or services. A limited partner may only contribute cash or property as part of the partnership capital.

*What does partnership property include?*

1. All property originally contributed by members of the firm.

2. All property subsequently acquired by the firm with partnership funds or services.

3. Any property, profits, or proceeds directly or indirectly acquired through the use of firm property, time, or knowledge.

*What rights do each of the partners have in the partnership property?*

Each partner has equal right to possess and use specific partnership property only for partnership purposes. For example, he may not use an automobile belonging to the firm for private purposes unless the other partners consent.

*What is the difference between partnership capital and partnership property?*

1. Partnership capital is fixed in amount and cannot be changed except by consent of all the partners. Partnership property, on the other hand, may vary in amount from time to time, and may be more or less the capital provided for the partnership.

2. Partnership capital may but does not necessarily include undivided profits. The assets of a partnership always include undivided profits.

3. Upon dissolution of the partnership, the firm's capital is repayable to each of the partners in proportion to the amounts contributed, before net assets are figured and distributed. In the absence of an agreement to the contrary, net assets are distributed to the members of the firm equally, regardless of unequal contributions of capital.

*How are loans or advances made by one partner to the firm regarded?*

As obligations to be repaid ahead of capital.

*May a partner convey his interest in the firm?*

Yes, if there is nothing in the partnership agreement to the contrary. Even if he does, however, such conveyance does not dissolve the partnership, nor does it entitle the assignee to interfere with the management of the partnership. All that such assignee is entitled to is to receive profits and surplus after the creditors of the firm have been satisfied.

*What are the rights and duties of one general partner with relation to another?*

Each partner has the obligation (1) to be loyal to the firm's interests, (2) to exercise care and skill in the management of the partnership business, and (3) to keep accurate accounts of the firm's business and to have such books open for inspection to all the other partners. Each partner has the right (1) to share in the management and control of the firm's business and decisions and (2) to share profits and losses equally, regardless of unequal capital contributions.

*Is a partner entitled to extra compensation for extra services rendered by him for the firm?*

No, not unless the partnership agreement so provides.

*Is an agreement between two partners binding on third parties?*

Not unless the third party has knowledge of such an agreement.

*Which partnership acts require the unanimous consent of all the partners?*

1. Any assignment of the partnership property in trust for creditors or on the assignee's promise to pay the debts of the firm.

2. Any disposition of the good will of the business.

3. Any other act which would make it impossible to carry on the firm's business.

4. Allowing a creditor to enter a judgment against the firm without a law suit.

*While driving his automobile on firm business, a partner strikes and seriously cripples a pedestrian. Is each member of the firm individually liable?*

Yes.

*Is one partner criminally liable for the criminal acts of another partner?*

Only if the criminal act is done with his consent or approval, or if he aids and abets his partner in the commission of the crime.

*Do partners have the right to expel another partner from the firm?*

Not unless the partnership articles so provide. The same result can be achieved, however, by dissolving the firm and forming a new one from which the offending or undesirable member is excluded.

*What is meant by the "dissolution" of a partnership?*

The Uniform Partnership Act defines dissolution as "the change in the relation of the partners caused by any partner ceasing to be associated in the carrying on as distinguished from the winding up of a business."

*Is a partnership terminated upon its dissolution?*

No. A partnership is not terminated until partnership affairs are concluded.

*What is the effect of dissolving a partnership?*

The chief effect is that all authority of the partners ceases so far as new business is concerned. Upon dissolution, partners remain as trustees for the purpose of winding up the affairs of the firm— which means distributing the remaining assets after payment of the partnership debts.

*Suppose a surviving or liquidating partner continues the partner-ship or conducts new business not necessary to terminating the partnership?*

In that case, the surviving or liquidating partner will be charged, except to persons without knowledge or notice of the dissolution.

*Is a liquidating partner allowed compensation for liquidating services?*

Yes, if he has not dealt unfairly with the firm.

*How is a voluntary dissolution of a partnership brought about?*

**1.** By the terms of the original agreement, which may contain a date for the dissolution.

**2.** By subsequent agreement of the parties, or by any one party, subject to damages for the breach of the partnership agreement.

*May a partner withdraw any time he pleases?*

Yes, though he may have to pay damages for loss to the firm's business.

*Does one partner have to give other partners notice of his retirement?*

Yes. Such notice may be given either orally or in writing.

*How is involuntary dissolution brought about?*

**1.** By operation of law, as in the case of death or bankruptcy.

**2.** By judicial decree at the instance of one of the partners.

*What is the effect of dissolution upon the death of one of the partners?*

Upon the death of one partner, the latter's personal representative (his executor or administrator) stands in his place. As such, the personal representative has the right to require that the surviving partners wind up the firm's affairs and pay over to the estate of the deceased the latter's share of the assets and profits after payment of the firm's debts.

*For what reasons will a court decree a dissolution of a partnership?*

**1.** When one of the partners is insane or mentally incompetent.

**2.** When one of the partners is guilty of such gross misconduct as to seriously impair the firm's business.

**3.** When it is obvious that the firm is heading towards insolvency or bankruptcy.

*What are the usual partnership remedies?*

Suits between partners that in no way involve the partnership may be brought in an ordinary law court. In other cases the remedies are to demand an accounting with or without dissolution, to request an injunction against a specified act, or to ask that a receiver be appointed to conserve the firm's assets and wind up its affairs.

### What is a demand for an accounting?

This is a request before a court to determine a partner's interests and rights in the firm. It may be made either with or without a request for dissolution of the partnership.

### What is an injunction?

This is a judicial command, issued by a court of equity, that a partner or partners do or not do a specific act. It may be requested if it is feared that one of the partners will monopolize the firm or "doctor" its books.

### What is a receiver?

A receiver is an officer appointed by the court to conserve the assets and wind up the affairs of the firm. After his duties are discharged the receiver makes an accounting to the court.

### How are firm assets distributed when a partnership is dissolved?

They are distributed in the following order:

1. To creditors other than partners.
2. To partners for liabilities other than for capital and profits.
3. To partners for liabilities in respect to capital.
4. To partners for liabilities in respect to profits.

### Will a court decree dissolution if there have been persistent violations of the articles of partnership?

Yes.

### Will a court decree dissolution if the business has been abandoned by one of the partners?

Yes.

*Will a court decree dissolution if a partner has been excluded from participation?*

Yes.

*Will a court decree dissolution if a partner has been dishonest?*

Yes.

*Will a court decree dissolution if one of the partners is habitually drunk?*

Yes.

*Will a court decree dissolution if the partners cannot reconcile sharp differences?*

Yes.

*How are liabilities determined among partners?*

In the absence of an agreement the following rules apply:

**1.** Each partner must be repaid his contributions, whether by way of capital or advances to the partnership property.

**2.** Each partner is entitled to share equally in the profits and surplus remaining after all liabilities have been met, including those to partners.

**3.** Each partner must contribute to the losses sustained by the partnership, according to his share of the profits.

*Under what circumstances are partners personally liable for the debts of the firm?*

When the assets of the firm are insufficient to satisfy such debts.

*What is the liability of the partners when the firm goes bankrupt?*

The separate assets of all partners, as well as of the partnership estate, are called upon, no matter whether the individual members of the firm are adjudicated bankrupts.

*What is the purpose of limited or special partnerships?*

To achieve joint effort with limited responsibility.

*What should be specified in a limited partnership agreement?*

Since, under the Uniform Limited Partnership Act, a limited partnership is one formed by two or more persons having as members one or more general partners and one or more limited partners, the following should be included in a limited partnership agreement:

1. The name of the partnership.

2. The character of the business.

3. The location of the principal place of business.

4. The name and place of residence of each member, general and limited partners being respectively designated.

5. The term for which the partnership is to exist.

6. The amount of cash and a description of and the agreed value of the other property contributed by each limited partner.

7. The additional contributions, if any, agreed to be made by each limited partner at the times at which or events on the happening of which they shall be made.

8. The time, if agreed upon, when the contributions of each limited partner is to be returned.

9. The share of the profits or the other compensation by way of income which each limited partner shall receive by reason of his contribution.

10. The right, if given, of the partners to admit additional limited partners.

11. The right, if given, of one or more of the limited partners to priority over other limited partners as to contributions or as to compensation by way of income, and the nature of such priority.

12. The right, if given, of the remaining general partner or partners to continue the business on the death, retirement, or insanity of a general partner.

13. The right, if given, of a limited partner to demand and receive property other than cash in return for his contribution.

14. The right, if given, of a limited partner to substitute an assignee as contributor in his place, and the terms and conditions of the substitution.

*What is the purpose of such a certificate?*

To inform the public—especially creditors of the prospective firm—of the partner's limited liability, so that the public may be protected. The certificate should be filed with the clerk of the appropriate court, as provided by state law.

*May a limited partner's sole contribution be services?*

No. It may be either cash or property, but may not consist of services.

*Is an agreement to share profits on a pro rata basis, but losses only as to some partners a limited partnership?*

Yes.

*May a limited partnership contain the surname of a limited partner in the firm name?*

Not unless it is also the surname of a general partner.

*What right to the firm's profits does a limited partner have?*

He has a right to receive profits and compensation provided in the certificate, provided the rights of outside creditors are not jeopardized.

*Does a limited partner have a right to inspect the firm's books?*

Yes. He also has a right to demand an accounting.

*Does a limited partner have the right to a return of his capital contributions to the firm?*

Yes, if all firm members agree and provided, further, there is either a cancellation or amendment of the partnership certificate.

*Does a limited partner have a right to have the firm dissolved?*

Yes, when he is unable to obtain the return of his contribution, or when the other liabilities of the partnership have not been paid, or the partnership property is insufficient for their payment, and the limited partner would otherwise be entitled to the return of what he put into the firm.

*What is the liability of limited partners?*

Their chief liability is that their capital contributions are subject to the claims of the creditors of the firm.

*Under what circumstances may a limited partner be held liable as a general partner?*

1. If he allows his name to be used as part of the firm name.

2. If he takes an active part in the business.

*What distribution of profits or assets is made after dissolution of a limited partnership?*

The order of distribution is as follows:

1. To outside creditors in the order of priority provided by law.

2. To limited partners in respect to their share of the profits and other compensations by way of income on their contributions.

3. To limited partners in respect to their capital contributions.

4. To general partners other than for capital and profits, as well as advances, loans, etc.

5. To general partners in respect to profits.

6. To general partners in respect to capital.

CHAPTER 20

## CORPORATIONS

*What is a corporation?*

A corporation is a legal entity consisting of one or more natural persons, established by law, usually for some specific purpose, continued by a succession of members.

*What are some of the characteristics of a corporation?*

1. It has continuous succession; it is not subject to dissolution by the death, withdrawal, or legal disability of any of its individual members.

2. It may take and grant property and contract obligations, within the limits of its charter.

3. It may sue and be sued in its corporate name, in the same manner as an individual.

4. It may receive grants of privileges and immunities.

5. It confers on its members exemption from personal liability for the debts of the corporation beyond the amount of their respective shares.

6. It may buy and sell real estate.

7. It has power to use a common seal.

8. It has power to make by-laws.

9. It has power to transfer membership in the corporation without the consent of the other members.

*What are the advantages of the corporate form of business?*

One of the most important advantages is that the liability of each shareholder is limited to the amount of his subscription. Once the shareholder has paid for his stock, he is no longer liable either to the corporation itself or to the creditors of the corporation. In a

313

partnership, the liability is personal and unlimited; for example, creditors may collect their judgments out of the assets of any single partner, something that cannot occur in a corporation.

Another advantage is that the members of a corporation are not liable for the unauthorized acts of their associates. If anyone is liable, it is the corporation itself.

The corporate form also has a permanency afforded by no other type of business organization. When a partner or a sole proprietor dies, the business is dissolved and must be reorganized if it is to continue. The death of any officer or stockholder does not dissolve a corporation.

Finally, a corporation, because of its permanency, offers greater inducements for raising capital and borrowing money than a partnership. In this way, corporate shares can be more readily sold than shares in a similar but unincorporated business.

### What are the disadvantages of a corporation?

A corporation is burdened by high taxes and by the expense of franchise licenses needed to carry on the corporate business.

### What is an eleemosynary corporation?

A corporation formed to distribute the bounty of the founder in such manner as he has directed. Such corporations may be hospitals for the relief of the poor and the weak, colleges for the promotion of learning, and foundations for the support of persons engaged in literary pursuits. The term is generally synonymous with a charitable organization.

### What is a corporation sole?

A corporation which, by law, consists of but one member at any one time—as a bishop in England, for example.

### What is a foreign corporation?

This is a corporation created by legislation in a state other than the one in which its right to do business or own property is being considered. For example, a corporation created under the law of New York is a foreign corporation in Maryland.

*What is a nonprofit corporation?*

This is a corporation having no capital stock and not being operated for financial profit. Lodges, pleasure clubs, church organizations, etc., are examples.

*Are nonprofit or charitable corporations liable for the negligence of their employees?*

No, not when the person suing is a beneficiary of the charity. A charitable corporation is generally held liable to strangers for the negligence of its employees within the scope of their employment.

*What should be considered in determining the state of incorporation?*

In general, a corporation should be organized in the state in which its principal business is to be conducted, unless certain advantages and privileges needed for its operation can be acquired only under the laws of another state. Some of the most important matters to be considered are:

1. Fees and taxes.

2. Requirements as to the issuance of shares.

3. Convenience of operation, such as requirements as to qualifications and residence of directors, etc.

4. Ease of making corporate changes.

5. Limitations on the power of the corporation to declare dividends and to purchase its own shares and the shares of other corporations.

6. Liabilities imposed by statute on directors and shareholders for debts of the corporation, etc.

7. Right to remove cases to the federal courts.

*How is an ordinary business corporation organized?*

1. A lawyer drafts the articles of incorporation.

2. The corporation papers are signed by the requisite number of incorporators and their signatures acknowledged before a notary public.

3. The articles or certificate is filed or recorded with the Secre-tary of State and the organization fees paid.

4. A certified copy of the articles or certificate is filed or recorded with the clerk of the county in which the principal office is located.

5. Directors are elected and an organization meeting is held by the shareholders and directors.

6. A permit or license to do business is procured.

7. The Federal Securities Act is complied with.

*What should the articles or certificate of incorporation contain?*

1. The name of the corporation, which must not be in conflict with an existing name.

2. The purposes for which it is formed.

3. The authorized capital structure; that is, the number of shares and whether or not they shall have a par value, the different classes of shares, common or preferred, and the preferences and restrictions thereof.

4. The principal place of business or office.

5. The period of time for which the corporation is organized.

6. The number of directors, usually not less than three, with their names and addresses.

7. The names and addresses of the incorporators.

8. The amount of subscribed and paid-in capital with which the corporation proposes to do business.

9. The amount of indebtedness authorized, and limitation, if any, of stockholder's liability.

10. The execution and acknowledgment.

*What is the charter of a corporation?*

A charter is the contract between the state and the corporation and defines its powers. A corporation has only those powers ex-pressly contained in its charter, as well as those implied powers reasonably necessary to carry out the express powers.

*What should be contained in a corporate charter?*

1. The name of the proposed corporation.

2. The objects of the corporation.

3. The amount of capital stock.

4. The number and amount of shares.

5. The classes of stock.

6. The duration of life of the corporation.

7. The location of the principal office.

*Who issues the corporate charter?*

The state.

*What takes place at the first corporate meeting?*

After the issuance of the charter, stock subscribers come together and elect the board of directors. By-laws are adopted, or a committee is appointed to draw them up. The newly elected directors elect officers of the corporation and perform any other business that may be properly presented, such as propositions to exchange property or services for stock.

*What are the by-laws of a corporation?*

These are rules passed for the internal government of the corporation. They are alterable at the pleasure of the stockholders and are binding on them so long as they are regularly enacted. They must not be contrary to the law, the charter of the corporation, or to public policy.

*With what do by-laws deal?*

They are usually concerned with the duties and qualifications of directors and officers, terms of office, bonds of officers, dates of regular meetings, and how special meetings may be called.

*Who determines the by-laws of a corporation?*

Usually the stockholders, unless, by statute, power is delegated to the directors.

*A corporate charter is granted by the State of South Carolina. The corporators, who are authorized to act as directors until others shall be elected, assemble in Baltimore, pass resolutions of accept-*

*ance of the corporation and perform other acts necessary to orga-
nize the corporation. Has the corporation a legal existence?*

No. A corporation can have no legal existence outside the boundaries of the state by which it is created. To be effective, acceptance of the charter and organization under it must take place
within the State of South Carolina. Since the corporate proceedings took place in Maryland, they are void.

*Under a charter granted by the State of Maine, the corporators
meet in New York, where they organize and accept the charter,
electing officers and directors. The directors then meet in New York
and authorize the president and secretary to execute a mortgage
on the corporate property, which is done. Is this a good mortgage?*

No. The action of the corporators in meeting and electing officers
is a corporate act which could not take place outside the state of
incorporation. Hence, the directors being illegally chosen, the
mortgage is void.

*A state law requires, as a preliminary to incorporation, that articles
be filed with the clerk of the Court of Appeals and that a duplicate
copy be filed with the clerk of the judicial district. The duplicate is
not filed as required. Nevertheless, the business functions under
the corporate name. Creditors of the corporation file suit against
it. Can they recover against the corporation?*

No. Since the corporation lacked a charter and failed to comply
with the statutory requirements, no corporation legally existed.
Hence, the indebtedness is a personal one, not a corporate obligation.

*A subscriber to stock in a corporation to be formed takes an active
part in its organization, as well as in its management after organization. When the corporation files suit against him for his unpaid
subscription, he defends on the ground that the corporation was
not legally organized. Is this a good defense?*

No. A person who undertakes to form a corporation, later participating in its management, cannot dispute the existence of the
corporation, nor can he avoid liability on his stock subscription

in the pretended corporation when sued thereon, either by it or its creditors.

*A state law requires that the charter give the names of the incorporators. A charter is procured, however, which fails to provide such information. Has a valid corporation been formed?*

Yes. A corporation, defectively organized, may still have progressed to a point to give the company sufficient legal standing, as a corporate body, for it to transact business and incur liabilities. Compliance with the law has gone far enough, in this example, to enable the company to function as a corporation. Its members, therefore, would not personally be liable, only the corporation itself.

*You contract with an association of persons, becoming their creditor. You do so without any knowledge that they claim to be a corporation instead of partners, and there is nothing to put you on notice. As a matter of fact, the group of persons had organized themselves defectively as a corporation. You now seek to hold them as partners, there being no corporate assets. May you do so?*

Yes. You may sue the members as partners, showing that they failed to comply with the law under which they claim corporate existence.

*May a corporation adopt any name it please?*

Yes, as long as its name does not conflict with that of an existing concern. A corporation adopting a name already in use, for the purpose of attracting the other's business, may be restrained by injunction or be liable in damages.

*How is membership acquired in a corporation?*

In non-stock corporations, membership is regulated by the charter and the by-laws. Membership in stock corporations is determined by the ownership of one or more shares of the capital stock secured either (1) by subscription to the capital stock, before or after incorporation, (2) by purchase from the corporation or, (3) by transfer from the owner.

*What books should a corporation keep?*

The books of account that are regularly kept in any business.

Special corporate books: The *minute book,* containing the minutes of the corporation. The *stock certificate book,* consisting of a number of blank stock certificates in the form authorized by the directors numbered consecutively, attached to "stubs" containing corresponding serial numbers. When required, these certificates are detached from the stubs and filled in with the stockholder's name and the number of shares it represents, the stub being a record of the transaction. The *stock ledger,* showing the status of each shareholder in relation to the company. It contains the name of each recorded stockholder, alphabetically arranged, his address, the number of shares owned by him, the date and source of the transaction, the date of the disposition of any shares and to whom disposed, and how much stock remains in his credit. The *transfer book,* consisting of a series of blank transfer forms to be filled out and signed by the transferor or his agent. A *corporate calendar,* kept by the secretary, covering the entire year and indicating to him the days on which notices are to be sent, meetings held, taxes payable, when reports to state officers are due, etc.

*Has a stockholder a right to examine the books of the corporation?*

Yes. A stockholder has a right to inspect the books and papers of a corporation, either personally or by an agent, provided he does so for a proper purpose and at a proper time. Thus a stockholder showing a prima-facie case of fraud, and whose purpose is to obtain information to remedy the fraud, is entitled to inspect corporate books and papers. A stockholder has no right of inspection, however, if his purpose in making the examination is improper, hostile to the interests of the corporation, or merely frivolous.

*Of what does the capital of a corporation consist?*

The capital of a corporation consists of the funds, securities, credits, and property of any kind owned by the corporation. "Capital stock" and "capital" are virtually synonymous.

*What is capital stock?*

It is the amount of money or property subscribed and paid in by the shareholders or the amount authorized to be so paid in. In actual practice, the capital stock has come to present a corporation's total assets, so that the law insists that such stock be issued only in exchange for equivalent value. The capital stock always remains the same, unless changed by law. It does not necessarily indicate the value of the property of the corporation.

*What is authorized capital stock?*

This is the amount of stock a corporation is authorized to issue under its charter. The issued stock is that actually issued within the authorized limit.

*What does a share of stock represent?*

A share of stock is the right to partake in the surplus profits of a corporation and, upon the dissolution of the corporation, to partake of the fund representing as much of the capital stock as is not liable for the debts of the corporation.

*What is a stock certificate?*

It is written acknowledgment by the corporation of the interest of the holder in its property and franchises.

*What is a stock subscription?*

A stock subscription is an agreement to purchase at a certain price a certain number of shares of stock in an existing corporation. The subscription, when accepted, is a contract between the subscriber and the corporation. It is subject to the rules governing other kinds of contracts.

*What is the usual method of subscribing to stock in a corporation not yet formed?*

Generally, the procedure is for the parties to sign an agreement to form the corporation and take stock in it when organized.

*A railroad company is organized under a law which appoints commissioners to open books and receive stock subscriptions. You subscribe to some stock, your name being properly recorded in the books. Shortly afterwards, having changed your mind, you attempt to withdraw your subscription. May you do so?*

No. Your subscription is an offer to purchase stock on the terms set forth by the corporation. When that offer is accepted by the corporation, in this case the railroad company, a binding contract results and neither party may then withdraw from the agreement. The corporation's acceptance is indicated by having your subscription recorded in its books.

*A subscription to stock in a railroad company provides that one fourth shall be paid when the road is completed to a certain county line, the remainder to be paid in four equal monthly installments, provided the company establishes a depot on said road at a certain point. The road is completed to the specified county line, but the depot is not erected. Because of this, the subscriber seeks to cancel his subscription. May he do so?*

No. The completion of the road to the specified county line is a condition precedent to any liability on the subscription, being made so by the subscription agreement. The erection of the depot is an independent stipulation, not a condition precedent to liability on the subscription. Whether a particular stipulation is a condition precedent, or merely an independent stipulation, is a question of intention, the courts taking into consideration not only the words of the particular clause, but also the language of the entire contract, the situation of the parties, the nature of the act required, and the whole subject matter to which it relates.

*What is treasury stock?*

This is issued stock reacquired by the corporation and held in its treasury for possible reissuance.

*What is the difference between common and preferred stock?*

Preferred stock usually entitles the holder to preference over the holder of common stock, both in the participation of earnings and in the division of assets. For example, if there is a 7 per cent preferred stock, it must be paid 7 per cent before anything is paid on the common stock. Being stockholders, the owners of preferred shares are subject to all the liabilities of stockholders, including liability for corporate debts.

*What is "participating" preferred stock?*

Such stock not only entitles the holder to the preferences described in the above question, but also participates with the common stock in the earnings above the per cent agreed upon.

*What is meant by "watered" stock?*

This is stock issued gratuitously, or under an agreement by which the holder is to pay less than its par value, either in money, property, or services. Watered stock issued by a corporation is binding on it, and also binds stockholders who participate or acquiesce in the transaction. Dissenting stockholders, however, may sue to enjoin or cancel the issue of such stock. Again, if the watered stock is original stock, issued on subscription, the transaction is a fraud on creditors of the corporation, who deal with it on the faith of the stock being fully paid. Hence, if the corporation becomes insolvent, the original holders of such stock, and purchasers with notice, may be held liable for its par value to pay such creditors.

*It is agreed between a corporation and all its stockholders that only 25 per cent should be paid on their shares. Subsequently, the corporation seeks to collect the full value of its stock. May it do so?*

No. This is a perfectly valid agreement; it is as binding upon the company and its stockholders as if it were expressly authorized by charter. No suit, therefore, can be maintained by the corporation to collect the unpaid stock, since the shares were issued as fully paid and on a fair understanding.

*What is a blue-sky law?*

A law designed to prevent the sale of stock, the only assets of which are "blue sky." A blue-sky law provides for the registration of the proposed stock with the proper body, with the provision that the securities are not to be issued until so registered and passed upon and a license to sell is granted by the Federal Securities Commission. The effect of such a law, when properly enforced, is to regulate the sale of speculative securities, though the law does not actually forbid it.

*What does the Federal Securities Law provide?*

This act, passed by Congress in 1933, provides for full disclosure of the facts concerning securities offered for sale in interstate commerce or through the mails. Under the act, a registration must be filed with the Securities and Exchange Commission in Washington by the registrant, including financial statements, pertinent exhibits, and a copy of the "prospectus." The law prescribes certain penalties for failure to file a full and honest report.

### What is a dividend?

A dividend is a fund which the corporation has set apart from its profits to be divided among its members.

### Who declares a dividend?

The directors of a corporation. They have large discretionary powers over dividend declarations, and are therefore not accountable unless they abuse this discretion and act fraudulently, oppressively, or unreasonably.

### Who is entitled to a dividend?

Every stockholder of record at the time the dividend is declared, no matter when the profits were earned, and without regard to the length of time particular members may have been stockholders.

### May a stockholder bring suit against the corporation to compel it to declare a dividend when there is a surplus?

No. He can only bring suit after the dividend has been declared, for, until that time, no dividend is due. However, should the directors fraudulently fail to declare a dividend or act in obvious bad faith, a stockholder may go into a court of equity to compel the directors to declare a dividend. A stockholder may obtain an injunction, if he can secure no other relief, restraining or preventing the directors or other officers of the corporation from paying out money on purposes thought to be illegal.

### May a dividend be declared if there are no profits or surplus?

No, to do so is improper.

### An insolvent corporation declares a dividend. May creditors of the corporation recover such dividend?

Yes. The creditors may recover from each stockholder who has been paid a dividend, such dividend being considered a fraud on the creditors of the corporation.

*A dividend is declared in June, payable in August. In July, a stockholder transfers his stock to Bill. Is Bill entitled to the dividend?*

No.

*A corporation declares a dividend, to be paid to those stockholders who are registered as such on the books of the corporation. Jones, a former stockholder, has sold and assigned his stock to Collins before the declaration of the dividend, but the latter has not yet had the stock transferred to his name. As between Jones and Collins, who is entitled to the dividend?*

Collins. The rule is that a dividend is payable to the substantial owner of the shares at the time the dividend is declared.

*What constitutes a legal meeting of stockholders, so as to render the acts and vote of the majority binding?*

1. The meeting must be called by one having authority to call it. In the absence of a provision to the contrary, such authority exists in the directors or managing agents.

2. Notice of time and place of the meeting must be given to each stockholder, unless the time and place are definitely fixed by statute, charter, by-laws, or usage. But if all the stockholders are present, in person or by proxy, notice is waived.

3. If a special meeting is called, notice of the business to be transacted must be given to the stockholders.

4. The meeting must be held at a reasonable time and place.

5. It must be regularly and properly conducted.

6. If there is a provision that a certain number of stockholders shall constitute a quorum for the transaction of business, a smaller number cannot act. In the absence of express provision, no particular number is necessary to constitute a quorum.

*May a stockholder be prevented from attending a stockholders' meeting?*

No.

*Who is entitled to vote?*

Anyone whose name appears on the books of the corporation as a stockholder.

*If a stockholder cannot attend a meeting, does he lose his right to vote?*

No. He may vote by "proxy"—that is, he delegates or authorizes someone to vote his stock in a certain prescribed way.

*Do trustees, executors, and administrators have the right to vote?*

Yes. They may vote the stock they hold in trust.

*In general, what are the powers of majority stockholders?*

As a rule, each shareholder is bound by all acts and proceedings, within the scope of the powers and authority conferred by the charter, which are adopted by a vote of the majority of the corporation, duly taken in accordance with the law. However, if the charter grants to the board of directors, or to other agents, the power to manage the corporate affairs, the power is exclusive and cannot be controlled or interfered with by the stockholders, their remedy being to elect or appoint new directors or agents. At the same time, even the majority cannot bind the minority by acts *beyond* the corporation's authority, nor defeat or impair contract rights between the corporation and individual stockholders, nor act fraudulently or oppressively, as against the minority.

*In violation of its charter, a majority of the stockholders in a corporation sells, at a loss, several buildings belonging to the corporation. Is such a transaction binding on the corporation?*

No. Even a majority of stockholders have no power to bind the minority by any act or proceeding not within the powers conferred upon the corporation by its charter. In this case, a stockholder, on behalf of himself and other stockholders, may bring suit against the corporation in a court of equity. As a basis for the suit it must be shown (1) that some action, or threatened action, of the board of directors is beyond the authority conferred by the charter (as in the above example); or (2) that the transaction is so fraudulent as to result in serious injury to the corporation or to the interests of the other stockholders; or (3) that the board of directors, or a majority of them, are acting in their own interests, in a way destructive of the corporation itself, or of the other stockholders; or (4) that the majority of the stockholders themselves are oppressively and illegally pursuing a course in violation of the rights of the other shareholders. Finally, it must appear that the aggrieved stockholder or stockholders have exhausted all means, within the corporation itself, to obtain redress of alleged grievances.

*May stock be sold, mortgaged, or pledged as security?*

Yes. One who buys stock usually stands in the same position as the one from whom he bought it.

*How is stock transferred?*

Usually by indorsement and delivery of the stock certificate to the corporation or its agent.

*Stockholders of a corporation agree among themselves not to sell, pledge, or transfer their shares. Subsequently, a shareholder, in violation of this agreement, does sell his stock to a stranger. Is the transaction legal?*

Yes. An agreement between stockholders not to sell, pledge, or transfer their shares is an unreasonable restraint of trade and therefore void.

*May a stockholder sell or transfer his shares to an infant—that is, one under legal age?*

No, nor can he sell or transfer his stock to any person who is incapable in law of assuming liability with respect to shares, such as a lunatic, for example.

*Does a transferee of stock have a right to vote at stockholders' meetings before he has had his transfer registered?*

No. He also takes the risk, as against the corporation, of payment of the dividend to the person who appears as owner on the books of the corporation. Of course, the transferee would be entitled to recover dividends from the person so receiving them.

*What general powers do directors have?*

When the general management of a corporation is entrusted to a board of directors or other officers, they have the power to bind the corporation by any act or contract within the powers conferred upon them. However, they cannot effect any great or radical change in the organization without the assent of the stockholders, unless such power is expressly conferred. The board may delegate authority to a committee or to third persons to do acts for the company. They cannot delegate the exercise of a discretion vested in them.

*May a director vote upon any resolution in which he is personally interested?*

No.

*May a director profit by his relationship to the corporation?*

No. A director occupies a position of trust. He cannot use his position to make secret profits without a full and fair disclosure of the facts.

*A tool manufacturer sells some tools to a corporation of which he is a director, procuring the contract by his own vote. May the corporation cancel the contract?*

Yes. If a director, by his own vote, procures a contract with himself in which his own interests are opposed to the corporation, the contract may be set aside by the corporation or its stockholders. The law does not permit a director to place himself in a position where he may betray the interests of the corporation to his own advantage.

*Are directors and other officers of a corporation personally liable for losses sustained by the corporation?*

Ordinarily, directors are not personally liable for accidents, thefts, etc., if they have not been negligent, nor for mere mistakes or errors of judgment when they act in good faith and with ordinary care and diligence. However, they are personally liable if they willfully abuse their trust—as by exceeding their authority or the powers of the corporation or by misappropriating corporate funds. They are personally liable, too, when they are guilty of gross negligence and inattention to the duties of their office.

## How may a director be removed?

By the stockholders of the corporation. He cannot be removed by his co-directors.

## How may an officer of a corporation be removed?

Normally, a corporation has a right to remove an officer or agent, when there is a contract for a fixed term, only if he violates his contract or is incompetent. But it can, at any time, revoke the authority of an agent, although it may render itself liable for breach of contract by so doing. An agent or officer who is appointed by vote of the stockholders, or whose term of office is fixed by charter, cannot be removed by the directors, nor can his authority be revoked by them.

*Black, an investment broker, organizes and controls a number of corporations. He persuades his clients to invest in the worthless securities of these "dummy" corporations. A client whom he has bilked now seeks to hold Black personally liable. Black defends on the ground that the corporation should be sued, not he. Is he right?*

No. There is a sharp difference between the legal rights and responsibilities of a corporation and of its members. Contracts made by an officer of a corporation, for example, bind the corporation, not the officer individually. Corporate debts are not the debts of its members but the debts of the corporation. However, when the corporate form is used as a cloak to evade responsibility, the court will ignore the corporate form and fix responsibility as substantial justice requires. Black, therefore, would be liable individually.

*A corporation issues a stock certificate to Black. Black, claiming that it is fully paid for, sells it to a friend, who has no idea that actually the stock is not fully paid for. Is the friend liable to creditors of the corporation?*

No, since the friend lacked knowledge.

*You subscribe for stock of the par value of $1,000. You have paid $200 on the subscription when the corporation becomes insolvent. What can the creditors of the corporation collect from you?*

$800. Your indebtedness is a corporate asset from which the corporation may meet its obligations.

*The president of a banking corporation enters into a contract with cotton brokers for the purchase of cotton on the stock exchange. The brokers buy the cotton for the bank president who, after due notice, refuses to receive the cotton. No money has passed between the parties. Is the bank liable?*

No. The act of the president in contracting for the purchase of cotton is beyond the usual scope of banking business; the bank, therefore, would not be liable. Had the cotton been delivered, however, the bank would be liable.

*Black sues Smith for personal injuries resulting from a fall on a defective stairway in a corporation-owned building. Smith insists that the corporation be sued, not himself. Black contends, however, that the corporation holds title to the real estate merely as a subterfuge to relieve Smith, the real owner, from liability. The capital stock is $1,000, consisting of one hundred shares of a par value of $10 each, held by Smith and the members of his family. Who is liable, Smith or the corporation?*

The corporation. Organizing a corporation for the purpose of escaping general liability is perfectly lawful. Hence, Smith is not liable; the corporation is.

*Four men contract to organize a corporation. It is agreed that a fifth man, Black, shall receive fifty shares of stock for installing a bookkeeping system for the proposed corporation. The next day, the corporation is organized, all its stock being issued to the four organizers. After this, Black performs the services indicated but the corporation's officers refuse to deliver the promised shares of stock. Can they be compelled to do so?*

Yes. A corporation is not usually liable for services and expenses of its promoters in organization. In the present case, however, the evidence shows that the corporation adopted the contract, made by its organizers with Black, and therefore is bound by it.

*A promoter promises to pay you for services rendered prior to incorporation. After the corporation is formed, the promoter refuses to pay. You sue the corporation rather than the promoter, on the ground that the corporation benefited by his services. May you recover from the corporation?*

No. Prior to incorporation, a promoter is personally liable on contracts made by him, unless he is acting as agent for the shareholders—in which case the shareholders would be liable. The promoter cannot represent the corporation or bind it, since the corporation is still nonexistent. When the corporation comes into legal existence, it may ratify the contract—in which case the corporation will be bound.

*A railroad company buys a large office building, which it then rents to tenants. Is this a proper exercise of its corporate powers?*

Yes. Every corporation has a right to own as much property as is necessary to carry out its charter powers. In this case, it could be argued that the railroad company had an eye toward expansion. It could, therefore, erect a building to provide for such growth, although it was not then necessary.

*Does a corporation have the power to buy in its own shares?*

Yes, when no harm is done to its creditors. Such shares are known as treasury stock.

*May a corporation insure the lives of its officers?*

Yes.

*Does a corporation have power to sell its assets?*

Yes, if there is no dissent from the stockholders.

*May a stockholder object to a proposed merger or consolidation?*

Courts generally refuse to allow a small minority to block a sale of assets, especially when the sale is to the interest of the stockholders. A dissenting stockholder, however, has a right to have his shares appraised in the manner provided by statute, and to receive payment therefor.

*Under what circumstances may a receiver for a corporation be appointed?*

A receiver usually is appointed to take charge of the assets of a business when there is mismanagement or internal dissension in the corporation or when the corporation is insolvent or unable to pay its debts.

*The president of a corporation signs a contract for advertising space in a magazine, for one year, at $2,000 a month. The president has not been authorized by his board of directors to sign the contract, nor is it signed by the general manager or secretary of the corporation. When the corporation refuses to pay the bill, the magazine sues it. Who will win?*

The corporation. Whether a president or any other corporate officer has authority to do particular acts depends upon the powers conferred upon him, either by the charter, the by-laws, or by the directors. In the absence of such authority, the president has no intrinsic power to bind the corporation.

*The directors of a bank pass a resolution requiring that the books shall be opened under the direction of Atwell and Brown for further subscriptions to the stock of the bank. It is agreed that $5 shall be required on each share when the subscription is entered. Jones agrees to buy certain shares, arranging with Atwell and Brown that they take a note which Jones holds, then collect it, applying the proceeds to the payment of his subscription. Learning of the transaction, the bank refuses to issue Atwell and Brown certificates of stock in the amount of Jones's subscription. Can the bank be legally compelled to do so?*

No. Atwell and Brown exceeded the authority conferred upon them by the resolution. Having no authority to take anything but money for the stock, their act does not bind the bank, since it neither ratified nor affirmed the unauthorized transaction.

*A farmer and his wife subscribe for stock, mortgaging their farm on representations that the stock will prove a lucrative investment.*

*The stock goes down in value. The farmer and his wife now seek to repudiate the contract by returning the stock and obtaining the purchase price. Can they do so?*

No. Opinions as to the value of stock are not such representations as are ordinarily a basis for repudiation of a contract.

*The directors of a corporation issue a prospectus stating that the company has a franchise to use steam power instead of horses on its right of way. Brown, relying on the representations, applies for and is allotted shares in the company. The corporation builds street railways, but not obtaining the right to use steam power, it becomes insolvent. When Brown files suit against the corporation, it defends on the ground that the directors believed the truth of the assertion, although now they know it was false. Is this a good defense?*

Yes. Unless it is proved that the false statements were made knowingly, or without belief in their truth, or with reckless disregard as to their truth or falsity, the corporation would not be bound. It is sufficient if the directors were motivated by the honest belief that their representations were true.

*You buy certain stock on a secret condition, agreed to by the promoter, that you will not be bound unless certain other parties subscribe. When the other parties fail to subscribe, you seek to cancel your contract, alleging the secret condition which the promoter does not deny. May you cancel your agreement?*

No. The capital stock of a corporation represents a fund paid in by its subscribers and stockholders so that it may conduct its business and pay its obligations. In the above example, you are imposing a condition which, if enforced, may deplete the fund to which creditors have a right to look for the payment of their debts. Hence, such secret conditions are void, and the subscription may be enforced against you.

*Do directors have power to dissolve a corporation?*

No. It must be done by vote of the stockholders.

*How is a corporation dissolved?*

1. If of limited duration, by the expiration of the term of its existence, as fixed by charter or general law.

**2.** By the loss of all its members, or of an integral part of the corporation, by death or otherwise, if the charter or act of incorporation provides no way by which such loss may be supplied.

**3.** By the surrender of its corporate franchise to, and the acceptance by, the state authority.

**4.** By the forfeiture of its charter through the neglect of duties imposed or the abuse of the privileges conferred by it, the forfeiture being enforced by proper legal action.

CHAPTER 21

# TORTS

*What is a tort?*

A violation of a right not arising out of a contract.

*What is the subject matter of torts?*

The subject matter of torts, one of the larger branches of the law, includes negligence and automobile accidents (see separate chapters for each) trespass, assault, battery, seduction, alienation of affections, deceit, conspiracy, malicious prosecution, libel and slander, and the right of privacy, among others.

*Is everyone liable for his torts?*

As a general rule, yes. Infants, lunatics, and drunkards are generally held liable for their torts. However, when a tort or wrong requires the exercise of a mental element that is beyond the capability of the minor, as in malicious prosecution, the infant is relieved of liability.

*Is an employer liable for the torts of his employee?*

Yes, if the employee acts within the course and scope of his employment. The employee, however, is liable for his own torts. The same principle holds true of partnerships. If a tort such as defamation was committed on behalf and within the reasonable scope of the partnership business, all partners will be liable.

*May the federal government or a state government be sued for its torts?*

Yes, under many modern statutes. Under the Federal Tort Claims Act the United States government has assumed liability for negligent torts—automobile accidents, for example—of its employees, but not for nonnegligent torts such as false arrest.

*Is a husband, as such, liable for his wife's torts?*

No. The wife can be sued in a proper case and recovery had against her.

*Is a parent liable for torts committed by his child?*

A father is not liable for the torts of a child merely because he is the father. A parent may become liable if he aids or abets a child in the commission of a wrong, or if he approves or ratifies it after the wrong is committed. A father would be liable, for example, if he watched his child beat up another boy or if he encouraged him to do so. He would not be liable if the child, without the father's knowledge or consent, smashed a neighbor's window with a brick. A parent may also be liable if he entrusts a child with a dangerous instrument, such as a gun.

*In the law of torts, what is trespass?*

Trespass is a direct and immediate injury to the plaintiff's person or to his property by the wrongful act of the defendant. Trespass includes assault, battery, and false imprisonment.

*Does an action of trespass lie even if no damage occurred?*

Yes. When one person harmlessly crosses another's land, nominal damages only will be awarded.

*What is an assault?*

An assault is a *threatened* battery; an *actual* battery is the unlawful use of force or violence on the person of another. Both acts are not only civil wrongs, but crimes, for which the offender may be fined, jailed, or imprisoned. Actually, any touching of the person in an angry, vengeful, rude, or insolent manner constitutes a battery. An intent to do harm is not necessary, even though the intent to do harm is the essence of an assault. The essence of a battery is the unlawful interference with the person of the plaintiff, and a mistake in identity or an apology makes no difference. Finally, every battery is necessarily an assault, although not every assault terminates in a battery.

*Bob boards a crowded streetcar, dropping his fare in the box. The conductor fails to notice that Bob has paid his fare and demands that he deposit another coin. When Bob refuses, the conductor bodily removes him. Does Bob have a claim against the transit company?*

No. If a passenger refuses to pay his lawful fare or to give proper evidence that he has paid it, he may be ejected from the car. However, if Bob, through witnesses, could prove that he did in fact pay his fare and was therefore wrongfully removed from the car, he would have a valid claim against the company.

*You tell Betty, as a joke, that her husband has been killed in an automobile accident. The shock that this false statement gives Betty, a rather nervous woman, brings on a serious illness. Are you liable in damages to Betty?*

Yes, since you should have foreseen that the intended fright might cause Betty bodily injury. You would not be liable, however, if Betty suffered fright without bodily injury.

*As a practical joke on Archie, who is asleep on a beach, John holds a magnifying glass in such a way that the sun's rays are focused on Archie's head. He keeps this up until Archie awakens from the pain caused by the heat and compels him to stop. Archie's head is severely burned. Does he have a claim against John?*

Yes. John has committed a battery on Archie by intentionally burning him. That John did it as a joke does not excuse him.

*Henry calls Bert an "S.O.B." within the hearing of several people. Bert then strikes Henry, knocking him to the ground. Has Henry a remedy?*

Yes, he can file suit for assault and battery against Bert. A person who has been called a vile name cannot resort to force. The fact that Henry called Bert an odious name might reduce damages.

*In the course of an argument you angrily point an unloaded pistol at Bob and threaten to shoot him. The gun is empty and you know it, but Bob does not. Bob sues you. May he recover?*

Yes. Bob was put in fear of bodily harm, even though the gun was actually unloaded and the threat could not be carried out.

*Albert tells his dentist to extract a particular tooth. Having given Albert an anesthetic, the dentist discovers a cavity in an adjoining tooth and rightly concludes that it is the cause of the ache. He pulls the adjoining tooth. Does Albert have a cause of action against the dentist?*

Yes. Albert directed the dentist to extract one particular tooth. The fact that he would have consented to the extraction of a different tooth is immaterial. If the arrangement had been for the dentist to extract the tooth that in his opinion was the cause of Albert's pain, Albert would have no claim, since he gave his consent to the dentist's action. In the absence of such an arrangement, the dentist is liable. The same principle of law is true in surgical operations. An operation performed on a patient without his consent is actionable at law, since it is an invasion of the rights of another.

*Albert suffers from a disease of his right kidney. His physician advises him to submit to an operation for its removal, but Albert refuses. Later, Albert consents to another minor operation, and for that purpose, submits to anesthesia. The physician removes Albert's kidney. Does Albert have a claim against the physician?*

Yes. An unlawful battery against Albert's body has taken place.

*Jack, coming close to Ann, shakes a stick in her face and threatens to strike her, although he does not actually do so. Ann is frightened and, from the shock and fright, suffers a miscarriage. She files suit against Jack for damages. Does she have a claim?*

Yes. Jack has committed an assault by threatening Ann with violence and accompanying his threats with menacing gestures. Such conduct is actionable even though no physical injury results.

*Arthur, without justification, bursts into Betty's room in a hotel and uses violent and abusive language toward her. As a consequence of the nervous shock received through Arthur's conduct, Betty is made ill. Does she have a claim against Arthur?*

Yes. Mere insults and abuse do not amount to an assault if no violent touching is involved. In this case, however, Betty has suffered bodily harm.

*Albert, a small boy, throws a snowball at Bob. He hits Bob in the eye and causes him severe pain. May Bob, in retaliation, "beat up" Albert?*

No, not unless he believes that Albert will continue to throw snowballs at him. Should Albert do so, Bob has a right to use force to compel the boy to desist, an assault and battery having been committed.

*Ted owes John $10. He gives John a $20 bill, expecting John to give him $10 change. John insists on keeping the $20. Ted then takes the $20 bill back from John by force. Is he within his rights?*

Yes. Ted has the same right to use force to get his $20 bill back as he had to prevent Jack from taking it away in the first place.

*What is false imprisonment?*

False imprisonment is any unlawful detention of the person of another. The application of force is not essential. A false imprisonment may be committed by words alone or by personal violence. A person may be imprisoned without his knowledge, as when he is asleep, drunk, or unconscious. A mistake does not excuse the defendant. However, if the detention is reasonable, as distinguished from unreasonable, it is not unlawful. For example, a restaurant manager may reasonably detain a person to determine whether he has paid the bill.

*Albert is a patron in John's restaurant. As Albert is about to leave, John tells him to wait until an investigation is made to determine whether Albert has paid his bill. When it is learned that Albert did actually pay, he is allowed to go. Does Albert have a claim against John for false imprisonment?*

No, unless the jury finds that Albert was detained for an unreasonable time or in an unreasonable way.

*Andrew has a legal right to enter a certain building. To keep Andrew out, Bob locks all the doors and windows. When Andrew cannot get in, he sues Bob for false imprisonment. Can he recover?*

No. In an imprisonment a person must be confined. In this case Andrew is not confined, since he is at liberty to go anywhere in the world—except the particular place from which he is barred.

*John is asleep in a room, high above the ground, from which there is only one means of exit, a door. Bob, knowing John is in the room, locks the door from the outside, although he has no legal authority to do so. Before John awakes, Bob unlocks the door; when John is ready to leave, he is able to do so. Later, John, learning that Bob locked him in the room, files suit against him. Can he recover?*

No. If John had tried to get out and had been unable to do so because he was locked in, he would have had a claim against Bob, but since John was unaware of any restraint, he could suffer no injury for which he could be compensated.

*Albert, age eight, in company with a group of other boys, repeatedly plays on the lumber pile Bob keeps on his land. Bob has often ordered the boys off the premises, Albert himself having been ejected several times. Seeing the boys on the pile of lumber, Bob picks up a stick and runs toward them, shaking the stick and shouting to them, "Get out of there." Albert, frightened, runs out into the nearby street. There he is struck by a passing automobile that is being operated with reasonable care. Is Bob liable in damages?*

No. Albert is a trespasser, and Bob may employ reasonable force, if necessary, to expel a trespasser from the premises, though he cannot kill him or inflict serious bodily harm on him.

*Albert, holding a cane, is standing on the road. Bob, a one-legged man, flourishes a knife and threatens to attack Albert. Albert stands his ground and, when Bob comes close, strikes Bob's leg with the cane. Bob falls to the ground and is bruised. Albert could have avoided the whole incident by going into his house a short distance away and locking the door. Is he liable to Bob for damages?*

No. One may use such force in self-defense as appears reasonably necessary under the circumstances.

*Albert attacks Bob upon the street. Bob raises his cane to ward off Albert's attack and, in so doing, strikes Chester, a bystander. Is Albert or Bob liable in damages?*

Albert, because he is the proximate cause of Chester's injuries.

*Jack is a guest at the Craggy Hotel. At Jack's invitation, Bob goes to the hotel, visits Jack in his room, and plays cards for money. Gambling is a criminal offense in this particular state. The elevator shaft in the hotel is in a dark place and, on leaving, Bob sustains injuries by falling into the open elevator shaft when he thinks he is stepping into the elevator itself. Does Bob have a claim against the hotel?*

No. An inkeeper has an obligation to guests to use due care to keep the premises reasonably safe and to discover and remove dangerous conditions. He owes the same duty to one who comes on proper business with a hotel guest—as, for example, to a merchant who comes to inspect a salesman's samples or to a friend who comes to pay a social call. In this case, however, Bob has come for an unlawful purpose, not on proper business with the hotel or the guest; therefore he cannot claim the benefit of the duty owed an invited guest whose business is lawful. Bob is a mere trespasser to whom the hotel owes no duty save to refrain from actively injuring him.

*A boy gains admission to a circus by crawling under the canvas. While seated with the paying patrons, he is injured by the negligence of one of the clowns who explodes a giant cracker near the audience. Is the circus liable for the boy's injuries?*

Yes. In conducting its activities the circus has a duty to exercise reasonable care to avoid causing bodily harm to those even wrongfully on the premises.

*Henry enter's Donald's farm and refuses to leave. What can Donald do?*

He can use a reasonable amount of force to put Henry off his land. He cannot attack Henry unless Henry actively resists him.

*You own a flock of chickens. Your neighbor, who lives across the road from you, has a freshly planted garden. Although your yard is enclosed by a fence, your chickens get out, go into your neighbor's garden, and cause considerable damage before they can be removed. Your neighbor now seeks to hold you liable. Can he?*

Yes. The rule is that an owner of animals is liable for trespass committed by them, even though he uses due care to keep them restrained.

*What is seduction?*

Seduction is the act of a man who induces a woman to surrender her chastity. If the girl is under the statutory age, she cannot give her consent, and the man may be charged with statutory rape, a serious crime. Seduction also includes the right of the father to recover damages for the daughter's loss of chastity and for any consequent shame and mortification. Though the right to sue is generally the right of the father, an unmarried female may sue for her own seduction in some states.

*A state law declares that any man having sexual intercourse with a girl under eighteen years of age, not his wife, is guilty of rape, regardless of whether the girl consents. The law is silent on the subject of civil liability. Albert has intercourse with Barbara, who is under eighteen, but with her consent. Does Barbara have a claim for damages against Albert?*

Yes. The law is designed to protect young girls from the consequences of their own acts.

*What is deceit?*

Deceit is a false representation of a material fact that the defendant knew or should have known to be false, on which the plaintiff relied to his damage. Damage must be proved by the plaintiff.

*Robert, a broker, buys a farm through his agent, the agent telling him that the farm is a sound investment. Later, needing money, Robert decides to sell the farm. He has never seen the property, but he tells Henry, an inexperienced young man who has just inherited some money, that the farm contains good corn land, is a sound investment, and will provide Henry with an income. Henry, without further investigation, relies on Robert's recommendation and buys the farm for $20,000. It is not good corn land and is worth only $12,500. Henry now seeks to recover his money. Will he succeed?*

Yes. Robert misrepresented the facts. He had never seen the farm and therefore knew nothing of it; yet he stated specifically that it was good corn land.

*What is malicious prosecution?*

Malicious prosecution results when a person, with malice and without probable cause, institutes a criminal prosecution against another.

*What must a person prove to support an action for malicious prosecution?*

1. He must show that there was an actual criminal prosecution that resulted in the arrest of the defendant.

2. He must show that the defendant instigated the action.

3. He must show that the defendant was animated by malice, or had no legal justification or excuse.

4. He must show lack of probable cause. Probable cause is a reasonable ground of suspicion, supported by circumstances, sufficiently strong to warrant a reasonably prudent man's believing that the person accused is guilty of the offense with which he is charged.

*Out of pure spite you cause the arrest of a neighbor. He is tried and acquitted before the magistrate. Can you be sued for malicious prosecution?*

Yes.

*What is defamation?*

Defamation is anything that holds one up to hatred, contempt, disgrace, or ridicule, that causes one to be shunned and avoided, or that tends to injure one in his occupation. Defamation is either slander or libel, the former being oral and the latter written.

*For which slanders is no proof of damage necessary?*

One such defamation, known legally as a slander *per se*, is any false and unprivileged publication that charges one with having committed, or with having been indicted, convicted, or punished for, a crime involving moral turpitude (immorality) or that imputes to the plaintiff the existence of an infectious, contagious, or loathesome disease. Other slanders *per se* in which the plaintiff does not have to prove that he has been specially damaged are those publications that tend to injure a man in his business or that impute unchastity to a woman and, in some states, to a man. A false accusation of adultery is slanderous *per se*.

### What is the important element in defamation?

The fact of publication to a third party. It is the damage to the plaintiff's character or reputation in the eyes of others that is the essential ingredient of slander. There is no publication if the otherwise slanderous words were spoken in jest and were so understood by the plaintiff and any others present.

### What is a privileged communication?

The discharge of an official duty without fear of an action for defamation. Certain publications, otherwise slanderous, are held to be absolutely privileged; that is, immune from suit, the public necessity outweighing the private advantage to the person whose reputation may be injured. A judge may slander a witness or a defendant on trial without being subjected to a damage suit. Any legislative, judicial, or other proceeding authorized by law is also privileged.

### Which communications are conditionally privileged?

**1.** Those in which the maker and the receiver have a common interest, as when a club publishes a letter to its members charging that the plaintiff was short in his accounts.

**2.** Those in which the person interested is so related to another that it may be reasonably inferred that the communication was innocently made, as when a brother makes a communication to a sister.

**3.** Those in which the person interested has requested another to give information, as in an answer to a request for a recommendation of a prospective employee.

### Upon what does the conditional privilege depend?

That the defamation is made without malice or that the defamer was acting without a proper motive to defamation.

*What is fair comment?*

It is the right and privilege of everyone to comment fairly and honestly on any matter of public interest, including plays, movies, books, art, or a candidate for public office. The essence of fair comment is that the person making the criticism must not be motivated by ill will toward the person and he must not use the excuse of criticism to accomplish a slander.

*Carl told John that Henry had a veneral disease. Has Henry any right of action against Carl?*

Yes, an action in slander, since Carl's statement was defamatory.

*Peter, having a grudge against the Rider Company, told a number of people that the Rider Company, Hardware Jobbers, were insolvent. The charge was false. Has the Rider Company a right of action against Peter?*

Yes. If Peter's statement injured the Rider Company's credit standing, the latter could sue and recover damages for slander.

*What are the defenses to a charge of slander?*

1. Consent.

2. Truth, although some courts require, in addition, that the publication was made for a justifiable end and from good motives.

3. Retraction. Though retraction is not a defense as such, some state laws allow a newspaper to make a retraction when the publication was without malice and under a mistake of fact.

*What is the right to privacy?*

The right to be let alone. An unauthorized use of a photograph for advertising or distasteful publicity is an invasion of one's right to privacy. In such cases no proof of special damages is necessary; the law will presume damage.

*Albert goes to a hospital for an appendectomy and is taken to the operating room. By a mistake of the hospital staff, the surgeon who is to operate on Albert is given the record of Henry. Henry's rec-*

*ord calls for an operation upon a tumor on his back. The surgeon
makes an incision in Albert's back before the error is discovered.
Is the surgeon liable?*

Yes. The unauthorized operation is an invasion of the patient's
privacy, and the surgeon is held accountable for it.

## CHAPTER 22

# NEGLIGENCE

*What is negligence?*

Negligence is the failure to exercise that degree of care which an ordinarily careful and prudent person would exercise under similar circumstances.

*What is meant by "proximate cause"?*

That cause of an injury which, in natural and continuous sequence, unbroken by an efficient intervening cause, produces the injury and without which the accident would not have occurred. Stripped of legal jargon, proximate is "near" as distinguished from "far"; "close" as distinguished from "remote."

*Why is it important to understand the meaning of proximate cause?*

Because in a negligence action the plaintiff cannot recover if he cannot prove that the defendant was the proximate cause of his injuries.

*Within what time from the date of an accident can one file suit?*

Generally, within three years.

*What are the defenses to a charge of negligence?*

1. Assumption of risk. The plaintiff is precluded from recovery because the law presumes that he knew a peril or danger was to be encountered and that he was willing to undertake it. This occurs, for example, when a baseball fan attends a ball game and is struck by a fly ball. The spectator is said to assume the normal risks that are likely to follow from attendance at the ball park.

2. Imputed negligence. The plaintiff is precluded from recovery because negligence may be legally imputed to him. For example, when a driver exceeds the speed limit and his guest neither cau-

tions the driver to slow down nor threatens to get out of the car unless the driver does slow down, the guest's failure to act will, in many states, bar him from recovering damages against the driver should the latter be negligently involved in an accident.

3. Contributory negligence. The plaintiff is precluded from recovery because his failure to exercise ordinary care concurred with the negligence of the defendant, thus contributing to the injury as a proximate cause. If one automobile driver is speeding and the other fails to yield the right of way, both may be said to be contributorily negligent, and so both will be barred from recovery for damages to each other.

4. Comparative negligence. Here the legal principle, adopted in a number of states is that a verdict should be apportioned according to the faults of the parties. If the plaintiff is 20 per cent negligent, he is allowed to recover 80 per cent, whereas in contributory negligence he would be barred from recovery if he were only one per cent contributorily negligent.

*Is there any defense against a charge that the plaintiff was guilty of contributing to his own accident?*

Yes. Under the doctrine of "the last clear chance" a defendant will still be liable if he was aware of the plaintiff's peril, or was unaware of it through carelessness, and had the opportunity to avert the accident. If, for example, a motorist is stalled on the railroad tracks through no fault of his own and a train smashes into the car when the engineer could have stopped the train, the railroad might still be held guilty of negligence, because it had "a last clear chance" to avoid the accident. The "last clear chance" doctrine does not apply, however, when the negligence is coincident and concurring or when both parties are actively and simultaneously negligent.

*When alighting from a bus, you slip and injure yourself. Do you have a claim against the transit company?*

No. To obtain a settlement or to win a law suit, it must be shown that the bus operator was careless or reckless. A case of negligence may be made out, for example, when it is proved that the bus started off with a "sudden, violent, and unusual jerk." Or that the operator carelessly closed the door on the claimant's leg, or that there was some oily substance on the platform steps that caused the claimant to fall. Before there can be a recovery in a personal injury case, two things must be proved: first, that the party asserting a claim, the plaintiff, sustained some injury; and second, that the party against whom a claim is being made, the defendant, was guilty of negligence or carelessness in causing the accident. If there is an injury without negligence, there can be no legal recovery, though settlements occasionally are made to avoid the nuisance of a lawsuit. Similarly, if there is negligence without an injury, the claimant again has no valid claim.

*You buy a bottle of peroxide which, when you uncork it, explodes and causes you personal injuries. Against whom do you have a claim?*

You may sue the manufacturer. You may also have a claim against the retailer if you can prove that he was negligent in selling the peroxide to you.

*You buy a heating pad which, through faulty construction, gives off an excessive amount of heat, causing a severe burn. Against whom do you have a claim?*

Both the manufacturer and the seller of the heating pad are liable.

*At a seaside resort, a beach umbrella, blown through the air, strikes and injures Bob. Is the resort liable?*

Yes. The danger of such a happening should reasonably have been foreseen by the management.

*Your wife goes to a beauty shop to get a permanent wave. In the course of the treatment she suffers scalp burns. Is the beauty shop owner liable in damages?*

Yes. A beauty shop proprietor has a duty to exercise the care that a reasonably prudent and skillful person engaged in the same calling would exercise under the same or similar circumstances.

*You buy a soft drink from a confectionary store. While drinking its contents, you discover that a small mouse has somehow gotten into the bottle. You become ill and seek to recover damages against the manufacturer. Can you?*

Yes. A manufacturer of beverages is liable to the consumer for any injuries resulting from impurities in the beverage. However, if the manufacturer can prove (as he usually does) that he used the care, skill, and diligence in and about the manufacturing and bottling of the soft drink that a reasonably careful, skillful, and diligent person engaged in a similar business would use, that is all the law requires and the plaintiff is barred from recovery.

*Jones manufactures and places on the market a patent medicine. The dose prescribed on the bottle contains mercury in poisonous quantities. You purchase a bottle of the medicine, and your wife, taking the prescribed dose, is made seriously ill. Is the manufacturer liable to your wife?*

Yes. The negligence of the manufacturer consists in the fact that the dosage labeled on the bottle is misleading.

*You are a customer in a department store. You walk through the aisles, looking at goods displayed on the counters. While doing so, you stumble over an obstruction which you could have seen had you been looking at the floor instead of at the goods on the counter. Is the department store liable?*

Yes. You are entitled to rely on your belief that the aisle is reasonably safe for patrons of the store.

*While walking down the stairway of a department store, you slip, falling on your back. May the department store he held liable?*

No. The department store or its servants must have been negligent in some way before liability can be established. If, for example, your falling was caused by the existence of an oily substance that the employees of the store negligently failed to remove, the store would be liable.

*While walking down the aisle of a motion picture theater, you stumble and fall over a piece of torn carpet. You are injured. Is the theater liable?*

Yes, if you can show that the condition of the carpet was known to the owner of the theater or that it had existed for such a length of time that the theater owner should have known of it.

*John, who operates a hotel, employs Bill, as a plumber, to install
a shower bath. Bill negligently transposes the handles so that the
hot water pipe is labeled "cold." A guest, deceived by the label,
turns on the hot water and is scalded. Is the hotel liable?*

Yes. John is as liable as if he had done the work himself instead
of entrusting it to the plumber.

*Your dentist fails to remove part of the root of a tooth extracted
by him. He tells you, however, that he has done so. As a result,
your jaw becomes infected and you are hospitalized for a few
weeks. Can the dentist be charged with negligence?*

Yes. Dentists have been held liable when the improper treatment
of a cavity after extraction results in infection; when unsterilized
instruments have been used; when an impacted tooth has been
improperly removed; when several healthy teeth have been unnecessarily removed; and when the flow of blood from an artery
after an extraction has not been stanched. A dentist, like a physician, is not liable, however, for errors of judgment when the proper
treatment is reasonably in doubt.

*Albert and Bob are players on opposite sides in a football game.
In the course of the game, Bob tackles Albert and injures him.
Does Albert have a claim?*

No. The law infers that Albert, by participating in the game, has
consented to the risks that go with it.

*You invite Bob to your house for dinner. As Bob starts to ring your
doorbell, his leg goes through the porch floor. The defective condition of the porch is unknown to you. Are you liable to Bob?*

No. Bob can recover only for such defects as are known to the
occupant of the house. You have no duty to inspect for concealed
dangers. If Bob does sue you, you can defend yourself on the
ground that you did not know the porch floor was defective. If
evidence is produced to the contrary, the question becomes one
of fact to be resolved by a jury or by the court sitting as a jury. The
burden of proof is on Bob to show that you had knowledge of the
defect. If he can offer no such evidence, he will lose his case.

*You lend Bob your automobile to go for a ride. The car is defective, and while Bob is driving it, he is injured. You do not know of the defect. Does Bob have a claim against you?*

No. If you had loaned the car with a hidden defect to Bob, for a consideration, you would have been liable. But one who lends a car without receiving anything of value in return (the consideration) is not liable—except for defects of which he knows and which he should recognize as making the car dangerous to use.

*The Skyland Motor Company sells automobiles that are assembled from parts purchased from other manufacturers. The Skyland Company buys the chassis, including the brakes, from the Detroit Company. Through the Detroit Company's negligence, the brakes in one car are defective. The Skyland Company could have discovered the defect had a reasonable inspection been made; but once the car is assembled, the defect is not discoverable unless the entire car is torn down. The Skyland Company sells the car to the Johnson Company, a dealer in automobiles, which in turn sells it to Peters, a customer. While Peters is driving the car carefully, he collides with Jones's automobile, which is also being driven carefully. Jones is hurt because of the defective brakes. Against whom does Jones have a claim?*

The Detroit Company. Peters is not liable because he was driving carefully. The Detroit Company is responsible for the accident, since it allowed the car to go out with defective brakes, the proximate cause of the collision.

*A boiler insurance company, as part of its service, undertakes to inspect your boiler. It issues a certificate that the boiler is fit for use. Relying upon this certificate, you use the boiler. It explodes, because of a defect which a reasonably careful inspection would have disclosed. The explosion wrecks the adjacent building and causes the occupants therein bodily harm. Who is liable?*

The boiler insurance company. If it is part of a person's business or profession to give information or advice regarding matters upon which the personal safety of another depends, he must exercise reasonable care that the information is sufficiently accurate to insure the safety of such persons. The boiler company was negligent in failing to find a defect which could have been discovered.

*Albert's house contains a mass of oil-soaked rags in a corner of his basement. The rags take fire spontaneously, the fire spreading to Bob's house next door. Is Albert liable to Bob for the partial destruction of his home?*

Yes. Albert would be charged with knowledge of the combustible quality of the rags, although he may be actually ignorant of that fact.

*A strong swimmer sees a man floundering in deep water. Not knowing the man's identity, he goes to his rescue. When he discovers that the drowning man is a man whom he hates, the swimmer turns away, letting the other man drown. Is the swimmer liable in damages?*

No. A person is under no legal duty to aid or to protect another who has fallen into peril through no fault of the former.

*You see a blind man about to step into the street in front of an approaching automobile. You could prevent him from doing so, by word or touch, without delaying your own progress. Yet you do not do so. The blind man is run over and hurt. Can you be held liable?*

No. There is no legal duty imposed on you to go to the blind man's rescue.

*Jack operates a private sanitarium for the insane. Through the negligence of the guards employed by him, a homicidal maniac escapes and attacks Bob, a stranger. Is the hospital liable?*

Yes. One who voluntarily takes charge of a person who he knows, or should know, is likely to cause bodily harm to others if not controlled is liable in damages to the person harmed.

*Jack, a guest in your house, is seriously ill and in need of immediate medical attention. You call your physician on the telephone; he promises to come immediately, thereby causing you not to summon other medical aid. The physician neglects to come until several hours later. As a result, Jack's illness is aggravated. Is the physician liable?*

Yes. He is liable in damages for the aggravation of the illness. Jack had a right to rely on the promise that the physician would come promptly. The latter was negligent in failing to come as promised, or, at the very least, in failing to notify Jack that he would be tardy so that another physician might be called.

*A mining company knows that children in the neighborhood are in the habit of playing around the mouth of a pit. One of the employees of the company leaves a cartridge of blasting powder lying in a shed which the children, to the knowledge of the company, have used as a playhouse. Youngsters, coming to play, find the cartridge and use it as a plaything. They cause it to explode, the explosion injuring one of the children. Is the mining company liable?*

Yes. The company officials knew that the children were likely to trespass around the mouth of the pit. Knowingly to leave dynamite about under such circumstances constitutes negligence.

*A manufacturing company permits the children of its workmen to enter the factory in order to bring their fathers' lunches to them. A daughter of one of the employees comes into the factory for this purpose. While there, she is hurt, because some of the workmen of the company work carelessly. Is the company liable for injuries sustained by the daughter?*

Yes. In the above case, the daughter is legally called a "licensee," that is, a person privileged to enter or remain upon land with the landlord's consent, whether given by invitation or permission. To such persons the company would be liable for bodily harm caused by the workmen's failure to carry on their activities with reasonable care.

*During rush hours, the passengers on a streetcar are accustomed to crowd into it in a way likely to cause injury. The company fails to provide a sufficient staff of guards to prevent this practice. A passenger, hurt during a rush hour, files a claim against the street railway company. Is the company liable?*

Yes. The company, knowing of the crowded condition, must take active steps to prevent it. If a passenger is hurt as a result of the company's failure to provide the necessary guards, it will be liable.

*Jack employs a building contractor to build a row of houses according to certain plans and specifications supplied by Jack. These plans require material and workmanship so cheap and inferior that any competent builder would realize that houses so built might collapse at any time. The contractor builds the houses according to the plans and specifications. One of the homes collapses, thereby causing an injury to a prospective purchaser. Is the contractor liable?*

Yes. Liability is based on the fact that the contractor knew that the house would not be reasonably safe. When, nevertheless, he went ahead and erected it, he made himself liable to those lawfully on the premises who might be injured.

*While moving his household goods, Albert throws out of his window a heavy parcel, intending it to fall into a waiting cart. Before doing so, he calls out, "Watch out below." His aim misses, however, and the parcel falls onto the sidewalk. It strikes a pedestrian who did not hear the warning because his attention was directed to other matters. Is Albert liable to the pedestrian?*

Yes. The fact that Albert shouted a warning does not relieve him from liability. In throwing the parcel out of the window he acted in a reckless manner, and he must assume the responsibility for the consequences of his act. Albert should have waited until the sidewalk was actually clear of pedestrians before throwing out the parcel.

*A blind man walks along a sidewalk in which there is a hole. A normal man would see the hole and avoid it, but the blind man stumbles and falls as a consequence of stepping into it. Does he have a claim against the city for his injuries, assuming that the city paved the walk?*

Yes. The law makes allowance for physical defects that prevent a person's seeing or acting as a normal person would.

*While crossing a street at night, you step into a hole, fall, and break your arm. Do you have a claim against the city?*

Yes, if you can show that the hole or defect was in the street for a sufficiently long time that the city could have had notice of the defect, thus affording it an opportunity to repair it.

*Suppose the accident had occurred in the daytime. Would you still have a claim?*

Yes, but not a strong one. The principle is that, in the daytime, you could have avoided the hole if you had looked. A failure to look might make you guilty of contributing to the accident.

*A young girl is a train passenger, holding a ticket to Philadelphia. Falling asleep, she is carried beyond her station. The conductor asks her for additional fare, but having no money, she is unable to pay it. The conductor at once stops the train and puts the girl off at an isolated spot near the camp of a construction gang. It is a notorious fact that many members of this gang are of a rough and violent character. The girl is ravished by a member of this gang. Is the railroad liable?*

Yes. The railroad is guilty of negligence in ejecting the girl at a place which it knew, or should have known, was dangerous, thus affording an opportunity for misconduct.

*A telegraph company receives a message sent by Johnson, a wholesaler, calling for the delivery of five hundred bicycles. The message, reading "five bicycles," is delivered to the bicycle manufacturer who fills the order for five bicycles. As a result of the altered telegram, Johnson is unable to fill his five hundred orders. Does he have a claim against the telegraph company?*

Yes. A message must be delivered exactly as furnished. A telegraph company is liable for any damages resulting from an alteration.

*An engineer of a locomotive is driving it with the throttle open. On rounding a curve he sees a trespasser lying on the track a quarter of a mile away. The train runs over the man, killing him. Is the railroad liable?*

Yes. The engineer, by slackening the speed, could have stopped the train in time without injury to its passengers. In failing to do so, the engineer was guilty of negligence.

*Through the negligence of a railroad company, Bob sustains a compound fracture of his leg. Despite proper medical attention,*

*Bob never regains the full use of his leg. After his doctors have advised him that he can walk again, the bad condition of his leg causes him to fall and break his arm while crossing a pavement which, had his leg been normal, he would have traversed safely. Bob now seeks to recover damages against the railroad both for the injury to his leg and for his broken arm. Can he?*

Yes. If a company is liable for an injury that impairs the physical condition of a person's body, it is also liable for harm sustained in a later accident that would not have occurred had the person's bodily efficiency not been impaired.

*Cindy was seriously hurt and lay unconscious on the street. A doctor amputated her arm in order to save her life. Is the doctor liable to Cindy?*

No. Cindy's life was in danger, and the doctor is excused if he acted in good faith.

*Jack, without charge, lent to his neighbor, Ted, his stepladder, knowing it to be defective. Ted falls and injures himself. Is Jack liable?*

Yes.

*You negotiate to buy a business and send your accountant to go over the books. Your accountant reports that the assets of the business are worth $18,000. You pay $18,000 for the business. Shortly thereafter you discover that the assets are worth only $12,000. Against whom do you have a claim, if anyone?*

Your claim is only against your accountant. An accountant is generally held to a degree of care and vigilance commensurate with the standards of skill and efficiency ordinarily employed by those engaged in that profession. Since he was careless in reporting the actual amount of assets, and since your purchase of the business was based on his figures, your claim would be against him. You would have no claim against the seller.

*While you are on a jet-propelled plane flying between San Francisco and New York, the plane hits an air pocket. You are thrown into the air; your luggage falls into the aisle; a tray of food, which you were eating, is upset and ruins your clothes; and you sustain cuts about your face and scalp. Is the airline liable?*

No. An air carrier is not an insurer of passengers or of their safety. It is only liable for negligence on its part, although it is required, as a common carrier, to exercise the highest degree of care consistent with the nature of the undertaking. If it could be shown that the accident was unavoidable and that the pilot exercised as much care as possible under the circumstances, you would be barred from recovery.

*You are a passenger on a plane which, as a result of a bomb planted by some unknown person, explodes in mid-air. Half the passengers lose their lives. Fortunately, you escape with only minor injuries. Would you, or the representatives of the passengers who were fatally injured, have a claim against the airline?*

No. An air carrier is only responsible for the negligence of its pilot and its employees. The mere happening of an accident or of the explosion of a bomb is not negligence that would make the airline liable either for death or for injuries.

*While visiting an amusement park, you approach a caged bear too closely and are clawed by the animal. Is the owner of the amusement park liable?*

Probably not. The fact that you placed yourself in a position of danger would probably preclude you from recovering against the owner of the amusement park.

*While visiting an amusement park, you seat your six-year-old child on a carousel. After a minute or so your child is thrown from the carousel and seriously hurt. Do you have a claim against the owner of the amusement park?*

No. The owner of the carousel has a duty only to keep the device in a safe condition. If he can prove, as he usually can, that the machinery was operating satisfactorily, then you as a parent would be guilty of contributory negligence by placing the child in a position of danger, precluding your recovery from the owner.

*While at an amusement park, you take a ride on a roller coaster. During the ride the roller-coaster car gives a sudden jerk, the strap*

*buckled around your waist breaks, and you are hurled to the*
*ground and seriously injured. Is there any liability on the part of*
*the owner of the amusement park?*

Yes. Negligence consists in the failure to provide an adequate
safety strap. When the car's jerk caused the strap to break, a
prima-facie case of negligence was made out against the owner of
the amusement park, allowing you to recover damages.

*You attend a baseball game during which you are struck on the*
*shoulder by a foul ball. Do you have a claim for damages?*

No. The owners of a baseball park are not insurers of the safety
of the spectators. They discharge their duty of reasonable care
if they provide wire netting or similar screening in at least part
of the grandstand, so that those who desire such protection can
secure it. To sit in the bleachers without such protection is to do
so at your own peril. However, a person who attends a baseball
contest and is unfamiliar with the game may have a claim for
damages if he is struck by a foul ball, since he may not have been
aware of the hazards involved.

*While on a golf course, you are struck by a ball hit by a player*
*who does not call out "Fore" before hitting it. You are struck on*
*the head, knocked unconscious, and receive permanent injuries.*
*Do you have a claim against the player whose ball hit you?*

Only if you can prove negligence on the part of the golfer. Negligence may be implied, however, if a golfer fails to give timely
warning upon hitting the ball or if, without due care or consideration, he strikes the ball into a dense crowd. Failure to call out
"fore" in a voice loud enough for the other golfers to hear and to
warn persons in the probable line of the ball's flight may also be
evidence of negligence.

*While on your lawn, you are bitten by your neighbor's dog. You*
*had always thought it was a friendly animal. Do you have a claim?*

Only if the animal had a previous record of viciousness, known
to the owner, could you recover damages. Since the dog was
known to be friendly, he did not have such a vicious disposition as
to make his owner liable.

*You ride up in an automatic elevator to visit your friend. As it reaches the second floor, it drops back to the first-floor level. The impact injures you seriously. Is the owner of the building liable?*

Yes. The mere happening of the accident shifts to the defendant the burden of proof that he was not negligent in the care and maintenance of the elevator. To relieve himself of liability, he would have to prove and convince a jury that he had had the elevator inspected and that he had given it reasonable care and maintenance. Unless he could establish all these facts, the chances are you would be able to collect damages.

*You are a passenger on a ferry boat during a heavy fog. You are injured when the boat collides with another vessel. Can you successfully assert a claim?*

Yes. The owner of a ferry boat is held to the highest degree of care consistent with the nature of his undertaking. If the pilot could not operate during the fog, he should not have left the pier. The fact that he ventured out under such a hazard would make the owners liable for any negligence on his part.

*While at a filling station getting gasoline, your car is set ablaze because an overflow of gas runs from the tank onto the concrete floor. Do you have a claim against the filling-station owner?*

Yes. It was the filling-station attendant's duty to make sure that the hose through which the gasoline passed was securely fastened to the car before he allowed any fluid to flow from the pump, and to take every precaution to prevent any overflow. Since the overflow was caused by the attendant's carelessness, he, as well as the station owner, would be held liable for any injuries sustained.

*While attending a professional football game, the stand in which you are seated collapses. Do you have a claim against the owner of the stadium?*

Yes. Your ticket for the football game was an implied contract that the stand was reasonably fit and proper for your use. Although it is true that the owners are not insurers of the safety of the spectators who come upon their premises, they do owe them the highest degree of care. Since the chances are that the stadium was structurally defective or was not kept in proper repair, a suit for negligence could be successfully maintained against the owners and recovery for damages would be allowed.

*You enter a Turkish bath and slip on a step made hazardous by the presence of soapy water. Can you recover against the owner of the establishment?*

No. The owner of a Turkish bath is only held to the exercise of reasonable care. A patron should anticipate that the water on the floor of the bath might be slippery or soapy, one of the calculated risks assumed upon entry into a Turkish bath.

*You buy a bottle of soft drink from your neighborhood grocer. On returning home, you open the bottle, pour out most of the contents in a large glass, and consume half of it. When you put down the glass, you notice several bugs swimming around in the bottle. You suffer no ill effects. Do you have a claim against either the grocer or the bottling company?*

On the facts, you have a claim against neither. To assert a claim for negligence, you first have to prove the existence of a foreign substance negligently allowed to enter the bottle, and, second, some injury as a result of drinking the contaminated contents. Since you did not become ill or otherwise suffer an injury, you would have no claim.

*You take a prescription issued by your family physician to your neighborhood pharmacist. The prescription calls for three different ingredients. Temporarily out of one of the ingredients, the pharmacist substitutes one he thinks has the same medicinal value, and which he honestly believes is harmless. You take the medicine and become quite ill. Calling in your family physician, you explain what occurred. He learns from the pharmacist that one ingredient was substituted for another. Do you have a claim against the druggist?*

Yes. A pharmacist is not allowed to substitute his judgment for that of a physician; nor is he allowed to substitute one ingredient for another. Should he do so, and be discovered, the pharmacist not only may be sued for malpractice but stands a good chance of having his license revoked.

*Your physician writes out a prescription for digitalis, which is filled by your druggist. You become seriously ill. It turns out that the physician prescribed an excessive dosage. Is the pharmacist liable?*

Both the physician and the druggist are liable, the former for prescribing an excessive dosage, the latter for filling the prescription when he knew the dosage to be dangerous. The pharmacist relieves himself of liability on any questionable prescription if he verifies the dosage of the ingredients in the prescription by phoning the attending physician.

CHAPTER 23

AUTOMOBILE ACCIDENTS

*What should you do if you are involved in an automobile accident?*

**1.** Obtain the names and addresses of all or as many witnesses as possible.

**2.** Immediately notify your insurance company or your attorney, if you have one—the sooner, the better—so that he may make a thorough investigation as quickly as possible.

**3.** If injured, call your regular attending physician.

**4.** Do not sign any statement without the advice of your counsel; do not sign any statement presented to you by a claim adjuster or insurance adjuster.

**5.** If at all possible, arrange to have photographs taken of the damaged automobile, as well as of the skid marks or other physical evidence, including the point of impact between the two vehicles.

*What damages are you entitled to if you are injured or otherwise negligently hurt in an automobile accident?*

You are entitled to compensation for all wages or salary lost because of your accident and to compensation for your pain and suffering. The former damages are known as "out-of-pocket expenses" and include, besides income lost, medical, hospital, and surgical bills and any other expenses that may be a direct result of your injury and treatment. The phrase "pain and suffering" is much more loosely interpreted, and compensation depends, in part, on the nature and extent of the injuries and on whether they are permanent in nature. This is why it is always desirable, in all accident cases, to employ counsel to represent you, since they are in a much better position to determine what damages to ask for any given injury. Many an overanxious claimant has settled a claim for a back injury for a fraction of what an experienced attorney might have procured because the claimant did not fully

363

understand the nature of his injuries or that the symptoms might recur weeks or even months later.

*You proceed to cross a street at an intersection with a traffic signal in your favor. The signal changes to red before you finish crossing. As you are halfway over, you are struck by an automobile that is being operated within the speed limits. Can you recover from the driver?*

Yes. The green light gives the pedestrian the right of way. He continues to have the right of way even when the traffic signal changes while he is crossing. The motorist is therefore guilty of negligence in striking the pedestrian, since he deprived the pedestrian of his right of way.

*You invite a friend for a ride in your automobile and proceed to drive at high speed in a moderate-speed zone. Your friend protests that you are going much too fast and pleads that you slow down, but you brush his protests aside. Soon you are involved in an accident in which your companion is injured. Are you liable for damages to the passenger of your car?*

Yes. Had your friend acquiesced in your violation of the speed law, he would have been guilty of contributory negligence and forfeited his claim for damages. Since he did protest against the excessive speed, he would, if the court believed his testimony, be in a strong position to collect damages.

*Before purchasing a used car, you test the brakes and find them to be in sound operating condition. You buy the automobile. The very next day, while you are driving, the brakes suddenly fail and you are involved in an accident with another vehicle. Would you be liable, assuming you were not otherwise negligent?*

No. Since you had tested the brakes before buying the car and had found them satisfactory, you could not be held responsible for their concealed defect. You would have a claim against the seller of the automobile for damages to your own car caused by the defective brakes.

*While driving on a downgrade, you suddenly apply your brakes to avoid striking a small child who darts across the road. The inci-*

*dent causes your car to turn over, injuring your passenger on the front seat. The child escapes unharmed. Have you been negligent so that the passenger can collect damages against you?*

No. From the facts there is no indication of negligence. In attempting to avoid striking the child by applying your brakes, you did only what the law says you have a right to do.

*While pursuing the driver of a stolen automobile, a motorcycle policeman crosses an intersection at a high rate of speed and strikes a pedestrian who is crossing the street properly. Is the officer liable to the pedestrian in damages?*

Yes. The mere fact that an officer is in the pursuit of his public duty does not relieve him from operating his vehicle with care. Driving at an excessive rate of speed so as to strike a pedestrian at an intersection is evidence of negligence, allowing the pedestrian to recover damages.

*You lend your automobile to a friend to go on a special trip. While on the highway, he is involved in an accident with another automobile as the result of his negligence. Would you, as owner, be liable in damages to the operator of the other vehicle?*

No, in most states. In some states the owner would be liable for the negligence of a driver operating his car irrespective of whether it was for his own benefit or for the pleasure of the driver.

*Your employer asks you to deliver some groceries to a customer and return to the store promptly. After making the delivery, you decide to stop off to see a friend who lives in another part of the town. En route you strike a small child as a result of your negligent driving. Would the owner of the car be liable in damages?*

No. The test is whether you had so deviated from your duties at the time of the accident that you can no longer be considered as acting within the scope of your employment. Since you were on a mission completely unconnected with your errand, you—not your employer—would be liable in damages for any negligence. Had the accident occurred while you were either proceeding to or returning from the errand, your employer could have been held, but since it did not, you yourself would be responsible.

*A reporter for a local newspaper is involved in an accident while en route to a fire in his own automobile. The injured person sues the newspaper instead of the reporter. Can he recover?*

Yes. Here the reporter was obviously acting within the scope of his employment, and it is immaterial that at the time of the accident he was using his own car instead of his employer's.

*Your automobile stalls on the streetcar tracks, even though you are driving slowly. The operator of an approaching streetcar fails to keep a lookout, and a collision results. At the hearing it is brought out that the operator of the streetcar would have discovered your plight in time to have avoided the accident had he kept a sharp lookout. Do you have a claim, even though you placed yourself in a position of danger on the streetcar tracks?*

Yes. You did contribute to the happening of the accident by stalling on the streetcar tracks, but had the operator of the streetcar used due care, the accident could have been avoided. Therefore the streetcar company would be liable.

*While crossing a street, not at the intersection but in the middle of the block, a pedestrian is struck by a motorist who has exceeded the speed limit by five miles an hour. The pedestrian sustains a broken leg. Is he barred from recovering damages because he crossed in the middle of the block?*

No. While it is true that a pedestrian may cross a street wherever he pleases, he is held to a much higher degree of care if he does not cross the street at an intersection. The fact that the motorist exceeded the speed limit would probably convince a jury that it was he who actually caused the accident rather than the pedestrian crossing in the middle of the block.

*You invite a friend to take a drive in your new convertible. Your friend knows that you have had a couple of drinks too many, but nevertheless accepts your invitation. An accident occurs as a result of your intoxication, and your friend is seriously injured. Are you liable?*

No. In accepting your offer, your friend assumed the risk. Since your intoxication was the proximate cause of the accident, the passenger would be barred from recovery.

*You park your automobile and leave your friend, who is intoxicated, in the car with the ignition key in place. During your brief absence, your friend drives the car away and wrecks it. Do you, as owner of the car, have a claim against him?*

No. In allowing an intoxicated person to remain in the car with the ignition key in place, you are guilty of contributory negligence. This would bar you from effectively asserting a claim.

*A three-year-old child runs across the street in the middle of the block and when about halfway across is struck by a motorist. The driver, just before impact, was manipulating the dials of his radio and his attention was momentarily diverted. The child had crossed in the middle of the block and between two parked automobiles. The child's parents sue the motorist. Can they recover?*

Probably. A three-year-old child cannot be held guilty of contributory negligence. If it could be proved that the motorist was diverted just before the impact, he would be held liable in damages, despite the fact that the child ran from between two parked cars. It is the motorist's negligence that is the proximate cause of the accident. Had the child been over four years of age, the question of whether he had contributed to the happening of the accident by his own carelessness would have had to be considered by the jury; but since the child was three, no negligence can be imputed to him.

*You violate a traffic ordinance by parking your car on the wrong side of the street. A five-year-old child runs from behind your parked vehicle and is killed by a passing motorist, through no fault of the driver. The evidence indicates that if your car had been legally parked, facing in the opposite direction, the obstacle to the child's vision and that of the driver of the second automobile would have been as great as it was with your car illegally parked. Do the child's parents have a claim against you?*

No. It is plain that parking your car on the wrong side of the street was not the proximate cause of the accident. Since a five-year-old child running from behind a parked vehicle is not in the favored position of a three-year-old, he would probably be charged with negligence so as to preclude his recovery.

*You are seated on a doorstep. In front of you children are playing ball on the sidewalk. Bert is driving his car down the street at a legal speed. Although he sees the children, he does not slacken his speed or bring his car under more perfect control. One of the youngsters darts into the street in pursuit of the ball. Realizing that Bert will be unable to stop his automobile in time to avoid running down the child, you rush forward and pull the youngster out of danger. In doing so, you slip and fall under the car, which runs over you, breaking your leg. Do you have a claim against the driver of the automobile?*

Yes. Bert was obliged both to slacken his speed and to observe a higher degree of care when he first saw the children. He was negligent in not doing the first, and since your injuries were caused by your attempt to prevent the child from being injured, you would have a claim against him.

*You allow a sixteen-year-old boy to drive your automobile, knowing that he has never driven one before. He drives the car with you in it. While doing so, he causes a collision in which the other driver is injured. The driver files suit against you. Can he recover?*

Yes. The fact that you allowed a sixteen-year-old youngster to operate your automobile, knowing that he has never operated one before, is certainly strong evidence of negligence. Under these facts, it is likely that damages would be obtained against you.

*You hail a taxicab and tell the driver you have but ten minutes to catch your train, directing him to ignore all traffic signals. You offer him $10 if he will get you to the station in time to catch your train. While the driver is speeding, the cab collides with another vehicle, causing personal injuries to the driver of the other car. Are you liable?*

Both you and the taxicab driver would be liable—you because you knew, or should have known, that obedience to your orders was likely to cause injury, and the taxicab driver in following your instructions to violate the law. If you had been injured in the accident, you would be barred from recovery against the cab company because of your own contributory negligence.

*You are negligently run down by a motorist and sustain a fractured leg. A short time thereafter the motorist becomes insane. May he still be sued for damages?*

Yes. Insanity is no defense for an automobile accident, even if it were proved that the motorist was actually insane at the time of the accident.

*While driving your car carefully along a public highway, you accidentally go over a fairly large hole, and a tire blows out. The car goes into a ditch, and your wife strikes her head against the windshield. You are uninjured. Does your wife have a claim against the city?*

Yes. The city or state is guilty of negligence in allowing a large hole to remain unrepaired. Your case would be stronger, however, if the accident happened at night, since then you would have been unable actually to see the hole before striking it. Even during the day, however, you would have a claim, but your case might be weakened because you had a better opportunity to see the hole and so avoid it. In addition to a claim for personal injuries, you could also recover for the damage to your tire.

*You are driving your automobile on a public highway, but you are not carrying an operator's permit, nor do you have license plates attached to your car. You are driving with reasonable care when, through no fault of your own, the car falls through an unsafe bridge, although unknown to you to be unsafe. You are seriously injured. The hazardous condition of the bridge is the result of the city's negligence, the city officials having had sufficient notice of the defect. Would the city be liable?*

Yes. While it is true that you violated the law by not having either an operator's permit or license tags, the fact is that the car would have fallen through the bridge whether it bore plates or not.

*You park your automobile unlawfully on a street where no parking is allowed at any time. A second parked car runs into your car because its owner failed to set the emergency brake. Do you have a claim against the owner of the other vehicle?*

Yes. The negligence lies in the failure of the operator of the second vehicle to set his emergency brake, and he would therefore be responsible for any damages caused to any vehicle. The fact that your car was illegally parked would not preclude you from recovery in a civil action, the traffic violation being a criminal offense.

*While driving an automobile at night on the highway, a driver strikes a pedestrian crossing at an intersection. Actually, he was unable to see the pedestrian because he was blinded by the headlights of a vehicle coming in the opposite direction. Is he relieved of responsibility because he was blinded by the headlights of the other car?*

No. At an intersection a pedestrian has the right of way to which a motorist must yield. However, in this case he was prevented from seeing the pedestrian because be was blinded by the headlights of the vehicle approaching from the opposite direction. If the motorist could convince a jury, by some disinterested witness, that he was in fact blinded by the headlights, he might succeed in barring the claim of the injured pedestrian. But since the pedestrian has the right of way, he is in a much stronger position to assert his claim. The motorist's unsupported word on what took place would probably be unconvincing to the average jury.

*While driving your automobile, you come to a stop sign and stop. A few seconds later you attempt to cross the boulevard and are struck by another automobile. You contend that you obeyed the law by stopping at the sign, and that it wasn't your fault that you were struck since the motorist on the boulevard was coming from your left. Are you correct?*

No. To attempt to cross a road or a boulevard from a stop sign is to do so at your peril. A favored driver has a right to assume that the unfavored motorist will yield the right of way up to the moment of impact.

*To avoid striking a child who runs in front of your car, you apply your brakes quickly and bring your car to a complete halt. An automobile directly in back of you crashes into your car. Can you recover from the owner of the second car?*

Yes. A motorist is obliged to have his car under control at all times. His running into your car indicates that he did not have his car under control, and he is therefore presumed negligent.

*Your wife is a passenger in your automobile. You are involved in a collision with a second car because of your negligence. Does your wife have a claim against you?*

No. A wife cannot sue her husband, nor a husband his wife, for negligence of either, since the law presumes there would be too much opportunity for fraud or collusion. A brother may sue a sister, and a sister a brother.

*You park your automobile in front of your house and set the emergency brake. A few minutes later you are informed that your car "ran away" and crashed into a street light, causing $75 worth of damage. Are you responsible?*

If the accident was due to defective brakes and you had failed to check them recently, you would be responsible. If you had had them checked, you would be relieved of liability.

*You have your car parked in your driveway so that it obstructs the sidewalk. Wishing to pass, a pedestrian politely asks you to move your car, which you refuse to do. Attempting to walk around your automobile, the pedestrian slips and injures himself. Does he have a claim against you?*

Yes. Your refusal to move the car, as well as your violation of an ordinance in blocking the sidewalk, would be considered the proximate cause of the accident.

*While crossing the street at an intersection, you walk into the side of an automobile and sustain personal injuries. Is the owner of the car liable?*

No. To recover, one must have exercised due care. Walking into the side of an automobile suggests a lack of such care.

*While crossing the street on a rainy, windy day, with an umbrella over your head, you are struck by an automobile you did not see or hear approaching. Would you be able to collect for your injuries?*

No, since you were guilty of contributory negligence in crossing the way you did.

*You are driving on a highway at night within the prescribed speed limit. Suddenly a man emerges from the woods alongside the road, runs directly into the path of your car, and is injured. Are you liable in damages?*

No. Since there is no negligence on your part, the accident would be considered legally unavoidable. Had you been speeding, the injured pedestrian could have recovered from you.

*You drive your automobile while drunk, and are involved in an accident, even though you were not negligent. Would you be liable in damages to the pedestrian because of your drunken driving?*

No. The test is whether you were negligent, not whether you were driving while intoxicated. Since you were not negligent, there would be no liability. You would be fined for drunken driving, however.

*A mail truck runs into your automobile through no fault of yours. Can you sue the United States Government?*

Yes. Until recently a suit against the United States government could only be instituted by seeking permission from the government. Since the passing of the Federal Tort Claims Act, suit can now be filed without such consent.

*You park your car close to a corner, but not on the streetcar tracks. A streetcar rounding the corner strikes your automobile because you are parked too close to the car tracks. Would the transit company be liable?*

Yes. It was the duty of the operator of the streetcar to make certain that he had proper clearance before attempting to make the turn.

*You carry liability insurance as required by your state. You cross over the border into Mexico with your automobile, and are involved in an accident. Would your policy cover you in Mexico?*

No, not unless arrangements were made with your insurance company satisfactory to the Mexican government before you crossed into Mexico. The usual method of securing protection is to obtain insurance in an American border town before entering Mexico.

*Who has the right of way at an intersection—a motorist or a cyclist?*

The usual right-of-way rule applies to both; that is, the vehicle on the right has the right of way over a vehicle approaching on the left. The same rule applies to a person on horseback and to a person driving animals on a road.

*You operate your automobile on a downgrade where children are coasting on their sleds. You injure one of them. You set up as a defense that you are not responsible for the accident, since the road is no place for coasting and such coasting should be done on private property or on the sidewalk. Is your contention legally sound?*

No. A motorist must use reasonable care to avoid injury to those coasting on snow-covered highways.

*The bus on which you are a passenger is involved in an accident with an automobile that carelessly runs into the bus while the bus is proceeding carefully along its route. As a result of the collision, you sustain serious injuries. Because the motorist is uninsured, you assert a claim against the bus company. Will you be able to collect from them?*

No. A bus company is not an insurer of your safety, and unless you can prove negligence against them, you could not recover. Your claim, therefore, would be against the uninsured motorist—for whatever it was worth.

*While driving your automobile carefully, you have a sudden heart attack, your car careening into an automobile and damaging it. Actually, you were completely unaware that you had any trouble with your heart. Can the owner of the damaged car recover damages from you?*

No. For the owner of the damaged car to collect damages, there must be some evidence of negligence on your part. Since you were unaware of any damage to your heart, there can be no recovery.

*A husband drove his wife's automobile on a trip to the cemetery where his mother was buried. The husband proceeded, without directions from his wife, to visit his brother. Returning from his brother's house, the husband was involved in an accident resulting in injuries to the rider of a motorcycle. Would the husband, wife, or both be liable in damages to the driver of the motorcycle, assuming negligence on the part of the husband in operating the automobile?*

Only the husband would be liable, since at the time of the accident he was not on his wife's business, but on business of his own.

*After his son's operator's license was revoked, a father allowed him to use the family automobile, as the result of which the youngster struck a pedestrian through his negligent driving. The pedestrian enters suit against the father. Would he be liable in damages?*

Yes. Since the father knew that his son's license had been revoked, it was negligence on his part to permit the youngster to drive the car.

*In violation of an ordinance, a truck is proceeding along a highway without a taillight. A motorist crashes into the rear of the truck. In defense, the motorist alleges that the accident was caused by the truck driver's failure to have his taillight on so that the rear of the truck would have been visible. Is his defense valid?*

No. If the motorist had been reasonably observant, he would have spotted the rear of the truck with his own headlights and so could have avoided running into the truck in the first place.

*A truck driver, stopping at a traffic signal, gives a lift to a waiting pedestrian. Shortly thereafter the truck, through the negligence of its driver, is involved in an accident in which the rider is seriously injured. The rider seeks to recover against the owner of the truck instead of the operator. Can he do so?*

No. The operator of the truck had no authority to invite anyone to ride with him. Under these conditions, the only person from whom recovery could be had would be the driver of the truck himself. If, on the other hand, the driver is clothed with apparent authority to invite or allow persons to enter the truck, the owner would be liable.

*A pedestrian stands on the curb in a grassy area in the middle of a two-way boulevard. The night is rainy and misty. She stoops to retrieve her purse, which had fallen onto the highway, and is struck by an automobile. May she recover damages?*

No, since she was guilty of contributory negligence.

*A drunk attempts to cross a street at an intersection, and in doing so is struck by a passing automobile. The motorist's attorney pleads in defense that he was not negligent, since the pedestrian was drunk at the time he was struck. How would the court rule in this case?*

The court would probably overrule the motorist's contention. Drunk or sober, every pedestrian has the right of way at an intersection not marked by a traffic signal. Despite the fact that the pedestrian in this case was intoxicated, he still had the right of way, and if the motorist knew, or by the exercise of reasonable care should have known, that the pedestrian was drunk, he owed the man an even higher degree of care.

*Dan invites Paul, his guest, to take a drive in his automobile. Paul accepts the invitation. Due to Dan's negligence in handling the car, it collides with a truck and Paul is hurt. Paul now seeks to hold Dan liable. May he?*

Yes, in the absence of a state law to the contrary. Dan owes Paul reasonable care in driving the automobile, even though Paul is a guest and not a paid passenger. In at least half the states, however, by statute a guest may recover only when the driver has been guilty of "gross negligence," "recklessness," or "willful or wanton misconduct."

*In the above case, suppose that Paul has been hurt by the combined negligence of Dan and the truck driver. Could Paul recover against both?*

Yes.

*Paul, a youngster of three years, is left unattended on a busy street by his parents. He suffers injuries when struck by an automobile. Do Paul's parents have a claim against the driver, assuming the latter is negligent?*

Yes. Paul is too young to be held responsible for his parents' carelessness in leaving him unattended.

*You permit your chauffeur, who is in the habit of driving at an excessive rate of speed, to use your car to take his family to the seashore. While driving the car for this purpose, the chauffeur drives recklessly, injuring Paul, a pedestrian. Against whom has Paul a claim?*

Against both you and the chauffeur. You are negligent in permitting him to have the car when you know his habit of excessive speed. For whatever it is worth, the chauffeur may also be held liable.

*Bill attempts to drive his automobile across a track in full view of an approaching locomotive. He believes that he has ample time to cross, but he misjudges the train's speed. His car is struck by the locomotive, and Bill sustains serious injuries. He seeks to collect damages from the railroad. Can he?*

No. By driving across the track in full view of an approaching locomotive, Bill is guilty of contributory negligence. His duty is to "stop, look, and listen" before proceeding. By failing to do so he assumes the risk involved.

CHAPTER 24

## HANDLING YOUR OWN ACCIDENT CASE

*What can you do if you are involved in an accident case?*

There are two things you can do if you get hurt in an accident. One is to call in an experienced negligence lawyer who will handle the case for a share of whatever amount is obtained by way of suit or settlement. The other is to attempt to settle your own case, dealing with the other party or insurance company without the assistance of a lawyer.

*What are the advantages of each method?*

Each procedure has certain advantages. By calling in an experienced personal-injury or negligence attorney you absolve yourself of all trouble and responsibility. A competent lawyer, for example, will make a complete investigation of the facts in order to determine liability—that is, whether the defendant has been legally guilty of such carelessness or negligence as to make him responsible for damages. Your lawyer will interview witnesses, have photographs taken when necessary, obtain copies of the accident report filed with the motor vehicle commission, see that you are examined by physicians or surgeons who will give you the benefit of any medical doubt, and calculate what your injuries, pain, and suffering are worth. He will negotiate with the claims adjuster until he arrives at a satisfactory settlement or is forced to file suit and try the case before a judge and jury. In many states it may take several years before the trial is actually reached. Of course, where the injuries are serious and permanent, where the matter of liability is in doubt, and where you have neither the temperament nor the skill to handle your own accident case, you are far better off calling in a skilled attorney and paying him a portion of what you receive by way of settlement or suit. There is the added advantage that in case he loses, you don't have to pay him at all.

*Can you give some examples of accident cases one could handle one's self?*

There are many such cases. Let's say you are driving home from work and are stopped at a red traffic signal. The first thing you know a car has crashed into the rear end of your automobile with such force that you are thrown to the right side of your car, twisting and straining your back in the process. When you gather your wits together, you painfully get out of the car, obtain the name and address of the operator of the other vehicle, together with the name of his insurance carrier, and notice there is considerable property damage to your car. No policeman is in sight.

Another example is that you are in a supermarket doing the family shopping. While walking down the aisle you stumble over a box protruding from the lower shelf and find yourself on the floor writhing in pain from a sprained ankle. You are helped to your feet by a clerk who calls the manager. The manager takes your name and address.

These are types of cases where you may have much to gain and little to lose if you try to settle your own case. In fact, if you have average intelligence and can follow a few simple rules, there is no reason why you can't handle the matter yourself. If you do, you may save yourself considerable time and money.

*What do lawyers charge in handling an accident case?*

In personal-injury cases a lawyer will usually charge about one-third of the amount recovered if the case is settled without suit; 40 percent if the case goes to court; and 50 percent if he has to take an appeal. What the actual fee is going to be depends on the arrangements you make as incorporated in the power of attorney you sign when you authorize your lawyer to act on your behalf. You should read the power of attorney very carefully before you sign so that you know exactly what the charges will be.

*Is the attorney's fee based on the gross or net amount of the settlement?*

This depends on the arrangements you make with him. Let's assume, for example, that you have signed a power of attorney in which you agree to give your counsel one-third of the total amount received. The amount received is $1500. Under this arrangement you get $1,000, your lawyer $500. But what about the actual losses and expenses you have incurred in connection with your accident? You have lost two weeks from work at $150 per week, have a medical bill of $100, plus property damage of $98. Under the power of attorney all these expenses will have to be paid by you, reducing your net share from the accident to $502 instead of $1,000.

*Do all lawyers do this?*

No. Some lawyers will first deduct all expenses from the amount of settlement then charge one-third or whatever fee is agreed upon of the net amount. Done this way, your special damages or out-of-pocket expense of $498 will be deducted from the $1,500 leaving a net of $1,002 to be divided, one-third to your counsel, the remainder to you. Obviously you have fared better with the second arrangement.

*What kind of cases, then, should one attempt to handle?*

In the simple personal-injury or property damage, as explained above, it may be advantageous to try for a settlement yourself. For one thing you save an attorney's fee which, as we've seen, is likely to be substantial. And in dealing directly with an insurance company, you may be able to obtain a quicker settlement. Some lawyers, in their anxiety to build up a case and therefore get as much money as possible, tend to exaggerate the nature and extent of the injuries. They suggest that the client stay home from work unnecessarily and run up excessive medical and other bills. More valid reasons why some attorneys postpone settlements are that their offices are too busy to properly and promptly process their client's claims. They also require a lapse of time to determine whether or not there's going to be any residual permanent disability. To settle a case prematurely, without knowing how much permanent damage there will be and how it will affect a client's wage earning capacity—as well as the pain and suffering he may have to endure for an indefinite period, could be disastrous to the individual though profitable to the insurance carrier. So, where the injuries are serious and involve a question of permanent disability, the client should allow an experienced personal-injury attorney to handle the case. In the long run he will be far better off even if he does have to pay a fee.

*What should you remember if you are going to file a claim?*

To recover damages in any negligence case—whether handled by you or your attorney—you must prove both negligence and injuries. One without the other is insufficient. Before you file a claim be reasonably certain that the defendant (the party against whom you are asserting a claim) has been negligent or careless and that you yourself have been relatively free of fault. Next, obtain the names and addresses of witnesses to the accident. If at all possible, get your witnesses to give you a simple statement of what they saw, preferably in their own handwriting. The number of witnesses is relatively unimportant. What counts is their quality, reputation, character, and freedom from bias.

*What should you do if your injuries prevent you from obtaining witnesses?*

If you are trying to settle the case yourself and the injuries prevent you from obtaining witnesses, call in a professional investigator listed under "Investigators" in the yellow pages of your telephone directory and have him make the investigation for you, including the taking of necessary photographs. Obtaining such evidence is exceedingly helpful. If, for example, you are struck by an automobile while crossing at an intersection and claim you had the green light, which the motorist hotly disputes, your case is weakened unless you can back up your statement with eyewitnesses.

*What is the next step?*

If you are handling the case yourself, write to the defendant or insurance carrier, or both, or have someone write in your behalf, stating in simple language that as a result of the negligence or carelessness of the defendant you have been hurt on a certain date at a certain place. If by the end of two or three weeks no one has been in touch with you, write again. Insurance carriers are normally just as eager to reach a settlement as you are. If you do not hear from anyone after a couple of months, get in touch with your lawyer.

*What about the injuries?*

Make sure they receive prompt and proper attention. For minor injuries your own physician should normally be adequate. If you are taken to a hospital for emergency treatment, obtain a copy of the hospital report. Also obtain a copy of the police report as well as a copy of the report sent to the motor vehicle commission.

When the injuries are serious, you or your physician should consult a specialist. If, for example, you have suffered a badly twisted ankle or a broken arm, you will require the specialized services of an orthopedic surgeon.

*What if the insurance investigator asks for a written statement as to how the accident occurred?*

You should not sign any such statement. The insurance investigator will have made his own investigation and will determine, from all the facts and witnesses, whether or not there is any liability on the part of the defendant whom he represents. By signing a statement you may be providing the insurance company with ammunition it may use against you.

*Should you try to settle your claim before the physician discharges you?*

No. Before considering settlement you should have been discharged by your physician and/or surgeon and have in your possession medical reports from either or both of them. The reports should clearly indicate the nature and extent of your injuries, whether or not you have been cured or merely reached your maximum medical improvement, the percentage of permanent or residual disability, if any, the number of treatments or visits, whether or not you will have pain and suffering in the future, and the amount of the medical, surgical, hospital, drug bills, taxi fares, and other legitimate expenses paid for by you as a result of the accident.

*How much should you ask for in settling a claim yourself?*

In attempting to settle the ordinary, run-of-the-mill case yourself —where there are no permanent injuries—add your special damages or expenses up to and including the time you will have been fully recovered and multiply the figure by three or four. This will give you a rough idea of what your case is worth in terms of settlement. If your loss of wages, medical, and other expenses runs to one thousand dollars, a reasonable settlement would be in the neighborhood of three or four thousand dollars. If you are a housewife who had no lost wages but have had extensive pain and suffering in addition to a physical injury, the settlement figure might be somewhat less.

*What factors affect the value of a personal injury claim?*

1. Whether or not you have a prior record of existing claims or injuries; in short whether or not you are claim prone.

2. Your appearance, personality, and the impression you make.

3. Your educational and cultural background.

4. Whether you live in a large city or rural area. If the former, your chances of getting more are substantially greater.

5. Whether you are under medical treatment for several months or more, or merely for a few days.

6. Whether the negligence or liability is clear or doubtful; if the latter, the chances are you will get less.

*Do you have to comply with the insurance company's request that you be examined by one of their physicians?*

While you do not have to comply at the early stages of the proceedings, the defendant does have a right to have you examined by one of his physicians. Insurance company physicians tend, in general, to minimize injuries of plaintiffs, just as plaintiffs tend to exaggerate the value of their claims. Usually a compromise is worked out based on the often conflicting reports of the two physicians.

*What if you and the claims adjuster can't agree on an offer of settlement?*

If you feel the offer made to you does not adequately compensate for your injuries and expenses, you would be wise to consult an experienced negligence or personal-injury attorney. Explain the facts to him, what you have been offered, and why you think you should get more. Bear in mind that you will have to pay an attorney's fee, which may not leave you any better off in the long run. Some lawyers, if convinced you have a good case, will charge only a percentage over and above what you yourself have been offered. Others will still insist on a portion of the entire amount recovered, including the sum you have been already offered.

*What is the effect of signing a release?*

In signing a release for a personal-injury claim, you in effect relinquish all future claims you may have against the defendant arising from the injury forming the basis of the settlement. This is true even if the injuries become worse in the future, or the pain and suffering continues for a much greater period than anticipated. Setting aside a release is extremely difficult. So do not sign unless you are convinced that the amount of money received is, under all the circumstances, fair and reasonable. Finally, in cases where the injury is truly serious or the damage likely to be permanent such as a head or knee injury or a face that has been burned or scarred and requires plastic surgery—to mention only a few possibilities—you should never try to settle your own case. To do so invites almost certain financial loss and legal complications beyond the scope of the average person.

*Does conviction in a traffic court preclude your recovering damages in a civil suit?*

Not necessarily. The fact that you are convicted or acquitted in a traffic court is inadmissible in a civil court, although the evidence given in a traffic court proceeding may be introduced to contradict your testimony in the civil case.

*What should you do in case of an automobile accident?*

1. Give whatever aid and assistance you can to those who are injured by calling either the police or an ambulance. Under no circumstances should you leave the scene of the accident without identifying yourself. To do so is usually a criminal offense as well as damaging in a civil suit.

2. If the police arrive, avoid any arguments, which may leave a bad taste in their mouths. You do not have to sign any statements as to how the accident occurred; hence make as few admissions as possible. Be sure you obtain the investigating officer's name and badge number for future identification.

3. If at all possible get the names and addresses of witnesses favorable to your version of the accident.

4. Notify your insurance carrier immediately that you have been involved in an accident—especially if it is a serious one; if the accident is a minor one, involving no injuries and little property damage, try to settle the case yourself.

5. As soon as possible make a sketch of the scene of the accident, showing the direction in which each car was traveling, whether or

not there was a traffic signal, the length and position of the skid marks. All this may prove valuable later on in settling the question of liability and thus the question of damages.

6. Do not accept any payments from the motorist at fault unless you are positive there are no personal injuries involved and that the amount offered more than compensates for the property damage.

7. If at all possible, call a professional photographer or investigator and arrange to have photographs made not only of the scene of the accident, including the skid marks, but of the damaged vehicles themselves. Proving the point of impact between automobiles is often important in determining who caused the accident. If unable to have photographs taken immediately, arrange to have them taken at the garage or filling station to which the car has been removed.

8. If taken to a hospital for emergency treatment, obtain the name of the hospital as well as the name of the attending physician and, if possible, the preliminary diagnosis.

9. As soon as possible obtain estimates from at least two reliable mechanics as to the cost of repairs. If you were driving a Cadillac, go to several Cadillac dealers for an estimate. If a Ford go to several Ford dealers, especially if your car is relatively new. You are not obliged to have your car repaired by a second or third rate mechanic. The insurance carrier also has a right to obtain an estimate of damages from one of their mechanics, provided his work is first rate.

10. If your car is brand new and you suspect that the accident may be due to some inherent defect in the car itself, do not have the car repaired until you first obtain an expert opinion. Remember, that an original defect in the automobile may allow you or your attorney to file suit against the manufacturer of the car.

### Should you employ an attorney in a traffic court case?

For the average parking ticket your best bet is to pay and forget about it. For moving violations such as running through a red light you might be able to handle the matter yourself provided you can prove by reliable witnesses, such as passengers in your car, that you did not, in fact, run through the red light. In a traffic court violation the burden is on the police to prove the case beyond a reasonable doubt. If you can produce witnesses to negate the officer's testimony, chances are the charge will be dismissed, especially if you have previously had a good record. In more serious cases such as drunken driving or accidents involving personal injuries where your driver's license may be revoked or suspended, an experienced lawyer should represent you at the hearing. Where the injuries warrant, a good lawyer will employ a stenographer to take down a verbatim account of the proceedings for future use in either settlement or suit. Whenever there is any doubt as to whether or not you should employ counsel in a traffic court matter, the doubt should be resolved affirmatively.

## CHAPTER 25

# BANKRUPTCY

*What is the nature and purpose of the National Bankruptcy Act?*

To give creditors an equal opportunity to share in a debtor's property in proportion to their claims and to allow honest but insolvent debtors an opportunity to make a fresh start in life.

*What is the difference between bankruptcy and insolvency?*

Bankruptcy is a legal status; insolvency is a financial status. A person is not bankrupt in a legal sense until declared so in a bankruptcy court, which is always a federal court.

Insolvency, on the other hand, merely means the inability to meet one's debts as they mature. For example, one may be worth $100,000 in frozen assets and yet be unable to meet a $10,000 note when it becomes due. In the equity sense, such a person is insolvent, not bankrupt.

There is another sense in which insolvent is used under the National Bankruptcy Act: a person is insolvent if the total amount of his assets is not, at a fair valuation, sufficient to pay his debts. If, for example, a person's entire assets amount to $50,000 and his liabilities to $60,000, he is insolvent—in the bankruptcy sense of the term.

Still another distinction may be made: there are numerous state insolvency acts, but only one bankruptcy act. The essence of a bankruptcy law is to compel a debtor to surrender his assets for the benefits of his creditors, after which the debtor is discharged from bankruptcy and is able to make a fresh start. State insolvency laws cannot compel a debtor to make an involuntary surrender of all his assets for the general benefit of his creditors; nor may state insolvency laws grant a discharge to a debtor in the way that the National Bankruptcy Act allows.

*Who has jurisdiction in bankruptcy matters?*

The federal courts, under the U. S. Constitution. Such courts consist of judges and referees. The judge has full authority not only on matters of original jurisdiction, but also on appeals from the referee.

*What is the function of the referee in bankruptcy?*

A referee is both a judicial officer and an administrative officer; he is appointed by the U. S. district court for a period of two years. A referee's function is to pass on matters referred to him by the U. S. district court judge, either before or after adjudication. If a bankruptcy matter is referred to the referee by the court, the referee has complete jurisdiction of the proceedings. He may grant or deny a discharge or adjudicate or dismiss a petition.

*What are the administrative duties of the referee?*

1. To examine all schedules of property and lists of creditors filed by bankrupts.

2. To furnish information concerning bankrupt estates to all parties in interest.

3. To give notices to creditors.

4. To make up the record in each case.

5. To conduct hearings.

6. To keep and transmit to the clerks the records of all proceedings in bankrupt estates.

7. To declare dividends for the benefit of the creditors, when possible.

*What is the difference between a referee and a trustee?*

A referee functions chiefly as the court itself. A trustee functions primarily on behalf of the creditors. A referee is both a judicial and administrative officer of the court. A trustee is merely an administrative officer.

*How are bankruptcy proceedings begun?*

On a voluntary bankruptcy, by petition to the U. S. district court asking that the petitioner be declared a bankrupt. This procedure applies both to individuals and to business firms. In an involuntary bankruptcy, a creditor files a petition requesting that the individual or firm be declared bankrupt.

*Who may file a voluntary petition?*

Anyone—except municipal, railroad, insurance, or banking corporations.

*Is it necessary that the petitioner owe any fixed minimum of debt?*

No.

*Who may file an involuntary petition in bankruptcy?*

Three or more creditors who have provable claims against any person amounting to $500 or more may file an involuntary petition. If there are less than twelve creditors any one whose claim or claims exceed $500 may file the petition.

*Against whom may an involuntary petition be filed?*

Any natural person, except one earning $1,500 or less, or any business firm that owes debts of $1,000 or more, may be forced into involuntary bankruptcy. Under the Bankruptcy Act farmers, building and loan associations, or municipal, railroad, insurance, or banking corporations are exempt, since other legal statutes cover such cases.

*How does the Bankruptcy Act treat a partnership?*

As an entity, separate from the partners. Actually, an involuntary petition may be filed against either the partnership or the individual general partners or both. The petition may be filed either before or after dissolution of the firm, but not after a final settlement of partnership affairs.

*Where and how are bankruptcy petitions filed?*

In the office of the clerk of the United States district court. A voluntary petition must be accompanied by a schedule of the petitioner's property, under oath, showing among other things:

1. The amount and the kinds of property.
2. The location of the property.
3. The value of the property.
4. The names of creditors, together with their residences and the amounts due each.

*What are the proceedings in a voluntary bankruptcy?*

Voluntary bankruptcy proceedings are begun by a petition, accompanied by schedules of assets and liabilities, in which the petitioner requests that he be given a discharge. The schedules, executed in triplicate, under oath, are filed in the office of the district court having jurisdiction where the bankrupt lives or has his place of business. Immediately upon his filing a voluntary petition, the petitioner is adjudicated a bankrupt, after which the procedure is similar to that for those who file involuntary proceedings after adjudication.

*What are the proceedings in an involuntary bankruptcy?*

In an involuntary bankruptcy a creditor or creditors file a petition stating that within the preceding four months the alleged bankrupt has committed one or more acts of bankruptcy. The alleged bankrupt is served with a subpoena, equivalent to a summons, which is returnable within ten days. The alleged bankrupt has a specified time (five days after the return day) in which to file his answer under oath.

*What happens if the alleged bankrupt fails to file an answer?*

If the petition is in proper form, he is adjudicated a bankrupt.

*What if he denies the allegations of the petition?*

He may have a trial by jury on the issues. If the jury sustains the allegations of the petition, the debtor is declared or adjudged a bankrupt; otherwise, the petition is dismissed.

*What are the acts of bankruptcy?*

A debtor may be adjudged a bankrupt if he has committed any one of the following acts within the four months immediately preceding the filing of the petition:

1. He has transferred or concealed property for the purpose of defrauding creditors.

2. While insolvent, he gave a preference to a creditor. Any act of the debtor that enables a creditor to obtain payment of a larger percentage of his debt than other creditors constitutes a preference.

3. While insolvent, he permitted a creditor to obtain a lien and failed to vacate such lien.

4. He has made a general assignment for the benefit of creditors.

5. While insolvent, or while unable to pay his debts as they matured, he procured or permitted the appointment of a trustee or receiver for his property.

6. He has admitted, in writing, his inability to pay his debts and his willingness to be adjudged a bankrupt.

*What is the function of a receiver or marshal?*

To protect and preserve the debtor's property pending adjudication. A receiver in bankruptcy will be appointed when assets are perishable or unprotected, or likely to be wasted or destroyed, stolen, secreted, or turned over to favored creditors. A receiver or marshal has authority to take over premises and continue to occupy them under an existing lease.

*How is a receivership terminated?*

By the appointment of a trustee in bankruptcy or by the dismissal of the bankruptcy petition.

*What happens if the debtor is adjudicated a bankrupt?*

The bankrupt's estate is administered and distributed. The creditors elect a trustee to act on their behalf—under the general supervision of the referee—to convert the bankrupt's estate into money and make the distribution—after necessary fees and expenses—in a certain order of priority.

*When is the first meeting of the creditors held?*

Not less than ten days, nor more than thirty days, after the adjudication of bankruptcy, the referee calls for and presides over the first meeting of the creditors. At this meeting the creditors file "proofs of claim," which may or may not be allowed by the referee.

*Within what time may creditors file their proofs of claim?*

Within six months after adjudication, but only those creditors whose claims have been allowed may vote at such meetings.

*What happens if the creditors do not elect a trustee?*

If the creditors fail to elect or appoint a trustee the referee appoints one. The creditors also have a right to appoint a creditors' committee to consult with the trustee.

*What are the duties of a trustee?*

As already pointed out, his chief responsibility is to reduce all the assets of the bankrupt to cash for eventual distribution to the creditors. His other duties are:

1. To examine the bankrupt.
2. To set aside voidable preferences, transfers, and liens.
3. To assume or to reject contracts on behalf of the estate.
4. To bring or to defend actions on behalf of the estate.
5. To account for the estate.

*Why does a trustee examine the bankrupt?*

To make certain that the bankrupt has not withheld any property that should go into the estate and that he has not been guilty of a voidable preference.

*What is a voidable preference?*

The making, by the bankrupt, of an unlawful preference of one creditor over another, as by transferring his property for an inadequate consideration or by allowing a lien to be placed on his property for the benefit of a favored creditor. A preference may be rescinded by the trustee or referee:

1. If there has been a transfer.
2. If the alleged bankrupt was insolvent at the time of the transfer.
3. If the transfer was made within four months before the filing of the petition or after the filing and before adjudication.
4. If the creditor obtained a greater percentage of his debt than other creditors of the same class.
5. If the transferee had reason to believe that the person making the transfer (the transferor) was insolvent at the time of the transfer.

*Within what period does a trustee have the right to assume or reject a contract?*

He may assume or reject, within sixty days after adjudication, any executory contract, that is, one that remains to be fulfilled. If the bankrupt has received the benefit of the contract, the agreement is a valid claim against the estate and may not be rejected.

*What about actions by or against a trustee?*

A trustee may bring any court action on behalf of the estate; he may be sued by alleged creditors who wish to enforce their rights and claims.

*What duty does a trustee have to account?*

A trustee must give an accounting of his management of the bankrupt's estate within the first month of his appointment; thereafter, he must give an accounting every two months; he must also give a final accounting fifteen days before the day fixed for the final meeting.

*Should a bankrupt employ counsel to represent him?*

Yes, so that he may be advised of his legal rights. However, the court may examine any fee paid to the bankrupt's counsel, and if the court thinks the fee excessive, it may require such excess to be turned over to the bankrupt's estate as an unlawful preference.

*What exemptions are generally allowed to a bankrupt?*

Every state allows to a bankrupt various exemptions under its laws, and these exemptions are recognized by the National Bankruptcy Act. Although the amounts and kinds of exemptions vary from state to state, they include, in general, wearing apparel, jewelry, a certain amount of wages, and certain occupational exemptions such as growing crops, tools, and implements of trade.

*What jewelry would be generally exempt?*

A wedding ring would be, but not a diamond ring.

*Would a bankrupt's piano be exempt?*

Yes, if it is used principally to give lessons.

*What about insurance policies?*

Property insurance is regarded as a part of the bankrupt's estate and is not exempt. On life insurance there are conflicting decisions—if the bankrupt is himself the policyholder and the policy has a cash surrender value, the insurance would not normally be exempt.

*What happens to property acquired by a bankrupt after the filing of a petition but before adjudication?*

It belongs to the bankrupt, not to the estate. The bankrupt's estate includes only that property owned by him at the time the petition was filed and that property preferentially transferred by him within four months prior to the filing of the petition.

*Two weeks after a bankrupt files a petition his mother gives him $10,000. To whom does the money belong?*

To the bankrupt. He may do what he pleases with it.

*What are the general duties of the bankrupt?*

1. To attend all necessary meetings called by the trustee or referee.
2. To obey court orders.
3. To verify proofs of claim and report any irregularities.
4. To execute and deliver all necessary papers.
5. To submit a preliminary statement of his affairs.
6. To submit himself to examination by court-appointed officials.

*What happens if the bankrupt commits a bankruptcy offense?*

He is liable to arrest and imprisonment.

*What happens if the bankrupt dies or becomes insane?*

The estate continues to be administered, to the extent possible, as if the bankrupt had not died or become insane.

*Within what time must a creditor file a proof of his claim?*

Within six months after the first date set for the first meeting of creditors. If he does not, his claim is lost.

*What are the distinctions between a secured, a preferred and a general creditor?*

A *secured creditor* is one "who has security for his debt upon the property of the bankrupt of a nature to be assignable under this Act or who owns such a debt for which some endorser, surety, or other person secondarily liable for the bankrupt has such security upon the bankrupt's assets." A *preferred creditor* is one who has been given a preference. A *general creditor* is one who has no security or priority.

*What are the rights of secured creditors?*

They may resort to their security in satisfaction of their claims. Should there be anything left after the claim is satisfied, the surplus goes to the trustee in bankruptcy.

*Which debts are accorded priority over the claims of general creditors?*

1. Actual and necessary expenses of preserving the estate after the filing of the petition, including court costs and attorney's fees.

2. Wage claims, not to exceed $600 to each claimant, servant, clerk, or traveling or city salesman on salary or commissioned basis.

3. Costs and expenses of creditors for successfully opposing or revoking a bankrupt's discharge.

4. Tax claims.

5. Debts entitled to priority by federal law, and rent due and owing for actual use and occupancy.

*What happens if a landlord becomes bankrupt?*

His leasehold interest goes to the trustee in bankruptcy; the tenant's rights are unaffected.

*What happens to the landlord's claim for rent due and unpaid at the time of the tenant's bankruptcy?*

The claim for such rent is a fixed liability and is provable as such.

*What happens when a partnership is declared bankrupt?*

The separate assets of all partners, as well as the partnership property, are drawn into bankruptcy. The bankruptcy of one individual partner, however, does not draw in partnership property, unless the remaining partners consent or unless the bankrupt partner is the sole surviving partner and has control of the firm's assets.

*Does the bankruptcy of a corporation make the officers, stockholders, directors, and officers liable to creditors?*

No.

*What is a dividend in bankruptcy?*

It is a proportion of the assets of the bankrupt's estate that is made available for distribution to the creditors. Such dividends are declared by the referee and paid by the trustee. They are generally paid within thirty days after the first date set for the first meeting of creditors.

*How is a bankrupt discharged?*

By a United States district court, acting on the advice of the referee.

*What will bar a bankrupt from receiving his discharge?*

A bankrupt will not receive his discharge:

1. If it is proved that he has committed a bankruptcy offense.

2. If there is evidence that he has destroyed, multilated, or failed to keep necessary books and records, unless in the opinion of the court the acts were justified.

3. If he has made false statements.

4. If he has removed, destroyed, or concealed assets.

5. If he has been discharged from bankruptcy within the preceding six years.

6. If he refuses to obey a court order or to answer a material question.

7. If he fails to explain a loss or deficiency.

*Which debts survive as obligations even with the bankrupt's discharge.*

1. Taxes—federal, state, county, and local.

2. Liability for obtaining money or property by false pretenses.

3. Liability for willful and malicious injury to persons or property, such as a judgment for assault and battery.

4. Liability for support of wife or child, including liability for alimony.

5. Liability for seduction or breach of promise.

6. Debts created by fraud or embezzlement in a confidential or fiduciary relationship.

*What is the penalty for committing an infraction of the bankruptcy laws?*

Imprisonment for not more than five years or a fine of not more than $5,000 or both. All those who aid and abet a bankrupt to commit an offense, including attorneys and accountants, are liable to the same punishment, as principals, and not as accessories.

*Which offenses are so punishable?*

1. The concealment from the receiver, custodian, or other officer of any property belonging to the bankrupt estate.

2. The making of a false oath or account in relation to any bankrupt proceeding.

3. The presenting, under oath, of any false claim against the bankrupt estate, either personally or by attorney.

4. The receiving of property from a bankrupt, after the filing of a petition, with the intent to defeat the purpose of the bankruptcy law.

5. The receiving of, or attempt to receive, any money or property for acting or forbearing to act in any proceeding under the Bankruptcy Act.

6. The concealing or transferring of property in violation of the Bankruptcy Act.

7. The destroying, mutilating, or falsifying of records affecting the affairs of the bankrupt.

8. The withholding of any document affecting the property or affairs of the bankrupt.

## What is an "arrangement"?

Under the Bankruptcy Act, an arrangement is "any plan of a debtor for the settlement, satisfaction, or extension of the time of payment of his unsecured debts, upon any terms." The purpose of an arrangement is to effect a compromise with unsecured creditors by offering them a settlement as good as they would have under the Bankruptcy Act, without the delay and expense that a full bankruptcy proceeding involves. An arrangement may be effected either during the course of a bankruptcy proceeding or without any proceeding in bankruptcy at all.

## Who may take advantage of an arrangement?

Anyone who may become a bankrupt.

## What is the procedure for an arrangement?

1. A petition is filed by the debtor in the U. S. district court.

2. Upon the filing of the petition, the court may refer the matter to a referee, appoint a receiver, continue the debtor in possession, or, when a trustee has already been appointed, continue such trustee in possession.

3. Creditors then file their claims against the debtor and either accept or reject the proposed arrangement.

4. The arrangement, even if approved by the creditors, must also be approved by the court.

## What are the normal costs for filing a petition in bankruptcy?

Aside from attorney's fees, about $45.

CHAPTER 26

## CIVIL LIBERTIES

*What is the difference between civil liberties and civil rights?*

Civil liberties refers to those freedoms guaranteed to the people by the first ten amendments to the federal Constitution, popularly known as the Bill of Rights. Civil rights usually refers, at least in contemporary social history, to the efforts of Negro Americans to gain and enjoy their full legal rights under the Constitution. Specifically, civil rights refers to the various laws passed by the Congress to implement and strengthen the constitutional rights of Negro Americans. (See chapter 27.)

*Do the states also have bills of rights?*

Many states have a bill of rights in their own constitution. But in the field of civil liberties and civil rights, the federal Constitution as interpreted by the U. S. Supreme Court is supreme, even against individual states.

*What does the First Amendment guarantee?*

The First Amendment reads as follows: "Congress shall make no law respecting an establishment of religion, or prohibiting the free exercise thereof; or abridging the freedom of speech, or of the press; or the right of the people peaceably to assemble, and to petition the government for a redress of grievances." In essence the First Amendment provides a safeguard against the oppression of minorities by a majority.

*Didn't our ancestors establish freedom of religion even before the adoption of the federal Constitution?*

No. The First Amendment was a victory for such liberal statesmen as Jefferson and Madison, who insisted that the right to religious freedom included the right not to have any religion at all.

398

*Was the 1963 Supreme Court decision an attack on religion?*

No. This decision, which banned the saying of prayers and the reading of the Bible in public schools, merely continued the separation of church and state on which this government was founded. In the majority opinion Justice Hugo L. Black wrote, "It is neither sacrilegious nor antireligious to say that each separate government in this country should stay out of the business of writing or sanctioning official prayers and leave that purely religious function to the people themselves and to those the people choose to look to for religious guidance."

*What of all in the Bill of Rights is considered to be most fundamental in a democratic society?*

The right to freedom of speech. Without full freedom of speech and press, we cannot intelligently discuss controversial issues or find out what the will of the majority is. A democracy thrives on open discussion, whereas in totalitarian states free speech and press, as well as freedom of religion, are the first rights to be suppressed.

Many of the present day riots and sit-ins involve serious constitutional questions. There are those who claim that anything radicals, leftists, and revolutionaries do—even to taking over a college—is not in violation of their constitutional rights. Others insist that the right to express one's views—even the most critical—does not give one the right to incite a riot or otherwise take the law into his own hands.

*Does the right to freedom of speech also include the right to remain silent?*

Yes. In *West Virginia Board of Education* v. *Barnette* the court held that a child did not have to salute the flag if doing so violated his conscience or that of his parents.

*May a speaker use inflammatory words to denounce an ethnic group?*

Ordinarily a speaker may denounce anyone he pleases, including minority groups and even the U. S. President. It is the duty of the police to prevent violence in the audience, if at all possible by means other than stopping the speaker. This is what free speech means in a free society. In a democratic society even the most unpopular views and opinions should be given a hearing.

*Is there such a thing as an absolute freedom of speech or press?*

No. Justice Oliver Wendell Holmes said, "The most stringent protection of free speech would not protect a man in falsely shouting fire in a theater and causing a panic." There are certain limitations on the absolute right of freedom of speech and press. No one has a constitutional right to slander or libel another, to urge people to commit crimes, to commit perjury.

*What about group libel laws, that is, denouncing entire groups such as Jews, Negroes, Nazis, etc.?*

In *Beauharnais* v. *Illinois* (1952) the Supreme Court sustained a conviction under a group libel law, after debating the rights of an individual under the First Amendment versus the right of a group not to be libeled or defamed.

*How can freedom of speech and press be legally abridged?*

In time of war or grave national emergency Congress may find it in the public interest to establish censorship to prevent vital information from reaching enemy hands. But what may be necessary in wartime or in a national crisis should be resisted in peacetime, for with the erosion of our civil liberties go our rights as free men in a democracy.

In 1919 Justice Holmes formulated what has become known as the "clear and present danger" test. Speaking for a unanimous court Justice Holmes declared that a conspiracy to obstruct the draft in 1917 was such a "clear and present danger" that the government had a right to place a restraint on freedom of speech.

*Does the Constitution forbid acts which are dangerous but not "present"?*

Yes. In *Dennis* v. *United States* (1951) the Supreme Court upheld the conviction of certain Communist party leaders under the Smith Act of 1940. The reasoning of the Court was that advocacy of a revolution was a criminal offense, even when no tangible action was proven.

*Is the censoring of movies, books, and plays a violation of the constitutional rights of free speech and free press?*

To a large extent, yes. The legal fact is that all states forbid obscenity and make the publication of obscene matter a crime. The difficulty is in determining what is obscene.

In *Roth* v. *United States* the Supreme Court defined obscene material as that "which deals with sex in a manner appealing to 'prurient interest,' which arouses lustful thoughts." The material must be prurient to the average person, applying contemporary community standards, and must be prurient as a whole rather than in isolated parts. Sex and obscenity are not synonymous, and the portrayal of sex in art, literature, and scientific works is not itself sufficient reason to deny material the constitutional protection of freedom of speech and press.

*How may government legally regulate free speech?*

A city may regulate times and places at which massive demonstrations will be allowed. It may also forbid the use of sound trucks. However, an ordinance forbidding the use of circulars or handbills to prevent littering the streets would be a violation of the First Amendment.

A community may not arbitrarily refuse a permit for either a demonstration or parade, since to do so would violate the right to assemble peacefully. An ordinance must set out clear criteria for officials to follow; otherwise they would have power to grant permits for causes they approve and refuse permits for causes they dislike.

*What is freedom of assembly and petition?*

The right to assemble peaceably and to petition the government is closely akin to the rights of freedom of speech and press. Negro Americans have attempted to assert these rights in demonstrations and sit-ins, and they have had their plight as second-class citizens dramatized when they have been mauled, beaten, and jailed.

*What does the Second Amendment provide?*

It provides that "the right of the people to keep and bear arms shall not be infringed."

*What does the Third Amendment provide?*

This amendment provides that "no soldier shall in time of peace be quartered in any house without the consent of the owner, nor in time of war but in a manner to be prescribed by law."

*What does the Fourth Amendment provide?*

Provision (4) protects a witness against self-incrimination but exposes him to public ridicule and possible loss of employment rather than criminal prosecution.

*What does the Fifth Amendment provide?*

It provides that (1) no person shall be held to answer for a capital or otherwise infamous crime, unless on a presentment or indictment of a grand jury; (2) no person shall be tried twice for the same criminal offense; (3) no person shall be compelled in any criminal case to be a witness against himself; (4) no person shall be deprived of life, liberty, or property, without due process of law; and (5) private property shall not be taken for public use without just compensation.

*What are the provisions of the Sixth Amendment?*

In all criminal prosecutions the accused shall enjoy the right to a speedy and public trial by an impartial jury. The accused is to be informed of the nature and cause of the accusation; he is to be confronted with the witnesses against him; he is to have compulsory process for obtaining witnesses in his favor; and he is to have the assistance of counsel for his defense.

*What does the Eighth Amendment provide?*

It states: "Excessive bail shall not be required, nor excessive fines imposed, nor cruel and unusual punishments inflicted."

*What civil liberties are guaranteed by the Thirteenth Amendment?*

This Amendment abolishes slavery and involuntary servitude, except as punishment for a crime for which the accused shall have been convicted. It also outlaws forced labor contracts.

*What does the Fourteenth Amendment provide?*

No state shall make or enforce any law that shall abridge the privileges or immunities of citizens of the United States; nor shall any state deprive any person of life, liberty, or property without due process of law; nor deny to any person within its jurisdiction the equal protection of the laws.

*How does the Fifteenth Amendment affect civil liberties?*

This amendment asserts that the right of citizens of the United States to vote shall not be denied or abridged by the United States or by any state on account of race, color, or previous condition of servitude.

The provisions of this amendment are one of the greatest bulwarks of the Negro people's campaign for equal rights. Some states have violated the spirit, if not the letter, of the amendment by enacting various laws requiring certain property or educational qualifications of prospective voters. These tests have often been administered in such a manner that millions of Negroes have been barred from registering or voting in state or federal elections.

*How does the Nineteenth Amendment affect civil rights?*

It extends the suffrage to women.

*What provisions of the original Constitution affect civil rights?*

Article I, section 10, states: "The privilege of the writ of habeas corpus shall not be suspended, unless when in cases of rebellion or invasion the public safety may require it." This article also forbids the passage of a bill of attainder or ex post facto law.

*What is a bill of attainder?*

A bill of attainder is a law that punishes a person without trial.

*What is an ex post facto law?*

An ex post facto law makes criminal an act that, when it was committed, was not criminal or imposes a new punishment for an act that, when it was committed, merited a different punishment.

*To what extent has the Supreme Court refused to allow further segregation of the Negro and white races?*

Until recently the Supreme Court, following precedent, had ruled that racial segregation was permissible—as long as equal accommodations were provided. In its historic decision of 1954 the Court repudiated that doctrine and declared segregation of the races in the public schools to be unconstitutional. Now, in addition to ending segregation in the public schools, the Court, by various decisions, has held that no state may compel segregation in public parks or bathing beaches, on public golf courses, in colleges supported by public funds, or at athletic events.

*What is meant by "due process of law"?*

The constitutional guarantee of due process of law means, roughly, that no governmental body may deprive anyone of his life, liberty, or property without a fair and impartial trial or hearing held publicly. It is an assurance that the government will be administered by laws, not by the arbitrary will of men who condemn without a hearing.

*Is evidence obtained by wiretapping admissible at trial under federal law?*

In several cases the federal courts have held that evidence illegally obtained is inadmissible in a federal case. Since wiretapping violates the accused's privilege against self-incrimination, as guaranteed in the Fifth Amendment, evidence so obtained is illegal and inadmissible.

*Is such evidence admissible in a state criminal case?*

Yes, since the privilege against self-incrimination contained in the Fifth Amendment is not binding on the states. Thirty-three states forbid wiretapping, but many of them exempt police officers from the prohibition. In New York, for example, a police officer is allowed to tap wires, but only on a warrant showing reasonable grounds for believing that evidence of a crime may thus be obtained.

*Have any attempts been made to induce Congress to change the wiretapping law?*

Legislation sponsored by the U. S. Attorney General and introduced in Congress would allow the Attorney General to issue wiretapping orders in national security cases involving sedition, espionage, and unauthorized disclosure of information on atomic secrets. The proposed bill also calls for court-authorized wiretapping by federal agents in the investigation of murders, kidnapings, gambling, and narcotics traffic.

*Why is the writ of habeas corpus so important?*

It is important because a person deprived of his liberty may secure, by this writ, a judicial determination whether such restraint is illegal. The writ, one of the oldest in Anglo-American law, may be suspended when martial law has been declared and the courts closed.

*Is habeas corpus a substitute for appeal?*

No. The primary purpose of the writ is to test the legality of a person's detention. An individual held in jail without bail may apply for the writ and have his case brought before a judge to determine the legality of the detention. Any prisoner by this writ may test the legality of his imprisonment, including an alien held for deportation proceedings. In recent years the scope of the writ has been enlarged by the Supreme Court. It may now be used in any case in which the prisoner's constitutional rights have been disregarded, as, for example, when the state has failed to provide a prisoner with counsel.

*Does the provision against double jeopardy contained in the Fifth Amendment apply only to federal law?*

No. The constitutions of forty-five states contain a similar provision. The states that have no such provision are Connecticut, Maryland, Massachusetts, North Carolina, and Vermont.

*Does double jeopardy mean that a state cannot convict a person for an offense that is both a state crime and a federal crime?*

No. This was actually done during the Prohibition era, when violators were prosecuted by both federal and state governments.

*Can a man be acquitted of rape and then be charged with assault with intent to commit rape, a lesser offense?*

No. Conviction or acquittal of a crime that includes lesser offenses will generally bar prosecution for the lesser offense.

*Can a man convicted of assault with intent to kill be tried later for murder if the victim dies?*

Yes, since the new circumstance has altered the nature of the defendant's criminal conduct.

*When is a defendant first placed in jeopardy so that he may later avail himself of the privilege of double jeopardy?*

Assuming no defects in the indictment, as soon as the jury is impaneled.

*May a judge after fining a prisoner later change the sentence to imprisonment?*

No, since this would constitute double jeopardy.

*What rights does a police officer have after he has made a lawful arrest?*

He has the right to search the prisoner and to seize those articles that are connected with the crime. Such articles might be the instrument of a crime, such as a gun or knife, or the spoils of a crime, such as money or jewelry.

*Does the privilege against self-incrimination apply only in criminal cases?*

No. By extension, a witness may say, "I refuse to answer on the ground that an answer might tend to incriminate or degrade me," in grand jury investigations, Congressional hearings, bankruptcy proceedings, and even in civil suits when an answer to a question might tend to establish his criminal liability.

*May a federal judge comment upon a witness's pleading the Fifth Amendment?*

No. Nor may any judge state that a refusal to testify creates a presumption of guilt.

*May the privilege against self-incrimination be waived?*

Yes. The privilege may also be forfeited if it is not claimed at the very outset of the questioning.

*What are the elements of due process?*

**1.** The defendant must receive due notice of the charge against him, including a bill of particulars describing the exact nature of the charge and the time and place where it is alleged to have taken place.

**2.** There must be an atmosphere in which a fair and impartial trial may be had. Such an environment is patently lacking if the judge is obviously biased or prejudiced or if Negro jurors are deliberately and systematically excluded by the state when a Negro is on trial.

**3.** Confessions extorted by fraud, trickery, or third degree methods must be excluded from evidence.

*Is a trial by jury guaranteed in all cases?*

The requirement is binding on the federal government, but not on state governments. In many states the defendant in a criminal case is allowed to waive a jury trial.

*Is it a violation of a defendant's constitutional rights if no member of his race is on the jury?*

No. It is only the systematic and deliberate exclusion of Negroes, laborers, or women that is a violation of the Constitution.

*If a person is arrested and cannot afford to employ counsel, what should he do?*

He should request the court to appoint counsel for him. Charged with a federal violation, an accused is entitled to counsel, even if the federal court must appoint one to represent him gratis. The accused is entitled to representation by counsel, whether or not he can afford one, at every stage of the proceedings.

*Is the right to counsel in state courts as extensive as in federal courts?*

Prior to the decision in *Gideon* v. *Wainwright* (1962) the Supreme Court of the United States had taken the position that the Sixth Amendment's guaranty of right to counsel applied only to federal courts. In the Gideon case the Court completely overthrew this doctrine, declaring that the right to counsel is absolute and applies to state courts equally with federal courts.

*May states reject the right to counsel in noncapital cases, that is, those cases for which the penalty is not death?*

Under Supreme Court decisions the defendant is entitled to counsel in virtually every type of criminal case, if he lacks means to employ an attorney himself.

## CHAPTER 27

## THE NEGRO AND CIVIL RIGHTS

Criminal penalties are provided for injuring or interfering with a person exercising specific rights—including the right to vote, serve on a jury, participate in government or government aided programs, work, attend school or college, and enjoy public accommodations.

In addition, the Act provides penalties for manufacturing or teaching the use of firearms or explosives for use in a civil disorder.

### What is the Civil Rights Act of 1964?

On July 2, 1964, President Johnson signed into law an act designed to implement and strengthen the constitutional rights of nearly twenty million Negroes. It is perhaps the most important legislation of its kind ever passed by the United States Congress.

### What does the law seek to accomplish?

To assure to all citizens, regardless of race, color, religion, or national origin, their equal rights in voting; access to hotels, restaurants, theaters, libraries, and parks; education; federally assisted programs; and employment. To accomplish these aims, the law gave the Justice Department additional powers, established an Equal Employment Opportunity Commission and a six-man Community Relations Service, and extended the life of the U.S. Civil Rights Commission.

### What is the Civil Rights Act of 1968?

This law supplements that of 1964. It forbids discrimination in the sale or rental of eighty percent of all housing. Covered are housing built with federal assistance; all multiple units except for owner-occupied dwellings of four units or less; single family houses in real estate developments not owned by private individuals; and privately owned single family homes sold or rented by real estate agents. The ban against discrimination also applies to financing and brokerage services.

*What is the basis of the constitutionality of these laws?*

The Civil Rights Acts of 1964 and 1968 are based on the commerce clause (Article I, Section 8) of the Constitution, which gives Congress the power to legislate over interstate commerce; the Fourteenth Amendment, which safeguards the rights of citizens against state denial of equal protection of the law; and the Fifteenth Amendment, which protects the right to vote. Both the Fourteenth and Fifteenth Amendments authorize appropriate legislation by Congress to enforce them.

*Who is covered by the law?*

The law protects the individual rights of all persons, whether they are citizens of the United States or simply visiting our country.

*Which facilities are covered by the law?*

All facilities publicly owned by a city, county, state, or the national government.

The following privately owned facilities are mentioned in the law: (1) restaurants, cafeterias, lunchrooms, soda fountains, gasoline stations, motion picture houses, theaters, concert halls, sports arenas, and all hotels, motels, or lodging houses except those which are owner-occupied with five or less units for rent; (2) any facility principally engaged in selling food for consumption on the premises (this includes facilities located in retail stores and gas stations); (3) any place of exhibition or entertainment.

Facilities located within a place of public accommodation such as a barbershop within a hotel are covered, whereas a separate barbershop is not covered.

There is no clear federal ruling at the time of this writing about noncovered establishments containing covered facilities, as an apartment house (not covered) with public dining room (covered).

*What will prevent motel owners, restaurants, etc., from converting their establishments into private clubs?*

To qualify, they must become bona-fide clubs. "Instant membership" is not valid.

*Are rest rooms in gas stations and motels, etc., now open to members of all races?*

Yes.

*Are separate white and colored facilities legal in facilities covered by public accommodations section?*

No.

*Are public parks and public buildings allowed to provide separate but equal rest-room facilities?*

No.

*Does the Civil Rights Law effect individually owned beauty and barbershops?*

No, unless they are located within a covered facility such as a hotel.

*If you have a stag bar, must you, under the law, serve a woman?*

No. The public accommodations section does not mention sex.

*Does the law effect private clubs, social clubs, swimming clubs, key clubs, etc.?*

Bona-fide private clubs are specifically exempted. However, on June 2, 1969, the United States Supreme Court held that recreation clubs or clubs privately owned and operated for profit are not entitled to the private club exemption of the 1964 Civil Rights Act.

*Which facilities are not covered under the public accommodations section?*

Private clubs such as fraternal organizations, college sororities and fraternities, and religious organizations (except when private clubs serve patrons of covered establishments, such as hotels).

*Does the federal government provide any financial assistance to schools trying to carry out desegregation plans?*

The law provides that financial and technical assistance shall be provided to school boards to deal with problems resulting from the desegregation of schools, including provisions for the training of teachers. The law prohibits the use of federal funds for the busing of children to secure racial balance in public schools.

*Does this law mean that all private schools and private colleges must integrate?*

No. It says that schools which are wholly or predominately operated with public funds must not discriminate. This would not include private or religious schools.

*Certain counties may wish to revamp their public school system to avoid civil rights provisions. Is this possible?*

The law does not cover this, but the courts have already decided that Prince Edward County, Virginia, must provide public school; for all students who wish to attend.

*Does the law provide that busing must be done to eliminate de facto segregation in northern cities where neighborhood schools are often all white or all Negro?*

The law does not permit the federal government to order transportation of students to provide racial balance in the schools and forbids the use of federal money for such purposes.

*Are parochial and private schools covered by this law?*

No.

*Is it legal for college applications to continue to ask for information on race or religion?*

There is no prohibition as to questions about race or religion.

*Does this bill cover "quota systems" in graduate schools supported by public funds?*

Quota systems for members of various races or religions is prohibited under the law, insofar as public schools and universities are concerned and in programs financed by the federal government.

*Does the act force all public schools to integrate?*

No. The act does not force all public schools to integrate, but discriminatory practices are now specifically forbidden. Under this act, the U. S. Attorney General is permitted to sue where there is evidence of discriminatory practices.

*What protection is provided for equal employment opportunity?*

Employers, labor unions, and employment agencies whose activities affect interstate or foreign commerce, or the production of goods for interstate or foreign commerce, are prohibited by the law from discriminating on the basis of race, creed, color, or national origin. In addition, any discrimination on the basis of sex alone is outlawed.

Coverage originally included only employers and unions with one hundred or more employees or members, but the restriction dropped by stages until 1969. Now having twenty-five employees or members brings the organization under the law.

An Equal Employment Opportunity Commission was established to make investigations and attempt to voluntarily settle complaints. When this procedure fails to result in settlement, the Commission is authorized to file suit in a court of law to enforce the principle of nondiscrimination.

The law excludes from coverage anyone denied employment by reason of being a communist.

*What is the Equal Employment Opportunity Commission?*

The law created a bipartisan commission of five men to administer the equal employment section of the law. The Commission investigates charges of job or union discrimination and attempts through conciliation to resolve disputes.

*May you indicate on application blanks and want ads the color or sex of the employee you are now seeking?*

No, unless your business is *not* covered by the act or unless the job *requires* someone of a particular race, religion or sex.

*Does this law mean that a person of inferior training and ability must be hired to fill a quota of Negro employees?*

No. The employer still may set all reasonable hiring standards. There are no "quotas" and no one is required to be let go to make room for another.

*Is a company now required to pay equal salary in one state for the same job done in another state for more or less?*

This is not within the provisions of the act, but an employer, all other things being equal, may not discriminate with respect to compensation paid his employees compared to the prevailing rates within the same locality.

*If a complainant is upheld, must he be hired and the man who filled the job in the meantime be fired?*

If a person is found to have lost his job or not been hired (by a company covered under this law) for reasons of race, color, creed, religion, sex, or national origin, he must be employed by the discriminating company. It is left up to the employer to decide whether to let the replacement go.

*Must a corporation employing over one hundred persons have an equal balance of employees according to race, color, sex, or creed?*

The act does not permit the federal government to require an employer or union to hire or accept for membership a quota of employees from any particular minority. But discrimination for reasons of race, religion, sex, or national origin is forbidden.

*Can a person be refused a job because he is a Communist or atheist?*

Yes, as to the first; no, as to the second.

*What provision does the new law make for women's rights?*

Women's rights are guaranteed in the employment section of the law. They may not be discriminated against because of their sex, except where the nature of the employment demands the hiring of men.

*Who or what group determines hiring standards?*

Hiring standards for performance are determined by employer or union or both. There may be *no* discrimination in hiring for reasons of race, color, sex, creed, or national origin.

*Can labor unions keep members of minority groups out of apprenticeship training programs?*

No. The law forbids labor unions to practice discrimination in qualifications for membership or participation in training programs.

*Are employment agencies able to engage in job referrals that are discriminatory in order to get around the law?*

No. Job referrals by employment agencies may not be discriminatory.

*Does this law affect the seniority of labor union members?*

No. The act protects the seniority of labor union members, and government rulings may not destroy job seniority in any way.

*If a white man loses his job because a Negro is hired, and he believes he is being discriminated against, to whom does he complain?*

The Commission on Interracial Problems and Relations.

*Does the law apply to Communists and atheists?*

Communists are not protected under the employment section. There is nothing in the act, as finally passed, about atheists.

*What enforcement is provided for the Civil Rights Law?*

The Attorney General is empowered to initiate or intervene in suits aimed at desegregating public facilities other than schools—such as parks, libraries, hospitals, and playgrounds—where the injured party is unable to pursue the remedy. He is also authorized to intervene in private actions brought by persons seeking relief from a denial of equal protection of the law because of race, color, creed, or national origin.

*What are the duties of the Attorney General?*

The Attorney General is permitted to sue to prevent discriminatory practices in public education when the students or the parents involved are unable to bring suit, and when he considers the suit important to the orderly programs of desegregation. In *voting cases* he is empowered to ask the chief judge of the circuit court, within twenty days of the complaint, to empanel a three-judge court to act immediately. The Attorney General also is authorized to bring civil action when he "has a reasonable cause to believe" that a person or group of persons is engaged in a pattern of practice of resistance to public accommodations and employment provisions of the act and can assume court costs where necessary.

*Can the Attorney General come into a community and charge an individual with violation of this law?*

No. The Attorney General can intervene only if he has received a complaint or has been called in by state or court authorities. The Attorney General cannot act independently except in cases of publicly owned facilities. He also must establish in the courts that there is a pattern of discrimination.

*Is the Attorney General the only one responsible for the effectiveness of this act?*

No. The Secretary of Commerce is administratively responsible for the Community Relations Service in the areas of public accommodation. The Equal Employment Opportunities Commission is responsible for conciliation in the areas of employment.

*How is the U. S. Civil Rights Commission set up and how does it operate?*

The act extends the life of the Civil Rights Commission (established in 1957) and gives it authority to serve as a national clearing house for information on denials of the equal protection of the laws and to investigate vote frauds.

*What happens to a person in a covered place of public accommodation who refuses to serve patrons for reasons of race, color, creed, or national origin?*

The person refusing service is liable to civil suit if the person denied chooses to bring suit.

*Will the F.B.I. enforce this law?*

No, the F.B.I. is only investigative. It has no enforcement powers.

*If you reside in a state (or county) that has no local civil rights protection laws, what do you do?*

Where there is no local law, individuals may go immediately to the federal court or to the local offices of the Attorney General of the United States. The matter may then be referred by the court to the Community Relations Service of the United States for voluntary compliance. After a maximum of 120 days, if no agreement has been reached, the matter is referred again to the court for action.

*Isn't it too expensive for minority groups to prove discrimination in the courts?*

No, the machinery of government operates for the victim of discrimination. The law provides that the court may appoint a lawyer and assess court costs and attorney fees against the person found guilty of violating the law.

*If you have an establishment not covered by the law, and it is disturbed by pickets, can you order them away?*

You may ask them to leave, but peaceful picketing is specifically allowed under the Constitution.

*What is the Community Relations Service?*

It is established by this law under the Department of Commerce to help communities resolve racial disputes. The service has no power of compulsion or law enforcement and cannot file suits.

*Can the Equal Opportunities Commission file suits?*

No, it only conciliates and mediates.

*How, under this act, are public facilities made available to all without sit-ins, wade-ins, and demonstrations?*

The act has a section on publicly owned facilities such as parks, beaches, golf courses, and playgrounds. The Justice Department, upon receipt of complaint, can sue to secure public use of these facilities.

*If a person is denied service on the basis of race, color, creed, or national origin, what can he do?*

He can report this discriminating practice to the State Commission on Interracial Problems and Relations, which will refer complaints to the proper agency for investigation and, if necessary, see that a complaint is filed in court.

*Which takes precedence, state and local civil rights laws, or the federal act?*

Federal law always takes precedence over local laws; but contained in this federal law is the stipulation that local machinery, when it exists, must be used first. If there is no local law, or if such local laws are not enforced or are in conflict with the federal law, the federal act will be applied.

*How are individuals penalized for violating the provisions of the law?*

There are no specific penalties in the law. Violators are ordered to cease discriminating. If they refuse to obey the order of the court, they are dealt with by the courts in the normal manner of contempt proceedings. The law states that the penalty for contempt is $1,000 or six months in prison, to be determined by judge or jury.

*Are there any penalties for bringing false charges or complaints against a person?*

Yes. Under *other laws*, complainants found guilty of "willful intent" to falsify are subjected to five years imprisonment or $10,000 fine.

*If you file a complaint with the proper state agency and no action has been taken, what can you do?*

To file proper action you must either send a registered letter or appear in person at the proper state agency. If, at the end of thirty days, there has been no action, then go to either the federal court or to the Attorney General of the United States. If there is no local law, go directly to the federal court or to the Attorney General's office. The court may refer the case to the Federal Community Relations Service and would give them a maximum of 120 days to effect conciliation.

*What can the courts do to enforce the law?*

1. Courts can provide injunction relief by ordering compliance.

2. Courts can refer cases to the Community Relations Service for conciliation.

3. Courts can refer cases to the Community Relations Service for conciliation. Give thirty days' notice to the state authority.

4. Either an individual or the Attorney General's office can file civil suit in the courts, charging that rights have been denied.

5. Courts can order contempt proceedings.

6. Courts can impose penalties of six months' imprisonment or $1,000 fine.

*What procedure do you follow if you live in one of the "exempted counties" where the state equal accommodations law does not apply?*

1. You may institute action in a federal court without first going to any state authority.

2. You may go to the State Commission on Interracial Problems and Relations.

3. If the federal court thinks it is of general public importance, it may permit the Attorney General to join in the action with you.

4. If you wish to sue under the federal law and pay your own legal fees, you are free to do so.

*Can anyone violating any part of the act be brought to trial without a jury?*

No. Jury trials, if requested, are provided for by the act.

*Are you allowed to use private guards to keep Negroes out of privately owned establishments?*

If the facility is covered by the act, no. If the facility is not covered by the act, it is not prohibited, but discriminatory practices are not enforceable by state or local officials.

*Will it be legal to "sit-in" or test a privately owned business to verify complaints or to pressure for service?*

There is nothing in the act which says you cannot verify complaints or pressure for service as long as the "pressure" is in accordance with existing laws regarding picketing, etc.

*Is the federal government empowered to send police to enforce the act in states which are reluctant to enforce it?*

The Attorney General has said that the federal government does not have this power. However, this is being contested by a group of knowledgeable constitutional lawyers of leading law schools. Thus, this is now in dispute.

*What protection is provided voting rights in federal elections?*

To further protect voting rights in federal elections, the law prohibits (1) the application of different tests, standards, etc., to white and colored voters and (2) the denial of registration for immaterial errors in applications. It requires all literacy tests to be given in writing or transcribed. To expedite handling of cases filed under the 1957 and 1960 Civil Rights Acts, it authorizes the Attorney General or a defendant to ask for trial by a three-judge court, with direct appeal to the U. S. Supreme Court. In any such proceeding it establishes a presumption of literacy for those who have completed the sixth grade.

*If one cannot read or write, can one be denied the right to vote?*

Yes. Literacy tests are allowed by the law, but there is a rebuttable presumption of literacy if a person has a sixth-grade education.

*Does the act guarantee the right to vote in all elections?*

No. The law only says you cannot be denied the right to vote in national elections (President, Congressmen, Senators) if you are otherwise qualified.

*Can there be one set of voter qualifications for Negroes and another for whites?*

The act prohibits unequal application of voting registration requirements in national elections. It prohibits registrars or registration officials from applying different standards to white and Negro applicants.

*If a birth certificate has some errors on it, can the individual be denied the right to vote?*

The law prohibits the denial of the right to vote because of immaterial errors or omissions on records of applications.

*Is the poll tax illegal?*

The poll tax is illegal in federal elections by reason of the passage of the Twenty-third Amendment to the Constitution of the United States.

*Is discrimination in housing prohibited?*

Yes. It is covered by the Civil Rights Act of 1968, described at the beginning of this chapter.

*How does this law affect my right to sell my home to the person of my choice? To rent my home to the person of my choice?*

The acts in no way affect the sale, rental, or leasing of owner-occupied dwellings of four units or less by the owner himself without an agent.

*Must the builder of a federally financed housing development sell his new homes to whoever wishes to buy?*

There is nothing in the law that would require the sale of a house to any buyer, whatever the financing. However, an executive order in 1962 requires that federally assisted building developments must have "open occupancy" clauses. These require rental or sale to anyone, regardless of race, creed, or color.

*If you have a government-insured loan on your boarding house, will you have to rent to anyone?*

The act states that federal insurance and guaranteed loan programs are exempted from the act.

*Is it true that boarding houses serving permanent residents must give lodging to all?*

No. Boarding houses occupied by "residents" rather than "transients" (travelers) are not covered in this act. Furthermore, any owner-occupied house with five or less rooms for rent is exempted, even if it serves transients.

*Will it be possible to have "restricted" housing developments or "restricted" apartments?*

Racially discriminating covenants have been ruled by the courts to be "judicially unenforceable"; that is, they will not be upheld in court.

*If urban renewal funds are used for private building, will there be a requirement for open occupancy?*

Under Title VI, the law requires open occupancy, and an earlier act of Congress makes open occupancy a requirement for the use of urban renewal funds.

*Is it illegal for a white person to marry a Negro?*

No. State statutes which forbade miscegenation are now invalid. They have been interpreted by the courts as unconstitutional.

*Are banks permitted to lend money to persons or firms of their choice?*

Yes. The act makes no mention of this.

*Does the Civil Rights Law mean one has to take a Negro into one's home?*

No. There is absolutely nothing in the act which says you have to have anyone in your home you do not want.

*Do professional men have to attend anyone who requests service?*

The law does not cover doctors, lawyers, bankers, or other professional men.

*What definitions of the following terms will be used to interpret the meaning of the law: transient, discrimination, racial imbalance?*

The act does not provide any definitions of the terms transient, discrimination, or racial imbalance. All of them are subject to court interpretation.

*How does the law affect nondiscrimination in federally assisted programs?*

It would prohibit discrimination in any program or activity receiving federal assistance under grant, contract, or loan. It directs federal agencies to establish programs of compliance and would authorize denial of funds to those programs that discriminate. But any denial is subject to judicial review. A hearing is guaranteed before funds are cut off, and a report to Congress is also required before funds can be denied. Presidential approval is required before any general cut-off of funds is approved.

*Can Congress hold up the funds of a contractor doing government work who fails to employ Negroes?*

The law permits the halting of funds to federally aided programs in which racial discrimination is allowed to persist. The act prohibits racial discrimination under any program or activity receiving federal assistance except insurance and loan guarantee programs. For example, requests for federal aid for a new hospital, school, airport, or other public facility would be denied if the party making the request refused to observe nondiscriminatory requirements. Any cut-off of federal funds is subject to review by the courts.

## Chapter 28

## CRIMINAL LAW

*What is a crime?*

A crime is a violation of law punishable at the instance of the government as a public wrong. Basic to criminal law is the distinguishing of a crime—a public wrong, or injury to the peace and good order of society—from a tort—a private wrong, or injury to a private citizen. While one act, such as assault and battery, may at the same time constitute a tort and a crime, only the criminal aspect is taken into full account in prosecuting the one who committed the wrong.

*What is an infamous crime?*

The term now means an offense that makes the offender liable to an infamous punishment, such as a disqualification from holding public office or imprisonment in a state prison or penitentiary.

*What is a capital crime?*

Any offense for which the death penalty may be inflicted.

*How are crimes classified?*

As treasons, felonies, and misdemeanors.

*What constitutes treason?*

The United States Constitution provides that treason against the United States shall consist only in levying war against them or in adhering to their enemies, giving them aid and comfort. The Constitution further provides that no person shall be convicted of treason unless on the testimony of two witnesses to the same overt act or on confession in open court. Congress may declare the punishment of treason, but no attainder of treason shall work corruption of blood or forfeiture, except during the life of the person attainted. Statutes provide for the punishment of treason, as defined, with death or imprisonment and fine.

## What is a felony?

Originally a felony was an offense punishable with death or with forfeiture of estate. Felonies included arson, burglary, larceny, robbery, murder and manslaughter, sodomy, mayhem, as well as breach of prison, rescue and escape in the case of prisoners held for a felony. Under modern statutes felony includes any offense punishable by imprisonment in a state prison or penitentiary.

## What is a misdemeanor?

The word "misdemeanor" denotes all crimes less than a felony. Punishment for a misdemeanor is confinement in a jail rather than in a state prison.

## In criminal law what is meant by "attempt"?

An attempt is an endeavor to commit an offense of any grade or to cause or to procure its commission by another by means of solicitation or incitement. It is a misdemeanor.

## Is every person punishable for the crimes he commits?

No. Friendly foreign sovereigns and their attendants and their ambassadors, diplomatic agents, and public ministers, along with their attendants, households, and retinue, are exempt from arrest, entry of their houses, or subjection to the process of the law of the country visited.

Ships of war belonging to foreign nations are exempt from the local jurisdiction of the country whose ports they are permitted to visit; however, merchant ships and their crews are not so exempt.

## Are members of Congress immune to arrest?

No. They may be subject to arrest and prosecution on criminal charges under either state or federal authority.

*To what extent are minors liable for their crimes?*

A person under seven years of age is conclusively presumed to be incapable of committing a crime. Between seven and fourteen a person is presumed incapable of committing a crime, and the presumption can only be overcome by clear and strong proof of actual criminal capacity; that is, of the person's ability to understand the nature of the transaction in question and to know its wrongfulness.

A male infant under fourteen is conclusively presumed incapable of the commission of rape or of an attempt to rape.

In offenses involving the power to contract, or the like, the guilt cannot attach to a minor because of the civil disqualifications of infancy.

*Can a corporation be convicted of a crime?*

Yes. The acts of a corporation, strictly speaking, are the acts of the individuals who, as its agents or officers, execute its powers; and these individuals are punishable as principals for any criminal transaction in which they engage in the course of the conduct of corporate affairs.

A corporation is also liable to prosecution and punishment, by fine and sequestration of property or by loss of franchise, for acts of its servants or of agents assuming to act for it in the exercise of corporate functions. Among the offenses so punishable are violations of liquor, license, and revenue laws; keeping a disorderly house; permitting gambling; publishing a libel; and contempt of court.

*To what extent is insanity a defense to criminal liability?*

Insanity is a defense if, at the time of the commission of an alleged crime, the perpetrator labors under any form of disorder or mental unsoundness that deprives him of a sane appreciation of right and wrong with reference to the particular transaction or of the nature and quality of the act or that renders him unable to refrain from doing the act.

*To what extent is drunkenness a defense?*

Liability to punishment is not ordinarily affected by mere voluntary intoxication; but whenever any particular intent, purpose, or state of mind is an element of the crime charged, or of its degree, the fact of intoxication must be taken into consideration. If intoxication is involuntary, as when it is produced accidentally or by the connivance of another, there is no liability to punishment.

## To what extent is ignorance a defense?

Ignorance of the law is immaterial to the question of guilt, unless a crime is of such nature that it requires a special intent, in which case any ignorance that precludes the entertaining of the requisite intent operates as an excuse. For example, there can be no larceny without fraudulent or dishonest intent; hence one who takes a thing under an honest mistake of legal right does not incur guilt.

Ignorance or a mistake of fact on any matter essential to guilt exempts from criminal liability one whose conduct was free from fault or gross negligence. Thus a minor who voted illegally, but who in good faith thought himself to be of proper age, would not be punishable. On the other hand, it is no defense to statutory rape to assert that the accused did not know the girl was under the age of consent.

## Who are the parties to a crime?

The principal, or actual perpetrator, and any accomplices and accessories. Every person in any manner concerned in the commission of a crime is an accomplice, or *particeps criminis,* and incurs the guilt of that crime. If several persons act in concert, performing different parts together constituting the crime, each is chargeable with the complete felony or misdemeanor, as the case may be. The participation must be actual, voluntary, and intentional. There is no criminal liability, for example, if one is so drunk, or otherwise affected, as to be unable to appreciate what the perpetrators are doing; nor is there any criminal liability if one is merely present at the commission of an offense.

An accessory before the fact is one who instigates the commission of a felony that is afterward, in pursuance of the instigation, committed in his absence. If the instigator is present, he is a principal.

An accessory after the fact is one who, knowing a felony to have been committed by another, aids or assists him, in hindrance of public justice, to avoid or escape arrest, trial, or punishment for the offense.

*What are assault and battery?*

A battery is an unlawful beating, or any actual physical force or violence unlawfully applied to the person of another. If the force is only attempted, without actual contact or touching, the offense is assault. An action that tends to create in another the fear that force or violence is about to be applied to him constitutes an assault. The consent of the injured person to a battery is immaterial; a beating or the infliction of injury to one's person cannot be licensed. Battery may be committed by any sort of physical touch, including such acts as jostling, throwing a missile or water on a person, or spitting on him. The touching need not be done with the hand or with anything held in it; it may be done by pushing any other person, by pushing anything against the person, or by setting a dog on him. As a practical matter, the word "assault" is also used to include battery.

*What is an aggravated assault?*

An assault may be accompanied by various circumstances of aggravation. Such assaults are distinct crimes and as such are subject to greater punishment than so-called common assaults. Modern statutes generally describe assault with intent to murder, rob, or rape or assault with a deadly weapon as aggravated assault.

*What is homicide?*

Homicide refers to the killing of one human being by another. For an act to be a homicide, it must involve the destruction of human life at any time after actual birth.

*How are homicides classified?*

A homicide is "culpable" or "felonious," unless it is committed under exceptional circumstances of excuse or justification.

*What exceptional circumstances will reduce felonious homicide to manslaughter?*

1. If a homicide results from merely unlawful conduct or neglect of duty without an intent to inflict death or injury likely to prove fatal, the homicide is manslaughter.

2. If the act causing death is due wholly to the heat of overwhelm-

ing passion caused by adequate provocation, the homicide is manslaughter.

### What is murder in the first degree?

A homicide perpetrated by means of poison or by laying in wait or by any other kind of willful, deliberate, and premeditated killing, or a homicide committed in the perpetration or attempted perpetration of arson, rape, robbery, or burglary, is murder in the first degree.

### What is murder in the second degree?

An unlawful killing without premeditation is murder in the second degree. If the homicide is committed with the intent to kill —but the intent did not exist until the moment of the act—it is murder in the second degree. Murder committed in a sudden fit of passion is murder in the second degree. Murder in the first degree often carries the death penalty; murder in the second degree does not.

### What is the difference between manslaughter and murder?

Manslaughter, a less serious offense than murder, is a killing without malice or intent, as in the heat of passion or by gross negligence. For example, a pedestrian who is run over and killed by a drunken automobile driver is the victim of manslaughter.

### Under what circumstances is the taking of a human life justifiable?

In lawful warfare, in the execution of sentences of capital punishment, or under military law or military orders. One is also justified in using such reasonable means within one's power as may in any particular case be apparently necessary for the security and protection of one's person or property, even to the extent of taking another's life.

### What is false imprisonment?

False imprisonment is the restraint of one's freedom without authority of law, whether it be in a prison, in a dwelling, on a highway, or at any other place whatever. Kidnaping is essentially false imprisonment aggravated by the carrying of the kidnaped person to some other place. Kidnaping is both a federal crime punishable by death and a state crime.

### What is abduction?

Abduction is the wrongful taking away of a person by means of fraud, persuasion, or violence. For example, a child is abducted when he is wrongfully taken from the care and custody of his parent or guardian.

### What is the difference between adultery and fornication?

Adultery is the voluntary sexual intercourse of a married person with one who is not the husband or wife. Fornication is the unlawful sexual knowledge of one unmarried person by another, whether the latter is married or not. Both offenses are misdemeanors, but they are rarely punished.

### What is incest?

Incest is sexual intercourse or cohabitation between persons related to each other in a degree within which marriage is prohibited by law, as between an uncle and his niece.

### What is bigamy?

Bigamy is the act of one who, having a husband or wife living, marries a second person. It is not bigamy if the husband or wife has been absent for a certain period—usually seven years—and the party who remarries does not know whether the absent party is living. A belief that the former wife or husband is dead, or that a former marriage was legally dissolved, does not constitute a defense to a charge of bigamy.

### What is abortion?

Abortion is the expulsion of a human fetus prematurely, or before it is capable of sustaining life. The procuring of an abortion is a misdemeanor.

### What is rape?

Rape is the unlawful carnal knowledge (sexual intercourse) by a man of a woman by force and against her consent. A rape is by force and against the woman's consent if her actual resistance is overcome by violence, if her submission is extorted through fear of bodily hurt, or if she is, to the knowledge of the perpetrator, to such an extent of unsound mind, or unconscious from sleep, alcohol, or drugs, as to be incapable of giving her consent. A male infant under fourteen years of age is conclusively presumed incapable of rape or attempted rape. A husband cannot rape his wife.

### What is statutory rape?

By statute girls under a certain age cannot give their consent to sexual intercourse. A man who has intercourse with a girl under that age exposes himself to the charge of statutory rape. The penalty may be death or life imprisonment.

### What is sodomy?

Sodomy, or buggery, is sexual intercourse by human beings either with each other against the order of nature or with an animal. Homosexuality is often punished under sodomy statutes. Sodomy, under our outmoded laws, may also be committed by a husband and wife who engage in various forms of oral intercourse.

### What is arson?

Arson is the willful and malicious burning of the dwelling of another. The dwelling or some part of it must be consumed by fire. By statute the offense includes the burning of virtually all other buildings, as well as a dwelling, and sometimes includes the burning of one's own house. The building may be any outhouse which, though not contiguous to the dwelling or under the same roof, is still within the curtilage or same common fence as the mansion house itself, and it may be a barn, stable, cow shed, dairy house, or the like. It is even a felony at common law to burn a barn unconnected with the house if it has corn or hay in it.

The burning, to constitute arson, must be both willful and malicious; but if willful, it is presumed to be malicious, although the contrary may be proved. If a homicide results from an attempt to commit arson, even though unintentionally, the crime is murder.

### What is burglary?

Burglary is the breaking and entering of the house of another in the nighttime with an intent to commit a felony. It does not matter whether the felony is actually committed. In general, the burglary must be committed in a house actually occupied as a dwelling. However, if the owner is absent but intends to return, although no one resides in the house in his absence, it is still his mansion house and the crime is burglary. By dwelling house is meant the house usually occupied by the person there residing and his family. It must be a permanent structure, and it is sufficient if part of the structure only is used as a home. A burglary may be committed in a church. One cannot commit burglary to one's own dwelling house.

The act must be done at night to constitute burglary; that is, when by the light of the sun the face or countenance of another cannot be clearly discerned, but the light referred to does not apply to moonlight, which is reflected sunlight.

The breaking and entering may be done on different nights, but both must be in the nighttime. There must be both breaking and entering, and both must be with felonious intent. The removal of any part of the house, or of the fastenings provided to secure it, is a breaking. Breaking includes knocking out a pane of glass, taking out nails or other fasteners, cutting and tearing down a netting at a window, raising the latch or picking open the lock with a false key, putting back the lock of a door or the fastening of a window by an instrument, turning the key when the door is locked on the inside, picking a lock, or lowering windows fastened only by a wedge or weight. But removing a loose plank in a partition wall has been held not to be a breaking. The further raising of a window sash already partly open to admit the person has also been held not to be a breaking. But the breaking of an inner door only will be sufficient to constitute a burglarious breaking. There may also be constructive breaking, as when entry is gained by fraud, conspiracy, or threats, which will be as effectual in making out a charge of burglary as an actual breaking.

The least entry with all or any part of the body, hand, or foot or with any instrument or weapon, if for the purpose of committing a felony, is sufficient to constitute the offense.

The intent to commit a felony is a necessary part of the crime, and the jury must determine whether the intent existed. The actual commission of a felony will furnish prima-facie evidence that the intent to commit a felony existed at the time of the breaking and entering. If the breaking and entering is with an intent to commit a trespass or a misdemeanor simply, and no felony is committed, the offense is not burglary.

Many states, by special law, have broadened burglary to include shops, stores, warehouses, and so on. Burglary may now be committed during the day as well as at night.

## What is meant by the term "false pretense"?

A false statement or misrepresentation made with fraudulent intent constitutes false pretense. Not every false representation or statement is a false pretense in a criminal sense. To be a crime the misrepresentation must have been made with fraudulent design to obtain money, goods, wares, or merchandise, and it must relate either to past events or to existing facts. Representations of future transactions may amount to a promise or covenant or warranty but not to a false pretense.

The pretense must be such as would lead one to give credit upon a false assumption that there is a basis for credit. And it is only necessary that one of several pretenses be false if, without that one, the credit would have been given or the property delivered. The false pretense, however, must have occurred before the contract was completed and the goods delivered. An intent to cheat or defraud must exist, and the intent may be inferred from a false representation. It is not necessary that the party defrauded should sustain loss, unless by statute obtaining goods is made part of the crime.

## What is counterfeiting?

The unlawful forging, copying, or imitating of that which is original or genuine to deceive or defraud another. Counterfeiting is usually applied to the unlawful printing or imitation of money.

## What is forgery?

Forgery is the fraudulent making or altering of a writing to the prejudice of another man's right. Fraudulently securing a true signature to a false instrument, or one not intended by the signer, is forgery. For example, if one is requested to draw a will for a sick person in a particular way and instead of doing so one inserts legacies other than those directed and procures the signature of the sick person to the will so made, without revealing to him the insertion of the additional legacies, he is guilty of forgery.

Making an instrument in a fictitious name or in the name of a person not existing is a forgery; the making of an instrument in one's own name and representing it to be the instrument of another of the same name when there is no such person would seem to be forgery. In the drawing of a will, the fraudulent omission of a legacy that one is directed to insert, so causing material alteration in a bequest to another, will be a forgery.

Signing the name of another to a note with an addition over the signer's own name stating that it was done by the other's authority will not constitute forgery, though no authority was given. Forgery may be committed by simply changing the second initial of a name.

Forgery may be complete without a publication or circulation of the forged instrument. It is forgery to falsify or falsely make records and other matters of a public nature, as a parish register or a letter in the name of a magistrate or of the warden of a prison directing the discharge of a prisoner.

A letter of recommendation of a person as a man of property and pecuniary responsibility, a guarantee of payment for goods delivered, a testimony of character, or a railway pass or ticket may all be forged. It is forgery to fraudulently attest or falsely make a deed or will or to falsely sign or endorse one's name on a promissory note, check, or bill of exchange. There may be forgery of a printed or engraved instrument as well as a written one, but it must be of some document or writing. Printing an artist's name in the corner of a picture to falsely represent it as an original picture by the artist is said not to be forgery.

There must be an intent to defraud another to constitute forgery, but it is not necessary that one should have been actually injured, and it is sufficient if the instrument forged might have proved prejudicial. By statute in most states, some acts are made forgery that would not be so at common law.

To utter or publish a forged instrument is to assert and declare directly or indirectly by words or actions that the instrument is good. It is not necessary that it should be passed in order to complete the uttering.

### What is conspiracy?

Conspiracy is a combination of two or more persons by some concerted action to accomplish a criminal or unlawful purpose or to accomplish by criminal and unlawful means a purpose not unlawful.

The conspiracy or unlawful combination is itself a criminal offense and is punishable whether the object of the conspiracy is accomplished or not. It is not necessary that any person actually be injured by the conspiracy or that any act at all be done toward carrying out the intended plan. It is not necessary that the thing proposed to be done be itself criminal.

A combination to destroy one's reputation by a verbal report is indictable, though the verbal report itself would not be; so is a combination between two or more whereby the goods of one may be disposed of to the other or to a third person for the purpose of defeating creditors; so is a combination to go to a theater and hiss an actor or to prosecute one for the purpose of extorting money from him.

A combination of two or more to falsely charge one with poisoning another or with being the father of a bastard child, or to induce a girl by false statement to leave her parents' home with a view to facilitating her prostitution, or to affect the price of public stocks by false rumors, or to prevent competition at an auction, or to coerce workmen to quit work, or to injure one in his trade or business or profession, or with the object of benefiting themselves to the prejudice of the public or the oppression of individuals, such prejudice or oppression being the natural or necessary consequence of the proposed acts, is a conspiracy.

The declaration or statement of one conspirator made while acting in the common design is evidence against all. But if it is made after the accomplishment of the intended purpose and after the concert of action is ended, it is evidence only against the one making it.

If retail dealers combine and refuse to purchase from wholesalers, unless they discontinue to sell to brokers, this is unlawful, and those injuring the business of the broker by so doing may be held for damages resulting from the destruction of his business.

### What does the term "larceny" cover?

The wrongful and fraudulent taking and carrying away of the personal goods of another with the felonious intent to make them the property of the taker without the owner's consent. The distinction between grand and petit larceny has been abolished in most places. In some places, however, the penalty is different depending upon whether the larceny is of goods valued at more or less than a given sum.

The taking of goods must be against the consent of the owner, and the property of the owner in the goods may be general or absolute, or it may be special, that is, it may be in his hands as bailee or for the exercise of some particular function or right or duty in connection therewith. There will be no larceny if consent to the taking was given, though the contrary is true if the consent is obtained by fraud. Neither will there be larceny if the taking is under claim of right, that is, if the party honestly believes that the property belongs to him or that he has a right to take it even though he does not actually have such right.

It is not larceny if one comes rightfully into possession of an article and appropriates it to his own use. To meet such cases, statute laws have been quite commonly passed making larceny by bailee or trustee, and certain embezzlements, criminal. Mere custody has been construed not to be possession, the dominion over a property being of a very limited character. In cases where custody only of the property has been parted with by the owner there may be, it seems, such a taking and carrying away by the custodian as will constitute larceny.

The taking must be in the county where the criminal is to be charged, but by construction of law there is a fresh taking in every county into which the thief carries the stolen goods. He may be tried wherever caught with the stolen property in his possession, if it is within the state where the theft took place. To constitute a taking the property must be actually removed, but a slight removal only is necessary if it is actually taken into possession.

No larceny can be committed of things affixed to the soil, but if actually severed by the owner, a third person, or the thief himself as a separate transaction, it then becomes a subject of larceny. The article must have some value, even though it is slight.

Possession of the fruits of the crime soon after its commission is evidence of guilt if unexplained either by direct evidence or by attending circumstances or by showing the character and habits of life of the possessor or otherwise. The longer the time elapsing before discovery of the stolen article, the weaker this presumption, particularly if the goods are of such character as frequently change hands.

Where conviction depends alone upon the evidence of the possession of the stolen goods, the possession proven should be exclusive. For example, if the goods should be found in a house in which other persons reside capable of committing the larceny, this would be insufficient to prove guilty possession unless coupled with other proof of suspicious circumstances against the defendant. The presumption of guilt arising from possession is much greater if the possession consists of fruits of a series of thefts, or if it consists of the multiplicity of miscellaneous articles, or if it is of a kind of value inconsistent with the means and station of the party accused, or if the party has suddenly and otherwise inexplicably acquired means or has an unusual amount of money to spend.

This rule of presumption of guilt from possession of stolen property, however, must be exercised with caution and should never be applied when there is reasonable ground to conclude that the witness may be mistaken, or when from any cause the identity of the stolen article with that found in the possession of the accused is not clearly and satisfactorily established, because of the danger of convicting innocent persons. Usually, however, there are corroborative or explanatory circumstances to be proven in support of this presumption of guilt arising from possession. This may arise either in the conduct of the party or otherwise, as when he has secreted the property or falsely denied possession of it or cannot in a credible manner give consistent accounts thereof, or when he has attempted to dispose of it at an unreasonably low price, or when instruments of crime are found in his possession. These and many other circumstances will aid the presumption of guilt.

## What is libel?

Libel is any malicious defamation expressed in printing or writing and intended to blacken either the memory of one who is dead or the reputation of one who is living and expose him to public hatred, contempt, or ridicule. The person guilty may be proceeded against by indictment or may be sued for damages.

Slander when spoken is not a subject of indictment, but if it is written or printed, it becomes a libel and is a subject of indictment.

It is a libel to fix a gallows at a man's door, burn him in effigy, or exhibit him in any ignominious manner. It is a libel to publish a ludicrous story in a newspaper, if it tends to ridicule a person, even though he told the same story himself.

The sale of each copy of a book or paper containing the libel is a distinct publication and a separate offense. The publication must be malicious, and evidence of the malice may be either expressed or implied; and when a man publishes a writing that on its face is libelous, the law presumes a malicious intent and it is unnecessary to prove other circumstances showing malice. Though he does not know of the publication of a libel in his paper, the managing editor is nevertheless responsible. Criticism of a book is not libelous so long as it does not impugn the character of the author or contain misstatements of facts set forth in the book. Alleging falsely that one is "slippery," for example, is libelous. Communications to merchants impugning the credit of another merchant by alleging that he does not pay his debts, and deterring others from dealing with him are libelous, if not true. Statements made in affidavits and in similar legal proceedings, though injurious, are nevertheless not libelous.

### What is perjury?

Perjury is the swearing willfully, absolutely, and falsely, under oath, in a matter material to the issue. In general, perjury may be committed in case of an affirmation as well.

To constitute perjury the oath must be taken and the falsehood asserted with deliberation and with consciousness of the nature of the statement made, for if made through inadvertence, surprise, or mistake of the import of the question, there is no corrupt motive. If one swears willfully and deliberately to a matter which he rashly believes but which is false, and which he has no probable cause for believing, he is guilty of perjury. Even if one, intending to deceive, asserts what may happen to be true, without a knowledge of the fact, the accidental truth of his evidence will not excuse him.

Before a person can be convicted of perjury it must appear that the oath or affirmation was administered by one having competent authority to do so in the particular case, and an oath before a private person or before an officer having no jurisdiction is no crime. The proceeding must be before one who is in some way entrusted with the administration of justice, and the testimony must be in respect to a matter regularly before him. The assertion must be absolute.

Another necessary element in perjury is that the oath must be material to the issue. If the facts sworn to are foreign to the matter in the question, there can be no perjury; yet questions on cross-examination asked for the proper purpose of testing the credibility of the witness, as, for example, whether he has ever been convicted of a felony, are considered material.

*What is subornation of perjury?*

It is the offense of procuring another to make such false oath as would constitute perjury in the principal.

*What is meant by "receiving stolen goods"?*

One who has received stolen goods knowing them to have been stolen is criminally responsible. An aider or abettor in the stealing cannot be regarded as a receiver, for he is a party to the theft itself. If the goods are found in the house of a man who is not the thief prima facie, he is a receiver, though if found in the room of a boarder in the house, this would not be true. The actual manual possession or touching of the goods by the defendant is not needed to make him a receiver. It is sufficient if they are in the possession of his agent or of one over whom he has control, so that they will be forthcoming on his order.

The defendant must know the goods to have been stolen or it must appear that the circumstances under which he obtained them were such that a person of ordinary understanding and prudence must have been satisfied that they were stolen. This would be the case if he should receive watches, jewelry, large quantities of money, bundles of clothes of various kinds, and the like, from boys or persons destitute or without means of acquiring them, or if brought to him at untimely hours, or if offered far below their value, or if obvious falsehood is resorted to by the thief to account for possession of them.

*What is robbery?*

The felonious and forcible taking of goods or money, to any value, from the person of another against his will by violence or by putting him in fear. The violence necessary to this crime, however, is not confined to an actual assault of the person by beating and knocking him down or forcibly wresting the thing away from him. Whatever goes to intimidate by apprehension of personal violence or by fear of life, with a view to compelling the delivery of property, is sufficient. The "taking from the person" need not be in its strictly literal sense, for the taking may be from the person's presence when it is done with violence and against his consent.

The violence and putting in fear need not concur; if a man is knocked down and robbed while unconscious, the offense is still robbery. If one is put in fear by threats and then robbed, no other violence is necessary to constitute the crime, though the violence or putting in fear may be at the time of the act or immediately preceding.

It has been held that the snatching of an article by a sudden pull, even though a momentary force is exerted, is not such violence as would constitute a robbery, though if there is any struggle or disruption, the offense is robbery. There is no robbery if the property is taken under a bona-fide claim of right and not with a view to wrongfully taking another's property.

### What is meant by "compounding crimes"?

A party immediately aggrieved who agrees with a thief or other felon not to prosecute is compounding a felony. Merely taking back the stolen goods is no offense, unless the owner agrees not to prosecute. A mere failure to prosecute is not compounding a felony, but the accepting of a promissory note signed by the thief as a consideration for not prosecuting is sufficient to constitute the offense and to render one guilty. Compounding felonies is criminal. So is compounding misdemeanors when the injury is done to an individual who would have a right to recover in a civil suit, as in a case of embezzlement. When the offense is serious in character or of a notably public nature, no agreement to stifle a prosecution is valid. Generally, it may be said that when a prosecution has been instituted and there is evidence to support the charge, there should be no settlement of the case except by express permission of the court. No recovery can be had in any agreement or obligation given for compounding felonies or misdemeanors when the compounding of such misdemeanors is illegal.

### What is blackmail?

It is extortion by threats, either oral or written, with the intent to compel the person threatened to do some act against his will that threatens that person with bodily harm, humiliation, ridicule, or disgrace.

*What is breach of prison?*

The act of breaking out of jail or prison with intent to escape. The escape from custody of a person lawfully arrested is also breach of prison.

*What is bribery?*

Bribery is the receiving or offering of any undue reward, by or to any person whose ordinary profession or business relates to the administration of public justice, to influence his behavior and incline him to act contrary to his duty and the known rules of honesty and integrity. It now applies to persons in almost all official positions, as well as to the giving or taking of a reward in connection with voting at public elections. To constitute the offense it is not necessary that the person sought to be bribed should even have a right to vote at all. Even an *attempt* to bribe is criminal.

A contract procured by bribery is void. Merely paying one in an official position for his time, and for loss occasioned in his own business from attending a meeting in order to vote in favor of a contract with the one paying for such loss of time, etc., will vitiate the contract, unless, at least, such vote was not necessary to the passage of the resolution awarding the contract.

*What is extortion?*

By criminal extortion is meant the unlawful taking by any officer, by reason of or through his office, of any money or thing of value that is not due him or that is more than is due or that is due at a later time. To constitute the crime, money or something of actual value must be received. The taking of a promissory note that is void is not sufficient to constitute an extortion, for it has no value. The note will not be enforceable, at least that part of it which was for an extortionate fee or compensation. An officer may not take money other than regular fees for the performance of his duty, even though the taking is within the exercise of a discretionary power.

The word "extortion" has a more extended popular meaning than that indicated above. If money or some other valuable thing is extorted by one not an officer, by way of blackmail or other species of coercion, the injured person has a right of action to recover it from the offender.

### What is criminal negligence?

Acting in such a reckless and dangerous manner as to constitute an utter disregard for human life. An automobile driver, operating a car under the influence of liquor, who strikes and injures a pedestrian is guilty of criminal negligence. So is a driver who operates his car at sixty miles an hour in a thirty mile an hour zone in a congested area.

### What is embezzlement?

Embezzlement is the misappropriation of funds or goods that come into a person's hands lawfully. A salesman who fails to turn over funds to his employer is guilty of embezzlement, since the original taking of the money was lawful.

## Chapter 29

## CRIMINAL PROCEDURE

*What is an arrest?*

An arrest is made when one person takes another into custody for the real or pretended purpose of bringing the arrestee before a court or official to answer a criminal charge.

*Is every restraint by a peace officer a technical arrest?*

No. A police officer who detains a motorist for the purpose of checking his driver's license imposes a restraint, but not an arrest.

*Under what circumstances may an arrest be made without a warrant?*

A private citizen may arrest a felon without a warrant when a felony or serious crime has been committed and he has reasonable grounds to suspect that the person he arrests has committed the crime. A private citizen may also arrest another person without a warrant if he suspects that a felony has been committed, if such is actually the case. A private citizen may arrest without a warrant when a felony or breach of the peace is committed in his presence. He may also arrest another person to prevent a breach of the peace or a felony from taking place.

*May a private citizen arrest another without a warrant in the case of misdemeanors?*

Yes, in some states, provided the misdemeanor is committed in his presence.

*What liability does a private citizen assume if the accused is later acquitted or found not guilty?*

He runs the risk of being sued for false imprisonment.

*Under what circumstances may a police officer make an arrest without a warrant?*

**1.** If a felony has been committed and the officer reasonably suspects that the arrestee committed it.

**2.** When a felony or breach of the peace is committed, or is about to be committed, in the presence of the officer.

*May a police officer call upon a private citizen to help make an arrest?*

Yes. The person aiding in the arrest is protected if he reasonably believes that the officer has the authority to make the arrest. A citizen who fails or refuses to aid a police officer may be guilty of a misdemeanor.

*What is a warrant?*

A warrant is an order, issued by a magistrate or other official, commanding a peace officer to arrest a certain person accused of a certain crime. To be effective every warrant:

**1.** Must be in writing and be issued in the name of the state.

**2.** Must set forth the nature of the offense.

**3.** Must command that the accused be arrested and brought before the magistrate who issues the warrant or before any magistrate convenient in the case.

**4.** Must specify the name of the accused and describe him with reasonable certainty.

**5.** Must state the date and place of issuance.

**6.** Must be signed by the issuing magistrate or official and designate his title.

*What is a bench warrant?*

A bench warrant is simply a warrant issued by a judge rather than by a justice of the peace or other magistrate.

*May an arrest, with or without a warrant, be made at any time of the day or night and on any day of the week?*

Yes.

*May a police officer use deadly force to prevent the escape of a person charged with a misdemeanor?*

No.

*May a police officer use deadly force to prevent the escape of a person charged with a felony?*

There is a conflict of authority on this.

*May a police officer pursue the accused into another state and make the arrest there?*

Yes. According to the Uniform Act on Fresh Pursuit, when such an arrest is made, the person so arrested shall be taken before a magistrate of the county in which the apprehension took place. After a preliminary hearing by the magistrate, he may be held a reasonable time, pending the issuance of an extradition warrant. If the magistrate should determine that the arrest is unlawful, he must discharge the person accused.

*What is extradition?*

According to the United States Constitution "a person charged in any state with treason, felony, or other crime, who shall flee from justice and be found in another state, shall, on demand of the executive authority of the state from which he fled, be delivered up, to be removed to the state having jurisdiction of the crime."

*What are the essential requirements of an extradition?*

1. That the person to be extradited be a fugitive from justice in the demanding state.

2. That the fugitive be charged with a crime in the demanding state.

3. That the executive authority of the demanding state demand delivery of the fugitive and accompany the demand with a copy of the indictment or other form of accusation.

4. That the demanding executive have the indictment when the demand is made.

*What is the first thing a person arrested should do?*

Request permission, at the police station where he is to be booked, to phone his attorney.

*Is the accused under any compulsion to make any statement to the police?*

No. Nor should he volunteer any information before his counsel arrives, and then only with the counsel present.

*Should the accused volunteer to take a so-called lie detector test?*

No. The results of such a "test" are not admissible in a court of law. Under no circumstances should the accused allow himself to be subjected to such a test without the full knowledge of his counsel.

*What is the purpose of a preliminary hearing before a magistrate?*

To protect the accused from standing trial when there is no probable cause to believe that he is guilty of the offense charged.

*Does the accused have the right to have counsel present at the preliminary hearing?*

Not only does he have the right, he should insist on it. Too much stress cannot be laid on the fact that the accused should retain counsel immediately upon his arrest, and at every stage of the proceedings. If the accused does not have counsel by the time of the preliminary hearing, he should request a postponement until he is able to obtain such counsel.

*May the accused waive the preliminary hearing?*

Yes, but he should do so only on the advice of his attorney.

*What happens at the preliminary hearing?*

If the magistrate finds that the state has failed to produce sufficient evidence linking the accused with the crime charged, he may dismiss the accused. If, on the other hand, he finds that the state has made out a prima-facie (at first view) case, he may admit the accused to bail.

*Does the defendant's discharge at a preliminary hearing prevent the state from later trying him on an identical charge?*

No. The weight of authority is that such a discharge does not expose the accused to double jeopardy.

*What is bail?*

Bail is the security given for the release of a person who is in legal custody. Bail insures that the accused will appear before a court or magistrate as required in the bail bond or recognizance.

*What is the purpose of bail?*

To prevent the accused from being confined indefinitely while awaiting trial.

*Does the accused have a right in all cases to be released on bail before conviction?*

Yes, except in those cases for which death may be the penalty on conviction.

*What about bail after conviction for a crime?*

In some states it is a matter of right only if the sentence is a fine. In all other states bail following conviction is a matter of discretion with the judge.

*How does bail operate?*

Bail operates through bail bondsmen, most of whom are licensed and regulated by the fifty states. The accused pays the bondsman a fee based on the amount of bail set by the magistrate or judge. A common practice is to charge a defendant ten percent of the amount of bail set. If bail is $5,000, the accused or his friends and relatives must put up $500 as a cash premium. Bond rates vary from state to state. In some the usual premium is five percent of the first $1,000 of bail, four percent of the second $1,000, and three percent for each $1,000 above that. Often the bondsman insists on additional collateral as insurance that the defendant will appear in court on schedule. The amount of bail depends in large measure on the gravity of the charge. It is usually the attorney for the accused who arranges for the release of the defendant through a professional bondsman.

### What happens if the defendant fails to appear for trial?

If he fails to appear when scheduled, the case may be continued for a reasonable period to allow him to appear. If when the case is again called the defendant does not appear, the bail is forfeited and a warrant for his arrest is issued.

### What is meant by release on the defendant's own recognizance?

Simply that the accused is trusted, for one reason or another, to appear for trial without bail. It is usually granted when the offense is either minor or the reputation of the accused is so good that there is little question in the judge's mind about the defendant's appearance.

### What happens if you witness a crime?

If the police know you are a witness, you will be expected to identify the accused, appear at the preliminary police hearing, at the grand jury hearing, and finally at the trial itself. If you witness a crime—murder or robbery for example—and the police are not at the scene, you have a public duty to report the alleged crime to the police as promptly as possible. Many people, unfortunately, are reluctant to do so for fear of getting involved, but if the administration of justice is not to break down, witnesses to all crimes must accept their responsibility to step forward.

### What is a subpoena?

A subpoena is a court order requesting your appearance at some trial, usually as a witness, sometimes a reluctant one. It is never wise to ignore a subpoena. A refusal to obey one usually results in the issuance of an arrest warrant. Failure to testify as a witness may invite a charge of contempt of court unless the witness pleads self-incrimination, that his testimony will lead to his own indictment. This he may do on constitutional grounds either on the advice of his own counsel or that of the presiding judge.

### Can a witness be held in jail?

Yes, if the police have reason to believe that the witness for one reason or another will not appear in court.

## Under what circumstances can the police search your home?

Before he can legally search, a police officer must first obtain a warrant from a judge. The search warrant will not be issued unless the officer swears that he has probable cause for believing that certain *specific* evidence of a crime will be found at a *certain* place. Probable cause is more than mere guesswork. It is the action that a normally cautious man would take under similar circumstances; it is not a license for a general fishing expedition.

## What procedure must a police officer follow if he appears with a search warrant?

He must identify himself, show you a copy of the warrant, and allow you sufficient time to read it.

## What are no-knock laws?

Congress passed a no-knock law in 1968 and many states have followed suit. The aim was to prevent an accused from destroying evidence which might implicate him, such as drugs or gambling slips. Under no-knock provisions a policeman with a warrant has a right to break into a house without warning to prevent the disposal of incriminating evidence. The no-knock rule may also be applied when it is obvious that the police officer's life might be endangered were he to identify himself.

## May you resist an officer even if you know there is no criminal evidence in your home?

Not if he has a warrant. To resist an officer who has either a warrant for your arrest or a search warrant is in itself a crime. Your only alternative if you feel your constitutional rights have been violated is to tell the officer that you protest the search—in front of a witness if at all possible—and then take legal action against the policeman. Of course, you may allow a police officer to search your home without a warrant by waiving your constitutional rights. If you do, any criminal evidence found on the premises may be used against you. A minor may not give such assent. Premises include not only homes but apartments and motels. Where a police officer has reasonable cause for believing that evidence of a specific crime may be located in an automobile or boat, he has a right to search without a warrant. This is on the understandable theory that the fugitive may escape before a warrant could be obtained.

## What rights do the police have to stop and frisk an individual?

They have this right only if they reasonably suspect that the individual is about to commit a crime. Thus one suspected of attempting to commit a robbery or murder or any other serious crime may be stopped and frisked, and arrested if a gun or burglary tools are found on him. The "stop" must be limited to asking the suspect what he is doing in the area and to properly identify himself. The "frisk" must be limited to patting down the suspect's clothing to reveal any concealed weapons such as guns, knives, or clubs.

## Are most arrests made with warrants?

No. Obviously if a policeman sees a crime being committed—or has reasonable cause for believing that the accused actually committed the crime even if later it turns out otherwise—he can make the arrest without a warrant. Otherwise many criminals would escape before a warrant could be issued. The arrest, however, must be based on more than mere suspicion. A policeman may arrest without a warrant if he hears over his police radio that a suspect of a given description has just killed a man and fled in a certain automobile bearing certain license plates. He has no right to round up a number of individuals, without appropriate warrants, merely because they happened to be in the vicinity of the crime. Incidentally, you should under no circumstances resist a lawful arrest—nor even what you may consider an illegal one. Your proper remedy is to employ counsel to protect your legal rights. In carrying out his duties a policeman has a right to use as much force as is necessary, even to the use of his gun, where circumstances warrant.

## What are your rights when a policeman does make an arrest?

Under United States Supreme Court decisions, especially as the result of the Miranda case, an arresting officer is duty bound to inform you of your constitutional rights. Many police departments use the so-called Miranda card, which they ask the suspect to read and sign. A typical card may read as follows:

1. You are under arrest. Before we ask you any questions, you must

understand what your rights are.

2. You have the right to remain silent. You are not required to say anything to us at any time or to answer any questions. Anything you say may be used against you in court.

3. You have a right to talk to a lawyer for advice before we question you and to have him with you during questioning.

4. If you cannot afford a lawyer and want one, an attorney will be provided you.

5. If you want to answer questions now without a lawyer present, you still have the right to stop answering at any time. You also have the right to stop answering at any time until you talk to your lawyer.

### WAIVER

1. Have you read or had read to you the warning as to your rights?
2. Do you understand these rights?
3. Do you wish to answer any questions?
4. Do you wish to have an attorney present during questioning?
5. Signature of defendant on line below

_____

6. Time _____
7. _____Date
8. Signature of officer _____
9. Signature of witness _____


*What should you do about such a card if arrested?*

Refuse to sign it altogether and insist on being allowed to call an attorney when you arrive at the police station for booking.

*Is it true that when arrested you have the right to make only one telephone call for your attorney?*

No. You have the right to make as many calls as necessary to obtain counsel. Unhappily, some police stations do not always accord this privilege to the accused. But the right to make as many telephone calls as necessary to obtain counsel and to inform your closest relative of your arrest nevertheless remains.

*What happens to a suspect when taken to a police station?*

The police have the right to book him, that is enter his name, address, and the crime of which he is accused in their register or charge book. They also have the right to fingerprint and photograph him and search his clothes and body including injection scars to determine whether or not he uses narcotics. Evidence found as a result of such a search may be used against him. He may even be placed in a line-up for identification in connection with the crime he is accused of, but he is entitled to have an attorney present at the line-up.

*What is meant by plea bargaining?*

This is a process by which the accused—ordinarily by and with the advice and consent of his counsel—pleads guilty to a lesser offense than the crime for which he is charged and hence receives a lesser sentence. Plea bargaining or "copping a plea" is generally done by the accused's counsel with the consent and approval of the prosecuting attorney, and sometimes with the approval of the judge. The theory is that plea bargaining often saves the state the expense of a long drawn out trial which may or may not convict the defendant of the more serious crime. If the state, for example, cannot prove willful, premeditated murder, it may be willing to accept a plea of second degree murder. If the defendant is charged with burglary and there is a question of sufficient evidence to convict, the state may accept a plea of guilty to a lesser offense, such as larceny. Of course, plea bargaining should be reserved only in those cases where there is little or no doubt about the defendant's guilt.

*How is an accused person charged with a crime?*

The accused may be charged by (1) indictment, (2) presentment, (3) information, or (4) complaint.

*What is an indictment?*

An indictment is a written accusation of a crime presented to a court, on oath, by a grand jury. It is usually drawn by the public prosecutor and referred to a grand jury. If the grand jury finds sufficient evidence of a crime, it reports a "true bill of indictment" and presents it to the court.

## What is a presentment?

A presentment is a written accusation initiated by a grand jury and presented to a court for the purpose of having an indictment drawn and submitted to a grand jury.

## What is an information?

An information is a written accusation of a crime drawn and filed in a court by the public prosecutor without the intervention of a grand jury.

## What is a complaint?

A complaint is a written accusation of a crime made on oath by a private citizen.

## What is the function of a grand jury?

To return indictments in criminal cases and/or to investigate matters on its own initiative for possible criminal action.

## How is a grand jury selected?

A federal grand jury consists of sixteen to twenty-three persons. In the various states the number ranges from five to twenty-three, the latter number being the most popular. Jurors are selected either by lot from tax rolls or election registration lists or by the discretionary choice exercised by certain officials. Most states require that jury lists be prepared by commissioners or other officials and that both grand jurors and petit jurors be selected therefrom. The federal Constitution forbids the systematic exclusion of the members of any race from a grand jury.

## On what grounds may the validity of a grand jury be challenged?

Both the defendant and the state may challenge a grand jury on the ground that was not properly selected by law. Challenges to individual grand jurors may be made on the ground that they are prejudiced or that they are not legally qualified to act.

## Does a grand jury decide the guilt or innocence of a defendant?

No. A grand jury decides only that a prima-facie case stands against the defendant—unless explained by him and his witnesses.

It is for this reason that grand juries usually hear only the witnesses for the state and such other witnesses as they may choose to hear.

*Who is permitted to be present at the proceedings of a grand jury?*

During the taking of testimony, only the defendant, the prosecutor, the witnesses, the reporter, and the jurors. No one other than the jurors is allowed to be present while the grand jury is deliberating. The members of the grand jury, of course, are sworn to secrecy.

*How many jurors must agree before an indictment is endorsed by the foreman and presented to the court as a true bill?*

When the jury is composed of sixteen to twenty-three persons, twelve must agree before a true bill is returned. If less than twelve agree, the bill is endorsed "not a true bill" and no criminal conviction can be based on it.

*What is an arraignment?*

An arraignment is the formal bringing of the defendant into a court of law where the charge against him is stated and he is asked how he wishes to plead. When two or more persons are accused in the same indictment, they may be arraigned together or separately, at the discretion of the trial judge. The accused may also waive the arraignment. The arraignment usually takes place before the trial itself, on a separate day set aside especially for arraignments. If the defendant is not ready to plead at the arraignment, or has failed to employ counsel, he may ask for, and usually receive, a continuance.

*What pleas are available to a defendant?*

A defendant may plead (1) guilty, (2) not guilty, (3) former jeopardy, (4) insanity, (5) alibi, or (6) *nolo contendere.*

*What is the effect of a plea of guilty?*

The effect of such a plea is to obviate the need for a trial on the issues. On a guilty plea, if accepted by the court, testimony may

be restricted to such evidence only as will give the court sufficient
background to pass sentence.

## What is the effect of a plea of not guilty?

A plea of not guilty leads to a complete trial based on the issues.
If a defendant fails to plead, refuses to plead, or stands mute when
the accusation is read, the trial judge frequently enters a plea of
not guilty so that the accused may have the benefit of a full trial.

## What is meant by former jeopardy?

This is a plea by a defendant that he cannot be convicted for the
offense charged because he has been once before in jeopardy of
conviction for the same offense.

## What is the effect of a plea of insanity?

A plea of insanity is in effect a plea of guilty with extenuating circumstances, the circumstance being that at the time of the commission of the crime the defendant did not know the difference
between right and wrong, or that he acted because of an irresist-
ible impulse. Many states require that insanity, as a question of
fact, be considered by the jury and be proved by a preponderance
of the evidence.

## What is the effect of an alibi?

While an alibi is technically not a plea, it has the effect of one,
since it helps to frame the issues on which the accused will be
tried.

## What is nolo contendere?

Nolo contendere (literally, "I do not wish to contend") is notice
by a defendant that he will not contend with the government or
state. It is neither a plea of guilty nor a plea of not guilty. The
advantage of nolo contendere over a plea of guilty is that nolo
contendere is an implied confession of guilt for the purposes of
the case only; it cannot be used against the defendant in another,
collateral criminal proceeding.

### What is a motion to quash?

It is a motion to have the indictment or information set aside on any of the following grounds:

1. The facts alleged do not constitute a crime.
2. The indictment is vague and uncertain.
3. The indictment is defective in its form.
4. The grand jury proceedings were defective.
5. There was error in the summoning or selecting of the grand jury.
6. The indictment contains matter that constitutes a good defense to the charge.

### What is venue?

Venue is the place where a cause may be heard and determined by a court having jurisdiction.

### What is change of venue?

It is the right of a defendant, subject to the discretion of the court, to request a change in the place where a trial will be held. By a change of venue the trial is transferred from the county where the crime was committed to another county. A change of venue is requested when the defendant believes his rights to a fair and impartial trial will be violated in the county having original jurisdiction.

### What is a trial by jury?

A trial by jury is a trial before a judge and jury composed of twelve men and women selected from the county in which the offense was committed. (Some states provide for six-man juries.) The evidence to convict or to acquit the accused is presented by the prosecutor and by counsel for the defendant. It is the function of the jury only to decide issues of fact, matters of law being determined by the trial judge.

### What happens if the right to a trial by jury is waived by a defendant?

In such a case the judge decides both questions of law and questions of fact.

*How may a defendant challenge a jury?*

A defendant may challenge individual jurors for cause on the ground of interest, prejudice, or other legal disqualification. Both the state and the defendant have, in addition, a number of peremptory challenges by which a juror may be removed from the panel without cause; that is, no reason need be given for refusing to allow him to serve on the jury.

*Does every accused person have a right to counsel?*

Yes. The modern tendency is, in a proper case, to have the defendant represented by counsel at every step of the proceedings, even if he cannot afford to hire an attorney. Courts increasingly recognize that a failure to provide counsel for a defendant when he cannot find or afford it, especially in a serious criminal matter, is a gross violation of his constitutional rights.

*What other rights does the accused have?*

1. He has the right to a public trial.

2. He has the right to be confronted by his accusers.

3. He has the right to be present at all stages of the trial of his case.

*What is the order of procedure at a trial in a criminal case?*

1. The selection and swearing in of the jury.

2. The opening statement for the state by the prosecuting attorney.

3. The opening statement for the defendant.

4. Introduction of the state's evidence.

5. Introduction of the defendant's evidence.

6. Rebutting evidence by either the state or the defendant or both.

7. The argument by the state.

8. The closing argument by the defendant.

9. The closing argument by the state.

10. Instructions to the jury by the judge on the applicable law.

11. Deliberation by the jury followed by a verdict or by the dismissal of the jury if the jurors fail to agree on a verdict.

12. Judgment by the court.

13. Sentencing.

*What is the purpose of a motion for a new trial?*

To correct any injustice done by the verdict in the original trial. A motion for a new trial is usually granted if the original trial was unfair or grossly prejudicial to the defendant, or if new evidence that was unavailable during the original trial has been discovered. A motion for a new trial is commonly made and denied before an appeal to a higher court is allowed.

*What are the grounds for the granting of a new trial?*

A new trial may be granted:

1. If a felony prosecution was begun and completed in the defendant's absence and to his prejudice.

2. If the verdict was decided by lot, in which case prejudice is assumed.

3. If there is newly discovered evidence.

4. If the verdict is against the law or the evidence.

5. If the jury received evidence out of court.

6. If there was misconduct on the part of the jury or the prosecutor.

7. If the court erred in instructing the jury.

*Within what time may the defendant file a motion for a new trial?*

Usually within three to five days.

*What is meant by "judgment"?*

It is the adjudication by the court that the defendant is "guilty" or "not guilty" of the offense charged in the accusation.

*What is "sentence"?*

Sentence is a pronouncement by the court of the penalty imposed on a defendant for the crime of which he has been found guilty. If the statute imposes a penalty of from one to three years for a certain offense, it is the duty of the judge to decide exactly what the penalty shall be. In many cases the judge, before he passes sentence, will refer the case to the probation department for a detailed review of the background of the convicted man. Thus a first offender is likely to receive a much lighter sentence than a hardened criminal. An embezzler who has made restitution is more likely to receive leniency than one who has not. Many first offenders who have good backgrounds and are considered good risks may be given suspended sentences or placed on probation for a given period, with the understanding that they will be sentenced to prison if they get into further legal difficulties or violate their probation.

*What remedies does a person have after he has been convicted and sentenced?*

1. He may appeal his case within the period prescribed by law, usually within sixty days.

2. He may file a writ of habeas corpus. The function of such a writ is to effect release from an illegal detention, as from a void sentence. Before sentence is pronounced, the writ may challenge the jurisdiction of a court or the denial of the defendant's being admitted to bail. However, the writ cannot be used to review a case, no matter how serious the errors of law may be. For this, either a motion for a new trial or an appeal to a higher court is the proper procedure.

*What is parole?*

Parole is the conditional release of a prisoner *after* he has begun to serve his sentence, conditional upon his fulfilling the terms of his parole. For the violation of parole, the offender may be returned to prison to serve out the unexpired portion of his sentence.

## Chapter 30

## SOCIAL SECURITY

*What is social security?*

The basic idea of social security is simple. During working years employees, their employers, and self-employed people pay social security contributions which are pooled in special trust funds. When earnings stop or are reduced because the worker retires, dies, or becomes disabled, monthly cash benefits are paid to replace part of the earnings the family has lost.

Part of the contributions made go into a separate hospital insurance trust fund so that when workers and their dependents reach sixty-five they will have help in paying their hospital bills. Voluntary medical insurance, also available to people sixty-five or over, helps pay doctors' bills and other medical expenses. This program is financed out of premiums shared half-and-half by the older people who sign up and by the federal government.

Nine out of ten working people in the United States are now building protection for themselves and their families under the social security program.

*What amount of work is required before you are eligible for benefits?*

To get monthly cash payments for yourself and your family, or for your survivors to get payments in case of your death, you must have credit for a certain amount of work under social security. The credit may have been earned any time after 1936.

Most employees get credit for one-fourth of a year of work if they are paid $50 or more in covered wages in a calendar quarter. Four quarters are counted for any year in which a self-employed person's income is $400 or more. A worker who receives farm wages gets credit for one-fourth of a year of work for each $100 of covered wages per year up to $400.

You can be fully insured, depending on the total amount of credit you have for work under social security, and you can be currently insured, depending on the amount you had in the last

460

three years. The table given later on page 411 shows which kinds of cash benefits may be paid if you are fully insured and which kinds may be paid if you are currently insured.

If you stop working under social security before you have earned enough credit to be insured, no cash benefits will be paid to you. Earnings already credited will remain on your social security record; if you later return to covered work, regardless of your age, all your covered earnings will be considered.

*How much credit must you have to be fully insured?*

Just how much credit you must have to be fully insured depends upon the year you reach sixty-five if you are a man, or sixty-two if you are a woman, or upon the date of your death or disability.

The credit is measured in quarter-year units of work called quarters of coverage, but for convenience the following table is given in years. If you have questions, people in your social security office will be glad to give you further details. You are fully insured if you have credit for at least as many years as shown on the appropriate line.

| If you reach 65 (62 if a woman) or die or become disabled in— | You will be fully insured if you have credit for this much work |
|---|---|
| 1965 | 3½ years |
| 1967 | 4 |
| 1969 | 4½ |
| 1971 | 5 |
| 1975 | 6 |
| 1979 | 7 |
| 1983 | 8 |
| 1987 | 9 |
| 1991 or later | 10 |

If you become disabled or die before reaching sixty-five (sixty-two for a woman), you are fully insured if you have credit for one-fourth of a year of work for each year after 1950 up to the year of disability or death. In counting the number of years after 1950, omit years before you were twenty-two.

No one is fully insured with credit for less than one and one-half years of work and no one needs more than ten years of work to be fully insured. Having a fully insured status, however, means only that certain kinds of cash benefits may be payable—it does not determine the amount. The amount will depend on your average earnings.

*When are you currently insured?*

You will be currently insured if you have social security credit for at least one and one-half years of work within the three years before you die or become entitled to retirement benefits.

*How is the amount of benefits figured?*

The amount of your monthly retirement or disability benefit is based on your average earnings under social security over a period of years. The amount of the monthly payments to your dependents or to your survivors in case of your death also depends on your average earnings.

The exact amount of your benefit cannot be figured until there is an application for benefits. This is because all of your earnings up to the time of the application may be considered in figuring your benefit. The Social Security Administration will, of course, figure your exact benefit at that time.

You can estimate the amount of the benefit, however, by following the steps given below.

1. Count the number of years to be used in figuring your average earnings as follows:

   *a)* If you were born before 1930, start with 1956.

   If you were born after 1929, start with the year you reached twenty-seven.

   *b)* Count your starting year and each year up until (but not including)

   the year you reach sixty-five, if you are a man;

   the year you reach sixty-two, if you are a woman;

   the year the worker becomes disabled or dies, for disability or death benefits.

   (NOTE: At least five years of earnings must be used to figure retirement benefits and at least two years to figure disability or survivor benefits.)

2. List the amount of earnings for all years beginning with 1951. (Include earnings in the year of death or the year disability began.) Do not count *more than* $3,600 for each year 1951 through 1954), $4,200 for each year 1955 through 1958, $4,800 for each year 1959 through 1965, $6,600 for 1966 and 1967, $7,800 for 1968 through 1971, and $9,000 for 1972 and after.

3. Cross off your list the years of lowest earnings until the number remaining is the same as your answer to step 1. (It may be necessary to leave on your list years in which you had no earnings.)

4. Add up the earnings for the years left on your list and divide by the number of years you used (your answer to step 1).

The result is your average yearly earnings covered by social security over this period.

Look in the table at the end of the chapter and estimate your benefit from the examples shown there.

If you work after you start receiving benefits and your added earnings result in higher benefits, your benefit will be automatically refigured after the additional earnings are credited to your record.

*Are there payments for people not eligible for social security?*

Special payments of $58 a month ($87 for a couple) can be made under the social security program to certain people seventy-two and over who are not eligible for social security benefits. These payments are intended to assure some regular income for older people who had little or no opportunity to earn social security protection during their working years.

People who reach seventy-two in 1968 or later need credit for some work under social security to be eligible for special payments. Those who reach seventy-two in 1968 need credit for three-fourths of a year of work under social security. The amount of work credit needed increases gradually each year for people reaching seventy-two after 1968, until it is the same as that required for retirement benefits. (This will be in 1970 for men and 1972 for women.)

The special payments are not made for any month for which the person receives payments under a federally-aided public assistance program. The special payments are reduced by the amount of any other governmental pension, retirement benefit, or annuity.

Payments to people who have credit for less than three-fourths of a year of work under social security are made from general revenues, not from social security trust funds.

*What benefits are available if you become disabled before sixty-five?*

If you become disabled before sixty-five, you and certain members of your family may be eligible for benefits.

Do not wait too long after you are disabled to apply for benefits; if you wait more than a year, you may lose benefits. Payments may begin with the seventh full month of disability.

If you are found eligible for disability insurance benefits, you will remain eligible as long as you are disabled. When you reach sixty-five, your benefit will be changed to retirement payments at the same rate.

*What are the requirements for a person to be considered disabled?*

A person is considered disabled only if he has a severe physical or mental condition which:
  *a*) Prevents him from working, and
  *b*) Is expected to last (or has lasted) for at least twelve months or is expected to result in death.

A person with a severe medical condition could be eligible even if he manages to do a little work.

*How much social security credit must you have for disability payments?*

If you become disabled before you are twenty-four, you need credit for one and one-half years of work in the three years before you become disabled.

If you become disabled between twenty-four and thirty-one, you need social security credits for half the time after you are twenty-one and before your become disabled.

To get disability benefits if you become disabled at thirty-one or later, you must be fully insured and have credit for five years of work in the ten years just before you become disabled.

*What is the amount of your disability benefits?*

The amount of your monthly disability payment is generally the same as the retirement benefit you would get if you were sixty-five. Figure your average earnings if you had reached sixty-five (sixty-two for a woman) at the time you become disabled. If you are a disabled widow, surviving divorced wife, or dependent widower, the amount of your benefit is figured from what your spouse would have received.

Everyone who applies for social security disability benefits is referred for possible services to his state rehabilitation agency. These services help many people to return to productive employment. Social security often helps pay the cost of services provided to applicants by rehabilitation agencies.

For more information about the disability benefits for blind people, disabled widows, disabled surviving divorced wives, and disabled dependent widowers, get in touch with your social security office.

*What payments can be made to certain dependents when the worker gets retirement or disability benefits, or when he dies?*

Dependents who may receive monthly payments are:

Unmarried children under eighteen, or between eighteen and twenty-two if they are full-time students;

Unmarried children eighteen or over who were severely disabled before they reached eighteen and who continue to be disabled;

A wife or widow, regardless of her age, if she is caring for a child under eighteen or disabled and the child gets payments based on the worker's record;

A wife sixty-two or widow sixty or older, even if there are no children entitled to payments;

A widow fifty or older (or dependent widower fifty or older) who becomes disabled not later than seven years after the death of the worker or, in the case of a widow, not later than seven years after the end of her entitlement to benefits as a widow with a child in her care;

A dependent husband or widower sixty-two or over;

Dependent parents sixty-two or over after a worker dies.

In addition to monthly benefits, a lump-sum payment may be made after the worker's death.

Children are now considered dependent on both their mothers and their fathers, and they may become eligible for benefits when either parent becomes entitled to retirement or disability benefits or dies.

Payments may also be made under certain conditions to a divorced wife at sixty-two or a surviving divorced wife at sixty (or a disabled surviving divorced wife fifty or older). To qualify for benefits, a divorced wife must have been married to the worker for twenty years and also meet certain support requirements. Benefits also can be paid a dependent surviving divorced wife at any age if she is caring for her deceased former husband's child under eighteen or disabled who is entitled to benefits. For more information about this provision, get in touch with your social security office.

Monthly payments to the wife or dependent husband of a person entitled to retirement or disability payments generally cannot be made until the marriage has been in effect at least one year, unless the couple are parents of a child. Payments can be made to the widow, stepchild, or dependent widower of a deceased worker if the marriage lasted nine months or longer; or in the case of death in line of duty in the uniformed services, and in the case of accidental death, if the marriage lasted for three months, under special circumstances.

### How are cash benefits calculated?

Cash benefits to your dependents, and to your survivors in case of your death, are figured from the amount of your retirement or disability benefit.

Permanently reduced benefits are received by:

Workers and their wives who choose to start receiving retirement benefits while they are between sixty-two and sixty-five;

Widows who choose to start receiving benefits between sixty and sixty-two;

Disabled widows and disabled dependent widowers fifty or older who receive benefits before they reach sixty-two.

The amount of the reduction depends on the number of months they receive benefits before they reach sixty-five (sixty-two for widows and disabled dependent widowers). On the average, people who choose to get benefits early will collect about the same value in total benefits over the years, but in smaller installments to take account of the longer period during which they will be paid.

If a person could be entitled to monthly benefits based on the social security records of two or more workers, he will receive no more than the largest of the benefits.

The lump-sum payment at a worker's death is ordinarily three times the amount of his monthly retirement benefit at sixty-five, or $255, whichever is the less.

Social security benefits you receive are not subject to federal income tax.

## TYPES OF CASH BENEFITS

This table shows the principal types of payments and the insured status needed for each.

### Retirement

| Monthly payment to | If you are |
| --- | --- |
| *You as a retired worker and your wife and child | Fully insured |
| Your dependent husband 62 or over | Fully insured |

## Survivors

| *Monthly payment to your* | *If at death you are* |
|---|---|
| *Widow 60 or over or disabled widow 50-59 | Fully insured |
| *Widow (regardless of age) if caring for your child who is under 18 or disabled and is entitled to benefits | Either fully or currently insured |
| Dependent child | Either fully or currently insured |
| Dependent widower 62 or over and disabled dependent widower 50-61 | Fully insured |
| Dependent parent at 62 | Fully insured |
| *Lump sum death payment* | Either fully or currently insured |

## Disability

| *Monthly payments to* | *If you are* |
|---|---|
| You and your dependents if you are disabled | Fully insured and if you meet requirements explained on page 409 |

* Under certain conditions, payments can also be made to your divorced wife or surviving divorced wife.

## What must you do before payments can start?

An application must be filed. When you are nearing sixty-five or if you become disabled, get in touch with your social security office.

It is important for you to inquire at your social security office two or three months before you reach sixty-five, not only for the possibility of retirement benefits, but also for Medicare benefits, which are available whether or not you retire. If you wait until the month you reach sixty-five to apply for the medical insurance part of Medicare, you will lose at least one month of protection. It is always to your advantage to apply before you reach sixty-five, even if you do not plan to retire. If you have high earnings which would increase the amount of your benefit in the year you are sixty-five or later, your benefit amount will be refigured. You will always be sure of receiving benefits at the highest possible rate.

When a person who has worked under the social security law dies, some member of his family should get in touch with the social security office.

If you cannot come to the social security office—perhaps because you are housebound or hospitalized—write or telephone. A social security representative can arrange to visit you.

Long delay in filing an application can cause loss of some benefits, since back payments for monthly cash benefits can be made for no more than twelve months.

An application for a lump-sum death payment must usually be made within two years of the worker's death.

When you apply for social security benefits, bring your own social security card or a record of your number and, if your claim is based on the earnings of another person, his card or a record of the number.

*What proof will be required?*

You will need proof of your age. If you have a birth certificate or a baptismal certificate made at or shortly after your birth, bring it with you when you apply. If you are applying for wife's or widow's benefits, bring your marriage certificate. If your children are eligible, bring their birth certificates.

Bring your form W-2 wage and tax statement for the previous year or, if you are self-employed, a copy of your last federal income tax return.

Proof that the applicant was being supported by the insured person is required before benefits can be paid to a parent after the death of a working son or daughter, or to a husband or widower whose working wife has retired, become disabled, or died. Generally, this proof must be furnished within two years after the worker dies or, in the case of husband's benefits, within two years after his wife applies for cash benefits.

*Should you delay applying because you do not have all these proofs?*

No. When you apply, the people in your social security office can tell you about other proofs that may be used.

Suppose you apply for retirement or survivor payments and supply all of the necessary information. If four to six weeks go by after the time you thought your benefits should start and you do not hear about your claim, get in touch with your social security office. There are special procedures for speeding payments in these cases, and your social security officer will be glad to do everything possible to prevent delays in your payments.

Under the law social security records are confidential. Information from your record may not be disclosed without proper authorization.

## How do future earnings affect your social security payments?

When you apply for retirement or survivors insurance benefits, your social security staff will explain how any future earnings you may have will affect your payments and when and how to report your later earnings to the Social Security Administration. If you earn $1,680 or less in a year, you get all the benefits.

If you earn more than $1,680 in a year while you are under seventy-two, the general rule is that $1 in benefits to you (and your family) will be withheld for each $2 you earn from $1,680 to $2,-880. In addition $1 in benefits will be withheld for each $1 of earnings over $2,880.

*Exception to the general rule:* Regardless of total earnings in a year, benefits are payable for any month in which you neither earn wages of more than $140 nor perform substantial services in self-employment.

*The decision as to whether you are performing substantial services in self-employment depends on the time you devote to your business, the kind of services you perform, how your services compare with those you performed in past years, and other circumstances of your particular case.*

Benefits are also payable for all months in which you are seventy-two or older, regardless of the amount of your earnings in those months.

Your earnings as a retired worker may affect your own and your dependents' rights to benefits. If you get payments as a dependent or survivor, your earnings will affect only your benefit and not those of other members of the family.

## Which earnings must be counted?

Earnings from work of any kind must be counted, whether or not the work is covered by social security. (There is one exception: tips amounting to less than $20 a month with any one employer are not counted.) Total wages (not just take-home pay) and all net earnings from self-employment must be added together in figuring your earnings for the year. However, income from savings, investments, pensions, insurance, or royalties you receive after sixty-five because of copyrights or patents you obtained before sixty-five does not affect your benefits and should not be counted in your earnings for this purpose.

In the year in which your benefits start and the year your benefits end, your earnings for the entire year are counted in determining the amount of benefits that can be paid.

Earnings after you reach seventy-two will not cause any deductions from your benefits for months in which you are seventy-two or over. However, earnings for the entire year in which you reach seventy-two count in figuring what benefits are due you for months before you are seventy-two.

For more information about how working after you apply for benefits will affect your retirement or survivors payments, inquire at your social security office.

*Do special rules affect the payment of benefits to people outside the United States?*

Yes. If you intend to go outside the United States for thirty days or more while you are receiving benefits, ask your social security office for leaflet no. SSA-609.

If you are not a citizen or national of the United States, your absence from this country may affect your right to benefits. The people in your social security office will be glad to explain these provisions to you.

*Under what circumstances will monthly payments be discontinued?*

When monthly payments are begun, they continue until they are stopped for one of the reasons given below. If any of these occurs, it must be promptly reported to the Social Security Administration.

*Marriage*—Benefits for a child, an aged dependent parent, a disabled dependent widower, a divorced wife, a disabled widow, or widow receiving mother's benefits generally stop when the beneficiary marries a person who is not also getting social security dependent's or survivor's benefits.

There is an exception for the widow who remarries after reaching age 60. If she could have qualified for benefits on her deceased husband's record, she may still get benefits on that record. She would qualify for one-half of her deceased husband's retirement benefit, or (at sixty-two) for the amount of the wife's benefit on her later husband's record, whichever is larger. A similar provision applies to widowers who remarry after sixty-two.

*Divorce*—Payments to a wife or a dependent husband generally end if a divorce is granted. However, if a wife sixty-two or older and her husband are divorced, benefits to the wife may continue if the marriage lasted at least twenty continuous years before the divorce. (If a wife under sixty-five and her husband are divorced after twenty continuous years of marriage, she may receive benefits at sixty-two or later providing certain conditions are met. For more information, get in touch with any social security office.)

*No child in her care*—Payment to a wife under sixty-two or to a widow or surviving divorced wife under sixty will generally stop when she no longer has in her care a child under eighteen or disabled. A widow or surviving divorced wife who is fifty or over and is severely disabled should get in touch with her social security office for information about any benefits that may be payable.

*Child reaches eighteen*—When a child reaches age eighteen, his payments stop unless he is

Disabled (if so, he and his mother may be eligible for benefits for as long as he is disabled), or

A full-time, unmarried student (if so, he may be eligible for benefits until he reaches twenty-two).

*Adoption*—When a child is adopted, his payments end unless he is adopted by his stepparent, grandparent, aunt, uncle, brother, or sister after the death of the person on whose record he is receiving benefits.

*Death*—When any person receiving monthly benefits dies, his or her payments end.

*Disability benefits*—When the benefits payable to a person stop because he is no longer disabled, the benefits payable to his dependents also stop.

If payments end because of any of these reasons, the last check due is the one for the month before the event.

## Who is eligible under Medicare?

Nearly all people sixty-five and over are eligible for health insurance protection under Medicare, including some people who do not have enough credit for work covered by social security to qualify for monthly cash benefits.

There are two parts to Medicare, hospital insurance and, for those who choose, medical insurance.

If you are sixty-five or over and are entitled to social security or railroad retirement benefits, you are automatically eligible for hospital insurance; if you are not entitled to either of these benefits, you should ask about hospital insurance and medical insurance at your social security office.

Nearly everyone who reached sixty-five before 1968 is eligible for hospital insurance, including people not eligible for cash social security benefits.

If you reached sixty-five in 1968 or later and are not eligible for cash benefits, you will need some work credit to qualify for hospital insurance benefits. The amount of credit needed depends on your age. Eventually the amount of work required for hospital insurance will be the same as for social security cash benefits.

After you establish your eligibility, you receive a health insurance card which shows that you have hospital insurance, medical insurance, or both.

*What hospital and post-hospital costs are paid?*

Hospital insurance will pay the cost of covered services for the following hospital and follow-up care:

Up to ninety days of hospital care in a participating hospital during a "benefit period."[1] For the first sixty days of care, your hospital insurance will pay for covered service except for the first $60 of expenses.[2] For the sixty-first through the ninetieth day of care, hospital insurance pays for all covered services, except for $15 a day.

You also have a sixty-day "lifetime reserve" which can be used after you have exhausted your ninety days of hospital care in a benefit period. "Lifetime reserve" days are not replaced after you use them. Hospital insurance pays all but $30 a day of your covered expenses during the reserve days.

Up to 100 days of care in a participating extended care facilities (a skilled nursing home or special part of a hospital which meets the requirements of the law) during each benefit period. Your hospital insurance will pay for all covered services for the first twenty

---

[1] A benefit period (or spell of illness) starts on the first day you receive covered services as a bed patient in a hospital or extended care facility. It does not end until for 60 consecutive days you have not been a bed patient in any hospital or skilled nursing home.

[2] Once you have taken care of the first $40 of hospital expenses in each benefit period, you don't have to pay it again, even if you have to go back in a hospital more than once in that same benefit period.

days of care and all but $7.50 daily for the next eighty. You will be covered for extended care facility services only if you have been in the hospital for at least three days in a row and you enter the facility within fourteen days after you leave the hospital.

Up to 100 home health visits by nurses or other health workers from a participating home health agency (but not doctors) in the 365 days following your release from a hospital (after at least a three-day stay) or from an extended care facility.

*Is everyone covered automatically under Medicare?*

No. The medical insurance part of Medicare is voluntary and no one is covered automatically. You will receive this protection only if you sign up for it within a specified period.

You will have protection at the earliest possible time if you enroll during the three-month period just before the month you reach sixty-five. You may also enroll the month you reach sixty-five and during the three following months, but your protection will not start until one to three months after you enroll.

If you do not enroll during your first enrollment period, you will have another opportunity during the first three months of each year for the three years after you had your first chance to enroll. However, if you wait, you may have to pay a higher premium for the same protection, and your coverage will not begin until three to six months after you enroll.

Medical insurance is financed with monthly premiums paid by people sixty-five or over who have signed up for this insurance. The government matches these premiums dollar for dollar. Since July 1971 the medical insurance premium has been $5.60 a month. Once you enroll for medical insurance, you do not have to do anything to keep your protection. It continues from year to year without any action.

If you wish to drop your medical insurance, you may give notice to do so at any time. Your medical insurance protection will stop at the end of the calendar quarter following the quarter you give notice.

*What will your medical insurance pay?*

Generally, your medical insurance will pay eighty percent of the reasonable charges for the following services after the first $50 in each calendar year:

Physicians' and surgeons' services, no matter where you receive the services—in the doctor's office, in a clinic, in a hospital, or at home.

Laboratory and radiology services of physicians when you are a bed patient in a hospital. The full reasonable charge (100 percent) will be paid, instead of eighty percent.

Home health services even if you have not been in a hospital—up to 100 visits during a calendar year.

A number of other medical and health services, such as diagnostic tests, surgical dressings and splints, and rental or purchase of medical equipment.

Outpatient physical therapy services—whether or not you are home-bound—furnished under supervision of a participating hospital, extended care facility, home health agency, approved clinic, rehabilitation agency, or public health agency.

All outpatient services of a participating hospital, including diagnostic tests or treatment.

Certain services by podiatrists (but not routine foot care or treatment of flat feet or partial dislocations).

*How are benefits paid for?*

Federal retirement, survivors, and disability benefits, and hospital insurance benefits are paid for by contributions based on earnings covered under social security.

If you are employed, you and your employer share the responsibility of paying contributions. If you are self-employed, you pay contributions for retirement, survivors, and disability insurance at a slightly lower rate than the combined rate for an employee and his employer. However, the hospital insurance contribution rate is the same for the employer, the employee, and the self-employed person.

As long as you have earnings that are covered by the law, you continue to pay contributions regardless of your age and even if you are receiving social security benefits.

*How are social security contributions collected?*

If you are employed, your contribution is deducted from your wages each payday. Your employer sends it, with an equal amount as his own share of the contribution, to the Internal Revenue Service.

## CONTRIBUTION RATE SCHEDULE FOR EMPLOYEES AND EMPLOYERS (EACH)

| | PERCENT OF COVERED EARNINGS | | |
| Years | For Retirement, Survivors, and Disability Insurance | For Hospital Insurance | TOTAL |
| --- | --- | --- | --- |
| 1968 | 3.8 | 0.6 | 4.4 |
| 1969-70 | 4.2 | .6 | 4.8 |
| 1971-72 | 4.6 | .6 | 5.2 |
| 1973-75 | 5.0 | .65 | 5.65 |
| 1976-79 | 5.15 | .7 | 5.85 |
| 1980-86 | 5.15 | .8 | 5.95 |
| 1987 and after | 5.15 | .9 | 6.05 |

## CONTRIBUTION RATE SCHEDULE FOR SELF-EMPLOYED PEOPLE

| | PERCENT OF COVERED EARNINGS | | |
| Years | For Retirement Survivors, and Disability Insurance | For Hospital Insurance | TOTAL |
| --- | --- | --- | --- |
| 1968 | 5.8 | 0.6 | 6.4 |
| 1969-70 | 6.3 | .6 | 6.9 |
| 1971-72 | 6.9 | .6 | 7.5 |
| 1973-75 | 7.0 | .65 | 7.65 |
| 1976-79 | 7.0 | .7 | 7.7 |
| 1980-86 | 7.0 | .8 | 7.8 |
| 1987 and after | 7.0 | .9 | 7.9 |

If you are self-employed and your net earnings are $400 or more in a year, you must report your earnings and pay your self-employment contribution each year when you file your individual income tax return. This is true even if you owe no income tax.

Your wages and self-employment income are entered on your individual record by the Social Security Administration. This record of your earnings will be used to determine your eligibility for benefits and the amount of cash benefits you will receive.

The maximum amount of earnings that can count for social security and on which you pay social security contributions is shown in the following table:

| Year | Amount |
|------|--------|
| 1937-50 | $3,000 |
| 1951-54 | 3,600 |
| 1955-58 | 4,200 |
| 1959-65 | 4,800 |
| 1966-67 | 6,600 |
| 1968-71 | 7,800 |
| 1972 and after | 9,000 |

*What happens if amounts higher than the maximums are reported to your social security record?*

Earnings over the maximums may have been reported to your social security record and may appear on your earnings statement, but cannot be used to figure your benefit rate.

When you work for more than one employer in a year and pay social security contributions on wages over $9,000, you may claim a refund of the excess contributions on your income tax return for that year. If you work for only one employer and he deducts too much in contributions, you should apply to the employer for a refund. A refund is made only when more than the required amount of contributions has been paid. Questions about contributions or refunds should be directed to the Internal Revenue Service.

*How are social security contributions invested?*

Social security contributions for retirement, survivors, and disability insurance go into the Federal Old-Age and Survivors Insurance Trust Fund and the Federal Disability Insurance Trust Fund. They are used to pay the benefits and administrative expenses of these programs and may be used for no other purpose.

There are two other trust funds—(1) a Federal Hospital Insurance Trust Fund into which hospital insurance contributions are placed and out of which hospital insurance benefits and administrative expenses are paid, and (2) a Federal Supplementary Medical Insurance Trust Fund into which the enrollees' premiums along with the government's matching contributions are placed and out of which the benefits and administrative costs of the medical insurance program are paid.

Funds not required for current benefit payments and expenses are invested in interest-bearing U. S. Government securities.

*Are all social security costs financed by contributions?*

No. Certain benefit costs are financed from general funds of the

U. S. Treasury, including (1) the cost of hospital insurance benefits for people who are uninsured for cash social security benefits, (2) the government's share of the cost for supplementary medical insurance, and (3) cash payments for certain uninsured people seventy-two and over.

## Is everyone covered under social security?

Almost every kind of employment and self-employment is covered by social security. Some occupations, however, are covered only if certain conditions are met.

## How does social security affect a farmer?

You receive social security credit as a farm operator or rancher if your net earnings from self-employment are $400 or more in a year. You must report your net earnings from self-employment as a part of your income tax return.

If your gross earnings from farming in a year are between $600 and $2,400, you may report two-thirds of your gross earnings, instead of your net earnings, for social security purposes. If your gross earnings from farming are more than $2,400 and your net earnings are less than $1,600, you may report $1,600 for social security purposes.

If you rent your farm land to someone else, you receive social security credits for your rental income if you "materially participate" in the actual production of farm commodities or the management of production.

## How does social security affect farm employees?

When you work for a farmer, a ranch operator, or a farm labor crew leader, you earn social secuity credits:

*a*) If the employer pays you $150 or more in cash during the year for farm work, or

*b*) If you do farm work for the employer on twenty or more days during a year for cash wages figured on a time basis (rather than on a piece-rate basis).

Household workers employed on a farm or ranch operated for profit are covered under the same rules as other farm employees.

For more information about farm labor crews and the conditions under which the farmer or the crew leader is the employer, get leaflet no. 15 from your social security office.

*How does social security affect the clergy?*

A clergyman reports his income and makes his tax contributions as if he were self-employed, even though he may be working as an employee.

Earnings from services as a clergyman are automatically covered unless the clergyman files an application to have them excluded, stating that he is conscientiously opposed by reason of religious principles to receiving social security benefits based on services as a clergyman. He may complete form 4361 and file it with the Internal Revenue Service. This form may be secured at any social security office or at any Internal Revenue Service office. Once this form is filed it cannot be withdrawn.

Members of religious orders who have taken a vow of poverty are not covered by social security.

For more information about social security coverage for clergymen, ask for a copy of leaflet no. 9 at your social security office.

*How does social security affect employment of family members?*

Work done by a parent as an employee of his son or daughter in the course of the son's or daughter's trade or business is covered by the law. Domestic work in the household of a son or daughter is not covered unless special conditions are met.

Work for a parent by a daughter or son (also a stepchild, adopted, or foster child) under twenty-one is not covered. Also not covered is any work performed by a wife for her husband or by a husband for his wife.

*How does social security affect domestic workers?*

A domestic worker's cash wages (including transportation expenses if paid in cash) for work in a private household are covered by the law if they amount to $50 or more from one employer in a calendar quarter. If you employ a household worker who will come under the law and you are not receiving the forms for making the earnings reports, ask your social security office or your Internal Revenue Service office for a copy of leaflet no. 21. This leaflet explains how to get the forms and make the reports.

*Are tips included as social security income?*

Cash tips amounting to $20 or more in a month with one employer are covered by social security. You must give your employer a written report of the amount of your tips within ten days after the month in which you receive them. Your employer will collect your contributions due on these tips from other wages he owes you or from funds you turn over to him for that purpose. Otherwise, your contribution must be paid by you to the Internal Revenue Service.

Your employer includes your tips reported to him along with your other wages in his social security wage reports and on form W-2, but he does not have to match your social security contribution on the tips.

If your report is late or incomplete, you will be liable for your social security contribution on tips not reported, and you may also be subject to a penalty in an amount equal to one-half of that contribution. If you receive tips, you can get further information at your social security office.

*How does social security affect employees of non-profit organizations?*

Employees of non-profit organizations operated exclusively for religious, charitable, scientific, literary, educational, or humane purposes, or for testing for public safety, may be covered by the social security law if:

*a*) The organization waives its exemption from payment of social security contributions by filing a certificate (form SS-15) with the Internal Revenue Service, and

*b*) Those employees who wish to be covered indicate their desire to participate by signing the form SS-15a that goes with the certificate.

Employees who sign the form and employees who are hired or rehired after the calendar quarter in which the waiver certificate is filed are covered. If any employee of a non-profit organization earns wages of less than $50 in a quarter, his wages for that quarter are not covered.

*How does social security affect government employees?*

State and local government employees may be covered by social security under voluntary agreements between the individual state and the federal government.

Most employees of the federal government not covered by their own staff retirement system are covered by social security.

*How does social security affect members of the uniformed services of the United States?*

Active duty or active duty for training you perform as a member of the uniformed services of the United States after 1956 counts toward social security protection for you and your family. Your basic pay is credited to your social security record.

Credits in addition to military basic pay, generally amounting to $100 for each month of active duty, after 1967 count toward social security. No additional deductions will be made from your pay for these credits.

Social security credits of $160 a month are given to most veterans who served after September 15, 1940, and before 1957. When credits are given, they count the same as wages in civilian employment. These credits are not actually listed on your record, but if they would affect your benefit, the people in the social security office will ask for proof of your military service when an application is filed.

*How about earnings from railroad work?*

Earnings from railroad work are reported to the Railroad Retirement Board and not to the Social Security Administration. Your social security record will not include any work you may have done for a railroad.

Benefits based on work for a railroad are ordinarily paid by the Railroad Retirement Board. However, if you have less than 120 months (ten years) of railroad service when you retire or become disabled, your earnings for railroad work after 1936 are considered in figuring your disability or retirement payments under the social security law.

A retired worker who has at least 120 months of railroad service and who has also done enough work under social security to qualify for social security benefits may receive retirement benefits under both railroad retirement and social security.

Survivors of a worker can be entitled under one system only, either railroad retirement or social security, even though the worker may have been entitled during his lifetime under both. Regardless of which program will pay the benefits, records of the deceased worker's railroad earnings after 1936 and his earnings under social security will be combined to determine payments to survivors.

Railroad workers or their survivors can get further information from the nearest social security or railroad retirement office, or they may write to the Railroad Retirement Board, 844 Rush Street, Chicago, Illinois 60611.

## What about U. S. citizens working abroad?

U. S. citizens with American employers in foreign countries or aboard vessels or aircraft of foreign registry are covered by social security. Seamen and airmen employed on American vessels or aircraft are usually covered regardless of citizenship.

U. S. citizens working abroad for a foreign subsidiary of an American corporation may be covered if the parent firm makes an agreement with the secretary of the treasury to see that social security contributions are paid for all U. S. citizens employed abroad by the foreign subsidiary.

## What about foreign citizens working in the United States?

Agricultural work performed by foreign workers admitted to the United States on a temporary basis to do agricultural work is not covered.

Work performed by foreign nationals temporarily in the United States to study, teach, conduct research, etc. under a foreign exchange program is not covered under social security if it is performed to carry out the purpose for which they were admitted to the country.

## How important is a social security number?

You must have a social security number if your work is covered by the social security law or if you receive certain kinds of taxable income. Your social security number is also used for income tax purposes. Show your card to each of your employers when you start to work. Upon request, show it to anyone who pays you income that must be reported.

## Where can you get a social security card and number?

You can get a social security card at any social security office. The number on your card is used to keep a record of your earnings and of any benefits to which you and your dependents become entitled. You need only one social security number during your lifetime. Notify your social security office if you ever get more than one number.

*What happens if you change your name or lose your social security card?*

If you change your name, or if you lose your social security card, go to a social security office to get a card showing your new name or a duplicate of the card you lost.

*Are employers required to give you receipts for the social security contributions they deduct from your pay?*

Yes. They do this at the end of each year and also when you stop working for them. These receipts, such as form W-2, will help you check on your social security record. They show the amount of your wages that counts for social security. For most kinds of work, your wages paid in forms other than cash—for instance, the value of meals or living quarters—must be included. For domestic work in a private household or for farm work, only cash wages count.

You should keep a record of the amount of self-employment income you have reported.

*Can you find out what earnings are reported on your social security record?*

From time to time make sure your earnings have been correctly reported. This is especially important if you have frequently changed jobs. Simply ask your social security office for a postcard form to use in requesting a copy of your record. Complete, sign, and mail it.

*What if your records do not agree with the amounts shown on the statement you get from Social Security?*

Get in touch wih your social security office promptly. If you write, give your social security number, the periods of work in question, your pay in each period, and your employer's name and address. If the earnings in question were from self-employment, include the date your tax return was filed and the address of the Internal Revenue Service office to which the return was sent.

*Is there any procedure for a hearing if the Social Security Administration does not allow a claim that your records should show additional earnings?*

If you feel that a decision made on your claim is not correct, ask the Social Security Administration to reconsider it. If you are then still dissatisfied, you may ask for a hearing by a hearing examiner of the Bureau of Hearings and Appeals. If you are not satisfied that the decision of the hearing examiner is correct, you may request a review by the Appeals Council. The Social Security Administration makes no charge for any of these appeals. You may, however, choose to be represented by a person of your own choice, and he may charge you a fee. The amount of such a fee is limited and must be approved by the Social Security Administration.

Someone in your social security office will explain how you may appeal and will help you get your claim reconsidered or help you request a hearing. If you are still not satisfied, you may take your case to the federal courts.

*Where are social security offices found?*

The Social Security Administration has over 750 offices conveniently located throughout the country. These offices have representatives who regularly visit neighboring communities.

For the address of your nearest social security office, look in the telephone directory under Social Security Administration, or ask at the post office.

*What are the monthly benefits for eligible persons with various average yearly earnings?*

The table on page 486 will help you estimate your benefits after you have figured your earnings according to the steps outlined on pages 462 and 463.

*What are the latest changes in social security legislation?*

In October 1972 the social security program was affected by amendments to the law. Here are some of the highlights of that legislation.

Widow age sixty or over—Many will get higher monthly checks. Those who first received a widow's benefit at age sixty-five or later will get one hundred percent of the husband's benefit. The previous maximum was 82.5 percent. Many of those who first received widow's benefits before sixty-five will also get an increase but generally bringing them less than one hundred percent of the husband's benefit.

If you are a widow eligible for an increase, it will automatically be included in your check for February 1973.

If you are a widow age sixty or over getting checks only on your own wage record and not as a widow, get in touch with your social security office to determine whether you are eligible for a higher benefit based on your husband's wage record.

Recipient who works—Under the new law the more you earn the higher your total income will be. You will never have more than one dollar in benefits withheld for each two dollars of earnings, and you can earn as much as $2,100 annually without having any benefits withheld. Regardless of your total earnings in 1973 you will receive a check for any month in which you neither earn wages of more than $175 nor perform substantial services in self-employment.

Remember, the old law still applies to any earnings in 1972; one dollar in benefits withheld for each two dollars in earnings over $1,680 up to $2,880, and one dollar withheld for every one dollar over $2,880. The monthly limit was $140.

Disability—The new law provides Medicare coverage starting July 1, 1973, for those who have received disability checks two years or more by that date. If you are getting disability checks now, you will be sent more information about Medicare.

However, if you are a widow fifty years or older who was severely disabled the last two years but did not file a claim based on disability because you were getting checks as a mother caring for young or disabled children, you will have to apply for disabled widow's benefits to be eligible for Medicare.

Effective in 1973 the annual deductible amount for the medical insurance part of Medicare is sixty dollars instead of the fifty dollars under the old law. This means that after you have incurred sixty dollars in doctor bills or other covered expenses in one year, medical insurance will pay eighty percent of the reasonable charges for the rest of the year.

Medicare will now pay the full reasonable cost of home health care (after the annual sixty dollars deductible) instead of eighty percent as before.

Medical insurance will also cover certain colostomy supplies and, starting July 1, 1973, some services by independent physical therapists and certain limited chiropractic services.

Chronic kidney disease—Those under sixty-five who need continual hemodialysis treatment for kidney disease or require a kidney transplant will be covered by Medicare beginning July 1, 1973. Those who worked long enough under social security to be insured, those getting monthly benefits, and the wives or husbands and dependent children of insured people and beneficiaries are eligible.

Special minimum benefit—The new law provides a special minimum benefit at retirement for those who have worked under social security for more than twenty years. For a worker retiring at sixty-five with twenty-five years of coverage the minimum will be $127.50 a month; with thirty or more years of coverage the minimum will be $170.

Military wage credits—The new law grants additional social security credits of $100 for each month of active military service from 1957 through 1967. If you are getting benefits and you were in the armed forces during that period or were a survivor of someone who served in those years, get in touch with your local social security office.

## EXAMPLES OF MONTHLY CASH PAYMENTS

| Average yearly earnings after 1950* | $923 or less | $3,000 | $4,200 | $5,400 | $6,600 | $7,800 | $9,000 |
|---|---|---|---|---|---|---|---|
| Retired worker 65 or older<br>Disabled worker under 65 | $ 84.50 | $174.80 | $213.30 | $250.60 | $288.40 | $331.00 | $354.50 |
| Wife 65 or older | 42.30 | 87.40 | 106.70 | 125.30 | 144.20 | 165.50 | 177.30 |
| Retired worker at 62 | 67.60 | 139.00 | 170.70 | 200.50 | 230.80 | 264.80 | 283.60 |
| Wife at 62, no child | 31.80 | 65.60 | 80.10 | 94.00 | 108.20 | 124.20 | 133.00 |
| Widow at 60 | 73.30 | 125.10 | 152.60 | 179.30 | 206.30 | 236.70 | 253.50 |
| Widow or widower at 62 | 84.50 | 144.30 | 176.00 | 206.80 | 238.00 | 273.10 | 292.50 |
| Disabled widow at 50 | 51.30 | 87.50 | 106.80 | 125.50 | 144.30 | 165.60 | 177.30 |
| Wife under 65 and one child | 42.30 | 92.50 | 157.40 | 217.30 | 233.90 | 248.30 | 265.90 |
| Widowed mother and one child | 126.80 | 262.20 | 320.00 | 376.60 | 432.60 | 496.60 | 531.80 |
| Widowed mother and two children | 126.80 | 267.30 | 370.70 | 467.90 | 522.30 | 579.30 | 620.40 |
| One child of retired or disabled worker | 42.30 | 87.40 | 106.70 | 125.30 | 144.20 | 165.50 | 177.30 |
| One surviving child | 84.50 | 131.10 | 160.00 | 188.00 | 216.30 | 248.30 | 265.90 |
| Maximum family payment | 126.80 | 267.30 | 370.70 | 467.90 | 522.30 | 579.30 | 620.40 |

* Generally, average earnings covered by social security are figured from 1951 until the worker reaches retirement age, becomes disabled, or dies. The maximum benefit for a retired worker in 1972 is $259.40 a month, based on average yearly earnings of $5,652. The higher benefits shown in the chart, based on average earnings shown in the columns on the right, generally will not be payable until later.

486

## CHAPTER 31

## VETERANS BENEFITS

*Are veterans entitled to automobiles or other conveyances?*

Yes, veterans of World War II, Korean Conflict, post-Korean period, and current servicemen are eligible as follows:

1. World War II and Korean Conflict servicemen (discharged under other than dishonorable conditions) as well as persons currently on active duty, suffering from service-connected loss or permanent loss of use of one or both hands or feet, or permanent impairment of vision of both eyes to a prescribed degree.

2. Service after January 31, 1955, and discharged or retired. Same as above plus the requirement that the qualifying disability must be shown to have been the direct result of the performance of active duty.

Payment is made by the Veterans Administration of an amount not to exceed $2,800 toward the purchase price of an automobile or other conveyance, excluding adaptive equipment. This equipment will be maintained or replaced. Adaptive equipment on automobiles previously acquired because of service-connected disability will also be maintained or replaced. Payment is made to the seller, not to the veteran.

*What compensation are veterans entitled to?*

Veterans of Spanish-American War, Mexican Border Campaign, World War I, World War II, Korean Conflict, Vietnam era, and peacetime service with service-connected disabilities are eligible if they were disabled by injury or disease incurred in or aggravated by active service in line of duty during wartime or peacetime service and discharged or separated under other than dishonorable conditions.

Veterans found eligible for wartime disability compensation are entitled to monthly payments. These range from $25 for ten percent degree of disability to $450 for one hundred percent disability.

*Compensation for Service-Connected Disability*

|  |  | Wartime rate |
|--|--|-------------:|
| (a) | 10 percent | $ 25 |
| (b) | 20 percent | 46 |
| (c) | 30 percent | 70 |
| (d) | 40 percent | 96 |
| (e) | 50 percent | 135 |
| (f) | 60 percent | 163 |
| (g) | 70 percent | 193 |
| (h) | 80 percent | 223 |
| (i) | 90 percent | 250 |
| (j) | Total disability | 450 |

In addition, specific rates up to $1,120 per month are paid when the eligible veteran is adjudged to have suffered certain specific severe disabilities. These are all decided on an individual basis. Compensation at eighty percent of the wartime rates is paid for disabilities incurred under non-extra-hazardous conditions during peacetime. Veterans whose service-connected disabilities are rated at fifty percent or more are entitled to additional allowances for dependents at the same ratio that the degree of disability bears to one hundred percent.

## Who are eligible for pensions?

Veterans of Mexican Border Campaign, World War I, World War II, Korean Conflict period, and Vietnam era with nonservice-connected disabilities. Eligible are wartime veterans discharged under other than dishonorable disability, who are permanently and totally disabled from reasons not traceable to service. Veterans sixty-five years of age or older are considered permanently and totally disabled. Periods of wartime service for pension eligibility:

Mexican Border Campaign—May 9, 1916, to April 5, 1917, veterans who during such period served in Mexico or on the borders thereof or in the waters adjacent thereto.

World War I—April 6, 1917, to November 11, 1918; extended to April 1, 1920, for veterans who served in Russia; also extended through July 1, 1921, for veterans who had at least one day of service before November 12, 1918, and who served after November 11, 1918, and before July 2, 1921.

World War II—December 7, 1941, to December 31, 1946.

Korean Conflict—June 27, 1950, to January 31, 1955.

Vietnam era—August 5, 1964, to date to be determined later.

All veterans who came on the pension rolls on or after July 1, 1960, will receive pensions under the current system.

### Monthly Pension Rates for Veterans

| Income not more than: | Veteran alone | With one dependent | With two dependents | With three or more dependents |
|---|---|---|---|---|
| $ 300 | $130 | $140 | $145 | $150 |
| 400 | 127 | 140 | 145 | 150 |
| 500 | 124 | 140 | 145 | 150 |
| 600 | 121 | 138 | 143 | 148 |
| 700 | 118 | 136 | 141 | 146 |
| 800 | 115 | 134 | 139 | 144 |
| 900 | 112 | 132 | 137 | 142 |
| 1000 | 109 | 129 | 134 | 139 |
| 1100 | 105 | 126 | 131 | 136 |
| 1200 | 101 | 123 | 128 | 133 |
| 1300 | 97 | 120 | 125 | 130 |
| 1400 | 93 | 117 | 122 | 127 |
| 1500 | 89 | 114 | 119 | 124 |
| 1600 | 84 | 111 | 116 | 121 |
| 1700 | 79 | 108 | 113 | 118 |
| 1800 | 74 | 105 | 110 | 115 |
| 1900 | 68 | 102 | 107 | 112 |
| 2000 | 62 | 99 | 104 | 109 |
| 2100 | 56 | 96 | 101 | 106 |
| 2200 | 50 | 93 | 98 | 103 |
| 2300 | 43 | 90 | 95 | 100 |
| 2400 | 36 | 87 | 92 | 97 |
| 2500 | 29 | 84 | 89 | 94 |
| 2600 | 22 | 81 | 86 | 91 |
| 2700 | | 78 | 83 | 88 |
| 2800 | | 75 | 80 | 85 |
| 2900 | | 72 | 77 | 82 |
| 3000 | | 69 | 74 | 79 |
| 3100 | | 66 | 71 | 76 |
| 3200 | | 63 | 68 | 73 |
| 3300 | | 58 | 63 | 68 |
| 3400 | | 53 | 58 | 63 |
| 3500 | | 48 | 53 | 58 |
| 3600 | | 43 | 48 | 53 |
| 3700 | | 38 | 43 | 48 |
| 3800 | | 33 | 38 | 43 |

An applicable formula will reduce pension for every dollar of income above that shown in each level.

*How is income determined?*

Determination of a veteran's income is made by the Veterans Administration and includes the income received by him (less specific exclusions) and under certain circumstances income received by his spouse. The income cutoff figure, above which no pensions are paid, is $2,600 for a single veteran and $3,800 for veterans with dependents. Basic pension payments range from $150 monthly in the lowest brackets for a veteran with three dependents (or $130 monthly for a single veteran) down to $33 for a veteran with dependents ($22 for a single veteran) whose income is equal to the cutoff figures given above.

The size of a veteran's estate is also a determining factor for entitlement to pension. Certain unusual medical expenses (not reimbursed by insurance) may be excluded. Veterans within the income limits and in need of regular aid and attendance, including patients of nursing homes, will receive $110 a month or if housebound $44 a month additional.

*Is a veteran's pension reduced while hospitalized?*

Yes. The pension of a hospitalized veteran without a wife or child is reduced to an amount not in excess of $30 a month after two full calendar months of care. Full pension resumes following release from the hospital or VA maintenance, but the moneys reduced from his pension are not recoverable.

*What hospital benefits are provided?*

1. Veterans needing hospitalization because of injuries or disease incurred or aggravated in line of duty in active service have top priority for admission for treatment of the service-incurred or service-aggravated disability.

2. Veterans who were discharged or retired for disability incurred or aggravated in line of duty or who are receiving compensation, or would be eligible to receive compensation except for receipt of retirement pay, who need treatment for some ailment not connected with their service will be admitted as beds are available.

3. Veterans with service during any war or the post-Korean Conflict, veterans with peacetime service awarded the Medal of Honor, and any veterans who are sixty-five years of age or older who were not discharged or retired for disability, may apply for treatment of

a nonservice disability and may be admitted to Veterans Administration hospitals if (a) hospitalization is deemed necessary, (b) they state under oath, unless they are sixty-five years of age or older or in receipt of VA pension, that they are financially unable to defray the cost of the necessary hospital charges elsewhere, and (c) beds are available.

The VA may perform certain prehospital and posthospital medical service for nonservice-connected veteran patients on an outpatient basis. This applies only to veterans who are scheduled for admission to, or who were patients in, VA hospitals. It does not extend VA outpatient care to nonservice-connected veterans generally.

Veterans hospitalized in VA hospitals who have attained maximum hospitalization benefits and will require a protracted period of nursing home care may be furnished such care either in Veterans Administration facilities or in private nursing homes at VA expense. Normally, these veterans will be placed in private or community homes when it is reasonably certain that the aggregate requirement for care will not exceed six months. There is no time limit for veterans who were hospitalized primarily for service-connected conditions.

Apply to any VA office.

## How about Drug Treatment?

All veterans discharged or released from military service under conditions other than dishonorable are eligible. After hospitilization, veterans who receive drug treatment may become eligible for follow-up outpatient care. Patients are admitted to any VA hospital but specialized VA drug treatment centers are in the following cities: Atlanta; Baltimore; Battle Creek, Mich; Boston; Breckville, Ohio; Brentwood, Calif.; Brooklyn; Buffalo; Chicago; Denver; East Orange, N. J.; Houston; Indianapolis; Iowa City; Miami; Minneapolis; New Orleans; New York; North Little Rock; Oklahoma City; Omaha; Palo Alto, Calif; Philadelphia; Pittsburgh; Salem, Va.; Salt Lake City; Sepulveda, Calif.; St. Louis; Syracuse, N. Y.; Topeka, Kans.; Vancouver, Wash.; and Washington, D. C. In addition to the diversified centers listed above there are drug dependence rehabilitation units in VA psychiatric hospitals in the following cities: Albany; Albuquerque; American Lake, Wash.; Augusta, Ga.; Bay Pines, Fla.; Bedford, Mass.; Brockton, Mass.; Canandaigua, N. Y.; Coatesville, Pa.; Downey, Ill.; Gulfport, Miss.;

Hines, Ill.; Leavenworth, Kans.; Lexington, Ky.; Lyons, N. J.; Marion, Ind.; Memphis; Montrose, N.Y.; Nortyport, N. Y.; Perry Point, Md.; Pittsburgh (Psy.); San Juan; Sheridan, Wyo.; St. Cloud, Minn.; Temple, Tex.; Togus, Me.; Tucson; and Wood, Wis.

*What is domiciliary or home care?*

To provide care on an ambulatory self-care basis for veterans disabled by age or disease who are not in need of acute hospitalization and who do not need the skilled nursing services provided in nursing homes.

Eligibility is essentially the same as for VA hospital treatment. In addition, war veterans and post-Korean Conflict veterans must have disabilities that incapacitate them from earning a living but not so severe as to require hospitilization, and meet certain other requirements for residence in a domiciliary. Peacetime veterans must be permanently disabled, have been discharged for a disability incurred in line of duty or be receiving compensation for a service-incurred or service-aggravated disability or have been awarded the Medal of Honor, have no adequate means of support, be incapacitated from earning a living, and meet certain other requirements.

As a rule, transportation to a domiciliary at government expense is provided only for the initial admission.

Apply at any VA office. Prior approval needed for admission.

*What about outpatient medical treatment?*

The veteran must have been discharged or retired under conditions other than dishonorable and be in need of treatment for a disability incurred or aggravated in service. War veterans with total and permanent service-connected disabilities, those receiving aid and attendance or housebound allowances, Spanish-American War veterans and disabled veterans training under the Vocational Rehabilitation Act may be entitled to this treatment.

If medically indicated, VA may prescribe outpatient treatment for eligible veterans either before admission to or following discharge from a VA hospital. Drugs or medicine ordered on prescription may be furnished.

*How about outpatient dental treatment?*

Eligibility is generally the same as for outpatient medical treatment with the following conditions:

**1.** Those whose dental conditions or disabilities are service-connected and compensable in degree may apply at any time.

**2.** Those whose dental conditions or disabilities are service connected but not compensable in degree, and which are shown to have been in existence at time of discharge or release from active service, must apply to VA for outpatient dental care for the service-connected dental condition within one year after discharge or release. The one year is extended in certain cases.

**3.** Those with service-connected noncompensable dental conditions resulting from combat wounds or service injuries, former prisoners of war with service-connected noncompensable dental conditions, and those whose nonservice-connected dental conditions are found by VA to be directly related to or aggravating a service-connected condition, may apply at any time.

**4.** Disabled veterans training under the Vocational Rehabilitation Act and Spanish-American War veterans who need dental treatment may apply for and receive this type of treatment as needed.

*What benefits are provided for those requiring artificial devices or appliances?*

The veteran must meet the basic requirement for outpatient medical treatment, or be receiving hospital, domiciliary, or restoration care, and be in need of a prosthetic appliance for at least one of the following: (1) service-connected disabilities or adjunct conditions, (2) disabilities for which hospitalization has been authorized or disabilities associated with and aggravating the condition for which hospitalization was authorized, (3) when necessary as part of domiciliary or restoration care, (4) any disability for war veterans with total and permanent service-connected disabilities, or (5) when in receipt of special monthly compensation or increased pension based on the need for regular aid and attendance or for being permanently housebound.

*What about aid for the blind?*

Veterans must be entitled to compensation for any service-connected disability and be blind in both eyes, and must be war veterans with total and permanent service-connected disabilities or in receipt of increased pension based on the need for aid and attendance. The VA provides (1) approved electronic and mechanical aids to the blind and their necessary repair and replacement, (2) guide dogs including the expense of training the veterans to use the dog and the cost of the dog's medical attention.

*Who is eligible for GI educational training and what are the bill's provisions?*

Veterans who served and servicemen currently serving on active duty for more than 180 days, any part of which occurred after January 31, 1955, and who (a) were released under conditions other than dishonorable, (b) were discharged for a service-connected disability, or (c) continue on active duty are eligible under the Veterans Readjustment Benefits Act of 1966 as amended. The 181 days required active duty does not include any period when assigned full-time by the Armed Forces to a civilian institution for a course substantially the same as a course offered to civilians; serving as a cadet or midshipman at a service academy; or on active duty for training in the Army or Air National Guard or as a Reserve in the Army, Navy, Air Force, Marine Corps, or Coast Guard. Six-month enlistees under the reserve program authorized by Public Law 305, 84th Congress, are also excluded.

An educational institution approved for training may include any public or private elementary, high, vocational, correspondence, or business school, junior or teachers college, normal school, college or university, professional, scientific, or technical institution, or any other institution which furnishes education at the secondary school level or above.

Each eligible person may select a program of training at any educational institution or training establishment which will accept and retain him as a student trainee in any field or branch of knowledge which the institution finds him qualified to undertake. Educational and vocational counseling will be provided by the Veterans Administration upon request. Generally a program of education outside the United States may be pursued only at an approved educational institution of higher learning. A change from one program to another is permitted under some conditions.

Each eligible person is entitled to educational assistance for a period of one and one-half months or the equivalent in part-time training for each month or fraction of his service on active duty after January 31, 1955, but not to exceed thirty-six months. If he served eighteen months or more after that date and has been released under conditions satisfying his active duty obligation, he will be entitled to the full thirty-six months. The aggregate period of time for which a person may receive educational assistance under two or more laws administered by the Veterans Administration is forty-eight months. Veterans released from active duty after January 31, 1955, have eligibility for eight years after release or until May 31, 1974, whichever is later. For farm cooperative, apprentice or on-job training, or flight training, eligibility ceases eight years from date of last separation from service after January 31, 1955, or August 31, 1975, whichever is later. Allowance for a program of education pursued exclusively by correspondence and paid quarterly will be computed on the basis of the established charge paid by nonveterans for the same course or courses. Entitlement will be reduced at the rate of one month for each $175 paid to the veteran.

A cooperative program combines formalized education with training in a business or industrial establishment with emphasis on the institutional portion. An eligible veteran enrolled in an educational institution for a farm cooperative program consisting of institutional agricultural courses prescheduled to fall within forty-four weeks of any period of twelve consecutive months, must be concurrently engaged in agricultural employment which is considered to be related to the approved institutional courses. An eligible veteran may pursue, on a full-time basis only, an approved program of apprenticeship or other training on-the-job. Apprenticeship or on-job training programs must be approved by a state approving agency. The employer's wages shall be at least one-half of the wages paid for the specific job and shall be increased on a regular schedule until the veteran is receiving eighty-five percent of the wages for that job by at least the last full month of his training period, which cannot exceed two years. The two-year limitation does not apply to apprenticeships.

An eligible veteran may take an approved course of flight training generally accepted as necessary to attain a recognized vocational objective in the field of aviation or where recognized as ancillary to the pursuit of another vocation. He must first possess a valid private pilot's license and meet the medical requirements necessary for a commercial pilot's license. Educational assistance allowance for flight training is computed at the rate of ninety percent of the established charges for tuition and fees which nonveterans are required to pay. Flight training as a part of an approved college degree program is also available.

A veteran who must complete high school training or pass the G&D examination to qualify for higher education may receive educational assistance allowance without a charge against his basic entitlement. The law also permits additional secondary school training such as refresher courses or deficiency courses needed to qualify for admission to an appropriate educational institution. Veterans not completing the eighth grade may receive educational assistance allowance without a charge against basic entitlement.

*G.I. Bill Rates*

| | *No dependents* | *One dependent* | *Two dependents* | *Each Additional dependent* |
|---|---|---|---|---|
| Full-time | $175 | $205 | $230 | $13 |
| Three-quarter | 128 | 152 | 177 | 10 |
| Half-time | 81 | 100 | 114 | 7 |
| Cooperative | 141 | 167 | 192 | 10 |
| Apprenticeship on-job-training | | | | |
| 1st 6 mos | 108 | 120 | 133 | |
| 2nd 6 mos | 81 | 92 | 105 | |
| 3rd 6 mos | 54 | 66 | 79 | |
| 4th 6 mos | 27 | 39 | 52 | |
| Farm cooperative | | | | |
| full-time | 141 | 165 | 190 | 10 |
| three-quarter | 101 | 119 | 138 | 7 |
| half-time | 67 | 79 | 92 | 4 |
| Active duty; less than half-time | Tuition cost, not to exceed full-time rate of $175. | | | |
| Correspondence and flight | Monthly entitlement charge of $175. | | | |

Veterans or servicemen in post-secondary (above high school) training at educational institutions on a half-time or more basis, who need tutorial assistance may qualify for tutorial payments not to exceed $50 a month for a maximum of nine months with no charge against basic entitlement.

Servicemen with 181 days of active duty may pursue, without loss of basic entitlement, courses required for a high school diploma or any deficiency or refresher courses required for pursuit of an appropriate program of education or training. Servicemen may contact base education officers for information or application forms.

*Are there any restrictions?*

Yes. The educational allowance is not payable if the eligible person is on active duty and has his education paid for by the Armed Forces or the Department of Health, Education, and Welfare (for Public Health Service duty), or is a federal employee receiving his full salary and educational allowances under the Government Employees' Training Act.

*Who is eligible for vocational rehabilitation?*

Veterans who served in the Armed Forces during any of the four periods described below are eligible for vocational rehabilitation if all three of the following conditions are met:

1. They suffered a service-connected disability in active service which entitles them to compensation, or would but for receipt of retirement pay;

2. They were discharged or released under other than dishonorable conditions; and

3. The VA determines that they need vocational rehabilitation to overcome the handicap of their disabilities. Veterans whose disabilities were incurred in periods 2 and 4, described below, and whose disability ratings are less than thirty percent must show clearly that they have a pronounced employment handicap resulting from a service-connected disability.

The periods of service are:

1. World War II — the vocational rehabilitation training period was terminated for most veterans of World War II on July 25, 1956. Such period may be extended for certain seriously disabled veterans under certain conditions.

2. From World War II to the Korean Conflict, July 26, 1947, to June 26, 1950 — the termination date for training of this group of veterans was October 15, 1971, but may be extended to October 15, 1975, for those unable to enter and complete training by the basic termination date.

3. Korean Conflict, June 27, 1950, to January 31, 1955 — the termination date for those discharged before August 20, 1954, was August 20, 1963. For those discharged later the termination date is nine years after date of separation.

4. Post-Korean Conflict, February 1, 1955, to present. Includes

Vietnam era — for those who were discharged prior to October 15, 1962, the basic termination date was October 15, 1971. For those discharged later the basic termination date is nine years after the date of separation.

Eligible disabled veterans may get training up to a total of four years or its equivalent in part-time or combination of part-time and full-time training, and in some cases exceeding four years. Before a disabled veteran begins training, he will be provided vocational counseling to assist him in the selection of a suitable occupation and in the development of a vocational rehabilitation plan. Eligible veterans may (a) enroll in schools or colleges, (b) train on the job, (c) take institutional on-farm training, or (d) enter other programs which combine school and job training.

While in training and for two months after rehabilitation, eligible disabled veterans may receive subsistence allowances in addition to their disability compensation, plus tuition, books, and fees.

*New Rates—Vocational Rehabilitation Program*

|  | No dependents | One dependent | Two dependents |
|---|---|---|---|
| Full-time | $135 | $181 | $210 |
| Three-quarter | 98 | 133 | 156 |
| Half-time | 67 | 91 | 102 |
| On-farm, on-job-training or apprenticeship, full-time | 118 | 153 | 181 |

All these allowances will be increased by an additional $6 a month for each dependent in excess of two for veterans with less than fifty percent disability who are not entitled to added compensation for dependents.

*Are orphans, wives, and widows eligible for education assistance?*

Generally eligible are widows, wives, and children between eighteen and twenty-six years old of deceased and living veterans whose death or permanent and total disability was the result of service in the Armed Forces after the beginning of the Spanish-American War on April 28, 1898. Wives and children of servicemen missing in action, or prisoners of war, for more than ninety days are also eligible.

If eligible children under eighteen have (a) graduated from high school or (b) are above the age of compulsory school attendance, the VA may begin this schooling before they reach age eighteen. In some instances, handicapped children may begin a special vocational or restorative course as early as age fourteen. The period of eligibility for educational assistance of special restorative training ends on an eligible child's twenty-sixth birthday, plus any period of time after his eighteenth birthday which was required to process his application, unless extended under certain conditions.

Generally, the period of eligibility for a wife or widow extends to November 30, 1976, or eight years from the date the veteran was first found to have a service-connected total disability permanent in nature or from his date of death, whichever is later. For wives of servicemen missing in action or prisoners of war, eligibility extends to December 24, 1978 or eight years from the date the spouse was so listed, whichever is later.

The eligible child will receive VA educational or vocational counseling to assist him in the selection of a goal and the development of a program of education. After counseling an educational plan must be submitted by or for the eligible child showing the selected goal, the program of education, school or schools he plans to attend, and an estimate of the total cost of the education. The plan becomes part of the application. Counseling is available to wives and widows on request.

A child's marriage will be no barrier. A widow's remarriage terminates entitlement unless the remarriage is terminated by death or divorce.

Up to thirty-six months of schooling is provided or the equivalent of thirty-six months if enrolled part time. The aggregate entitlement to educational benefits may not exceed forty-eight months.

Training may be taken in schools and colleges only. On-the-job training, on-the-farm training, vocational flight training, and correspondence school training are prohibited. Training given by radio or open circuit television is prohibited except in certain instances. Training in foreign countries is not permitted except under special conditions. All courses must be approved by the designated state approving agency.

Monthly rates under this program are: full-time, $175; three-quarter-time, $128; and half-time, $81. Less than half-time is limited to tuition cost, not to exceed $175. Those enrolled in full-time cooperative courses—alternating classroom study and related experience on the job—will receive $141 a month. These allowances will be paid after the end of each month of school completed.

*What GI loans are available for homes, farms, businesses?*

Those qualified are veterans and eligible widows of World War II, Korean Conflict, post-Korean Conflict, Vietnam era; wives of servicemen officially listed as missing in action or captured for more than ninety days; and servicemen with at least 181 days of active duty. Loans are available to:

1. Purchase, construct, refinance, or improve a home.
2. Buy a farm, farmland, stock, feed and seed, farm machinery, other farm supplies, and equipment.
3. Purchase a mobile home (guaranteed loans only; no insured loans for mobile homes).
4. Buy a business or otherwise enable a veteran to undertake or expand a legitimate business venture, except that post-Korean Conflict veterans and servicemen still on active duty are not eligible for business loans nor insured loans unless at the time of application they had entitlement based on World War II or Korean Conflict service and no part of it had been used to obtain a GI loan.

Eligibility requirements for veterans of World War II: (a) active duty on or after September 16, 1940, and prior to July 26, 1947; (b) a discharge or separation under other than dishonorable conditions; and (c) at least ninety days' total service unless discharged earlier for service-connected disability. Eligibility requirements for veterans of the Korean Conflict are: (a) discharge or separation under other than dishonorable conditions; (b) active duty at any time on or after June 27, 1950, and prior to February 1, 1955; and (c) at least ninety days' total service unless discharged earlier for a service-connected disability. Eligibility requirements for post-Korean and Vietnam veterans are: (a) active duty for 181 days or more, any part of which occurred after January 31, 1955, and discharge or release from active duty after such date for a service-connected disability (six-month enlistees are not eligible since their service does not constitute active duty as defined in the governing law); and (b) servicemen who have served at least 181 days in active duty status, even though not discharged, while their service continues without a break.

Unremarried widows of men who served in World War II, the Korean Conflict or the post-Korean period (including the Vietnam era) and who died as a result of service-connected disabilities, and wives of servicemen on active duty who are officially listed as missing in action or prisoners of war and have been in such status for more than ninety days, are eligible for GI loans to acquire a home. Receipt by the wife of official notice that the husband is no longer listed as missing or captured ends entitlement.

Loan entitlement is no longer subject to an expiration date. The word "entitlement" means the guarantee or insurance benefits available to an eligible veteran. The maximum entitlement available to an eligible veteran is as follows:

1. $12,500 for home loans.

2. $4,000 for other real estate loans.

3. $2,000 for non-real estate loans.

4. A veteran who has the maximum entitlement for home loans is eligible for a loan to purchase a mobile home. The maximum is $10,000 for a mobile home only. It may go up to $17,500 when the loan includes site acquisition. Within these maximums the amount of such loan may not, however, exceed the figure established by the VA for the particular transaction. Use of the mobile home loan benefit will preclude the use of any other home loan benefit until the mobile home loan has been paid in full.

Eligible veterans must make their own arrangements for loans through the usual lending channels, such as banks, building and loan associations, mortgage loan companies, and the like. The lender making GI loans for the purchase of homes (not mobile homes), farm homes, condominium units, refinancing of existing mortgage loans or liens secured of record on a veteran's dwelling, or repairs and improvements to farm dwellings is guaranteed against loss up to sixty percent of the loan with a maximum guarantee of $12,500. On other loans VA guarantees the lender against loss up to fifty percent of the loan with a maximum guarantee of $4,000 on real estate and up to $2,000 on nonreal estate loans. On mobile home loans, the amount of guarantee is thirty percent of the loan. Maximum interest rate on GI loans may vary due to changes in the law and VA regulations. Once a loan is made, the interest remains the same for the life of the loan. In obtaining loans for the refinancing of existing mortgage loans or other liens of record veterans may pay discounts of reasonable amounts.

Instead of a VA guarantee some lenders prefer to use the VA insured loan program. The interest rate on insured realty loans will be in keeping with the governing law and VA regulations.

Post-Korean Conflict veterans are not eligible for insured loans unless at the time of application they had previous entitlement and no part of it was used to obtain a GI loan.

The loan terms are subject to negotiation between the veteran and the lender. The repayment period or maturity of GI home loans may be as long as thirty years. The VA does not require that a downpayment be made. However, the amount of a loan may not exceed the VA's determination of the home's reasonable value. If it does, the veteran must certify that he is paying the difference in cash without any supplementary borrowing. The statutory maximum maturity for a mobile loan is twelve years and thirty-two days. If site acquisition is also involved, the maturity may go up to fifteen years and thirty-two days. A cash down payment will be required in connection with such loans in an amount equal to the difference, if any, between the VA loan maximum and the cost to the veteran.

Closing costs must be paid in cash.

The VA protects veteran borrowers in the following ways:

1. Homes completed less than a year before acquisition with GI financing must meet or exceed VA minimum requirements for planning, construction, and general acceptability.

2. The VA may suspend from participation in the loan program those who take unfair advantage of veteran borrowers or decline to sell a new home to, or make a loan to, a credit worthy, eligible veteran because of his race, color, creed, or national origin.

3. On a new home the builder is required to give the veteran purchaser a one-year warranty that the home has been constructed in substantial conformity with VA approved plans and specifications. A similar warranty is required to be given to the veteran in respect to new mobile homes.

4. In some instances the VA may pay or otherwise compensate the veteran borrower for correction of serious structural defects which develop within four years of the time a home loan is guaranteed or made.

A veteran must certify that he intends to live in the home he is buying or improving with a GI loan both at the time of application and at the time of closing the loan. The same is true in respect to mobile homes.

Upon request to the VA when he sells residential property financed with a GI loan, an original veteran borrower may be released from liability to the government, provided the loan is current and the purchaser has obligated himself by contract to purchase the property and assume all of the veteran's liabilities and the VA is satisfied that the purchaser is a good risk. This release of liability does not mean that a veteran could have his GI home loan entitlement restored. The VA restores entitlement only where it no longer is liable to the lender on the guarantee and the veteran is otherwise eligible for restoration. The release of a veteran from liability to the government does not change the fact that the VA continues to remain liable on the guarantee.

In some rural or small community areas where the VA has determined that private mortgage financing is not generally available, direct loans may be secured. Consult local VA officials.

### What are wheelchair homes?

Certain disabled veterans of wartime or peacetime service may be entitled under certain conditions to a grant from VA for a "wheelchair home" especially adapted to their needs. VA grants not more than fifty percent, up to maximum of $12,500, to pay part of cost of building, buying, or remodeling such a home or paying indebtedness on such a home already acquired.

The veteran must have a service-connected disability due to war or peacetime service after April 30, 1898, entitling him to compensation for permanent and total disability due to:

**1.** Loss or loss of use of both lower extremities, such as to preclude locomotion without the aid of braces, crutches, canes, or a wheelchair.

**2.** Blindness in both eyes, having only light perception, plus loss or loss of use of one lower extremity.

**3.** Loss or loss of use of one lower extremity together with residuals of organic disease or injury which so affect the functions of balance as to preclude locomotion without resort to a wheelchair.

### What about GI life insurance?

VMLI has no bearing upon other government life insurance coverage. Under certain circumstances former policyholders who have been on continuous active duty may replace an expired term policy or replace or reinstate a permanent plan of insurance which was surrendered for its cash value, while in active service. The applicant must apply while he is in service or within 120 days following separation from service.

For veterans of World War I, World War II, Korean Conflict, Vietnam era, and peacetime service:

### Status of Life Insurance Programs

| Program | Beginning date | Ending date for new issues | Policy letter prefix |
|---|---|---|---|
| U.S. Government (USGLI) | May, 1919 | Apr. 25, 1951 | K |
| National Service (NSLI) | Oct. 8, 1940 | Apr. 25, 1951 | V,H |
| Veterans Special (VSLI) | Apr. 25, 1951 | Dec. 31, 1956 | RS,W |
| Service Disabled (SDVI) | Apr. 25, 1951 | Still open | RH |
| Veterans Reopened (VRI) | May 1, 1965 | May 2, 1966 | J,JR,JS |
| Servicemen's Group (SGLI) | Sept. 29, 1965 | Still open | — |
| Veteran's Mortgage (VMLI) | Aug. 11, 1971 | Still open | — |

The maximum amount of government life insurance, exclusive of SGLI and VMLI, that one can carry is $10,000. It is possible to carry as much as $15,000 of SGLI and an additional $10,000 government life insurance.

Veterans separated from service on or after April 25, 1951, with a service-connected disability but otherwise good health may apply to the VA for the special nonparticipating National Service Life Insurance within one year from the date VA notifies the veteran that his disability has been rated as service-connected. Effective June 25, 1970, lapsed term policies may be reinstated within five years from the date of lapse. However, NSLI on the Limited Convertible Term Plan (policy prefix W) may not be reinstated if the term period ended after the policyholder's fiftieth birthday. A five-year term policy which is not lapsed at the end of the term period is automatically renewed for an additional five-year period. The premium rate for each renewal is based on the attained age of the insured.

Lapsed permanent plan policies may be reinstated at any time except that J, JR, and JS policies must be reinstated within five years from date of lapse, and an endowment plan must be reinstated within the endowment period.

Any term policy which is in force may be converted to a permanent plan if requirements are met. However, NSLI policyholders are not eligible to convert to an endowment plan while totally disabled. An insured who is age sixty-five or older and has a five-year level premium term policy of USGLI in force by payment of premiums may exchange such policy for a Special Endowment at Age 96 Plan policy. Veterans with RS five-year term policies in force are eligible to exchange their policies for the Limited Convertible Five-Year Level Premium Term Plan before insurance age fifty or convert the RS term insurance to one of the permanent plans of insurance.

Effective May 1, 1965, NSLI policyholders may convert their term insurance or exchange their permanent plan policies for a new modified life plan through insurance age sixty. Premiums for this new plan insurance (other than those policies with a J, JR, or JS prefix) will remain level but the face value of the modified plan policy is automatically reduced by fifty percent at age sixty-five. The insured can replace the reduced half of his policy at the premium rate for his attained age on the ordinary life plan. Effective July 1, 1972, a new Modified Life Plan policy which will be automatically reduced by fifty percent at age seventy becomes available.

No new applications for in-service waiver of premiums were acceptable after December 31, 1956. Policyholders whose policies are still under the inservice waiver of premiums may continue the waiver as long as they remain in continuous active service and for 120 days thereafter. However, if a policyholder died on or after January 1, 1972, and the waiver was still in effect, an amount equal to the premiums, less dividends, waived on or after that date shall be placed as an indebtedness against the insurance, and unless otherwise paid, shall be deducted from the proceeds. This liberalization removes the bar against payment of DIC (dependency and indemnity compensation) to survivors of veterans who died while the NSLI and USGLI was in force under a 724 waiver. Policyholders may cancel their inservice waiver upon written request to the VA. The waiver may not be discontinued retroactively.

Dividends are payable to holders of K and V insurance only. After the end of the first policy year, provided premiums have been paid for at least one year, guaranteed values available include cash value, paid-up insurance, extended term insurance, and policy loan provision. Current interest on policy loans is five percent. Earlier loans at lower interest are not affected.

NSLI policyholders who become totally disabled and are likely to remain so for six or more months should consult the VA about their entitlement to premium waiver. USGLI policyholders who become totally and permanently disabled should consult the VA about their right to receive the proceeds of their policies in monthly payments. Full information about the total disability income provision which eligible policyholders may add to their policies is available from the VA office which maintains the policyholder's insurance records. The provision currently provides for a payment of $5.75 for USGLI and $10.00 for NSLI each month for each $1,000 of insurance in force, if the insured is determined by the Veterans Administration to be totally disabled prior to age sixty-five, without reducing the amount of insurance.

Special notice to J, JR, and JS policyholders—premiums on these policies may be raised or lowered from time to time depending on actual experience. A small administrative cost is included in each policy premium and this cost may also increase or decrease, based on experience.

### What is servicemen's group life insurance?

All members of the Armed Forces are automatically insured under Serviceman's Group Life Insurance (SGLI) with premiums deducted from their pay unless they decline in writing to be insured. Coverage is $15,000 unless the member elects $10,000 or $5,000. Before June 25, 1970, maximum amount was $10,000.

Members on full duty have protection for 120 days after separation, unless absent without leave for more than thirty-one days and not restored to duty with pay. Members with orders for less than thirty-one days are protected only during duty and while proceeding directly to and from duty. Reserve Officers Training Corps (ROTC) members are covered only during field training or practice cruises. Members totally disabled retain coverage for a year after separation or until total disability ceases—whichever is earlier.

The group coverage can be replaced, regardless of health, by individual policies issued by six hundred participating commercial companies if application is made and premiums paid before the end of 120 days. Duty based on orders that specify less than thirty-one days does not carry extension of coverage or the right to obtain individual policies except for those with service-incurred or aggravated disability, who have ninety days to obtain a policy. Veterans may contact their nearest VA regional office or write to the Office of Servicemen's Group Life Insurance, 212 Washington St., Newark, N. J. 07102.

### What is veterans mortgage life insurance?

Effective August 11, 1971, PL 92–95 established a program of group type mortgage life insurance for those veterans who have been granted or will be granted a specially adapted housing grant, primarily paraplegics. The law provides for a maximum of $30,000 insurance to cover a mortgage. Protection is automatic unless eligible veterans decline in writing or fail to respond to a final request for information on which their premiums can be based. Premiums are automatically deducted from VA benefit payments or paid direct, if the veteran does not draw compensation, and will continue until the mortgage (up to $30,000) has been liquidated or the home is sold, or until the veteran reaches age seventy or dies.

*What dependency and indemnity compensation (DIC) benefits are available and to whom?*

For survivors of deceased veterans of Spanish-American War, Mexican Border Campaign, World War I, World War II, Korean Conflict, Vietnam era, and peacetime service.

1. DIC payments are authorized for widows, unmarried children under eighteen (as well as certain helpless children and those between eighteen and twenty-three if attending a VA-approved school), and certain parents of servicemen or veterans who die on or after January 1, 1957, from: (a) a disease or injury incurred or aggravated in line of duty while on active duty or active duty for training; (b) an injury incurred or aggravated in line of duty while on inactive duty training; or (c) a disability otherwise compensable under laws administered by VA.

When a veteran dies on or after April 30, 1957, and before January 1, 1972, and there is an in-service waiver of insurance in effect, his survivors may elect DIC. When a veteran dies on or after January 1, 1972, and there is an in-service waiver of insurance in effect, DIC is the benefit payable to survivors. When such waivers are continued in effect at time of death, the insurance premiums which would have become payable from January 1, 1972, until the veteran's death will be offset from the amount of insurance proceeds payable.

2. Widows, children, and parents who are on the rolls or found to be eligible for death compensation by reason of a death occurring before January 1, 1957, may elect to receive DIC payments in lieu of death compensation. They cannot thereafter choose to receive death compensation.

A widow must have lived continuously with the veteran from

the time of marriage until the veteran's death, except where there was a separation due to the misconduct of, or procured by, the veteran without fault on the wife's part. Remarriage makes a widow ineligible based on the death of that veteran unless the purported remarriage was void, has been annulled, or terminates in death or divorce. A widow may also be ineligible if, after the death of the veteran, she has lived with another man and held herself out openly to the public to be his wife. Should such relationship terminate, she may reapply for benefits. If she meets the other qualifications, a woman who married a veteran without knowing that a legal impediment to the marriage existed may be eligible for compensation under certain conditions.

The DIC monthly rates range from $184 in case of an E-1 pay grade to $503 for an O-10 pay grade, with some higher payments in certain cases. There are additional payments for children and parents.

NOTE: The term widow includes the widower of a female veteran if he (1) is incapable of self-maintenance, and (2) was at the time of her death permanently incapable of self-support due to physical or mental disability.

*What are the DIC rates for widows?*

### DIC Widow Rates

| Pay grade | Monthly rate | Pay grade | Monthly rate |
|-----------|-------------|-----------|-------------|
| E-1 | $184 | W-4 | $262 |
| E-2 | 189 | O-1 | 232 |
| E-3 | 195 | O-2 | 240 |
| E-4 | 206 | O-3 | 257 |
| E-5 | 212 | O-4 | 272 |
| E-6 | 217 | O-5 | 299 |
| E-7 | 227 | O-6 | 337 |
| E-8 | 240 | O-7 | 365 |
| E-9 | 251[a] | O-8 | 399 |
| W-1 | 232 | O-9 | 429 |
| W-2 | 241 | O-10 | 469[b] |
| W-3 | 249 | | |

[a]If the veteran served as sergeant major of the Army, senior enlisted adviser of the Navy, chief master sergeant of the Air Force, or sergeant major of the Marine Corps at the applicable time designated by section 402 of this title, the widow's rate shall be $270.

[b]If the veteran served as Chairman of the Joint Chiefs of Staff, Chief of Staff of the Army, Chief of Naval Operations, Chief of Staff of the Air Force, or Commandant of the Marine Corps, at the applicable time designated by section 402 of this title, the widow's rate shall be $503.

Widows and parents qualified for either death compensation or DIC may be granted a special allowance for aid and attendance if they are patients in a nursing home, helpless or blind, or so nearly helpless or blind as to require the regular aid and attendance of another person. The allowance is $55 monthly payable in addition to the DIC or death compensation rate for which the eligible person qualifies.

The monthly rates of DIC for parents range from $10 to $100 based upon the income of the parents and whether there is only one parent, two parents not living together, or two parents together or remarried with spouse. The income limit for two parents together or remarried and with spouse is $3,800, that for one parent or two parents not together is $2,600.

*What death compensation benefits exist for survivors who died before January 1, 1957?*

Death compensation payments are authorized for widows, unmarried children under eighteen (or until twenty-three if attending a VA-approved school), helpless children, and dependent parents of servicemen or veterans who died before January 1, 1957, from a service-connected cause not the result of willful misconduct. If service-connected death occurred after service, the veteran's discharge must have been under conditions other than dishonorable. As explained in the preceding section on DIC payments, widows, children, and parents eligible for death compensation under this section may elect to receive DIC payments instead. They may not thereafter choose death compensation.

Children who become permanently incapable of self-support because of a mental or physical defect before reaching age eighteen may receive death compensation as long as the condition exists or until they marry.

Parents are held to be dependent for death compensation if their income is insufficient to provide reasonable maintenance for themselves and for members of their family under legal age. Proof of dependency must be submitted to VA upon application for death compensation under this section.

Monthly payments to eligible survivors at wartime rates are: $87 for widow only with higher amounts if there are eligible children; children only $67, $94, and $122 for one, two, or three children respectively with $23 for each additional child; and $75 for one dependent parent or $40 each for two dependent parents.

Lesser amounts are paid in peacetime rates. A widow who qualified for death compensation may be granted a special allowance
for aid and attendance if she is a patient in a nursing home; helpless or blind; or so nearly helpless or blind as to need or require the
regular aid and attendance of another person. The additional
allowance is $55 monthly, which is payable in addition to the
basic death compensation rate for which the widow otherwise
qualifies.

### What nonservice-connected death pension benefits are provided?

All widows and children (except those of Spanish-American War
veterans) who came on the pension rolls on or after July 1, 1960,
will receive pension under the current system. The veteran must
have had ninety days' service, unless discharged or retired sooner
for service-connected disability, and have been discharged under
conditions other than dishonorable. The widow must have lived
continuously with veteran from time of marriage until veteran's
death, except while there was a separation due to the misconduct
of, or procured by, the veteran without fault on the wife's part.
Remarriage following the death of the veteran makes the widow
ineligible for pension based on the death of that veteran unless the
purported remarriage is void or has been annulled or is terminated
by death or divorce. A widow may also be ineligible if after the
death of the veteran she has lived with another man and held herself out openly to the public to be his wife. Should such relationship terminate, she may reapply for benefits. If she meets the other
qualifications, a woman who married a veteran without knowing
that a legal impediment to the marriage existed may be eligible for
pension in certain cases.

### What are the eligibility requirements for widows and children?

Widows and unmarried children under age eighteen (age twenty-
three if attending a VA-approved school) of deceased veterans of
these wars or conflict may be eligible for pension if they meet the
applicable conditions below.

Otherwise qualified children who become permanently incapable of self-support because of a mental or physical defect before
reaching age eighteen may receive a pension as long as the condition exists or until they marry.

## Regular Pension (New Law)

| Income not more than | Widow | Widow and one child |
|---|---|---|
| $   300 | $87 | $104 |
| 400 | 86 | 104 |
| 500 | 85 | 104 |
| 600 | 84 | 104 |
| 700 | 81 | 103 |
| 800 | 78 | 102 |
| 900 | 75 | 101 |
| 1,000 | 72 | 100 |
| 1,100 | 69 | 99 |
| 1,200 | 66 | 98 |
| 1,300 | 63 | 97 |
| 1,400 | 60 | 96 |
| 1,500 | 57 | 94 |
| 1,600 | 54 | 92 |
| 1,700 | 51 | 90 |
| 1,800 | 48 | 88 |
| 1,900 | 45 | 86 |
| 2,000 | 41 | 84 |
| 2,100 | 37 | 82 |
| 2,200 | 33 | 80 |
| 2,300 | 29 | 78 |
| 2,400 | 25 | 76 |
| 2,500 | 21 | 74 |
| 2,600 | 17 | 72 |
| 2,700 | | 70 |
| 2,800 | | 67 |
| 2,900 | | 64 |
| 3,000 | | 61 |
| 3,100 | | 58 |
| 3,200 | | 55 |
| 3,300 | | 52 |
| 3,400 | | 49 |
| 3,500 | | 46 |
| 3,600 | | 43 |
| 3,700 | | 42 |
| 3,800 | | 42 |

An applicable formula will reduce pension for every dollar of income above that shown in each level. $17 is paid for each additional child. Where there is no eligible widow, a child may receive $42 a month with $17 added for each additional child and the total divided among them. A child is not entitled if his income, not counting his own earnings, exceeds $2,000.

Pension is not payable to those whose estates are so large that it is reasonable they look to the estates for maintenance. A widow who qualifies for pension may be granted a special allowance for aid and attendance if she is so severely disabled as to require the regular aid and attendance of another person. A widow of a Spanish American War veteran receives a death pension of $70 a month, or $75 if she was his wife during service. An additional $8.13 is paid for each child. An additional $55 is payable to a widow who is in need of the aid and attendance of another person or is a patient in a nursing home. Death pension of $73.13 per month is paid for one child where there is no widow, plus $8.13 for each additional child.

### To what extent is there reimbursement of burial expenses?

The deceased veteran must have been discharged under conditions other than dishonorable and have been either a wartime veteran of Korean Conflict or Vietnam era, or a peacetime veteran in receipt of service-connected compensation at time of death or discharge, or retired for disability incurred in line of duty.

### Who may claim reimbursement?

Undertaker, if unpaid, otherwise person who bore veteran's burial expenses. Payment not to exceed $250 is made toward veteran's burial expenses. Claim must be filed within two years after permanent burial or cremation. Additional costs of transportation of the remains may be allowed if the veteran died while hospitalized or domiciled in a VA hospital or domiciliary or at VA's expense, or died in transit at VA's expense to or from a hospital, domiciliary, or VA regional office.

### What about burial flags?

The deceased veteran must have been discharged under conditions other than dishonorable, and must have been either a wartime veteran or one who served after June 26, 1950, or a veteran who served at least one enlistment during peacetime, unless discharged or released sooner for disability incurred in line of duty. VA may also issue a flag for a veteran who is missing in action and is later presumed dead. An American flag drapes casket of veteran, after which it may be given to next of kin or close friend or associate of the deceased.

*Who is eligible for burial in national cemeteries?*

This service is administered by Department of the Army and Department of the Interior through superintendents of the various national cemeteries.

Burial is available in all national cemeteries having available grave space except Arlington to any deceased veteran of wartime or peacetime service whose last period of active service (other than for training) terminated honorably, by death or otherwise. Reservists who die while performing active duty for training also are eligible. Burial is also available to eligible veteran's wife, husband, widow, widower, minor children, and under certain conditions unmarried adult children.

Effective February 17, 1967, eligibility in Arlington is limited to the following:

1. Persons dying on active duty in the Armed Forces.

2. Retired members of the Army, Navy, Air Force, Marine Corps, or Coast Guard who have performed active federal service, are carried on official service retired lists, and who are eligible to receive compensation stemming from service in the Armed Forces.

3. Recipients of the Medal of Honor.

4. Persons otherwise eligible by reason of honorable military service who held elective office in the United States government or served on the Supreme Court or in the Cabinet or in an office compensated at level II under the Executive Salary Act.

5. The spouses, minor children, and dependent adult children of the persons listed in 1 through 4 above and persons already buried in Arlington.

Until the cemetery personnel have verified the decedent's eligibility for burial and notified the funeral director or the decedent's family that the tentative arrangements are confirmed, the remains should not be shipped to Arlington and the date, time, and place of interment should not be announced in newspapers.

Any VA office will provide information and other assistance in filing burial request applications. Applications should be made only at the time of death of the veteran or that of an eligible dependent by contacting the superintendent of the nearest national cemetery.

*Are headstones or grave markers provided?*

For Veterans of Spanish-American War, World War I, World War

II, Korean Conflict, Vietnam era, and peacetime service whose *last* period of active service (other than for training) terminated honorably by death or otherwise, a headstone or grave marker is available. Reservists who die while performing active duty for training also are eligible. Headstone or grave marker is provided without charge and shipped to the consignee designated. Applicants are cautioned to ensure the correctness of all information. The benefit does not apply to members of a veteran's family who are buried in a private cemetery.

Applications (DOD Form 1330) go to the Chief of Support Services of the Army, Washington, D.C. 20315. Any VA office will provide information and other assistance in filing applications.

*Are memorial markers and memorial plots available?*

A memorial headstone or marker may be furnished on application of a close relative recognized as the next of kin to commemorate any member of the Armed Forces of the United States who dies in the service and whose remains are not recovered and identified or are buried at sea. The memorial may be erected in a private cemetery in a plot provided by the applicant or in a memorial section of a national cemetery.

Applications (DOD Form 1330) for memorial markers go to the Chief of Support Services of the Army, Washington, D.C. 20315. Any VA office will provide information and other assistance in filing applications.

*What reemployment rights are included?*

1. For private employment a veteran must have left other than temporary employment to enter military service; must have served not more than five years after August 1, 1961, after leaving the employment to which he claims restoration, provided that any service over four years was at the request and for the convenience of the government; must have been separated honorably or under honorable conditions; and must be qualified to perform the duties of the job or, if disabled while in military service, some other job in employer's organization of comparable seniority, status, and pay.

2. For federal employment generally the same as for private employment.

*What is the nature of the benefit?*

Restoration in the position the veteran would have attained had he not been absent or in another position of like seniority, status, and pay, including all benefits falling due after reemployment which would have accrued by his seniority. Protection against discharge without cause for one year (six months in the case of a reservist or guardsman returning from initial active duty for training).

A veteran must apply to his preservice employer within ninety days after separation from active duty, or after release from hospitalization continuing for not more than a year immediately after active duty for training of at least three consecutive months. Reservists and national guardsmen returning from other types of military training duty must report back to their employer for the next regularly scheduled work period after their return home, allowing for hospitalization and necessary travel time.

## What is the aim of unemployment compensation?

The purpose of unemployment compensation for veterans is to provide a weekly income for a limited period of time to help veterans meet basic needs while searching for employment. The amount and duration of payments are governed by state laws with maximum payments generally ranging from $45 to $86 a week. Benefits are paid from federal funds. While state laws vary, all states require that veterans have ninety days or more continuous active service (unless separated earlier because of a service-connected disability) and be able to work and be available for work. Generally benefits are not paid to persons receiving certain educational assistance or vocational subsistence allowances from VA.

Veterans should apply immediately after leaving service at their nearest local state employment service office (*not* at the VA) and bring their DD Forms 214 to establish their type of separation from service.

## What job-finding assistance is available?

While the VA seeks to assist veterans who are seeking employment through job marts, on-the-job and apprenticeship training opportunities, etc., (which can be checked out at VA Regional Offices and U.S. Veterans Assistance Centers), the federal agency charged with employment assistance is the U.S. Department of Labor, which provides job counseling and employment placement services. These programs are administered through local veterans employment representatives in local state employment service offices where employment counseling and testing are provided. While these services are available to all, priority for referral to appropriate training programs and job openings is given to eligible veterans, with first consideration to the disabled veteran.

*What other non-VA benefits are provided?*

There are several benefits available to veterans and their dependents which are not administered by the Veterans Administration. These are summarized below with information on how to contact the proper agency.

1. Corrections of Military Records — Generally a request for correction must be filed within three years after the discovery of the alleged error or injustice. The veteran, his survivors, or his legal representative should write to the service concerned on Department of Defense Form DD-149, which may be obtained at any VA office.

2. Exchange and Commissary Privileges — Honorably discharged veterans with one-hundred percent service-connected disability, their dependents, and their unremarried wdows are entitled to unlimited exchange and commissary store privileges. Also covered are widows of veterans who were rated one-hundred percent service-connected disabled at time of death. Certification of eligibility and assistance with the application for Uniformed Services Identification and Privilege Card, DD Form 1172, may be obtained from your VA regional office.

3. Farm and Rural Loans — Supervised credit and management advice to farm and rural families unable to get sufficient credit from any other source may be obtained from the Farmers Home Administration, Department of Agriculture. Apply at local Farmers Home Administration offices generally located in county seat towns.

4. Federal Civil Service Preference — Many benefits for veterans seeking federal employment including the addition of points to passing scores in competitive examinations, waivers of physical requirements, restrictions of certain jobs to veterans, preference for retention in case of reduction in force, and similar advantageous procedures for veterans, unremarried widows, and mothers of deceased veterans are authorized by the U.S. Civil Service Com-

mission. Most large post offices will have civil service information or addresses where such information may be obtained.

5. FHA Home Mortgage Insurance for Veterans — Gives veterans certain advantages with respect to down payment requirements in obtaining FHA insured loans. Veterans eligible for VA loans should check advantages of both programs.

6. Manpower Retraining Programs — Veterans are given priority for referral to appropriate training programs in private or public schools and on-the-job in facilities of employers and other organizations. Training allowances, equivalent generally to weekly rate of unemployment compensation in trainee's state, may be supplemented by other amounts. The program is administered by (a) U.S. Department of Labor through state employment service agencies and (b) U.S. Department of Health, Education, and Welfare through state vocational education agencies.

7. Guaranty of Premiums on Commercial Life Insurance — The premiums and the interest due on eligible commercial life insurance policies, not exceeding $10,000 in any individual case, may be guaranteed by the government while the policyholder is on active military duty and for two years thereafter. Repayment must be made to the government for any amount paid insurers on account of the protected policy.

8. Naturalization Preference — Aliens with war service in U.S. Armed Forces who have been lawfully admitted to the United States for permanent residence or who at any time entered the Armed Forces while within the United States, the Canal Zone, American Samoa, or Swain's Island may have their naturalization authorized and expedited by eliminating certain requirements. Apply at nearest office of the Immigration and Naturalization Service. Former citizens who lost their citizenship by entering the armed forces of nations while allied with the United States during World War II may be naturalized under certain liberal conditions.

9. Review of Discharges — Within fifteen years after discharge, veterans may apply to a board of review with authority to change, correct, or modify any discharge or dismissal from the service that was *not* the result of a general court-martial and to direct issuance of a new discharge. The veteran, his surviving spouse, next of kin, or legal representative should write to the service concerned on Department of Defense Form DD-293, which can be obtained at any VA office.

10. Six Months' Death Gratuity — A sum equal to six months' pay

of the deceased but within specified limits is paid to the deceased veteran's spouse, children, or if designated by the deceased, parents, brothers, or sisters. Normally, this is paid as soon as possible by the command to which the deceased was attached. If not received within a reasonable time, application should be made to the service concerned. Persons must have died in service or within 120 days thereafter for specified reasons relating to military service.

11. Social Security Credits — Veterans with ninety days of active service since September 16, 1940, are given wage credits toward their earnings record. This was done differently during different time periods, some credits were gratuitous and others followed a contribution from basic pay. These credits, whether listed on earnings records or not, are counted when the veteran or his survivors make a claim for benefits. Further information may be obtained by visiting or writing the nearest Social Security district office. The address can be found under Social Security Administration in local phone books or obtained at local post offices.

*How can claims be expedited by veteran's families?*

To file a claim it is necessary to identify the veteran. If the veteran had ever filed a VA claim and his file number ("C" number) is known to his family, there will be no problem. Otherwise it will be necessary to establish his identity by submitting a copy of his discharge from service or his military service number or his branch of service and dates served. If not already on record in VA files, the following documents will be required:

1. The veteran's death certificate for all claims where the veteran died outside of service or outside of a VA hospital.

2. The veteran's marriage certificate where the claim is made by the widow or by or for his children.

3. The children's birth certificates, whether claim is made in the child's own right or by the widow.

4. The veteran's birth certificate if the parents of the veteran wish to establish eligibility.

The immediate benefits following the death of the veteran—a burial flag and burial in national cemeteries—can be secured with the aid of the undertaker handling the veteran's funeral. The undertaker's requests usually alert the VA insurance division so that an insurance claim form is automatically sent to the veteran's beneficiary. If the undertaker has not alerted the VA at the time of the veteran's death, families in the eastern half of the United States should send their insurance claim to the VA Center, 5000 Wissahickon Ave., Philadelphia, Pa. 19101. Families in the western half of the nation should address the VA Center, Fort Snelling, St. Paul, Minn. 55111. Be sure to send the complete name of the veteran and number of the policy or, if the number is unknown, identify the veteran by his file number, his military serial number, or the branch and dates of his military service. The undertaker will also assist in filing for reimbursement of burial expenses.

If the veteran's death was service-connected, the widow and minor children may be eligible for dependency and indemnity compensation (DIC). Nonservice-connected death may entitle the widow and veteran's minor children to pension payments. In certain cases, parents may be eligible for dependency and indemnity compensation.

Children of veterans who die or become permanently and totally disabled with service-connected disabilities or of servicemen who are missing in action or prisoners of war may be eligible for orphans education assistance. Widows of veterans who died as the result of service-connected disabilities are eligible for education assistance. Wives of veterans who are permanently and totally disabled with a service-connected disability or of servicemen who are missing in action or prisoners of war are eligible for educational assistance.

Unremarried widows of veterans of World War II, the Korean Conflict, or post-Korean period, whose deaths were service-connected, are eligible for a GI home loan. Wives of servicemen who are missing in action or prisoners of war are eligible for a GI home loan.

Death gratuity is paid by the Armed Services to widows, children, and if designated by the deceased, to parents, brothers, or sisters.

Wherever possible, veterans should acquaint their families with the location of their military records, the file number, and their insurance numbers to save delay.

## Where should one go for help?

For information or assistance in applying for veterans' benefits write, call, or visit one of the regional offices or local veterans' service organization representatives. Application for medical benefits may be made at any VA station with medical facilities.

If telephoning, many states have toll-free service to the VA from communities in the state. Consult your local directory or information assistance operator for the latest listing of these numbers. All other telephone numbers may be found in local telephone directories or obtained from the operator without charge.

GI life insurance is administered at the VA Centers in St. Paul or Philadelphia. For any information concerning a policy write directly to the VA Center administering it, giving the insured's policy number, if known. The insured's full name, date of birth, and service number should be given if the policy number is not known.

## Chapter 32

## WILLS

*What is a will?*

A will is an instrument by which a person makes a disposition of his property to take effect after his death.

*What property cannot be transferred by will?*

1. Pensions.

2. U.S. government savings bonds.

3. Dower and curtesy and right of election.

4. Life insurance policy proceeds.

5. Property mutually owned.

*What is meant by probating a will?*

To probate a will is to prove before some officer or tribunal, authorized by law, that the document offered is the last will and testament of the deceased person whose act it is alleged to be; that it has been executed, attested, and published as required by law; and that the testator was of sound and disposing mind. In short, when a will is probated, its validity is established. Until a will is duly probated or proved, courts will not recognize any powers of the one named in the will as executor, nor the claims of anyone under the will, such as a devisee or legatee. If probate is refused, it is presumed that the deceased died intestate; that is, without a will.

*What happens to your property if you die intestate?*

Instead of being disposed of according to your wishes, your property is distributed in accordance with the law of your particular state, which may be contrary to your express wishes. When you leave a will, your estate is managed by the executor named by you. When you die without a will, the court will appoint an administrator, usually your closest relative, who might not have been your personal choice had you made a will.

*What is a testator?*

A testator is a man who has made a will.

*What is a testatrix?*

A testatrix is a woman who has made a will.

*What is a codicil to a will?*

A codicil is a supplement or addition to a will, made by the testator or testatrix, by which the dispositions in the will are explained, added to, or altered.

*What is an heir?*

Originally, under the common law, the word "heir" meant any person who by law was entitled to an interest in the real property of one who died intestate, that is, without leaving a will. The decedent had no right to violate this rule of inheritance; he could not even attempt to dispose of his real property by will to deprive his heir or heirs of it. Such is no longer the case, and a decedent now may so dispose of his property, both real and personal, as to deprive his heirs at law of their interest in his estate.

*What is a devise?*

A devise is real property passing under a will—for example, a house.

*What is a devisee?*

A devisee is the person who takes real property under a will.

*What is a legacy?*

A legacy is personal property passing under a will, especially money.

*What is a legatee?*

A person who takes personal property under a will.

*What is a bequest?*

A bequest is any form of personal property passing under a will—a collection of books, a piano, etc.

*What is a beneficiary under a will?*

A person who receives a benefit or advantage under a will.

*What is meant by "personal representative" and "next of kin"?*

Personal representative generally refers to executors and administrators. Next of kin refers to all those related by blood to the decedent.

*What is the difference between an executor and administrator of a will?*

An executor is a person named in the will by the testator to carry out its provisions. An administrator is a person appointed by the court to administer the estate of the deceased if there is no will.

*In making a will, whom should you generally appoint as executor?*

Your attorney, if you have one, and your wife, husband, or child to act as co-executor with your lawyer. It is a good idea to include in your will an alternate executor, to be appointed upon the death of the executor named by you.

*May an executor refuse to accept appointment under a will?*

Yes.

*What should be done if the executor named in the will dies before the testator?*

A new executor should be named by the testator.

*What will be done if the executor dies after the testator?*

A new executor will be appointed by the court if the will does not provide an alternate.

*Who is usually appointed administrator?*

Ordinarily, preference is given in the following order: widow or widower; son or daughter; grandchild, father or mother, brother or sister; and finally, any other next of kin, preferably the one taking the largest share of the estate.

*What are some of the duties of an executor or administrator?*

1. To locate the will.
2. To bury the decedent.
3. To collect the testator's effects and preserve them from waste.
4. To probate the will and be appointed executor.
5. To keep accurate records of all estate transactions.
6. To open the safe deposit box.
7. To assume control of all personal property.
8. To do whatever is necessary to liquidate or to carry on the decedent's business.
9. To determine the debts that are due the estate and to see that they are paid.
10. To determine and to collect all assets due the estate.
11. To arrange for the collection of all insurance payable to the estate.
12. To make arrangements for the transfer of all stocks, bonds, and other securities from the name of the decedent to that of the executor.
13. To pay all taxes and other expenses of the estate.
14. To have all property, real and personal, appraised for tax purposes.
15. To defend the estate against any suits.
16. To pay all legacies to those named in the will.
17. To submit a final accounting to the court.

*How is an executor or an administrator paid?*

The executor or administrator is paid a commission that is deducted from the estate. Though statutes vary in the different states, the usual commission is up to 10 per cent of the value of the estate. The larger the estate, the smaller the percentage.

*May an executor or administrator be removed from office?*

Yes, if he reveals himself to be corrupt or manifestly incompetent.

*At what age is a person legally competent to make a will?*

**Alabama** The age is twenty-one for disposing of real estate and eighteen for disposing of personal property.

**Alaska** The age is twenty-one for both real and personal property.

**Arizona** The age is twenty-one for both real and personal property.

**Arkansas** Anyone of sound mind over eighteen can dispose of both real and personal property.

**California** A person must be eighteen years or over to dispose of real estate and personal property.

**Colorado** Anyone who has attained the age of eighteen may dispose of real or personal property.

**Connecticut** Anyone eighteen years old may make a valid will of both real and personal property.

**Delaware** The age is eighteen for both males and females for disposing of both real and personal property.

**District of Columbia** The age is twenty-one for males and eighteen for females.

**Florida** Those eighteen years of age may make a will disposing of both real estate and personal property.

**Georgia** The minimum age is fourteen years for disposing of both real and personal property.

**Hawaii** The age is twenty for both males and females.

**Idaho** The minimum age is eighteen for both classes of property.

**Illinois** Males and females must be eighteen to dispose of both real and personal property.

**Indiana** Those twenty-one years or over may will real and personal property.

**Iowa** Those twenty-one years or over may will real and personal property.

**Kansas** Those twenty-one years or over may will real and personal property.

**Kentucky** Those twenty-one years or over may will real and personal property.

**Louisiana** Any person sixteen years or over may make a will disposing of real and personal property.

**Maine**   The minimum age is twenty-one, but any married woman or widow of any age may dispose of real and personal property by will.

**Maryland**   The minimum age for men is twenty-one, for women eighteen, regarding both real and personal property.

**Massachusetts**   The minimum age is twenty-one years for disposal of both real and personal property.

**Michigan**   The minimum age is twenty-one years for disposal of both real and personal property.

**Minnesota**   Both male and female must be twenty-one years or over.

**Mississippi**   The minimum age is twenty-one for disposal of all property.

**Missouri**   Males must be twenty-one to will real property and eighteen for personal property; females must be twenty-one for both real and personal property.

**Montana**   Those over eighteen may dispose of real and personal property.

**Nebraska**   The minimum age is twenty-one for all kinds of wills, though a married woman, irrespective of age, may make a valid will.

**Nevada**   Real and personal property may be disposed of by those eighteen years and over.

**New Hampshire**   Males and females must be eighteen or married before disposing of property, both real and personal.

**New Jersey**   Any person over twenty-one may will real and personal property.

**New Mexico**   Any person over twenty-one may will real and personal property.

**New York**   The minimum age at which a person may will real property is twenty-one; the minimum age for willing personal property is eighteen.

**North Carolina**   The minimum age for real and personal property is twenty-one.

**North Dakota**   The minimum age is eighteen for disposing of both real and personal property.

**Ohio**   Twenty-one for both real and personal property.

**Oklahoma**   Eighteen for disposal of real and personal property.

**Oregon**   Permits disposition if twenty-one for both males and females.

**Pennsylvania** To dispose of any kind of property by will, one must be over twenty-one years of age.

**Puerto Rico** All persons under fourteen years are barred from making valid wills.

**Rhode Island** One must be twenty-one to will real and personal property.

**South Carolina** Anyone twenty-one years or over may will both real and personal property; fourteen-year-old males and twelve-year-old females may will only personal property.

**South Dakota** A person must be over eighteen to dispose of real and personal property.

**Tennessee** A will of real estate may be made only by those twenty-one or over; personal property, however, may be bequeathed by males fourteen years old and females over twelve years.

**Texas** One must be over twenty-one to dispose of real and personal property.

**Utah** Any person over eighteen may dispose of real and personal property.

**Vermont** One must be over twenty-one to dispose of real and personal property.

**Virginia** The person making a will of real and personal property must be twenty-one or over; those over eighteen may bequeath their personal possessions.

**Washington** The age for disposition of both real and personal property is twenty-one years of age or eighteen if married or in military service.

**West Virginia** Anyone except infants may dispose of both real and personal property.

**Wisconsin** Anyone over twenty-one, or any married woman over eighteen, may will real and personal property.

**Wyoming** Anyone over twenty-one may dispose of all his property by will.

*How many witnesses are required to execute a valid will?*

Two witnesses are required in Alabama, Alaska, Arizona, Arkansas, California, Colorado, Delaware, District of Columbia, Florida, Hawaii, Idaho, Illinois, Indiana, Iowa, Kansas, Kentucky, Maryland, Michigan, Minnesota, Mississippi, Missouri, Montana, Ne-

braska, Nevada, New Jersey, New Mexico, New York, North Caro-
lina, North Dakota, Ohio, Oklahoma, Oregon, Pennsylvania,
Rhode Island, South Dakota, Tennessee, Texas, Utah, Virginia,
Washington, West Virginia, Wisconsin, and Wyoming.

Three witnesses are required in Connecticut, Georgia, Louisiana, Maine, Massachusetts, New Hampshire, South Carolina,
Vermont, and Puerto Rico.

### What is a nuncupative will?

It is an oral will made during the last illness of the deceased, in the
presence of witnesses, respecting the disposition of his personal
property after death. Soldiers in actual service and mariners at sea
may verbally dispose of their wages and personal property to any
amount, provided they are in actual fear or peril of death, or in expectation of immediate death from an injury received that day.
Most states recognize some form of oral will.

### In which states are oral wills legal?

**Alabama**  An oral will is valid only when the personal property
bequeathed does not exceed $500. Such a will must be made
during the last illness of the deceased, at his dwelling or where
he resided ten days or more, except when the testator is taken
ill away from home and dies before his return. It must be shown
that the deceased called upon persons present, or some of them,
to bear witness that the statement is his will. Oral wills made by
soldiers and sailors in actual service or mariners at sea are also
valid in Alabama.

**Alaska**  An oral will is permitted if the deceased's words, or the
substance thereof, are reduced to writing within thirty days after they are spoken and the writing probated after fourteen days
and within six months after such words are spoken. Any mariner at sea or any soldier in military service may dispose verbally
of his wages or other personal property.

**Arizona**  An oral will is allowed if made in the last sickness of the
deceased, where the property does not exceed $50 in value.
Three competent witnesses must testify that the testator called
on some person to take notice and bear testimony that such is
his will, and that the testimony, of its substance, was reduced to

writing within six days after the making of such will. When this is done, the amount that may be disposed of is without limit.

**Arkansas** An oral will must be made at the time of the last illness of the deceased in the presence of at least two witnesses. The amount is limited to $500. Such a will must be proved not less than twenty days nor more than six months from the date thereof; it must be reduced to writing and signed by the witnesses within fifteen days after the will is made.

**California** The amount of an oral will is limited to $1,000. The will must be proved by two witnesses present at the time it was made, one of whom was asked by the testator, at the time, to bear witness that such was his will. In addition, the deceased must have been, at the time, in actual military service in the field or doing duty while at sea. Finally, the deceased must have been in actual contemplation, fear, or peril of death, or in expectation of immediate death from an injury received that same day. The verbal statement of the deceased must be reduced to writing within thirty days after the making.

**Delaware** An oral will is valid if confined to personal property not exceeding $200 in value. It must have been pronounced in the last illness of the deceased before two witnesses, be reduced to writing within three days, and be attested by the signatures of the witnesses, provided the testator dies before the expiration of the said three days or subsequently becomes incapable of making a will.

**District of Columbia** An oral will is invalid, except in the case of soldiers and sailors in actual military service who may dispose of wages and personal property by word of mouth. Such a will must be proved by two witnesses and reduced to writing within ten days after its making.

**Florida** An oral will must be proved by three witnesses present at the time of making. The oral will must have been made during the deceased's last sickness and be reduced to writing within six days of its making. Personal property only may be disposed of in this way.

**Georgia** An oral will must be made during the last illness of the deceased at the place where he resided for at least ten days preceding the declaration, except is case of sudden illness and death away from home. Three witnesses are necessary to prove such a will.

**Idaho**  An oral will must be reduced to writing within thirty days of its making. The will must be probated not less than fourteen days after the testator's death.

**Indiana**  An oral will must be made in the testator's last illness, be witnessed by at least two people, and be reduced to writing within fifteen days after the words are spoken. Such a will is valid only to extent of $100 worth of personal property.

**Iowa**  Personal property up to $300 may be disposed of by an oral will if witnessed by two competent persons. Those in actual military or naval service may dispose of all their personal estate orally.

**Kansas**  To be valid, an oral will must be reduced to writing and witnessed by two disinterested persons within ten days after the words are spoken. It must be proved that the testator called upon some person or persons present when the words were spoken to bear witness that the words were his last will.

**Kentucky**  Only a soldier in actual service or a mariner at sea may dispose of personal effects orally, provided it is done ten days before death, in the presence of two competent witnesses and reduced to writing within sixty days after the words are spoken.

**Louisiana**  An oral will must be witnessed in the presence of a notary public by three persons residing in the place where the will is executed, or by five persons not residing in the place.

**Maine**  An oral will is allowed when made in the last illness of the testator at his home or at the place where he resided ten days before making it. The maximum amount that may be disposed of in this way is $100. The will must be proved by three witnesses present at the time of making, who were requested by the testator to bear witness that such was his will. If the words are not reduced to writing within six days after being spoken, they must be proved in court within six months. A soldier in actual service or a mariner at sea may orally dispose of his personal estate.

**Maryland**  An oral will is valid only for soldiers in actual service or mariners at sea who may dispose of their wages, movables, and personal property.

**Massachusetts**  The rule is the same as for Maryland.

**Michigan**  The maximum amount that can be willed orally is $300. The will must be proved by two competent witnesses; this applies to soldiers in actual military service and to mariners on shipboard.

**Mississippi** An oral will is valid only when made during the testator's last illness. The maximum amount is $100, unless the will is proved by two witnesses whom the testator called to bear witness to his will. Such a will cannot be proved after six months unless reduced to writing within six days of speaking. There is a soldier and sailor provision.

**Missouri** The maximum amount to be disposed of may not exceed $200; it must be proved by two witnesses that the testator, in his last sickness, at his home, called some person to witness the will. Proof of such will must be given within six months after the words are spoken or the substance of the words reduced to writing within thirty days. Wills of soldiers and sailors are governed by the common law.

**Montana** An oral will is valid when proved by two witnesses present at the making thereof, one of whom, at least, must have been asked by the testator to bear witness that such was his will. The maximum value is set at $1,000. The testator at the time must have been in actual military or marine service, and the will must have been made in the expectation of immediate death from injury received that day. The will must be proved within six months after it was made, but not less than fourteen days after the death of the testator.

**Nebraska** The maximum amount that can be willed orally is $150. The will must be proved by three witnesses present at the making who were called by the testator to witness his oral will. The will must have been made during testator's last illness at home or while taken sick away from home. Unless reduced to writing within six days after the oral declaration, the will is not allowed. These rules are not applicable to soldiers in service and mariners on ships.

**Nevada** The maximum value that can be willed orally is $1,000. The will must be proved by two witnesses present at making thereof; it must be made during the testator's last illness and proved not less than fourteen days nor more than three months after the words are spoken.

**New Hampshire** The maximum value that can be willed orally is $100. The will must be declared in the presence of three witnesses who were requested by testator to bear witness thereto, or be made during testator's last illness, at his usual dwelling place or away from same if he is taken ill while away from home and dies before his return, or unless a memorandum of the oral will was reduced to writing within six days.

**New Jersey**  An oral will bequeathing personal property exceeding $80 is invalid unless it is proved by the oaths of at least three witness present at the making thereof and unless the testator requested the persons present to bear witness to his verbal will or words to that effect. The will must be made during the testator's last illness, in his house or where he was a resident for ten days or more, except when the deceased was surprised or taken sick while away from his home and died before returning to his dwelling place.

**New York**  Only soldiers in service and mariners at sea may bequeath personal property by oral will. Such a will must be made within the hearing of two persons and its execution proved by at least two witnesses.

**North Carolina**  An oral will must be proved by at least two witnesses present at the time it was made. The will must have been made during the testator's last sickness and in his own residence, or where he had previously resided.

**North Dakota**  The maximum amount that can be willed orally is $1,000. The will must be proved by two witnesses who were present at its making; the deceased must have been in actual military service in the field or doing duty on shipboard at sea; in either case, he must be in fear or peril of immediate death from an injury received the same day that the will was made.

**Ohio**  An oral will must be made in the last sickness of the testator; it must be reduced to writing and subscribed to by two competent witnesses within ten days after the verbal declaration.

**Oklahoma**  The maximum amount that can be willed orally is $1,000. The will must be proved by two witnesses who were present at the making thereof, one of whom was asked by the testator at the time to act as a witness. In addition, the testator must have been in actual military service in the field or doing duty on shipboard at sea and must have been in actual contemplation, fear, or peril of death, or in expectation of immediate death from an injury received that same day.

**Oregon**  Oral wills are valid only for soldiers in service and sailors at sea.

**Pennsylvania**  An oral will is valid only if made during testator's last illness, in his own home or one in which he resided for at least ten days before making it, or when he is taken sick while away from home and dies before returning. If the property bequeathed is over $100 in value, the oral will must be proved by two witnesses present at the time of the making thereof that the testator requested persons present to witness his will. The words spoken must be reduced to writing within six days after they are spoken, but no proof of the words spoken can be received after six months from the speaking thereof unless they are reduced to writing.

**South Carolina** An oral will disposing of personal property in excess of $50 is invalid unless proved by the oaths of three or more witnesses who were present when the will was made and requested by the testator to witness his will. The will must be made in the testator's last illness and in his house or place where he died. Proof of such will cannot be made after six months from the time the words were spoken unless reduced to writing within six days after the making of such will and then not after one year.

**South Dakota** The maximum amount that can be willed orally is $1,000. The will must be proved by two witnesses present at the time the words were spoken.

**Texas** An oral will is valid if made during the last illness of the deceased; it must be made at his home, unless he was taken sick away from home and died before returning. No oral will is allowed when the personal property bequeathed exceeds $30 in value unless proved by three credible witnesses. The will must be proved within fourteen days of the testator's death and not after six months from the date of speaking, unless committed to writing within six days therefrom.

**Utah** If the estate is not in excess of $1,000, an oral will may be admitted to probate at any time after deceased has been dead ten days and within six months after the words are spoken; the words must be reduced to writing within thirty days after they are spoken.

**Vermont** An oral will may not pass personal possessions exceeding $200 in value. A memorandum in writing must be made by a person present at the time of the making of said will within six days of the making of the oral will.

**Virginia** Only soldiers in military service and mariners at sea may dispose of personal property by oral will.

**Washington**  An oral will is allowed if the personal estate does not exceed $200. The will must be made during the testator's last illness and must be proved by two witnesses who were requested by the testator to witness his will. The will must be reduced to writing.

**West Virginia**  Only soldiers and sailors in actual service may dispost of personal property by an oral will.

**Wisconsin**  An oral will disposing of an estate in excess of $150 is of no effect unless proved by the oath of three witnesses, present when the will was made, who were requested by the testator to witness it. It must be made during the last illness of the testator, in his home or dwelling or where he resided for ten days prior to the making of the will, except when he was taken sick while absent from his home and died before returning.

*While on maneuvers, a soldier is fatally stricken with a heart attack. A few minutes before he dies, he tells the commanding officer that he wants his buddy to have his diamond ring. Is this a valid will?*

Yes. Oral wills of soldiers in actual service and sailors at sea are generally valid. In many states such wills are recognized as legal without any specified number of witnesses.

*What is a holographic will?*

A holographic will is one written *entirely* by the hand of the testator. It may be written in pencil or in ink, or partly in both. It may take the form of a letter or a notation or a note. It must be entirely written, signed, and dated by the testator. Not all states recognize such wills, nor are witnesses required in all jurisdictions that allow holographic wills. But as to this, see the following question.

*In which jurisdictions are holographic wills recognized as legal?*

Holographic wills are valid in the following states:

**Alaska**  No witnesses.
**Arizona**  No witnesses.
**Arkansas**  Three disinterested witnesses.
**California**  No witnesses.
**Idaho**  No witnesses.

**Kentucky**  No witnesses.

**Louisiana**  No witnesses.

**Mississippi**  No witnesses.

**Montana**  No witnesses.

**Nevada**  No witnesses.

**New York**  Holographic wills by soldiers or sailors while in actual military service, or by a mariner while at sea, are valid during the war. Such wills become unenforceable and invalid one year after the testator's discharge from military service, provided the testator still retains the capacity to execute a valid will. If, after his discharge from service, a testator still lacks such capacity, the holographic will is valid and enforceable until one year after the time capacity is regained.

**North Carolina**  It must appear that the will was found among the valuable papers of the testator. Testator's handwriting must be proved by three witnesses.

**North Dakota**  No witnesses.

**Oklahoma**  No witnesses.

**Pennsylvania**  No witnesses.

**Puerto Rico**  No witnesses.

**South Dakota**  No witnesses.

**Tennessee**  Substantially the same provisions are in force as in North Carolina.

**Texas**  No witnesses.

**Utah**  No witnesses.

**Virginia**  No witnesses.

**West Virginia**  No witnesses.

**Wyoming**  No witnesses.

*You write a letter to your sister in which, after referring to your land and your intention to build thereon, you tell her: "If I die or get killed in Texas, the place must belong to you and I would not want you to sell it." It this a valid will?*

Yes. This is a holographic will and is valid in those states in which such wills are legal.

*After a testator's death, a letter is found which reads as follows: "Many accidents may occur to me which might deprive my sisters of that protection which it would be my duty to afford; and in that event I must beg that you will attend to putting them in pos-*

*session of two thirds of what I may be worth, appropriating one third to Mrs. Jones and her child, in any manner that may appear most proper." Is this a valid will?*

Yes. A will may take the form of a letter if signed and properly witnessed.

*After Johnson's death, a paper is found which reads as follows: "This is good to Miss Ruby Cox for $600, as payment for care and attendance rendered by her to me in my last sickness; this $600 is to be collected out my estate, providing, however, I die a bachelor." Can Ruby collect the $600?*

Yes. This is a valid will, since it is conditioned on Johnson's dying a bachelor, and was not to take effect until after his death.

*To be valid, must a will be signed by the testator?*

Yes. It must be signed either by the testator or by some person in his presence, and at his express direction and request.

*Is a will otherwise valid if signed by a cross or mark?*

Yes. What constitutes a sufficient signature largely depends on the custom of the time and place, the habit of the individual, and the circumstances of the particular case.

*A testator, Robert Smith, begins to sign his name, writes the syllable "Rob," then desists because of physical weakness. Would his failure to complete his name make the entire will void?*

Yes. The testator must write all that he intended to write in order that there may be a sufficient signing. In this case, for example, it could be argued that the reason the testator did not complete his signature is that he changed his mind after writing "Rob."

*A will, written wholly in the handwriting of the testator, begins, "I, John Doe, declare this to be my last will." The testator's name appears nowhere else in the will. The will is enclosed in a sealed envelope on which is written, in the testator's handwriting. "My will. John Doe." Is this a valid will?*

No. Because it is not signed by the testator.

*What is meant by attestation?*

The attestation of a will is the witnessing of it at the request of the testator, the party making it, and the signing of one's name to it as a witness.

*An attorney who has drawn a will proposes to the testator that the attorney and his stenographer witness it. He calls his stenographer from an adjoining room into his office, where they both sign the will in the testator's presence and without objection from him. Is this a valid will?*

Yes. The general rule is that the testator must request the witnesses to attest the will. This request may be made either expressly by the testator or by another in his behalf, or may be inferred from his conduct and from all the facts and circumstances attending the witnessing. When the testator allowed the lawyer and his stenographer to witness the will, he gave his consent to their attestation.

*Must you reveal the contents of a will to the witnesses if you write it in your own hand?*

No. All you have to do is inform the necessary witnesses that you wish them to witness your will and that the document you show them is in fact your will.

*May one who is to be a beneficiary under a will be a witness to it?*

No. It is generally provided by statute that a bequest to a subscribing witness shall be void but that the will shall be otherwise valid.

*Is it necessary that witnesses see the testator sign the will?*

No, in the absence of a statutory requirement. However, it is frequently provided by statute that the testator shall either sign the will in the presence of witnesses or acknowledge his signature before them. Any words, acts, or conduct of the testator which, reasonably interpreted, amount to a recognition of the signature as his, in the presence of witnesses who are aware of such words, acts, or conduct, is a sufficient acknowledgment.

*A will is so folded that the testator's signature is invisible to the witnesses, who nevertheless, sign the document. Is this a sufficient acknowledgment of the testator's signature?*

No. The witnesses must see the testator's signature.

*Is it necessary that witnesses sign at the end of the will?*

No, not unless a statute specifically provides for it. The attestation need not be in any particular place, provided there is evidence that the witnesses, in signing their names, have the intention of attesting the document. To avoid any question, however, it is wise to have witnesses sign at the end of the will.

*Is it necessary that witnesses to a will sign it in the presence of the testator?*

Generally, yes. This requirement is met when the witnesses sign in such a way that the testator can see the act of attestation.

*While a testatrix is in one room, her will is signed by witnesses in an adjoining room. The testatrix can observe the signing of the will if she looks. Is this sufficient?*

Yes. If the witnesses are so situated that the testatrix can see them when they sign, it is immaterial where the witnesses are.

*Black is stone deaf. He executes his will in the office of his lawyer, who draws it in accordance with his instructions. The attorney brings in two secretaries to act as witnesses. After Black reads the will and signs it, the attorney shows him a pad on which he writes: "Is this your will, and do you wish Miss Smith and Miss Jones to witness it for you?" Black nods his head, whereupon the lawyer hands the will to the secretaries, who attest it, signing their names as witnesses. The secretaries see Black nod but do not see what is written on the pad. Is the will properly executed?*

Yes. Unless the statute expressly requires it, witnesses need not know the nature of the instrument they are signing; in this case, it is sufficient that they know they are witnessing some instrument which Black has signed and means to acknowledge as his own.

*An ailing testator signs his will, but before the witnesses can affix their signatures, he lapses into unconsciousness. The witnesses sign, nevertheless. Is such a will valid?*

No. The witnesses must sign in the testator's presence while he is conscious.

*What is meant by the capacity to make a will?*

What constitutes capacity to make a valid will is defined by the laws of the various states; by such laws all persons except infants and those of unsound mind have the capacity to execute a valid will.

*A person makes a will while suffering severely from cancer. Suit is later brought to upset the will on the ground that the testator lacked the capacity to make a valid will. Would the court, in the absence of other proof, permit the will to be upset?*

No. A capacity to make a will may exist, even though the testator is old, weak, and ill, even to the point of death, at the time he executes the will, as long as his mind functions normally.

*A testator suffers from an incurable disease that his physician ceases to treat because he can do nothing to arrest its progress. On the day the testator signs his will, he lies helpless in his bed, unable to carry on conversation or to understand questions put to him. Does he have the capacity to make a will?*

No. Here, obviously, the testator is unable to comprehend the significance of his act in signing the will. If proved, this fact will probably suffice to upset the document.

*A testator directs in his will that part of his intestines shall be made into violin strings and the rest of his body vitrified into lenses, explaining that he has an aversion to funeral pomp and wishes his body to be made useful to mankind. Are these eccentric instructions sufficient to upset a will on the ground that the testator lacks mental capacity?*

No. Mere eccentricity does not of itself amount to insanity, although it may properly be considered as bearing thereon.

*A testator who is chronically insane makes a will during a lucid interval. Is the will valid?*

Yes, although the existence of a lucid interval will be exceedingly difficult to prove. If, however, such a lucid interval can be proved, the will may be sustained.

*What constitutes "undue influence" in the writing of wills?*

The exercise of such influence over the testator as to control his mental operations, inducing him to dispose of his property in a way that he would not have done had he been left free to act according to his own wishes. Undue influence deprives the person making a will of his free agency, and if such influence is proved, the instrument will be upset. Mere advice, argument, or persuasion, which do not deprive the testator of his mental freedom, are not considered undue influence.

*What is the effect of a will obtained by undue influence?*

Such a will is void to the extent that it is the result of such influence.

*At the constant and repeated urgings of his wife, a testator who is ill makes a will leaving all his property to her and ignores completely his children by a former marriage. Is such a will valid?*

Probably not. It is true that the will was made voluntarily, but it was made clearly for the sake of the respite or peace of mind gained. Very likely such a will could be upset on the ground that it was obtained by undue influence.

*A son urges his mother to make a will in his behalf, which she later does. Is such a will considered to be obtained by undue influence?*

No. A son has a right to urge his mother to make a will in his behalf, and if the only effect of such promptings is to arouse her affections or to appeal to her sense of duty, they are unobjectionable.

*A bedridden testator is induced to make a certain will by his wife's threat to leave him if he refuses to do so. Is such a will considered to be obtained by undue influence?*

Yes.

*An aged and feeble testator makes a will that disinherits a faithful son at the demand of his wife, with whom the son has quarreled. Is such a will valid?*

No. In this case, the wife would be considered legally to have exercised undue influence over her husband.

*May a blind or deaf person make a valid will?*

Yes. Proof, however, must be given that the contents were made known to the testator.

*Black, a habitual drunkard, executes a will, properly witnessed, that leaves his property to his wife and children. Is such a will valid?*

Yes. Intoxication does not of itself invalidate a will. Courts incline to sustain a drunkard's will when it is just and natural and the circumstances of execution are favorable.

*A testator executes one will, then executes a second one. He later writes a third will in which he declares that the first shall be his last will if he dies before a given date; otherwise the second is to be his last will. Is such will (or series of wills) valid?*

Yes. Wills may be written to take effect in the alternative with reference to a stated contingency or happening of an event.

*In his will, a testator leaves a legacy of $1,000 to John, but he forgets to add John's last name. Is such a legacy good?*

Yes. Omissions may be supplied when the context of the will indicates a name or thing has been inadvertently left out. However, if both names of a legatee or devisee are omitted in the will, oral evidence as to their identity may not be introduced to supply the missing blanks. In this case evidence is admissible to establish the identity of John's last name.

*A will is read orally to a testator who intends that a legacy shall be given to a certain person. This legatee's name is unintentionally omitted in the will, the omission being unobserved by the testator. May the unnamed beneficiary claim a share under the will?*

When the contents of a will are actually communicated to the testator, the will takes effect as written, and no evidence can be received to add to or subtract from it. Hence, the unnamed beneficiary has no claim.

*May you cut off your spouse completely in a will?*

No, in most states. As a rule, you must leave your spouse, by will, at least the same part of the estate that she (or he) would have received if there had been no will. In many states, a wife may refuse to accept what has been provided for her in the will and take advantage of her statutory rights instead, unless she is given all the law requires. A spouse is generally entitled to one third of the decedent's estate.

*In which states may a husband disinherit his wife from any share in his real property?*

Alabama, Arizona, District of Columbia, Florida, Georgia, Michigan, North Carolina, North Dakota, South Carolina, South Dakota, Utah, and Wisconsin.

*In which states may a husband disinherit his wife from personal property?*

Alaska, Arizona, Delaware, Florida, Georgia, Michagan, New Jersey, North Carolina, North Dakota, Oregon, Rhode Island, South Carolina, South Dakota, Utah, and Wisconsin.

*In which states may a wife disinherit her husband from her real property?*

North Dakota and South Dakota.

*In which states may a wife disinherit her husband from personal property?*

Alaska, Delaware, Georgia, New Jersey, North Dakota, Oregon, Rhode Island, South Carolina, South Dakota, and Utah.

*A testator, on slight but insufficient proof, clings to the belief that his wife is unchaste and one of his daughters illegitimate. In his will, he completely disinherits that daughter. Can the will be upset?*

No. An ill-founded belief, not actually amounting to insanity, does not destroy a person's capacity to make a will. If one indulges in an aversion, however harsh, which is the conclusion of a reasoning mind, on evidence, no matter how slight or inaccurate, one's will cannot on that account be overturned or upset.

*What happens to the bequests in your will if there is not enough money in the net estate to pay them all?*

All the bequests are reduced proportionately, unless you have made specific provisions that some are to be preferred over others.

*A will provides that, after payment of the testator's debts, all the debts of his mother are to be paid out of "my estate." Is such a clause binding on the testator's heirs?*

No. Only the testator's debts need be paid.

*A testator leaves Black a valuable diamond ring. Black, however, dies before the testator, leaving two children. May Black's children claim the diamond ring after the testator's death?*

No. Black's heirs get nothing. The property will either pass under the residuary clause (a clause which passes the testator's estate left after payment of debts, costs of administration and specific bequests) or be distributed as intestate property—that is, as if no will had been made and in accordance with the laws of the testator's state.

*Two beneficiaries under a will enter into an agreement whereby one of them agrees that he will not contest its probate. Is such an agreement binding?*

Yes, if it is made with full knowledge of all the facts and risks involved.

*How may a will be revoked?*

A will may be revoked or canceled at the pleasure of the testator. Ordinarily, a will is revoked by mutilation, by a subsequent writing, or by certain changes in the circumstances and conditions of the testator, from which a revocation will be implied by law.

*May a written will be revoked orally?*

No.

*A testator, intending to destroy his will, throws it into a fire. The will, slightly singed, is snatched from the flames by another person. Is the will still valid?*

No. Any visible burning of the will, no matter how slight, if caused with the intent to revoke, is sufficient to constitute a revocation. Multilation which is one of the recognized methods of revoking a will, includes any impairment of the material upon which the will is written, such as tearing, burning, etc.

*A testator makes an unsuccessful attempt to burn his will. He dies a few minutes later. Has his will been revoked?*

No. Unsuccessful attempts to burn a will effect no revocation; neither does a burning of the envelope containing a will, providing the latter remains untouched.

*Black brings a will to a blind testator at the latter's request. The testator, after feeling the seals of the envelope in which the will is enclosed, requests Black to throw it into the fire. Black, pretending to do so, substitutes another paper for the will and calls the testator's attention to the odor and the crackling of the burning paper. The testator dies in the belief that his will has been revoked. Has it?*

No. The revocation must be in a manner prescribed by law.

*A testator tears up his will, under the mistaken impression that he had not properly executed it, and orders a new and similar writing to be made. He dies before executing it. May the torn instrument be introduced as the will?*

Yes. It is admissible on the ground that an intent to revoke was lacking, since the testator destroyed the will while laboring under a misapprehension.

*A testator excutes a will in duplicate, keeping one copy for himself and depositing the other with his bank. Shortly afterward, the testator destroys his copy of the will and dies before he can request the bank to destroy the copy it holds. Has the testator revoked the will?*

Yes. If a will is executed in duplicate, a mutilation by the testator of that part in his own custody constitutes a revocation of both copies. The law presumes that the mutilation of the one duplicate was done with the intent to revoke both copies.

*A testator, while sane, makes a valid will. He becomes insane and destroys the will. Is his will still good?*

Yes. As much mental capacity is required to revoke a will as to make one. The testator's insanity deprived him of the necessary intent to revoke.

*A testator executes two wills. He wishes to revoke one of them but destroys the wrong document by mistake. Does his act revoke the paper he intended as his will?*

No. There is no mutilation of the will, since the testator did not intend to revoke it, having torn it up erroneously.

*Does a mutilation of a will induced by undue influence constitute a revocation?*

No, since the testator is not acting of his own volition but under the influence of another.

*A testator cancels his signature and those of the subscribing witnesses, accompanying the act with this memorandum: "In consequence of the death of my wife it becomes necessary to make another will." He dies before the will is made. Is his first will revoked?*

Yes. The revocation of the will is absolute and complete, the testator clearly indicating such intention by canceling the signatures and leaving a memorandum to that effect.

*In his will, a testator leaves his house to a brother. A few weeks before the testator's death, he sells the house to a third party. Can the brother still claim the house?*

No. When the testator sold the house, the will was revoked—as far, at least, as the house was concerned.

*You make a will prior to your marriage. A few years after the marriage, a child is born. Is your will, executed before the marriage, valid?*

No. Marriage, followed by the birth of a child, absolutely revokes a will. Your wife and child will inherit your property in the manner prescribed by law in cases of intestacy, rather than in accordance with your personal wishes.

*You make a will after your marriage, but in it you mention nothing about children. A few years later, a child is born. Will your child inherit upon your death?*

Yes. In most states the birth of a child does not work the entire revocation of a prior will; it does so only to the extent of the interest that the child would have taken had there been no will. A wise precaution is to make a new will, or codicil, upon the birth of each child.

*A few years after his marriage, a testator adopts a child. Is his will revoked to the same extent as it would be if the child were born in wedlock?*

Yes, in many states. Giving a child the status of one born in wedlock by adoption has been held to revoke a prior will as effectually as would the birth of natural children of the marriage.

*What is the effect of the birth of illegitimate children upon a prior will?*

It depends wholly upon the statute of each particular state. As a rule, the birth of an illegitimate child after a will is executed has no effect if the child is not recognized or in some way made legitimate under the statute, and the illegitimate child will not inherit.

*A testator makes a will leaving all his property to his wife. A few years later he secures a divorce. Before he can make a new will he dies. Does the divorce revoke the will and prevent the ex-spouse from inheriting?*

No. Revocation of a previously executed will is not implied by law from the fact that the testator obtains a divorce. But when a divorce is accompanied by a property settlement, it is *sometimes* held that the change of circumstances is sufficient to cause an implied revocation of a prior will.

CHAPTER 33

## YOUR INCOME TAX RETURN

*What are the chances of your federal income tax being audited?*

About one in thirty-five, according to the Internal Revenue Service. The higher your income the greater the possibility your return will be given a thorough going over. If you earn $30,000 or more, the odds are one in five your return will be questioned by the jaundiced eye of an IRS auditor. Uncle Sam is in the business of collecting as much legal taxes as possible. He knows that while many of his nephews and nieces are relatively honest, some are not. And it is the latter he goes after.

All of us, of course, try to pay as little income tax as possible. There are many legal devices for doing so, some of which apply to the wealthy such as purchasing nontaxable municipal bonds or deducting oil depletion allowances. This is known as tax avoidance which simply means taking advantage of every loophole provided by the tax code, usually with the aid and support of a knowledgeable tax attorney.

There is a difference between tax avoidance and tax evasion. Tax avoidance takes advantage of the law and is legally allowable. Tax evasion, on the other hand, smacks of fraud, is illegal, and is likely to get you into trouble with the IRS. Tax evasion is avoiding taxes which are lawfully due, for example, when you claim deductions for nonexistent dependents or maintain that you contribute more than fifty percent to the support of your mother when you actually contribute only twenty-two percent, or when your entertainment or business expenses are shockingly out of line with your net income.

In making up your income tax return—whether of the federal or state variety—the burden is on you, the taxpayer, to support your claims. Your best bet in avoiding sleepless nights and questioning by the IRS is to file an honest return, backed up by documented records such as checks, receipts, and memorandums in diaries. If you make an honest mistake, all you may have to pay is the additional sum requested by the IRS plus interest. But if the mistake is made with intent to defraud, you may be subject to additional penalties.

*In a joint return are both husband and wife liable for mistakes?*

Yes. Even though a spouse did not examine the return, the fact that he or she signed it makes the spouse equally responsible. In short a wife cannot disclaim responsibility by insisting that she did not read the return. In any joint return both parties are liable not only for mistakes but for fraud.

*If there are mistakes in the return does the IRS look to the attorney or accountant who prepared the return or to the taxpayer?*

The primary liability is on the taxpayer, no matter who assists in the preparation of the return. However, if the attorney or accountant is part of a conspiracy to defraud the government, they may also be prosecuted.

*How does a taxpayer learn that his return is being audited?*

There are many ways. The simplest, perhaps, is to receive a form letter from the IRS announcing that your return is going to be examined. The letter usually requests that you supply the IRS with corroborative, written evidence supporting your claim for whatever is being questioned. Before supplying the IRS with such evidence you should consult either your tax attorney or accountant, and obtain their guidance and advice. Obviously, if you refuse or cannot supply the requested information, you may be in even deeper trouble. If there is no criminal intent to defraud, all that will happen is that your claim will be disallowed and you will be asked to pay the additional tax plus, possibly, a penalty and interest. If, on the other hand, you can substantiate your claim by records or receipts, that will be the end of the matter.

*Must you reply by mail to an IRS request for further information?*

No. If you feel you will do better with a private interview, you are entitled to ask for a conference. Contrary to legend most IRS agents are not interested in either persecuting or prosecuting you. In the main, they are honest, hardworking employees who have a thankless job to do and do it, for the most part, with patience and sympathy. Whether you should go alone or be accompanied by the individual who prepared your return is another question. In any case the latter should be consulted either before you write the IRS or visit their offices, especially if the return is a complicated one. Not infrequently the person who prepared the return is at fault. He may have made an arithmetical error; he may have made an unwarranted deduction based on a misunderstanding or mistake on the part of the tax attorney or accountant. If as a result of the latter's negligence you are compelled to pay any additional taxes, penalties, and/or interest, you may have a legal claim against the one who prepared your return.

*How else may an audit begin?*

An agent of the IRS may appear unexpectedly at your home or office to inform you that your return is being audited and proceed to ask questions. While this method is unusual, it does sometimes happen. When it does, you should make certain that the person purporting to be from the IRS is a bona fide agent and insist that he properly identify himself. But do not be belligerent! If the agent turns out to be from the Intelligence Division of the IRS, you should politely but firmly refuse to answer any questions without advice of competent counsel. To do otherwise may be self-incriminating. Nor should you turn over any receipts, documents, or books, unless your tax counsel approves.

*What happens in the case of most audits?*

In about eighty percent of the cases, audits are disposed of quickly. If you can not sustain a deduction or document an expense account, the agent will disallow the item claimed and add the additional tax plus any penalty or interest. Remember, the burden is always on you, the taxpayer, to sustain the statements made on the tax return. If the agent determines to his satisfaction that you have made an error or lack sufficient evidence to sustain a deduction, he will tell you so at once and figure out what you owe Uncle Sam. If you agree with him, you can then and there pay the additional charges. Alternatively, the agent may have to re-compute the entire return to determine the tax liability. In that case you will receive a letter stating the nature of the error and the new tax due, whether with or without interest and/or penalties. If you and your tax consultant are satisfied with the decision, you send a check for the additional money requested which brings the matter to an end.

*What if the taxpayer isn't satisfied with the decision?*

If you feel you have a case but had less than fair treatment, you may appeal to the IRS district conference by notifying the IRS that you do not accept the agent's findings. This should be done rarely, if at all, without the benefit of tax counsel. If, however, you and your tax counsel have appealed, you will receive a letter from the IRS offering several alternatives. If the amount claimed from you by the IRS as a tax deficiency is less than $2,500, you may in writing give your reasons for disagreeing with the agent who audited your return. If the tax deficiency is over $2,500, there is a more complicated form to answer. In any event, after you have submitted your written objections to the IRS findings, your case will have an impartial review by an IRS agent independent of the audit staff. The review member or board can 1) sustain the original agent's findings, 2) disregard them, or 3) work out some compromise satisfactory to both the taxpayer and the IRS. If you accept the findings of the conference staff, you sign a waiver, pay the taxes claimed, and the file is closed.

*What if you do not accept the findings of the district conference staff?*

The next step up the escalator is to request a hearing before the appellate conference. Similar to an appeals' court, the appellate conference consists of more experienced tax personnel who are invested with greater authority and discretion. They have a right to make settlements, usually in cases involving close points of tax law. Representing the government, the appellate conference takes into consideration the amounts involved, the tax issues at stake, and whether or not, in his opinion, the government could win its case if the taxpayer filed a suit for relief.

What happens is somewhat analogous to lawyers working out a compromise in a personal-injury case. For example, the plaintiff's attorney believes his client's injuries are worth $100,000. But since there is some question as to liability and jury verdicts are unpredictable, he is willing to accept less than the asking price. The insurance carrier, on the other hand, agrees the injuries are serious but contends that the plaintiff contributed as much to the cause of the accident as the defendant and legally is entitled to nothing. But since the insurance attorney agrees that the law is unclear and that his witnesses may not hold up in court, he is also willing to compromise. Both parties agree that a settlement of $50,000 is fair to all concerned. So it is with income tax matters on the appellate conference level.

However, while an attempt at some compromise may be and often is accomplished, it is not necessarily inevitable. The government may feel that its case is open and shut, may not want to set an undesirable precedent, or may want to establish new law. The taxpayer's past may have been unsavory. Whatever the reason, the appellate division may turn down the taxpayer's claim. However, if it decides to accept the taxpayer's claim, the IRS will draw up an agreement to be signed by the contending parties, and this will finally dispose of the matter.

*What happens if the taxpayer is overruled and still wants to appeal?*

If the tax liability is under $1,000, he can appeal to the Small Claims Court, a division of the United States Tax Court. Unlike state or city small claims courts, the federal one handles only tax cases. The taxpayer can appeal himself or can be represented by counsel. In either case the rules are relaxed and the atmosphere is informal; many cases are disposed of within an hour or two. To file an appeal to the Small Claims Court for a tax hearing send a $10 filing fee to the United States Tax Court, Box 70, Washington, D. C. 20044. The taxpayer then receives a petition, which he or his attorney must fill out within the ninety-day period allowed for appeals from the appellate conference. Hearings are held in most large cities, and it usually takes from four to six months for a case to be heard and disposed of.

*What happens if your tax liability exceeds the $1,000 limit?*

Your recourse then is to appeal to the federal court system, specifically, for a hearing before the Tax Court. You, through your attorney, file a petition within the ninety-day period for a hearing. If your claim is denied, your counsel can then file suit in either the United States District Court or the United States Court of Claims. In either case the hearings are held with all the formality of law; these are apt to be long drawn out and expensive legal proceedings and should be undertaken only when the amount involved is large and when the chances of victory are good. If you lose, you pay not only substantial legal and accounting fees but interest from the time you were first assessed for the tax deficiency.

*How does the IRS distinguish between various violations of the tax law?*

Penalties are based on the gravity of the offense and whether or not the fraud involved, if any, was civil or criminal.

*What is the penalty for a simple error, where no fraud is involved?*

If you claim a fifty percent automobile expense which is disallowed because of lack of supporting evidence, the usual penalty is six percent interest on the additional tax from the date it was originally due, plus the additional tax due because of the disallowance of your claim. For what the IRS considers negligence—that is, failing to keep records to support a claim or deduction—the penalty is five percent per month of the tax due up to a maximum of twenty-five percent.

*What is the penalty for failing to file an income tax return on schedule?*

The taxpayer is penalized five percent of the tax due for each month he fails to file the return, up to a maximum of twenty-five percent. If the taxpayer willfully fails to file a return with intent to defraud, he may be subject to criminal prosecution.

*What constitutes a civil fraud in filing an income tax return and what is the penalty?*

Judicial decisions have held that civil fraud is more than mere ignorance or negligence. There must be evidence of intent to defraud. A taxpayer who underestimates his income by some thirty or forty percent may be guilty of civil fraud, especially if there is a pattern of continuity. A taxpayer found guilty of civil fraud may be penalized almost double the amount of the tax deficiency.

*What is criminal fraud?*

Courts have determined that an evasion is criminal if the taxpayer willfully attempts to evade or defeat any tax, including the failure to file any return. It must be pointed out, however, that the distinction between a civil and criminal fraud is often difficult to define. A physician who earns a gross income of $100,000 and willfully reports a gross income of $50,000 with intent to defraud

Uncle Sam is subject to criminal prosecution. Roughly about one out of every eight fraud cases results in prosecution, and of these about half the offenders plead guilty.

*What happens when an IRS agent suspects the taxpayer of filing a fraudulent return?*

Under the IRS procedures the agent terminates his audit and turns over his findings to the Intelligence Division of the IRS for further investigation. Whenever a special agent is assigned a case, he must notify the taxpayer that he is conducting a criminal investigation and advise him of his constitutional rights, including the right against self-incrimination. In such cases a taxpayer is under no legal duty to make any statement to the special agent nor is he obliged to turn over any books, receipts, or memoranda. If the taxpayer is wise, he will immediately get in touch with an attorney experienced in tax matters, preferably one who has previously served as U. S. District Attorney or who was an associate in that office. The government must prove its case against the taxpayer through its own independent audit or investigation. It cannot do so by subpoenaing the taxpayer's books or records. However, once the taxpayer's books or records are placed in evidence, they may be attacked by the government. But as in any other criminal proceeding it is up to the government to prove the guilt of the taxpayer beyond a reasonable doubt.

*Is there any period of time in which the federal government must prosecute a tax fraud case?*

No. The statute of limitations does not apply to fraud cases, either criminal or civil. In effect, this means that the government can go back five, ten, or even twenty years in order to prove fraud and is not barred merely because of the lapse of time. A consequence of this is that the taxpayer should keep records and books as long as possible in case his return is audited. Lacking such books or records he may be unable to substantiate his tax claim and become subject to interest and penalties.

# Appendix I

## SAMPLE LEGAL FORMS*

Form 1

### AFFIDAVIT

State of _____ County _____, ss:
   Before me, the subscriber, a notary public for the City of
_____, State of _____, personally appeared
_____, who, being duly sworn, deposes and says
that [*here set forth clearly the matter sworn to*]

/s/ _____

Sworn and subscribed this _____ day of _____, 19_____

_____
                                     Notary Public

Form 2

### ACKNOWLEDGMENT

   STATE OF _____, CITY OF _____, to wit:

   I HEREBY CERTIFY, that on this _____ day of _____,
in the year 19_____, before me, the subscriber, a Notary Public of the City of _____, State of _____, personally appeared _____ and acknowledged the aforegoing deed to be his act.

_____
                                       Notary Public

---

* The forms in this appendix are intended to be used only as guides and as a matter of legal information.

FORM 3

## AGENCY CONTRACT WHEREBY A TRAVELING SALESMAN IS EMPLOYED

This agreement made this fifth day of October, 19_____ by and between John Smythe and Robert Blank, doing business under the name of The Skyland Company, witnesseth:

1. The said salesman shall enter the service of the said firm as a traveling salesman for them in their business of manufacturing toys for the period of one year from the 10th day of October 19_____, subject to the general control of said The Skyland Company.

2. The said salesman shall devote the whole of his time, attention and energies to the performance of his duties as such salesman, and shall not, either directly or indirectly, alone or in partnership, be connected with or concerned in any other business or pursuit whatsoever during the said term of one year.

3. The said salesman shall, subject to the control of the said firm, keep proper books of account and make due and correct entries of the price of all goods sold, and of all transactions and dealings of and in relation to the said business, and shall serve the firm diligently and according to his best abilities in all respects.

4. The fixed salary of the said salesman shall be six thousand dollars per annum, payable in equal weekly installments.

5. The reasonable traveling expenses and hotel bills of the said salesman, incurred in connection with the business of the said firm, shall be paid by the said firm, and the said firm shall from week to week pay the said salesman the said traveling expenses and hotel bills in addition to the said fixed salary.

/s/   Robert Blank
-------------------------------------------------
The Skyland Company

/s/   John Smythe
-------------------------------------------------
Salesman

/s/   Harry Roe
-------------------------------
Witness

FORM 4

## AN ANTENUPTIAL AGREEMENT OR MARRIAGE SETTLEMENT WHERE ALL PROPERTY IS TO BE HELD JOINTLY

This agreement entered into this fifth day of June, 19......., by and between Richard Roe and Jane Smith, witnesseth:

1. That the parties hereby agree to enter into the marriage relation and hereafter live together as husband and wife.

2. That all moneys or property hereafter acquired or accumulated by them, or either of them, shall be held in joint of equal ownership.

3. That each of the parties hereby grants, bargains, sells and conveys to the other an undivided one-half interest in all the property, real and personal, which he or she now owns, for the purpose and with the intent of vesting in both parties the joint ownership of all property at this date owned in severalty by either of them.

4. In case of the death of one of the above mentioned parties, all of said property shall, subject to the claims of creditors, vest absolutely in the survivors.

5. The consideration for this agreement is the marriage to be entered into pursuant to its terms and the mutual promises herein contained.

(Seal) *Jane Smith*
-------------------------------------------------
Jane Smith

(Seal) *Richard Roe*
-------------------------------------------------
Richard Roe

John Green
-----------------------
Witness

FORM 5

## FORM OF CHATTEL MORTGAGE

This chattel mortgage, made this 15th day of July, 19......., John Smith to Jane Doe, witnesseth: that for and in consideration of the sum of eight hundred dollars, the said John Smith doth hereby bargain and sell unto Jane Doe the following property: 19_____ Ford, station wagon, serial number 48,195, engine number AA 981764, provided, however, if the said John Smith shall pay the said Jane Doe the aforesaid sum of eight hundred dollars, with interest, on or before the 15th day of July, 19_____, then these presents shall be void. And it is also agreed that until default be made in the payment of the aforesaid sum of eight hundred dollars, with interest, the said John Smith shall possess the property hereby mortgaged. But in case of default, then the said John Smith does hereby declare his assent to the passage of a decree for the sale of the property hereby mortgaged, in accordance with the Code provisions provided therefor.

                          (Seal)    John Smith
                          ------------------------------------------
                                             Mortgagor
Jane Doe
------------------
   Witness


FORM 6


### CONFESSED JUDGMENT NOTE


$ _____ 19_____
_____ after date _____ promise to
pay to the order of _____
_____ Dollars
Payable at _____
Without defalcation, value received, with interest

    And further, _____ do hereby empower any Attorney of any Court of Record within the United States or elsewhere to appear for _____ and after one or more declarations filed, confess judgment against _____ as of any term for the above sum with Costs of suit and Attorney's commission of _____ per cent for collection and release of all errors, and without stay of execution and inquisition and extension upon any levy on real estate is hereby waived, and condemnation agreed to and the exemption of personal property from levy and sale on any execution hereon, is also hereby expressly waived, and no benefit of exemption be claimed under and by virtue of any exemption law now in force or which may be hereafter passed.

Witness _____ hand and seal _____ (Seal)

No. _____ Due _____            _____ (Seal)

FORM 7

## GENERAL BY-LAWS OF CORPORATION

### Annual Meeting

Section 1. The annual meeting of the stockholders of this company shall be held at the office of the corporation, in the City of Chicago, on the first Monday in January of each and every year, at 10 o'clock A.M. for the election of directors and such other business as may properly come before said meeting. Notice of the time, place and object of such meeting shall be given by publication thereof, at least once in each week for two successive weeks immediately preceding such meeting, in the manner required by the laws of the state, and by serving personally or by mailing at least ten days previous to such meeting, postage prepaid, a copy of such notice, addressed to each stockholder at his residence or place of business, as the same shall appear on the books of the corporation. No business other than that stated in such notice shall be transacted at such meeting without the unanimous consent of all the stockholders present thereat, in person or by proxy.

### Special Meetings

Section 2. Special meetings of stockholders, other than those regulated by statute, may be called at any time by a majority of the directors. It shall also be the duty of the president to call such meetings whenever requested in writing so to do, by stockholders owning 51 per cent of the capital stock. A notice of every special meeting, stating the time, place and object thereof, shall be given by mailing, postage prepaid, at least ten days before such meeting, a copy of such notice addressed to each stockholder at his postoffice address as the same appears on the books of the corporation.

## Quorum

Section 3. At all meetings of stockholders, there shall be present, either in person or by proxy, stockholders owning 51 per cent of the capital stock of the corporation, in order to constitute a quorum, except at special elections of directors pursuant to the laws of the state governing corporations.

## Voting Capacity

Section 4. At all annual meetings of stockholders the right of any stockholder to vote shall be governed and determined as prescribed in the laws of the state governing corporations.

## Postponed Annual Meeting

Section 5. If, for any reason, the annual meeting of stockholders shall not be held as hereinbefore provided, such annual meeting shall be called and conducted as prescribed in the laws of the state governing corporations.

## Registered Stockholders Only May Vote

Section 6. At all meetings of stockholders, only such persons shall be entitled to vote in person and by proxy who appear as stockholders upon the transfer books of the corporation for thirty days immediately preceding such meeting.

## Order of Business

Section 7. At the annual meetings of stockholders the following shall be the order of business, viz.:
1. Calling the roll.
2. Reading, notice and proof.
3. Report of officers.
4. Report of committees.
5. Unfinished business.

6. New business.
7. Election of directors.
8. Miscellaneous business.

## Manner of Voting

Section 8. At all meetings of stockholders all questions, except the question of an amendment to the by-laws, and the election of directors and inspectors of election, and all such other questions, the manner deciding which is specially regulated by statute, shall be determined by a majority vote of the stockholders present in person or by proxy; provided, however, that any qualified voter may demand a stock vote, and in that case, such stock vote shall immediately be taken, and each stockholder present, in person or by proxy, shall be entitled to one vote for each share of stock owned by him. All voting shall be viva voce, except that a stock vote shall be by ballot, each of which shall state the name of the stockholder voting and the number of shares owned by him, and in addition, if such ballot be cast by proxy, it shall also state the name of such proxy.

## Same

Section 9. At special meetings of stockholders, the provisions of the laws of the state governing corporations shall apply to the casting of all votes.

# Directors

## Election

Section 1. The directors of this corporation shall be elected by ballot, for the term of one year, at the annual meeting of stockholders, except as hereinafter otherwise provided for filling vacancies. The directors shall be chosen by a plurality of the votes of the stockholders, voting either in person or by proxy, at such annual election as provided by the laws of the state governing corporations.

## Vacancies

Section 2. Vacancies in the board of directors, occurring during the year, shall be filled for the unexpired term by a majority vote of the remaining directors at any special meeting called for that purpose, or at any regular meeting of the board.

## Death or Resignation of Entire Board

Section 3. In case the entire board of directors shall die or resign, any stockholder may call a special meeting in the same manner that the president may call such meetings, and directors for the unexpired term may be elected at such special meeting in the manner provided for their election at annual meetings.

## Rules and Regulations

Section 4. The board of directors may adopt such rules and regulations for the conduct of their meetings and management of the affairs of the corporation as they may deem proper, not inconsistent with the laws of the state of _____ _____, or these by-laws.

## Time of Meeting

Section 5. The board of directors shall meet on the first Monday of every month, and whenever called together by the president upon due notice given to each director. On the written request of any director, the secretary shall call a special meeting of the board.

## Committees

Section 6. All committees shall be appointed by the board of directors.

## Officers

### Appointment Term

Section 1. The board of directors, immediately after the annual meeting, shall choose one of their number by a majority vote to be president, and they shall also appoint a vice-president, secretary and treasurer. Each of such officers shall serve for the term of one year, or until the next annual election.

### Duties of President

Section 2. The president shall preside at all meetings of the board of directors, and shall act as temporary chairman at, and call to order all meetings of the stockholders. He shall sign certificates of stock, sign and execute all contracts in the name of the company, when authorized so to do by the board of directors; countersign all checks drawn by the treasurer; appoint and discharge agents and employees, subject to the approval of the board of directors; and he shall have the general management of the affairs of the corporation and perform all the duties incidental to his office.

### Duties of Vice-President

Section 3. The vice-president shall, in the absence or incapacity of the president, perform the duties of that officer.

### Duties of Treasurer

Section 4. The treasurer shall have the care and custody of all the funds and securities of the corporation, and deposit the same, in the name of the corporation, in such bank or banks as the director may elect; he shall sign all checks, drafts, notes and orders for the payment of money, which shall be countersigned by the president, and he shall pay out and dispose of the same under the direction of the president; he shall at all reasonable times exhibit his books and accounts to any director or stockholder of the company upon application at the office of the company during business hours; he shall sign all certificates of stock signed by the president; he shall give such bonds for the faithful performance of his duties as the board of directors may determine.

## Duties of Secretary

Section 5. The secretary shall keep the minutes of the board of directors, and also the minutes of the meetings of stockholders; he shall attend to the giving and serving of all notices of the company, and shall affix the seal of the company to all certificates of stock, when signed by the president and treasurer; he shall have charge of the certificate-book and such other books and papers as the board may direct; he shall attend to such correspondence as may be assigned to him, and perform all the duties incidental to his office. He shall also keep a stock-book, containing the names, alphabetically arranged, of all persons who are stockholders of the corporation, showing their places of residence, the number of shares of stock held by them respectively, the time when they respectively became the owners thereof, and the amount paid thereon, and such book shall be open for inspection as prescribed by the laws of the state governing corporations.

# Capital Stock

### Subscriptions—Payment

Section 1. Subscriptions to the capital stock must be paid to the treasurer at such time or times, and in such installments, as the board of directors may by resolution require. Any failure to pay an installment when required to be paid by the board of directors shall work a forfeiture of such shares of stock in arrears, pursuant to the laws of the state governing corporations.

### Certificates of Stock

Section 2. Certificates of stock shall be numbered and registered in the order they are issued, and shall be signed by the president or vice-president and by the secretary and treasurer, and the seal of the corporation shall be affixed thereto. All certificates shall be bound in a book, and shall be issued in consecutive order therefrom, and in the margin thereof shall be entered the name of the person owning the shares therein represented, the number of shares and the date thereof. All certificates exchanged or returned to the corporation shall be marked canceled, with the date of cancellation, by the secretary, and shall be immediately pasted in the certificate book opposite the memorandum of its issue.

## Transfers of Stock

Section 3. Transfers of shares shall only be made upon the books of the corporation by the holder in person, or by power of attorney duly executed and acknowledged and filed with the secretary of the corporation, and on the surrender of the certificate or certificates of such shares.

## Increase—Subscriptions

Section 4. Whenever the capital stock of the corporation is increased, each bona fide owner of its stock shall be entitled to purchase at par value thereof, an amount of stock in proportion to the number of shares of stock he owns in the corporation at the time of such increase.

## Dividends

Section 1. Dividends shall be declared and paid out of the surplus profits of the corporation as often and at such times as the board of directors may determine, and in accordance with the laws of the state governing corporations.

## Inspectors

Section 1. Two inspectors of election shall be elected at each annual meeting of stockholders to serve for one year, and if any inspector shall refuse to serve or shall not be present, the meeting may appoint an inspector in his place.

## Seal

Section 1. The seal of the corporation shall be in the form of a circle, and shall bear the name of the corporation and the year of its incorporation.

## Amendments

Section 1. These by-laws may be amended at any stockholders' meeting by a vote of the stockholders owning a majority of the stock, represented either in person or by proxy, provided the proposed amendment is inserted in the notice of such meeting. A copy of such amended by-law shall be sent to each stockholder within ten days after the adoption of the same.

By-laws are not required to be filed in any public office. After adoption they should be entered in the book of minutes of the corporation.

## Waiver of Notice

Section 1. Whenever, under the provisions of these by-laws or of any of the corporate laws, the stockholders or directors are authorized to hold any meeting after notice or after the lapse of any prescribed period of time, such meeting may be held without notice and without such lapse of time by a written waiver of such notice signed by every person entitled to notice.

FORM 8

## NOTICE OF FIRST MEETING

State of Maryland ⎫
                   ⎬ SS.
City of Baltimore  ⎭

You are hereby notified that the first meeting of the subscribers and corporators to the articles of incorporation and an agreement to associate themselves for the purpose of forming a corporation to be known by the name of Prints, Inc., dated on the 1 day of November, 19........, for the purpose of organizing said corporation by the election of directors, the adoption of by-laws, and the transaction of such other business as may properly come before the meeting, will be held at the office of John Blank in the city of Baltimore, state of Maryland, on the 10 day of December, 19........, at 10 o'clock A.M. of said day.

--------------------------------------------------
                                        Secretary

FORM 9

## GENERAL FORM OF PROXY TO VOTE STOCK

Know all Men by These Presents:

That John Smith ..................... does hereby constitute and appoint Harry Roe attorney and agent for John Smith, and in his name, place and stead to vote as ..................... proxy at the next election of Directors of the Swain Company, Inc., and for inspectors of election, according to the number of votes and upon the shares of stock he should be entitled to vote, if then personally present, and authorize him to act for me and in my name and stead, at the next meeting for the election of directors as fully as I could act if I were present, giving to said Harry Roe, agent and attorney, full power of substitution and revocation.

This proxy is to continue in force until the 10 day of May, 19........, unless sooner revoked.

--------------------------------------------------
                                        John Doe

---------------------------
        Witness

FORM 10

## ASSIGNMENT OF A COPYRIGHT OF A BOOK

[Note: *The person or firm receiving such an assignment should have it recorded with the Register of Copyrights within three months after the date thereof.*]

This agreement made this 10 day of June 19........, between Richard Roe, called the vendor, and the Brown Publishing Company, called the vendee, or purchaser, to wit:

Whereas the said vendor is the author and absolute proprietor of the copyright of a book entitled "VIEWS AND
NEWS," and has agreed with the said purchaser for the absolute sale to him of the said copyright, free from encumbrances, at the price of _____ dollars;

Now this agreement witnesseth, that in pursuance of the
said agreement, and in consideration of the sum of _____
dollars by the said purchaser to the said vendor now paid,
the receipt of which is hereby acknowledged, the said vendor
hereby assigns, and, as absolute owner, conveys unto the
said purchaser, his executors, administrators and assigns,
the unencumbered copyright of and the sole privilege of
printing all the said book or work entitled VIEWS AND NEWS,
and all future impressions of said work. To have, hold, exercise and enjoy the said copyright and premises unto the said
purchaser, his executors, administrators, and assigns, henceforth during the residue of the term of the said copyright now
unexpired, for his and their own use and benefit, but subject
always to such right as may now be subsisting in the pub-
lisher or proprietor of the last edition of the said book or
work to prevent the publication of any future edition of the
same until such last edition shall be out of print.

Witness our hands and seals.

(Seal)   Brown Publishing Company
-------------------------------------------------------------
                                      Purchaser

(Seal)   Richard Roe
-------------------------------------------------------------
                                      Vendor

FORM 11

## DEED

This indenture made on the _____ day of_____
A.D. One Thousand Nine Hundred _____ by and between
_____ of _____ party (or parties) of the first
part, and _____ of the County of _____
in the State of _____ party (or parties) of the second
part:

Witnesseth, that the said part _____ of the first part, in consideration of the sum of _____ dollars, to_____ _____ paid by the said part _____ of the second part, the receipt of which is hereby acknowledged do (or does) by these presents, grant, bargain and sell, convey and confirm, unto the said part _____ of the second part _____ heirs and assigns, the following described lots, tracts or parcels of land, lying between and situate in the County of _____ _____ and State of _____ to wit: All [*describe the property*]

To have and to hold the premises aforesaid, with all and singular the rights, privileges, appurtenances and immunities thereto belonging or in anywise appertaining until the said part _____ of the second part, and unto _____ heirs and assigns, forever, the said _____ hereby convenanting that they are (or he or she is) lawfully seized of an indefeasible Estate in Fee in the premises herein conveyed; that _____ _____ have (or has) good right to convey the same; that the said premises are free and clear of any encumbrances done or suffered by them (or him or her) or those under whom _____ claim _____ and that _____ will warrant and defend the title to the said premises unto the said part _____ of the second part, and unto _____ heirs and assigns, forever, against the lawful claims and demands of all persons whomsoever.

In Witness Whereof, the said part _____ of the first part has _____ hereunto set _____ hand _____ the day and year first above written.

-----------------------------------------------------

-----------------------------------------------------

Signed and delivered in the presence of us,

-----------------------------------------------------

-----------------------------------------------------

[*Add acknowledgment. For forms of acknowledgment to be added to deeds, see* Acknowledgment.]

FORM 12

## BILL FOR ABSOLUTE DIVORCE ON THE GROUND OF ADULTERY

Richard Roe                                      Circuit Court
    Complainant                                      of
        vs.                                  Baltimore City
Mary Roe
    Defendant

To the Honorable, the Judge of Said Court:
Your Orator, complaining, says:

1. That he and the defendant were married June 10, 19.........., in Baltimore, Maryland, in a religious ceremony.

2. That both your Orator and the Defendant have resided in the City of Baltimore, State of Maryland, for more than one year prior to the filing of this bill of complaint.

3. That one child was born of said marriage, namely, Jack Roe, whose age is six months.

4. That ever since their said marriage your Orator has behaved himself as a faithful, affectionate and kindly husband toward the said defendant.

5. That the said Defendant did on July 15, 19.........., commit adultery with a person whose name will be revealed at the hearing of the above mentioned cause and that said adultery took place in the City of Baltimore, State of Maryland.

6. That your Orator has not lived nor cohabited with the said defendant since he has discovered the said adultery, nor has he condoned, connived, nor forgiven such adultery.

TO THE END THEREFORE:

(1) That your Orator may be divorced a vinculo matrimonii from the defendant.

(2) That your Orator may be permitted to have the custody of the said infant child.

(3) That your Orator may have such other and further relief as his case may require.

And as in duty bound, etc.

------------------------------------------------
Solicitor for Complainant

Richard Roe
------------------------
Complainant

FORM 13

### SIGHT DRAFT

$ 1,000 _____ New York, N.Y. _____ June 15, _____ 1965

_____ At Sight _____ Pay to

the order of — — — — — — Jane Doe — — — — —

— — — — One Thousand and 00/100 — — — — — Dollars

Payable through the Planters Trust Company, New York, N.Y.

Value received and charge the same
to account of

THE SKYLAND TOY COMPANY, INC.

------------------------------------------------
James Blank, Treasurer

To _____
No _____

U.S. Bond.

FORM 14

### LEASE OF A HOUSE, WITH USE OF FURNITURE, PLATE, LINEN, ETC.

Agreement made this 15 day of May, 19____, between Henry White hereinafter called the landlord, of the one part, and John Hunt hereinafter called the tenant, of the other part. The landlord agrees to let and the tenant agrees to take the house situate and being No. 2440 Glenwood Park Ave., in the City of _____, State of _____, with the outbuildings, stable, garden, and appurtenances thereto belonging, together with the use of the fixtures, furniture, plate, linen, utensils and effects particularly mentioned in the schedule hereunder written; and also with the right to such produce of the garden as the tenant shall require for the use of himself and his household and establishment; and also with such attendance as is hereinafter mentioned, for the term of six calendar months commencing from the 15 day of May next, at the rent of $500.00 for the said term, payable in advance, upon the execution of this agreement. The landlord agrees to pay all rates, taxes and assessments, except gas and water rates, and to make at his own cost all repairs of the premises (except as hereinafter mentioned) which may be necessary during the term, upon being requested by the tenant so to do, and to leave or provide his servants, who shall reside in the house and attend upon the tenant, and also a gardener, and to pay the wages of such indoor servants and gardener. The tenant agrees to pay the said rent in manner aforesaid, and to leave the premises, including the said fixtures, furniture, plate, linen, utensils and effects, in as good state and condition in all respects as the same now are, reasonable wear and tear excepted, and to replace such of the same respectively as shall be broken, damaged, or missing, with other articles of the same pattern and equal value; and to permit the said indoor servants to reside in the house, and to provide them with proper and sufficient board and nourishment; and to bear all expenses of washing and mending all table or house linen which he shall use; and not to assign or underlet the premises, or any part thereof, without the previous consent of the landlord. Provided that if there shall be any breach by the tenant of the conditions herein contained, the landlord may re-enter upon any part of the premises in the name of the whole, and determine the tenancy without prejudice to his other remedies.

-------------------------------------------------------------
                                                     Landlord

-------------------------------------------------------------
                                                     Tenant

-------------------------------------------------
Witness

FORM 15

## LEASE OF PROPERTY—NEW YORK CITY LEASE

This indenture, made this 15 day of May, in the year one thousand nine hundred and _____, between Henry

White, hereinafter called the lessor, party of the first part, and John Hunt, hereinafter called the lessee, party of the second part:

Witnesseth: that the lessor has agreed to let and hereby does let and demise unto the lessee, and the lessee does hereby take and hire from the lessor, the Vacant Store, located at _____, to be used as drugstore for the term of five years, to commence on the 15 day of May, 19_____, and equal monthly installments of $300.00 each in advance on the fifteenth day of each month until said expiration of the term, but the said term shall be subject to the limitations hereinafter mentioned in paragraphs numbered tenth and eleventh.

The above letting is upon the following conditions and covenants, all and every one of which the lessee does covenant and agrees to and with the lessors to keep and perform:

1. To pay the rent at the times and in the manner herein provided.

2. To pay and discharge all debts of every kind, which, during the term hereby granted, may be imposed upon or grow out of or become a lien upon the said premises, or any part thereof, within thirty days after the same shall be payable.

3. To promptly comply with and execute, at the lessee's own cost and expense, all laws, rules, orders, ordinances and regulations of the city of New York or any of its boroughs, and of any and all of its departments and bureaus, and of the county and state authorities, and of the Board of Fire Underwriters, which shall impose any duty upon the lessors or the lessee with respect to the premises hereby demised or the use thereof.

4. To make and pay for all necessary repairs, including repairs to the roof and the exterior of said premises and to the sidewalks in front of the same, of whatsoever nature required to keep the premises in good order and condition during said term and, at the expiration of said term, to deliver up and surrender the said premises in as good state and condition as they were at the commencement of the said term, damages by fire not occasioned by the negligence of the lessee or the lessee's agents, and damages occasioned by the direct, sudden and violent action of the elements excepted.

5. To keep the sidewalk in front of said premises free from rubbish and encumbrances and to remove ice and snow therefrom with all diligence.

6. To permit the lessors and their agents to enter upon the premises or any part thereof, at all reasonable hours, for the purpose of examining the same or making such repairs or alterations as may be necessary for the safety or preservation thereof, and no claim or action for damages or set-off of rent by reason or on account of such entry, repairs or alterations, shall be made, had or allowed.

7. To permit the lessors or their agents to enter upon and show the premises to persons wishing to hire or purchase the same at all reasonable hours, and, during the three months next preceding the expiration of the term, to permit the usual notice "To Let" and, at any time, the notice "For Sale" to be placed upon the doors or walls of said premises, and remain thereon without hindrance or molestation.

8. To protect the lessors and save them harmless from any and all liability for any damage to any occupant of the said premises or to any other person, during the said term, occasioned by or resulting from the breakage, leakage or obstruction of the water, gas or soil pipes or of the roof or rain ducts, or other leakage or overflow in or about the said premises, or from any carelessness, negligence, or improper conduct on the part of the lessee or the lessee's agents, on, in or about the said premises or the sidewalk in front of the same, and the lessors shall not be liable for any damage, loss or injury to the person, property or effects of the lessee or any other person, suffered on, in or about the same by reason of any present, future, latent or other defects in the form, character or condition of said premises or any part or portion thereof, and the said rent shall not be diminished or withheld by reason or on account of any such loss or damages.

9. No alteration, addition or improvements shall be made in or to the premises without the consent of the lessors in writing, and all additions and improvements made by the lessee shall belong to the lessors.

10. If, during the term of this lease the demised premises shall be destroyed by fire, the elements, or any other cause,

or if they shall be so injured that they cannot be repaired with reasonable diligence within 6 months, then this lease shall cease and become null and void from the date of such damage or destruction and the lessee shall immediately surrender the premises to the lessors and shall pay rent only to the time of such surrender, and the foregoing provision of this paragraph shall be a limitation of this lease, but, if the premises shall be repairable within 6 months as aforesaid, then the lessors may repair the same with all reasonable speed, and the rent shall cease until such repairs shall be completed, provided, however, that this lease shall continue of full force and effect, unless the lessors shall neglect to commence such repairs within seven days after the lessee shall notify them of such damage, except as to the payment of rent, and provided, further, that in case any portion of the said premises shall, during the period of such repairs be fit for the purpose for which these premises are demised, then the rent shall be equitably apportioned and paid for the part so fit for occupancy. It is expressly agreed that the provisions of section 197 of the Real Property Law of the State of New York shall not apply to the estate hereby granted or to the premises hereby demised.

11. That the lessee will not assign this indenture or the estate or term hereby granted, or any part thereof, or let or underlet the said premises, or any part thereof, without the lessors' written consent thereto, or use the said premises, or any part thereof, for any purpose deemed extra-hazardous on account of fire, or contrary to law or good morals or to the city ordinances and regulations. It is expressly understood and agreed that the stipulations contained in this paragraph and in the paragraphs numbered 3 and 6 hereof, respectively, shall be limitations of this lease; and, in case of a violation of any one or more of such stipulations, this lease shall become null and void and the estate and term hereby granted shall cease and determine, but without prejudice of any right of action on the part of the lessors for damages for any such violations.

12. That, if the lessee, John Hunt shall neglect or fail to pay any tax, assessment, water rent or meter charges, or to make any of the repairs hereinbefore mentioned in paragraph

4, or, if any liability for damages or otherwise shall be imposed upon the lessors by reason of the failure of the lessee, John Hunt to observe or perform any covenant or condition herein contained, or, if by like reason the lessors shall be put to any other charges or expense, or any charge or lien shall be imposed on said premises, the lessors shall have the right and privilege, at their option, to pay such tax, assessment, water rent or meter charges, or pay for such repairs as they may make pursuant to the provisions contained in paragraph numbered 6 hereof, or to discharge such liability, charge or lien, or any portion thereof, with any interest or penalties thereon, and the amount of such tax, assessment, water rent or meter charges, and the amount paid for such repairs, and the amount paid by the lessors in discharging such liability, charge or lien, and in defraying such charges and expense shall, after notice thereof to the lessee, John Hunt, become rent, and the installment of rent next payable under the provisions of this lease shall be augmented by the amount so paid as aforesaid, and upon default of the lessee John Hunt in the payment of any intallment or installments of rent as thus augmented, in addition to all other appropriate remedies, summary proceedings for the removal of the lessee from the possession of the said premises for the nonpayment of the rent as thus augmented may be instituted and prosecuted by the lessors in the same manner as would be lawful in case of the nonpayment of the rent herein otherwise reserved.

13. If default be made in the observance or performance of any of the covenants or conditions of this lease, it shall be lawful for the lessors to re-enter and resume possession of said premises, and the same to have again, repossess and enjoy, or to dispossess and remove all persons and their goods and chattels therefrom without liability in law or equity for any damage caused by such removal. The lessee does hereby expressly waive the service of any notice in writing of intention to re-enter, as provided for in the third section of an act entitled "An Act to Abolish Distress for Rent," passed May 13, 1846. In case of such re-entry, or, if the premises become vacant, or the lessee is dispossessed by summary proceedings, the lessee John Hunt shall be liable for the

amount, which the rent hereby reserved would equal for the remainder of the term hereby granted, in the same manner as he would otherwise be liable for said rent, provided, however, that the lessors may relet the premises or any part thereof for the remainder of the term for the account of the lessee, John Hunt, and the lessee does expressly covenant and agree to pay and make good to the lessors any deficiency in the amount of rent and also expense of the lessors in re-entering and reletting.

14. That failure of the lessor to insist upon the strict performance of the terms, convenants, agreements and conditions herein contained, or any of them, shall not constitute or be construed as a waiver or relinquishment of the lessor's right to thereafter enforce any such term, covenant, agreement or condition, but the same shall continue in full force and effect.

The lessee herewith deposits with the lessors the sum of $100.00, the receipt whereof is hereby acknowledged, the same to be held by the lessors as security for the full and faithful performance and observance by the lessee of all the terms, covenants and conditions herein contained, and to be returned to the lessee as, when and provided that the lessee shall have fully performed and observed all of the said terms, covenants and conditions on his part to be performed and observed; and it is expressly understood and agreed that the sum so deposited is not an advance payment of or an account of the rent herein reserved, or any part of installment thereof, or a measure of the lessors' damages, and in no event shall the lessee be entitled to return or particular application of the sum or any part thereof, until the full end of the term hereby granted, and until a reasonable time and opportunity shall have been had thereafter to inspect the said premises for the purpose of determining whether the terms, covenants and conditions hereof have been fully performed and observed; and it is further agreed that the issuance of a warrant in summary proceedings shall not effect a cancellation of this lease so as to make sooner recoverable the said sum or any part thereof.

All of the aforesaid agreements, covenants and conditions should apply to and be binding upon the parties hereto, their

heirs, executors, administrators, successors, and assigns.
In witness whereof, we have set down our signatures.

---------------------------------------------------------------
                                      Lessor

---------------------------------------------------------------
                                      Lessee

---------------------------------------------------
                  Witness

In the Presence of Henry White,

In consideration of the letting of the premises above mentioned to the above-named Lessee, and the sum of One Dollar ($1.00) to him paid by the said Lessors, the undersigned, do hereby covenant and agree to and with the said lessors, their legal representatives and assigns, that if default shall at any time be made by the said lessee in the payment of the rent or the performance of the covenants above expressed on his part to be paid and performed, that he will well and truly pay the said rent, or any arrears thereof, that may remain due unto the said lessors, and also all damages that may arise in consequence of the nonperformance of said covenants, or either or any of them, without requiring notice of any such default from the said lessors.

Witness my hand and seal.

                  (Seal) -----------------------------------------------
                                      Guarantor

In the Presence of Henry White

FORM 16

## AGREEMENT TO LET FURNISHED APARTMENTS

Agreement made the 15 day of July, 19........, between Tom Smith, hereinafter called the lessor, of the one part, and John Roe, hereinafter called the lessee, of the other part.

The said lessor agrees to let, and the said lessee to take, the 5 rooms on the 1st floor of the dwelling-house situated at

450 Blue Ridge Avenue, in the County of ......................................,
.............................................; and also the furniture, articles and
effects now being in the said rooms respectively; and also the
other articles and things specified in the schedule hereunder
written, for the term of 1 year from the 15 day of July, 19........,
at the yearly rent of $2,500.00 payable quarterly. And the said
lessee hereby agrees to keep and preserve the said furniture
and effects, so far as reasonable wear will permit, in a proper
state and condition, and supply and replace any article that
may be destroyed, broken, or lost, by articles of a like kind
and of equal value; and on the expiration or sooner determination of the said term to deliver up to the said lessor the
said rooms, furniture and effects, or such articles as shall be
so substituted in the place of any of the said articles as shall
have been so destroyed or broken as aforesaid.

Witness the hands of the said parties.

-------------------------------------------------
Lessor

-------------------------------------------------
Lessee

FORM 17

## LEASE OF APARTMENT—MONTH TO MONTH TENANCY

This agreement, made and entered into this 1 day of October, 19........, between Harry Smith, party of the first part,
hereinafter called lessee. (It is mutually agreed by the parties
hereto, where either is mentioned herein, that same refers to
their heirs, executors, administrators, successors or assigns,
who are bound as fully and completely by the covenants
herein as the parties hereto.)

Witnesseth: That the said lessee has this day rented and
leased from said lessor the following described unfurnished
apartment: 4 Rooms, Kitchen and Bath, located at No. 10
Green Street, in the City of Cleveland, Ohio, for the term of 1
year, commencing on the 1 day of November, 19........, and
ending on the 1 day of November, 19 ........, for which the lessee

agrees to pay the lessor, at his office, promptly on the first day of each rental month, in advance, a monthly rental of $100.00; and on failure of lessee to pay same when due, all further rent under this contract shall immediately become due and payable, and the said lessor has the right, at his option, to declare this lease void, cancel the same, re-enter and take possession of the premises. Lessor, at his option, upon a breach of this contract, may card for rent and sublet the premises at the best price obtainable by reasonable effort, under private negotiations, and charge the balance, if any, between said price of subletting and the contract price to lessee and hold him therefor. Such subletting on the part of the lessor will not in any sense be a breach of the contract on the part of the lessor, but will be merely as agent for the lessee and to minimize the damage. Said lessor is not required, however, to let same for any other purpose than that specified herein. These rights of the lessor are cumulative and not restrictive of any other rights under the law, and failure on the part of lessor to avail himself of these privileges at any particular time shall not constitute a waiver of these rights.

It is further mutually agreed as follows:

1. Lessee hereby waives and renounces for himself and family any and all homestead and exemption rights he or they may have under or by virtue of the laws of the state, or the United States as against any liability that may accrue under this contract. Lessee agrees to pay all costs and 15 per cent attorney's fees on any part of said rental that may be collected by suit or by attorney after same has become due.

2. Lessee is to repair, at his own expense, any damage to water or steam pipes caused by freezing or any neglect on his part, also to be responsible for all damages to the property of lessor's other tenants in said building, if there by any, or to the adjoining buildings, caused by the overflow or breakage of waterworks in said premises, during the term of this lease. Lessee agrees not to sublet said premises, or any part thereof, without the written consent of said lessor, and will deliver said premises at the expiration of this lease in as good order and repair as when first received, natural wear and tear excepted.

3. Lessee hereby releases said lessor from any and all

damages to both person and property during the term of this contract.

4. Should the premises be destroyed or so damaged by fire as to become untenantable, this lease shall cease from the date of the fire.

5. Lessee is to make no changes of any nature in the above-named premises without first obtaining written consent from said lessor or his agent; and the lessor or his agents shall have the right to enter said premises at reasonable hours, to examine the same, make such repairs, additions or alterations as may be deemed necessary for the safety, comfort and preservation of said building, and to enter upon said premises at any time to repair or improve lessor's adjoining property, if any.

6. Lessee agrees not to permit any act which would vitiate or increase the fire insurance policy upon said property; to pay all electric light, heat, water, gas and power bills accruing against said property during the term of this contract, and to comply with all rules, orders, ordinances and regulations as attached hereto and of the city government of the City of Cleveland, in any and all of its departments.

7. In the event bankruptcy or state insolvency proceedings should be filed against lessee, his heirs or assigns, in any federal or state court, it shall give the right to said lessor, his heirs or assigns, at their option, to immediately declare this contract null and void, and to at once resume possession of the property. No receiver, trustee, or other judicial officer shall ever have any right, title or interest in or to the above-described property by virtue of this contract.

8. Lessor has the privilege of carding the above-described premises for rent or for sale at any time within thirty days previous to the expiration of this lease, and during the said time to exhibit said premises during reasonable hours.

In Witness Whereof, we have hereunto set our hands, this the day and year above written.

-------------------------------------------------
Lessor

-------------------------------------------------
Lessee

Form 18

## LEASE OF APARTMENT FOR A YEAR

Indenture made the 1 day of May 19_____, by and between Henry Smith, of _____, hereinafter called the lessor, which expression shall include his heirs, and assigns and John Green, of _____, hereinafter called the lessee, which expression shall include his executors, administrators, and assigns. The lessor doth hereby demise and let unto the lessee all those unfurnished rooms or apartments consisting of six rooms on the second floor of the dwelling house numbered 87 in Spruce Street, in City of San Francisco, California, together with the free use of the front entrance, the hall, staircase, and passageways leading to said rooms, the water closet and bathrooms, and part of the cellar for the storage of fuel. To hold the same from the 1 day of June next, for the term of one year, determinable, nevertheless, as hereinafter mentioned, yielding and paying therefor the annual rent of $2,500.00, which is to include all taxes and water rates (and furnace heat).

The lessor agrees that he will at all times keep the front entrance, hall, staircase, and passageways leading to said rooms, and also the water closet and bathroom, clean, dry, and free from noise and annoyance.

It is mutually agreed that the said lessee may quit the said rooms and apartments at any time on giving to the said lessor four weeks' notice of his intention so to do, and on paying a proportionate part of the said rent up to the time of quitting the same, and also that the said lessee shall be at liberty to terminate the said tenancy, and to quit the said rooms and apartments, on any breach of either, of the agreements herein contained on the part of the lessor to be performed.

----------------------------------------------------

Lessor

----------------------------------------------------

Lessee

FORM 19

## ASSIGNMENT OF A LEASE BY ENDORSEMENT

This agreement, made the 1 day of May, 19_____, between the within named Harry White, of _____, hereinafter called the vendor, of the one part, and John Smith, hereinafter called the purchaser, of the other part, witnesseth, that in consideration of One dollar ($1.00) to the said vendor paid by the said purchaser, and of the covenants of the said purchaser hereinafter contained, the said vendor doth hereby assign unto the said purchaser, his executors, administrators and assigns, all that tenement demised to the said vendor by the within-written lease, with all rights, easements and appurtenances as within mentioned; and all the estate, right, title and interest of the said vendor in and to the said premises.

To have and to hold the said premises unto the said purchaser, his executors, administrators and assigns, for the residue of the term granted by the within-written lease, at the rent thereby reserved, and subject to the covenants by the lessee and conditions therein contained, and thenceforth to be performed and observed by the said purchaser; and the said purchaser doth hereby for himself, his heirs, executors and administrators, covenant with the said vendor, his executors and administrators, that he and they will henceforth pay the rent reserved, and perform the covenants on the part of the lessee contained in said lease, and will keep the said vendor, his executors and administrators, indemnified against all actions, claims and liability for the non-payment of said rent, or breach of the said covenants, or any of them.

_____
Assignor

_____
Assignee

FORM 20

## LEASE FOR A TERM OF YEARS

This indenture, made the _____ day of _____, in the year of our Lord one thousand nine hundred and _____ between A.B., of _____, of the first part, and C.D., of _____, of the second part, witnesseth: That the said A.B., for and in consideration of the yearly rent and covenants hereinafter mentioned and reserved, on the part and behalf of the said C.D., his executors, administrators and assigns, to be paid, kept, and performed, hath demised, granted and leased, and by these presents doth demise, grant, and lease, unto the said C.D., his executors, administrators, and assigns, all that messuage and lot of ground, and all and singular the premises hereby demised, with the appurtenances, unto the said C.D., his executors, administrators, and assigns, from the _____ day of _____ next ensuing the date hereof, for and during the term of _____ years thence next ended; yielding and paying for the same unto the said A.B., his executors, administrators and assigns, the yearly rent or sum of _____ dollars, in four equal quarterly payments (or as the case may be) of_____ dollars each the first of which to be made on the _____ day of _____ next.

And the said C.D., for himself, his heirs, executors, and administrators, doth covenant, promise, and agree to and with the said A.B., his heirs, executors, administrators, and assigns, by these presents, that he, the said C.D., his heirs, executors, and administrators, shall and will well and truly pay or cause to be paid unto the said A.B., his heirs, executors, administrators, or assigns, the said yearly rent of _____ dollars, hereby reserved, on the several days and times hereinbefore mentioned and appointed for the payment thereof, according to the true intent and meaning of these presents. And the said A.B., for himself, his heirs, executors, and administrators, doth covenant, promise, and agree to and with the said C.D., his executors, administrators, and assigns (paying the rent and performing the covenants aforesaid), shall and may peaceably and quietly have, hold, use, occupy, possess and enjoy the said demised premises, with the appurtenances, during the term aforesaid, without the lawful let, suit, trouble, eviction, molestation, or interruption of the said A.B., his heirs or assigns, or any other person or persons whatsoever.

Witness the hands and seals of the said parties the day and year first above written.

A.B.   (Seal)
C.D.   (Seal)
Signed, sealed and delivered in the presence of
E.F.
G.H.

FORM 21

## TENANT TO LANDLORD OF DESIRE TO PURCHASE THE PREMISES UNDER OPTION

In pursuance of the power contained in a lease dated the 1 day of April, 19_____, and made between yourself of the one part, and myself of the other part, I desire and agree to purchase the premises comprised in the said indenture at the sum of $6,000.00; and I request you, on or before the expiration of sixty days from the date hereof, to deliver to me a good and sufficient deed of conveyance of said premises in accordance with the provision in said indenture.

------------------------------------------------
                                        Tenant

FORM 22

## TENANT TAKING OPTION FOR ANOTHER TERM

Philadelphia, Pennsylvania
1 day of April, 19_____

To Richard Roe:
By a certain lease executed on the 1 day of March, 19_____, between yourself of the one part and myself of the other part, you demised to me for a term of three years from the date thereof the premises which I now occupy, with the proviso that I should have the right and option to lease said premises for a like term on like conditions. In the exercise of the power reserved in said lease I hereby notify you of my intention to lease said premises for another term.

------------------------------------------------
                                        Tenant

FORM 23

## NOTICE BY TENANT OF INTENTION TO QUIT

I hereby give you notice that I shall quit and deliver up to you, on the 1 day of October next, the possession of all that dwelling house, with the garden and appurtenances thereto belonging, situate at 56 Ridge Road, now held by me of you.

Witness my hand this 1 day of September, 19 ........

-------------------------------------------------
                                         Tenant

FORM 24

## TENANT TO LANDLORD TO TERMINATE A LEASE CONTAINING AN OPTION FOR ANOTHER TERM

City of Baltimore, State of Maryland
1 day of March, 19........

To Richard Roe:

By that certain lease made between yourself of the one part and myself of the other part on the 1 day of April, 19........, the premises now occupied by me as your tenant were demised for a term of three years from the 1 day of April, 19........, with the provision that I should have the right and option to lease the said premises for a like term on the same conditions, and to give you notice if it should be my desire not to do so. In pursuance thereof, I hereby notify you that it is my intention to terminate said lease at the expiration thereof, on the 1 day of April, 19........, when I shall quit and deliver up to you the possession of the buildings and lands therein comprised.

-------------------------------------------------
                                         Tenant

FORM 25

## NOTICE TO TENANT TO MAKE REPAIRS

In pursuance of the stipulation contained in the lease made by me to you, dated the 1 day of May, 19........, whereby it was agreed that you should keep in good repair the premises described in said lease, which you now hold as my tenant (or which you lately held as my tenant), I hereby give you notice, and require you within thirty days from the date hereof, to put said premises in good repair, and particularly that you make in a workmanlike manner the several repairs mentioned in the schedule hereunder written (or mentioned in the specification by my architect hereunder written).

------------------------------------------

Landlord

FORM 26

## LANDLORD TO TENANT TO MAKE REPAIRS

I do hereby give you notice, and require you to put in good and tenantable repair the dwelling house and premises situate at 24 Ruby St., which you now hold under and by virtue of a certain indenture of lease executed by me to you, bearing date the 1 day of April, 19_____, pursuant to your covenant in such indenture of lease contained, and particularly that you fix and repair all broken windows on said premises.

------------------------------------------

Landlord

FORM 27

## LANDLORD TO TENANT TO QUIT FOR NONPAYMENT OF RENT

I hereby notify you to quit and deliver up, in ten days from this date, the premises now held by you as my tenant at No. 21 Orchard Street.

------------------------------------------

Landlord

FORM 28

## LANDLORD TO TENANT FROM YEAR TO YEAR TO QUIT

I hereby give you notice to quit, and deliver up to me on the 1 day of April next, the possession of all that dwelling house, with the garden and appurtenances thereto belonging, situate at 100 Globe Street, in the County of Calvert, which you now hold under me as tenant from year to year.

---

Landlord or Lessor

FORM 29

## LICENSE TO SUBLET A PART OF LEASED PREMISES

I, the undersigned, being the lessor named in a lease made between myself, of the one part, and John Smith, of _____ _____, the other part, do hereby consent that the said lessee may underlease a portion of the premises comprised in said lease, namely, one bedroom of said apartment, unto Harry White, of _____, for the whole remaining term of said lease, provided that this consent shall not authorize any further underletting, or parting wholly or partially with the possession of said premises, or any part thereof, or prejudice or affect any of the covenants, conditions, or provisions in the said lease contained except to the extent hereinbefore expressed.

Witness my hand the 1 day of July, 19_____.

---

Lessor

FORM 30

## LICENSE TO SUBLET

I, the undersigned, hereby consent that Richard Roe, lessee in a certain lease made by me to him, dated the 1 day of May, 19_____, for the term of five years, may underlease the premises demised to John Doe, for the term of one year. Provided that this license shall be restricted to the particular underlease hereby authorized, and the covenant in said lease made by me against assigning or underletting shall remain in full force and effect.

Dated the 10 day of May, 19_____.

---

Lessor

Form 31

## PLAN OF APARTMENT OWNERSHIP
## MASTER DEED

[Note: *Laws concerning condominiums vary from state to state with New York, Michigan, California, and Florida affording the buyer the greatest protection. In all cases, however, the prospective buyer should consult a competent attorney in order to be reasonably certain that he is getting what he is paying for.*]

In the City of _____, County of _____, and State of _____, on this _____ day of _____, 19_____, _____ _____, a corporation organized and existing under the laws of the _____ _____ of _____, whose principal office and domicile is situated in the City of _____ _____, State of _____, hereinafter referred to as Grantor represented in this Deed by its President, _____, who is fully empowered and qualified to execute this Deed on behalf of said corporation, does hereby state:

FIRST: That Grantor owns the following property situated in the City of _____, State of _____, which is described as follows:

and recorded in the Office of the Recorder of the County of _____, State of _____, in Book _____ of Deeds at page _____.

SECOND: That Grantor has constructed on the parcel of land described above a project known as _____ _____, according to the plans attached hereto as Exhibit "A" which were approved by the Planning Board of the City of _____, State of _____, on the _____ day of _____, 19_____, and which are made a part hereof.

THIRD: That the said project consists of a basement, a

ground floor and _____ upper floors. The ground floor will be used for commercial facilities, or other common purposes. The _____ upper floors consist of individual apartments all for residential purposes. The _____ upper floors are all capable of individual utilization on account of having their own exit to a common area and facility of the project, and the apartments will be sold to one or more owners, each owner obtaining a particular and exclusive property right thereto, hereinafter referred to as "family unit", and also an undivided interest in the general and/or restricted common areas and facilities of the project, as listed hereinafter in this Deed, necessary for their adequate use and enjoyment and hereinafter referred to as "general and/ or restricted common areas and facilities", all of the above in accordance with (identify the state law establishing apartment ownership).

FOURTH: That the aforesaid project has a total building area of _____ square feet, of which _____ square feet, will constitute family units, and _____ square feet will constitute general and/or restricted common areas and facilities.

FIFTH: That the family units and common areas and facilities of the project will be as follows:

1. Family Units—Upper Floors: In each of the _____ upper floors there are _____ family units. The said family units will be numbered consecutively from one to _____ on each floor. These numbers will be preceeded by the tenth which corresponds to each floor to wit: those of the first floor will bear the numbers "101", "102", et cetera; those of the second floor the numbers "201", "202", et cetera; and those of the higher floors will be numbered similarly according to the corresponding tenth of each floor. Hereinafter such family units will be referred to as Family Unit Type Number One, Family Unit Type Number Two, et cetera, respectively.

Each family unit is equipped with (describe equipment)

The family units are described hereinbelow. The measures

of the family unit include all of the outside walls and one half of the block partitions but exclude bearing walls.

(a) Family Unit Type Number One: It is a rectangular shaped apartment measuring _____ feet long and _____ feet wide, making a total area of _____ square feet, as specifically shown in Exhibit A of this Deed. Its boundaries are as follows:


Its main door has access to the corridor of the respective floor.

The family unit consists of the following rooms: a hall of _____ square feet, a living room of _____ square feet, a dining room of _____ square feet, a kitchen of _____ square feet, which includes the sinks, a _____ gas range, model _____ color _____; _____ bedrooms of _____ square feet, bathroom of _____ square feet. In addition, the family unit has a balcony facing _____ Street of _____ square feet. (A description of each type of family unit should follow as items (b), (c), (d), etc.).

2. Common Areas and Facilities:

(a) The parcel of land described in Paragraph First of this Deed.

(b) A basement as shown in Exhibit A attached hereto and consisting of _____ square feet.

(c) The following facilities located in the basement:


(d) Parking facilities as shown in Exhibit A attached hereto and consisting of _____ square feet.

(e) The ground floor as shown in Exhibit A attached and consisting of _____ square feet.

(f) The following facilities located in the ground floor:

(1) Commercial areas and facilities as shown in Exhibit A attached hereto, consisting of _____ square feet and described as follows:

(2) A lobby and facilities as shown in Exhibit A attached hereto, consisting of _____ square feet, and described as follows:

(3) _____.

(g) The following facilities located throughout the project and as shown in Exhibit A, attached hereto:

(1) _____ elevators.

(2) An elevator shaft of _____ square feet, for the _____ elevators extending from the ground floor up to the _____ floor.

(3) A stairway, referred to in this Deed as stairway "A," of _____ square feet, which leads from the ground floor to the roof of the project.

(4) A stairway, referred to in this Deed as stairway "B," of _____ square feet which leads from the open court to the _____ upper floor.

(5) A flue extending from the incinerator in the basement to the roof of the project. The said flue will have a hopper door in each one of the _____ upper floors for the disposal of garbage and rubbish, and will be fed from the janitor's room of each of the _____ upper floors.

(6) Water tank located on the roof of the project.

(7) Elevator penthouse with corresponding elevator equipment located on the roof of the project.

(8) Plumbing network throughout the project.

(9) Electric and telephone wiring network throughout the project.

(10) Necessary light, telephone and water public connections.

(11) The foundations and main walls of the project as described in the plans which form part of this Deed as Exhibit "A" hereof.

(h) The following facilities located in each one of the _____ upper floors and as shown in Exhibit A, attached hereto, are restricted common areas and facilities restricted to the family units of each respective floor:

(1) A lobby which gives access to the _____ eleva-

tors, to the family unit, to the janitor's room, to the corridor and to Stairway "A."

(2) A room for the use of the janitor.

(3) A corridor extending from the lobby to stairway "B."

SIXTH:

(a) That the title and interest of each owner of a family unit in the general common areas and facilities listed under letters (a) through (g) of subparagraph Two (2) of Paragraph Fifth, and their proportionate share in the profits and common expenses in the said general common areas and facilities, as well as the proportionate representation for voting purposes in the meeting of the Association of Owners of the _____ _____ Condominium is based on the proportionate value of each family unit to the total value of all family units as follows:

Family Unit Type Number One:

_____ percent based on a value of $ _____ for this apartment and a total value of $ _____ for all family units. (Here follows the proportionate value of Family Unit Type Number Two through Family Unit Type Number _____.)

(b) That the title and interest of each owner of the family units located on each of the _____ upper floors in the restricted common areas and facilities located in the respective floor and listed under letter (h) of said subparagraph Two (2) of Paragraph Fifth, and their proportionate share in the profits and common expenses in the said restricted common areas and facilities, as well as the proportionate representation for voting purposes with respect to the said restricted common areas and facilities in the meeting of the Association of Owners of the _____ Condominium is based on the proportionate value of each family unit to the total value of all family units located on its respective floor, as follows:

Family Unit Type Number One:

_____ percent

(Here follows the title and interest of the family unit owners of Family Units Type Number Two through Family Units Type Number _____, in the restricted common areas and facilities located in their respective floors.)

(c) The proportionate representation for voting purposes provided in (a) and (b) hereof may be limited in accordance with the provisions of the by-laws attached hereto as Exhibit "B."

SEVENTH: That the administration of _____
_____ Condominium consisting as aforesaid of the project and parcel of land described in paragraphs "FIRST" and "FIFTH" of this Deed shall be in accordance with the provisions of this Deed, and with the provisions of the By-Laws which are made a part of this Deed and are attached hereto as Exhibit B, and shall be subject to the terms of a Regulatory Agreement executed by the Association of Owners and the Commissioner of the Federal Housing Administration which is made a part hereof and is attached as Exhibit C.

EIGHTH: That as appears above a plan of apartment ownership is hereby constituted under and subject to the provisions of (identify the state law establishing apartment ownership)


so that the family units of the _____ upper floors may be conveyed and recorded as individual properties capable of independent use, on account of each having its own exit to a common area and facility of the project, each family unit owner having an exclusive and particular right over his respective family unit and in addition the specified undivided interest in the common areas and facilities and/or restricted common areas and facilities.

NINTH: That for the purposes of the recording fees to be imposed on the recordation of this Deed in the Book of Deeds, the value of the _____ Condominium is distributed as follows:

(a) Parcel of land described in Paragraph "FIRST" hereof is valued at _____ Dollars.

(b) The project described in Paragraphs "SECOND" and "THIRD" hereof is valued at _____ Dollars.

TENTH: That so long as the Grantor owns one or more of the family units, the Grantor shall be subject to the provisions of the Deed and of the Exhibits "A," "B" and "C" attached hereto; and the Grantor covenants to take no action which will adversely affect the rights of the Association with respect to assurances against latent defects in the project or other rights assigned to the Association, the members of such association and their successors in interest, as their interests may appear, by reason of the establishment of the condominium.

ELEVENTH: That the general and/or restricted common areas and facilities shall remain undivided and no owner shall bring any action for partition or division.

TWELFTH: That the percentage of the undivided interest in the general and/or restricted common areas and facilities established herein shall not be changed except with the unanimous consent of all of the owners expressed in amendment to this deed duly recorded.

THIRTEENTH: That the undivided interest in the general and/or restricted common areas and facilities shall not be separated from the unit to which it appertains and shall be deemed conveyed or encumbered with the unit even though such interest is not expressly mentioned or described in the conveyance or other instrument.

FOURTEENTH: That each owner shall comply with the provisions of this Deed, the By-Laws, decisions and resolutions of the Association of Owners or its representative, and the Regulatory Agreement, as lawfully amended from time to time, and failure to comply with any such provisions, decisions or resolutions, shall be grounds for an action to recover sums due, for damages, or for injunctive relief.

FIFTEENTH: That the dedication of the property to the Plan of Apartment Ownership herein shall not be revoked, or the property removed from the Plan of Apartment Ownership, or any of the provisions herein amended unless all of the owners and the mortgagees of all of the mortgages covering the units unanimously agree to such revocation, or amendment, or removal of the property from the Plan by duly recorded instruments.

SIXTEENTH: That no owner of a family unit may exempt himself from liability for his contribution towards the common expenses by waiver of the use or enjoyment of any of the general and/or restricted common areas and facilities or by the abandonment of his family unit.

SEVENTEENTH: That all present or future owners, tenants, future tenants, or any other person that might use the facilities of the project in any manner, are subject to the provisions of this Deed and that the mere acquisition or rental of any of the family units of the project or the mere act of occupancy of any of said units shall signify that the provisions of this Deed are accepted and ratified.

The respective "family units" shall not be rented by the owners thereof for transient or hotel purposes, which shall be defined as (a) rental for any period less than thirty (30) days; or (b) any rental if the occupants of the "family unit" are provided customary hotel services, such as room service for food and beverage, maid service, furnishing laundry and linen, and bellboy service. Other than the foregoing obligations, the owners of the respective "family units" shall have the absolute right to lease same provided that said lease is made subject to the covenants and restrictions contained in this Declaration and further subject to the By-Laws and Regulatory Agreement attached hereto.

EIGHTEENTH: That if the property subject to the Plan of Apartment Ownership is totally or substantially damaged or destroyed, the repair, reconstruction, or disposition of the property shall be as provided by _____ _____ (or in the absence of statute, insert the following: "an agreement approved by _____% of the votes".)

NINETEENTH: That, where a mortgagee or other purchaser of a family unit obtains title by reason of foreclosure of a mortgage covering a unit, such acquirer of title, his successors or assigns, shall not be liable for assessments by the association which became due prior to the acquisition of title by such acquirer, it being understood, however, that the above shall not be construed to prevent the Association from filing and claiming liens for such assessments and enforcing same as provided by law, and that such assessment liens shall be subordinate to such mortgage.

TWENTIETH: That in a voluntary conveyance of a family unit the grantee of the unit shall be jointly and severally liable with the grantor for all unpaid assessments by the Association against the latter for his share of the common expenses up to the time of the grant or conveyance without prejudice to the grantee's right to recover from the grantor the amounts paid by the grantee therefor. However, any such grantee shall be entitled to a statement from the manager or Board of Directors of the Association, as the case may be, setting forth the amount of the unpaid assessments against the grantor due the Association and such grantee shall not be liable for, nor shall the family unit conveyed be subject to a lien for, any unpaid assessments made by the Association against the grantor in excess of the amount therein set forth.

TWENTY-FIRST: That the Board of Directors of the Association of Owners, or the Management Agent, or Manager shall obtain and continue in effect blanket property insurance in form and amounts satisfactory to mortgagees holding first mortgages covering family units but without prejudice to the right of the owner of a family unit to obtain individual family unit insurance.

TWENTY-SECOND: That insurance premiums for any blanket insurance coverage shall be a common expense to be paid by monthly assessments levied by the Association of Owners; and that such payments shall be held in a separate escrow account of the Association of Owners and used solely for the payment of the blanket property insurance premiums as such premiums become due.

(Execution and Acknowledgement as Required by State Statute)

ENABLING DECLARATION
ESTABLISHING A PLAN FOR CONDOMINIUM
OWNERSHIP

[Note: *May be used in place of Master Deed, preceding form, where local law permits.*]

WHEREAS, _____, (hereinafter referred to as "Grantor") owns certain real property herein described; and

WHEREAS, said Grantor has improved said property by constructing thereon a _____ unit multifamily structure known as _____, said structure having been constructed in accordance with plans and specifications prepared by _____ _____, said plans being on record in the _____ of the City of _____, State of _____, and styled _____, FHA Project No. _____, and consisting of sheets _____ through _____, _____ through _____, etc., all inclusive; and

WHEREAS, said Grantor hereby establishes by this declaration a plan for the individual ownership of the real property estates consisting of the area or space contained in each of the apartment units in said multifamily structure, and the co-ownership by the individual and separate owners thereof, as tenants in common, of all of the remaining real property which is hereinafter defined and referred to herein as the "common areas and facilities."

NOW, THEREFORE, said Grantor, the fee owner of the following described real property, to-wit:

(Land description)

hereby makes the following declaration as to divisions, covenants, restrictions, limitations, conditions and uses to which the above described real property and improvements thereon, consisting of a _____ unit multifamily structure and appurtenances, may be put, hereby specifying that said declaration shall constitute covenants to run with the land and shall be binding on said Grantor, its successors and assigns, and all subsequent owners of all or any part of said real property and improvements, together with their grantees, successors, heirs, executors, administrators, devisees or assigns:

A. Said Grantor, in order to establish a plan of condominium ownership for the above-described property and improvements, hereby covenants and agrees that it hereby divides said real property into the following separate freehold estates:

1. The _____ separately designated and legally described freehold estates consisting of the spaces or areas, being the area or space contained in the perimeter walls of each of the _____ apartment units in said multifamily structure constructed on said property, said spaces being defined, and referred to herein, as "apartment spaces."

2. A freehold estate consisting of the remaining portion of the real property is described and referred to herein as the "common areas and facilities," which definition includes the multifamily structure and the property upon which it is located, and specifically includes, but is not limited to, the land, roof, main walls, slabs, elevator, elevator shaft, staircases, lobbies, halls, parking spaces, storage spaces, community and commercial facilities, swimming pool, pumps, water tank, trees, pavement, balconies, pipes, wires, conduits, air conditioners and ducts, or other public utility lines.

B. For the purpose of this declaration, the ownership of each "apartment space" shall include the respective undivided interest in the common areas and facilities specified and established in "E" hereof, and each "apartment space" together with the undivided interest is defined and hereinafter referred to as "family unit."

C. A portion of the "common areas and facilities" is hereby set aside and allocated for the restricted use of the respective "apartment spaces," as is hereinafter designated, and as shown on survey attached hereto, and said areas shall be known as "restricted common areas and facilities."

D. The _____ individual "apartment

spaces" hereby established and which shall be individually conveyed are described as follows:

(Legal description of apartment spaces)

E. The undivided interest in the "common areas and facilities" hereby established and which shall be conveyed with each respective "apartment space" is as follows:

(Apartment number—Percentage of undivided interest)

The above respective undivided interests established and to be conveyed with the respective "apartment spaces" as indicated above, cannot be changed, and said Grantor, its successors and assigns, and grantees, covenant and agree that the undivided interests in the "common areas and facilities" and the fee titles to the respective "apartment spaces" conveyed therewith, shall not be separated or separately conveyed, and each said undivided interest shall be deemed to be conveyed or encumbered with its respective "apartment space" even though the description in the instrument of conveyance or encumbrance may refer only to the fee title to the "apartment space."

F. The proportionate shares of the separate owners of the respective "family units" in the profits and common expenses in the "common areas and facilities," as well as their proportionate representation for voting purposes in the Association of Owners, is based on the proportionate value that each of the "family units," referred to herein, bears to the value of $ ........................... which represents the total value of all of the "family units." The value of the respective "family units," their respective interests for voting purposes, and their proportionate shares in the common profits and expenses shall be as follows:

(Family unit number—value—Proportionate representation for voting and share in common profits and expenses)

G. The "restricted common areas and facilities" allocated for the restricted uses of the respective "family units" are as follows:

FAMILY UNIT 1: That portion of the parking area designated as parking space No. 1; storage space No. 1; together with balcony adjoining the "apartment space" associated with family unit 1 on the south. Said restricted areas are further described, located, and shown on survey attached hereto.

H. That attached hereto and made a part hereof as Exhibit "A" is a survey consisting of _____ sheets as prepared by _____, dated _____.

I. Said Grantor, its successors and assigns, by this declaration, and all future owners of the "family units," by their acceptance of their deeds, covenant and agree as follows:

1. That the "common areas and facilities" shall remain undivided; and no owner shall bring any action for partition, it being agreed that this restriction is necessary in order to preserve the rights of the owners with respect to the operation and management of the condominium.

2. That the "apartment spaces" shall be occupied and used by the respective owners only as a private dwelling for the owner, his family, tenants and social guests and for no other purpose.

3. The owner of the respective "apartment spaces" shall not be deemed to own the undecorated and/or unfinished surfaces of the perimeter walls, floors and ceilings surrounding his respective "apartment space," nor shall said owner be deemed to own pipes, wires, conduits or other public utility lines running through said respective "apartment spaces" which are utilized for, or serve more than one "apartment space," except as tenants in common with the other "family unit" owners as heretofore provided in "E." Said owner, however, shall be deemed to own the walls and partitions which are contained in said owner's respective "apartment space," and also shall be deemed to own the inner decorated and/or finished surfaces of the perimeter walls, floors and ceilings, including plaster, paint, wallpaper, etc.

4. The owners of the respective "apartment spaces" agree that if any portion of the "common areas and facilities" encroaches upon the "apartment spaces," a valid easement

for the encroachment and for the maintenance of same, so long as it stands, shall and does exist. In the event the multi-family structure is partially or totally destroyed, and then re-built, the owners of "apartment spaces" agree that minor en-croachment of parts of the "common areas and facilities" due to construction shall be permitted and that valid easement for said encroachment and the maintenance thereof shall exist.

5. That an owner of a "family unit" shall automatically, upon becoming the owner of a "family unit or units," be a member of _____ hereinafter referred to as the "Association," and shall remain a member of said Association until such time as his owner-ship ceases for any reason, at which time his membership in said Association shall automatically cease.

6. That the owners of "family units" covenant and agree that the administration of the condominium shall be in ac-cordance with the provisions of this Declaration, the By-Laws of the Association which are made a part hereof and attached as Exhibit "B," and shall be subject to the terms of a Regu-latory Agreement executed by the Association and the Com-missioner of the Federal Housing Administration, which Agreement is made a part hereof and is attached as Exhibit "C."

7. That each owner, tenant or occupant of a "family unit" shall comply with the provisions of this Declaration, the By-Laws, decisions and resolutions of the Association or its representative, and the Regulatory Agreement, as lawfully amended from time to time, and failure to comply with any such provisions, decisions, or resolutions, shall be grounds for an action to recover sums due, for damages, or for in-junctive relief.

8. That this Declaration shall not be revoked or any of the provisions herein amended unless all of the owners and the mortgagees of all of the mortgages covering the "family units" unanimously agree to such revocation or amendment by duly recorded instruments.

9. That no owner of a "family unit" may exempt himself

from liability for his contribution towards the common expenses by waiver of the use or enjoyment of any of the common areas and facilities or by the abandonment of his "family unit."

J. All sums assessed by the Association but unpaid for the share of the common expenses chargeable to any family unit shall constitute a lien on such family unit prior to all other liens except only (1) tax liens on the family unit in favor of any assessing unit and special district, and (2) all sums unpaid on the first mortgage of record. Such lien may be foreclosed by suit by the manager or Board of Directors, acting on behalf of the owners of the family units, in like manner as a mortgage of real property. In any such foreclosure the family unit owner shall be required to pay a reasonable rental for the family unit, if so provided in the by-laws, and the plaintiff in such foreclosure action shall be entitled to the appointment of a receiver to collect the same. The manager or Board of Directors, acting on behalf of the owners of the family units, shall have power, unless prohibited herein, to bid in the unit at foreclosure sale, and to acquire and hold, lease, mortgage and convey the same. Suit to recover a money judgment for unpaid common expenses shall be maintainable without foreclosing or waiving the lien securing the same.

K. Where the mortgagee of a first mortgage of record or other purchaser of a family unit obtains title to the unit as a result of foreclosure of the first mortgage, such acquirer of title, his successors and assigns, shall not be liable for the share of the common expenses or assessments by the Association chargeable to such family unit which became due prior to the acquisition of title to such family unit by such acquirer. Such unpaid share of common expenses or assessments shall be deemed to be common expenses collectible from all of the family units including such acquirer, his successors and assigns.

L. The respective "family units" shall not be rented by the owners thereof for transient or hotel purposes, which shall be defined as (a) rental for any period less than thirty (30) days; or (b) any rental if the occupants of the "family unit" are provided customary hotel services, such as room service for food and beverage, maid service, furnishing laundry and linen, and bellboy service. Other than the foregoing obligations, the owners of the respective "family units" shall have the absolute right to lease same provided that said lease is made subject to the covenants and restrictions contained in this Declaration and further subject to the By-Laws and Regulatory Agreement attached hereto.

M. In the event the property subject to this Enabling Declaration is totally or substantially damaged or destroyed, the repair, reconstruction, or disposition of the property shall be as provided by _____. (In the absence of statute, insert the following: "an Agreement approved by _____% of the votes.")

N. In a voluntary conveyance of a family unit the grantee of the unit shall be jointly and severally liable with the grantor for all unpaid assessments by the Association against the latter for his share of the common expenses up to the time of the grant or conveyance, without prejudice to the grantee's right to recover from the grantor the amounts paid by the grantee therefor. However, any such grantee shall be entitled to a statement from the manager or Board of Directors of the Association, as the case may be, setting forth the amount of the unpaid assessments against the grantor due the Association and such grantee shall not be liable for, nor shall the family unit conveyed be subject to a lien for, any unpaid assessments made by the Association against the grantor in excess of the amount therein set forth.

O. All agreements and determinations lawfully made by the Association in accordance with the voting percentages established in the _____, this Declaration or in the By-Laws, shall be deemed to be binding on all owners of family units, their successors and assigns.

P. That the Board of Directors of the Association of Owners, or the Management Agent, or Manager shall obtain and continue in effect blanket property insurance in form and amounts satisfactory to mortgagees holding first mortgages covering family units but without prejudice to the right of the owner of a family unit to obtain individual family unit insurance.

Q. That insurance premiums for any blanket insurance coverage shall be a common expense to be paid by monthly assessments levied by the Association of Owners; and that such payments shall be held in a separate escrow account of the Association of Owners and used solely for the payment of the blanket property insurance premiums as such premiums become due.

R. That so long as said Grantor, its successors and assigns, owns one or more of the family units established and described herein, said Grantor, its successors and assigns shall be subject to the provisions of this Declaration and of Exhibits "A," "B," and "C" attached hereto; and said Grantor covenants to take no action which would adversely affect the rights of the Association with respect to assurances against latent defects in the property or other right assigned to the Association, the members of such association and their successors in interest, as their interests may appear, by reason of the establishment of the condominium.

S. The terms "Declaration" and "Condominium Ownership" as used herein shall mean and include the terms "Master Deed" and "Apartment Ownership" respectively.

(Execution and Acknowledgement in Accordance with Requirements of Jurisdiction)

FORM 32

BY-LAWS OF _____ CONDOMINIUM

# Article I

### Plan of Apartment Ownership

Section 1. Apartment Ownership. The project located at _____ Street, City of _____, State of _____, known as "_____ Condominium" is submitted to the provisions of _____

---------------------------------------------------------------- (identify state law establishing apartment ownership).

Section 2. By-Laws Applicability. The provisions of these By-Laws are applicable to the project. (The term "project" as used herein shall include the land.)

Section 3. Personal Application. All present or future owners, tenants, future tenants, or their employees, or any other person that might use the facilities of the project in any manner, are subject to the regulations set forth in these By-Laws and to the Regulatory Agreement, attached as Exhibit "C" to the recorded Plan of Apartment Ownership.

The mere acquisition or rental of any of the family units (hereinafter referred to as "units") of the project or the mere act of occupancy of any of said units will signify that these By-Laws and the provisions of the Regulatory Agreement are accepted, ratified, and will be complied with.

# Article II

## Voting, Majority of Owners, Quorum, Proxies

Section 1. Voting. Voting shall be on a percentage basis and the percentage of the vote to which the owner is entitled is the percentage assigned to the family unit or units in the Master Deed.

Section 2. Majority of Owners. As used in these By-Laws the term "majority of owners" shall mean those owners holding 51% of the votes in accordance with the percentages assigned in the Master Deed.

Section 3. Quorum. Except as otherwise provided in these By-Laws, the presence in person or by proxy of a "majority of owners" as defined in Section 2 of this Article shall constitute a quorum.

Section 4. Proxies. Votes may be cast in person or by proxy. Proxies must be filed with the Secretary before the appointed time of each meeting.

# Article III

## Administration

Section 1. Association Responsibilities. The owners of the units will constitute the Association of Owners (hereinafter referred to as "Association") who will have the responsibility of administering the project, approving the annual budget, establishing and collecting monthly assessments and arranging for the management of the project pursuant to an agreement, containing provisions relating to the duties, obligations, removal and compensation of the management agent. Except as otherwise provided, decisions and resolutions of the Association shall require approval by a majority of owners.

Section 2. Place of Meetings. Meetings of the Association shall be held at the principal office of the project or such other suitable place convenient to the owners as may be designated by the Board of Directors.

Section 3. Annual Meetings. The first annual meeting of the Association shall be held on _____ (Date). Thereafter, the annual meetings of the Association shall be held on the _____ (1st, 2nd, 3rd, 4th) _____ (Monday, Tuesday, Wednesday, etc.) of _____ (month) each succeeding year. At such meetings there shall be elected by ballot of the owners a Board of Directors in accordance with the requirements of Section 5 of Article IV of these By-Laws. The owners may also transact such other business of the Association as may properly come before them.

Section 4. Special Meetings. It shall be the duty of the President to call a special meeting of the owners as directed by resolution of the Board of Directors or upon a petition signed by a majority of the owners and having been presented to the Secretary, or at the request of the Federal Housing Commissioner or his duly authorized representative. The notice of any special meeting shall state the time and place of such meeting and the purpose thereof. No business shall be transacted at a special meeting except as stated in the notice unless by consent of four-fifths of the owners present, either in person or by proxy.

Section 5. Notice of Meetings. It shall be the duty of the Secretary to mail a notice of each annual or special meeting, stating the purpose thereof as well as the time and place where it is to be held, to each owner of record, at least 5 but not more than 10 days prior to such meeting. The mailing of a notice in the manner provided in this Section shall be considered notice served. Notices of all meetings shall be mailed to the Director of the local insuring office of the Federal Housing Administration.

Section 6. Adjourned Meetings. If any meeting of owners cannot be organized because a quorum has not attended, the owners who are present, either in person or by proxy, may adjourn the meeting to a time not less than forty-eight (48) hours from the time the original meeting was called.

Section 7. Order of Business. The order of business at all meetings of the owners of units shall be as follows:

(a) Roll call.
(b) Proof of notice of meeting or waiver of notice.
(c) Reading of minutes of preceding meeting.
(d) Reports of officers.
(e) Report of Federal Housing Administration representative, if present.
(f) Report of committees.
(g) Election of inspectors of election.
(h) Election of directors.
(i) Unfinished business.
(j) New business.

# Article IV

## Board of Directors

Section 1. Number and Qualification. The affairs of the Association shall be governed by a Board of Directors composed of _____ persons (an odd number not less than five), all of whom must be owners of units in the project.

Section 2. Powers and Duties. The Board of Directors shall have the powers and duties necessary for the administration of the affairs of the Association and may do all such acts and things as are not by law or by these By-Laws directed to be exercised and done by the owners.

Section 3. Other Duties. In addition to duties imposed by these By-Laws or by resolutions of the Association, the Board of Directors shall be responsible for the following:

(a) Care, upkeep and surveillance of the project and the common areas and facilities and the restricted common areas and facilities.

(b) Collection of monthly assessments from the owners.

(c) Designation and dismissal of the personnel necessary for the maintenance and operation of the project, the common areas and facilities and the restricted common areas and facilities.

Section 4. Management Agent. The Board of Directors may employ for the Association a management agent at a compensation established by the Board to perform such duties and services as the Board shall authorize including, but not limited to, the duties listed in Section 3 of this Article.

Section 5. Election and Term of Office. At the first annual meeting of the Association the term of office of two Directors shall be fixed for three (3) years. The term of office of two Directors shall be fixed at two (2) years, and the term of office of one Director shall be fixed at one (1) year. At the expiration of the initial term of office of each respective Director, his successor shall be elected to serve a term of three (3) years. The Directors shall hold office until their successors have been elected and hold their first meeting. (If a larger Board of Directors is contemplated, the terms of office should be established in a similar manner so that they will expire in different years.)

Section 6. Vacancies. Vacancies in the Board of Directors caused by any reason other than the removal of a Director by a vote of the Association shall be filled by vote of the majority of the remaining Directors, even though they may constitute less than a quorum; and each person so elected shall be a

Director until a successor is elected at the next annual meeting of the Association.

Section 7. Removal of Directors. At any regular or special meeting duly called, any one or more of the Directors may be removed with or without cause by a majority of the owners and a successor may then and there be elected to fill the vacancy thus created. Any Director whose removal has been proposed by the owners shall be given an opportunity to be heard at the meeting.

Section 8. Organization Meeting. The first meeting of a newly elected Board of Directors shall be held within ten (10) days of election at such place as shall be fixed by the Directors at the meeting at which such Directors were elected, and no notice shall be necessary to the newly elected Directors in order legally to constitute such meeting, providing a majority of the whole Board shall be present.

Section 9. Regular Meetings. Regular meetings of the Board of Directors may be held at such time and place as shall be determined, from time to time, by a majority of the Directors, but at least two such meetings shall be held during each fiscal year. Notice of regular meetings of the Board of Directors shall be given to each Director, personally or by mail, telephone or telegraph, at least three (3) days prior to the day named for such meeting.

Section 10. Special Meetings. Special meetings of the Board of Directors may be called by the President on three days notice to each Director, given personally or by mail, telephone or telegraph, which notice shall state the time, place (as hereinabove provided) and purpose of the meeting. Special meetings of the Board of Directors shall be called by the President or Secretary in like manner and on like notice on the written request of at least three Directors.

Section 11. Waiver of Notice. Before or at any meeting of the Board of Directors, any Director may, in writing, waive notice of such meeting and such waiver shall be deemed equivalent to the giving of such notice. Attendance by a Director at any meeting of the Board shall be a waiver of notice by him of the time and place thereof. If all the Directors are present at any meeting of the Board, no notice shall be required and any business may be transacted at such meeting.

Section 12. Board of Director's Quorum. At all meetings of the Board of Directors, a majority of the Directors shall constitute a quorum for the transaction of business, and the acts of the majority of the Directors present at a meeting at which a quorum is present shall be the acts of the Board of Directors. If, at any meeting of the Board of Directors, there be less than a quorum present, the majority of those present may adjourn the meeting from time to time. At any such adjourned meeting, any business which might have been transacted at the meeting as originally called may be transacted without further notice.

Section 13. Fidelity Bonds. The Board of Directors shall require that all officers and employees of the Association handling or responsible for Association funds shall furnish adequate fidelity bonds. The premiums on such bonds shall be paid by the Association.

# Article V

## Officers

Section 1. Designation. The principal officers of the Association shall be a President, a Vice President, a Secretary, and a Treasurer, all of whom shall be elected by and from the Board of Directors. The Directors may appoint an assistant treasurer, and an assistant secretary, and such other officers as in their judgment may be necessary. (In the case of an Association of one hundred owners or less the offices of Treasurer and Secretary may be filled by the same person.)

Section 2. Election of Officers. The officers of the Association shall be elected annually by the Board of Directors at the organization meeting of each new Board and shall hold office at the pleasure of the Board.

Section 3. Removal of Officers. Upon an affirmative vote of a majority of the members of the Board of Directors, any officer may be removed, either with or without cause, and his successor elected at any regular meeting of the Board of Directors, or at any special meeting of the Board called for such purpose.

Section 4. President. The President shall be the chief executive officer of the Association. He shall preside at all meetings of the Association and of the Board of Directors. He shall have all of the general powers and duties which are usually vested in the office of president of an Association, including but not limited to the power to appoint committees from among the owners from time to time as he may in his discretion decide is appropriate to assist in the conduct of the affairs of the Association.

Section 5. Vice President. The Vice President shall take the place of the President and perform his duties whenever the President shall be absent or unable to act. If neither the President nor the Vice President is able to act, the Board of Directors shall appoint some other member of the Board to so do on an interim basis. The Vice President shall also perform such other duties as shall from time to time be imposed upon him by the Board of Directors.

Section 6. Secretary. The Secretary shall keep the minutes of all meetings of the Board of Directors and the minutes of all meetings of the Association; he shall have charge of such books and papers as the Board of Directors may direct; and he shall, in general, perform all the duties incident to the office of Secretary.

Section 7. Treasurer. The Treasurer shall have responsibility for Association funds and securities and shall be responsible for keeping full and accurate accounts of all receipts and disbursements in books belonging to the Association. He shall be responsible for the deposit of all moneys and other valuable effects in the name, and to the credit, of the Association in such depositaries as may from time to time be designated by the Board of Directors.

# Article VI

## Obligations of the Owners

Section 1. Assessments. All owners are obligated to pay monthly assessments imposed by the Association to meet all project communal expenses, which may include a liability insurance policy premium and an insurance premium for a policy to cover repair and reconstruction work in case of hurricane, fire, earthquake or other hazard. The assessments shall be made pro rata according to the value of the unit owned, as stipulated in the Master Deed. Such assessments shall include monthly payments to a General Operating Reserve and a Reserve Fund for Replacements as required in the Regulatory Agreement attached as Exhibit "C" to the Plan of Apartment Ownership.

Section 2. Maintenance and Repair.

(a) Every owner must perform promptly all maintenance and repair work within his own unit, which if omitted would affect the project in its entirety or in a part belonging to other owners, being expressly responsible for the damages and liabilities that his failure to do so may engender.

(b) All the repairs of internal installations of the unit such as water, light, gas, power, sewage, telephones, air conditioners, sanitary installations, doors, windows, lamps and all other accessories belonging to the unit area shall be at the owner's expense.

(c) An owner shall reimburse the Association for any expenditures incurred in repairing or replacing any common area and facility damaged through his fault.

Section 3. Use of Family Units—Internal Changes.

(a) All units shall be utilized for residential purposes only.

(b) An owner shall not make structural modifications or alterations in his unit or installations located therein without previously notifying the Association in writing, through the Management Agent, if any, or through the President of the Board of Directors, if no management agent is employed. The Association shall have the obligation to answer within _____ days and failure to do so within the stipulated time shall mean that there is no objection to the proposed modification or alteration.

Section 4. Use of Common Areas and Facilities and Restricted Common Areas and Facilities.

(a) An owner shall not place or cause to be placed in the lobbies, vestibules, stairways, elevators and other project areas and facilities of a similar nature both common and restricted, any furniture, packages or objects of any kind. Such areas shall be used for no other purpose than for normal transit through them.

(b) The project shall have _____ elevators, _____ devoted to the transportation of the owners and their guests and _____ for freight service, or auxiliary purposes. Owners and tradesmen are expressly required to utilize exclusively a freight or service elevator for transporting packages, merchandise or any other object that may affect the comfort or well-being of the passengers of the elevator dedicated to the transportation of owners, residents and guests.

Section 5. Right of Entry.

(a) An owner shall grant the right of entry to the management agent or to any other person authorized by the Board of Directors or the Association in case of any emergency originating in or threatening his unit, whether the owner is present at the time or not.

(b) An owner shall permit other owners, or their representatives, when so required, to enter his unit for the purpose of performing installations, alterations or repairs to the mechanical or electrical services, provided that requests for entry are made in advance and that such entry is at a time convenient to the owner. In case of an emergency, such right of entry shall be immediate.

Section 6. Rules of Conduct.

(a) No resident of the project shall post any advertisements, or posters of any kind in or on the project except as authorized by the Association.

(b) Residents shall exercise extreme care about making noises or the use of musical instruments, radios, television and amplifiers that may disturb other residents. Keeping domestic animals will abide by the Municipal Sanitary Regulations.

(c) It is prohibited to hang garments, rugs, etc., from the windows or from any of the facades of the project.

(d) It is prohibited to dust rugs, etc., from the windows, or to clean rugs, etc., by beating on the exterior part of the project.

(e) It is prohibited to throw garbage or trash outside the disposal installations provided for such purposes in the service areas.

(f) No owner, resident or lessee shall install wiring for electrical or telephone installation, television antennae, machines or air conditioning units, etc., on the exterior of the project or that protrude through the walls or the roof of the project except as authorized by the Association.

# Article VII

## Amendments to Plan of Apartment Ownership

Section 1. By-Laws. These By-Laws may be amended by the Association in a duly constituted meeting for such purpose and no amendment shall take effect unless approved by owners representing at least 75% of the total value of all units in the project as shown in the Master Deed.

# Article VIII

## Mortgagees

Section 1. Notice to Association. An owner who mortgages his unit, shall notify the Association through the Management Agent, if any, or the President of the Board of Directors in the event there is no Management Agent, the name and address of his mortgagee; and the Association shall maintain such information in a book entitled "Mortgagees of Units."

Section 2. Notice of Unpaid Assessments. The Association shall at the request of a mortgagee of a unit report any unpaid assessments due from the owner of such unit.

## Article IX

### Compliance

These By-Laws are set forth to comply with the requirements of (identify state law establishing apartment ownership)

In case any of these By-Laws conflict with the provisions of said statute, it is hereby agreed and accepted that the provisions of the statute will apply.

FORM 33

### MODEL FORM OF SUBSCRIPTION AND PURCHASE AGREEMENT

Application No. _____
Family Unit No. _____
Project _____
Date _____

WHEREAS, _____ (hereinafter called Seller) is the owner of [or proposes to construct] a multifamily housing project known as
_____ located at _____
_____ and WHEREAS, the said project is proposed to be converted to a Condominium; And

WHEREAS, 80 percent of the total value of the family units in the project (or such lesser percent as may be approved by the Federal Housing Administration (hereinafter referred to as the FHA)) must be sold to purchasers approved by the FHA before its insurance of individual mortgages under Section 234(c) of the National Housing Act; and

WHEREAS, it will be necessary to establish an association of owners for the operation and regulation of the "common areas and facilities" of the Condominium;

BE IT AGREED AS FOLLOWS:

## 1. Subscription and Purchase Amount

I/We _____, in consideration of the mutual promises of other subscribers and other good and valuable considerations, and having a bona fide intention to reside in a unit in the above-referred-to project, hereby subscribe for participation in _____ (hereinafter called Association) and hereby agree to purchase the above-numbered family unit and the _____ percentage undivided interest in the common areas and facilities for the price of $_____, payable as follows: $_____ upon signing this agreement; $_____ within _____ days after date hereof and the balance at time of conveyance as provided in paragraph 3, hereof.

Seller hereby agrees that all sums received on account of the purchase of the family unit shall be held in trust and shall be placed in an escrow account with

_____ Bank under an escrow agreement, the terms of which are acceptable to the FHA. The escrow agreement shall provide that Seller shall not be entitled to receive any sums in the escrow until conveyance of title.

I/We hereby subscribe to the Plan of Apartment Ownership, Association By-Laws and Regulatory Agreement, copies of which are attached hereto and receipt of which is hereby acknowledged. I/We hereby agree that, in addition to the purchase price above mentioned, I/We will be liable for our proportionate share of the Association assessments as outlined in the By-Laws. I/We also agree that in addition to the above-mentioned purchase price we will pay to the Association at or before conveyance of title the sum of $_____, representing our proportionate share of the Association's required working capital.

## 2. Plan and Purpose

The Association will be established for the purpose of operating and maintaining the common areas and facilities of the Condominium. Each owner of a family unit in the Condominium will be a member of the Association and will be subject to the by-laws and regulations thereof. As set forth in the Plan of Apartment Ownership, the vote of each member will be based on the ratio of the value of the family unit(s) which he owns to the total value of the entire project.

The affairs of the Association will be conducted by a Board of Directors as provided for in the By-Laws.

### 3. Conveyance of Title

In consideration of this subscription the Seller agrees to convey to Subscriber good and marketable title to said family unit. Subscriber agrees to purchase said family unit from the Seller within thirty (30) days after Seller has notified Subscriber it is prepared to tender title and possession thereof to him for an amount equal to the purchase price. It is contemplated that the unpaid purchase price will be secured by an individual mortgage on the family unit insured by the FHA under Section 234. Subscriber may, however, pay this amount in cash or may elect to finance under a conventional uninsured mortgage. It is understood that Subscriber will, at the time title is conveyed to him, pay such closing costs as are customarily paid by the purchaser of comparable real estate in this jurisdiction and taxes, assessments and insurance will be adjusted to the date of closing. The FHA estimate of value of the above-described family unit is $_____.

### 4. Location of Project

The above-referred-to housing project will be located at _____ in the City of _____. Nearest public transportation in the form of (bus, streetcar, subway, train service) is available at the following points:

Churches, schools, shopping centers, playgrounds and other community facilities available to members of the project are located as follows:

### 5. Priority of Mortgage Lien

This Agreement and all rights hereunder are and at all

times shall be subject and subordinate to the lien of the mortgage and accompanying documents to be executed by the Subscriber to a lending institution and to be insured under Section 234 of the National Housing Act; and to any and all modifications, extensions, and renewals thereof; and to any mortgage or deed of trust made in place thereof.

## 6. Cancellation Rights

In the event Subscriber shall have died prior to his acquisition of title to the family unit, the Seller reserves the right to return such amount or amounts to Subscriber's estate or legal representative, and thereupon all rights of Subscriber shall cease and terminate without further liability on the part of the Seller.

It is understood that Subscriber's credit is subject to approval by the Federal Housing Administration. In the event the FHA determines that Subscriber does not meet its credit requirements for participation in this project or Subscriber is unable to obtain an FHA-insured mortgage thereupon within Seller shall have privilege_____ days from date hereof, of withdrawal from this contract and the Seller shall return to Subscriber all of the sums paid hereunder and this Agreement shall be deemed null and void and all of Subscriber's and Seller's rights shall cease and terminate without further liability on the part of either party.

If Subscriber within five (5) days after the execution of this Agreement notifies the Seller in writing that Subscriber wishes to withdraw from this Agreement, the amounts theretofore paid by him under this Agreement will be returned to him and thereupon all rights and liabilities of Subscriber hereunder shall cease and terminate. The right of the Subscriber to withdraw shall, however, expire unless exercised within such five- (5) day period, except that if title to the family unit is not conveyed to the Subscriber in accordance with FHA requirements on or before _____, the Subscriber and the Seller shall have the right to withdraw from this Agreement, in which event Seller shall return to Subscriber all sums paid hereunder and Subscriber's and Seller's rights shall cease and terminate without further liability on the part of either party.

If the Subscriber shall default in any of the payments or

obligations called for in this Agreement, and such default shall continue for fifteen (15) days after notice sent by registered mail by the Seller to the Subscriber at the address given below, then, forthwith at the option of the Seller, the Subscriber shall lose any and all rights under this Agreement, and any amount paid toward the purchase price may be retained by the Seller as liquidated damages, or may at the option of the Seller be returned less the Subscriber's proportionate share of expenses to be determined solely by the Seller.

The Seller, may, at its option, release the obligation of Subscriber under this Agreement in the event Subscriber shall secure another subscriber who is satisfactory to the Seller and to the Federal Housing Administration. This Agreement is not otherwise assignable.

### 7. Function of FHA in Connection with this Project

The FHA as insurer of the individual mortgage loan covering a family unit does not insure Subscriber against loss. The validity of title is the responsibility of the Seller and the parties to the mortgage transaction and not of the FHA. FHA has not examined or approved any advertising or informational material in connection with this project other than that contained in this Subscription and Purchase Agreement.

### 8. Oral Representations Not to be Relied Upon

This Agreement will supersede any and all understandings and agreements and constitutes the entire agreement between the parties and no oral representations or statements shall be considered a part hereof.

### 9. Types of Dwelling Units Available

Attached hereto as exhibit "A" is a listing of the various family units in connection with this project, showing types, cash down payment requirements, estimated monthly assessments by the Association and estimated monthly mortgage payments, inclusive of deposits for mortgage insurance premiums and taxes, which will be applicable in the event individual mortgages are insured under Section 234 of the National Housing Act.

## 10. Interim Occupancy on Rental Basis

You as a subscriber may, if you desire, move into the completed dwelling unit prior to conversion of the project to condominium ownership, provided the proposed Seller permits you to do so and the FHA approves such interim occupancy. If you do so, however, you should be mindful of the fact that prior to passage of title you will be occupying the premises merely as a tenant of the proposed Seller and you are therefore advised not to expend any sums for improvements without a written agreement and authority from the proposed Seller satisfactory to you as to the manner in which compensation or adjustments will be made for such expenditures in the event the conversion to condominium ownership does not ultimately materialize.

WITNESS:

---------------------------------------------------------
*(Subscriber)*

-------------------------------------------------    ---------------------------------------------------------
*(Subscriber)*

---------------------------------------------------------
*(Address)*

---------------------------------------------------------
*(Telephone)*

---------------------------------------------------------
*(Name of Corporation)*

---------------------------------------------------------
*(Address)*

---------------------------------------------------------
*(Telephone)*

---------------------------------------------------------
*(President or other Corporate Officer)*

---------------------------------------------------------
*(Address)*

---------------------------------------------------------
*(Telephone)*

FORM 34

## MODEL FORM OF
## MANAGEMENT AGREEMENT FOR CONDOMINIUMS

Agreement made this _____ day of _____,
19_____, between the _____
for the _____ Con-
dominium, hereafter called the "Association," organized and
established in accordance with the Plan of Apartment Ownership executed and recorded in the Office of the Recorder
of the County of _____, State of _____,
in Book of _____ Deeds at page
_____, having its principal office at _____,
and _____, having its principal
office at _____, hereinafter
called the "Agent."

### WITNESSETH:

In consideration of the terms, conditions, and covenants
hereinafter set forth, the parties hereto mutually agree as follows:

FIRST. (a) The Association hereby appoints the Agent, and
the Agent hereby accepts appointment, on the terms and conditions hereinafter provided, as exclusive managing agent of
the condominium known as _____,
located in the County of _____ State of
_____, and consisting of _____
dwelling units.

(b) The Agent fully understands that the function of the Association is the operation and management of the Condominium; and the Agent agrees, notwithstanding the authority
given to the Agent in this Agreement, to confer fully and freely
with the Directors of the Association in the performance of its
duties as herein set forth and to attend membership or Director's meetings at any time or times requested by the Association. It is further understood and agreed that the authority and
duties conferred upon the Agent hereunder are confined to
the common areas and facilities and the restricted common
areas and facilities as defined in the Plan of Apartment Ownership. Such authority and duties do not and shall not include

supervision or management of family units except as directed by the Association.

SECOND. In order to facilitate efficient operation, the Association shall furnish the Agent with a complete set of the plans and specifications of the Condominium as finally approved by the Federal Housing Administration, and with the aid of these documents and inspection made by competent personnel, the Agent will inform itself with respect to the layout, construction, location, character, plan and operation of the lighting, heating, plumbing, and ventilating systems, as well as elevators, if any, and other mechanical equipment in the Condominium. Copies of guarantees and warranties pertinent to the construction of the Condominium and in force at the time of the execution of this Agreement shall be furnished to the Agent.

THIRD. The Agent shall hire in its own name all managerial personnel necessary for the efficient discharge of the duties of the Agent hereunder. Compensation for the services of such employees shall be the responsibility of the Agent. Those employees of the Agent who handle or are responsible for the handling of the Association's monies shall, without expense to the Association, be bonded by a fidelity bond acceptable both to the Agent and the Association.

FOURTH. Under the personal and direct supervision of one of its principal officers, the Agent shall render services and perform duties as follows:

(a) On the basis of an operating schedule, job standards, and wage rates previously approved by the Association on the recommendation of the Agent, investigate, hire, pay, supervise, and discharge the personnel necessary to be employed in order properly to maintain and operate the Condominium. Such personnel shall in every instance be in the Association's and not in the Agent's employ. Compensation for the services of such employees (as evidenced by certified payrolls) shall be considered as operating expense of the Condominium.

(b) Immediately ascertain the general condition of the property, and if the accommodations there afforded have yet to be occupied for the first time, establish liaison with the general contractor to facilitate the completion by him of such corrective work, if any, as is yet to be done; also, cause an inventory to be taken of all furniture, office equipment, maintenance tools and supplies, including a determination as to the amount of fuel on hand.

(c) Coordinate the plans of owners of family units in the condominiums, hereinafter referred to as "Members" for moving their personal effects into the Condominium or out of it, with a view towards scheduling such movements so that there shall be a minimum of inconvenience to other Members.

(d) Maintain businesslike relations with Members whose service requests shall be received, considered and recorded in systematic fashion in order to show the action taken with respect to each. Complaints of a serious nature shall, after thorough investigation, be reported to the Association with appropriate recommendations. As part of a continuing program, secure full performance by the Members of all items and maintenance for which they are responsible.

(e) Collect all monthly assessments due from Members, all rents due from users of garage spaces and from users or lessees of other non-dwelling facilities in the Condominium; also, all sums due from concessionaires in consequence of the authorized operation of facilities in the Condominium maintained primarily for the benefit of the Members. The Association hereby authorizes the Agent to request, demand, collect, receive, and receipt for any and all charges or rents which may at any time be or become due to the Association and to take such action in the name of the Association by way of legal process or otherwise as may be required for the collection of delinquent monthly assessments. As a standard practice, the Agent shall furnish the Association with an itemized list of all delinquent accounts immediately following the tenth day of each month.

(f) Cause the buildings, appurtenances and grounds of the Condominium to be maintained according to standards acceptable to the Association, including but not limited to interior and exterior cleaning, painting, and decorating, plumbing, steamfitting, carpentry, and such other normal maintenance and repair work as may be necessary, subject to any limitations imposed by the Association in addition to those contained herein. For any one item of repair or replacement the expense incurred shall not exceed the sum of _____ _____ unless specifically authorized by the Association; excepting, however, that emergency repairs, involving manifest danger to life or property, or immediately necessary for the preservation and safety of the property, or for the safety of the Members, or required to avoid the suspension of any necessary service to the Condominium, may be made by the Agent irrespective of the cost limitation imposed by this paragraph. Notwithstanding this authority as to emergency repairs, it is understood and agreed that the Agent will, if at all possible, confer immediately with the Association regarding every such expenditure. The Agent shall not incur liabilities (direct or contingent) which will at any time exceed the aggregate of _____, or any liability maturing more than one year from the creation thereof, without first obtaining the approval of the Association.

(g) Take such action as may be necessary to comply promptly with any and all orders or requirements affecting the premises placed thereon by any federal, state, county, or municipal authority having jurisdiction thereover, and orders of the Board of Fire Underwriters or other similar bodies, subject to the same limitation contained in Paragraph (f) of this Article in connection with the making of repairs and alterations. The Agent, however, shall not take any action under this Paragraph (g) so long as the Association is contesting, or has affirmed its intention to contest any such order or requirement. The Agent shall promptly, and in no event later than 72 hours from the time of their receipt, notify the Association in writing of all such orders and notices of requirements.

(h) Subject to approval by the Association, make contracts for water, electricity, gas, fuel oil, telephone, vermin extermination, and other necessary services or such of them as the Association shall deem advisable. Also, place orders for such equipment, tools, appliances, materials and supplies as are necessary properly to maintain the Condominium. All such contracts and orders shall be made in the name of the Association and shall be subject to the limitations set forth in Paragraph (f) of this Article. When taking bids or issuing purchase orders, the Agent shall act at all times under the direction of the Association, and shall be under a duty to secure for and credit to the latter any discounts, commissions, or rebates obtainable as a result of such purchases.

(i) When authorized by the Association in writing, cause to be placed and kept in force all forms of insurance needed adequately to protect the Association, its members, and mortgagees holding mortgages covering family units, as their respective interests appear (or as required by law), including but not limited to workmen's compensation insurance, public liability insurance, boiler insurance, fire and extended coverage insurance, and burglary and theft insurance. All of the various types of insurance coverage required shall be placed with such companies, in such amounts, and with such beneficial interests appearing therein as shall be acceptable to the Association and to mortgagees holding mortgages covering family units. The Agent shall promptly investigate and make a full written report as to all accidents or claims for damage relating to the management, operation and maintenance of the Condominium, including any damage or destruction to the Condominium, the estimated cost of repair, and shall cooperate and make any and all reports required by any insurance company in connection therewith.

(j) From the funds collected and deposited in the special account hereinafter provided, cause to be disbursed regularly and punctually (1) salaries and any other compensation due and payable to the employees of the Association, and the taxes payable under paragraph (k) of this Article, (2) fire and other property insurance premiums and the amount specified in the Regulatory Agreement for allocation to the Reserve Fund for Replacements and to the General Operating Reserve, and (3) sums otherwise due and payable by the Association as operating expenses authorized to be incurred under the terms of this Agreement, including the Agent's commission. After disbursement in the order herein specified, any balance remaining in the special account may be disbursed or transferred from time to time, but only as specifically directed by the Association in writing, but such balance must be within the limits of the fidelity bond which shall be in an amount equal to the gross monthly collections.

(k) Working in conjunction with an accountant, prepare for execution and filing by the Association all forms, reports, and returns required by law in connection with unemployment insurance, workmen's compensation insurance, disability benefits, Social Security, and other similar taxes now in effect or hereafter imposed, and also requirements relating to the employment of personnel.

(l) Maintain a comprehensive system of office records, books, and accounts in a manner satisfactory to the Association and to the consenting parties, which records shall be subject to examination by their authorized agents at all reasonable hours. As a standard practice, the Agent shall render to the Association by not later than the tenth of each succeeding month a statement of receipts and disbursements as of the end of every month.

(m) On or about _____ and thereafter at least 60 days before the beginning of each new fiscal year, prepare with the assistance of an accountant, if need be, an operating budget setting forth an itemized statement of the anticipated receipts and disbursements for the new fiscal year based upon the then current schedule of monthly assessments, and taking into account the general condition of the Condominium. Each such budget, together with a statement from the Agent outlining a plan of operation and justifying the estimates made in every important particular, shall be submitted to the Association in final draft at least 30 days prior to the commencement of the annual period for which it has been made, and following its adoption by the Association, copies of it shall be made available, upon request, for submission to the consenting party. The budget shall serve as a supporting document for the schedule of monthly assessments proposed for the new fiscal year. It shall also constitute a major control under which the Agent shall operate, and there shall be no substantial variances therefrom, except such as may be sanctioned by the Association. By this is meant that no expenses may be incurred or commitments made by the Agent in connection with the maintenance and operation of the Condominium in excess of the amounts allocated to the various classifications of expense in the approved budget without the prior consent of the Association, except that, if necessary because of an emergency or lack of sufficient time to obtain such prior consent, an overrun may be experienced, provided it is brought promptly to the attention of the Association in writing.

(n) The Agent shall actively handle the renting of any garage spaces or other non-dwelling accommodation, arranging for the execution of such leases or permits as may be required.

(o) It shall be the duty of the Agent at all times during the term of this Agreement to operate and maintain the Condominium according to the highest standards achievable consistent with the overall plan of the Association and the interests of the consenting party. The Agent shall see that all Members are informed with respect to such rules, regulations and notices as may be promulgated by the Association from time to time. The Agent shall be expected to perform such other acts and deeds as are reasonable, necessary and proper in the discharge of its duties under this Agreement.

FIFTH.   Everything done by the Agent under the provisions of Article FOURTH shall be done as Agent of the Association, and all obligations or expenses incurred thereunder shall be for the account, on behalf, and at the expense of the Association, except that the Association shall not be obligated to pay the overhead expenses of the Agent's office. Any payments to be made by the Agent hereunder shall be made out of such sums as are available in the special account of the Association, or as may be provided by the Association. The Agent shall not be obliged to make any advance to or for the account of the Association or to pay any sum, except out of funds held or provided as aforesaid, nor shall the Agent be obliged to incur any liability or obligation for the account of the Association without assurance that the necessary funds for the discharge thereof will be provided.

SIXTH. The Agent shall establish and maintain, in a bank whose deposits are insured by the Federal Deposit Insurance Corporation and in a manner to indicate the custodial nature thereof, a separate bank account as Agent of the Association for the deposit of the monies of the Association, with authority to draw thereon for any payments to be made by the Agent to discharge any liabilities or obligations incurred pursuant to this Agreement, and for the payment of the Agent's fee, all of which payments shall be subject to the limitations in this Agreement.

SEVENTH. The sole compensation which the Agent shall be entitled to receive for all services performed under this Agreement shall be a fee computed and payable monthly in an amount equivalent to _____. (    %) of gross collections, exclusive of all surcharges.

EIGHTH. (a) Unless cancelled pursuant to section (b), (c), or (d) of this Article, this Agreement shall be in effect for a term of _____ from the date of execution, provided that in no event shall it be of any force and effect until there is endorsed hereon the consent of the consenting party.

(b) This Agreement may be terminated by mutual consent of the parties as of the end of any calendar month, but not without prior written notice to the consenting party.

(c) In the event a petition in bankruptcy is filed by or against Agent, or in the event that he shall make an assignment for the benefit of creditors or take advantage of any insolvency act, either party hereto may terminate this Agreement without notice to the other, but prompt advice of such action shall be given to the consenting party.

(d) It is expressly understood and agreed by and between the parties hereto that the Federal Housing Administration shall have the right to terminate this Agreement at the end of any calendar month, with or without cause, on 30 days' written notice to the Association and the Agent of its intention so to do. It is further understood and agreed that no liability shall attach to the Federal Housing Administration in the event of termination of this Agreement pursuant to this section.

(e) Upon termination, the contracting parties shall account to each other with respect to all matters outstanding as of the date of termination, and the Association shall furnish the Agent security, satisfactory to the Agent, against any outstanding obligations or liabilities which the Agent may have incurred hereunder.

NINTH. As used in this Agreement:

(a) The term "consenting party" shall mean the Federal Housing Administration acting through its Commissioner or his duly authorized representatives.

(b) The term "assessments" shall mean those monthly rates established by the Association which the Members are bound to pay as their share of the common expenses under the Master Plan of Apartment Ownership.

(c) The term "gross collections" shall mean all amounts actually collected by the Agent, either as assessments or as rents.

(d) The term "Association" as used herein shall mean an association, cooperative or corporation consisting of all of the owners of family units in the Condominium organized and existing under state law for the purpose of administering the Condominium established by the Plan of Apartment Ownership.

TENTH. (a) This Agreement, which is made subject and subordinate to all rights of the Federal Housing Administration as insurer of mortgages on family units in the Condominium, shall inure to the benefit of and constitute a binding obligation upon the contracting parties, their respective successors and assigns; and to the extent that it confers rights, privileges, and benefits upon the consenting party, the same shall be deemed to inure to its benefit, but without liability, in the same manner and with the same force and effect as though the Federal Housing Administration was a signatory to this Agreement.

(b) This Agreement shall constitute the entire Agreement between the contracting parties, and no variance or modification thereof shall be valid and enforceable, except by supplemental agreement in writing, executed and approved in the same manner as this Agreement.

(c) For the convenience of the parties, this Agreement has been executed in several counterparts, which are in all respects similar and each of which shall be deemed to be complete in itself so that any one may be introduced in evidence or used for any other purpose without the production of the other counterparts. Immediately following endorsement of the consenting parties, counterparts will be furnished to the consenting parties so that each may be advised of the rights, privileges, and benefits which this Agreement confers.

IN WITNESS WHEREOF, the parties hereto have executed this Agreement the day and year first above written.

---------------------------------------------------
*(Association)*

By ---------------------------------------------------

---------------------------------------------------
*(Agent)*

By ---------------------------------------------------

The Federal Housing Administration hereby consents to the foregoing Management Agreement and the Managing Agent designated therein.

Date: ---------------------------     ---------------------------------------------------
*(Federal Housing Commissioner)*

By ---------------------------------------------------
*(Authorized Agent)*

FORM 35

## LETTER OF CREDIT

The _____ National Bank of _____
Circular Letter of Credit
No. _____.

_____ U.S.A., _____ day of _____.

Gentlemen: We beg to introduce to you and commend to your courtesies _____, a specimen of whose signature appears in the accompanying list of correspondents.

Kindly provide _____, with such funds as may be required up to an aggregate amount of U.S. _____ _____ dollars (or the equivalent of same at current market rates for checks on New York) against _____ drafts drawn at sight on the _____ Bank of England, Ltd., London, the _____ Trust Company of New York, Paris, France.

We engage that such drafts negotiated by you before the _____ day of _____ will be duly honored.

The amount of each payment must be indorsed on this letter and each draft must bear the clause, "Drawn under letter of credit No. _____" of the _____ National Bank of _____, dated _____ day of _____ 19_____. The letter must be attached to the last draft drawn. We remain, dear sirs,

Yours faithfully,

_____
Vice-President

_____
Cashier

FORM 36

## MORTGAGE FORM

[Note: *The following form, it is believed, will supply all the information required to draft a mortgage for use anywhere in the United States or Canada. For forms of acknowledgments to be appended to the mortgages, see* Acknowledgments. *For forms of chattel mortgages, see* Chattel Mortgage.]

This indenture, made the _____ day of _____ A.D., 19_____, between _____ of the first part, and _____ of the second part: Whereas, the said _____ in and by his certain obligation of writing obligatory under his hand and seal duly executed, and bearing even date herewith, stands bound unto the said party of the second part, in the sum of _____ dollars conditioned for the payment of _____ dollars _____ year after the date thereof with interest at the rate of _____ per centum per annum from said date _____ without any fraud or further delay, as in and by them said recited obligation and condition thereof, relation to the same being had, may more fully and at large appear.

Now this indenture, witnesseth, that the said party of the first part, as well for and in consideration of the aforesaid debt or sum of _____ dollars and for the better securing the payment thereof, unto the said party of the second part, his executors, administrators and assigns, in discharge of the said obligation above recited, as for and in consideration of the further sum of one dollar in specie, well and truly paid to the said party of the first part, by the said party of the second part, at and before the sealing and delivery hereof, the receipt of which one dollar is hereby acknowledged has granted, bargained, sold, released and confirmed, and by these presents does grant, bargain, sell, release and confirm unto the said party of the second part, his heirs and assigns, all the premises. [*Describe the premises.*]

Together with all and singular, the buildings, improvements, woods, ways, rights, liberties, privileges, hereditaments and appurtenances, to the same belonging, or in anywise appertaining and the reversion and reversions, remainder and remainders, rents, issues and profits thereof: To have and to hold the said hereditaments and premises above granted, or intended so to be, with the appurtenances, unto the said party of the second part, his heirs and assigns forever.

Provided, however, and it is expressly agreed, that if at any time default shall be made in the payment of any installment of principal or interest for the space of _____ days after the same becomes due by the terms hereof, then and in such case, the whole principal debt and interest aforesaid, shall,

at the option of the said party of the second part, his executors or assigns, become due and payable immediately; and
the said party of the second part may at once proceed to collect the same by suit upon said obligation, or *scire facias*
hereon, any law, usage or custom, or anything herein contained to the contrary notwithstanding, and in such suit, or
upon such *scire facias,* judgment shall be recovered for the
said principal sum, and all interest then due, together with
_____ per cent on the whole amount thereof as attorney's
commission.

Provided always, nevertheless, that if the said _____
heirs, executors, administrators or assigns, do and shall well
and truly pay or cause to be paid unto the said party of the
second part, his executors, administrators or assigns, the
aforesaid debt or sum of _____ on the day and time
hereinbefore mentioned and appointed for the payment
thereof, together with lawful interest for the same, in like
money, in the way and manner hereinbefore specified therefor, without any fraud or further delay, and without any deduction, defalcation or abatement to be made, for or in respect of any taxes, charges or assessments whatsoever, that
then and from thenceforth, as well this present indenture, and
the estate hereby granted, as the said obligation above recited, shall cease, determine and become absolutely null and
void, to all intents and purposes, anything hereinbefore contained to the contrary thereof in anywise notwithstanding.

Witness our hands and seals.

_____ (Seal)

_____ (Seal)

_____ (Seal)

Test:

_____

FORM 37

### OPTION TO BUY REAL ESTATE

In consideration of the sum of Two hundred dollars
($200.00), receipt of which is hereby acknowledged, I hereby

agree to give John Jones the option to buy the following described real estate in the City of Chicago, State of Illinois, to wit: 2400 Martingale Street.

Said John Jones shall have the right to close this option at any time within thirty days from date, and I agree to execute to him or any person named by him, a good warranty deed to said real estate, and to furnish therefor an abstract of title showing said title to be perfect, upon demand therefor. Upon execution of said deed and abstract, I shall be paid the sum of Six thousand dollars ($6,000.00) as full payment of the purchase price of said real estate. I further agree neither to sell nor encumber said real estate during said term, and should I do so I hereby agree to pay the sum of Five hundred dollars ($500.00) to said John Jones as liquidated damages. Likewise, should I fail, neglect or refuse to make said deed, or to furnish said abstract as above provided, I hereby agree to pay to him as liquidated damages the sum of Five hundred dollars ($500.00). I waive all claims for damages for failure to close this option.

Dated October 10, 19_____.

--------------------------------------------------

(Seal)  /s/  John Doe

FORM 38

## NOTICE OF ELECTION TO EXERCISE OPTION

You are hereby notified that I elect to exercise my option to purchase 2400 Martingale Street, Chicago, Illinois, upon the terms and conditions specified in the agreement dated October 10, 19_____.

--------------------------------------------------

/s/  John Jones

FORM 39

## SIMPLE PARTNERSHIP AGREEMENT

This agreement made this 5 day of October, 19_____, by and between Jack Smith of the one part and of John Brown of the other part, witnesseth as follows: that the said parties hereby agree to become partners in the business of "wholesale hardware" under the firm name of Smith, Brown and Company, for the term of five years from the date hereof, upon the terms and conditions hereinafter stated, to wit:

1. That the business shall be carried on at number 510 Patton Avenue, in the City of Baltimore, State of Maryland, or at any other place that may hereafter be mutually agreed upon for that purpose.

2. That proper books of account shall be kept, and therein shall be duly entered, from time to time, all dealings, transactions, matters and things whatsoever in or relating to the said business; and each party shall have full and free access thereto at all times, but shall not remove the same from the premises.

3. That the capital requisite for carrying on the said business shall be advanced by the said partners in equal parts, and the said capital, and all such stock, implements and utensils in trade, purchased out of the partnership funds, as well as the gains and profits of the said business, shall belong to the said parties in equal parts.

4. That each party shall be at full liberty to draw three hundred dollars monthly for his own private use, on account, but not in excess of his presumptive share of the profits, so long as the said business shall be found profitable, and the capital advanced as aforesaid shall remain unfinished.

5. That neither party shall become bail or surety for any other person; nor lend, spend, give or make away with any part of the partnership property; or draw or accept any bill, note, or other security in the name of the said firm, except in due course of the said partnership business.

6. That an account of the stock, implements and utensils belonging to the said business, and of the book debts and capital shall be taken and a statement of the affairs of the said partnership be made yearly, to be computed from the date hereof, when the sums drawn by each party during the preceding year shall be charged to his share of the profits of the said business; but if, at the end of any one year of the said partnership, it shall be found to be unprofitable, the said partnership shall thereupon be dissolved, unless it shall be occasioned by some unavoidable loss or accidental circumstances.

7. That each party shall sign duplicate copies of each of such statement of affairs, and shall retain one of them for his own use; and another copy thereof shall be written in one of the partnership books, and likewise signed by each of them; such accounts shall not again be opened, unless some manifest error shall be discovered in either of them, within three months thereafter, and then so far only as respects the correcting of such error; and every such statement of affairs shall, in all other respects, be conclusive evidence between and binding on said parties.

8. That at the termination or expiration of the said partnership, by death or otherwise, a valuation and similar account of the stock, effects and capital, and good will, if any, of the said firm, shall be taken, stated, copied and signed in like manner and become equally conclusive; and the balance of such account then found to exist shall belong to the said parties in equal moieties and be realized and divided accordingly, and thereupon they shall execute mutual releases.

9. That all disputes and differences, if any, which shall arise between the said parties, shall be referred to and decided by two indifferent, competent persons in or well acquainted with the wholesale hardware business, one to be chosen by either party, or by an umpire to be chosen by the referees in the usual course in such or similar cases; and their or his decision shall, in all respects, be final and conclusive on both the said parties, and shall be given in writing within fifteen days next after such submission or within such further time, not exceeding thirty days, as they or he shall require.

10. That either party may terminate the partnership hereby created on breach of this agreement by the other of them, on giving unto the other of them six calendar months' notice thereof in writing.

Witness our hands and seal this fifth day of October, 19___.

(Seal) *Jack Smith*
Jack Smith

(Seal) *John Brown*
John Brown

Harry Green
**Witness**

Form 40

## ASSIGNMENT OF INTEREST IN PATENT

[Note: *To protect himself, the person to whom the patent is assigned should have it recorded in the Patent Office within three months from the date of the agreement.*]

Whereas I, Harry Green, of New York City, did obtain letters patent of the United States for an improvement in the mechanism of a power mower, which letters patent are numbered _____ and bear date the 10 day of October, 19_____, and whereas I am now the sole owner of said patent and of all rights under the same, and whereas Jack Smith of New York City is desirous of acquiring the entire interest in the same, now therefore to all whom it may concern, be it known that for and in consideration of the sum of five thousand dollars to me in hand paid, the receipt of which is hereby acknowledged, I, the said Harry Green, inventor, have sold, assigned and transferred, and by these presents do sell, assign and transfer unto the said Jack Smith, purchaser, the whole right, title, and interest in and to the said improvement in the power mower, and in and to the letters patent therefor aforesaid; the same to be held and enjoyed by the said Jack Smith for his own use and behoof, and for the use and behoof of his legal representatives, to the full end of the term for which said letters patent are or may be granted, as fully and entirely as the same would have been held and enjoyed by me had this assignment and sale not been made.

In testimony whereof I have hereunto set my hand and seal this 10 day of December, 19_____, in the presence of the two witnesses whose signatures appear below.

/s/ *Harry Green*
----------------------------------------------
                                  Harry Green

/s/ James Hawkins
----------------------------------------
            Witness

/s/ John Smith
----------------------------------------
            Witness

FORM 41

## PROMISSORY NOTE

Negotiable Note
Baltimore, _____, 19_____.

$200.00

Sixty days after date I promise to pay to the order of Harry Green two hundred dollars, without defalcation for value received.

_____
Jack Smith

FORM 42

## GENERAL POWER OF ATTORNEY

Know all Men by These Presents:

I, Richard Roe, residing in the City of Lexington, Ky., by these presents hereby make, constitute and appoint Henry Green, also of Lexington, Ky., my true and lawful attorney in fact for and in my name, place and stead, to [*here insert the power intended to be conferred, which should be stated in clear and precise language, as for example, to purchase a 19_____ Oldsmobile Station Wagon to cost not more than twelve hundred dollars*]

I hereby grant and give unto my said attorney in fact full authority and power to do and perform any and all other acts necessary or incident to the performance and execution of the powers herein expressly granted, with power to do and perform all acts authorized hereby, as fully to all intents and purposes as the grantor might or could do if personally present, with full power of substitution.

In testimony whereof I have set my hand and seal this fifth day of October, 19_____.

Richard Roe
_____
Grantor

Wilson Smith
_____
Witness

Archie Black
_____
Witness

FORM 43

## QUITCLAIM DEED

Know all men by these presents, that A.B.C., of the Borough of _____, in the County of _____, and State of _____, for and in consideration of the sum of _____ dollars, to me in hand paid, or secured to be paid, by D.E., of _____, and state aforesaid, the receipt whereof is hereby acknowledged, have remised, released, and quitclaimed, and by these presents do _____ remise, release, and quitclaim, unto the said D.E., and to his heirs and assigns, forever, all that, &c., [*here describe the premises*]. Together with all and singular the hereditaments and appurtenances thereunto belonging or in anywise appertaining, and the reversions, remainders, rents, issues, and profits thereof; and all the estate, right, title, interest, claim, or demand whatsoever of me, the said A.B.C., either in law or equity, of, in, and to the above-bargained premises. To have and to hold the same to the said D.E., and to his heirs and assigns, forever.

In witness whereof, I have hereunto set my hand and seal, this _____ day of _____, A.D., 19_____.

_____ (Seal)

Signed, sealed and delivered in the presence of

_____

_____

FORM 44

## RELEASE

[Note: *Never sign a release without first consulting an attorney.*]

Know all Men by These Presents:
That I, Jack Smith, do hereby remise, release and forever

discharge Frank Green, his heirs, executors and administrators of and from all and all manner of actions and causes of action, suits, debts, dues, accounts, bonds, covenants, contracts, agreements, judgments, claims and demands whatsoever in law or equity, which against the said Frank Green I ever had, now have, or which my heirs, executors, administrators or assigns, or any of them, hereafter can, shall, or may have, for or by reason of any cause, matter or thing whatsoever, from the beginning of the world to the date of these presents.

In Witness Whereof, I have hereunto set my hand and seal the 1 day of October, 19_____.

-----------------------------------------------------------------

Jack Smith

FORM 45

## BILL OF SALE OF RESTAURANT

This agreement witnesseth that Frank White, party of the first part, has this day sold, and does hereby sell and transfer to Jack Smith, party of the second part, the following described personal property located at 1010 East Bancroft Street, Baltimore, Maryland, to wit: [*here itemize completely the personal property sold*] and all fixtures and appurtenances belonging to and forming a part of what is known as Frank's Restaurant, located at the above address, including the good will of the first party thereto, for and in consideration of the sum of six thousand and three hundred dollars, payable as follows: three thousand dollars cash, the receipt of which is hereby acknowledged, and the balance to be evidenced by a promissory note of even date herewith in the sum of three thousand three hundred dollars, secured by a mortgage on said personal property. Said note payable one hundred dollars per month until the full amount of said note is paid, with interest at the rate of six per cent after maturity.

Immediate possession to be given said second party.

It is hereby understood and agreed that the said first party hereby conveys all his right, title and interest in and to the groceries and provisions, and the said second party is to assume the payment of any indebtedness thereon if there be any indebtedness thereon remaining unpaid on said goods taken and no more. The said first party warrants the title to the fixtures.

/s/ Frank White
-------------------------------------------------
                                   Vendor

/s/ John Jones
-------------------------------------
            Witness

Accepted this 4th day of October, 19_____.

/s/ Jack Smith
-------------------------------------------------
                                   Buyer

FORM 46

## CONDITIONAL SALES AGREEMENT

This agreement, made this first day of October, 19_____, between Richard Roe, called the vendor, and John Doe, called the vendee or buyer, witnesseth:

Whereas the vendor has this day delivered to and hereby agrees to sell to the vendee, for the sum of three hundred dollars, upon the conditions hereinafter set forth, the following personal property [*describe exactly the personal property to be sold*]

The vendee agreeing to and does receive said property, and to pay the vendor therefor, at his place of business said amount as follows, to wit:

The sum of one hundred dollars upon the execution hereof and the sum of twenty-five dollars on the first day of each and every week hereafter until the whole sum first above mentioned, or any judgment obtained therefor, is fully paid, when title to said property shall vest in the vendee; but until then title shall remain in the vendor.

It is further agreed that in the event of failure by the vendee to pay any installment, as it becomes due, or in case the vendee removes the property from his present residence or place of business, without the written consent of the vendor, or in case the property is destroyed in any manner, the whole of the said sum shall immediately become due, and the vendor may take possession of such property with or without legal process and sell the same according to law, in which case it is expressly understood and agreed the vendor may retain all installments previously paid as and for compensation for the use of said property by the vendee, and the vendee will pay any deficiency arising on account thereof together with the expense of retaking and sale thereof.

No verbal contract or agreement contrary to any of the terms conditioned in the foregoing contract has been made.

In witness whereof we have set our hands.

/s/  Richard Roe
-------------------------------------------------
                              Vendor

/s/  John Smith
-------------------------------------
                Witness

/s/  John Doe
-------------------------------------------------
                              Vendee

FORM 47

## CONTRACT FOR THE SALE OF A GROWING

## CROP OF FRUIT

This agreement made this 2 day of September, 19......, between Richard Roe, vendor, and Jack Smith, purchaser, witnesseth:

It is agreed that the vendor will sell and the purchaser will buy all that crop of apples growing on the trees of the vendor's orchard, situate in Worcester County, Georgia, for the sum of fifteen hundred dollars, of which five hundred dollars shall be paid before any part of the crop is gathered, and the purchaser shall not be at liberty, without the consent of the vendor, to remove from the premises any part of the crop not paid for until the purchase price thereof is paid.

The fruit shall be gathered when suffcently mature for gathering, and the purchaser and his workmen shall have, for the purpose of gathering and taking the fruit, full liberty to enter upon the said orchard and trees with ladders and other necessary appliances.

/s/ Richard Roe
---------------------------------------------
Vendor

/s/ Jack Smith
---------------------------------------------
Purchaser

/s/ John Doe
-----------------------------------
Witness

FORM 48

## CONTRACT FOR THE SALE OF A HOUSE

[Note: *The following agreement is merely a contract whereby one party agrees to buy and the other to sell a house. It is not a deed which represents the completed transaction.*]

This agreement, made this _____ day of _____ 19_____, between Richard Roe, hereinafter called the vendor or seller, of the one part, and Jack Smith, hereinafter called the purchaser, of the other part, witnesseth:

That the said Richard Roe, vendor, hereby agrees to sell to the purchaser, who agrees to purchase, for the sum of six thousand dollars, the fee simple, in possession, free from all incumbrances, of and in all that dwelling house and land belonging thereto situate on 25 Arch Avenue, Yonkers, New York, heretofore in the occupation of said vendor, all which said premises are delineated on a plan here to be annexed and signed by the parties hereto; together with all the rights, easements and appurtenances thereto belonging; which said premises are sold and purchased upon and subject to the following terms and conditions:

1. That the purchaser shall take, and on the completion of the purchase pay for, the fixtures and fittings in the said dwelling house and buildings, and specified in the schedule hereto annexed, at the valuation therein mentioned.

2. That on payment of the purchase money, and the value of said fixtures and fittings, the vendor shall execute a proper

conveyance of the property according to the stipulations herein contained, which conveyance shall be prepared by and at the expense of the vendor, and sent to the said purchaser for approval fifteen days prior to _____, 19_____.

3. That the purchaser shall pay to the said vendor, upon the execution of these presents, a deposit of five hundred dollars on and in part of his purchase-money, and pay him the residue thereof on the _____ day of _____, 19_____, when the purchase shall be completed.

4. That if from any cause whatever, the purchase shall be delayed beyond _____, 19_____, the purchaser shall thenceforth be entitled to the rents and profits of the property and shall pay interest at the rate of 6 per cent per annum on the purchase-money till the completion of the purchase.

5. That if any obstacle or difficulty shall arise in respect to the title, the completion of the purchase, or otherwise, the vendor shall be at full liberty, at any time, to abandon this contract on returning the deposit money only to the purchaser.

6. That if the purchaser shall refuse or neglect to complete his purchase at the time hereby appointed, his deposit money shall be absolutely forfeited to the vendor, who shall be at full liberty, at any time afterward, to resell the property, either by public aution or private contract; and the deficiency, if any, occasioned thereby, together with all losses, damages and expenses of and attending the same, shall be borne and paid by the purchaser, but any increase in the price obtained at such sale shall belong to the vendor.

7. That time in all respects shall be of the essence of this contract.

In witness whereof we have hereunder set our hands and seals.

Jack Smith
--------------------------------------------
                              Purchaser

Richard Roe
--------------------------------------------
                              Vendor or Seller

Harry Black
------------------------------------
          Witness

FORM 49

## FORMS OF BILLS OF SALE

[Note: *If the bill of sale is to be recorded, add a proper acknowledgment, for forms of which see* Acknowledgment.]

### Short Form

Know all men by these presents, that I, Jack Smith, of _____ in consideration of one hundred dollars, to me paid by Harry Green, of the same place, have bargained and sold to said Harry Green, the following goods and chattels, to wit: one gray horse, one wagon, and three cows.

Witness my hand seal, this fifth day of _____, A.D., 19_____.

Jack Smith

Signed, sealed and delivered in presence of

A.B.

C.D.

[*If the horse is to be warranted the following may be inserted.*]

And I do hereby warrant the said horse to be sound in every respect, to be free from vice, well broken, kind and gentle in single and in double harness, and under saddle; and I do covenant for myself, my heirs, executors and administrators, with the said Harry Green, to warrant and defend the sale of the said horse unto the said Harry Green, his executors, administrators, and assigns, from and against all and every person or persons, whomsoever lawfully claiming, or to claim the same.

### General Form

Know all men by these presents, that _____ of _____ in the county of _____ and state of _____ part _____ of the first part, for and in consideration of the sum of _____ dollars, to _____ in hand paid by _____ of

_____, part _____ of the second part, the
receipt of which is hereby acknowledged, do _____ hereby
grant, bargain and sell unto the said part _____ of the second part, _____ heirs and assigns, the following goods and
chattels, to wit: [*state what and describe it*]

To have and to hold, all and singular, the said _____
_____ unto the said part _____ of the second part, _____
heirs and assigns forever. And the said part _____ of the
first part, for _____ heirs, executors and administrators, do
_____ hereby covenant to and with the said part _____
of the second part, and _____ assigns, that _____
lawfully possessed of the same goods and chattels as of
_____ own property, that the same are free from all encumbrances, and that _____ will warrant and defend
the same to the said part _____ of the second part, and
_____ assigns, against the lawful claims and demands
of all persons.

In witness whereof, the said part _____ of the first
part ha___ hereunto set _____ hand _____ and seal _____
this _____ day of _____ A.D., 19_____.

Signed, sealed and delivered in presence of

_____ (Seal)

_____ (Seal)

Form 50

AGREEMENT FOR SALE OF LEASE, FIXTURES, AND GOOD
WILL OF BUSINESS

Agreement entered into this 1 day of March, 19_____, between Jack Smith, hereinafter called the vendor, for himself,
his heirs, executors and administrators, of the one part, and
Harry Green, hereinafter called the purchaser, for himself,
his heirs, executors and administrators, of the other part.

1. The said vendor doth hereby agree with the said purchaser to sell and assign unto him the said purchaser, all
the workshop, warehouses, buildings and premises, situate,
4605 Riverside Road, whereon the said vendor has for several
years past carried on the trade or business of Toy Manufacturer, and which he now holds for the residue of a term of

five years, under an indenture of lease dated the 1 day of March, 19_____, made between Richard Roe as lessor, of the one part and the said vendor as lessee, of the other part; as also all the fixtures, engines, machinery, utensils, tools and implements used or employed in carrying on the said trade or business, together with the said business and the good will of the same.

2. In consideration whereof, the said purchaser doth hereby agree with the said vendor to purchase the residue of the said term in the said premises, as also the said fixtures, engines, machinery, utensils and implements used or employed in carrying on the said trade or business in or upon the said premises, together with the said business, and the good will thereof, upon the terms and conditions hereafter mentioned.

3. It is mutually declared and agreed by and between the said vendor and purchaser that if the attorney of the said purchaser shall approve of the title of the said vendor the said vendor will, on the 15 day of April next, at the cost of the said purchaser, by proper deed of assignment, assign the said lease, workshop, warehouses, buildings, and premises, with all usual and proper covenants, unto the said purchaser, his executors, administrators, and assigns, for all the residue of the said term of five years; and also all the fixtures, engines, machinery, utensils, tools and implements employed in carrying on the said trade or business in or upon the said premises; and which said deed of assignment, in addition to the usual and ordinary covenants, shall also contain a covenant on the part of the said vendor that he will from time to time and at all times hereafter, recommend the said purchaser to all the customers of him the said vendor, and use his utmost endeavors to induce them to deal with the said purchaser; and that the said vendor shall not, at any time hereafter, either directly or indirectly, alone or in partnership with any other person or persons whomsoever, carry on the trade or business of a Toy Manufacturer at Riverside Road, or any other place or places within the distance of twenty miles thereof.

4. Immediately upon the execution of the said deed of assignment, the said purchaser shall pay unto the said vendor the sum of $10,000.00 as for the purchase of the residue of the said term in the said workshop, warehouse, buildings, and

premises, and for the purchase of the said trade or business, and the good will thereof. Also, within the space of three months, a valuation shall be made and taken of the said fixtures, engines, machinery, utensils, tools and implements, by two indifferent persons, one to be chosen by the said vendor, and the other to be chosen by the said purchaser, who, previously to their entering on their reference, shall choose an umpire between them, whose decision, in case the said referees shall not agree, shall be binding on both parties; and in case either of the said parties shall refuse to name a referee within seven days after request by the other party, then the referee named by the other party may proceed along, and his award shall be conclusive on both parties.

5. The said purchaser shall pay or secure unto the said vendor the amount of such valuation by four equal installments, at three, six, nine and twelve calendar months. Further, the said vendor shall remain in the possession of all and singular the said premises which are hereby agreed to be assigned, with full and free liberty to have, hold, use and enjoy the same in the same manner as heretofore, up to the 1 day of April next; and shall pay and discharge all rents, rates, taxes and other outgoings up to that period, on which day the possession of all the said premises shall be delivered to the said purchaser.

In witness whereof we have set down our signatures.

---------------------------------------------------------------
Purchaser

---------------------------------------------------------------
Vendor

---------------------------------------------------
Witness

FORM 51

RETAIL INSTALLMENT SALES AGREEMENT Acct. No. _____
UNDER MARYLAND ACTS OF 1941, CHAPTER 851
(CONDITIONAL SALES CONTRACT)

AGREEMENT, made this _____ day of _____ 19_____,
between _____
whose place of residence is _____
and whose post office address is _____

Maryland, herein called "Seller," and _____
_____ whose place of residence is _____
_____ and whose post office address is _____
_____ Maryland, herein called "Buyer."

WITNESSETH that Seller hereby sells to Buyer, and the latter buys from the former, the merchandise hereinafter set forth at the price and on the terms hereinafter specified.

### Description of Goods Purchased

----------------------------------------------------------------
----------------------------------------------------------------
----------------------------------------------------------------
----------------------------------------------------------------

The additional terms of this contract are:—

   1. The cash price of the merchandise sold is   $_____

   2. The charge for _____ is   $_____
     (Indicate delivery, installation, repair and other service items for which additional charge is made)

   3. The total cash price is                $_____
     (The sum of Items 1 and 2)

   4. The amount of buyer's down payment is, in cash      $_____
     and in merchandise as follows:
                     valued at   $_____   $_____
     (The down payment shall be forfeited entirely if the Buyer refuses to accept delivery of the merchandise sold to the Buyer under this contract; the Buyer being entitled to delivery of such merchandise before making further payments)

   5. The unpaid balance of the cash price is   $_____
     (Item 3 less Item 4)

   6. The premium on the policy, if any, insuring this merchandise against loss by fire, etc. is   $_____
     (The amount of this insurance, if any, is the same amount as to the total cash price owing by the Buyer, it expires on the date upon which the final installment is payable, as hereinafter indicated, and is payable jointly to the Buyer and the Seller)

7. Notary fees and recording charges are      $.............

8. The principal balance owed is      $.............

(The sum of Items 8 and 9)

It is agreed that this balance shall be payable by Buyer to Seller in ............ consecutive installments of $............. each and finally $............. . These installments shall be payable on the ............ day of every week/month after the date upon which this contract is signed by the Buyer. It is agreed that Seller, or its assigns, may also collect from the Buyer a delinquency and collection charge for default in the payment of this contract or any installment thereof, where such default has continued for a period of ten days; such charge equalling five per cent of the amount of the installments in default or the sum of five dollars, whichever is the lesser. In addition to such delinquency and collection charge, the Buyer shall be obligated to pay the attorney's fees, not exceeding fifteen per cent of the amount due and payable under this contract, where this contract is referred to an attorney, not a salaried employee of the holder of this contract, for collection, plus the court costs.

Title and ownership of said merchandise is to remain in Seller, or its assigns, until all of the payments herein required to be made by Buyer have been made, whereupon full ownership shall pass to Buyer. Should Buyer fail to make any of said payments at the time when due, as herein set forth, or to comply with any of the other agreements herein set forth, Buyer agrees to return said merchandise to Seller, or its assigns, who may repossess said merchandise if not returned.

The Buyer agrees to take good care of said merchandise and to be responsible for its loss by theft, fire or other casualty, and to keep the same at _____, Maryland. The Buyer further agrees that he will not change the place of keeping said merchandise without first securing the assent of the Seller, in writing.

No other collateral security has been taken by Seller from Buyer for the performance of Buyer's obligations.

No statement or representation shall be binding on the Seller unless it be in writing and signed by the Seller or the Seller's authorized agent.

The Seller reserves the right to cancel this contract before said merchandise has been delivered to the Buyer; where-upon any deposit or down payment made on account of it shall be returned to the Buyer.

Subsequent purchases may be added to this contract by mutual agreement, upon terms acceptable to the Buyer and the Seller.

The term "Seller" and the term "Buyer," as used through-out this contract, include the plural number when more than one.

## Notice to Buyer

1. You are entitled to a copy of this agreement at the time you sign it.
2. Under the State Law regulating installment sales, you have certain rights, among others:
   (1) to pay off the full amount due in advance and obtain a partial rebate of the finance charge;
   (2) to redeem the property if repossessed for a default;
   (3) to require, under certain conditions, a resale of the property if repossessed.

---------------------------------, 19--------
Date of Signing by Buyer

-----------------------------------------------

-----------------------------------------------

Buyer's Signature

-----------------------------, 19--------
Date of Signing by Seller

-----------------------------------------------

By -----------------------------------------------.

Seller's Signature

Buyer hereby acknowledges delivery to Buyer this ----------
day of ------------------, 19--------, of a copy of this agreement signed by Seller.

-----------------------------------------------

-----------------------------------------------

Buyer's Signature

Witness:

-----------------------------------------------

## Landlord's Waiver

The undersigned landlord of the premises known as _____ in _____, Maryland, hereby waives, renounces, relinquishes and releases any or all rights of distraint such landlord may now or hereafter have, in respect of the merchandise sold to the Buyer under the foregoing contract, until the title to such merchandise becomes vested in the Buyer; this being a condition precedent to the execution of such contract and the delivery of such merchandise by the Seller.

_____

By _____
Landlord's Signature

FORM 52

## RECEIPT FOR PAYMENT

Baltimore, Md., _____ 19_____.

Received of _____ the sum of $_____
Buyer

being a payment or deposit made by the Buyer on account of the purchase of goods this day selected by the Buyer and proposed to be itemized and incorporated in a prospective conditional or installment sales agreement.

If the Buyer has signed such agreement, but has not received an exact copy of it signed by the Seller within fifteen days after the date of the Buyer's signature, then such agreement shall be void without any action by the Buyer, and the Seller shall immediately refund to the Buyer all payments and deposits theretofore made; or

Until the Buyer signs such agreement and receives a copy of it signed by the Seller, the Buyer has an unconditional right to cancel such agreement and to receive the immediate refund of all payments and deposits made on account of, or in contemplation of it. A request for such refund shall operate to cancel such agreement.

This receipt is non-negotiable and non-transferable.

_____

FORM 53

## PETITION AND STATEMENT FOR AN INDIVIDUAL APPLYING FOR A TRADEMARK, INCLUDING OATH OF INDIVIDUAL MAKING APPLICATION

To the Commissioner of Patents:

Richard Roe, a citizen of the United States of America, residing at New York City in the State of New York, and doing business at 180 Madison Avenue, has adopted and used the trademark shown in the accompanying drawing for canned fruits and vegetables in Class _____, food and ingredients of foods, and presents herewith _____ specimens or facsimiles showing the trademark as actually used by applicant upon the goods, and requests that the same be registered in the United States Patent Office in accordance with the Act of _____ day of _____, 19_____, as amended. The trademark has been continuously used and applied to said goods in applicant's business since March 4, 19_____. The trademark is applied or affixed to the goods, or to the package containing the same, by placing thereon a printed label on which the trademark is shown.

/s/ Richard Roe
-----------------------------------------
Applicant's full signature

State of New York
City of New York

Richard Roe, being duly sworn, deposes and says that he is the applicant named in the foregoing statement, that he believes the foregoing statement is true; that he believes himself to be the owner of the trademark sought to be registered; that no other person, firm, corporation or association, to the best of his knowledge and belief, has the right to use said trademark in the United States, either in the identical form or in any such near resemblance thereto as might be calculated to deceive; that said trademark is used by the United States and foreign nations or Indian Tribes; that the description and drawing presented truly represent the trademark sought to be registered; that the specimens (or facsimiles) show the trademark as actually used upon the goods.

/s/ Richard Roe
-----------------------------------------
Full signature of applicant

FORM 54

## SEARCH WARRANT

State of Maryland, City of Baltimore:

To any Sheriff of said City:

Whereas complaint has been made before the subscribed, a justice of the peace for said City, upon oath of Richard Roe, that the following goods and chattels of him, said Richard Roe, namely one 19_____ Oldsmobile stationwagon, mist green, Md. license 46-284, was, on the 10th day of October, 19_____, feloniously stolen, taken and carried away, at the City aforesaid, and that he has just and reasonable cause to suspect and believe and does suspect and believe, that said goods and chattels, or a part thereof, are concealed in garage at 2406 Ridge Avenue in said City: You are, therefore, commanded forthwith to make diligent search in said described place for said goods and chattels, and if the same or any part thereof be found, to secure them and bring the person or persons in whose custody they are found before me or some other justice of the peace for said County, to be dealt with according to law; and have you there this writ.

Dated this 12th day of October, 19_____.

-------------------------------------------------
Justice of the Peace

FORM 55

## SEPARATION AGREEMENT, ALLOWING THE WIFE AN ANNUITY DURING THEIR JOINT LIVES

[Note: *To be binding, this agreement must relate to a separation that has already taken place, or is to take place immediately. If it relates to a separation to take place some time in the future, the agreement is void as against public policy.*]

This agreement made this 30th day of October, 19_____, by and between Richard Roe, husband, party of the first part, and Mary Roe, wife, party of the second part, witnesseth:

Whereas unhappy differences have arisen between the said husband and wife, by reason of which they have agreed to live separate and apart from each other for the future, and to enter into the following agreement contained herein, as follows:

1. It shall be lawful for the said wife, at all times hereafter, to live separate and apart from the said husband, and free from his marital control and authority, as if she were sole and unmarried, and to reside from time to time at such place as she may deem proper, without any interference whatever on the part of the said husband.

2. Neither of them, the said husband and wife, shall molest the other of them, nor compel, nor endeavor to compel, the other of them to cohabit or dwell with him or her by any legal proceeding for restitution of conjugal rights, or otherwise howsoever.

3. Neither of them, the said husband and wife, shall take any proceedings against the other of them to obtain a divorce or judicial separation in respect of any misconduct which has heretofore taken place, or is alleged to have taken place, on the part of the other of them.

4. The husband shall, during the joint lives of himself and the said wife, pay to her, the said wife, the sum of $6,000.00 per annum as her separate estate, but so that she shall not have power to anticipate the same, in quarterly payments on the quarter days, the first payment to be made November 15, 19_____.

5. All the wearing apparel and personal ornaments of the said wife, and all movable personal property belonging to the said wife, now in her possession, shall belong to the said wife as her separate estate, independently of the said husband. All the property of the said wife, both real and personal now held by her, or which shall hereafter come to her, shall be and remain her sole and separate property, free from all rights of the said husband, with full power to her to convey, assign, or deal with her said property.

6. On the death of the said wife in the lifetime of the said husband, all her separate estate, whether real or personal, which she shall not have disposed of in her lifetime or by will, shall, subject to her debts and engagements, go and belong to the persons or person who would have become entitled thereto if the said husband had died in the lifetime of the said wife.

7. If the said wife shall die in the lifetime of the said hus-

band, he shall permit her to be proved, or administration upon her personal estate and effects to be taken out by the persons or person who would have been entitled to do so had the said husband died in her lifetime.

8. The said wife shall have the sole custody and control of Jim and Louise, infant children, and of their education and bringing up, until they respectively attain the age of sixteen years, without any interference whatsoever on the part of the husband.

9. The said husband further agrees to pay unto the wife for the support and maintenance of the aforementioned children of the parties the additional sum of $3,000.00 per annum, to be paid in quarterly installments, the first installment to be payable November 15, 19_____, until each child reaches the age of twenty-one years, or remains unmarried.

10. The said husband and wife shall respectively, at all convenient and reasonable times have access to and communication with the children or child for the time being living with or under the control of the other of them.

11. The said wife, her heirs, executors and administrators, shall at all times hereafter keep indemnified the said husband, his heirs, executors and administrators, from all debts and liabilities, heretofore or hereafter to be contracted or incurred by the said wife, and from all actions, proceedings, claims, and demands, costs, damages, and expenses whatsoever in respect of such debts and liabilities, or any of them.

12. In case the said husband shall be obliged to pay any sum or sums of money for or on account of any debt or liability heretofore or hereafter contracted or incurred by the said wife, or in case the said wife shall at any time take any proceedings against him, the said husband, for restitution of conjugal rights or otherwise for compelling him to cohabit with her, or shall at any time directly or indirectly molest the said husband, then and in any such case the said annuity of $6,000.00 shall cease to be payable.

13. In case the said husband shall at any time or times hereafter be called upon to pay or discharge, and shall actually pay or discharge, any debt or liability heretofore or hereafter contracted or incurred by the said wife, then and in every such case it shall be lawful for the said husband, at his option, instead of availing himself of the rights secured to

him by the preceding paragraph, to deduct and retain out of the said annuity the amount which he shall have so paid, together with all costs and expenses.

14. Each of them, the said husband and wife, or their respective heirs, executors or administrators, shall at any time execute and do all such assurances and things as the other of them, his or her heirs, executors, administrators or assigns shall reasonably require for the purpose of giving full effect to these presents, and the covenants, agreements and provisions herein contained.

15. Provided always, and it is hereby agreed, that if the said husband and wife shall be reconciled and return to cohabitation, or if their marriage shall be dissolved, then and in such case all the covenants and provisions herein contained shall be void, but without prejudice to any act of the parties hereto in respect of any antecedent breach of any of the covenants or provisions herein contained.

Witness our hands and seals this 30th day of October, 19___.

(Seal)  /s/  Richard Roe
-----------------------------------------------------------------
                                        Husband

(Seal)  /s/  Mary Roe
-----------------------------------------------------------------
                                        Wife

/s/  Jack Wilson
--------------------------------------------
            Witness


FORM 56


## WILL


I, Richard Roe, a resident of the City of New York, State of New York, and residing therein at 16 Ridge Road, being over the age of twenty-one (21) years and of sound and disposing mind and memory, and not acting under duress, menace, fraud or undue influence of any person whomsoever, do make, publish and declare this my last will and testament, in the manner following to wit:

1. I direct that all my debts, including my funeral expenses, expense of my last illness and the expenses of the administration of my estate, be paid by my executor, hereinafter

named, out of the first moneys coming into its hands and available therefor.

2. I hereby declare that I am married; that my wife's name is Mary Roe; and that I have but two (2) children, a son, Joseph, and a daughter, Louise.

3. I give, devise and bequeath all of the rest and residue of my property, after the payment of the debts and expenses provided for in paragraph 1 hereof, whether such property be real, personal or mixed, or whatsoever kind or character and wheresoever situated, to my wife.

4. I hereby nominate and appoint the State Bank of New York the executor of this, my last will and testament.

Lastly, I hereby revoke all former wills and codicils to wills heretofore by me made.

In Witness Whereof, I have hereunto set my hand and seal this 10 day of November, 19_____.

_____ (Seal)

Richard Roe

The foregoing instrument, consisting of one (1) page besides this, was, at the date hereof, by said Richard Roe, signed, sealed and published as and declared to be his last will and testament, in the presence of us, who at his request and in his presence and in the presence of each other, have signed our names as witnesses hereto.

Witness

_____

Residing at 206 New Road

_____

Witness

Residing at 96 Palm Avenue

FORM 57

## PETITION FOR WRIT OF HABEAS CORPUS

To the Judge of the Baltimore City Court:

The petition of Richard Roe respectfully shows that he was illegally restrained of his liberty by Warden of the Baltimore City Jail. Your petitioner, therefore, prays that the writ of habeas corpus issue, commanding said Warden to produce before this Honorable Court, the body of your petitioner, to abide such direction as may be given in the premises.

---------------------------------------------------------------
Petitioner

FORM 58

### WRIT OF HABEAS CORPUS

State of Maryland:

To Warden, Baltimore City Jail:

You are commanded to have the body of Richard Roe, detained under your custody, as it is said, together with the cause of his detention, by whatsoever name he be called, before the Baltimore City Court, immediately after receipt of this writ to submit to and receive what shall be considered and determined in that behalf; and have you there this writ. Issued this 15th day of October, 19_____.

---------------------------------------------------------------
Clerk

(Seal of Court)

# Appendix II

## GLOSSARY OF LEGAL TERMS

### A

**Abet**—To encourage, stir up, or excite one to commit a crime.

**Abettor**—One who aids in the commission of a crime.

**Abeyance**—In the law of estates, expectation, waiting, suspense in law. An estate is in abeyance when there is no person in existence in whom an inheritance can vest.

**Abrogate**—To annul a law by an act of the same power that made it; to repeal.

**Abscond**—To hide or conceal one's self. Applied to one who hides to avoid legal process.

**Absolute conveyance**—A conveyance by which the right or property in a thing is transferred, free of any condition or qualification.

**Absolute estate**—An estate in lands not subject to any condition.

**Absolute property**—Full and complete ownership of chattels in possession.

**Abstract of title**—An abstract or summary of the most important parts of the deeds and other instruments, arranged usually in chronological order and intended to show the origin, course, and incidents of the title, without the necessity of referring to the deeds themselves.

**Abuttals**—The buttings and boundings of lands, east, west, north, and south, showing on what other lands, highways, or places they abut, or are limited and bounded.

**Acceptance of a bill of exchange**—The act by which the person (called the drawee), on whom a bill of exchange is drawn, assents to the request of the drawer to pay it, or engages or makes himself liable to pay it, when due.

**Acceptor**—The party who accepts a bill of exchange, and who is the principal debtor, the drawer being the surety.

**Accessory**—One who, without being present at the commission of a felonious offense, becomes guilty of such offense, not as a chief actor, but as a participator, as by command, advice, instigation, or concealment, either before or after the fact or commission; a *particeps criminis*.

**Accessory after the fact**—One who, knowing a felony to have been

661

committed by another, receives, relieves, comforts, or assists the felon.

**Accessory before the fact**—One who, being absent at the time a crime is committed, yet procures, counsels, or commands another to commit it.

**Accident**—An event that takes place without one's foresight or expectation.

**Accommodation paper**—A bill or note drawn, accepted, or endorsed by one person for another, there being no consideration between them, for the sole purpose of raising money upon it, for the accommodation of one or both of them.

**Accomplice**—An associate in a crime who co-operates, aids, or assists in committing it.

**Accord**—An agreement, consent, or concurrence.

**Accumulative legacy**—A legacy given in addition to another given by the same instrument or by another instrument.

**Acknowledgment**—The act by which a party who has executed an instrument declares or acknowledges it before a competent officer to be his or her act and deed.

**Acquittal**—A deliverance or setting free from a criminal charge by the process of trial at law; the verdict of a jury pronouncing the party not guilty.

**Act of God**—An inevitable accident or casualty, such as lightning, tempests, perils of the sea, or earthquake.

*Actio ex contractu*—An action of contract.

**Action**—The formal means or method of pursuing and recovering one's rights in a court of justice.

**Actionable**—That which can legally be made the ground or subject of an action. Also applied to slanderous words uttered or published of another.

**Ademption**—Of a legacy, the taking away from the party to whom it has been given, arising from a supposed alteration in the testator's intention.

**Administer**—To take charge and dispose of the personal property of an intestate, or testator having no executor.

**Administration**—The management and disposition of the estate of an intestate, or of a testator having no executor.

**Administration** *cum testamento annexo*—Administration granted when a testator has made a will without naming any executors, or when the executors who are named in the will are incompetent to act or refuse to act, or in case of the death of the executors or their survivors.

**Administration** *de bonis non,* or *de bonis non administratis*—Administration granted for the purpose of administering such of the goods of a deceased person as were not administered by the former executor or administrator.

**Administration** *durante in absentia*—Administration granted during the absence of an executor.

**Administration** *durante minore aetate*—Administration granted during the minority of an executor.

**Administrator**—A manager or conductor of affairs, especially the affairs of another, in his name or behalf.

**Administratrix**—A female who administers, or to whom the right of administration has been granted.

**Adoption**—A taking or choosing of another's child as one's own.

**Adult**—One who is of full age; usually, by statute, twenty-one for males, eighteen for females.

**Advancement**—A payment of money, or a settlement of real estate, made by a parent to or for a child in advance or anticipation of the share to which such child would be entitled after the parent's death.

**Adversary system**—The legal procedure in which each side presents opposing and conflicting views of a case in order to pin guilt or responsibility on one of the parties.

**Adverse possession**—The possession of lands for a certain length of time in opposition to the title of another.

**Advocate**—One who is called upon to assist or defend another.

**Affiant**—A person making an affidavit.

**Affidavit**—A written statement, made on oath, sworn before some person legally authorized to administer it.

**Agency**—The relation between principal and agent.

**Agent**—One who acts for another.

**Alibi**—A word used to express a defense to a criminal prosecution, in which the party accused, in order to prove that he could not have committed the crime with which he is charged, offers evidence to show that he was in another place at the time.

**Alien**—A person born in another or foreign country, as distinguished from a native or natural-born subject or citizen.

**Alienate**—To convey or transfer.

**Alimony**—An allowance made to a wife out of the husband's estate.

**Allegation**—Statement or pleading.

**Ambiguity**—Doubtfulness, uncertainty, or obscurity of meaning.

**Amicable action**—An action begun and carried on according to a mutual understanding and arrangement.

**Amicus curiae**—A friend of the court, usually an attorney appointed to assist the court in arriving at a decision.

**Annexation**—The adding or fastening of chattels to the freehold, which gives them the character of fixtures.

**Annuity**—A yearly payment of a certain sum of money.

**Answer**—Any pleading (except a demurrer, by which a party claims that he is not bound to answer) framed to meet a previous pleading.

**Appeal**—The removal of a cause from an inferior to a superior court for the purpose of re-examination or review.

**Appearance**—The coming into court of either of the parties to an action.

**Appellee**—The party against whom an appeal is made.

**Apportionment**—The distribution of a claim or charge among persons having different interests or shares, in proportion to their interests or shares in the subject matter to which it attaches.

**Appropriation**—The application of a sum of money paid by a debtor to his creditor to one or more of several debts due from the former to the latter.

**Appurtenant**—Accessory or incident to.

**Arbitration**—The investigation of a matter in dispute between contending parties pursuant to an agreement (usually in writing) termed a submission.

**Arraign**—to call a prisoner to the bar of the court to answer the matter charged against him in an indictment.

**Arrears**—Money remaining unpaid after it has become due.

**Arrest**—To stop or detain a person and restrain his liberty until he complies with some legal order. To stop or stay a legal proceeding, particularly a judgment of a court, by some rule or order of the same court.

**Arrest of judgment**—The act of refusing to render judgment in an action at law, after verdict, for some matter appearing on the face of the record which would render the judgment, if given, erroneous or reversible.

**Arson**—The malicious and willful burning of the property of another.

**Artificial persons**—Persons created by law as distinguished from natural persons. A corporation is an example of an artificial person.

**Assault**—An intentional attempt, by violence, to do bodily injury to another.

**Assent**—Agreement to, or approval of, an act or thing done.

**Assign**—To transfer, as to assign property or some interest therein.

**Assignee**—A person to whom some right or property is assigned, transferred, or made over by another.

**Assignment**—A transfer of any property.

**Assignor**—One who makes an assignment.

**Assumpsit**—A form of action brought in matters relating to contracts.

**Attachment**—A taking or seizing of a person or property by virtue of a legal process.

**Attainder**—The extinction of civil rights and capacities that takes place whenever a person who has committed treason or felony receives sentence of death for his crime.

**Attempt**—An endeavor to commit an offense, carried beyond mere preparation, but falling short of actual commission.

**Attest**—To witness or testify.

**Attestation**—The act of witnessing the signature of a deed or other instrument, and subscribing the name of the witness in testimony of such fact.

**Attestation clause**—The memorandum or form of words at the end of an instrument, immediately preceding and over the names of the attesting witnesses, importing that they have attested its execution in due form.

**Attorney at law**—One licensed to practice law.

**Authentication**—The act of giving legal authority to a statute, record, or other written instrument, or to a certified copy thereof, to render it legally admissible in evidence.

**Award**—The judgment or decision respecting any matter in dispute to an arbitrator.

## B

**Bail**—The security given for releasing a person from legal custody.

**Bailee**—A person to whom goods are delivered or bailed for a certain purpose.

**Bailiff**—A sheriff's officer or deputy.

**Bailment**—A delivery of goods in trust upon a contract that the trust shall be faithfully executed by the bailee.

**Bailor**—The party who bails or delivers the goods to another in the contract of bailment.

**Banc**—A meeting of all the judges of a court.

**Bank note**—A promissory note issued by a bank, payable to the bearer on demand, and intended for circulation as money.

**Bankrupt**—Any person who fails, or becomes unable, to pay his just debts.

**Bar**—The place in court that counsellors or advocates occupy while addressing the court or jury, and where prisoners are brought for the purpose of being arraigned or sentenced.

**Bargain and sale**—The word "bargain" means the arrangement of the terms upon which the one party sells and the other buys. The word "sale" expresses the completion of the contract, at which title passes from the seller to the buyer.

**Barrister**—A lawyer; in England, one who tries a case.

**Battery**—The unlawful beating of another.

**Bench**—The judges themselves, as occupying the judgment seat in courts.

**Bench warrant**—An order issued by a judge for the arrest of someone suspected of a crime or of contempt of court.

**Bequeath**—To give personal property by will.

**Bequest**—A gift of personal property by will; a gift of a legacy.

**Bill**—1. A formal written statement of complaint to a court of justice, as a bill of privilege, a bill of equity, and a bill of indictment. 2. A record or written statement of proceedings in an action, as a bill of exceptions. 3. A written statement of the terms of a contract, or specifications of the items of a demand, or counterdemand, as a bill of exchange, a bill single and penal, a bill of lading, a bill of sale, a bill of credit, and a bill of particulars. 4. A draft of an act of the legislature before it becomes a law; a proposal or projected law. A draft of an act presented to the legislature, but not enacted. 5. A solemn and formal written declaration of popular rights and liberties, promulgated on certain extraordinary occasions, as the Bill of Rights in English history.

**Bill of attainder**—An act of the legislature depriving a person of his property if he is found guilty of treason or felony. Such bills are forbidden by the U.S. Constitution and by the individual states.

**Bill of costs**—A statement in writing of the items composing the amount of the costs awarded a plaintiff or defendant in an action or other judicial proceeding.

**Bill of exceptions**—A formal statement in writing of exceptions taken to an opinion, a decision, or a direction of a judge delivered during the trial of a cause.

**Bill of exchange**—A written order or request by one person to another, for the payment of money absolutely, and at all events.

**Bill of indictment**—A written accusation of one or more persons of some crime or misdemeanor, preferred to, and presented upon oath by, a grand jury.

**Bill of lading**—A written statement by a common carrier to one sending goods by him that the goods have been received by him for transportation with the terms of shipment; it is both a receipt and a contract.

**Bill of particulars**—A written statement or specification of the particulars of the demand for which an action at law is brought.

**Bill of rights**—A formal and public declaration or assertion, in writing, of popular rights and liberties, usually expressed in the form of a statute, or promulgated on occasions of revolution, or the establishment of new forms of government or constitutions.

**Bill of sale**—A deed or writing under seal evidencing the sale of personal property and conveying the title to it.

**Bills of credit**—Promissory notes or bills issued by a state government, exclusively on the credit of the state, and intended to circulate through the community for its ordinary purposes as money redeemable at a future day, and for the payment of which the faith of the state is pledged.

**Binder**—In insurance a binder is intended to provide temporary coverage to the insured; in real estate a binder is an agreement where buyer and seller declare their intent to purchase a piece of property.

**Blackmail**—Money extorted from one by threats of exposure.

**Black endorsement**—An endorsement that does not name a particular person as the one to whom payment is to be made; it consists of the endorser's name only.

**Bona fide**—In good faith.

**Bona fide purchaser**—A purchaser in good faith.

**Bond**—A deed or instrument, under seal, by which a person binds or obliges himself, his heirs, executors, and administrators to pay a certain sum of money to another.

**Bondsman**—One who provides bond or surety for another.

**Bottomry**—An agreement entered into by the owner of a ship, or by the master as the owner's agent, whereby, in consideration of a sum of money advanced for the ship, the borrower undertakes to repay the same with interest if the ship terminates her voyage successfully and binds or hypothecates the ship for the performance of the contract.

**Boundary**—A line or object indicating the limit or farthest extent of a tract of land or territory.

**Breach**—The breaking or violating of a law, right, or duty, either by commission or omission.

**Breach of covenant**—The nonperformance of any covenant agreed to be performed or the doing of any act covenanted not to be done.

**Breach of peace**—The offense of breaking or disturbing the public peace by riotous, forcible, or unlawful proceeding.

**Breach of prison**—The offense of actually and forcibly breaking a prison or jail with intent to escape.

**Breaking**—In the law of burglary, a substantial and forcible irruption, as by breaking or taking out the glass of a window or otherwise opening it, by picking a lock or opening it with a key, by lifting up the latch of a door, or by unloosening any other fastening that the owner has provided.

**Bribery**—The taking of any undue reward by a judge, juror, or other person concerned in the administration of justice, or the taking of any undue reward by any public officer.

**Brief**—An abridgment of a plaintiff's or defendant's case prepared by his attorney.

**Broker**—One who transacts business for another; commonly, one who deals in corporation stocks.

**Burden of proof**—The duty of proving a fact or facts in dispute on an issue raised between the parties in a cause.

**Burglary**—The crime of breaking and entering into a building.

**By-laws**—Laws or regulations made by a corporation for its own government.

# C

**Canon law**—The rules and regulations by which the Roman Catholic Church is governed. Canon law has no standing in civil or criminal courts.

**Capital stock**—The amount of money, as distinguished from property, contributed or advanced by the stockholders of a company or corporation for the purposes of the corporation.

**Caveat emptor**—"Let the buyer beware." The expression applies to cases in which the thing sold is before the buyer and he examines it.

**Chain of title**—In real estate indicates the owners of a piece of land or property from the beginning to the present time.

**Challenge**—An objection to a juror made by legal counsel. No reason need be given for peremptory challenges, which are limited in number; challenges for cause, such as bias, are unlimited.

**Change of venue**—The transfer of a case from one jurisdiction to another, usually made to receive a fairer trial. Granting a change of venue is usually discretionary with the presiding judge.

**Charge**—1. An incumbrance or lien upon a land; a duty or liability attached to, or an obligation imposed upon, a person. 2. An address by the presiding judge to a jury after a case has been closed on both sides, summing up the testimony by the respective parties and instructing the jury in matters of law.

**Charter**—A written instrument under seal containing the evidence of things done between man and man. A conveyance of lands; a contract, covenant, or other sealed instrument.

**Chattel**—Any kind of personal property.

**Chattel mortgage**—A conditional sale of personal property, which becomes void upon the happening of a certain event; chiefly used as the security for the payment of money.

**Check**—A written order for money claims upon a bank, and payable immediately.

**Chose in action**—A thing in action, of which one has not the possession or actual enjoyment, but only a right to it or a right to demand it by action at law.

**Chose in possession**—A thing in possession, as distinguished from a thing in action. Taxes and customs, if paid, are a chose in possession; if unpaid, a chose in action.

**Circuit**—A civil division of a country, state, or kingdom for the more convenient administration of justice.

**Circumstantial evidence**—Evidence from circumstances, as distinguished from direct and positive proof.

**Citation**—An official call or notice to appear in court.

**Civil action**—An action brought to recover some civil right, or to obtain redress for some wrong, not a crime or misdemeanor.

**Civil injury**—An infringment of some civil right, which may be redressed or compensated, as distinguished from a crime, which is a subject for punishment.

**Civil law**—The system of law of ancient Rome.

**Civil liberty**—The liberty of a member of society, restrained by human laws only as is necessary and expedient for the general advantage of the public.

**Clemency**—An act by an executive or judge which reduces the penalty for a crime, after the defendant has been convicted. In some cases the clemency may result in the release of the prisoner.

**Client**—One who employs or retains an attorney.

**Closing**—The act by which a piece of real estate is transferred from the seller to the buyer.

**Code**—A collection or compilation of laws by public authority.

**Code Civil**—A code of law prepared under the direction of Napoleon and promulgated in 1804 as the civil law of France.

**Codicil**—A supplement to a will.

**Cognizance**—An official notice; the right or power to deal with a matter judicially.

**Collateral**—Property pledged as security for the performance of a contract.

**Collateral heirs**—Heirs coming in, on, or from the side.

**Collusion**—A deceitful agreement or compact between two or more persons, as in a divorce suit where the grounds for divorce are agreed upon to eliminate the possibility of a contest.

**Co-maker**—A person who by his signature guarantees the payment of a note, contract, or debt in case the original signer defaults.

**Common carrier**—One who as a business undertakes for hire to transport from place to place passengers or goods of all who choose to employ him.

**Common law**—The whole body of the law of England, as distinguished from the civil and canon laws. That branch of the law of England which does not owe its origin to parliamentary enactment. The common law is the common jurisprudence of the people of the United States. It was brought by them as colonists from England and established here, insofar as it was adaptable to our institutions and circumstances.

**Common nuisance**—A nuisance affecting the public; distinguished from a private nuisance, which is confined in its effects to particular individuals.

**Community property**—A system which exists in eight states in which all property acquired during marriage belongs equally to husband and wife. Community property states include Arizona, California, Idaho, Louisiana, Nevada, New Mexico, Texas, and Washington. Inheritances by either party during marriage are not considered community property.

**Commutation**—The change of a punishment from a greater to a lesser, as from hanging to imprisonment.

**Competency**—Applied to witnesses, it signifies legal ability to be received and examined on the trial of a cause.

**Complainant**—One who complains of another by instituting legal proceedings against him.

**Complaint**—An accusation or charge against a person as having committed an alleged injury or offense.

**Compounding a felony**—The taking of a reward for forbearing to prosecute a felony.

**Compromise**—Any adjustment by mutual concession of matters in dispute without resort to law.

**Conclusive evidence**—Evidence which, in its nature, does not admit of explanation or contradiction.

**Condemnation**—The taking of private property by legal proceedings for public use.

**Condominium**—An apartment building in which the apartments are owned individually like houses, and for which taxes and interest are deductible on income tax returns.

**Condonation**—The forgiving by a husband or wife of a breach of marital duties on the part of the other.

**Confession**—Acknowledgment of guilt or agency.

**Confession and avoidance**—The admission of the truth of a statement of fact contained in the pleading of the opposite party, coupled with the allegation of a new fact, which obviates or repels its legal effect and thus avoids it. A pleading framed upon this principle is called a pleading in confession and avoidance, or by way of confession and avoidance.

**Conflict of laws**—The conflict between the municipal laws of different countries or states.

**Consanguinity**—Relationship by blood, such as parent and child.

**Consent**—A concurrence of wills. An agreement as to something to be done or proposed to be done.

**Consideration**—The price or motive of a contract, without which no contract is binding.

**Consign**—To send or transmit goods to someone for sale.

**Consignee**—The person to whom goods are consigned, shipped, or otherwise transmitted.

**Consortium**—Mutual duties owed by one spouse to another, including support and sexual intercourse.

**Conspiracy**—Any confederacy of two or more persons to injure an individual or to do any other unlawful act or acts prejudical to the community.

**Constructive fraud**—Fraud inferred by law, as distinguished from positive, actual, or intentional fraud.

**Constructive larceny**—Larceny made out by construction, or inferred from the acts of a party, where the taking itself was not apparently felonious.

**Constructive notice**—Notice inferred by law, as distinguished from actual or formal notice. Actual notice to a party's attorney is constructive notice to the party himself.

**Constructive trust**—A trust raised by construction of law or arising by operation of law, as distinguished from an express trust.

**Contempt**—A disobedience of the rules, orders, or process of a court of justice or a disturbance or interruption of its proceedings. Those in contempt may be punished by fine or imprisonment or both.

**Continuance**—The adjournment of the proceedings in a cause from one day or one term to another.

**Contra**—The opposition of cases cited as establishing opposite doctrines.

**Contract**—An agreement, for a sufficient consideration, to do or not to do a particular thing.

**Contract of sale**—A contract by which one of the contracting parties, called the seller, enters into an obligation to the other, called the buyer.

**Contribution**—The making-up of a loss sustained to one of their number by several parties jointly interested or indebted; a payment made by one for the benefit of all.

**Conversion**—An appropriation of property belonging to another.

**Convey**—To transfer property, or title to property, by an instrument in writing. In a stricter sense, to transfer by deed or instrument under seal.

**Conveyance**—An instrument in writing by which property or title to property is transferred from one person to another.

**Conveyancing**—The business or practice of preparing conveyances, especially of real estate, including the investigation of titles, the preparation of abstracts, etc.

**Convict**—To find guilty of an offense, usually by the verdict of a jury.

**Conviction**—The finding a person guilty of an offense with which he has been charged, either by the verdict of a jury or on his own confession.

**Cooperative**—In a cooperative apartment house the individual has a stock ownership in the building and the right of occupancy to a specific unit. In a co-op each individual is dependent on the solvency of the other unit dwellers. If a number of units become empty, the co-op dwellers' costs increase.

**Copyright**—The exclusive right which the law allows an author (or a person purchasing from an author) of printing, publishing and selling a written composition for twenty-eight years. A copyright may be renewed for an additional period of twenty-eight years.

**Coroner**—One authorized to investigate a death under suspicious or mysterious circumstances. A coroner may be also authorized to empanel a jury to aid him in arriving at a verdict.

**Corporation**—An artificial person or being endowed by law with the capacity of perpetual succession.

**Corpus**—A body; a human body.

**Corpus delicti**—The body, a substance, or foundation of an offense.

**Corpus juris**—A body of law.

**Co-signer**—A person who by his signature guarantees the payment of a note, contract, or debt in case the original signer defaults.

**Costs**—The expenses which are incurred either in the prosecution or defense of an action or in any other proceeding at law or in equity.

**Counsel**—A lawyer who assists his client with advice and pleads for him in open court.

**Counsellor, counsellor at law**—A licensed attorney whose occupation and office is to give counsel or advice on the management of suits and other legal business.

**Count**—A single accusation in an indictment or information. There may be a number of counts against a defendant each charging him with a separate offense.

**Counterclaim**—One debt or claim to set off another.

**Court**—A tribunal established for the public administration of justice.

**Court martial**—A court held in the military and naval services for the trial and punishment of offenses against the regulations of the service.

**Court of record**—A court where the acts and judicial proceedings are permanently recorded and which has power to fine and imprison for contempt of its authority.

**Covenant**—The agreement or consent of two or more by deed in writing, sealed and delivered, whereby either or one of the parties promises to the other that something is done or will be done.

**Covenant in law**—A covenant implied by law from certain words in a deed which do not express it.

**Covenant real**—A covenant in a deed binding the heirs of the convenanter and passing to assignees or to the purchaser.

**Covenant running with land**—A covenant which goes with the land (conveyed by the deed in which it is expressed), as being annexed to the estate, and which cannot be separated from the land or transferred without it.

**Coverture**—The legal state of being a married woman.

**Creditor**—One who gives or has given credit to another.

**Creditor's bill**—A bill in equity filed by creditors for an account of the assets and a settlement of the estate of a decedent.

**Crime**—An act committed or omitted in violation of a public law that either forbids or commands it.

**Criminal**—One who commits a crime.

**Criminal law**—That branch or division of law which treats of crimes and their punishments.

**Criminate**—To expose a person to a criminal charge. A witness cannot be compelled to answer any question that has a tendency to incriminate him.

**Cross action**—An action on the same subject matter (as on the same contract) brought by a party sued against the party who has sued him.

**Cross bill**—A bill filed by a defendant, in a suit in equity, and frequently in bills of divorce, against the plaintiff or complainant in order to obtain some relief against him.

**Cross-examination**—The examination of a witness by the party opposed to the party who has first or directly examined him, in order to test the truth of such first or direct examination.

**Cruelty**—Such conduct on the part of one spouse toward the other as affords a reasonable apprehension of bodily injury. It is usually considered grounds for a divorce.

**Curtesy**—An estate to which a man is by law entitled on the death of his wife, in the lands of which she was seised during the marriage in fee simple or fee tail, provided he had issue by her, born alive during the marriage and capable of inheriting her estate.

# D

**Damage**—A loss, hurt, or hindrance sustained by a party in his estate or person.

**Damage feasant** or **faisant**—Applied to a person's cattle or beasts found on another's land, doing damage by treading down the grass, grain, etc.

**Damages**—Money compensation or satisfaction for an injury, usually given at law, but sometimes in equity.

**Debt**—A sum of money due by certain and express agreement.

**Debt of record**—A debt which appears to be due by the evidence of a court of record, as by a judgment or recognizance.

**Deceit**—A subtle trick or device; fraud.

**Declaration**—A plaintiff's statement in writing of the circumstances that constitute his cause of action.

**Declaration of intention**—The act by which an alien declares, before a court of record, that he intends to become a citizen of the United States.

**Declaration of trust**—A declaration by a party who has made a conveyance to another that the subject conveyed is to be held in trust.

**Declaratory judgment**—A judgment establishing the rights of the parties and making binding declarations of their respective rights but granting no consequential relief.

**Declaratory statute**—A statute that, instead of introducing a new law, only declares what is the existing law; the object of declaratory statute is to remove doubts that have arisen on the subject.

**Decree**—The judgment of a court of equity or admiralty.

**Dedication**—The appropriation of private property to public use, either by a formal or express act on the part of the owner or by acts from which an appropriation may be legally presumed.

**Deed**—A writing under seal used to transfer property, usually real estate.

**Defamation**—The offense of injuring a person's character, fame, or reputation, either by writing or by words.

**Default**—Failure to fulfill a legal obligation, such as the failure to pay rent when due.

**Defendant**—The party denying, opposing, resisting, or contesting an action.

**Defense**—A denial, by the defendant in an action at law, of the truth or validity of a plaintiff's complaint.

**Delinquent**—An account that is overdue; a minor who has violated a law or is accused of such.

**Delivery**—One of the essential requisites to the validity of a deed.

**Demise**—A conveyance of an estate to another for life, for years, or at will—most commonly, for years.

**Demur**—To object to the pleading of the opposite party as insufficient to sustain his action or defense and to refer the pleading to the court to judge whether it ought to be answered.

**Demurrage**—The detention of a vessel beyond the time allowed by the charter party for loading or unloading or for sailing. The allowance or payment made for such detention or delay.

**Demurrer**—An allegation of a defendant which, admitting the matters of fact alleged by the bill to be true, shows that, as they are set forth, they are insufficient for the plaintiff to proceed upon or to obligate the defendant to answer.

**Depose**—To state or testify under oath, the statement or testimony being set forth in writing.

**Deposition**—The testimony of a witness under oath or affirmation, taken down in writing, before a judicial officer.

**Deputy**—A person appointed, designated, or deputed to act for another.

**Descent**—The title by which a man, on the death of his ancestor, acquires his estate by right of representation, as his heir at law.

**Desertion**—The act of forsaking, deserting, or abandoning a person for whom one is legally bound to provide, as a wife or husband.

**Detainer**—The withholding of possession of another's goods.

**Devise**—A gift or disposition of lands or other real property by a last will and testament.

**Disability**—Incapacity to do a legal act.

**Disaffirm**—To disclaim being bound by a former act.

**Disbar**—To expel an attorney from the bar to forbid him to practice law.

**Discharge**—A setting free; a clearing, acquittance, release, or delivery.

**Disfranchise, bill of**—To deprive or divest certain places or persons of any privilege, freedom, liberty, or franchise.

**Dismiss**—To send away, to send out of court; to dispose of finally.

**Disorderly conduct**—Unruly behavior thought menacing to public safety or morality.

**Estate in severalty**—An estate held by a person in his own right only.

**Estoppel**—An impediment, or bar, by which a man is precluded in law from alleging or denying a fact, in consequence of his own previous act, allegation, or denial to the contrary.

**Eviction**—The recovery of lands, etc., by form of law.

**Evidence**—Proof, either written or unwritten, of facts in issue between parties.

**Executed contract**—A contract that transfers the possession of a thing, together with the right to it.

**Executory contract**—A contract which is to be executed at some future time.

**Ex parte**—Of or from one side or party. An order made by a court upon the application of one of the parties to an action without notice to the other.

**Ex post facto**—A law which makes an act retroactively a crime which was not a crime when the act was performed. Ex post facto laws are forbidden by the United States Constitution.

**Extortion**—An unlawful or violent wringing of money from another.

**Extenuating circumstances**—Facts tending to lessen the severity of punishment.

**Extradition**—Delivery, by one nation or state to another, of fugitives from justice, in pursuance of a law or treaty.

## F

**Factor**—A mercantile or commercial agent who buys and sells goods for others on commission.

**False arrest**—The unlawful detention of a person for which an action for damages may ensue.

**False imprisonment**—An unlawful restraint of liberty.

**False pretense**—False statements or representations made with intent to defraud for the purpose of obtaining money or property.

**Fee simple**—An absolute estate of inheritance, which a person holds inheritable to him and his heirs forever.

**Fee tail**—The division of ownership of land into two estates, one part going to the donee, the other remaining in the donor.

**Felony**—An offense punishable by death or by imprisonment in a state prison.

**Fiduciary**—Relating to, founded upon, or having the quality of a trust or confidence.

**Distrain**—To take and keep the property of another as a pledge to compel the performance of some duty, such as the payment of rent, the performance of services, or an appearance in court.

**Distress**—The taking of personal property from the possession of a wrongdoer into the custody of the party injured to procure a satisfaction for a wrong committed, as for nonpayment of rent.

**Distribution**—Commonly used to express the division of the personal effects of an intestate among his widow and children or next of kin.

**Divorce**—The separation of husband and wife by the operation of law.

**Docket**—In some states, the list or calendar of causes ready for hearing or trial, prepared by clerks for the use of courts.

**Domicile**—The place where a person has his home, accompanied with positive or presumptive proof of an intention to remain there for an unlimited time.

**Domicile of origin**—That which arises from a man's birth and connections.

**Donor**—The party making a donation.

**Double jeopardy**—Being tried twice for the same offense. Forbidden by the United States Constitution.

**Dower**—That portion (usually one third) of a man's lands and tenements to which his widow is entitled, to have and hold for the term of her natural life.

**Drawee**—The person to whom a bill of exchange is addressed, or on whom it is drawn.

**Drawer**—The person who draws a bill of exchange.

**Due bill**—A brief written acknowledgment of a debt, usually in the following words: "Due A.B. ——— dollars (payable on demand). Dated, etc., C.D." It is not made payable to order like a promissory note.

**Due process of law**—A right guaranteed by federal and state constitutions that no person shall be deprived of his life, liberty, or property without exhaustive legal proceedings.

**Duress**—Personal restraint or fear of personal injury or imprisonment; it nullifies all contracts into which it enters.

**Dwelling house**—In the law of burglary, a house in which the occupier and his family usually reside.

**Dying declarations**—Declarations made when the party is at the point of death and the mind is presumably induced by the most powerful considerations to speak the truth.

# E

**Earnest**—A part of the price of goods sold or a portion of the goods themselves, delivered by one of the parties to a contract of sale to the other, in order to bind the contract.

**Easement**—A liberty, privilege, or advantage in land, without profit, existing distinct from an ownership of the soil.

**Ejectment**—An action that lies to recover the possession of lands, with damages and costs for their being wrongfully withheld.

**Eleemosynary**—Charitable.

**Emancipation**—The freedom of a minor from parental control, allowing the former to retain his earnings and choose his own home.

**Embezzlement**—The fraudulent appropriation to one's own use or benefit of property or money entrusted to him by another.

**Emblements**—The profit of sown land; the crops and growing crops of corn or grain.

**Eminent domain**—The ultimate right of a sovereign power to appropriate for public purposes not only the public property but the private property of all the citizens within the territorial sovereignty.

**Endorse**—To write one's name on the back of a bill, note, or check.

**Endorsee**—The party in whose favor a bill of exchange, promissory note, or check is endorsed.

**Endorsement**—The writing of the name of the payee, or holder of a bill, note or check, on the back of it, by which the property in it is assigned and transferred.

**Endorsement in blank**—An endorsement consisting merely of the signature of the party making it.

**Endorsement in full**—An endorsement which mentions the name of the person in whose favor it is made, thus "Pay A.B., on order, C.D."

**Endorser**—The party by whom a bill of exchange, a promissory note, or check is endorsed.

**Enticement**—Persuading someone to commit an illegal act.

**Entrapment**—The act of a police or government official who persuades one to commit a crime he ordinarily would not have committed.

**Equitable estate**—An estate for whose use or benefit lands are held in trust by another, the latter having the legal estate; also, the estate of a mortgagor after the mortgage has become forfeited by nonpayment and before it has been foreclosed.

**Equitable mortgage**—A mortage arising in equity, from the transactions of the parties, without any deed or express contract for that special purpose.

**Equity**—A system supplemental to law, qualifying or correcting it in extreme cases.

**Escheat**—The reverting of land to the state on the death of the owner without lawful heirs.

**Escrow**—The turning over of a paper or money to a third person to be held by him until certain conditions are performed as agreed upon by the original contracting parties.

**Estate**—The interest which anyone has in lands or in any other subject of property.

**Estate at will**—A species of estate less than freehold in which lands and tenements are let by one man to another, to have and to hold at the will of the lessor.

**Estate by curtesy**—A species of life estate that a man is, by law entitled to claim on the death of his wife.

**Estate for life**—A freehold estate, not of inheritance, which man has, to hold for the term of his own life or for that of any oth person.

**Estate for years**—A species of estate less than freehold in wh a man has an interest in lands and tenements, and a possess thereof by virtue of such interest, for some fixed and determi period of time.

**Estate in common**—An estate in lands held by two or more sons, with interest accruing under different titles or accruing der the same title but at different periods.

**Estate in dower**—A species of life estate that a woman is, by entitled to claim on the death of her husband.

**Estate in fee simple**—An estate to a man and his heirs fc the entire and absolute interest and property in land.

**Estate in joint tenancy**—An estate in lands or tenements g to two or more persons, to hold in fee simple, fee tail, for years or at will.

**Estate in remainder**—An estate limited to take effect an joyed after another estate is determined.

**Estate in reversion**—A species of estate in expectancy, cr operation of law. It is the residue of an estate left in th to begin in possession after the determination of some estate granted out by him.

**Distrain**—To take and keep the property of another as a pledge to compel the performance of some duty, such as the payment of rent, the performance of services, or an appearance in court.

**Distress**—The taking of personal property from the possession of a wrongdoer into the custody of the party injured to procure a satisfaction for a wrong committed, as for nonpayment of rent.

**Distribution**—Commonly used to express the division of the personal effects of an intestate among his widow and children or next of kin.

**Divorce**—The separation of husband and wife by the operation of law.

**Docket**—In some states, the list or calendar of causes ready for hearing or trial, prepared by clerks for the use of courts.

**Domicile**—The place where a person has his home, accompanied with positive or presumptive proof of an intention to remain there for an unlimited time.

**Domicile of origin**—That which arises from a man's birth and connections.

**Donor**—The party making a donation.

**Double jeopardy**—Being tried twice for the same offense. Forbidden by the United States Constitution.

**Dower**—That portion (usually one third) of a man's lands and tenements to which his widow is entitled, to have and hold for the term of her natural life.

**Drawee**—The person to whom a bill of exchange is addressed, or on whom it is drawn.

**Drawer**—The person who draws a bill of exchange.

**Due bill**—A brief written acknowledgment of a debt, usually in the following words: "Due A.B. —— dollars (payable on demand). Dated, etc., C.D." It is not made payable to order like a promissory note.

**Due process of law**—A right guaranteed by federal and state constitutions that no person shall be deprived of his life, liberty, or property without exhaustive legal proceedings.

**Duress**—Personal restraint or fear of personal injury or imprisonment; it nullifies all contracts into which it enters.

**Dwelling house**—In the law of burglary, a house in which the occupier and his family usually reside.

**Dying declarations**—Declarations made when the party is at the point of death and the mind is presumably induced by the most powerful considerations to speak the truth.

# E

**Earnest**—A part of the price of goods sold or a portion of the goods themselves, delivered by one of the parties to a contract of sale to the other, in order to bind the contract.

**Easement**—A liberty, privilege, or advantage in land, without profit, existing distinct from an ownership of the soil.

**Ejectment**—An action that lies to recover the possession of lands, with damages and costs for their being wrongfully withheld.

**Eleemosynary**—Charitable.

**Emancipation**—The freedom of a minor from parental control, allowing the former to retain his earnings and choose his own home.

**Embezzlement**—The fraudulent appropriation to one's own use or benefit of property or money entrusted to him by another.

**Emblements**—The profit of sown land; the crops and growing crops of corn or grain.

**Eminent domain**—The ultimate right of a sovereign power to appropriate for public purposes not only the public property but the private property of all the citizens within the territorial sovereignty.

**Endorse**—To write one's name on the back of a bill, note, or check.

**Endorsee**—The party in whose favor a bill of exchange, promissory note, or check is endorsed.

**Endorsement**—The writing of the name of the payee, or holder of a bill, note or check, on the back of it, by which the property in it is assigned and transferred.

**Endorsement in blank**—An endorsement consisting merely of the signature of the party making it.

**Endorsement in full**—An endorsement which mentions the name of the person in whose favor it is made, thus "Pay A.B., on order, C.D."

**Endorser**—The party by whom a bill of exchange, a promissory note, or check is endorsed.

**Enticement**—Persuading someone to commit an illegal act.

**Entrapment**—The act of a police or government official who persuades one to commit a crime he ordinarily would not have committed.

**Equitable estate**—An estate for whose use or benefit lands are held in trust by another, the latter having the legal estate; also, the estate of a mortgagor after the mortgage has become forfeited by nonpayment and before it has been foreclosed.

**Equitable mortgage**—A mortage arising in equity, from the transactions of the parties, without any deed or express contract for that special purpose.

**Equity**—A system supplemental to law, qualifying or correcting it in extreme cases.

**Escheat**—The reverting of land to the state on the death of the owner without lawful heirs.

**Escrow**—The turning over of a paper or money to a third person to be held by him until certain conditions are performed as agreed upon by the original contracting parties.

**Estate**—The interest which anyone has in lands or in any other subject of property.

**Estate at will**—A species of estate less than freehold in which lands and tenements are let by one man to another, to have and to hold at the will of the lessor.

**Estate by curtesy**—A species of life estate that a man is, by law, entitled to claim on the death of his wife.

**Estate for life**—A freehold estate, not of inheritance, which a man has, to hold for the term of his own life or for that of any other person.

**Estate for years**—A species of estate less than freehold in which a man has an interest in lands and tenements, and a possession thereof by virtue of such interest, for some fixed and determinate period of time.

**Estate in common**—An estate in lands held by two or more persons, with interest accruing under different titles or accruing under the same title but at different periods.

**Estate in dower**—A species of life estate that a woman is, by law, entitled to claim on the death of her husband.

**Estate in fee simple**—An estate to a man and his heirs forever; the entire and absolute interest and property in land.

**Estate in joint tenancy**—An estate in lands or tenements granted to two or more persons, to hold in fee simple, fee tail, for life, for years or at will.

**Estate in remainder**—An estate limited to take effect and be enjoyed after another estate is determined.

**Estate in reversion**—A species of estate in expectancy, created by operation of law. It is the residue of an estate left in the grantor, to begin in possession after the determination of some particular estate granted out by him.

**Estate in severalty**—An estate held by a person in his own right only.

**Estoppel**—An impediment, or bar, by which a man is precluded in law from alleging or denying a fact, in consequence of his own previous act, allegation, or denial to the contrary.

**Eviction**—The recovery of lands, etc., by form of law.

**Evidence**—Proof, either written or unwritten, of facts in issue between parties.

**Executed contract**—A contract that transfers the possession of a thing, together with the right to it.

**Executory contract**—A contract which is to be executed at some future time.

**Ex parte**—Of or from one side or party. An order made by a court upon the application of one of the parties to an action without notice to the other.

**Ex post facto**—A law which makes an act retroactively a crime which was not a crime when the act was performed. Ex post facto laws are forbidden by the United States Constitution.

**Extortion**—An unlawful or violent wringing of money from another.

**Extenuating circumstances**—Facts tending to lessen the severity of punishment.

**Extradition**—Delivery, by one nation or state to another, of fugitives from justice, in pursuance of a law or treaty.

## F

**Factor**—A mercantile or commercial agent who buys and sells goods for others on commission.

**False arrest**—The unlawful detention of a person for which an action for damages may ensue.

**False imprisonment**—An unlawful restraint of liberty.

**False pretense**—False statements or representations made with intent to defraud for the purpose of obtaining money or property.

**Fee simple**—An absolute estate of inheritance, which a person holds inheritable to him and his heirs forever.

**Fee tail**—The division of ownership of land into two estates, one part going to the donee, the other remaining in the donor.

**Felony**—An offense punishable by death or by imprisonment in a state prison.

**Fiduciary**—Relating to, founded upon, or having the quality of a trust or confidence.